EMPRESS *of* IRELAND
THE STORY OF AN EDWARDIAN LINER

EMPRESS STEAMERS

EMPRESS *of* IRELAND
THE STORY OF AN EDWARDIAN LINER

Derek Grout

For 'DV' – who gave me courage and reasons to go on, all those years ago.
You proved that miracles appear in the strangest of places. How could I ever
forget? *Gracias, querida*.

And for the shadows who danced, and still do, on Dufferin Terrace.

TEMPUS

First published 2001

PUBLISHED IN THE UNITED KINGDOM BY:

Tempus Publishing Ltd
The Mill, Brimscombe Port
Stroud, Gloucestershire GL5 2QG
www.tempus-publishing.com

PUBLISHED IN THE UNITED STATES OF AMERICA BY:

Arcadia Publishing Inc.
A division of Tempus Publishing Inc.
2 Cumberland Street
Charleston, SC 29401
(Tel: 1-888-313-2665)
www.arcadiapublishing.com

Tempus books are available in France and Germany
from the following addresses:

Tempus Publishing Group   Tempus Publishing Group
21 Avenue de la République   Gustav-Adolf-Straße 3
37300 Joué-lès-Tours   99084 Erfurt
FRANCE   GERMANY

British Library Cataloguing in Publication Data.
A catalogue record for this book is available from the British Library.

ISBN 0 7524 2135 2

Typesetting and origination by Tempus Publishing.
PRINTED AND BOUND IN GREAT BRITAIN.

Contents

Acknowledgments

This book could not have been written without the contributions of literally hundreds of people in North America, Europe and Australia. To all of them I owe an immense debt of gratitude, for generously sharing their stories and family histories, their knowledge and talents and making this book possible. And, in several cases, for opening their private collections of *Empress* memorabilia, ephemera, photographs and artifacts, without which this story would be incomplete. *Empress* collectors, I found, were happy to share their things with me, and a common refrain was 'I'm glad someone is actually going to see this stuff!' So, to all of the collectors – you know who you are – a great thank you.

Many people who helped me did so in the performance of their jobs, and in numerous cases their support went far beyond what I had any right to expect. Thanks to all of you. If I have omitted anyone in the following list, I hope you will accept my sincerest apologies.

Susan Amos; Brian Avery; Raymond Beaulieu; Arthur Blundell; Denise Boivin; Chris Castravelli; Gordon Cornthwaite; Lorraine (Chapman) Cox; Brian Craik; Guy D'Astous; Jack Dahlstrom; Wayne Dutcher; Charles Garneau; Ted Grout; Eunice Gulbraa; Albert Gurinskas; Brad Hanna; Renee Harten; Dominique Jacquemin; Greg Johnson; Roger Jordan; Ian Kinder; Patricia Kirby; Marjorie Kohli; Richard Kudrna; Barry Lambe; Linda Larsen; Dan Lindsay; Andreas von Mach; Nikki McConnell; Ken Mikla; Mike Nunn; Bob O'Hara; Bernard Reeves; Mark Reynolds; Pierre Saint-Laurent; Lady Flora Saltoun; Jill Saward and Gavin Drake; Bill Schleihauf; Carol Sheldon; Patrick Smith; Sheila Taipale; Joan Thornley; Peter Tumilty; Jean-Pierre Vallée; Helena Vandeweerd; Dorothy (Cornthwaite) Varney; Maureen Venzi; Louise Weymouth; David Zeni; and Roy – (name withheld).

Also, to the following institutions and people:

The Royal Archives (Pamela Clark); University of Sussex (Fiona Arthur and Dorothy Sheridan); The National Trust (Margaret Willes); National Library of Australia (Graeme Powell, Valerie Helson and Susan Thomas); Cornwall Record Office (Colin Edwards); King's College (London); Fegans (David Waller); Maritime History Archive of Memorial University (Paula Marshall); National Maritime Museum; McLennan-Redpath Library of McGill University; Pointe Claire Public Library (Joni Crosby-Boyd); Bibliothèque de l'Assemblée nationale; Archives nationales du Québec (Jacques Morin); Edmonton *Journal* (Edith Kirby); DeGolyer Library of Southern Methodist University (Cammie Vitale-Schuman); National Library of Canada (Sharon Shipley); Canadian Pacific Archives (Stephen Lyons); Maritime Museum of British Columbia (Lynn Wright); Musée de la mer de Pointe-au-Père (Annemarie Bourassa and Yves Tremblay); Manitoba Archives (Scott Reid); Salvation Army's George Scott Railton Heritage Centre (Karl Larson and Ira Barrow); Salvation Army International Heritage Centre (John Hughes); National Archives of Canada (Ross MacKay, Martha Marleau, and Martin Tétreault); Canadian War Museum (Carol Reid); Provincial Archives of New Brunswick (Wanda Lyons); Transport Canada (Dragana Markovic); Royal Liverpool Seamen's Orphan Institution (Linda Gidman); Public Record Office; Maritime Museum of the Great Lakes; and the Merseyside Maritime Museum (Rachel Mulhearn, Karen Howard and Margaret Evans).

I am grateful to the following for permission to quote material:

Her Majesty Queen Elizabeth II for the diary entries of the Duke and Duchess of Connaught; A.P. Watts Ltd. on behalf of the National Trust for Places of Historical Interest or Natural Beauty for extracts from Rudyard Kipling's *Letters to the Family (Notes on a Recent Trip to Canada)* and *Something of Myself*; the University of Sussex and The National Trust for Places of Historical Interest or Natural Beauty for extracts from the letters of Rudyard Kipling; Lord Gowrie PC for the letter and draft autobiography of the first Earl of Gowrie; Sir Richard Carew Pole and the Cornwall Record Office for extracts from the diary of Lady Beatrice Pole-Carew; Mary Symon for the letters of Sir Josiah Symon; Canon Michael Saward for extracts from Captain Henry Kendall's *Adventures on the High Seas*; The Scout Association for extracts from the diary of Lord Baden-Powell; the National Archives of Canada for the diary of William Lyon Mackenzie King; Graham Baker for the letters of Florence Morgan; Miles Clark for the letters of Glenn Clark; Geoffrey Whiteley and the Black Dyke Band for portions of the diary of John Arthur Wood; Fegans for extracts of James Fegan's writings from *Loving and Serving*; Patricia Hope for the letters of Frank and Hetty Brooks; Brian Jones for the postcards of Henry Brown; John Owen for the memoirs of his father, steward Arthur Owen; The Salvation Army International Heritage Centre in London for extracts from *War Cry*; Noel Owens for the diary of Edith Jackson; Watchtower Bible and Tract Society of New York, Inc. for the letter of Charles Taze Russell; Maj. Ira Barrow of the Salvation Army's George Scott Railton Heritage Centre in Toronto for Capt. Edward Dodd's message and the postcard of Maj. George Attwell; the Manitoba Archives for the oral history recordings of Donald Craw; Helga (Israelson) Pearson for the story of Josephine Israelson; Yves Tremblay and Musée de la mer de Pointe-au-Père for extracts from certain letters of Henry Kendall; Tom Tumilty for the letter of Bernard Tumilty; and Joyce Gould for *A Trip on the Empress 1912*.

Special thanks are due to my wife Margaret for her patience and, for months on end, for putting up with the piles of paper that never seemed to get any smaller.

I owe a significant debt to Marion Kelch, Alberta playwright and *Empress* zealot, who interviewed former *Empress* passengers in Alberta and provided copies of ephemera and memorabilia to help illustrate the text. Her tireless energy and enthusiasm for this project helped make this book come alive.

And also to longtime *Empress* diver Philippe Beaudry, for generous access to his unparalleled collection of *Empress* ephemera and CPR nautical memorabilia, who happily shared with the author stories and anecdotes from half a lifetime's work.

Stephen Brooks, another *Empress* diver, also provided valuable illustrations and material at the last minute, for which I am very grateful. David Saint-Pierre, whose collection of *Empress* photographs is second to none, gave freely of his time and knowledge, and provided some of the key photos for this book.

Nancy Krajewsky deserves special mention for her critical reading of an early draft of the manuscript.

I am grateful to Susan Bashford who first proposed this book, and Campbell McCutcheon, my editor at Tempus Publishing, whose patience and skill helped make it a reality.

Finally, above all, a special thank you to the former *Empress* passengers whose recollections are still undimmed after all these years, and whose words have shed new light on the *Empress of Ireland*: Mary (Hill) McCullough; Joyce (Thompson) Gould; Bernard Blades; Vera (Knight) Way; and Gladys (French) Smith. You have spoken for all those who can no longer speak, and helped us touch the past.

Derek Grout
Montreal, Canada
October 2001

Introduction

Most books about the RMS *Empress of Ireland* focus, perhaps naturally, on the last fatal voyage in May 1914 that resulted in Canada's worst maritime disaster and the deaths of over a thousand people. Such books typically introduce a rich cast of characters – passengers and crew – and we follow their thoughts and actions over the last hours of the doomed ship's ninety-sixth voyage. At the end, the fate of each character is revealed to the reader, whose final impressions are a sense of great sorrow and tragedy, of families broken apart and lives needlessly lost.

Such an approach works well on the whole, but there are problems.

First, the ship sank in just fourteen chaotic minutes, some nine hours after leaving Quebec City, and so lacks the opportunity for high drama and legend that *Titanic* inspired. On the St Lawrence there were no gentlemanly cries of 'Women and children first!' There is nothing to make one proud, as Churchill was in 1912, that the strict observance of the great traditions of the sea reflected nothing but honour upon British civilization. On 29 May 1914, in the dark of night, it was a free-for-all, and surviving the *Empress* was, at best, a matter of luck.

Second, while the *Empress* carried some 'names', they were not in the same league as *Titanic*'s Col. John Jacob Astor, Isidor Straus and Benjamin Guggenheim and, hence, generate less interest. John Brinnin, writing in 1971, cruelly dismissed the passengers of the *Empress* as 'nothing better than… a lot of middle-class Anglo-Saxons and a long roster of Salvation Army officers and executives from one end of Canada to the other.'

Third, such an approach tends to ignore the fact that this ship, unlike *Titanic* which sank on her maiden voyage, actually *had* a history. She was a working vessel and between 1906 and 1914 she and her twin sister made an important contribution to the social and economic history of Canada, carrying tens of thousands of immigrants to lives in the New World. With the tragedy of May 1914, it becomes easy to overlook the notion of the *Empress* as a cheerful and popular ship, changing many lives for the better, carrying settlers, newlyweds and mothers with children to fathers who had already gone ahead.

Fourth, we get no feeling for how the *Empress of Ireland* and her crew related to the people and the ports they called home, both in England and Canada.

Fifth, apart from Henry Kendall, her last master, one learns almost nothing about the men who commanded the pride of the Canadian Pacific's Atlantic service. Who were they, how did they come to this vessel, and where did they go later?

Last, despite a mass of detail about the ship, one does not have enough information to form a firm opinion as to what it was *really* like aboard the *Empress of Ireland*. Were the beds soft? Was the food good? Were the stewards friendly? How did she handle in rough seas? What changes, if any, took place over time?

This book seeks to answer some of these questions.

In the Edwardian era, an age distinguished by mobility, global communications and a growing middle class, the *Empress of Ireland* transported a marvelous cross-section of people from all walks of life: businessmen, Olympic athletes, British and Japanese royalty, landed gentry, prelates, scientists and physicians, artists, diplomats, soldiers, war heroes (including three VCs), future Nobel laureates, politicians, actors, tourists, day labourers, farmers, students, and servants. Though it was they who defined the ship and helped gave it life, there was a certain reciprocity at work. In many cases the ship helped define their lives.

The years before the First World War were a time of high literacy rates in western Europe and the Americas and, fortunately for the historian, a number of these people recorded their impressions for posterity. Also fortunately for the historian, the history of the *Empress of Ireland* is a finite one, spanning ninety-five completed transatlantic round-trip voyages over eight years. It is thus easier to treat compared to, say, the career of her sister, the *Empress of Britain,* which ended in 1929. Nonetheless it is still an amazingly complex story, defined by the thousands of people whose lives all had this ship, even if little else, in common.

This book therefore takes a different approach and is intended to complement previous works on the *Empress*. I have tried to fill out the history of the ship using wherever possible the first-hand accounts of passengers and crew. From a variety of sources, not just maritime museums, a representative selection of letters, diaries, postcards and interviews show how people felt about their trip aboard the ship and describe their activities. Such sources offer an unparalleled glimpse into a rarefied world of power and privilege, and into the common, everyday world of second and third class passengers.

Who better, after all, to tell part of the *Empress*' story than those who were there, who marvelled at the sight of icebergs, shivered in the dank fogs off Newfoundland, gathered around the piano for an impromptu sing-along, stood on decks plunging and rolling in the North Atlantic swells, and inhaled the mixture of coal smoke and salt tang? Reading their contemporary accounts or interviewing them 85-plus years later, one has a sense of adventure and wonder.

Their stories and recollections give back to the *Empress* a life and energy that has somehow been missing from narratives that focus on the disaster. One suddenly sees her in a new light, for she is no longer a ship of tragedy and death. By some feat of magic she has been transformed into a place of excitement, laughter and music, and one can forget for a moment the crumpled hull on the bottom of the St Lawrence.

That such an approach has not been tried before is hardly surprising, given the difficulty of locating original material and securing the permissions necessary to reproduce it. As well, I have used contemporary newspaper and other sources to provide additional details of what it was like to travel aboard one of the premier vessels serving eastern Canada in the golden age of steamships.

This book does not attempt to recount the details of every voyage made by the *Empress*, even though Henry Kendall claimed that 'One voyage is never the same as any other, even though the same seas be traversed and the same landfalls made.' To reconstruct every voyage would be Herculean in nature and would add little to our overall understanding of the ship. Instead I have used selected material to convey a general impression of what it was like to travel and work on the ship.

I have drawn on the resources of libraries and archives on three continents, as well as the papers and collective family memories of a score of individuals, for the history of the *Empress of Ireland* is also to be found in attics and heirloom cabinets. It is remarkable that so much has survived, and what may be ferreted out with luck, patience and some skill – in that order.

Again somewhat differently, I have not focused much attention on artifacts raised from the *Empress* and preserved in two maritime museums in Quebec and by hundreds of individuals. Such objects – brass portholes, bridge telephones, intact beer bottles, floor tiles, dinner plates – all are interesting in their own right and certainly have a story to tell about the *Empress*. But they can tell little about the people who sailed or worked the ship, and to me this is an important distinction. History is, I believe, largely about people and their times, less so about objects or artifacts.

To do justice to the *Empress* and the context of her times, this book considers a host of related topics as well, including the ocean mail service, European immigration, and other vessels like the *Empress of Britain* and various Allan Line boats. Lack of space precludes anything more than a superficial look at these areas.

Marine engineers and techno-junkies will probably be disappointed in this volume, for I have tended to focus on the history of the ship rather than the minutiae of its technology. This is not my specialty and this work is aimed at a wider audience.

Without doubt many more stories of the ship still lie buried in family documents in England, Canada and the United States. The author therefore invites readers with further *Empress* material and photographs to communicate with him through the publisher.

In practice, a similar history could be constructed for any one of the dozen-odd steamships plying the North Atlantic routes to Canada during the Edwardian era. None of these would match the romance and tragedy surrounding the *Empress of Ireland*, for liners lost at sea have a singular mystique, and they have acquired a special following among the public at large.

In *Forgotten Empress*, David Zeni expressed the hope that others would improve and build upon his research. This I have tried to do. I can only hope this book does adequate justice to the memory and the story of this great ship.

In the text I have used 'Empress' to mean the *Empress of Ireland*. To avoid confusion, I refer to *Empress of Britain*, her sister ship, by the full name, although contemporary newspapers often referred to the vessels as simply the *Ireland* and the *Britain*.

Readers will note that many of the newspaper sources are from English-language dailies in eastern Canada, notably Montreal and Quebec City. In a bilingual province with French-language papers in both cities I had a selection of sources from which to choose. If I have selected more from English newspapers, I did so for two reasons. First, the English press had better day-to-day coverage of the shipping world in many, though not all, instances relating to the *Empress*. And, more importantly, the *Empress* crew integrated themselves into the English community in Quebec City, whose activities were reported in the local English papers.

I have also tended to use Canadian, rather than British newspapers, for the simple reason that the two *Empresses* were the premier liners serving eastern Canada at the time and they received more coverage in the Canadian press than in Liverpool, where they were just two of many fine vessels calling that city their home port.

I have kept the names of places as they were commonly used in 1914 (*e.g.* Father Point rather than Pointe-au-Père) and I have also retained the old Imperial measures, rather than convert them to modern metric equivalents. Military ranks and titles of persons referred to in the text are correct for the time. References to 'miles' are nautical miles (equivalent to 6,080 feet, 1.15 statute miles, or 1.852 kilometers) unless the context is plainly otherwise. Also as a matter of convention, I have used RMS *Empress of Ireland*, even though contemporary accounts often used SS *Empress of Ireland*. 'Company' refers, of course, to the Canadian Pacific Railway. 'Starboard' and 'port' are used, rather than 'right' and 'left' respectively, as this was the practice of the day in the British and American merchant services. References to 'Quebec' generally refer to Quebec City, *La vieille capitale* – the Ancient Capital, rather than the province.

Gold-based currencies in the pre-First World War period did not fluctuate much. In 1911, for example, £1 was equal to $4.85 in Canadian or American currency, the latter two being essentially at par. Apart from one or two instances, I have not made sterling/dollar conversions in the text. As a *very* rough approximation, multiply pre-1914 sterling prices by 45 to obtain the equivalent in pounds in the year 2001. For dollar amounts, the multiplier is approximately 20. Thus, for example, a donation of £10 to the *Empress* relief fund would be equivalent to a donation today of £450, and a one-way second class *Empress* ticket costing $45 would be about the same as $900. (Note: the multiplication does not work if pre-1914 sterling amounts are first converted to dollars.) For those unfamiliar with Britain's pre-decimal currency, the pound was divided into twenty shillings, with each shilling further divided into twelve pence. The penny itself was divided into half-pennies and farthings.

It should also be noted that the dialogue in the text has not been 'novelized.' Any words shown as a direct quote by an individual are his or her precise words.

Last, despite the formal titles of 'Saloon' or 'First Cabin,' 'Second Saloon' or 'Second Cabin' (for the CPR used all four), I have used the simpler and less pretentious descriptions of first and second class. These terms sound better to a modern reader, and they were often employed by newspapers of the era including, on occasion, even the staid *Times* of London. Third class, though often mistakenly termed 'steerage' by newspapers and, on occasion, the CPR and passengers themselves, was in fact a decided improvement over the old steerage accommodations.

As every historian knows, there are always maddening inconsistencies between various versions of events, sometimes even for the most basic facts. While every effort has been made to check and re-check the facts in this work against the most reliable contemporary sources, careful readers will notice that this history does not agree in all respects with other works on the *Empress* which may have used other source material.

1
The World of the *Empress of Ireland*

The ribbon of blacktop stretches arrow-straight to the horizon, crossing a succession of close-cropped fields of wheat, hay and corn. Reapers and combines kick up billows of dust as they gather the abundant golden harvest. The air is crisp and the sky a surreal shade of blue, punctuated by fleecy clouds. It is September in the year 2000 and the trees have started to change colour, the brilliant annual rite of fall that heralds the approach of winter here on the eastern edge of the Canadian prairies.

The road is almost empty on this sun-splashed day, and there is little to occupy my mind as the Manitoba scenery slowly unwinds. Leaving Winnipeg and heading southwest, I pass through a succession of small farming towns, each marked by a grain elevator.

If the *Empress of Ireland* has a tangible legacy, it is to be found on the Canadian prairies. Scattered on a thousand-mile arc reaching westward to the Rocky Mountains, the names of hundreds of villages and hamlets betray the origins of their founders who arrived in the great wave of immigration at the beginning of the twentieth century. The settlers – British, German, Scandinavian, Russian, Austro-Hungarian – arrived on ships like the *Empress*, and faint echoes of those vessels can still be found here, fifteen hundred miles and more from the St Lawrence.

I slow for Carman, population twenty-eight hundred. It is a typical Manitoba town with wide streets overhung by shade trees, neat homes, low-rise buildings, a school, various banks, a scattering of churches, a couple of restaurants. And, in the middle of town, a modern two-story brick building, home to a number of senior citizens.

One of these is Mary (Hill) McCullough, who travelled aboard the *Empress* as a young girl and has agreed to be interviewed for this book. She greets me with a smile and ushers me into a tidy apartment, introducing me to her daughter Patricia who has stopped by for the morning. Mary is frail with age and walks with a cane, but she is full of life and possesses a good sense of humour, despite her athritis and gout

I arrange my papers and set up a tape recorder on the dining table. 'I knew you were coming,' the ninety-five-year-old calls from the kitchen, 'so I baked a cake.' Her blue eyes twinkle with amusement as she cuts a slice and pours tea into a china cup, proudly refusing any help. The tape recorder is switched on and our conversation begins, dealing at first with Mary's early background. At first I am apprehensive, for memories are fallible, fading and distorting with the passage of time. After a few moments, I relax. It is clear that Mary has been blessed with an extraordinary memory. And that her trip in the *Empress* made a great impression, for she recalls the events of long ago with clarity and precision.

I scribble untidy notes, hoping the cassette recorder is working properly. Mary is a witness, a living link to the *Empress of Ireland*. When she speaks, it is on behalf of the 186,848 people who were once *Empress* passengers. She may be the only one left now, I think. Later, against all odds, I will find other former passengers whose stories will add to this narrative but, at this moment, Mary is my only direct tie to the ship. An hour passes in an eyeblink… then two. I change cassettes and our wide-ranging discussion resumes. Mary's animated voice sweeps away the veil of time and takes me back to a long-vanished world… The Edwardian era… *La belle époque*… regardless of the label, historians have always had trouble with the first fifteen years of the turbulent twentieth century.

Looking back, it was easy for North Americans and Europeans to characterize the beginning of the century as a golden age, the last romantic years. It was a time when everything seemed simpler and

Left: *Mary Hill, aged five, prior to emigrating to Canada aboard the* Empress *on 3 June 1910. (Voyage 47W) (Mary Hill McCullough)* Right: *Mary Hill, in the summer of 2000. (photograph by Institutional Promotions of Canada Ltd)*

more ordered – an age of innocence. The pace of life was slower and people knew and were content to keep their places in society. Such nostalgic over-simplifications are probably a deliberate distortion of memory, a reaction to the horrors that would later unfold and make those first years seem so calm in comparison. What Talleyrand had said of 1789 was repeated after the Great War had blighted Europe, that those who were not alive in 1914 would never know how sweet life could be.

In reality the Edwardian era, which began with the accession of Victoria's eldest son in 1901 and ended with a fatal gunshot in the obscure Bosnian town of Sarajevo in June 1914, was anything but simple. Nor, in many respects, was it much different than later decades of this troubled century. It was called an era of peace, *Pax Britannica*, yet it gave rise to the First World War. It was a time of order, but bred social chaos. It was a time of great optimism, in which the seeds of pessimism found root. It projected an illusion of stability and permanence, and was blown away in the whirlwind of war. The period has a curiously 'modern' feel about it, for it has more in common with the latter half of the twentieth century than the 1880s, which preceded it by only two decades. John Maynard Keynes, writing about Europe before 1914, noted that:

> The inhabitant of London could order by telephone, sipping his morning tea in bed, the various products of the whole earth, in such quantity as he might see fit, and reasonably expect their early delivery upon his doorstep; he could adventure his wealth in the natural resources and new enterprises of any quarter of the world.

It was a time of great innovation and social upheaval, counterbalanced by the stifling weight of conservatism and social convention. It was a time of justice and injustice, simple patriotism, colonies

Mary (Hill) McCullough and the author examining a sample of teak decking from the Empress of Ireland, *autumn 2000. (Author's collection)*

and spheres of influence, and European empires that spanned the globe. The Great Powers fought small-scale wars in far-away places, signed interlocking alliances and made an uneasy peace among themselves. It was a time when, with a few exceptions, a ruling class governed by right of birth rather than by merit, although the progressive views of a rising middle class had seriously to be reckoned with for the first time.

The political landscape has changed almost beyond recognition in the past eighty-five years, when something recognizable as democracy existed only in a handful of nations, led by the United States. Empires were the rule rather than the exception and, by 1910, Europeans controlled eighty-five percent of the world's land surface. Largest by far of the empires was the British, which extended over eleven million square miles, one-quarter of the globe, and included 400 million people, one-fourth of the world's population. The empires are gone now, mourned by few, though the last to be dismembered was the Russian Empire, which endured in various guises until the early 1990s.

Empires were more than just about colonies and markets for finished goods from the parent country. The empires arose also from a firm belief in the cultural superiority of Europeans over the rest of mankind, and that enlightened Europeans had an obligation to bring the blessings of 'civilization' to 'backward' peoples. Lord Curzon once described the British Empire as the greatest instrument for good that the world had seen, but it was Bombay-born Rudyard Kipling who put it better: '…to carry light and civilization into the dark places of the world, to touch the mind of Asia and of Africa with the ethical ideas of Europe.'

The century opened with a war in South Africa, a revolt in China that was soon quelled with the aid of an international peacekeeping mission, and a host of brush-fire wars. As the first fifteen years of the new century unfolded, localized wars broke out in Europe as well. Italy provoked a war with Turkey in 1911 and wrested control of the latter's North African provinces. Greece and other Balkan

RMS Empress of Ireland *underway. Davidson Brothers 'Real Photographic' series postcard, c.1908. This is an oversized postcard and measures 10¼ x 5⅛ inches. (Sheila Taipale)*

states fought two wars in 1912 and 1913 over the question of former Turkish territories and access to the sea. Such disputes, when they threatened to get out of hand, were settled by sensible diplomats around a conference table when the main powers – Britain, France, Germany, Austria-Hungary, and Russia – had had enough.

Some of the main socio-political causes of the Edwardian era seem, with the benefit of hindsight, to be so right and self-evident that one wonders why they generated such heated opposition at the time. The enfranchisement of women in Britain, for example, took so long and generated such emotions that one is led to speculate what might have been accomplished had this not consumed so much of the national attention and polarized a generation.

To almost everyone on both sides of the Atlantic, it was an age of wonder and optimism. North Americans and Europeans had good reason to fall in love with technology, for hardly a day seemed to pass without some breathtaking advance in almost every field of human endeavor, and the future appeared limitless. As *The Oxford History of the Twentieth Century* notes, for the first time advances in technology seemed to promise mankind freedom from the timeless scourges of poverty, disease, famine and war. Paradoxically, these hopes for the future were offset by fears stemming from the apparent disintegration of traditional values and social structure, the same factors which had held societies together in the face of just such scourges in the past.

After depression had blighted the 1890s, the Edwardian era offered prosperity to many, a direct result of improvements in the standard of living caused by industrial growth and technology. Technology had become synonymous with progress, and the watchwords of the period seemed to be 'bigger', 'better', 'faster' – in everything.

Speed became a new pleasure. The year 1901 saw the Paris-to-Berlin auto race won by a car with pneumatic tires at an average speed of 44.5mph, and that same year over a thousand Americans were killed in motoring accidents. A Stanley Steamer set a record at Daytona in 1906 of 127.66mph and the 1907 Paris-Peking automobile rally was won by two Italians and, as the Edwardian era drew to a close, events like the French Grand Prix motor race attracted thousands of spectators.

The typical male Briton in 1900 was better housed, better fed, better paid, better educated (with free basic schooling) and better represented in politics than his forebears could have imagined.

Despite this, huge problems remained to be overcome. In 1902 just nine percent of boys were still in school at the age of fourteen, and only one in 200 would go to university. Britain had over a million paupers in 1908, and the same number of able-bodied Britons were without work. One British study showed that thirty percent of townspeople and forty percent of rural inhabitants were living in poverty in the pre-war period. Despite a burgeoning population and a global empire, there were simply not enough jobs in Britain. Unskilled men raced for spades at building sites, while on the docks men fought for work discs thrown from a foreman's cage.

Coal, steam, iron and railrways, the drivers of growth in the nineteenth century, were about to be replaced. In the early years of the new century, the foundations for the future were established: oil, electricity, telephones, wireless and radio, internal combustion engines, air travel, plastics, synthetic fabrics, genetics, and sub-atomic physics. Even rocketry, for American Robert Goddard first proposed in 1909 a rocket fueled by hydrogen and liquid oxygen.

Almost overnight, cities everywhere were transformed. Homes and industries were wired for electricity, and the electric light and a host of labour-saving devices changed the world in ways that few inventions before or since have done. In places like New York and Chicago, new buildings called skyscrapers were being erected. Made possible by the nineteenth century developments of elevators and steel girders, in 1902 New York's 'Flatiron' building became the world's tallest structure, supplanted in 1909 by the fifty-story Metropolitan Life tower, itself replaced by the sixty-story Woolworth Building in 1913, which would retain its title for seventeen years.

City streets and country roads were being taken over by motor cars, an innovation most urban dwellers first welcomed as a way to get rid of horses. Festoons of wires announced that the telephone had become as indispensable in the home as in the place of business. By 1907 more than six million telephones were in service in the United States, and the Bell companies would shortly embark on the first trans-continental telephone network.

Despite the technology, the era witnessed its share of natural disasters and accidents. Newspaper headlines from the period show the Edwardian era was little different than our own in this respect. The San Francisco earthquake (1906), sinking of submarines like the German *U-3* (1911) and the British *A-3* (1912) all have their modern parallels, as do the era's train wrecks, mining disasters, air crashes, typhoons and hurricanes, volcanic eruptions, auto accidents, epidemics, famine and flooding.

Other stories as well from the era seem to be lifted from the newspapers of our own time: large-scale emigration of Russian Jews to the United States and the Holy Land; clashes between Arabs and Jews in Palestine; ethnic and religious conflict between Serbs and Albanians in the Balkans; international disaster relief and peacekeeping missions; launch of a new Zeppelin in Germany; sectarian violence in Northern Ireland; breakup of US business giants under anti-trust legislation; the Dalai Lama fleeing to India ahead of Chinese troops; and, sadly, school shootings.

New forms of popular entertainment emerged as well. Thanks to the development of moving pictures in 1895 by the Lumière brothers in France, people flocked to newly built picture palaces, and film production companies were starting to make full-length movies. The western had become suddenly popular with *The Great Train Robbery* and spawned a genre of movies that would last into the twenty-first century. In 1907 the first film makers moved to a pleasant suburb of Los Angeles named Hollywood, lured by a good climate, abundant sunshine and cheap land.

Sound recording gave birth to another new industry, bringing music into the daily lives of millions through hand-cranked gramophones. Records by international stars like Enrico Caruso were soon selling a million copies each.

Fads swept Europe and the Americas at intervals. The tango arrived about 1911, an import from Buenos Aires, and was considered daring and slightly scandalous. That same year, hotel guests in London danced to the syncopated rhythms of ragtime, imported from America. Postcard collecting became an international craze on both sides of the Atlantic, and family postcard albums were the second most important book after the Bible in many households, kept in the parlor so they could be shown to guests.

In the skies were the latest wonders of the age, airships and airplanes. In Germany Count Zeppelin was perfecting lighter than air dirigibles filled with hydrogen, while two inventive bicycle mechanics from Ohio first flew in December 1903 on a sandy hilltop off the North Carolina coast. Progress in the new field of aviation would be rapid, and the first primitive helicopter flew briefly in France in 1907. Frenchman Louis Blériot flew from Calais to Dover in 1909, ending the historic isolation of the British Isles, and the first aeronautical map was published in 1911 showing air routes across France. In 1911 the altitude record was set at 13,800 feet by Frenchman Roland Garros. Two years later it was 20,000 feet. In 1913 Garros astounded the world by flying from France to Tunisia, some 468 miles in eight hours, thus becoming the first man to cross the Mediterranean by plane, while that same year in Russia Igor Sikorsky built and flew a giant four-engine aircraft he called *Le Grand*. Aviation became a military weapon for the first time, when Italian airmen in 1911 dropped bombs in Libya against Turkish troops.

The epicentre of the world was London, the largest and richest city in the world, with a population of 6.6 million. Bragged *The Times* in 1913, 'London is no longer the capital of Britain, but of the world.' And so it seemed.

It was the financial and banking capital of the world, where companies and nations went to raise money. Over the previous fifty years Britain had created, almost single-handedly, the first truly global economy whose underpinnings were railroads, steamships, canals and the telegraph. Sea routes, essential for the worldwide trade of raw materials and finished goods, were protected by the Royal Navy and, by 1914, Britain owned about one-half the world's merchant steam tonnage.

Money flowed around the world on a scale not seen before, thanks to stable currencies and convertibility based on the gold standard. British savings financed mines, railroads and other infrastructure projects in all parts of the world, so that these areas could, in turn, produce food for British workers and raw material for British factories. By 1913 more than one-third of British wealth was invested overseas in the Dominions, Canada, Australia, New Zealand and South Africa.

Transcontinental railroads, first in the US, later in Canada, and finally the trans-Siberian in 1904, interconnected with steamships to provide fast links between countries and continents.

Tying this global economy together were two essential communications links: the postal service, and a worldwide network of undersea cables and wireless telegraph stations. At long last the tyranny of distance had been conquered; the latest news from London could be flashed around the world at the speed of light and appear in the next morning's paper.

London was also the social capital of the world, for the political and social worlds were closely intertwined. It was an era of glorious, conspicuous consumption, where the wealthy lavished fortunes on a dizzying season of entertainment and diversion. The rich flaunted their wealth openly. They built homes that looked like chateaux, equipped with the latest comforts and conveniences like electricity, running water, water closet, telephone, central hot-water heating, icebox, vacuum cleaners, gas range with oven, electric washing machine, and early air conditioners, all staffed by a small army of domestics who earned a pittance. Things were enough out of hand that by 1913 even *The Times* condemned 'The craze for costly and luxurious living which has wrought so much mischief in England in recent years.'

Such displays were intended to convey to 'decent people' the assurance that everything was for the best in the best of all possible worlds. For the affluent, it was a beautiful epoch, one that seemed destined to last forever. Stefan Zweig, in *The World of Yesterday*, wrote: 'No one thought of wars, revolutions and upheavals. Radicalism and violence were unthinkable in that age of reason.' Though describing Austria-Hungary, he could have been writing for any western nation of the era.

London was also a place for Americans to spend their money and, if possible, marry off their daughters to titled aristocrats. New York, the American metropolis of 3.4 million in 1900, if anyone in Europe condescended to note, was considered a brash upstart, filled with American millionaires and the poor of Europe, who had fled the slums of Europe for the slums of America.

The Edwardian era was an overdressed world, where a gentleman could not even think of going out without his walking stick and kid gloves. If a gentleman believed in anything, one later writer commented, it was in the value of the pound sterling, Savile Row tailors, and an Oxford accent.

European Royals and their friends moved in well-ordered social circles: taking the waters at Marienbad, the races at Longchamps and Ascot, the Royal Box at Wimbledon, vacations at Biarritz or Cannes, regatta week at Cowes. Grand hotels sprang up all over the continent to cater to their tastes, and even today places like The Ritz and The Savoy in London, along with The Plaza in New York, impart an echo of the Edwardian era. The carefree comings and goings of the titled and the famous were printed in the Court Circular and social page of *The Times*, and were devoured avidly by a public obsessed with wealth and position, the same way people of the 1990s followed the lives of rock and movie stars.

London also dominated the literary world, a magnet that attracted to its stages the most celebrated actors and writers of the day.

Society, particularly in the United Kingdom, was highly stratified, with little movement possible between the different classes. But change was in the air, and during this time in Europe and America the first halting steps were taken to bridge the gap between rich and poor. Progressive legislation for old age and sickness insurance was adopted, along with collective bargaining procedures in a variety of countries. Anti-trust legislation and the rise of democratic unions would curb the worst abuses of capitalism.

In America, things were different and, as now, money proved to be the great equalizer, and there was plenty of that filtering through all levels of society. The American *Review of Reviews* announced gravely that the decade had 'witnessed more money-making than any other in history.' The nouveau riche in New York, who had amassed fortunes in oil, railroads, mining and shipping, were admitted to the highest levels of society, although somewhat grudgingly at first by the old establishment.

Paris, a city of three million, had become the centre of art and fashion, and was the liveliest, most vibrant city in Europe. Londoners went to Paris to enjoy themselves, away from the social conventions and restrictions of England. In nightclubs like Moulin Rouge, dancers performed the frenzied can-can, a dance whose roots came from seedy Montmartre.

In this period some of Earth's last frontiers were conquered. American Robert Peary reached the North Pole in 1909, while in 1911 Norwegian explorer Roald Amundsen beat Briton Robert Falcon Scott to the South Pole by a matter of days.

On both sides of the Atlantic, with increased leisure time and disposable income, professional and amateur sports flourished as never before. Golf and tennis, formerly the preserve of the rich, blossomed into middle-class crazes. In Britain, association football (soccer) had become firmly entrenched as a new religion for the masses, with matches at every conceivable level, while North Americans followed baseball and a variety of other sports.

In almost every country stark contrasts and paradoxes existed, a reflection of societies in rapid transition. In this period of low or non-existent taxes, it was possible to amass staggering wealth, yet most European nations had large numbers of urban poor whose ranks were swelled by successive waves of migration from farms to factories.

It was possible to find examples of great individual philanthropy. In the United States, Scottish-born industrialist Andrew Carnegie retired in 1901 and began to give away his fortune of $350 million. So great was the sum that by the time of his death in 1919 he had not succeeded.

On every side a host of conflicting ideologies competed loudly, sometimes violently, for attention. Anarchists, nihilists, Marxists, social democrats, liberals, conservatives, monarchists, republicans, militarists, Zionists, secularists, advocates of universal suffrage, prohibitionists, pacifists, free-trade advocates and so on... each one a thread in a complex social tapestry.

Although almost no one recognized it at the time, the balance of power had shifted from the Old to the New World. By 1900 the American economy was already, by far, the world leader. The brash American republic of seventy-six million people had half the world's railway mileage, shipped half its freight, extracted one-half of its oil, mined a third of its gold, and forged one-third of its steel. In the decade from 1900 to 1910, the annual industrial growth rate in United States was almost seven times that of Britain. By 1910 American steel production had surpassed that of Britain, France and Germany combined. Two years later, the industrial output of the United States exceeded the three main European nations combined.

Within Europe itself the balance was shifting. Though Britain had pioneered the Industrial Revolution, as the twentieth century progressed Germany had become the leading European industrial power, so that by 1913 Germany outproduced Britain in steel and iron, and nearly matched Britain in coal output. The German Empire, despite its ultraconservative monarch, Wilhelm II, emerged on the world's stage as the most modern and progressive nation in Europe.

American businessmen proved they were ready to compete on the global stage, and US companies began setting up offices and plants in Britain, Germany and Russia, something their British counterparts had done with reluctance, if at all.

In Detroit a visionary named Henry Ford revolutionized the auto business (and industrial production in general) by introducing a moving assembly line and strict interchangeability of parts. His company introduced its universal car, the Model T, in 1908, as he put it, 'for the great multitude, constructed of the best materials after the simplest designs modern engineering can devise, so low in price that no man making a good salary will be unable to own one.' By 1914 the Ford Motor Company would make over 300,000 cars a years in the United States, more than half of US vehicle production that year. In 1914 the car sold for $550, thirty-five percent less than in 1908.

Oil, discovered in quantity in Texas and Oklahoma in the early years of the century, was discovered in Persia in 1908. By 1913 a 135-mile pipeline connected the oil fields to a refinery on Abadan Island and the following year the production company signed a contract to supply the Royal Navy.

On the oceans of the world, things were changing as well. Sail had long since yielded to steam on the North Atlantic, and had been in decline since 1843 when *Great Britain* became the first transatlantic passenger steamship to be driven by a screw propeller. Each year larger and faster cargo and passenger vessels were launched, and they revolutionized trans-oceanic transportation in the same way jumbo jets changed the world of aviation seventy years later. Freight and insurance rates fell, journey times were reduced and schedules became more regular and less dependent on the whims of weather. The more rates fell, the more goods were shipped, requiring more vessels.

Like hotels, the great liners became ever more luxurious for a discriminating clientele. Indeed, the ships came to resemble giant floating hotels, rivaling anything ashore in terms of luxury and cuisine, catering to clients who preferred to forget they were even on a ship. Luxury became an end in itself, the means to attract the wealthy with sybaritic cuisine, ever-larger cabins and the latest in comforts, like hot and cold running water and private bathrooms. Such ships were a calculated blend of art and technology, the marvels of the age and the largest man-made moving objects ever made. In terms of technology they were the equivalent of the Space Shuttle or the International Space Station to later generations.

Refrigeration on ships changed the nature of global trade. By 1900 New Zealand was exporting more than four million frozen sheep and lamb carcasses to Britain, while Australia, a longtime exporter of wool, could now ship meat and vegetables. Argentina, long an exporter of hides and bones, became one of the world's greatest exporters of beef.

On the Atlantic, capturing the symbolic Blue Riband for the fastest crossing became a matter of national prestige, and vessels were built as much for speed as anything else. Cunard, which had lost the title in 1889, regained it in May 1893 with *Campania*'s passage of 5 days 17 hours and 27 minutes between Sandy Hook and Queenstown, though she later lost it to her sister *Lucania*. Things had come a long way since Cunard's *Britannia* set a new record in 1840 between Liverpool and Halifax: 12 days and 10 hours.

With their country's aspirations to become a major maritime nation, German companies determined to make their mark in the North Atlantic and a full-fledged speed contest ensued. Germans were elated when Norddeutscher Lloyd's (NDL) *Kaiser Wilhelm der Grosse*, the first four-stack liner, wrested both the east – and westbound – Blue Ribands from *Lucania* in September 1897.

Britons chafed as Hamburg-Amerika's new *Deutschland* broke the old records in August 1900, in turn broken by NDL's *Kaiser Wilhelm II* in 1903, thus seeming to herald a new era of German domination of the seas, formerly an all-British preserve. British pride was saved when, in 1907, Cunard's turbine-powered greyhounds of the Atlantic, the superliners *Lusitania* and, later, *Mauretania* set new records of their own. *Mauretania*'s would stand for the next twenty years, with speeds in excess of twenty-six knots.

In a military sense, Britain's Royal Navy ruled supreme, not having been defeated in almost a hundred years. It was the navy, Britain's senior service, that maintained the trading routes which bound the global empire together. The Royal Navy pioneered the switch from coal to oil as a fuel, having signed long-term contracts with the Anglo-Persian producer, though by 1914 the conversion was not yet complete. Mercantile shipping fleets were far slower to convert, as a result of the costs involved. By 1914 just three percent of the world's steam tonnage burned oil, and significant numbers of coal-fired vessels would be found on the world's oceans for the next thirty years.

Powerplants were in a state of evolution as well. The merits of steam turbines, developed by Charles Parsons, were proven in 1897 when *Turbinia*, the world's first steam-turbine vessel, reached the unthinkable speed of 34.5 knots. The battleship HMS *Dreadnought* was equipped with turbines by a visionary Royal Navy, though the new powerplants were slowly taken up in commercial steamships. As with coal, merchant fleets continued to be equipped with the older reciprocating steam engines for many years. In 1906, for example, British yards launched just twelve turbine commercial vessels, compared to 803 powered by conventional reciprocating engines. The diesel, mainstay of today's shipping fleets, was in its infancy. In 1910 Hamburg-Amerika, having tested the concept on a small cargo boat, was scaling up to two larger steamers with 3,000hp engines, capable of 12 knots, though the first motor vessel built in Britain, *Jutlandia*, was not constructed until 1912.

New construction techniques for steel vessels were introduced in this period. In Britain Joseph Isherwood patented a technique of longitudinal framing, and the first vessel constructed using the Isherwood System was the *Paul Paix* in 1908. This new system gave great fore-and-aft strength to a hull and, as we shall see, it has an important role to play in this narrative. The Isherwood system differed considerably from conventional ship construction. In most ships, the frames that supported the outside plating stood vertically, at right angles to the keel. With the Isherwood design, they ran longitudinally from stem to stern, almost parallel to the water line. The result was an extraordinarily strong vessel, designed to withstand head-on impacts with little or no damage.

Above all, the Edwardian era survives in modern memory as a time of great movements of people from the Old to the New World. With the advent of regular passenger steam service in the 1880s, it was now fast, safe, convenient and relatively inexpensive to travel to places like the Americas, Australia and Africa.

The world was in motion like never before, and the period from 1900 to 1914 witnessed a massive hemorrhage of people from Europe to all corners of the globe. The United States was the main destination of European emigrants, inspired by Emma Lazarus' famed exhortation 'Give me your tired, your hungry, your huddled masses yearning to be free,' and the shipping lanes between Europe and North America carried more people and freight than the rest of the world's oceans together.

In the United States, the new arrivals transformed the northern cities, manned the factories and sparked a ten-year boom, though they were not always welcomed. The year 1905 marked a watershed in US immigration. For the first time more than a million people entered the United States. Between 1903 and 1914 the number of new arrivals was never less than three-quarters of a million people annually, so that the country's population increased 17% between 1900 and 1910, from 76 to 92 million. In states like Wisconsin, fully one-quarter of the populace was foreign born. Overall, one American in seven had been born abroad, and in cities like New York, Boston, Detroit and Chicago, three-quarters of the inhabitants consisted of immigrants and their American-born children.

In Canada a parallel immigration took place. In the decade between 1901 and 1911 the population of Britain's first Dominion rose from more than five million to just over seven million. Two million new Canadians, most of humble origin and limited means, added new ethnic dimensions to the country and helped re-define the nation and its sense of identity.

Canada actively sought out new immigrants in Europe, though many European nations, apart from Britain, were hostile to Canadian immigration agents and tried with various degrees of success to limit the outflow of their citizens. Most successful in this respect was France. Suspicious of the newly united Germany, its rising population and economic strength, the Third Republic curtailed emigration. Just thirty thousand of the 1.5 million immigrants to Canada in the decade 1901-1911 were French-speaking.

Immigrants to Canada were markedly different than those to the United States. A 1911 study showed that for 1909, almost 79% of immigrants to Canada were from northwestern Europe, compared to just 27% for the United States. In that year Canada welcomed two Britons for every person from the Continent; the US received two Britons for every thirteen persons from Continental Europe. Between 1900 and 1910, Canada had admitted almost one in four of its population. In the same period, the US admitted 8.4 million – one in eight of its population.

In terms of education, one in ten immigrants to Canada were illiterate; for the United States, the ratio was three in ten. In terms of religion, Protestant immigrants to Canada outnumbered Catholics by three to one, almost exactly the converse of the US

'A new star has risen upon the horizon,' Canada's Prime Minister Wilfrid Laurier had proclaimed. 'And it is toward that star that every immigrant… now turns his gaze.' And come they did in those years, lured by a westerner, Clifford Sifton who, as Minister of the Interior, staged the largest and most successful campaign to attract immigrants in Canada's history. His ministry sent out millions of pamphlets in a dozen European languages that promoted the virtues of farming in Canada, though not a single pamphlet mentioned problems like drought, hail, grasshoppers or wheat rust.

The Last, Best West was a typical pamphlet title (printed in eight languages), while another pamphlet of 1909 famously proclaimed 'The 20th century is the century of Canada.' There were others: *Canada, The Land of Opportunity*; *Alberta Red, the Winter Wheat; Canada as seen through Scottish Eyes*; and *Domestic Servant Pamphlet* are just four of a host of titles. In response, the immigrants arrived in tens of thousands each year from every corner of Europe. By 1905, for the first time in half a century, Canada was out-drawing the United States as the preferred destination of British emigrants. The Canadian Immigration Office on Charing Cross Road, London, measured its success by the fact that in 1900 just 1,200 from the British Isles settled in Canada. Five years later that number reached more than 65,000, and peaked in 1912-1913, when 150,000 Britons flooded into Canada, three-quarters of them from England.

The lure of free land made Canada the fastest growing country in the world in the decade from 1901 to 1911. Immigrants made the country rich with a five-fold increase in wheat production, turning Canada into one of the world's breadbaskets with its No.1 hard wheat. Prairie cities like Calgary, Edmonton and Regina that had not existed until the railway pushed westward in the 1880s, grew more than ten-fold in the decade between 1901 and 1911, while Winnipeg trebled its population to 136,000.

In the good years there was no scarcity of jobs, even for those who didn't want to farm. Railways, the largest employers in the country, pushed branch lines into remote areas. Mining boomed with gold

A MESSAGE FROM HOME.

This card
a simple
message
bears
Across the
ocean blue,
To show that
though we're far apart
My thoughts oft turn to you

And I
wish you
Health
and Fortune
No matter
where you roam
And a speedy return
to the ones you love
In England - Home sweet Home.

A typical card showing an Empress, *sent from the UK to a Canadian immigrant.*

and silver strikes and the timber business of British Columbia needed loggers. Ontario and Quebec hydro projects needed trainloads of labourers and factories demanded skilled workers and craftsmen.

In Britain, a number of organizations actively promoted emigration as a solution to the country's problems of overcrowding and unemployment. Emigration was a safety valve, helping to rid the nation of excess population while binding the colonies ever more firmly to the mother country. A variety of such organizations sprang up: the British Women's Emigration Association, Girls' Friendly Society, Self-Help Emigration Society, Church of England's Waifs and Strays Society, and the Empire Emigration Society – to name but a few. The Woman's Domestic Guild sent over prospective domestic servants, while London's East End Immigration Society helped the poor of the capital. Often such organizations paid the passages for fit males, and helped them find jobs in Canada, and trusted in their honesty to repay the cost of the trip once they had landed on their feet. Most times they were not disappointed.

Among the largest of the organizations was the Salvation Army, which provided guidance to would-be emigrants in its *Emigration Gazette*, conducted parties and organized special sailings. For many of the indigent, the Army provided funding. So numerous were the emigrants assisted by the Salvation Army – more than 150,000 by 1914 – that it was able to charter its own vessels. In the autumn of 1907, for example, the Army chartered ten vessels for the coming year to transport immigrants to Canada, using the Allan and Dominion Lines.

Groups like the Salvation Army helped their emigrants to find work in the new country. For women and girls, this usually meant domestic work, for in 1911 almost forty percent of Britain's working women were domestic servants.

Children had been brought to Canada from Britain ever since the 1830s. In the early years of the twentieth century, the best known of the British organizations specializing in children was Doctor Barnardo's homes, which sent an average of a thousand boys and girls annually. Another was the Fegan agency, which sent about a hundred boys each year to its homes in Toronto and Brandon. British children were well received in Canada. Farmers and householders were able to secure help at reasonable wages, while many childless homes were brightened by the adoption of little children. By the time child emigration to Canada ended in the 1930s, more than 80,000 British children had come to Canada.

The migration from Europe was a win-win for everyone in a multi-sided equation. Governments in Europe lost political, religious or economic undesirables, shipping companies filled steerage and third class berths with paying passengers in such numbers as to make the rest of the operation profitable, landless emigrants and unemployed workers could start new lives, and countries like Canada and the United States got the healthy, strong people they desperately needed to grow their economies.

The Canadian Pacific Railway, too, played an important role in opening up the country, quite apart from completing Canada's first transcontinental railroad in 1885. Having acquired millions of acres of land in Manitoba, Saskatchewan and Alberta from the Dominion government, the railroad recognized the need to build farming settlements along the line, whose passengers and freight would contribute to the railway traffic. The CPR thus began a massive promotional effort in Britain and on the continent, placing advertisements in newspapers and periodicals, inviting farmers and groups to contact it about the opportunities in Canada.

The Canadian Pacific was one of the first great business conglomerates, already far more than a railway. It was the largest private landowner in the British Empire, owned a string of fine hotels between the Atlantic and Pacific Oceans in Canada, operated its own telegraph system, money-order and express company, owned over a thousand grain elevators in western Canada, along with a fleet of steamships.

In an arid area of Alberta, known as the Palliser Triangle and centred around present day Strathmore, thirty-five miles east of Calgary in the Bow Valley, the company began a large scale irrigation project in 1904 and set up a 2,000-acre Demonstration Farm to show would-be settlers how to farm the dry lands. The farm was an instant success, raising various types of livestock, and even included gardens and greenhouses that soon began to supply the needs of the railway's dining cars and hotels between Winnipeg and Vancouver.

By 1906 the company had spent over a million dollars digging over 170 miles of canals and 800 miles of distribution ditches. The money was recouped by selling the land for between $18 and $25 per acre, about double the price of un-irrigated land. And the company had plenty of land; in all, more than three million acres, of which only 110,000 were irrigated by 1906.

Having proven that irrigated land could support mixed agriculture, immigrants swarmed into the region, often staying at the Demonstration Farm to learn the latest techniques in dry-land farming. The company focused its efforts on attracting English emigrants with money, for the land was not free, and even offered ready-made farms, which included a modest house and barn, along with livestock. One ad in the spring of 1914 promised '...on each a comfortable house and barn have been erected. A portion of each farm has been ploughed, disced, harrowed, and seeded with suitable crops; the land fenced and a well dug.' Payments could be stretched over twenty years. Only a company of the size and prestige of the Canadian Pacific could have persuaded people to leave their homes in England and, sight unseen, commit to a plot of land in a foreign country.

The scheme, broadened to Alberta, Saskatchewan and British Columbia, was a success. The company's ready-made farms, promoted in British news magazines, struck a responsive note. In May 1912, on a single ship, the company brought more than 500 families to such instant farms, but settlers soon realized that the 80-acre farms were not always large enough to support a family.

In the great migration of the era, the Canadian Pacific played another role as well. Of importance to this narrative, the company began to offer transatlantic passenger service in 1903 when it acquired fifteen of the best vessels of the Elder Dempster Line. With these ships the company could now feed its rail service and offer passengers from England a through service to the Orient via Canada.

Though passage tickets were inexpensive, the sheer number of emigrants made this portion of the transatlantic business the most profitable for shipping lines, and its revenues partially subsidized the first and second class passages.

Despite the westward flood of people from Europe there was a good two-way traffic across the Atlantic. Shipowners were very successful in promoting travel to Europe. With a growing middle class, mass tourism to Europe became a real possibility for many Americans and Canadians and, in this era of multi-national corporations, business travellers were avidly courted. Though their numbers were never large, their companies were able to pay well for superior accommodations, and represented a profitable market segment for the shipping lines. Oceanic travel had become so inexpensive and fast that it was possible for many homesick immigrants to contemplate a quick trip back to the Old Country for Christmas, and the passenger companies developed special holiday prices designed to fill otherwise empty vessels.

Other factors played a part in swelling transatlantic traffic. When the First Balkan War erupted in late 1912, transatlantic vessels that December were filled with Bulgarians returning for military service. A similar event would occur in the summer of 1914 when war clouds again threatened, and German and Austro-Hungarian reservists sailed home on neutral US vessels.

Wages were high in the United States compared to Europe, and the gap widened in 1914 when Henry Ford began paying his workers the unprecedented sum of five dollars a day, double their previous wage. High wages and low ticket prices made it possible for many Europeans to work in the United States and return to their homes in the off season or at times of plant shutdowns.

Though the year 1905 was an extraordinary year, it was entirely typical of the Edwardian period.

Albert Einstein, a German whose name was not yet a household word, published five definitive papers in the prestigious journal *Annalen der Physik* while working in the Swiss Patent Office. The last of these short papers, on the special theory of relativity, postulated the equivalence of energy and matter, though the practical meaning of this would only become apparent forty years later with the explosion of an atomic bomb in the New Mexico desert.

In the world of art, astute collectors in Russia and the United States were buying works by Impressionist and Post-impressionist French artists, although it was not until 1910 that a show of Impressionists in London cemented the artists' reputations. In 1905 the Paris *Salon d'Automne* featured an explosion of color by a group whose members included Henri Matisse. Georges Braque, another member, would go on to develop cubism along with Pablo Picasso. In New York, American photographer Alfred Stieglitz was beginning to establish photography as an art form and opened a gallery on Fifth Avenue.

In literature, Arthur Conan Doyle yielded to public demand and published *The Return of Sherlock Holmes*. Zane Grey, the great storyteller of the American West, wrote *The Spirit of the Border*, thus beginning a series of more than fifty novels, and English novelist E.M. Forster completed *Where Angels Fear to Tread*. Jack London, whose fame had been assured by *The Call of the Wild* in 1903, published three books in 1905. In England, Beatrix Potter whose career as a writer of children's books began in 1902 with *The Tale of Peter Rabbit*, published *The Tale of Mrs Tiggy-Winkle*, while Bram Stoker was in the process of completing *Dracula*. A German musician named Albert Schweitzer published a seminal work on Bach, though Schweitzer himself would gain lasting fame by serving as a doctor in French West Africa. Philosopher George Santayana wrote the first of his five-volume work entitled *The Life of Reason*.

On the stage, James Barrie's *Peter Pan*, having made its stage debut in London the year before, opened on Broadway featuring an elfin actress named Maude Adams in the title role. In Pittsburgh the world's first regular movie theatre opened its doors, followed by thousands of others around the world.

In the world of music Claude Debussy completed the impressionistic *La Mer*. Richard Strauss' opera *Salome* premiered in Dresden, and Hungarian Franz Lehar's operetta *The Merry Widow* opened in Vienna. John Philip Sousa, the American 'March King' whose music has not dimmed in popularity, made his third successful European tour and completed his operetta *The Free Lance*.

Walter Gropius and Frank Lloyd Wright were in the process of transforming architecture with their novel principles.

The first motor omnibus, the 'bus' of today, began regular service in London, and the world's first drive-in gas station opened in St Louis. Radium was first tested as a cure for cancer. Rayon, the first synthetic textile capable of being woven and dyed, was commercially produced in Coventry. The first nickelodeon opened (in Pittsburgh), along with the first pizzeria in the United States in New York. In sport, the dimple-faced golf ball was patented, while baseball's second World Series was held, the New York Giants defeating the Philadelphia Athletics, four games to one. The British tennis team defeated the United States 5-0 to capture the Davis Cup, and The All England Croquet and Lawn Tennis Club, whose grass-court championship had been first played in 1877, saw May Sutton of the United States capture the Ladies' Singles title, the first overseas tennis champion at Wimbledon. The Mens' Singles was won for the fourth year in a row by Hugh ('Laurie') Doherty, who also took the Mens Doubles and would later be inducted into the International Tennis Hall of Fame.

Caterpillar tractors were first developed, and the Simplon tunnel under the Alps was completed. The chemical fire extinguisher was invented and, in Paris, Alfred Binet and Theodore Simon devised a system to measure aptitude. The show-business newspaper *Variety* was first printed and Parisians began to ride the subway. The Audubon Society, Rotary Club and the Automobile Association were founded.

In Russia it was a year of disasters. In May the Russian navy was utterly defeated by the Japanese in a famous engagement in the Tsushima Strait. Anti-Jewish pogroms took place in a score of cities and, in Odessa, the celebrated mutiny of the battleship *Potemkin*. In October, workers in St Petersburg formed the first '*Soviet*', or council, to direct strikers.

In Canada, Alberta and Saskatchewan became provinces, and the German Kaiser stirred up the first Moroccan crisis between France and Germany by visiting the city of Tangier.

The people destined to play leading roles in the middle twentieth century were mostly active. Mohandas Gandhi was a British-trained lawyer in South Africa, working for social justice, though still a year away from his first campaign of passive resistance against anti-Indian racial policies in South Africa.

Winston Churchill, a journalist in the Boer War who had escaped from Boer captivity, was in his first term in the House of Commons, the beginning a fifty-year career of public service, and was about to be named Under-Secretary of State for the Colonies.

Franklin Roosevelt, attending Columbia Law School, married Eleanor. His uncle, Theodore Roosevelt, was President of the United States and would win the 1906 Nobel Prize for brokering a peace treaty between Russia and Japan, thus ending a war that had humiliated the Russians on land and sea.

Dwight Eisenhower, fifteen that year, was a high school sophomore in Abilene, Kansas. Lieutenant Douglas MacArthur, serving in the Philippines, received an appointment as aide-de-camp to his father, the US military attaché in Tokyo. Harry S. Truman was making a hundred dollars a month as an assistant bank teller and had joined the Missouri National Guard as a private, while George Patton was a struggling cadet at West Point.

Josef Dugashvili and Vladimir Ilyich Ulyanov were both members of the underground Social Democratic Workers Party in Russia. They would become known later around the world as Josef Stalin and Vladimir Lenin.

In the provincial Austrian town of Steyr sixteen-year-old Adolf Hitler was finishing school, having shown no great aptitude for academic study. A Viennese doctor named Sigmund Freud, whose first

The Empress *at Liverpool landing stage.*

published work was *The Interpretation of Dreams* in 1900, was laying the foundations of the new branch of medicine called psychiatry and published *Humour and the Unconscious* in that year.

In Russian Poland, an ardent Zionist named David Ben-Gurion continued his political activities in Warsaw, while a seven-year-old girl in the Russian city of Pinsk prepared to join her father and emigrate to the United States. History would know her later as Golda Meir.

And, in the village of Shaoshan in China's Hunan province, the future Chairman of the People's Republic of China, Mao Zedong, was a twelve-year-old, completing primary school while living on his parents' three-acre farm.

On the military scene, the battleship HMS *Dreadnought* was being fitted out in a Portsmouth dockyard. When launched in February 1906 she would be the fastest and most powerful warship in the world. Equipped only with large-calibre guns, she made every other warship in the world obsolete overnight. The ship and her sisters, all termed 'dreadnoughts' in honour of this pioneering vessel, would trigger an arms race with Germany and contribute to the powderkeg that was primed to explode in 1914.

In December of 1905, Count Alfred von Schlieffen, anticipating that Germany would one day have to fight a two-front war against Russia and France, finalized the General Staff's plan for an invasion of France through neutral Belgium, intending to knock France out by a swift and decisive blow. The failure of the Schlieffen Plan in the autumn of 1914 would lead to a four-year stalemate on the Western Front.

In Scotland, in the tiny county of Clackmannan, tenant farmer John Hill and his wife Elizabeth celebrated the arrival of their daughter Mary on 6 May, a sister for twelve-year-old Lizzie and two-year-old Jane.

Also in Scotland, in this year of nineteen hundred and five, the hulls of two graceful ships began to take shape on the south bank of the River Clyde, a few miles from the heart of Glasgow. Designated by their builder, the Fairfield Shipbuilding & Engineering Company, as Hulls 442 and 443, they were just two of the 815 commercial steamships destined to be launched from shipyards in the United Kingdom the following year, amounting to some 1.8 million tons gross.

At that time Glasgow was the second-largest shipbuilding centre in the United Kingdom, after Newcastle-upon-Tyne, and in 1906 the city accounted for more than 330,000 tons of ship construction, only slightly behind Newcastle's 385,000 tons. So highly regarded were British shipyards that nearly two-thirds of the world's merchant steamships launched in 1906 were built in the United Kingdom. And, if considering sea-going steel steamers of 3,000 tons gross and upward, the fraction rose to over eighty percent.

The two hulls at Govan would become, respectively, the *Empress of Britain* and the *Empress of Ireland*. Smaller, less opulently appointed and not as fast as the vessels on the New York run, they would, nonetheless, be the pride of the Canadian Pacific Railway Company's Atlantic Service, the fastest and most luxurious way to travel between Liverpool and Canada.

It is with the second of these vessels that this book concerns itself.

An early view of the Empress of Ireland *c.1907.*

2
'The Very Last Word in Shipbuilding'

When the CPR's famous red-and-white checkered burgee, or house flag, was first raised on board *Lake Champlain* at Liverpool on April 6, 1903, it marked the dawn of a new era of passenger transportation on the North Atlantic. Just two months earlier the company had purchased eight passenger and seven cargo vessels from the Elder Dempster Company for Canadian service. None of these vessels was particularly fast, for 12-13 knots was typical, but it *was* a beginning on the Atlantic for the storied railway that already owned fifty-four vessels of various types, and had built up a flourishing Pacific shipping business. It was an astute move for the railway. In a single stroke it had eliminated a competitor and acquired a viable Atlantic operation, along with a number of capable, experienced personnel.

It was the personnel that would prove to be the best part of the transaction. Some Elder Dempster masters and officers, already familiar with the North Atlantic route to Canada, would rise to high rank in the CPR, and all five future *Empress* commanders were acquired in the deal.

The Atlantic route was the last link in the company's 11,841-mile Liverpool-to-Hong Kong chain, the so-called 'all-red route', though speeches of men like Sir Thomas Shaughnessy, President of the CPR, made it clear that the concept of an all-British route had less to do with imperial policy or patriotism, and more to do with profits.

With its entry into the Atlantic, the CPR could transport immigrants to Canada in its own ships, move them across the country on the railroad, and sell them land which it had acquired for free from the federal government as part of the deal for constructing the transcontinental railroad. And, with its network of agents in England and on the continent, it could collect a bonus from the federal government for each new immigrant it recruited and brought to Canada.

Only one problem remained. The company's vessels were slow and there was no way it could secure mail contracts, with their generous subsidies, from the Canadian or British governments. Not, that is, while the Allan Line operated its new, fast turbine steamers on the routes to Canada.

Accordingly, the CPR developed its own specifications and preliminary designs, then placed an order in December 1904 with the Fairfield Shipbuilding & Engineering Company of Govan for two 20-knot liners, under a fixed-price contract. The price of each vessel was £375,000, or about $1.8 million (the equivalent of about £16 million pounds in today's currency). The CPR got a bargain, for Fairfield was determined to secure the future business of the railway, and kept its profit to something under three percent, in anticipation of further orders. In comparison to other noted passenger ships of the era, the CPR got into the business relatively inexpensively. *Lusitania* cost Cunard £1.25 million, and *Titanic* £1.5 million, though both were considerably larger and faster. *Titanic*, for example, was 882 feet long and had a displacement of 46,239 gross tons; *Lusitania* was 780 feet and 30,396 tons.

Fairfield was one of the best-known names on the Clyde, a company that had commenced its shipbuilding activities in 1864 with the three-masted sail and steam *McGregor Laird*, though it had begun as a specialty engineering firm in 1834. It was a highly qualified company, having constructed everything from battleships for the Royal Navy to cargo and passenger vessels and steam yachts for royalty. Its operations on the Clyde were vertically integrated in a fashion unimaginable today. Fairfield's skilled craftsmen and artisans constructed the ships and virtually everything that went into them, from the massive steam engines and boilers to custom-made furniture and cabinetry. In 1905, shipbuilding was a labour-intensive business, and over seven thousand men laboured to

Canadian Pacific brochure cover. (Canadian Pacific Archives Image No. BR.127) complete the two ships ordered by the CPR, for delivery had been specified for eighteen months after contract signature.

In terms of marine technology the two new CPR liners broke no new ground. The railway company was one that sought to mitigate risk and it showed little inclination to follow the Allan Line into the field of turbine powerplants. Instead it selected tried and proven coal-fired reciprocating engines. Arthur Piers, the former secretary to Sir William Van Horne who had been promoted to General Manager of the company's steamship services, spoke to the Montreal *Gazette* in August 1905 after a lengthy trip to England, the bulk of it being spent around the Clyde. 'From all I can learn,' Piers said, ' turbines are still in the experimental stage.' It wasn't true of course, and Piers should have known better, but it mattered little. He then described the engines to be fitted into the ships as 'the best piece of work ever turned out on the Clyde.'

The names of the two hulls at Govan appeared to be settled, for Piers also announced in the same interview that they would be named *Empress of Germany* and *Empress of Austria*, and would be 'by far the finest steamships in the St Lawrence trade.'

Somewhere in the CPR, reason later prevailed. Though relations between Britain and Austria had always been good, the bombastic and bellicose nature of King Edward VII's mercurial nephew, Emperor Wilhelm II of Germany, led the company to reconsider its position. Quietly, Hulls 442 and 443 at the Fairfield yard were renamed *Empress of Britain* and *Empress of Ireland* respectively.

In the late autumn of 1905 once the name change became known, someone was overheard to comment to a CPR official that Ireland had never had an empress. 'Is that right?' retorted the quick-thinking official. 'Then now we'll give her one.'

The twin sisters were virtually identical, with a length of 548.9 feet. Each had a total of eight decks, and were built to Lloyd's three-deck and shelter-deck 100 A1 class. During their construction, surveyors from the Board of Trade and Lloyd's were on site at the Fairfield yard to determine at every stage whether there were any failures or defects that required alteration or addition, and to ensure that proper construction standards were being followed. If the surveyors found a problem, it was brought to the attention of the builder, and corrected. After completion, the *Empresses* were classed as passenger vessels by the Board of Trade, and certified by Lloyd's as Class ★100 A1, the star indicating that the ships had been surveyed during construction, and not merely after they had been built. It was the highest classification available under Lloyd's rules. The process of certification was costlier, but it translated directly into reduced insurance premiums and increased peace of mind for the CPR.

So similar were the two ships that only an expert could tell them apart at a distance. At the stern, there were differences in the propeller warning signs. On some decks the small signs advising that certain portions of the ship were restricted to crew members differed and, at the bow of the *Empress*, the first two portholes of the crew's quarters on Shelter deck were protected by steel bars.

The hull of the *Empress of Ireland* was of steel, with bottom and top sides hydraulic-riveted. The steel used in the *Empress* was of different thicknesses. Hull plating was seven-eighths of an inch thick, while the Shelter and Upper decks were nine-twentieths of an inch. Main and Lower decks were one-twentieth of an inch less. A cellular double-bottom was fitted virtually the whole length of the ship, 4ft 6in in depth and 47ft in breadth at its widest part.

CPR promotional literature assured travellers that 'Every known proven device to insure safety, speed, comfort and luxury, has been introduced in their construction and appointments.' Another promotional piece claimed 'They are big graceful ships, well proportioned, built to meet every possible requirement of the service.'

During construction the press took considerable interest in the CPR's newest liners. *The Times* informed its readers 'Everything in their equipment is of the most modern pattern, advantage having been taken of the very latest improvements. These comprise many new features for the comfort of passengers and protection of perishable freight.' The former wasn't strictly true but few readers, apart

First Class grand staircase, between the Lower Promenade and Saloon decks. 'We got down at the end of the stairs ... where we wouldn't be hardly seen and watch those fancy ladies all dressed up' – Mary (Hill) McCullough. (David Saint-Pierre)

from marine specialists, would have known better. The Glasgow correspondent of one marine journal, quoted later by the CPR, which displayed no reticence in quoting a third-party half-truth, summarized the two new ships by saying, 'From stem to stern and from keel to truck, these ships are the very last word in shipbuilding.'

The *Empress of Ireland* is best thought of as a three-deck shelter deck vessel, with Promenade, Upper Promenade and Boat deck above. The shortened decks of the upper structure were carried to a greater length than usual with this type of vessel, permitting greater areas in the saloons and other public rooms. Below the Shelter deck, in descending order, were the Upper, Main, Lower and Orlop decks. Only the Shelter, Upper, Main and Lower decks extended the full length of the ship.

Boat deck, in addition to accommodating the ship's lifeboats of different types, held a spacious deck house for the captain and other deck officers, with a chart room, wheelhouse and a navigating bridge extending the full width of the ship. The *Empress* could be steered from three positions on the bridge and two positions aft. Above the officers' deck house was the upper navigating bridge with the usual steering wheel, compass and searchlight. Aft of the wheelhouse, under the second funnel, was a firemen's shelter, a place for the men of the engine room to come for a moment of fresh, cool air. From here a ladder led directly to the boiler room. It was this ladder which explains in part how many of the engine room staff on duty at the time of the ship's sinking managed to escape.

Upper Promenade deck, immediately below Boat deck, was devoted to the accommodation of first class passengers, in a series of outside single and *en suite* rooms, each with baths and lavatories. Its deck house offered sheltered recesses for deck chairs. On each side of the deck was a clear promenade 18½ feet wide; one circuit around the deck was approximately one-eighth of a mile. Midships on this deck was the first class Music Room, which had a grand piano and a fireplace. This deck was connected to the Lower Promenade and Saloon decks by a grand staircase of polished teak, and lit by an overhead glass dome.

Lower Promenade deck extended to the stern of the *Empress*, and was also given over to first class cabins. As on Upper Promenade, there was a clear walking area 18½ feet wide, and recesses in the deck house formed sheltered areas for passengers using deck chairs. The Library (open to first and second class passengers) was situated at the forward end of the deck house; midships was the Café and, at the after end, 170 feet from the stern, the first class Smoking Room. Only outside cabins, single and *en suite*, were provided on this deck. The Marconi wireless shack was initially located at the base of the mast on this deck. Later in the *Empress'* career the wireless shack was moved to the after portion of Boat Deck, where it was located just forward of the engine room skylight.

Saloon (or **Shelter) deck** held the first class Dining Saloon (capacity 304), and a small dining room for children in first class. As well, it held the kitchens, second class Dining Saloon (capacity 296), Smoking Room and the Social Hall (which the Montreal *Gazette* described as 'roomy' and 'extremely comfortable looking'). Forward of the first class dining saloon were twenty-four first class staterooms, twelve of which were inside rooms, although they were provided with outside light and ventilation. Midships on the starboard side was the purser's office and, at the stern, a small hospital, divided into male and female halves with four beds each. This deck featured a promenade for second class passengers.

It was via the gangway doors on Saloon deck that passengers normally boarded the ship. There were four gangway doors, two on each side of the *Empress*. The forward doors, used by first and second class passengers, led to the main staircase. The after door was used by third class passengers.

The forward portion of the Saloon deck was open, and used by third class passengers as an area for games. 'We have the fo'castle,' wrote one third class passenger in 1907, 'with a high and low open deck, besides our covered promenade.' In some respects this deck was better than the upper decks, further aft, for it was less exposed to the smoke and fly ash belching out of the twin funnels.

Next came **Upper deck**, one of the most varied in terms of usage. It had first and second class cabins, along with the first class barber shop, mail room, third class ladies' lounge (with a piano) and third class smoke room, a second class children's nursery, the third class children's play area which featured a sand pit, crew accommodations and storage.

Main deck was occupied with second class cabins, which CPR literature described as 'large, well-ventilated, and excellently furnished.' All of the 569 staterooms on board had high ceilings, which helped to overcome a sense of claustrophobia. This deck also held the third class dining room, seating 302 at one time. The dining room also had a piano and was the scene of concerts in the evening. Forward of the third class dining room were a number of third class cabins capable of holding from two to six persons. Where mahogany and other rare woods were used in the upper decks, Canadian maple was used in third class to relieve the monotony of bare steel.

Lower deck was given over to the engine room, storage and, at the forward end, accommodation for third class passengers or cargo.

The lowest, **Orlop deck**, was used for cargo and storage.

Vertical spacing between the steel decks at midships was eight feet, with the exception of Lower Promenade, which was eight and a half feet above Shelter deck. This extra six inches helped to impart a feeling of spaciousness to the first and second class dining saloons on Shelter deck. In all, the Boat deck was 45½ ft above the designated waterline, which was 27½ ft above the keel, while Lower deck was three feet below the waterline.

Four decks were equipped with circular portholes (or 'sidelights' as they were sometimes termed) of various sizes and containing clear glass. Measured at midships, the lower edges of the portholes on

CPR Atlantic Services, a typical advertisement, Quebec Chronicle, *7 August 1906.*

Saloon deck were 27ft above the waterline; Upper, 19ft; Main, 11ft; and Lower, a mere 5ft. Portholes on Lower deck were 10in in diameter, and had plugs and hinged cast-iron covers. Those on Main deck, one level higher, were also 10in, except in the third class dining room, where they were 12in. Upper deck had 12in diameter portholes, while those on the Saloon deck were 14in and 16in. The 16in portholes were found in the first class dining saloon, though these were covered by decorative panels. In the deck houses above Lower Promenade deck, there were rectangular sliding or hinged windows measuring approximately 20in x14in and fitted with clear glass

Each of the five passenger decks had a number of bath rooms and lavatories, arranged so that the occupants of each cabin had only a short distance to go to their bath. Only in a handful of first class cabins were there built-in bath and toilet facilities. In first class, every section of ten rooms had a 'splendidly equipped bathroom.' Second and third classes made do with less luxurious facilities.

Some of the *Empress'* public rooms merit a short description, for they were a successful blend of elegance and comfort.

The first class Dining Saloon was 58ft long, and extended the full width of the ship, some $65\frac{1}{2}$ft, and was capable of seating all first class passengers at once. Sixteen horseshoe-shaped tables, suitable for families and parties travelling together, were arranged in alcoves along each side of the room. Four sets of fore-and-aft tables occupied the central portion of the dining saloon, with the captain's table located in the middle on the port side. Paneling in the room was of mahogany, with cream enamel walls and carved moldings of dull gold. The ceiling was flat white and gold. Upholstery was crimson leather or velvet. Dining tables were equipped with side-guards in the event of rough weather.

In the centre of the dining saloon was a large oval, opening into the Café on the Lower Promenade, one deck above.

The two dining saloons were separated by the kitchen and pantries, with a single galley area serving both saloons and that for third class, two decks below.

The second class Dining Saloon was also finely furnished in mahogany, though less ornately than in first class. Swinging doors at the after end led to the second class Social Hall, whose walls were lined with sofas. Further aft was the second class smoking room.

The Café on Lower Promenade deck, where light refreshments could be had at any time of the day, was paneled in waxed Italian walnut and richly appointed throughout. Also on the same deck, the Library was finished in panels of polished Spanish mahogany, and featured easy chairs and cushioned nooks in green velvet and carpeting to match. There were writing tables and a fine collection of books designed to appeal to discriminating readers, the whole having a 'most home-like and attractive appearance.' At the aft end of the deck, the first class Smoking Room was finished in slightly fumed oak and, as the company promised, 'special attention has been paid to ventilation.'

The Music Room on Upper Promenade deck, which had been designed by William Flockhart of London, featured a fine central glass dome springing from a central column that doubled as an air vent. The shaft was paneled in satinwood while the dome was made to resemble the spreading petals of a flower. Cosy corners and an open fireplace made first class passengers feel at home.

First class passengers in an alcove of the Dining Saloon from a CPR brochure. (David Saint-Pierre)

In the *Empress*, the real innovation was the accommodation of third class passengers in cabins. However plain they seemed in comparison to first and second class, the concept of cabin accommodation for third class, rather than dormitories, helped transform the transport of Atlantic immigrants. Enthused the *Gazette* in May 1906 after the *Empress of Britain* arrived in Quebec on her maiden voyage: 'The third-class accommodation of old has been revolutionized in the present vessel… [T]he old order of discomfort which formerly reigned in the steerage department has been swept away, and in its place there is cleanliness and comfort. There is even a roped off sand playground for the little children. The rooms are large and well kept, and the bathrooms are ample and bright.'

A correspondent of *The Times* had similar good things to say, finding that the *Empresses* marked 'a new and better era in the treatment of persons belonging to the emigrant class.'

When specifications for the *Empress* were first drawn up, she was expected to carry 310 first, 468 second, 494 third, and 270 fourth class (or steerage) passengers, for a total of 1,542. However, that changed with the abolition of steerage. The exact number of passengers that could be accommodated aboard the *Empress* is a matter of conjecture. There are few sources that agree, and even the CPR's published information varies from one document to another. In round numbers the best estimates are 350 first, 350 second, and 1,000 third class passengers. These numbers are cited for the maiden voyage of the *Empress of Britain* and in the 1906 Rate Sheet. The confusion arises in part because some passenger spaces in the *Empress* were modular in nature. The fore-part of Lower deck, for example, could accommodate either cargo or third class passengers, and on Upper deck certain cabins could be switched between first and second class depending on the requirements for a particular crossing.

SAILORS' CONCERT
— IN THE —
Y. M. C. A. HALL,
ST. JOHN STREET.
TUESDAY, AT 8 P.M.

Sailors Free.   Civilians 10c.
PROGRAMME
Mrs. T. P. Ross
Independant Order of Good Templars.
Officers and Sailors of Empress of Ireland
and other ships.

*Sailors' Concert advertisement, Quebec
Chronicle, 6 August 1906.*

Approximate passenger accommodation capacities by deck are shown in the following table:

	1st class	2nd class	3rd class
Boat	none	none	none
Upper Promenade	120	none	none
Lower Promenade	92	none	none
Shelter (*or* Saloon)	98	none	none
Upper	134 1st *or* 2nd		
	plus	100	none
Main	none	234 2nd *or* 3rd	
		plus	430
Lower	none	none	328
Orlop	none	none	none

Confusion arose as well because the *Empress* was required, after the *Titanic* sinking, to carry sufficient lifeboats for all on board. A survey on 15 May 1914 found there were forty lifeboats of various types, sufficient for 1,860 persons. (In fact, the surveyor missed two lifeboats). As the assumed crew strength in the survey was 372 (itself low by almost fifty persons), it left space for 1,488 passengers, even though a total of 1,532 berths were fitted.

In third class, despite there being 758 fixed berths, she was only licensed to carry 714 third class passengers. This number was routinely exceeded.

As will be seen in Appendix 1 there were several occasions in her career, even after 1912, when the *Empress of Ireland* exceeded 1,488 passengers. In some cases, infants slept with their mothers, and it was possible for two half-price children to occupy the same bed, so the 'actual' number of passengers that could be accommodated is somewhat flexible.

If officers were well accommodated in the *Empress,* in the highest and brightest quarters in the ship, crew quarters were far more modest. Crew members were housed in different areas of the ship, often in close proximity to passengers. Junior engineers were on the port side of Upper deck, along with a number of stewards, with a stairway to an open space on the aft part of the Shelter deck. Firemen and greasers shared the after end of Upper deck; cooks, bakers and the interpreter were on the after port side. Seamen and firemen were in the forecastle of the ship on Shelter deck.

In terms of safety appliances, the *Empress* carried a total of forty-two lifeboats, and a large supply of lifebelts. From the Emigration Surveyor's Certificate of 15 May 1914, the *Empress* carried the following lifeboats:

16	steel boats under davits, accommodating	764 persons
20	wood and canvas Engelhardt boats, accommodating	920 persons
4	wood and canvas Berthon boats, accommodating	176 persons
40	boats, accommodating	1,860 persons

Inexplicably the Board of Trade Surveyor missed two additional Berthon boats, having a further capacity of 105 persons. This mistake may have arisen because the Surveyor did not realize there were two boats, not one, under covers.

The steel lifeboats, eight on each side of the ship, were under davits. There were fourteen on Boat deck and two at the after end of the Lower Promenade deck. They were distinguished by odd numbers on the starboard side, and even numbers on the port side. Under each steel boat was placed a collapsible Englehardt boat, and four more were stowed on the after Lower Promenade deck. Two 28ft collapsible Berthon boats were on the Boat deck on each side of the engine room skylight; two more were under covers on each side of the wireless shack on Boat Deck.

The ship's Passenger Certificate of 15 February 1914 showed the same number of boats, having also missed the two Berthon boats. However, it arrived at different passenger capacities than the 15 May Survey. The sixteen steel boats were shown to hold 752 persons, while the four Berthon boats held a total of 188 persons. Though the total capacity was still the same, the difference, according to a document attached to a subpoena for the 1914 Mersey Inquiry, 'seems to have arisen in the calculations as to the cubic contents in feet of each boat.'

Including the two uncounted Berthon boats, the *Empress'* lifeboats had a total capacity of 1,948 persons.

Prior to the summer of 1912, the *Empress* carried just sixteen steel lifeboats on davits, accommodating 764 persons. After the Board of Trade revised the rules concerning lifeboats, following *Titanic's* loss, the davits were lengthened, in order to raise the steel boats. Beneath each one was placed an Englehardt collapsible boat.

The Emigrant Certificate issued on 15 May 1914 showed the *Empress* carried 2,212 lifebelts, plus 150 for children. However, the 15 February 1914 Passenger Certificate declared she carried 1,950 adult life jackets and 150 for children. No explanation for the discrepancy was ever offered. Lifebelts for first and second class were kept in racks in the cabins or, in a few cases, on the wardrobes. In third class, lifebelts were stored in overhead racks. Lifebelts for crew and officers were stored in their respective quarters. Lifebelts were made of canvas and cork to Board of Trade standards, and were stamped as such.

There were eleven watertight compartments in the *Empress*, formed by ten transverse watertight bulkheads that terminated in each case at Upper deck. These bulkheads, numbered in sequence from the bow, were constructed in accordance with the recommendations of the Board of Trade's Bulkhead Committee of 1891. This meant that the bulkheads were so placed that any two adjacent compartments might be flooded when floating at the mean draught of $27\frac{1}{2}$ft, without sinking the ship below the margin of safety line drawn below the Upper deck, as recommended by the Committee. Even in 1906 very few ships were fully compliant with the recommendation drawn up fifteen years earlier, though it should be noted it was merely a recommendation and not a legal requirement.

Some sources claim the *Empress* had ten watertight compartments, perhaps feeling that the storage space in front of the No.1 (or 'collision') bulkhead did not properly warrant the title 'watertight compartment'.

Bulkheads 3 through 10 were pierced by a total of twenty-four watertight doors, which had to be closed in order to maintain their integrity. Watertight doors came in two forms: horizontal sliding doors worked by rack-and-pinion gear, and vertical sliding doors. In all cases, they were manually opened and closed by a hand crank, an operation that required one person per door. These handles, or 'keys', were located adjacent to the gearing. Doors on lower decks were operated by designated engine room staff; on higher decks, by stewards. Closing the doors took just three or four seconds in the engine room, but it took three and a half to four minutes to close the other doors, according to testimony in 1914 by Hugh Staunton, CPR's superintendent of life-saving appliances.

The actual mechanisms for the doors were located on the deck above. Thus, for example, the watertight door on Lower deck between the two engine rooms was activated by the crank in the third class dining saloon on Main deck. In this respect the design of the *Empress* was somewhat out of date, for some newer vessels were fitted with hydraulic or electric systems which made it possible to close all watertight doors simultaneously from the bridge by one man.

The location and types of watertight doors is shown below:

Bulkhead No.	Frame No.	Hold	Orlop deck	Lower deck	Main deck
1	229	none	none	none	none
2	211	none	none	none	none
3	189	none	none	none	2, horiz.
4	166	none	none	1, horiz.	2, horiz.
5	127	1, vert.	none	2, horiz.	2, horiz.
6	88	1, vert.	none	2, horiz.	1, horiz.
7	57 & 65	none	1, horiz.	none	2, horiz.
8	47	2, horiz.	none	none	2, horiz.
9	29	none	none	none	2, horiz.
10	14	none	1, horiz.	none	none

To move the 18,000-ton deadweight mass of the *Empress*, two massive reciprocating quadruple-expansion engines, designed and constructed at Fairfield, were installed. They developed 18,000 indicated horsepower at eighty-one revolutions per minute, and offered great torque at low rpms. There were four cylinders per engine, with bore diameters of 36in, 52in, 75in and 108in. The stroke was 69in. Counter-balancing was on the Yarrow, Schlick and Tweedy system, which reduced engine vibration to a minimum, a phenomenon commented upon favourably by passengers on the *Empress of Britain*'s maiden voyage.

Steam at an operating pressure of 220psi was supplied by nine boilers in two boiler rooms. Of the nine, six were double-ended and three single-ended, and used the Howden system of forced draught. The forward boiler room contained three double-ended boilers forward and one single-ended boiler aft. The after boiler room held three double-ended boilers aft and two single-ended boilers forward.

Like most ships of the day, the *Empress* burned bituminous coal, and had a capacity of 4,000 tons, though on a normal six-day voyage of some 2,650 miles the ship would burn about 2,400 tons. Fairfield specifications called for coal consumption of 1.37 lbs/IHP/hr or about 410 pounds per minute.

Coal was stored in six massive bunkers. Two side bunkers ran along each side of the hull, and were 175ft long and 14ft wide. Four other bunkers were transversely arranged.

Steering was by a balanced rudder operated by two steering engines on the telemotor principle, the steering gear being underwater to meet the British Admiralty's requirements that it be approached either from above deck or from the shaft tunnels. The rudder was modified in 1907 by increasing its area from 185 to 227 square feet.

Ventilation and heating of the interior spaces was accomplished by a 'Thermo tank' system. Air was drawn from the open into the so-called Thermo tanks, where it was brought to any desired temperature, and then forced along pipes to the cabins. Each cabin had an outlet that could be controlled by the occupant. CPR literature promised that the air in each compartment would be changed every ten minutes, 'thus avoiding offensive odours and liability to sea-sickness.' In the winter of 1911 Sir William Van Horne, in first class, wrote: 'The ventilation and temperature are just right and everybody is pleased.'

Everybody, that is, who mattered. In third class, it was another story. Observed one 1907 eastbound traveller of his June crossing: 'Ugh! but it is cold. No heat in the third class apartments.' Even later, when electric heaters were added to first class cabins, there was no mention of any improvement to third class.

The *Empress* had two novel safety features. One was a standard 1.5kW Marconi wireless transmitter which was fitted as part of her original equipment, and which allowed the ship to communicate with shore stations and other similarly equipped ships. The second was a receiver for the submarine bell signaling system. The idea behind the latter system was simple. Underwater transmitters were set up at dangerous points as a safety measure, and would emit sound waves that travelled great distances in water. The receiving equipment on the *Empress* collected these sound waves when they struck the hull and relayed them to the bridge.

There was only one problem. By early 1908 in Canada there were only four such submarine bell stations on the Atlantic coast, with one at Saint John and another at Chebucto Head off Halifax. Over the next years the Canadian government added more signals in the St Lawrence, one of the last being a bell buoy off Fame Point. The bell would be rung at irregular intervals by the rocking motion of the buoy.

For those who feared seasickness, the *Empress* was fitted with deep V-shaped bilge keels. A CPR 1906 Rate Sheet promised that these were 'to promote steadiness at sea' and another brochure claimed the ship was 'remarkably steady in rough weather.' The number of *Empress* passengers who were seasick makes one wonder how effective the bilge keels really were.

In all, the *Empress of Ireland* was a fine vessel, appreciated and liked by those who worked in her or sailed as passengers. John Forster, in the autumn of 1909 after three years in command of the *Empress*, described his ship in glowing terms to an accident investigation board: 'She is more fully equipped than any vessel I have been on.'

In 1911 *Railway and Travel Monthly* contended that the two *Empresses* were 'something beyond the highest point hitherto touched in travel to Canada… To form a true conception of the cabins and magnificently appointed assembly halls, one must dismiss all previous notions of such accommodation.'

And a correspondent of *The Times*, who had sailed in her early in 1906, praised the fine first class dining saloon, the Café ('much frequented for afternoon tea'), and the delightful music room. In all, he said, it would be difficult to find a more cheerful or popular ship.

RMS *Empress of Ireland* at a Glance

Official number:	123972
Hull number:	443
Registered owner:	Canadian Pacific Railway Company
Registry:	United Kingdom
Home port:	Liverpool
Builder:	Fairfield Shipbuilding & Engineering Company, Limited, Govan, Scotland
Designer:	Dr Francis Elgar (1845-1909)
Type:	shelter deck type, having a straight stem and elliptical stern. Four complete steel decks, *viz*. Shelter, Upper, Main and Lower decks all ran from stem to stern. Orlop deck fitted before and abaft the machinery spaces. Lower Promenade, Upper Promenade and Boat decks above the shelter deck. Vertical spacing (at midships) between decks: 8ft, with the exception of Lower Promenade, which was 8.5ft above Shelter deck.
Keel laid:	10 April 1905
Construction standard:	Lloyd's Class ★100 A1
Launched:	27 Jan 1906

Maiden voyage:	29 June 1906 Liverpool to Quebec City
Cost:	£375,000 under fixed-price contract, plus £4,611 of CPR-ordered extras
Dimensions:	548.9ft x 65.75ft x 36.7ft depth
Molded depth to Upper deck:	40ft
Draught, mean:	27.5ft
Draught, deep load:	31ft $1\frac{3}{4}$in
Displacement:	22,191 tons; at deep load draught, 26,000 tons
Gross registered tonnage:	14,191 (see Note 1)
Net registered tonnage:	8,028.17, after deducting 6,162.28 tons for propelling power and crew space
Hull:	steel plating; thickness: seven-eighths of an inch; decks: Shelter and Upper decks: 9/20 of an inch; Main and Lower decks, $\frac{2}{5}$ of an inch
Double bottom:	cellular, 4ft 6in in depth, 47ft in breadth at its widest point; extended from a point 35ft aft of the stem to 54ft forward of the stern post
Waterline:	27.5ft above underside of keel, at midships
Rivets used:	approximately 1.1 million
Holds:	6
Cargo capacity:	approximately 5,000 tons; total under deck deadweight, 9,941 tons
Engines:	2
Type:	quadruple expansion, reciprocating; constructed by builder
Horsepower:	18,000 IHP @ 81rpm
Cranks:	4 per engine
Cylinders:	4 per engine; bore diameter (inches): 36, 52, 75 and 108; stroke (inches): 69
Balancing:	Yarrow, Schlick and Tweedy system
Boilers:	double-ended: 6; single-ended: 3; working at 220psi
Capacity:	Approximately 4000 tons in bunkers
Fuel:	coal, bituminous
Consumption:	1.37lbs/IHP/hr; in a six-day voyage of some 2,650 miles, the *Empress* would normally consume approximately 2,400 tons
Screws:	2; four blades each; diameter, 20ft 6in; weight, 20 tons; clockwise revolution for forward
Steering:	balanced rudder operated by two steering engines on the telemotor principle
Rudder:	single plate, partially balanced; area 185 sq. ft.; increased in 1907 to 227 sq.ft; steel thickness, $1\frac{1}{4}$in
Speed	(knots): maximum, 20; normal, 18
Crew:	typically about 420
Passenger capacity:	350 first class, 350 second, 1,000 third (though figures vary widely)
Lifeboats:	total, 42; steel, under davits: 16; Englehardt, wood and canvas: 20; Berthon, wood and canvas, 6; total capacity, 1,948 persons
Watertight compartments:	11
Watertight bulkheads:	10
Watertight doors:	24
Lifebelts:	1,950 for adults and 150 for children (Passenger Certificate, 15 February 1914 (Emigration Certificate of 15 May 1914 shows 2,212 for adults, and 150 for children)
Ballast, water:	1,522 tons in cellular double bottom, and 1,950 tons in deep tanks
Metacentric height:	$40\frac{1}{2}$in (at 28 May 1914). (see Note 2)

Notes:

1. Gross registered tonnage is a measurement of volume, not weight. One gross registered ton is equal to 100 cu. ft. of a ship's internal space. The gross registered tonnage of a ship is arrived at by ascertaining the total internal capacity (measured in cubic feet) below the upper deck, and also of all enclosed spaces or deck houses above it and dividing the result by 100. For example, 1,450,000 cu.ft. divided by 100 equals 14,500 tons, gross registered tonnage.

2. The metacentric height is a measure of the stability of a ship; a reduction of the metacentric height reduces the stability of the ship. Before extra lifeboats were placed aboard Empress in 1912, the metacentric height was $42\frac{1}{2}$ inches. A reduction of two inches was not considered significant from a safety point of view by Percy Hillhouse, one of Fairfield's naval architects.

3
The 'Township' and its Operation

For more than a hundred years, writers have used terms like 'floating palace' to describe transatlantic liners, each bigger and more opulent than its predecessor. Such a description is wholly accurate, for palaces they were indeed, filled with novelty and wonders. So too was the *Empress of Ireland*, though on a more modest scale than the great liners plying the busy North Atlantic route to New York, and not as fast. Nonetheless, until 1914 when the Allan Line introduced its new *Calgarian* (another Fairfield vessel) and *Alsatian*, the two Canadian Pacific *Empresses* were the fastest and most luxurious ships on the Canada-Britain run. They offered value for money and solid comfort, rather than sybaritic excess. And that seemed to be precisely what those who travelled the route to Canada were looking for.

In truth, 'palace' actually understates the case, for a ship is much more complex than that. Leave it to *Empress of Ireland* passenger Rudyard Kipling, who inspected the ship from top to bottom, to come up with a better description: the 'township.'

This is far closer to reality. Transatlantic liners were self-contained towns in miniature, each a microcosm of Edwardian society and a reflection of the era. There were complete refrigeration and heating plants, along with an electrical plant. On board the township a variety of 'inhabitants' were thrown together for the duration of the voyage. Classes were carefully segregated, as on land, each being restricted to certain spaces or areas of the ship. Mirroring life ashore, there was even a teeming underclass, third class, whose numbers on the Atlantic routes supported the others.

The township of the *Empress of Ireland* featured a doctor (and nurse) with a small clinic, an 'excellent' 650-volume library, café, music room, gift shop, a variety of bars, print shop, post office and mailboxes, telegraph office, barber shop, exercise room, interpreter, a purser's office which functioned as a bank and currency exchange, a railway ticket office, musicians and an entertainment troupe. There were scheduled religious services, play areas for children that even included a sandbox for third class, cricket pitch, movie screening area, at least two soccer teams and one cricket team, along with a large assortment of 'tradesmen' to support the whole enterprise: butchers, electricians, carpenter, barber, butchers, plumber, bakers, cooks – to name but a few.

For the information of its 'citizens' a free newspaper, the *Empress Daily News*, was published on board. It contained a mix of news of the outside world, relayed by wireless, along with notices of various ship-board activities and CPR promotional stories.

And, as in any town, children were born aboard the *Empress* and people of all ages died aboard her (Appendix 5). In common with other ships of the day, the *Empress* lacked a morgue. Anyone who died during the course of a voyage was accorded the traditional burial at sea, usually presided over by the master. Fearing the possible spread of infectious diseases in the close quarters of the ship, the deceased were generally buried within twelve hours of death.

The township was presided over by a master with sole and unquestioned authority. Though his powers had eroded by the early years of the twentieth century, under English maritime law the ship's master still had absolute authority in all matters relating to the navigation of the ship. Answering only to the ship's owners, he was required to exercise reasonable skill, care and diligence in the performance of his duties. He alone was responsible for the safety of his vessel and all those in her, and was entitled to do anything reasonable to ensure their safety, comfort and convenience. As a ship's master was unable to call in officers of the law to assist him, he was invested with special powers over every person

Playing cricket, Lower Promenade deck. 'We played cricket this m[ornin]g 1&2nd class. BD Zalter a success as a bowler but no luck with the bat. John played for 2nd class but his keenness is greater then his skill!' – Alexander Hore-Ruthven (Stephen Brooks)

on board his vessel – officers, crew, and passengers alike, who were required to obey his lawful orders. The master could bury them at sea if they died, conduct religious services, and arrest and confine them (as did the master of the Allan Line's *Victorian*) for trial ashore if they failed to obey his commands. Though some sources claim that the master of a British vessel could marry two passengers, provided the marriage was entered in the log, the Official Log Book reminded masters that they 'have no power to perform the marriage ceremony on board their vessels, and that if such ceremony is performed by them the marriage will not be a legal one.'

Responsible not only for proper navigation of his vessel, the master was also accountable for proper operation of the other departments aboard ship, including the Engine and Victualing Departments.

Ship's Company

In late May 1914, the nominal crew complement of the *Empress* was about four hundred and fifteen, including the master. Of this number, just eleven were women – ten stewardesses and one matron. Over the years the *Empress*' crew complement had undergone a slight increase. In June 1906 the announced crew strength was 373. A year later this had grown to 398, as additional amenities and services for passengers were added. By October 1909 the number had risen to 420, with the addition of a translator and, possibly, musicians.

The number of crewmen increased with the size and speed of the ship, and greater passenger capacity. The CPR's *Lake Champlain*, acquired from Elder Dempster in 1903, was 446 feet in length and carried about 1,350 passengers. The ship, built in 1900, had a total crew of just 163, broken down as follows: Deck Department: 46; Engine, 37; Catering and Stewards: 80. The speed and luxury of the *Empress* carried a price in terms of increased manpower.

On any crossing, the actual number of crew would fluctuate slightly, with last-minute sicknesses and desertions. In such cases, the company tried to find spur-of-the-moment replacements to ensure that

Stewards and cooks of the Empress, *May 1914 from the Montreal* Daily Star, *29 May 1914. The man standing with his hands on the life preserver is Second Steward Alexander Craik. (National Library of Canada, neg. NL11427)*

neither the ship's operating ability nor service to passengers was compromised.

On Voyage 42W, for example, departing Liverpool on 8 October 1909, the crew numbered 408 from a nominal roll of 420. On Voyage 50W in 1910, arriving in Quebec City, the crew strength was 415. On voyage 96E, the last trip, seven men deserted the *Empress* in Quebec and the CPR seems to have replaced just five of them. Captain Henry Kendall testified at the Inquiry that a total of 413 was 'about correct' when the *Empress* arrived at Quebec on 22 May 1914. That number consisted of 59 (including officers) in the Deck Department, 132 in the Engine Department, and 222 in the Victualing Department.

There was considerable discussion at the Inquiry as to the actual number of crew on the last outbound passage. Kendall testified that the number was 420, though elsewhere in the testimony there was reference to 372 hands, a number that was obviously too low. As well, the Inquiry seems to have missed several names.

The organization aboard the *Empress of Ireland* was wholly typical of passenger vessels of the period. As an example, assuming a complement of 420, the crew can be broken down by Department as follows for the 96th voyage eastbound:

Deck Dept.	59 (including officers)
Engine Room Dept.	130
Victualing Dept.	222
Total	411
Add:	4 (supernumerary engineers, ex-*Empress of Asia*)
	5 (musicians)
Total	420

A list of the crew of the 96th voyage eastbound and their positions is given in Appendix 8.

Deck Department

The Deck Department, the least numerous of the three divisions, was in charge of the ship's navigation, *i.e.* its actual running and operation. It usually comes as a surprise to a layman that in a ship like the *Empress of Ireland*, there were just six officers, in addition to the master. These men were in command of the ship, and officers of other departments aboard the *Empress* were subject to the master or his designated subordinate. The number of officers does not appear to have changed over time. Captain John Forster testified in October 1909 that there were six officers carried aboard the ship. It took relatively few officers to run a large liner. *Aquitania* had just seven in addition to the captain and staff captain, while *Titanic* had seven in addition to the captain.

The six Deck officers of the *Empress*, in descending authority, were Chief, First, Second, Extra Second, Third, and Fourth Officers. These men were all highly qualified individuals who aspired one day to their own commands. Of the six, four held Master's certificates and two held Mate's certificates.

Watches for deck officers were four hours on, and eight hours off. This was a 'normal' watch for vessels of almost every class and nationality. On board the *Empress*, commencing at noon, the day was divided into six equal periods of four hours. Watches were 'afternoon' (noon to 4:00 p.m.); 'dog watch' (4:00 to 8:00 p.m.); 'first' (8:00 p.m. to midnight); 'middle' (midnight to 4:00 a.m.); 'morning' (4:00 to 8:00 a.m.); and 'forenoon' (8:00 a.m. to noon). Each half-hour period of the watch was marked by 'bells'. Thus, four bells in the afternoon watch was 2:00 p.m.

In the Deck Department, only the master did not stand a watch, it being presumed that he was always in charge of the ship and would be on the bridge whenever required, for as long as necessary. During heavy weather, approaching land, making or leaving a port, or in other situations, the master would be found on the bridge directing his officers and ensuring the safety of his vessel, passengers and crew.

The Chief Officer, reporting directly to the master, was the effective head of the Deck Department and in charge of its routine work. The First Officer was primarily in charge of watchkeeping, navigation, and safe stowage of cargo and baggage, while the Second Officer was responsible for watchkeeping, navigational appliances, life-saving equipment, etc. The junior officers, whose number increased with the size of the vessel, assisted the senior officers and were in control of the *Empress* for their designated watch periods.

Officers on watch on the bridge were paired, usually a senior officer with a less experienced man. On the last voyage, for example, the First and Third Officers were teamed for the watch. A typical bridge watch consisted of two officers, two Quartermasters (QMs), and a bridge boy (or messenger). On deck, there would have been about twenty-five hands including two lookouts.

Quartermaster	4	AB	24
Officers' Steward	1	Deck Boy	1
Donkeyman	1	Master-at-Arms	1
Marconi Operator	2	Surgeon	1
Seaman	2	Boatswain	1
OS	10	Boatswain's Mate	1

In addition to the Captain and the six deck officers identified above, the Department included the above forty-nine positions.

The Surgeon was authorized (in the words of an *Empress* passenger list from August 1911) to 'make customary charges, subject to the approval of the Commander, for treating any passengers at their request for any illness not originating on board the ship. In the case of sickness contracted on board, no charge will be made and medicine will be provided free.' The surgeon accompanied the master on the daily inspection of the *Empress*. He was also responsible for making a daily general inspection of the passengers on board, and at least once a detailed examination of each immigrant on board, and attesting to this in the manifest.

Officers of the Empress, *taken on the Lower Promenade deck while the ship was being turned around at Quebec, 20-26 June 1913 (Voyage 85). Second row, right to left: Frank Hamilton (ticket agent), indicated by arrow); L.B. Thain (Surgeon); William Sampson (Chief Engineer); John Forster (Master); Edward Jones (First Officer); Roger Williams (Second Officer); Charles Moore (Third Officer). A year later, only the surgeon and John Forster had left the* Empress. *(Saint John* Standard, *2 June 1914)*

Births and deaths took place aboard the *Empress* with regularity. When a death occurred, the surgeon was required to enter details in the manifest and the Official Log, along with the cause of death.

Quartermasters were responsible for steering the ship in response to helm orders issued by an officer or pilot on the bridge. On each four-hour watch, two QMs were on duty on the bridge. Each would have a shift (or 'trick', as it was termed) of two hours at the wheel, and two hours standing by. When instructed by an officer, a QM would perform other duties as well, such as streaming the log (*i.e.* measuring the ship's speed by lowering a patent log over the side).

It should be noted here that in the British merchant marine and Royal Navy, steering commands at the time were issued to QMs as *helm*, not rudder, orders. Thus, the officer on the bridge, if he wanted the *Empress* to turn two points to starboard, would order the helm to *port*. This was a holdover from the days of sail and represents a point of confusion for many modern readers, for such orders are the exact opposite of what one would expect.

The transition to rudder orders began over a century ago, beginning with the Swedish Navy in 1872, but the rate of change in tradition-bound maritime services was glacial. Although the United States Navy made the change in 1914, US merchant vessels did not complete the transition until the mid-1930s, and it was only in 1933 that Royal Navy and British merchant vessels abandoned the old practice.

Crew's concert troupe, Empress of Ireland, *early 1914, from the Montreal* Daily Star, *30 May 1914.*

Orders were also given in terms of 'points', not much used in today's maritime world. In fact, a point was $11\frac{1}{4}$degrees, the compass being divided into 32 points instead of 360°. Boxing the compass, *i.e.* correctly naming all thirty-two points in order, was one of the first requirements of basic seamanship for any deck rating.

Another practice that was changing was the use of 'right' and 'left' instead of the traditional 'starboard' and 'port'. In 1914 the US Navy used the former while the merchant service continued with the latter.

The Master-at-Arms was responsible for general police duties. Aboard the *Empress*, he would have been in charge of overseeing deportees from Canada to ensure they did not escape custody, and that they did not pose a danger to other passengers. And, if the master issued any charges, the Master-at-Arms would have been responsible for enforcing them. Arrests of stewards, for example, sometimes occurred aboard CPR vessels, for reasons like petty theft of passengers' belongings or company property. In such cases, the Master-at-Arms would confine the accused offender until he could be delivered into the hands of a competent authority ashore.

Occasionally offenses on board could be more serious. On 11 August 1911, fifty-seven first and second class stewards aboard the Allan Line's *Victorian* were charged with mutiny for refusing to serve breakfast and luncheon to passengers, and the stewards were jailed on the ship's arrival at Montreal. That particular incident was settled at the end of the month when, at the suggestion of the court in Montreal, each of the stewards filed up to Captain Outram, saluted, and acknowledged his regret for the occurrence.

Though a short-lived mutiny by three crewmen occurred in the CPR's *Mount Temple* in October 1913, there is no known mutiny aboard the *Empress*, and no instance of petty theft requiring intervention by the Master-at-Arms.

The Boatswain was a petty officer with immediate charge over all deck hands, and was also generally responsible for lifeboats, anchors, cables, cordage, and cargo gear. He was assisted by a Boatswain's Mate.

The Donkeyman was in charge of the small steam engine that supplied steam to auxiliaries and heat when the *Empress* was in port and her main boilers were not fired up.

Seamen were divided into two types: Able-Bodied or ABs, which initials were generally placed after a seaman's name on the Crew List, and Ordinary Seaman (OS).

Engine Department

The Engine Department of the *Empress* was a world unto itself, presided over by the Chief Engineer who reported to the master. Between 1906 and 1914, there had been only one Chief Engineer, William Sampson, whose career as a ship's engineer spanned more than thirty-four years.

Under Sampson's supervision, the Engine Department was responsible for all mechanical and electrical systems on board the *Empress*. This included all aspects of propulsion and steering, and other matters of an engineering nature, such as electricity, refrigeration, heating, and ventilation. *Rule 136* of the CPR's instructions to officers also required the Chief Engineer to ensure the watertight doors in his department were kept in good working order.

Under Sampson were eleven subordinate engineers of various grades, each with special responsibilities and having different levels of experience. Engineering positions were licensed, and a typical progression was often upward from fireman, after obtaining the first license. The number of subordinate engineers does not seem to have changed over time. In 1909 Captain John Forster testified there were fifteen engineers and that eleven of them were fully certified.

Typical responsibilities in the Engine Department were as follows:

Senior Second Engineer	in charge of the starboard engine
Senior Fourth Engineer	in charge of the port engine
Fifth Engineer	made entries in the department's scrap log
Eighth Engineer	took the timings for the log from a clock at his watch position.

In terms of seniority, and using the 96th voyage as an example, there were: 1 Chief Engineer; 1 Senior Second; 3 Junior Second; 1 Junior Third; 1 Senior Fourth; 1 Junior Fourth; 1 Senior Fifth; 1 Seventh; 1 Eighth; and 1 Junior Ninth Engineer. Note, though, that the above does not include the four temporary engineers from the *Empress of Asia*. Including these four men, who were merely working their passage across the Atlantic, makes a total of fifteen licensed engineers under Sampson for the last trip.

Engineering officers required administrative as well as mechanical skills. The Department was the single largest part of the *Empress*' running expenses, with coal accounting for as much as forty percent of the ship's total operating costs. If the Engineering staff did not maintain the two reciprocating engines at peak performance, consumption of coal by the *Empress* would have become excessive, and costs would have soared.

Though numbers fluctuated from one trip to another, the normal complement of the Engine Department was approximately 135 positions, as follows:

Chief Engineer	1	Trimmer	45
Engineers (var. grades)	11	Greaser	18
Engineer's Boy	1	Electrician	2
Eng. Steward	2	Plumber	1
Fireman	52	Carpenter	2

At the 1914 Inquiry, conflicting evidence was offered concerning the exact number of engineering staff. Chief Engineer William Sampson stated there were eighteen officers, consisting of himself, fifteen engineers, and two electricians. In addition there were eighteen greasers, six leading firemen, and the remainder being divided between firemen and trimmers, making a total of 135 men for the Department.

Elsewhere, the Inquiry's report shows a total of twelve engineers, of whom eleven held first-class certificates , though only four were credited with such certificates in the Articles. The presence in the

Empress on the 96th eastbound crossing of four engineers from the *Empress of Asia* tended to confuse matters as well, for these men were working their passage back to Britain aboard the ship and were not part of the permanent crew.

While most of the above Engine Department positions are self-explanatory, three require some explanation.

A Greaser (sometimes called an 'oiler') was an unlicensed member of the Department who, as the name suggests, oiled and greased bearings and moving parts of the main engines, auxiliary motors and electric motors.

The duties of a Fireman (sometimes called a 'stoker') consisted of shoveling coal from locations where it was dumped, into the furnace, and spreading the coal in such a way to make the fire burn most efficiently. He also had to rake and slice the fires at periodic intervals, and clean the fire box of accumulated ash and clinkers. In *The Only Way to Cross*, John Maxtone-Graham paints a grim picture of the back-breaking, mind-numbing work of the stoker, leaving little doubt why these men were the most frequent deserters from the *Empress*. After arriving at Quebec on 22 May 1914, for example, five of the seven men who jumped ship were firemen; the remaining two were trimmers.

Trimmers occupied the lowest positions in the engine room hierarchy. These men worked inside the various coal bunkers in the *Empress*, shoveling and piling coal so that it would spill down the chutes and be available to the firemen. The work of a trimmer got more strenuous as the voyage progressed, for coal in the bunkers was moved entirely by shovel and wheelbarrow. As the coal nearest the chutes was consumed, the coal from further away in the bunkers had to be shifted to the chutes.

Typically in the *Empress*, coal would be taken from the lower bunkers at the beginning of a voyage. As these bunkers were slowly emptied, coal would spill down through traps from the upper bunkers into the lower. As the coal spilled freely downwards only in the area around the hatches, trimmers inside the bunkers would ensure that it fell into the lower bunkers.

Firemen, trimmers and greasers formed what was commonly called 'The Black Gang.' In British ships of the era, the black gangs were traditionally drawn from Liverpool's Irish community, and the *Empress* was no exception. Though not writing specifically of the *Empress*, Henry Kendall claimed that '…Liverpool firemen have always been, for tamelessness, in a class by themselves.' The rough men of the black gangs were the unsung heroes of every Atlantic passenger steamship, for the massive engines and boilers required a small army of men, feeding soft, bituminous coal into the boilers to generate steam and drive the massive propeller shafts. The black gangs were the foundation on which a shipping company's prosperity rested. They were the lowest paid and the hardest working men aboard any coal-burning vessel. They were completely unappreciated and few people realized that without them, the ships would have come to a halt.

The conditions of appalling heat and noise in the Engine Department are best thought of as one form of hell. Commented the *New York Times* in 1908: 'The withering heat of the stoke hole fries the working strength out of a fireman in four hours.' 'Soul destroying' was Maxtone-Graham's apt description of the work performed by firemen, adding that 'Both owner and master relied on the endurance, brawn and skill of those awesome men who kept up the steam.' Robert Ballard observed that hands would become blistered and blackened from the searing heat during the course of a watch.

The Canadian Pacific offered *Empress* passengers the opportunity to inspect their vessel. One first class woman passenger in the summer of 1908 wrote 'engine room wonderful', though one suspects she was taken by the massive propelling machinery and did not linger long enough to notice the conditions under which the black gang worked.

On a single *Empress* crossing the black gang typically shoveled their way through almost 2,500 tons of coal, equivalent to some 250 train cars.

Despite the strenuous nature of the work in the Engine Department, it was not only the preserve of young men. A list of crew members returned to England after the sinking of the *Empress* shows that the oldest of the black gang survivors was Patrick D'Arcy, 51, and there were many more in the same age bracket.

R.M.S. " Empress of Ireland " arriving at Quebec

The Empress *arriving at Quebec. (Stephen Brooks)*

The need for such a large crew in the Engine Department stemmed directly from the use of coal as a fuel. Coal was very labour-intensive at all stages: loading aboard ship, moving, and shoveling to feed the ever-hungry boilers. Moreover, it had to be trimmed, properly stoked and sliced to ensure maximum combustion and, after burning, the ashes had to be dumped overboard.

On a typical watch in the Engine Department of the *Empress* there were something like forty men at work: in the engine room, three engineers and five greasers; in the stokeroom, 2 engineers, 15 firemen, 12 trimmers, and 2 leading hands.

Chief Engineer William Sampson stood no watch; he was available whenever required. A 'double watch' was kept in the engine room of the *Empress* from the time she left Quebec to the time she was clear of land. The term 'double watch' is somewhat misleading, for it does not mean that twice the normal number of men were on duty at the same time. In reality, it meant that a senior engineer was on standby in case of problems.

The work in the Engine Department changed radically with the use of oil, a switch pioneered by the Royal Navy early in the twentieth century. When the *Empress of Britain* was converted to oil in 1919, an immediate result was a reduction in the number of firemen from 120 to just twenty-seven. There was a similar dramatic reduction in the RMS *Olympic*: 246 to sixty. When Cunard's *Mauretania* was converted in 1921, the numbers declined from 318 to just ninety, and almost immediately justified the conversion cost of £250,000.

Conversion to oil thus reduced direct operating costs (labour and food) and shortened the vessel's turnaround time in port, for oil could be pumped aboard far faster than coal could be manhandled from lighters or railcars alongside the ship. Two further benefits were realized as well. The reduced crew complement meant that additional space could be used to accommodate a greater number of passengers. And speed could be increased, since oil had a greater energy content than the same weight of coal. Even for a venerable liner like *Mauretania* in 1921, the improvement in performance was remarkable.

Victualing Department

This department, under the Chief Steward Augustus Gaade, was the largest aboard the *Empress*, its 220-plus members accounting for more than half of the ship's company. It was responsible for all aspects of passenger comfort. It included pursers, stewards and stewardesses, linenkeepers, bell boys, cooks, bakers, butchers, and a host of others, as well as the kitchen staff – all of whom, in one way or another, contributed to the running of the passenger-oriented aspects of the ship. Many of the Victualing Department staff rarely came in contact with passengers; others spent virtually their entire working day performing services for the travelling public.

However, the Department played an important role in shaping the reputation of the *Empress of Ireland* and, ultimately, its revenues. Good service meant passenger satisfaction, and satisfied passengers spread the word about the company and its Atlantic *Empresses*.

The Victualing Department in May 1914 consisted of 225 members, shown below:

Chief Steward	1	Printer	2
Purser	1	Writer	2
Asst. Purser	2	Boots	3
Stewards	33	Lamp Trimmer	1
Asst Stewards	100	Inspector	1
Stewardesses	10	Ticket Agent	1
Matron	1	Musicians	5
Linenkeeper	1	Chef	1
Bell Boy	6	Cook	21
Barkeeper	2	Pantryman	10
Interpreter	1	Kitchen porter	1
Bugler	1	Baker	6
Storekeeper	2	Butcher	4
Barber	2	Scullion	4

A brief explanation of some of the above positions is useful.

'Boots' was the man responsible for shining passengers' shoes in first and second class. As they worked at night, polishing the footwear passengers left outside their cabin doors, the men also functioned as night watchmen between the hours of 11 p.m. and 6 a.m. They made periodic rounds and checked to ensure that night lights were on, and answered infrequent night calls from the occasional sleepless passenger. It appears they also telephoned the bridge every half-hour to report that all was well. Chief and Second Stewards visited the passenger compartments at night on occasion to make sure that the night watchmen were alert. Lights were extinguished in the first class saloon at 11 p.m., the Café and Music Room at 11:30 p.m., and the Smoke Room at midnight. The bar closed at 11 p.m.

A bugler was used to summon first class passengers for meals and to provide the necessary signals for boat and fire drills.

Five professional musicians provided entertainment in first and second class.

Two writers helped produce the *Empress'* on-board daily newspaper. They would edit wireless reports to fit the paper, as well as add stories about the ship, travel in general, and on-board events.

The two printers were kept busy producing the newspaper, along with menus, entertainment programmes, and a variety of other items required for the running of the ship or information of passengers.

In general the staff of the Victualing Department did not stand regular watches. Instead, they had defined periods of duty, after which they were excused. Bell Boy Arthur Owen in 1909, for example, worked from

ALEXANDER CRAIK.

R.M.S. " *Empress of Ireland.*"

5:15 a.m. until 11:00 p.m., with one hour off, and every second evening he finished after dinner. Second class steward Frank Harrison, who survived the sinking, had a duty day that ended at 10:00 p.m.

In terms of workload, second class bedroom steward Frank Harrison in May 1914 was responsible for seeing to the needs of passengers in sixteen cabins, Nos 400 to 430, on the starboard side of Upper Deck. Even at maximum loading that represented some sixty-four passengers of mixed sexes and ages. Bedroom steward Edward William Braine, in 1909, was responsible for ten first class bedrooms on Lower Promenade Deck.

Even though passenger loads could fluctuate widely from one voyage to another, or between the westbound and eastbound crossings of the same voyage, staff numbers remained almost constant in the Victualing Department. When the ship had a light passenger load, the crew had a bit of a respite, although tasks were redistributed to ensure that all hands were kept occupied. As well, a good number of the men were also detailed to operate watertight doors, fire hoses or lifeboats, and these jobs were necessary regardless of the number of passengers.

Stewards and others for the Victualing Department could be recruited easily enough in the teeming British cities of the era. What the CPR looked for in particular were capable, calm men with outgoing personalities. They had to adapt to life at sea in close confines with others and had to be comfortable with prolonged absences from their families. Above all, the company needed men who could get along well with passengers, who could provide the kind of service that passengers expected aboard the pride of the CPR's Atlantic fleet. And, if a crewman had some other skill, for example the ability to carry a tune or play an instrument, that was a useful attribute. Such skills would further ensure that passengers were well entertained while at sea for six days. There were some twenty men who, in addition to their regular duties, served as members of the *Empress'* concert troupe.

In addition to their regular jobs as stewards, many in the Victualing Department had extra responsibilities in the event of emergencies. Some men were detailed to man a particular watertight door, while others were assigned to a particular lifeboat. Such tasks were well organized. As Chief Steward Augustus Gaade testified at the 1914 Inquiry, 'They pick the men out and this list is made out before the ship leaves port in Liverpool, and posted up so that every man may know what his station is. Exactly the same with the … extinguishers; everything is made out on large lists and a man knows exactly where to go to.' With respect to bulkhead doors, Gaade was asked if any men were specifically delegated to close them. He answered, 'There is a list made out and posted up on a notice board in the pantry so that every man can see it.'

Chief Steward Gaade was responsible for provisioning the *Empress* before she sailed, for overseeing the preparation of all food and drink served on board, and the passenger accommodations. His was a complex job, requiring great organizational skills and a deft human touch in dealing with demanding passengers. In each port Gaade needed to ensure that adequate supplies of food and beverage were ordered on arrival, and delivered before the next sailing. And, once on board, the fresh and canned supplies had to be properly stored, prepared and served.

The purser was in charge of the ship's general administration, and was, in effect, the on-board accountant and chief clerk, as well as being the person to whom passengers went with a problem. He and two assistants filled out passenger and freight manifests, crew lists, and other required documents. Every crew member

Steward Arthur Owen, left, and Assistant Steward Harold
'Curly' Tunstall, right, aboard the Empress of Ireland,
c.1910. Tunstall, who died in the sinking in May 1914, was a
featured vocalist in many Empress *concerts. (John Owen)*

had a Certificate of Discharge book which contained details of his sea service, along with a report on the person's character, which was filled in and signed off by an officer. Books for the 420-odd *Empress* crew members had to be kept up to date by the purser's office for each voyage, and returned to the crew member on the ship's return to Liverpool.

The purser was also authorized 'for the convenience of passengers, to exchange a limited amount of English, Canadian, and American money.' The purser's office contained a safe in which passengers were invited to deposit money and other valuables for safekeeping during the voyage. There was no charge for the service.

Of the various tasks assigned the purser, the most time-consuming – in this pre-computer era, when all work was done manually – was the preparation of passenger manifests. This was no small job, when the *Empress* routinely carried over a thousand passengers, most of whom would have to be seen personally by the staff. Manifests required a good deal of information about each passenger to be obtained and transcribed correctly onto the sheets that would later be submitted to the port authorities. Some degree of urgency was attached to preparing the manifests. Once the *Empress* arrived off Halifax or Rimouski on a westbound crossing the manifests had to be ready for the civil and medical examiners. And, on returning to Liverpool, the paperwork had to be ready for British authorities.

Crew Turnover

In terms of crew turnover, a best estimate is that between 1906 and 1914 the crew complement of the *Empress* turned over about 2.5-3 times, thus making a total of about 1,000 to 1,300 persons who served in the ship during her eight-year career. Expressed another way, it means that on average there were eight to ten new faces among the crew at the start of each voyage.

There were many, mostly in the Engine Department, whose service in the *Empress* would be measured in terms of a few voyages. The work was hard and more than a few men from the black gang deserted in Canada, lured by higher wages ashore and less arduous working conditions.

Of eight members of the firemen's band of 1908, not one remained in the *Empress* by May 1914; of eleven stewards who performed as singers at a 1908 concert, just one remained aboard the ship in 1914.

Only a detailed analysis of the Crew Agreements (all held in the Public Record Office in London) for the ninety-six *Empress* voyages would reveal the exact number of men and women who served in the *Empress* between 1906 and 1914. Such research is beyond the scope of this present work.

Some men, notably Chief Steward Augustus Gaade, made every one of the *Empress* voyages between 1906 and May 1914, and always in that capacity. Others, like Chief Engineer William Sampson, had similar long periods of service in the *Empress*. Irish-born Sampson, who had been an engineer since 1880, joined the ship in March 1906 during her fitting-out period at Govan and made every voyage.

Other stalwarts were Second Class Smoking Room Steward George Willis who made ninety-four of ninety-six voyages in the *Empress* and Thomas Williams, Chief Second Class Steward, who served seven years and seven months in her.

Nurse-Stewardess Alice Riddell was another longtime crew member. Giving up her position as Nurse-in-charge at Glasgow's Fever Hospital, she joined the *Empress* on the second voyage in 1906 and made every voyage thereafter. While doctors came and went, Alice Riddell became a fixture aboard the ship. Her duties as stewardess were on Upper Deck and over the years she became known to thousands of first class passengers. To passengers of any class afflicted with seasickness or something more permanent, she became an angel of mercy, dispensing aspirin and good advice, though the most common complaint she treated at sea was coal-ash in the eye, a problem that would disappear only when passenger ships converted to oil. One of just eleven women in the crew, Alice Riddell died on 29 May 1914. Her body was one of those identified.

Officers, on the other hand, rotated on and off the *Empress*, gaining experience in a variety of Canadian Pacific ships. Some, though, spent considerable time aboard the *Empress*. Mansfield Richard Steede began aboard the *Empress* as second officer and, by May 1914, was chief officer, destined one day for his own command on the North Atlantic. That would never happen: Steede died with the vessel he had served in so well.

Henry Kendall also rotated through the *Empress*, serving from 1907-1908 as chief officer under John Forster before getting his own ship. Only in May 1914 did Kendall return to the *Empress*, this time as master.

Uniform Regulations

Like most passenger lines of the era, the Canadian Pacific had standards of dress for all personnel aboard its vessels. While earlier dress regulations existed, the following is based on the amended uniform regulations which appeared in 1914 in a twelve-page handbook that outlined the uniforms to be worn by officers and crew members at sea and while on duty in port. Loosely based on Royal Navy norms, the instructions touched in painstaking detail on every aspect of clothing from cap to boots and specified when the various uniforms were appropriate.

Commanders were directed to see that the orders were carried out, and that uniforms were 'clean and neat and that all officers are properly and similarly dressed.' In keeping with the times, a certain formality was expected of all crew members. Officers of the Deck Department might have as many as three uniforms: full, undress and, for those who dined in the saloon with passengers, a mess dress, though full and mess dress were not required on purely cargo vessels. Ranks could be distinguished by the number of rows of gold lace on the sleeve of the full dress coat, the master having four rows one-half inch in width, the two centre rows forming a cross diamond. Gloves were also required, brown buckskin or dogskin, and white gloves on special occasions. The necktie was 'Black always.'

The commander's cap was similar to that of a captain in the Royal Navy, with a blue cloth peak embroidered with gold oak leaves and having the company's badge in a gold wreath, surmounted by a crown. White cap covers were to be used between 1 May and 30 September.

Senior members of the Deck Department (*e.g.* boatswain and mate, carpenter, and QMs) were dressed differently than ABs and Ordinary Seamen. And, while most crew members, including officers, had to supply their own uniforms, QMs had their uniforms supplied free after six months' service. ABs and OSs were required to wear a cap with a ribbon (the latter known as a 'tally') in which the ship's name was worked in gold thread.

Gold cuff braid was one way to distinguish among officers, provided one knew what to look for. Some members of the crew had their titles worked in gilt wire in $\frac{1}{4}$-inch letters on both sides of the collar, and one could thus identify the electrician, various levels of stewards, bugler, interpreter, master-at-arms, and barber.

Chief Engineer William Sampson wore a blue, double-breasted coat, with cuffs trimmed with four rows of half-inch gold lace, with purple cloth between the rows, and the other engineers could similarly be distinguished by their cuffs. Given the working conditions below decks, the company made one concession: 'Full dress is not obligatory in the Engine Department except for Chief and Senior Engineers.'

Standards were rigorous for those who came in contact with the passengers. Chief Steward Augustus Gaade wore a standard blue serge, double-breasted jacket with five silver buttons (of which four were to be buttoned), and cuffs trimmed with two rows of $\frac{1}{4}$-inch silver braid. When in the dining saloon at mealtimes, he wore mess dress, the cuffs again denoting his position. His cap was standard, and he was entitled to the silver CPR cap badge. Lesser ranks of stewards had their own uniforms, each subtly different.

Stewardesses, the only women in the crew, had two uniforms, as follows:

Morning dress – Blue print, of approved pattern, with collar, cuffs, and cap, and linen aprons. Aprons at top to have Company's flag at each corner.

Afternoon dress – Navy blue serge. Plain round bodice, fastened in front with buttons according to height, of approved pattern for Stewardesses, plain skirt clear of the ground, collar of dress to stand up, sleeves quite plain. Linen turned-down collars, cuffs, and cap, as per Company's pattern. Short muslin apron, as per pattern, with house flag worked on bands at points of shoulders. For warm weather, the dress may be of blue jean instead of serge.

Salaries, Tipping and Purchasing Power

In May 1914 Henry Kendall was paid £850 (about $4,250) per year as master of the *Empress of Ireland*, and had room and board paid while aboard ship. This was a very substantial salary for the day. As might be expected, that salary was more than junior captains of the CPR were paid. In fact, *Empress* masters were the highest paid men in the CPR fleet. As Captain John Thomas Walsh, the company's Marine Superintendent, testified, 'Suitability and ability and seniority lead them to the *Empresses*, and the *Empresses* are our best.'

As a point of comparison James Murray, who turned the *Empress* over to Henry Kendall in May 1914 and left the employment of the CPR to become Harbour Master at Quebec was paid $4,000 per year in his new position.

British masters were typically paid somewhat less than their counterparts aboard German vessels, who also shared in the earnings of their vessels. Some British vessels paid their masters a bonus if the ship operated without incident over the year, but this does not seem to have been the CPR's practice.

Chief Engineer William Sampson probably received about $2,000 per year, roughly the same as his counterpart in a German liner. While some British engineers received a bonus if their engines ran without accident for the year, the CPR does not seem to have followed this practice.

Shipping companies were not known as the best-paying employers. A junior officer in the British mercantile marine, according to a 1909 article in the *New York Times*, earned about $600 a year, from which he had to purchase his uniform. The article went on to observe that this was hardly sufficient, and that the junior officer 'who walks the bridge while his seniors eat has barely carfare left for himself.'

Third Class Menu, 25 April 1910 (Voyage 45E). (Marion Kelch)

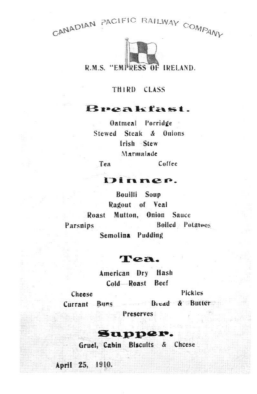

CANADIAN PACIFIC RAILWAY COMPANY

R.M.S. "EMPRESS OF IRELAND.

THIRD CLASS

Breakfast.

Oatmeal Porridge
Stewed Steak & Onions
Irish Stew
Marmalade
Tea   Coffee

Dinner.

Bouilli Soup
Ragout of Veal
Roast Mutton, Onion Sauce
Parsnips   Boiled Potatoes
Semolina Pudding

Tea.

American Dry Hash
Cold Roast Beef
Cheese   Pickles
Currant Buns   Bread & Butter
Preserves

Supper.

Gruel, Cabin Biscuits & Cheese

April 25, 1910.

Though it dealt specifically with the *Lusitania*, a September 1909 newspaper article offered some useful points for comparison. At that time, for a single Liverpool to New York passage, the captain and his six officers were paid just $99.42. Of that 'munificent' sum, the master earned $40.41; the chief officer, $14.55; first officer, $12.13; second, $9.70; third and extra third, $8.08 each; and the fourth officer, $6.47. Though none of these sums were high, most other Cunard officers earned even less. Ironically, captains of freighters made more than masters of passenger vessels, who were entrusted with the lives of thousands of people and vessels that were far more costly.

Put another way, just *one* first class fare (a minimum of $127.50) for the *Lusitania* paid the salaries of all her deck officers, with enough left over for the wages of two quartermasters, two firemen and two stewards, along with a couple of bellboys or a stewardess.

In 1913 the *Empress* made thirteen complete voyages, or twenty-six individual crossings. Assuming that Captain John Forster earned the same as Henry Kendall, $4,250, the amount per passage thus worked out to $163.46. Although wages had increased between 1909 and 1913, it must also be borne in mind that *Lusitania* made more voyages in a year than did the *Empress of Ireland*.

On a monthly basis, the following salaries for 1909 were probably typical for *Empress* officers, though actual pay depended on the length of service in a particular grade. A chief officer's salary peaked at $110 per month, where it remained until he was promoted to master. Monthly salary ($) after three months in the position:

Chief officer	90	Third officer	50
First officer	75	Fourth officer	40
Second officer	60		

The following table illustrates predominant wage rates per month (in shillings) for British crewmen engaged in passenger vessels between England and the east coast of North America, and the progression in their wages over time.

	1908	1910	1911
Able Seaman	80-90	80-90	90-100
Fireman	90-110	90-110	100-120
Trimmer	80-100	80-100	90-110
First Mate	285	285	310
Second Mate	220	220	250
Third Mate	185	215	215
Boatswain	115	125	135
Carpenter	150	150	155
First Engineer	375	385	380
Second Engineer	290	290	295
Third Engineer	230	230	250

Lower down on the scale in the *Empress* were the various grades of stewards who came in daily contact with passengers. A 1910 article in the *New York Times* stated that stewards were paid about $20 per month, out of which they paid for uniform and washing. Room and board were included in the wage. This number seems about right. Assistant Steward William Hughes, whose service in the *Empress* began in 1911, earned $11 per month, plus tips. Arthur Owen, a Bell Boy in 1909, was paid £3 16s per month, plus tips.

The 'plus tips' is important, for staff who performed services for passengers could easily earn gratuities that often amounted to more than the basic salary. Owen noted later, 'I received lots of tips and was thrilled to go home with pockets full of silver and gold.'

Seamen of the era were not well paid, though they did manage to get increases as a result of industrial action in Britain in 1911. The CPR's John Walsh, testifying at the Mersey Inquiry, reflected a prevailing attitude. '…[T]he leading seamen,' he said, 'after a certain number of years' service, if they behave themselves well and get a stripe or a badge, they get a little more, I think five shillings a month.' Even by the standards of the day it was a pittance.

When the *Empress* returned to Liverpool at the conclusion of a voyage, the crew's wages would be paid, and their discharge books were returned to them once they had signed off the crew agreement for that particular voyage. Those who wished to sign on for the next voyage would then be invited to do so. For officers and crew, there was never a guarantee they would be hired on for the next voyage.

Following a long-standing practice, when a ship was lost, the wages of all crew members, including the master, were halted, though the crew were entitled to compensation earned up until that time.

Almost at the bottom of the pay scale were the black gang, who performed the hardest physical tasks and received the lowest pay. And, since they never came in contact with passengers, they received no tips.

Tips were a sore spot with passengers and crew alike. Interviewed by the New York *Sun* in 1910, one English passenger observed, 'The practice of tipping is becoming a very great nuisance on some liners, where you can rarely ask a question without having to pay for an answer.' He complained, 'The amount of tipping done on a liner is out of all proportion to that in a hotel', and went on to blame American travellers for overly extravagant tips. Only the small fraction of stewards who served first class passengers were happy with the system. Others, serving second or third class travellers got proportionately less (if anything at all) and many in the Victualing Department, who worked out of sight of passengers, got nothing.

Some smaller lines had tried to discourage tipping altogether, but passengers could not seem to break the habit. Other passenger lines had tried to pool tips and share them among all the stewards who contributed to passengers' well-being. This was not a success either. Greater numbers of stewards in the newer vessels merely meant lower individual revenues. That led, in turn, to a short-lived movement among stewards for an increase in basic salary and abolishing tips altogether.

Liverpool shipping representatives, sensitive to the charge that the companies did not pay stewards a fair wage, observed that stewards were paid in accordance with the market value of the work they did. 'It is useful but not skilled work,' one said somewhat disparagingly, and added there was little prospect of abolishing the tip. He was right.

One union official noted that the rate of pay of a steward when at sea worked out to about a penny an hour, and stewards could spend as much as four months ashore due to sailing schedules. Stewards on the New York run also grumbled that the public had an exaggerated idea of the amount they made in tips. In a 1910 article in the *New York Times*, stewards lamented that many men and women simply walked ashore at the end of a voyage without giving a cent to the men who had attended them for a week on board. What was worse, they complained, it was always worse on the *westbound* trip, because American tourists, having spent all their money abroad, economized by cutting out the steward's tips on the voyage home.

Salary figures for *Empress* crew members, in isolation, mean almost nothing. To be meaningful, they need to be compared to other salaries, and considered in the context of what things actually cost in the Edwardian era.

The average wage in England for a labourer in 1914 was about 30s a week or about $7.50. Wages in Canada were always higher than in England, where manpower was abundant. In 1908 a teacher in Canada received about $850 per year, while a manual labourer was paid about $400 per year. In 1910 the Grand Trunk Railway in Canada paid its conductors $100-140 per month, and baggage handlers $60-85 per month. Yard foremen received $3.10 to $3.60 per day. Using these points of comparison, salaries of the *Empress* crewmen, despite the fact room and board were included, were low in comparison to other salaries in England, and considerably lower than in North America.

Prices, though, were very reasonable. In 1914 England, for example, 4 ½d bought a pint of beer, plus potato pie, cheese and pickle, and a twist of tobacco. A decent house in Leicester could be rented for 3s 6d per week, and in London's Faulkener Hotel by Charing Cross Road a room with bath cost 8s 6d – and that included a four-course lunch *and* a six-course dinner. By this standard, even the relatively low wages of the *Empress* crew were enough to support families back in Liverpool. Their families didn't live well, but they survived.

Unions and the Empress Crew

The Edwardian era was a time of growing unionism, and militant dockworkers and sailors in Britain were at the leading edge of the struggle for workers' rights and decent wages. Virtually every member of the *Empress*' crew, including the master and officers, were members of a union or an association. The vast majority belonged to the National Sailors' and Firemens' Union of Great Britain and Ireland. This was a large union, with over 90,000 members, and it claimed to represent between ninety and ninety-five percent of the sailors and firemen on British merchant vessels.

Represented at the Mersey Inquiry by its counsel, George Gibsone, the Union used the Inquiry to urge that the number of able-bodied seamen be increased, to two per lifeboat, since firemen and stewards were not trained in boat work. The *Empress*, Gibsone noted, had only nineteen ABs to look after forty-two boats, and the union made a clear distinction between ABs and ordinary seamen.

Other British-based unions had members in the *Empress* as well. The National Union of Ships' Stewards, Cooks, Butchers and Bakers represented a separate and populous constituency aboard passenger vessels. Engineering officers belonged to the Mercantile Marine Engineers' Association, though this was not a full-fledged union.

Even deck officers were unionized. In 1904 the Shipmasters' & Officers' Federation represented more than 6,000 members of the merchant marine service, although in 1912 a new union was formed, the National Union of Masters and Mates.

Canadian Pacific Rules

Almost every aspect of the navigation and discipline aboard the *Empress* was covered in a small handbook prepared by the company for the guidance of its masters and officers. The document appears to have been revised at intervals over the years, for the Mersey Inquiry was informed at one point that the rules were 'in proof.'

Some rules of interest to this narrative were the following:

Rule 23: The Commander, accompanied by the Doctor, Purser, and Chief Steward (and in the engine rooms by the Chief Engineer), will, unless weather conditions render it impracticable or unless the ship is in narrow waters, when the Chief Officer will act as Deputy, hold a complete inspection of all parts of the ship each day at ten-thirty a.m. During this inspection, all members of the crew detailed for watertight doors will be at stations, and all doors will be opened and closed. Notices must be posted in the passengers' quarters to this effect, with a request that complaints be made to the Commander. The Chief Steward will daily visit every stateroom whether occupied or not.

Rule 44: In fog or snow, speed is always to be reduced. Watertight doors are to be ready to be closed instantly, and every possible precaution taken for the safety of the ship. When to the eastward of Longitude 11 West or to the westward of Longitude 51 West, and whenever in proximity to the land, frequent soundings must be taken.

Rule 50: The Commander will see that at all times in foggy weather or in falling snow hands are stationed to close instantly all watertight doors which are not already closed. All self-closing doors will be kept closed. If at any time fog or snow shut down in the Gulf of St Lawrence or St Lawrence river, the same special precaution must at once be taken, entry being made in the ship's log book and in the engineer's log book of the time of opening and closing.

Rule 67: The cargo side ports will be opened whenever possible for purposes of ventilation, gratings being invariably shipped. These ports will be in the charge of the carpenter, and must only be opened by the instructions of the Commander or Chief Officer. The most careful attention must be given to the coaling ports below the upper deck. They will be in charge of the carpenter, acting under the instructions of the chief officer. Closing of ports before sailing must be entered in the log.

Rule 130: In the event of fog or thick weather and in narrow waters, orders will be issued from the bridge to stand by to close all watertight doors between engine rooms and boiler rooms and in bunkers. All self-closing doors will always be kept closed.

Rule 193: Before the ship proceeds to sea at the commencement of any voyage the Commander, assisted by the Chief Officer, Chief Engineer, Purser, and Chief Steward, will prepare a Fire and Boat Station Bill, appointing every man to his proper post, and the utmost care must be taken that every man on board knows his station and duty. Copies of the 'Bill' will be posted in a conspicuous place in the forecastle, engine rooms and stewards' and foremens' quarters.

Inspections and Drills

Inspections and drills were a routine part of daily life aboard the *Empress*, required either by law or by the CPR Rules, and served to make her an efficient, safe and well-run vessel.

As a British-flagged vessel the *Empress of Ireland* was subject to the *Merchant Shipping Acts* of 1894 and 1906, and the various rules and regulations made thereunder. Section 427 of the 1894 *Act* gave the Board of Trade power to make rules for life-saving appliances.

The *Empress* carried more than twelve passengers and was therefore classed as a passenger steamer.

She also carried more than fifty steerage passengers and was thus also classed as an Emigrant ship and she was engaged in the foreign trade. Consequently she fell under Class 1 for Foreign-Going Passenger Steamers. Certain rules applied to the ship, the three most important being:

> *Rule A*, that the ship had to carry sufficient lifeboats for the total passengers carried or the certified capacity, whichever was greater;
> *Rule F*, that ships between 400 and 600 feet in length had to carry at least eighteen approved life buoys;
> *Rule G*, that one approved life jacket or other approved article of buoyancy suitable to be worn on the body should be carried for each person on board, and that a sufficient proportion of the life jackets should be of a size suitable for children.

The *Empress* was subject to periodic inspections to ensure that she complied with the applicable regulations then in force and, having passed such inspections, was issued either a Passengers' Certificate or an Emigration Certificate by the Board of Trade.

A typical inspection, that conducted by the Emigration Officer at Liverpool on 15 May 1914 is described below in detail in Chapter 5.

The *Empress* was also inspected in February 1914 and issued a Passenger Certificate on that occasion.

In accordance with *Rule 23*, the master of the Empress conducted a daily inspection at 10:30 a.m. It was a thorough inspection, for the captain went through every part of the ship with a small entourage of officers. If a problem was found, someone was delegated to attend to it. In many cases, visitors were invited along, for the CPR was proud of its ships and had nothing to hide. Rudyard Kipling reported, 'I went all over her with the Captain at Inspection this morning,' and others were accorded a similar privilege.

Chief Steward Augustus Gaade was, by virtue of his position, a member of the inspection party. At the Inquiry he confirmed that the inspection was made every day and discussed the watertight doors. '[E]very morning,' he testified, 'at quarter to eleven, the doors are inspected… and the steward who is in charge of the second class goes with us until we finish with his doors, and the steward from the third class goes with us also until his doors are closed.'

Subsequent testimony showed that the inspection party was accompanied by Chief Engineer Sampson, as *Rule 23* required, and that the daily door drill was witnessed by him or, in his infrequent absence, by the senior second engineer.

Other inspections were performed as well, though these did not require the presence of a deck officer. Chief Steward Gaade visited every stateroom, occupied or not, on a daily basis as required by *Rule 23*. Stewards went to each cabin under their charge and ensured that the portholes were closed and screwed down with a special key by the time they went off duty at night, usually around ten o'clock. This particular duty was not always completely executed. In Mary Hill's cabin in 1910 one of the bunks got wet from an open porthole, and testimony at the 1914 Inquiry leaves some doubt that all portholes were closed the night of the disaster.

Boat drill (also called 'Deck Drill') was conducted by the crew prior to leaving each port, their specific responsibilities having been posted in advance in different sections of the ship. This suggests that *Empress* passengers were not assigned to specific lifeboats, and that no boat drills were conducted with the passengers actually on board, wearing their life vests and assembling at their designated lifeboat. Whether such additional steps would have saved lives in 1914 is a moot point.

Notices with emergency signals were posted in each pantry. A long blast of the siren, for example, meant that the men should attend to their watertight bulkhead doors and close them, then proceed to their boats. Those men not charged with a door were required to go straight to their boats. Despite being equipped with a steam whistle and siren, unusual in passenger steamers of the day, only the

Empress' siren would be used to signal an emergency such as 'Abandon Ship'.

In the summer of 1911, during turnaround of the *Empress of Britain* in Quebec, a journalist named Jane McPherson who was staying at the CPR's Chateau Frontenac Hotel overlooking the harbour, visited the ship. She and her aunt witnessed the lifesaving drills and described the activities thus:

> It just happened that we had the privilege of seeing the crew being put through their usual life saving drill, which takes place every Thursday when these boats are in port. Every man on board is mustered, and is instructed in case of accident what he should do and where he must report for service. It is very interesting to see the life boats manned, lowered and rowed around the ship, also to see the great collision mat quickly put over an imaginary hole in the side of the ship, and to watch the men rush with hose, buckets and blankets to put out an imaginary fire. There was no hesitating or inattention, every man seemed to understand just what was expected of him and performed his part with precision and pride.
>
> In this safety drill the watertight compartments are closed and opened a number of times to test their mechanism and to see if they are working properly. All of the life boats are kept provisioned with biscuits and water enough to last several days.
>
> The *Empresses* also have a powerful searchlight, which is always ready for service when required.

Turnaround

The last passenger walking down the gangway of the *Empress* marked the beginning of a five-day process known as the 'turnaround', a massive logistical exercise in which the ship was made ready for her next crossing. During that time a myriad of tasks had to be accomplished, for the *Empress* had to be re-supplied with fresh and frozen meat and fish, fruits, vegetables, and the ingredients to bake fresh bread, pies, pastries and other delights, beer, wine, and spirits, along with fuel, potable water and other consumable items. Every department aboard ship had its tasks to perform during this hectic period.

Sailors cleaned and inspected equipment, scraped, painted and polished the ship's brightwork, so that she gleamed as brightly as on the June day in 1906 when she had been delivered to her owners.

The Victualing Department had a mountain of dirty linens and laundry to send ashore for cleaning and ironing, probably upwards of 20,000 items that needed to be returned on time and stowed. Cabin stewards cleaned their assigned cabins and public areas of the ship, getting everything ready for the next wave of passengers who had a right to expect everything would be perfect. In third class, the cabin staff burned the straw bedding, and new straw and sheets were provided.

It was in the Engine Department where the most grueling tasks lay. Boilers and furnaces were allowed to go cold, whereupon they were inspected minutely from the interior to comply with regulations from the Board of Trade. They were cleaned and de-scaled to ensure optimum fuel efficiency. Coal was the single largest expense item in the Engine Department, and anything that increased the ability of the furnaces to turn coal into motive power was important to the company.

As well, the two massive engines were rigourously inspected. The engineers disassembled, cleaned, replaced, repaired if required, and oiled various components.

And, in the worst and most time-consuming job of all, some 2,400 tons of bituminous coal had to be manhandled aboard and properly stowed in the bunkers. This was a messy business, for the soft coal generated clouds of greasy dust that left a black film on everything. Once the last of the coal had been loaded aboard, the decks were hosed down. Then the staff went around and carefully removed all traces of dust from the ship. Brass was polished to a mirror shine, windows washed and everything put into shipshape order.

In Liverpool the chronometers were removed and taken to an optician for adjustment and calibration.

The Empress of Ireland *at the Landing Stage, Liverpool. (*Illustrated London News*)*

Though the turnaround normally took five days, it could be done in less. Thus, if the *Empress* had been delayed at sea for some reason, she could still mange to get away on the planned sailing date if the crew put in an extra effort.

A five-day turnaround was about normal for vessels on the Canada-England routes, though it was longer than for ships on the prestige run to New York. In December 1910 *Mauretania* made headlines by sailing from Britain to New York and back in twelve days, having turned around in New York in just 48 hours.

The turnaround process would be speeded up in later years once vessels had been converted to oil. Unlike coal, oil could be pumped directly aboard and into the bunkers.

Despite the work involved in turnaround, there is ample evidence to prove that the crew of the *Empress* had enough free time to participate in the social life of the ports in Canada which they called home.

Coal and Coaling

Coal was the single largest expense item for the *Empress of Ireland*, in the same way that jet fuel is the largest expense item for an airliner. As a point of rough comparison, the full fuel capacity of a Boeing 747-400 is 216,824 litres, representing a cost to the airline of some C$87,000 (using prices current in February 2000). For comparison, the *Empress* carried 4,000 tons of coal (though she used about 2,400 tons on a single crossing). With coal at Quebec valued at about $3.75 a ton in 1912, the coal aboard the ship was valued at $15,000 (assuming she was fully coaled). Converting this to today's dollars gives an equivalent of about C$300,000.

The *Empress*, like all ships of the day, burned bituminous coal, found in abundance in many parts of the world. In Canada coal for the *Empress* probably came from Nova Scotia's Cape Breton Island, which were the closest mines to the *Empress*' Canadian ports. The Cape Breton mines, first worked in the 1720s, produced more than half of the coal used in Canada. Steamship coal was usually provided under annual contracts, and prices fluctuated from year to year. In 1912 'Dominion'-grade coal in Sydney, Cape Breton, was priced at $3.50 per ton at the ship, up from $3.25 a year earlier. With shipping costs, the coal probably cost $3.75 in Quebec. Coal in Canada was generally remote from the end users, and shipping it to market added significantly to its cost.

At Quebec, the Dominion Coal Company rented storage space at the docks from the government, where it stored (in 1906) some 13,000 tons of coal. From these stocks it supplied ships in the navigation season, homes in winter, and businesses and steam plants year-round.

In Britain coal was abundant and came from various regions of the country. Supplying shipping companies at Liverpool was a very competitive business, due to the volumes of coal required by the large shipping lines. Steamship companies often contracted for coal directly with the colliery, with the contract typically calling for weekly delivery of a fixed amount of coal, often specified as the best hards and the best smalls. Using London prices as a guide for Liverpool, the price in 1912 for Best Durham unscreened was 16s 3d per ton, and this increased the next year to 19s 6d. In 1913, filling the *Empress'* bunkers in her home port would have cost roughly £4,100, or some £164,000 in today's money.

Coal prices in Britain had been increasing steadily for two decades, so that coal in 1913 was roughly $2\frac{1}{2}$ times its price in 1893. This was a great concern to ship owners. Anything which pushed up the price of coal had an immediate impact on operating expenses, and meant owners had to increase fares or reduce profits. And, because in the Edwardian era British imports and exports moved mostly by sea, coal hikes could trigger a round of price increases that rippled through the economy. Not much has changed today. OPEC price increases affect trucking firms and airlines, and have the same inflationary tendencies.

Coal consumption for the *Empress* was estimated by Fairfield to be 1.37 lbs/IHP/hr. Using a figure of 18,000 indicated horsepower, this means the *Empress* burned 24,660 pounds (or 12.3 tons) per hour. Over the course of a six-day trip, she would consume about 2,400 tons, a fraction of the 1,000 tons per day required by *Lusitania* and *Mauretania*.

Every single pound of those 2,400 tons had to be loaded aboard by hand. 'Coaling' it was called, and it was a slow, back-breaking, dirty job.

Typically, coal for the *Empress* arrived at the dock in rail cars or lighters. It was then shoveled by hand onto elevators which raised it from the rail car or lighter to coaling ports located along both sides of the ship below Upper deck. The ports had removable covers and led, via chutes, to the bunkers, or storage areas. Once the coal had been poured into the chutes, itself a noisy process as the coal tumbled down the iron chutes, it had to be distributed evenly in the bunkers, the largest of which stretched along the inside hull of the ship.

Once coaling was over, the carpenter sealed the coaling ports to prevent the entry of seawater into the bunkers. Coaling ports were secured by studs screwed down from outside the hull. *Rule 67* required this to be done under the supervision of the chief officer, and the sealing of the ports was entered in the ship's log. That done, the cabin staff could begin to clean up the thick residue of coal dust.

Coaling in other ports was probably similar, except that the *Empress* may have been coaled exclusively by lighter. In this case, she would be boomed out from the pier and lighters would come alongside so that their coal could be taken aboard.

Provisioning the township

An incredible variety of fresh and preserved provisions found their way into the *Empress* in the two days prior to each departure. With a typical load of 1,000 passengers and 420 crew, the chefs in the *Empress* could expect to serve something over 25,000 meals during the six-day voyage. And, while those in third class were fairly easy to please and their meals were straightforward, passengers in first and second class expected – and got – food that would rival the meals served in any first class hotel ashore.

Even for a voyage of seven days, the *Empress* carried enough fresh provisions for about twelve days, and enough non-perishable staples for a month. By law the *Empress* was required to carry sufficient food stocks for twenty-eight days at sea, in case of a problem.

Using a 1908 summary of the provisions required for a single 7½-day passage of Hamburg-Amerika's *Amerika*, we can pro-rate the German ship's numbers and arrive at an estimate of the foodstuffs required for a single crossing of the *Empress*. Assuming 1,100 passengers and 400 crew in the *Empress* (compared to a total of 4,000 in *Amerika*) and a typical voyage of six days, we arrive at the following:

9,600 pounds of beef, lamb, mutton, veal and pork
2,250 pounds of game and poultry
1,050 pounds of fresh fish
75 pounds of smoked fish
2,250 pounds of fresh fruit
24 cases of oranges
10,800 eggs
3,600 pounds of bread (to be baked at sea)
1,350 pounds of canned meats
540 pounds of salted meat
725 pounds of ham, sausage, smoked meat, and tongue
270 pounds of bacon
750 pounds of butter
675 pounds of cooking butter
540 pounds of cheese
7,500 pounds of flour
2,250 pounds of rice
600 cans of vegetables
615 pounds of coffee
400 pounds of tea
1,200 quarts of milk and cream
525 pounds of sugar
plus bottled water, and a variety of beers, wines and spirits.

Supplies in such quantities would have been available only from the same shore-based provisioners that served the best hotels in Liverpool, Quebec, Saint John and Halifax, and represented a significant business.

Meals

Meals were at set times aboard the *Empress*, though these varied by class.

In first class, where the dining saloon was large enough to accommodate all first class passengers at a single sitting, breakfast was from 8:30 to 10:00 a.m. Luncheon was served at 1:00 p.m., and dinner at 7:00 p.m. Beef tea was served on deck in late morning, afternoon tea at 4:00 p.m., and stewards would bring snacks if requested.

First class passengers were expected to make seating arrangements in advance with the steward. Children were not permitted to eat in the first class saloon unless they had paid full fare; otherwise, they ate in a separate (and nicely appointed) dining room, also on Shelter deck.

Meal times for second class were slightly different than for first, in order to ease the work in the single galley which served both dining saloons. Breakfast was offered at from 7:30, luncheon at 12:00 p.m. and dinner at 6:00 p.m. Tea or soup was served at 11:00 in the morning, with afternoon tea at 4:00 p.m. Depending on the number of passengers, two sittings might be required.

In third class breakfast was probably served at 8:00 a.m. The main meal, dinner, was served at midday, followed by afternoon tea. 'Supper' – which hardly deserved the name, as it typically consisted of gruel, biscuits and cheese, was served late, around 9:00 p.m. by one 1907 account, though on most crossings there were probably two meal sittings due to the number of third class passengers.

In terms of the quality of the food, most *Empress* passengers pronounced it very good, regardless of the class they travelled. Rudyard Kipling called the food in first class 'Not bad', and one passenger even complained in a postcard that there was too much of it. Another first class passenger in 1908 described the food as 'good' and added '…I have done nothing but eat non-stop since we left.' Food in third class tended to be somewhat repetitive and bland, but an American college student in 1907 called the third class dinner 'splendid', though lamenting that 'the tea and coffee are awful!' A Canadian clergyman in 1910 in third class called the food 'good, well cooked, and varied each day.'

Four Thousand Meals A Day
Three separate galleys, all located on Saloon deck, served first, second and third class passengers. On a typical day at sea, over four thousand meals were prepared. Under the supervision of the chief chef, more than thirty men laboured in the galleys. After an 'open house' was held aboard the *Empress* in November 1906, a reporter from the Saint John *Globe* described the kitchens.

'…none of those who were fortunate enough to view the kitchens could have failed to remark the ingenious devices by which the huge task of feeding over three thousand people upon shipboard is accomplished. With all the marvellous facility and ease by which this is accomplished the cuisine of the floating table is such as only the leading hotels on shore can rival. By means of the electric lift which connects the storerooms with the kitchen is conveyed every staple and delicacy known to the tables of the best hotels.
It will be seen that the work of catering to the large and diverse assemblage on a great liner is one which calls for something very special in the line of cooking devices. Nowhere can a better or more up-to-date system of this kind be seen than in the culinary department of the *Empress of Ireland*.

Electrical and steam power plays an important part in the cooking outfit. A button pressed, or a belt slipped on, and any desired part of the mechanism is working in a manner which produces the finished article in the shortest space of time which science has been able to accomplish – a time which will probably cut in half, at least, that which the operation consumes in the best shore kitchen. On board the trans-Atlantic liners the rare old English custom is pursued of serving five meals a day. The kitchen is in large measure the dispensary of curatives, too, and the numerous extra orders, in addition to the regular meals, make time a very serious consideration in the sea-going kitchen.

On the outer edge of the works is the pantry, where a regular host of plates, cups, saucers and all kinds of dishes are stored in a continuous row of wooden cabinets with copper tops, known as 'presses.' Each press is fitted with sliding shelves perforated to allow the moisture to percolate, and no space is wasted. When the dishes are taken from the mechanical washers they are placed in rows, and as each apartment of the presses is heated by steam, the dishes are dry when needed. The washers from which they have come consist of two huge round tin vessels, each with a capacity of fifteen gallons. Inside is a revolving stand which holds the dishes. A touch turns on the power, fresh water is kept pouring in, and in a jiffy these capable machines are ready for another load.

Adjacent to the china presses are the egg boilers. The chef who may wish to boil an egg with these does not have to worry himself lest they boil too soft or too hard. He places the eggs in a certain one of a row of large copper spoons, drops the latter into the water, and when the eggs have boiled the proper time – two minutes – three minutes – the spoon bobs up serenely and holds its burden out of the way of harm.

In the pantry are several of the numerous 'jamberees' – eight or ten gallon copper tanks in which tea, coffee, soup and the like are heated by steam, and drawn off in the desired quantity. As for the dishes which are not in the presses, because of their being required more frequently, these are slung by the handles on long rods attached to the roof, where they sway and adjust themselves to the rocking of the heaviest seas.

In the main section of the department stands the great range, twenty feet long, ten feet wide, an affair of wonderful possibilities and powers. It is built upon a double plan, each side corresponding to its mate. When the vessel is in port only one side is put to use. At one end are the capacious broiling ovens, where the grills, steaks and toasts are prepared. Charcoal is spread over a space five feet square, and over this glowing layer the preparation can be grilled to a nice shade of intensity. Between this portion and the roasting end, intervenes the main section, which is at once a mixing table and a cooker. In the burnished copper cauldrons which form part of its equipment, soup, stews, and the like are concocted in quantities such as ten or twelve gallons at a time. One end of the monster range is devoted to the roasting department of the culinary art. Here, in a huge cavern, are located the revolving spits, operated by electricity. Big iron hoops, these are, whose hooks are capable of holding a half dozen large roasts at a time. Both the heat and the speed of turning may be easily regulated, the former through a clever arrangement of wire frames, and the spit is much more satisfactory than the old-time turnspit or dog. The chef turns the button, and the 'juice' does the rest.

In the bakery is found a solid block of ovens, in which eighteen large sheets of bread, cake or pastry may be in process of baking at the same time. Speed is sought for in the bakery, too. This end is largely accomplished by the steam dough tester, where the much-used power is used to force the dough into the proper consistency. The tester is a large steel box, with compartments. It receives the dough in the baking tray, and when it is 'just right' these are popped across into the oven. To trace the bread still father back in its evolution, we are introduced to another room, where the dough is mixed. There are some pretty successful mechanical dough mixers on the market now, but what will the housewife say to one which works by steam power and mixes a barrel of flour in the remarkable time of eight minutes? This trick is accomplished by means of a revolving arrangement, something on the plan of an ice-cream freezer. When the bread is ready for the table it is stowed in a small room whose shelves have to hold sufficient of the food to supply three thousand persons with fresh bread daily.

The use of steam as a cook is brought to a climax in a great steel cooker, ten feet by five in surface, and five feet high – a device which holds the record for rapid cooking. Steam circulates through its numerous departments, which may each contain a different dish, and cooks them all in half the ordinary time, or in less. A large ham is a small thing for this cooker to handle in two hours, while it prepares potatoes thoroughly in fifteen minutes. In accordance with the space-saving spirit of the whole, the top is fitted with a varied assortment of cooking dishes.

It would hardly be supposed that in proximity to all these time, labour, and space-saving devices the old-fashioned hand method of cutting cold meats and bread would be tolerated. It is, in fact, replaced by a machine which works on the principle of a rotary saw. As fast as the loaf is shoved along a heavy revolving steel disk sings through it, severing the slice with greater accuracy than the most mathematical housewife could dare to hope for.

Speaking of housewives, it is said that a great many of those who see the marine kitchen find it very hard to reconcile themselves to the common terra firma variety. They quite envy the lot of the chefs who go down to the sea in ships.

Winter Overhaul

In the post-Christmas period there was a natural drop-off in the numbers of passengers who needed (or wanted) to travel the North Atlantic. While business people still needed to travel in first or second class, fewer emigrants made the voyage, and their numbers could be met with reduced sailings. Shipping lines like the CPR, Allan and Cunard therefore used the winter period to give their North Atlantic vessels an overhaul for, after a year of service on the toughest ocean in the world, most vessels required more than just preventive maintenance.

The *Empress of Ireland* skipped a sailing in January 1907, her first winter. She departed Liverpool on 14 December 1906 (Voyage 7W) and did not leave again until 8 February 1907. In her absence, the CPR adjusted the sailings of its other vessels or directed passengers to the Allan Line. The CPR made sure its two Atlantic *Empresses* were not out of service at the same time. Once the *Empress of Ireland* returned to work in February, her sister went to Liverpool for her overhaul.

Thereafter, a winter overhaul for the *Empress* was a regular occurrence, though it varied in terms of duration and timing, perhaps from the need to accommodate a similar overhaul of the *Empress of Britain*. In 1907-1908, a short overhaul appears to have taken place in January, with the sailing date pushed back by 10-14 days. There was no interruption in the ship's departures for 1908-1909, perhaps because the company felt that growing passenger traffic warranted keeping her in service. In the winter of 1909-1910 the *Empress* was in dry dock for three months for repairs following an accident, ample time for work that might have been neglected the previous winter.

For the 1910-1911 season, the January departure was stretched about ten days. The following winter the *Empress* skipped a January sailing, slipped two weeks in 1912-1913, and skipped a sailing in January 1914. Thanks to its close relationship with the Allan Line, the CPR had a variety of options to move its passenger traffic during the overhaul periods. In January and February of 1914, for example, it chartered *Corsican* and *Scotian* while the two *Empresses* were being overhauled.

Wireless

If the CPR had been reluctant to adopt new propulsion technology for its *Empresses*, it had no such qualms in terms of communications capability. Perhaps as a result of its experience with radio in *Lake Champlain*, an Elder Dempster vessel which was the first British merchant ship to be equipped with wireless in May 1901 and was acquired by the CPR in 1903, the *Empress of Ireland* had been equipped with the Marconi wireless system as part of her original equipment.

It was an astute decision, for the wireless apparatus could be used to make money for the company, while improving safety aboard ship. With wireless, the *Empress* could receive weather and other reports from shore stations as well as from other similarly equipped vessels within range. Communications were sometimes erratic, and service could be interrupted by thunderstorms.

Radio communication was still in its infancy and the equipment was primitive in comparison to what would come later. The wireless apparatus in the *Empress* had a transmitting range of only about 250 miles, though it had a receiving range several times that distance. The system was upgraded in 1909 to a standard 1.5 kW apparatus, suitable for longer range transmission. That meant it could remain in constant communication with a Marconi shore station, starting with Poldhu in Cornwall and switching later to Cape Cod, for a westbound passage. As well, it was fitted with a complete emergency gear. It may have been at this time, during the upgrade, that the wireless shack was moved from the Lower Promenade to Boat Deck.

By 1909 the masters of the two Atlantic *Empresses* had standing orders from the CPR to communicate with the company's management by wireless at the last possible moment before their ships passed out of range.

There was money to be made from the Marconi system by sending and receiving telegrams for passengers. A telegram to an *Empress* passenger could be broadcast by shore stations and received

The Wireless shack, Empress of Ireland. *'Well you go in there and find a young man all surrounded by most wonderful telegraph instruments which buzz and click and spit out long blue sparks.' – Rudyard Kipling (Stephen Brooks)*

aboard the ship. Equally, once the ship had come within transmission distance of a shore station, outgoing messages could be sent.

Like all shipboard wireless stations, the system in the *Empress* was owned by the Marconi company. For some vessels, Marconi rented the equipment to the shipowner. More often, it was installed by Marconi and paid for by the passenger telegram traffic. This latter arrangement probably prevailed in the *Empress*, since there was sufficient passenger telegram traffic to pay for the system.

Marconi installed the equipment, paid the salaries of the two operators, and transmitted official ship's business messages for free. In exchange, the CPR provided the physical space, room and board for the operators, and electrical power for the equipment. Money from sending passengers' telegrams was collected by the company and remitted to Marconi.

The *Empress* carried two Marconi operators, as did all British ships of the day, a senior and a junior. Both held first-class British government certificates, and were employees of the Marconi company, though they were subject, like everyone else aboard, to the master's orders. Operators were not assigned to a ship on a permanent basis; like other crew members they signed on for a particular voyage.

Watches in the radio shack were different than for other crewmen. The operators stood watches of six hours, with six hours off, compared to four hours on for other crew, and the wireless shack was manned around the clock. Each wireless operator had his own three-letter call sign. That for Ronald

Ferguson, for example, senior operator on the last voyage of the *Empress*, was 'MPB'.

Rates in 1909 for the service were as follows:

– to the United Kingdom: 10d per word, no minimum; every word in the text, signature and address were counted, and land lines were extra;

– ship-to-ship: 8d per word, no minimum, and all words were counted as above;

– to Canada, via the Marconi stations at Quebec, Grosse Ile or Rimouski, or relayed from another ship: 2s 1d for ten words, with each additional word at $1\frac{1}{2}$d. Using other Marconi stations increased the cost significantly: 4s 2d for ten words, with each additional word at 3d.

One 1907 first class passenger termed the rates 'very inexpensive,' a viewpoint someone in third class might not have agreed with. Traffic volumes at some of the Marconi stations could be quite low. Henry Kendall noted that in 1910 the wireless station at Father Point transmitted only a few hundred words a week.

Rates

Rates on the *Empress* varied by direction, season and, of course, by class. As well the CPR sometimes offered promotional rates, for example at Christmas or to attract immigrants. Company policy, from which even Thomas Shaughnessy did not deviate, stipulated that no discounts or reduced fares on the Atlantic steamers would be offered as favours, as was sometimes done for rail trips. The only exception to this ironclad rule was to allow CPR directors and their families a 50% discount on steamship tickets.

However, with the booking of a certain number of passengers as a group, the company gave free round-trip passage to the group leaders.

First Class

First class offered a complex variety of possible accommodations, depending on the configuration of the room and the number of persons in the room.

In her maiden season of 1906 the most expensive accommodation in the *Empress* was for an eastbound crossing between 1 May and 16 July, with a return between 1 August and 31 October. In this high-season period, an *en suite* room (of which there were just eight) on Upper Promenade deck cost $450 for one person, $500 for two persons, and $550 for three. Other rooms on this deck went for as 'little' as $195 for single occupancy.

As one went lower in the ship, prices were correspondingly reduced. On Lower Promenade deck, first class rooms ranged from $500 (for single occupancy, *en suite* outside room, with bath and toilet) to $175, depending on the type of room and location. If one were willing to accept an inside room on this deck, the rate was $150 for one adult, $100 each for two adults, and $80 each for three adults.

On Shelter (or Saloon) deck, outside rooms were $175 per single adult, and inside single rooms as low as $135.

By travelling off-peak, one could realize substantial reductions. The same *en suite* room on Upper Promenade deck that had cost $450 in high season was reduced to $350 – though that was still considerably more than most men earned in six months!

Children under ten were charged half fare. An infant under twelve months travelled free but, if there was more than one in a party, each additional infant paid half fare. Servants, if berthed in special servants' rooms in the *Empress*, were charged $65.

Each adult first class passenger was allowed twenty cubic feet of baggage free. Excess baggage was charged at the rate of 25 cents per cubic foot. All baggage was to be marked 'WANTED' or 'NOT WANTED', using special labels for the purpose. To each piece of luggage was also affixed a label bearing the first letter of the passenger's name. This made for easy sorting on arrival, as all bags bearing the same letter would be placed together. Steamer trunks required for the voyage by first class passen-

Afternoon tea on Promenade deck of the Empress of Ireland, Railway and Travel Monthly, *April 1911.*

gers could not exceed 3ft 6in length, 12in depth, and 24in width. As first and second class cabins were limited in size, passengers in these two classes could also label their trunk 'BAGGAGE ROOM' if they felt they would need it during the passage. In this case the trunk would be stored in special rooms on Upper deck, rather than being stored in the hold.

A steamer trunk of the era typically contained 6.5 cu.ft. Thus a first class passenger could travel with three trunks without paying excess baggage charges. It should be remembered that a first class passenger was expected to maintain certain standards and had a role to play while aboard the *Empress*. That role *required* an amazing variety of formal clothing, uniforms, and hats for the voyage itself, in addition to whatever was necessary for the rest of the passenger's trip. Life itself in the Edwardian era was an overdressed pageant and, while males might hope to get by with relatively few outfits, for women it was completely different. Convention dictated that she have a variety of fancy gowns, one for each night, in addition to all the other outfits required during the day. Still, one trusts that three trunks was surely enough for all but the most punctilious traveller.

Baggage, on later voyages, was separated by class and stowed in different holds. It took the CPR a couple of *Empress* crossings to realize that considerable time (and effort) could be saved at the destination by segregating the baggage in advance, rather than sorting it all on arrival.

Round-trip tickets were available at the combined eastward and westward rates, less a discount of ten percent on the return portion only. The CPR had a reciprocal arrangement with Cunard, so that each company accepted the other's tickets, provided space was available.

First class *Empress* passengers with through tickets to London were transferred with their baggage from the Landing Stage at Liverpool to the train station at no additional charge. Deck chairs were provided free of charge.

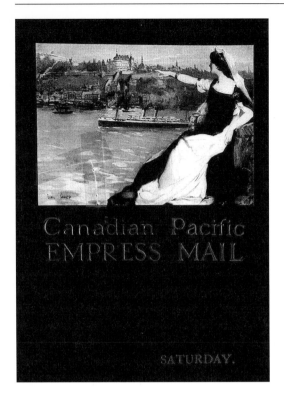

Cover of the 'Canadian Pacific Empress Mail', the generic diary and newsletter sold by the company. The Marconigrams in the centre page date this example to Saturday 7 October 1911. (Maureen Venzi)

Even the $450 first class suite was a bargain compared to what was available on the big liners out of New York. *Lusitania*'s palatial Regal Suites went for $4,000 – one way!

Second Class

Second class passengers were accommodated on Upper and Main decks, at adult fares ranging from $45.00 to $47.50 one way, and $85.50 to $90.25 return, according to location. Unlike first class, no allowance was made for season. If two persons occupied a 3- or 4-berth room, the rate was two and a half adult fares.

Baggage allowance for second class passengers was the same as first class, 20 cu.ft free, though excess was charged at 18 cents per cubic foot. The same size restrictions as first class were imposed on 'WANTED' steamer trunks.

The *Empresses* also carried pets for their first and second class owners. Dogs, for example, were carried to England for $10, but only if the owner had a license from the British Board of Agriculture certifying that the animal was free of rabies.

Bicycles and baby carriages were also carried for first and second class, though at the owner's risk, for a fee of $2.50 each, which one *Empress* passenger in 1907 termed 'exorbitant and senseless' and managed to avoid paying. The Rate Sheet suggested these items be crated. As in first class, deck chairs were provided free.

In an era that prided itself on personal service, the CPR provided some additional services for its first and second class passengers in the *Empress*. Immediately on landing at Liverpool, any mail for passengers would be brought on board and could be obtained from the library stewards. A similar arrangement was in place for arrival at Rimouski. Any further letters could be obtained at the company's ticket office at the wharf at Quebec.

Recognizing that letters and telegrams for passengers might not always connect with the ship at Rimouski and Liverpool, the company was prepared to forward them. Thus it requested first and second class passengers 'to give the Purser their name and address on the card for the purpose which will be found in the cabin or can be obtained at Purser's office.'

Third Class

It was in third class aboard the *Empress of Ireland* where the Canadian Pacific made the most money, simply due to the numbers of passengers carried. The company's Rate Sheet stated that third class rates included 'the use of bedding, eating, and drinking utensils free of charge' and promised that third class passengers would be comfortably berthed in closed rooms. 'Good food and attendance' were also promised. Deck chairs, though, were not provided for third class travellers.

Rates varied with the passenger's final destination. Eastbound from Quebec, for example, to Liverpool or London was (in 1906) $28.75. Infants were free; children over one and under 12 were charged half-fare. Infants to Continental destinations were charged $1.00, and $3.00 to Scandinavian or Finnish ports. Westbound rates were similar. Liverpool (or London) to Quebec was $28.75 per adult. From Scandinavian ports to Canada the fare was $35 ($38 for Stockholm), but this included free room and board in the CPR's lodgings in England, free baggage transfer, and meals on North Sea steamers. Fares from Finnish ports, depending on the distance from England, varied from $38.00 to $42.25.

Scandinavian passengers often signed a contact with the company for passage to Liverpool, and subsequent transportation to Canada by ship, and onward travel by rail. Passengers with contracts were issued two tickets, one for the trip to Liverpool, and the second for passage to Canada. The contract itself could not be used in place of the tickets.

Third class passengers over twelve were allowed just 10 cu.ft of baggage free, with excess being charged at $12\frac{1}{2}$ cents per cubic foot. Children over one were allowed 5 cu.ft.

Emigrants prevented by illness from travelling aboard their designated vessel were allowed to proceed by a subsequent steamer. If an emigrant were prevented from departing by the police, the fare would be returned.

Compared to its other Atlantic steamers, the CPR charged a premium for travelling on the two *Empresses*. In third class, for example, the rate from Quebec to Liverpool dropped from $28.75 in the *Empress* to $26.50 in the company's slower (but perfectly adequate) *Lake Champlain* or *Lake Erie*. Westbound rates similarly were reduced, from $28.75 to $27.50 for the same voyage.

For second class passengers, an adult single fare in a 4-berth room in *Lake Champlain* or *Lake Erie* was $42.50 eastbound or westbound on the Upper deck, compared to $45-47.50 in the *Empress*.

Over time, rates changed. There were any number of reasons – increases in coal prices and crew wages (low though these were) had to be passed on to customers. As well, rates could decrease in order to lure passengers from a competitor or help fill a vessel at a slow time of the year.

On occasion there were discounts for special purposes. In March 1907 the CPR advertised a rate reduction for British Columbia-bound immigrants, for the purpose of promoting settlement on the west coast. The company advertised a rate of one and one-fifth cents per mile between Liverpool to Vancouver. While the old rates had been $80.75 in the *Empress* steamships, and $79.50 in the company's other boats, the reduction lowered rates to $68.00 and $66.75 respectively.

Revenues

With the luxury and romance surrounding the *Empress* township, it is easy to forget that, like all trans-atlantic liners, she was constructed for a specific purpose. She had been launched not solely for prestige, but to move passengers, mail and freight for her owners – and, most importantly, to do so at a profit.

In the case of the CPR, other considerations came into play as well, for the company had first gotten into the steamship business to feed the railway network – already the world's largest – with passengers and freight, and to provide a continuing service for the railway's customers. And, as the CPR was also in the western land business, its ships could bring out settlers who would buy farms and ship their produce on the railway.

It is interesting to consider the revenues to the CPR from a single trip of the *Empress of Ireland*, and to show the relative 'value' of each class of passengers to the company.

Detail from the cover of the 'Canadian Pacific Empress Mail', the generic diary and newsletter sold by the company. The allegorical painting by noted American artist Cyrus Cuneo (1879-1916) depicts Canada welcoming the Empress in Quebec. Commissioned by the Canadian Pacific, Cuneo executed a number of works in Canada for the company. Many of these were lost when the CPR's London offices were destroyed in 1940 by German bombs. (Maureen Venzi)

Using Voyage 12W (the Earl Grey and Prince Fushimi crossing) as an example, the *Empress* arrived in Quebec on 7 June 1907 with 1,503 passengers. These were distributed as follows:

First class:	adults: 176;	children: 6;	infants: 2
Second class:	adults: 375;	children: 63;	infants: 21
Third class:	adults: 684;	children: 152;	infants: 24.

As a *rough* approximation, assume each adult in first class paid $100, children $50, and infants travelled for free. For second class, assume adults paid $45, children $22.50, and infants free. In third class, assume adults paid $28.75 (the minimum) and children $14.50, with infants travelling free.

Revenues by class are approximately:	First class:	$17,900
	Second class	$18,292
	Third class	$21,869
	Total	$58,061

To these passenger revenues should be added three further amounts.
First, the Canadian mail subsidy, amounting to one-half of the £3,000 per round trip, or about $7,500.
Second, the British subsidy for the Orient mails. Each one-way trip between Liverpool and Hong

Kong was worth $17,305 to the CPR. Apportioning 40% to each of the two ocean legs, this means the Atlantic *Empress* crossing was worth $6,920.

And, third, an amount for the carriage of freight. In this case, as no manifest has survived, it is impossible to hazard a guess as to the freight revenues.

However, it is possible to say that the CPR realized revenues in excess of $72,000 from this particular westbound crossing.

Routes and Ports

It is 2,633 miles from Liverpool via the Strait of Belle Isle to Quebec City, the ancient capital of Quebec and the St Lawrence gateway to Canada. Lying between Labrador and Newfoundland, and connecting the open Atlantic to the Gulf of St Lawrence, the Strait of Belle Isle is seventy-eight miles long and varies between ten and seventeen miles in width. The frigid Labrador Current sweeps into the Strait from the north, thus favouring an extended period of ice cover and restricting commercial navigation to the five months between June and late November.

Even in this period, floating ice and fog make navigation difficult, and numbers of *Empress* passengers wrote about severe fog conditions that required the ship to slow or even stop, with its horn blaring to warn other ships of its presence. Vessels in the Strait relied on land-based wireless stations to report weather conditions, as well as other wireless-equipped ships in the vicinity.

Caution and prudence were always hallmarks of the CPR. Though the company had acquired the Elder Dempster vessels in February 1903, it refused to allow its masters permission to use Belle Isle Strait, the so-called northern route, until the *Empress of Britain* made the passage on a trip to Liverpool in late August 1906. The CPR Rate Sheet for the summer of 1906 was still promising 'the steamships take the Southern Route (via Cape Race), adopted on account of safety.'

One reason for the company's change of heart was economic. A memo of 5 July from Thomas Shaughnessy to Arthur Piers observed that the company's use of the Cape Race route, instead of Belle Isle, represented some 20,000 miles of additional sea travel for the company's Atlantic steamships, or the equivalent of about seventy days extra at sea. That meant corresponding increases in wages, fuel, provisions and insurance. 'I want to discuss this subject with you on your return,' Shaughnessy commented.

In most years, ocean-going vessels did not attempt to use the Straits until late June. Even then, conditions were not ideal. In 1909, the master of the steamer *Devona*, the first vessel through the Straits that year, reported '…clear of field ice, but many bergs at Belle Isle and in as far as Cape Norman. Struck open field ice sixty miles east of Belle Isle and passed through twelve miles of it.'

Over the years, masters of vessels learned to exercise extreme caution in the waters around Belle Isle. Even so, accidents still happened with regularity. In June 1861 the Allan steamer *Canadian* sank after striking an iceberg off Belle Isle, a prelude to the *Titanic*. In September 1907 the Allan's *Mongolian* collided with the Thomson Line's *Hurona* in the vicinity of the straits, with both ships badly damaged, each limping more than seven hundred miles back to Quebec. The summer of 1908 saw *Monmouth* strike an iceberg in the Straits – her master at the time being Henry Kendall. In August 1912, just four months after *Titanic*, the Allan's *Corsican* struck an iceberg in the region east of Belle Isle. Damaged in the slow-speed collision, she continued on to Liverpool at reduced speed, assisted by *Lake Champlain* whose master happened to be Henry Kendall. And in the Gulf of St Lawrence, the *Empress of Britain* rammed and sank a collier in fog in July 1912.

For the so-called Summer Schedule to Quebec City, an alternative to Belle Isle was the Gulf of St Lawrence, following a track between Cape Ray at the southwest corner of Newfoundland and Cape Breton, Nova Scotia. This southern route added some two hundred miles to the voyage, making a total of 2,801 miles to Quebec, but it was safer and easier. Once clear of Cape Race at the south end of Newfoundland's Avalon Peninsula, the *Empress* could begin the great-circle track towards the Irish coast. Even this route had its hazards. Fog off the Grand Banks was notorious and icebergs were a

The Land of Promise by Frank Craig, 1908, showing third class passengers on the port side of Shelter deck. Craig travelled to Quebec aboard the Empress *(Voyage 26W) in July 1908. The drawing was later used by the CPR in its generic diary and newsletter. (Maureen Venzi)*

menace as well. In May 1909 the CPR's *Lake Champlain* struck a berg off Cape Race and, in July the same year, *Montrose*, bound for Montreal, had a similar accident in the same place.

The choice of route was left to the discretion of the master of the *Empress*. From newspaper and other accounts, her masters selected the southern route more frequently than one would expect. Sometimes there was another reason for selecting the southern route: in 1907 and 1908, Canadian mails were landed at Sydney, on Cape Breton Island.

Icebergs were a danger in spring and well into the summer months in the open ocean south and east of Newfoundland. As a result, the *Empress* sometimes took a more southerly track to avoid the worst of the icefields. April 1912 is a good example, for ice was unusually far south for that time of year, and ships bound to New York and Halifax took the southern route. On 26 April the *Empress of Britain* struck an iceberg in broad daylight less than 250 miles from where *Titanic* had been lost. With 1,400 passengers aboard, many understandably nervous, remembering the loss of *Titanic* less than two weeks before, the *Empress of Britain* was steaming slowly in thick fog when she struck a glancing blow. Lookouts had seen the berg in time and engines were fully reversed. The *New York Times* commented: 'In all Canadian ships there is one man on the lookout in the crow's nest and one in the foc'sle head, where it has been proved by experience an iceberg can be sighted quicker than from the crow's nest or the bridge.'

On 24 May 1914 Canadian Northern's *Royal Edward*, bound from Montreal for Bristol, struck a berg while going dead slow in dense fog 110 miles east of Cape Race. Not seriously damaged, she was able to proceed to England.

At the 1909 Inquiry, Captain Forster testified that in fog, his practice in the *Empress* was to remain on the bridge with the two watch officers, with lookouts at the stem and crow's nest, and a double watch in the engine room. With the crow's nest some 64ft above the water, visibility on a clear day would be about eight and a half miles; a lookout on the forecastle head, some 40ft above the waterline, would see just over seven miles.

When the CPR placed its order for the two sister *Empresses* in December 1904, it automatically restricted its choice of port on the St Lawrence to Quebec, though the company does not seem to have recognized it at the time. As late as November 1905 *The Times* still stated that the new *Empresses* would sail between Liverpool and Montreal, and it was only three months later that Quebec was confirmed as the summer terminus.

The reason for this restriction was simple. The *Empress of Ireland*, with a draught of 31ft 1¾in, could not navigate up the existing channel between Quebec City and Montreal. Even the port of Quebec presented obstacles to the *Empress* in the early years, for there were two important shoals below the city. If the ship did not arrive off the Crane Island flats at high water, she had to wait until the tide had turned. Similarly, the St Thomas Shoal which, until dredged in 1908, offered only 24ft of water at low tide.

With prodigious efforts, the Canadian government succeeded in deepening the channel between Quebec and Montreal to 31ft 11in by July 1913. Still, that wasn't quite deep enough for the newest ships. When the Allan Line introduced *Calgarian* and *Alsatian* the following year, they were obliged to terminate at Quebec for the same reason as the *Empresses*, eight years earlier.

Despite its importance to the country as a whole, the St Lawrence was not well lit until about 1908, when the last series of range lights was installed by the federal government.

In the winter months – roughly late November to late April – when the St Lawrence was blocked by ice in the pre-icebreaker days, the *Empresses* were forced to abandon Quebec. The CPR arranged its schedules so that the *Empress of Ireland* was never the first passenger liner to venture up the St Lawrence, nor the last to clear the Gulf before the water froze.

Only after the *Empress* had been in service for three months in 1906 did the CPR begin to address the question of a winter terminus with any seriousness. Not until the autumn of that year did Marine Superintendent John Walsh make an inspection tour of the docking and other facilities at Atlantic Canada's two major ports, Halifax (Nova Scotia) and Saint John (New Brunswick).

Walsh, born in 1871 in Chichester, England, of Irish parents, had been Superintendent with Elder Dempster in Liverpool, and was one of a number of talented individuals that the Canadian Pacific acquired when it had bought the Beaver Line and Elder Dempster's Atlantic vessels in 1903. His name, like several others in this narrative, would be closely linked to the *Empress* on numerous occasions throughout her career.

It was already late in the season when Walsh made his tour, for ice would close the St Lawrence route in less than two months, and the company needed to plan the schedules for its two new vessels. Walsh made up his mind quickly, recommending Saint John as the winter terminus.

Neither port was perfect, though Saint John merely represented the lesser of two evils and it was also a known entity, since the CPR and most other shipping lines were already using the port for Canadian winter traffic. However, before the *Empresses* could consider using the port, some hasty dredging work needed to be done at the CPR's Sand Point berths, to accommodate the deeper-draught vessels, and the rail connections needed to be upgraded.

Saint John, halfway up the Bay of Fundy, had two serious problems. It was prone to some of the highest tides in the world. Vessels like the *Empress* could dock at the pier only in accordance with the tide cycle. There were two docking 'windows' each day, extending from two hours before high tide, to two hours after. These windows tended to create traffic jams in the comparatively cramped harbour and incoming vessels were obliged to wait in deep water until the tide had turned.

The port's second problem was continual silting. The necessary dredging work began almost immediately, though it was not completed until a few days before the *Empress* first arrived in Saint John in November 1906.

Halifax had a better natural harbour, over a mile wide and six miles in length. It had a greater water depth than Saint John and was closer to Liverpool (2,534 miles) but lacked the immigration facilities to handle large numbers of people. As well, the CPR could not obtain running rights on the old government-owned Intercolonial Railway from Halifax, while it could use its own rail network from Saint John, a port it had served since 1889 with a short route through Maine.

Halifax was also a greater distance from Montreal, roughly a twenty-hour train trip by express train, compared to eleven hours for Saint John. Despite the fact that Saint John was her final destination in the winter months, Halifax was the mail point. The *Empress*, when inbound from Liverpool, briefly entered Halifax to drop off the mails. And, on occasion, to disembark some first class passengers who had this option.

Ideally, the Halifax stop did not take long. In April 1910 the Montreal *Gazette* noted that the *Empress* had arrived at 11:40 a.m. at Halifax and sailed for Saint John at 12:35 p.m. On other occasions the process took far longer, due to port delays and weather, frustrating passengers and the CPR alike.

Having cleared Halifax, the westbound *Empress* headed southward along the Nova Scotian coast, around Cape Sable, into the Bay of Fundy and thence to Saint John, a total distance of some two hundred and seventy miles. A similar arrangement took place on the eastbound voyage as well, with the *Empress* arriving in Halifax to connect with the mail train from Montreal. Sometimes the *Empress* failed to drop the Canadian mails at Halifax. In such cases the mail was sorted and postmarked at Saint John.

Empress passengers must have chafed at the additional delay occasioned by the stop at Halifax. The change of course for Halifax added an extra four to five hours steaming time, and the leg from Halifax to Saint John consumed the better part of a day, and the route from Liverpool to Saint John, at 2,700 miles, was already long enough. Worse, it was almost all open sea in the North Atlantic in winter – never a good combination for those who were prone to seasickness.

Most winter journeys to Saint John took seven days, rather than the usual six to Quebec, and it could hardly have been as enjoyable as the summertime run up the St Lawrence, with the last two days of the trip being sheltered in the Gulf of St Lawrence. The only offsetting factor was that the Civil and Medical examiners from Immigration could come aboard at Halifax and complete their work before the *Empress* docked at Saint John. Once at the wharf in Saint John, passengers could be swiftly disembarked onto waiting trains.

The winter port changed in the autumn of 1913 when the CPR abruptly announced it had selected Halifax as the winter terminus for its two *Empresses*, and the Allan Line announced a similar transfer for two of its vessels. On 5 December 1913 the *Empress of Ireland* docked at Halifax, and she would call the Nova Scotian capital her Canadian home port until May of 1914.

The three Canadian home ports of the *Empresses* were a study in contrasts. Quebec City, with a 1911 population of 79,000 was the largest of three, and a gateway to the continent. It was the country's seventh-largest city, an interesting and sophisticated amalgam of French and English cultures superimposed on one another. Halifax and Saint John, whose respective populations of 47,000 and 43,000 made them the Dominion's eighth- and ninth-largest cities, were typical eastern seaboard ports. Ice-free year-round, fishing and shipping gave them a dual focus, and they shared more in common with American cities like Boston and Portland than with Quebec. Both Quebec and Halifax were garrison cities where the military had been closely woven into the city's fabric for a century and a half.

Although Liverpool was her port of registry and English terminus, the *Empress*' route to and from the Lancashire port changed over time. In the summer of 1906, Moville in County Donegal in Ireland was the mail point, and the *Empress* took the northerly route around Ireland to pick up or drop off mail. 'North about' it was called, with the westbound *Empress* keeping her namesake island to port. Once Moville was dropped as a mail terminal later in the summer, the *Empress* generally (though not always) took the southerly route around Ireland, though the CPR vessels did not stop at Queenstown as did the New York-bound boats.

Although Cunard experimented unsuccessfully with other British ports besides Liverpool, and Canadian Northern served England by way of Avonmouth near Bristol, and others lines offered service direct to the port of London, the Canadian Pacific seems never to have contemplated a move from the great Lancashire port.

Liverpool, located at the mouth of the Mersey River, was one of the busiest ports in the world, the city through which one-quarter of Britain's maritime trade passed, along with more passengers than all other British ports combined. The city, which called itself the second-greatest port in the world, was a relatively new port, for its first docks had not been constructed until 1715. The Mersey River was prone to tide differentials of as much as thirty-three feet. In that respect, Liverpool was similar to Saint John, for the Bay of Fundy records some of the highest tides in the world.

On her approach to the Mersey, the *Empress* would pick up a pilot at the bar-ship, some thirteen miles from the Landing Stage where her passengers would be disembarked. The bar-ship marked the notorious Mersey Bar, a treacherous bank of sand and silt that obstructed the entrance to the river at low water.

In 1890, when dredging of the Bar began so that larger ships could be accommodated at Liverpool, the depth of water was just eleven feet at dead low water of spring tides, *i.e.* when the moon was new or full. No aspiring world-class port could restrict its traffic to shallow draught vessels, so dredging began in earnest. Despite constant work, by the end of 1912 no ship drawing more than 31ft could get over the Bar at low water. Depending on her draft, the outbound *Empress* would sometimes be forced to wait for the tide before she could venture into the harbour. Sir Sandford Fleming recorded a wait of four hours in 1909, and on one occasion early in 1907 the inbound *Empress* grounded and later refloated without damage.

A buoyed channel over the Bar, some 1,500 feet wide, led into the Mersey via the Queen's or Crosby Channels, and thence to the Landing Stage. The *Empress*, along with all transatlantic liners, moored at a floating dock known as the Landing Stage. It was the only dock lying in the Mersey, and a floating dock was the only practical solution to the river's great tide differentials. The first such floating structure had been constructed in 1847 but, by the early twentieth century, the Landing Stage was an immense structure, half a mile in length with a paved surface, and dated from 1876. Almost 200 iron pontoons were connected to the riverbank by mooring chains, booms and swivel joints anchored in the river wall. Seven bridges (one of which was for cattle) connected the Landing Stage to the mainland and the adjacent rail station. As its deck was just six to eight feet above the water, moveable gangways and high-level bridges were used for large liners. A number of low buildings completed the appearance of the Landing Stage. These housed post, telegraph and telephone offices, refreshment rooms, Customs examining rooms and shipping offices.

So busy was the port and so much in demand was space along the Landing Stage that the *Empress* had only a short time in which to load and unload her passengers. Maxtone-Graham notes that inbound passengers from Canada surged off the vessel in only an hour.

Coaling, victualing and other operations took place usually inside one of Liverpool's basin harbours, which could only be entered and exited at the high tide.

On sailing days, the *Empress* would be brought out into the Mersey and moored. Third class passengers were then brought out to the waiting liner by tenders, ferrying back and forth to the ship. Once they were all aboard, the *Empress* was brought alongside the Landing Stage to embark her first and second class passengers. In some cases, depending on the number of vessels scheduled to sail, third class passengers were also embarked directly from the Landing Stage.

The *Empress* normally made the trip between Liverpool and Quebec in six days, of which four were spent on the open sea and two traversing the Gulf of St Lawrence and the river. 'Only Four Days Open

Sea' was an inspired marketing slogan for the CPR's publicity posters, for it played on the fears of passengers who were afraid they might be seasick. Even four days must have seemed an eternity to many as the *Empress* ploughed her way through the swells, for the North Atlantic has long been regarded as the most grueling of the great oceans, and the *Empress*, by many accounts, pitched and rolled in heavy seas.

The slogan conveniently obscured the fact that there were faster ways across the Atlantic than the CPR's service to Quebec. Although Liverpool to New York – at 3,030 miles – was longer, the prestige ships on that run were larger and faster than the *Empress of Ireland*. Cunard's speedsters *Mauretania* and *Lusitania* were designed for speeds in excess of 25 knots, and routinely made the crossing in under five days.

The St Lawrence route was attractive to more than just Canadian passengers. Thanks to the CPR's excellent rail connections, returning Americans and US-bound immigrants destined for midwest points could easily get to Chicago, St Louis and Minneapolis.

Pilots and Fees

At the conclusion of the oceanic portion of her trip, the *Empress* was dependent on the services of a pilot experienced with the local waters. In the St Lawrence, the westbound *Empress* picked up her pilot at Father Point, on the south shore and just three miles downriver from Rimouski, a town of 3,000 on the Intercolonial Railway linking Quebec City and Halifax. Once aboard, the pilot stayed with the ship all the way to Quebec, where the St Lawrence narrowed to a width of just 1,314 yards. Eastbound, the pilot took her as far as Father Point and then went ashore in the pilot boat. The St Lawrence was a tricky body of water, with strong currents and reefs that spelled disaster for careless or unlucky navigators. Even the most modern of navigational aids and the services of a pilot were no guarantee against loss, as the Allan's *Bavarian* proved in 1905. Stranded at Wye Rock and too badly damaged to be refloated, she was later broken up where she lay. When the *Empress* began service in the summer of 1906, *Bavarian* was still there, a stark reminder of the river's perils.

Pilots on the lower St Lawrence were members of the Corporation of Pilots, whose members were accredited as pilots for and below the harbour of Quebec. Until 1914 the Corporation was an independent body, but in that year legislation was enacted making them responsible to the Minister of Marine and Fisheries. In addition to the safe pilotage of boats, pilots were expected to report to the Superintendent of Pilotage any defects in buoys or lights between Quebec and the lower St Lawrence. Each season prior to the opening of navigation, pilots were tested by a local doctor for sight and color vision. Pilots were ranked by seniority, and took ships on a simple rotational basis, the so-called *tour-de-rôle*. Fees earned by pilots were pooled and then divided among them.

However, shipping companies had the right to request the exclusive services of one pilot from the Minister of Marine. In such cases, the pilot did not become an employee of the shipping company, for he remained a member of the Corporation.

For its two *Empresses* the CPR had arranged for the services of Adélard Bernier. As Captain Walsh testified at the Mersey Inquiry, to be selected by the CPR was regarded as a 'distinct honour and distinct advantage.' Bernier, fifty-four in the spring of 1914, was a resident of Quebec and he had been a pilot on the St Lawrence since 1888. He had been dedicated to the Elder Dempster Line since 1897 and transferred to the CPR vessels when the latter purchased Elder Dempster's ships. From 1906 onward, his sole responsibility was the two *Empress* liners. He had steadily worked his way up the Corporation's seniority list. In 1906/07, he was 84th of 103 pilots. By 1909 he was 73rd of 92, and made twenty inbound and nineteen outbound trips between Father Point and Quebec. A year later, he was 66th of 84 and made forty trips. With retirements obligatory at age sixty-five, and apprentice pilots added, Bernier continued to advance. He was 62nd of 80 for 1911 (thirty-six trips), and 54th of 70 in 1914.

The Empress *at port. (Stephen Brooks)*

Other shipping companies all had 'their' designated pilots. In 1914, to mention a few examples, the Dominion Coal Company had nine – although Louis Lapierre, pilot of the *Alden* which passed the *Empress* on the night of 28 May and who testified at the Mersey Inquiry, was a *tour-de-rôle* pilot. The Donaldson Line had two dedicated pilots; the Allan Line had four, and the CPR had two others besides Bernier. In 1914, of seventy active pilots, almost half were dedicated to a particular line.

Rates for pilotage at Quebec, per foot of draught, are shown in the table below.

FROM	TO	May 1 to Nov. 10	Nov. 11 to Nov. 19
Father Point	Quebec	$3.87	$4.95
Quebec	Father Point	$3.40	$4.46

The *Empress*, fully laden and outbound from Quebec on 28 May 1914, would have paid pilotage fees of $94.35. This is based on a mean draught of 27ft 9in for testimony at the Inquiry showed a fore-end draught of 26ft 10in and an aft-end draught of 28ft 10in. Interestingly, by the time she arrived off Rimouski, the *Empress* would have risen nine inches in the water, resulting from a change in water density and consumption of a portion of her coal supply.

Inbound to Quebec in mid-summer, assuming a mean draught of 26ft 7in, pilotage fees from Father Point to Quebec would have been about $108.

Large vessels today no longer stop at Father Point to pick up or discharge the Quebec pilot, the last pilot having left in 1959. The route up the river now takes such ships along the north shore and pilots are discharged near Les Escoumins, near the mouth of the Saguenay River. The 1909 lighthouse, one of the tallest in Canada, and buildings of the former pilot station at Father Point have been converted to a museum dedicated to the *Empress of Ireland*.

Unlike at Quebec, the CPR does not seem to have had a dedicated pilot at either of the two winter ports for the *Empress*. The pilot for Saint John, first winter home of the *Empress*, came aboard a few miles out of the port. The Halifax pilot came aboard in the pilot boat while the ship was about five miles out from the harbour. Both ports had their special problems. The fine natural harbour of Halifax had difficult approaches, and the waters around the port still hold the remains of many vessels of the era which came to grief while approaching or leaving port. *Mount Temple* was driven ashore in December 1907 off Halifax, and the Bay of Fundy had trapped her share of wayward ships, including the Allan's *Castilian* in 1899.

Saint John was a tricky port to enter, despite the straight-in approach to the dock. In addition to the tides, currents could often be misleading. A surface current on a rising tide could be outward, for example, while concealing a strong inward current a few feet below the surface.

Pilot fees in Saint John were based on the vessel's draught and the distance she had been piloted. For the *Empress*, assuming a pilot only for the 1st district (Partridge Island) and a mean draft of 26ft 7in after a transatlantic crossing, the incoming pilot fee in 1908 would have been $54, based on a charge of $2 per foot of draught.

Outbound, assuming she was fully laden for the trip to Liverpool and drawing 27ft 9in, the fee would have been $49, based on a rate of $1.75 per foot.

On occasion, Saint John pilots boarded their intended vessel in Halifax and brought her around to Saint John. The *Globe* recorded in November 1906 the departure for Halifax by train of Pilot Doyle so that he could meet the incoming Allan liner *Parisian*.

Pilot rates at Halifax were based on the tonnage of the vessel. Assuming a net registered tonnage of 8,028 for the *Empress*, the inbound fee in 1908 would have been $66.60, based on a flat fee of $21.60 for the first 600 tons, and 60 cents for each increment of 100 tons thereafter. Outbound, the fee would have been $35.70, based on a flat fee of $13.20 for the first 600 tons, and 30 cents for every 100-ton increment. Outward pilotage was compulsory for all vessels of 200 tons and upward.

For Liverpool, compulsory inward pilotage extended from the Middle Mouse, on the coast of the Isle of Anglesey, to the River Mersey. Compulsory outward pilotage extended for a shorter distance, from the Mersey to the Fairway Buoys on the sea channels of the river. Pilotage was mandatory for all vessels of 100 tons and over.

Pilotage fees at Liverpool were based on a vessel's draught, with fees about 8s per foot inward and outward. Although both 'rotary' and 'appropriated' pilots were on the roster of 177 pilots (in 1909) at Liverpool, there is no evidence to confirm whether the CPR *Empresses* had dedicated pilots.

Schedules

Sailing dates for the CPR's Atlantic Service vessels were printed in newspapers, passenger lists, rate sheets and elsewhere. In each case they were carefully marked SUBJECT TO CHANGE WITHOUT NOTICE, often in small print, for ships' schedules could not be pinned down with precision. On the whole, though, between 1906 and 1914 the CPR adhered very well to the published sailing dates for the *Empress*.

In practice, the two *Empresses* left opposite sides of the Atlantic at about the same time, passed each other in mid-ocean, and – in theory – docked at about the same time, though weather, tides, and other factors helped determine whether the ship arrived at its expected time. And, while the two *Empresses* passed each other in mid-ocean, the two other CPR liners assigned to the Liverpool route were just coming into port. In effect, the company had established a virtual shuttle service across the Atlantic.

With one or two exceptions, the *Empresses* proved to be highly reliable in terms of schedules. The Montreal *Gazette* commented on this in the autumn of 1910, mentioning '…the clockwork regularity with which the… *Empress* steamers have been arriving and leaving from this side. Since the opening of navigation… their time of arrival at Quebec has been within forty minutes of 3:30 Thursday afternoons and their departure has not varied ten minutes from 3:30 p.m. of the following Friday.'

Pilot Adélard Bernier (1861-1921), the only man designated by the Canadian Pacific to pilot the Empress *bothways between Quebec City and Father Point. (Musée de la mer de Pointe-au-Père)*

A change came in 1913 when the Friday departure from Quebec City was changed to Thursday.

Boat trains were an essential part of the overall operation, for they took passengers to their onward destinations and – more importantly for the CPR – brought them to the *Empress*. In England, the London & North Western Railway ran a train from Euston at noon on sailing days, arriving at Liverpool's Riverside station about four hours later. A similar train met the arriving *Empress* and took incoming passengers to London.

The one-way fares to London were quoted by the CPR as $7.08 for first-class; round trip, $14.16. Second class, one way was $5.05, and round trip $8.83. Third class was $4.05. These fares remained constant between 1906 and 1914.

'Empress Specials' linked Quebec City in the summer season to Montreal and vice versa. In the winter, with the change of port, the trains connected to Saint John or Halifax. The special trains generally consisted of first and second class coaches, dining and parlor cars. As many as three trains were required to meet the arriving *Empress*, and separate trains were used to transport first, second and third class passengers, as each of these groups was respectively processed through immigration.

The westbound CPR trains were through-trains for immigrants. Thus there was no need to change trains in Montreal, a relief to those with families and heavy baggage. As sailing times varied over the years, train schedules were changed appropriately. In 1906 and 1907, for example, a special steamship express left Windsor Station in Montreal at 8:40 a.m. on sailing days and arrived at Quebec at 1:00 p.m., alongside the ship. That left plenty of time, for departure was set for 3:00 p.m. From 1909 to 1911, the train left at 9:45 a.m. on sailing day.

Ship's Performance

Although in her trials the *Empress* reached speeds in excess of 20 knots, her usual cruising speed was about 18 knots. On occasion, she was capable of more. The ship's best noon-to-noon daily run was 465 knots, which yields a sustained average over twenty-four hours of 19.375 knots. Henry Kendall testified that at full ahead, the *Empress* made 17 or 18 knots; at half-speed, 12 knots; and dead slow, about five knots. At full speed, the engines would have been turning at about 75 rpm; at half-speed, 50 rpm. When the Engine Room received a signal for fog, steam pressure was reduced from 220 psi to 200.

Though 18-20 knots was a very respectable speed for a liner with reciprocating engines, Cunard's *Mauretania* could reach 29 knots, half-again as fast as the *Empress*, enabling it to set a westbound record to New York of 4 days 14 hours and 38 minutes in 1909. Such higher speeds carried a heavy price. Marine engineers in 1908 reckoned that for the increase in speed of a single knot an hour, or 24 knots per day, to a 25-knot vessel, it would be necessary to add 16,000 horsepower, 30ft to the length, and an additional 1,255 tons of coal, along with eighty more engineering staff.

In terms of accelerating the *Empress*, with a displacement weight of some 18,000 tons, performance left something to be desired. Captain James Murray testified at the Mersey Inquiry that it took about half an hour for the ship to reach a speed of 17 knots from a standstill.

If reaching cruise speed was a slow process, stopping the ship was not. Early in the 1914 Inquiry some discussion took place concerning the performance of the *Empress*. Henry Kendall was examined by Butler Aspinall, lead counsel for the CPR, as follows:

Mr Aspinall: In the event of your ship travelling at full speed and your stopping and putting
                    your engines astern, in what space of time does she become stationary in the
                    water?
Kendall: In about two minutes.
Mr Aspinall: And what distance does she travel in the water?
Kendall: About two lengths.

Kendall was sure of his facts, for he had tested the ship only three weeks before while off the Welsh coast. His testimony was corroborated by First Officer Edward Jones, who had seen Murray perform the same experiment in the same location. Murray also confirmed the time as being two minutes and fifteen seconds.

Further questioning of Captain Kendall revealed that when the engines were put hard astern and the helm was not touched, the *Empress* kept her heading, this being one of the differences between a twin- and a single-screw vessel.

Timekeeping

Accurate timekeeping aboard any vessel was of critical importance for navigation, and clocks aboard the *Empress* were set from a chronometer. Asked at the Mersey Inquiry where he got his time from and what he knew about its accuracy, Henry Kendall replied: 'We correct our times by three chronometers we have on board our ship, which are always at Greenwich mean time.' A few minutes later, on further questioning, Kendall provided further details:

Kendall: Our time is from three chronometers on board the ship, which differ one-
                    fifth of a second per day. They are taken on shore every time we are in
                    Liverpool and handed to an optician, and are brought back on board again
                    twelve hours before the ship sails, and the time is absolutely accurate.
Mr Haight: They are never put forward or back?
Kendall: They are never touched. We couldn't touch them if we wanted to.

With her eastward and westward passages, it was necessary to adjust the ship's time as she passed through five time zones between Liverpool and Quebec (four, for Halifax and Saint John). On westbound trips, the *Empress* lost time, and shipboard clocks were set back each day, at midnight. Eastbound, the *Empress* gained time, and clocks were advanced. The daily adjustment depended, naturally, on the speed of the ship. On a westbound crossing, the following adjustments were typical:

Day 1   35 minutes retarded
Day 2   55 minutes
Day 3   55 minutes
Day 4   60 minutes
Day 5   60 minutes
Day 6   35 minutes.

Empress Daily News *and Diaries*

Both *Empress* vessels offered a free on-board newspaper called the *'Empress' Daily News*. The idea of a ship's daily paper, with the latest news by wireless, was an early Allan Line innovation that the CPR later copied. So popular was the concept that by early 1909 wireless newspapers were published on at least thirty Atlantic liners serving Canadian and US ports.

On the maiden voyage of the *Empress*, an on-board paper titled *Sea Gull* was published; the name changed at a later date. In the CPR Archives are two examples of the paper from the *Empress of Ireland*, from 23 May and 26 May 1910 (Voyage 46E, from Quebec to Liverpool). The National Archives of Canada has an *Empress of Britain* paper from January 1910.

They were printed on good-quality paper stock, measuring $5\frac{7}{8}$in x $8\frac{3}{4}$in, although there may have been slight variations in size between the two sister ships. Each issue contained eight pages and was bound by two centre staples. The two centre pages consisted of current news flashes (including sports scores and selected stock prices) from the Associated Press. News items in the 23 May edition were received from Marconi's Cape Cod station; in that of the 26th, from Poldhu, Cornwall. The standards of the paper were very high, although there were occasional minor typographical errors.

Unlike the Allan Line, the CPR did not allow any third-party advertising in its shipboard papers. Front pages carried various promotions for the CPR's Atlantic service and London-Hong Kong service. Inside pages held a mixture of illustrated travel-oriented articles (*e.g.* 'Venetian School of Painting' or 'Goldfields of the Far North'), witticisms (one example: *It was never meant that lazy people should reach the top of the ladder – there would be no place for them to sit down*), and a timely piece on the reappearance of Halley's Comet, along with the CPR's sailing schedule for the next seven months.

Some of the articles were reused from one voyage to the next. With the long voyage cycles, few passengers would even notice. As well, stories could be shared between the two sister ships; the Halley's Comet piece appeared on both ships.

Evidence suggests that the free onboard newspaper may have been given only to first class passengers. Second class passengers could purchase a daily diary *cum* information booklet entitled *Canadian Pacific Empress Mail*. There was one booklet per day, the idea being that a passenger would purchase a series of six or seven for the whole trip.

One specimen from Saturday, 7 October 1911 measured $6\frac{1}{8}$in x 9in and consisted of twelve pages, the first of which was blank and headed 'Diary of my voyage to Canada: Saturday.' On this page the passenger could enter details of the day's activities. Two centre pages carried the day's Marconigram news. Other pages contained short articles on the provinces of New Brunswick and Nova Scotia, portions of a 1908 speech by the then Prince of Wales on modern communications, another article on 'Poultry Farming for Girls', a poem entitled 'In Apple Picking Time', along with various CPR promotions.

Much of the diary was probably pre-printed ashore, including the cover with a color painting by the American Cyrus Cuneo showing an allegorical representation of Canada welcoming the *Empress* to Quebec City. Only the centre pages with the day's wireless news would have been printed on the

C.P.R.R.M.S. "Empress of Ireland" and Water Front, Quebec

The Empress *at the Breakwater, Quebec. (Stephen Brooks)*

Empress. The rest of the articles and artwork – different for each day – were date-insensitive, and could be easily re-used from one voyage to the next.

Entertainment

Before radio and television people were accustomed to entertaining themselves. In third class on the *Empress*, it was largely up to passengers to entertain each other with games, impromptu sing-alongs around the piano in the sitting room, or walking the decks. Of course, there were the old standbys to help pass the tedium of a voyage – drinking, smoking, and a variety of card games and games of chance. Wrote one third class passenger in 1907, 'The men's smoker… is a refrigerator with all windows open. Twenty or thirty smoked bacons hang around in there, constantly playing cards or drinking watery beer.' Regardless of one's native language, one could always find a game to join or a conversation to enter.

For the numerous children in third class there were deck games in fine weather. Photographs from around 1910 depict boys playing leapfrog, and women and girls skipping, both activities being observed by a deck crowded with passengers. And, in third class there was also a sandbox, recalled with fondness by one *Empress* passenger when interviewed ninety years later.

Third class had two pianos, one in the ladies' sitting room on Upper deck, and another in the third class dining room on Main deck. Over the years both of these would have tempted many pianists, and the rooms must have echoed with everything from the classics of Chopin and Liszt to the latest ragtime hits of Scott Joplin. Many people would have travelled with a favourite instrument – violins, concertinas and harmonicas were all compact enough – and they would have been swiftly unpacked with the hope of finding others of like mind. One 1910 traveller noted that the third class dining saloon was the scene of concerts in the evening.

In first and second class, shipboard entertainment was more formalized. The ship's twenty-one member concert troupe offered recitals, and five professional musicians were on hand to provide background music when necessary, and for light concerts.

By tradition, a gala evening was held in first class on the last night at sea, with entertainers and a master of ceremonies recruited from among the first class passengers and supplemented by crew members if necessary. Second class had a similar evening, typically on the fourth night of the crossing, held in the second class dining room. These events were not held earlier, so that most passengers would have acquired their sea-legs in time for the party. First class passengers could, if they wished, attend the second class concert, although the converse does not seem to have occurred.

Passengers could also pass the time with more traditional pursuits, including reading, writing letters (on *Empress of Ireland* stationery) and card games, such as the newly popular auction bridge. The Library, open to both first and second class, was stocked with books and a selection of current periodicals and newspapers. Walking the decks was another popular activity, and the Duke of Connaught in 1911 was reported as being one of the first ones out on deck in the morning, for his daily walk. One circuit of the Upper Promenade deck equaled one-eighth of a mile.

Good weather offered the opportunity for other forms of diversion for first and second class passengers. The *Empress* featured a cricket pitch in a protected deck area, and there are photographs of deck golf (played like shuffleboard around a 'course') and deck quoits (akin to horseshoes, but using circles of rope) being played on Boat deck.

Movies (or 'cinematographs' as they were called) were shown on the *Empress*, using a hand-cranked carbon-arc projector. Musk notes that films were shown aboard *Empress of Britain* as early as 1910, possibly the first movies aboard a ship anywhere. Research for this book proved that movies were also shown in the *Empress of Ireland* no later than June 1911.

In calm weather first class passengers could also avail themselves of a billiard table, though its location has never been ascertained.

Divine Services

On westbound crossings, *Empress* passengers were fairly homogeneous, being English or Scandinavian, predominantly Protestants of various denominations. Eastbound the mix was more eclectic, with an assortment of religions and languages.

A first class passenger list from October 1911 shows that Divine Service was held at 10:45 a.m. on Sunday in the saloon. Although this was an area normally reserved for first class, second class passengers were not barred from attending and one such passenger recorded in her diary that she sat just behind the Duke of Connaught and his party. However, second class passengers had their own Sunday evening service in the second class saloon. Services would have been conducted by a clergyman who happened to be aboard. In the unlikely event there was none, for passenger lists and manifests show many members of the clergy, the master or a senior officer would have read a short service.

Services could take place at other times as well. One 1913 letter records how a Salvation Army 'meeting' was conducted on a Monday evening in the second class dining saloon ('…very nice and we had some lovely hymns.')

Third class services were held in the dining room at 8:30 a.m. on Sunday, with a variety of clergymen given an opportunity to participate. Third class eastbound represented the greatest variety of religions: Anglicans from England, Lutherans from Germany and Scandinavia, Eastern Orthodox, Jews, and Roman Catholics, all speaking a polyglot of languages from English and Italian to Hungarian and Ukrainian.

In October 1909 the company installed small altars in all its ships so that, henceforth, priests making the crossing could say mass and all religious festivals could be properly observed.

Immigration

By far the most important ocean port for immigrant arrivals to Canada was Quebec, which accounted for over one-half of the total. April and May were the busiest months, as might be expected, and it was not unusual for three or four vessels to arrive close together, depositing as many as 3,500 people in four

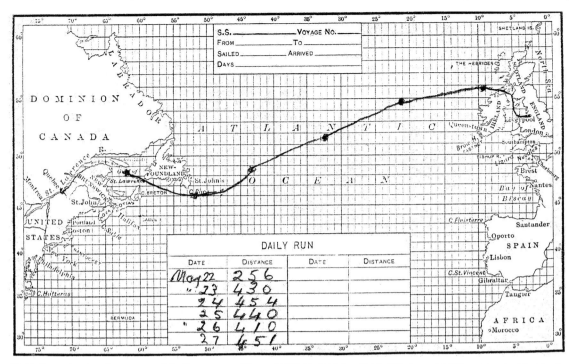

Daily Run, showing the progress of the Empress *on Voyage 37W, 22-27 May 1909. Edwin and Millicent Lambe filled in the ship's daily run and her course on this page in their second class passenger list. Details of the daily run and noontime position were posted at the purser's office. (Barry Lambe)*

hours. Even in the dead of winter the flow of immigrants into the ice-free ports of Halifax and Saint John never stopped.

Regardless of the port of entry, the process of arrival and screening was essentially the same. It could be a terrifying experience, worse than the roughest sea passage, for the results of the immigration inspection determined each would-be immigrant's fate. Whether destined to Canada or the United States, all aliens and British settlers were examined to determine their physical ability, health, character, and whether they had enough money to support themselves and not become a public burden. In order to expedite matters, the Canadian government allowed the US government to set up immigration inspection posts for those whose ultimate destination was the United States, having earlier realized that settlers headed for many western states preferred the St Lawrence route and a quick rail connection. In a *quid pro quo*, a reciprocal arrangement existed for would-be Canadians who arrived at the major US ports of entry on the eastern seaboard.

In Quebec, although the US and Canadian immigration inspection posts were adjacent to one another on the Breakwater, the procedures followed were quite different. In 1907 a Montreal *Daily Star* reporter followed one group of immigrants arriving in Quebec in a CPR vessel and described what he had seen. Apart from the fact that this particular group – 'a motley lot', the reporter termed them – had arrived from the continent, their experiences would be wholly typical of an *Empress* arrival.

The immigrants, being landed from the steamer on the Breakwater, are sent into the enclosures surrounding the sheds. Those intended for Canadian points are directed to the larger enclosure, while those who seek homes in the United States go to the smaller enclosure on the eastern end of the pier.

Second Class Programme of Entertainment, 11 August 1908 (Voyage 27W). (Philippe Beaudry)

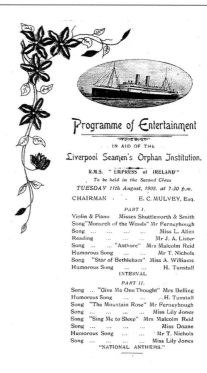

Programme of Entertainment

IN AID OF THE

Liverpool Seamen's Orphan Institution.

R.M.S. " EMPRESS of IRELAND"

To be held in the Second Class

TUESDAY 11th August, 1908. at 7-30 p.m.

CHAIRMAN - E. C. MULVEY, Esq.

PART I.

Violin & Piano   Misses Shuttleworth & Smith
Song "Monarch of the Woods" Mr Ferneyhough
Song ... ...   Miss L. Allen
Reading ... ...   Mr J. A. Lister
Song ... ... "Asthore" Mrs Malcolm Reid
Humorous Song ... ...   Mr T. Nichols
Song "Star of Bethleham" Miss A. Williams
Humorous Song ... ...   H. Tunstall

INTERVAL

PART II.

Song ... "Give Me One Thought" Mrs Belling
Humorous Song ... ...H. Tunstall
Song "The Mountain Rose" Mr Ferneyhough
Song ... ...   Miss Lily Jones
Song "Sing Me to Sleep" Mrs Malcolm Reid
Song ... ...   Miss Doane
Humorous Song ... ...   Mr T. Nichols
Song ... ...   Miss Lily Jones

"NATIONAL ANTHEMS."

The examination at both sheds began at the same time, and both were concluded at the same time – 11 o'clock that night. The United States inspectors required the same time to examine two hundred immigrants as the Canadian inspectors needed to pass thirteen hundred.

When spoken to upon the difference, Mr Doyle, who is Chief Inspector of the Canadian side, answered, 'Oh well, we're human over here. It would be too bad to refuse a refuge to a man who is in good health, even if he has little money.'

'There is no sentiment here,' said Mr Harrison, the chief on the United States side, to whom the difference was pointed out. 'These people are to be future citizens, and it is intended that they shall be good citizens and not likely to become public charges.'

The Canadian government seeks a good character from each immigrant landing, a certificate of health and some evidence of sufficient money to pay further transportation and to remain away from the public charities. The United States government desires similar evidence, but it is exacted in a far sterner manner.

Sometimes it looks as if charity had died, and that these poor humans were but so much live freight, from which the best could be selected, and the culls rejected.

In both sides the examination is to cover practically the same ground, general health and absence of disease. The immigrants are supplied with vaccination certificates… and these must be handed in with other necessary papers. The immigrant walks towards the doctor, who is at once enabled to determine whether there is any deformity. Then there is a hasty glance at the head, after which the eyes are examined for tracoma.

Afterwards the immigrant is passed along to determine his financial ability and to seek from him data for statistical information.

On the United States side the man, or woman, must show all his, or her, money. On the Canadian side it is sufficient to show ten dollars to secure the termination of the examination. The reason for the Canadian government's lack of curiosity regarding a man's money is that it was considered rather unsafe to compel a man who was carrying any considerable amount to reveal it to his fellows.

Each emigrant was inspected by a doctor on arrival and could be held in quarantine or rejected outright. Rejection by the Canadian inspectors could be for any one of 121 reasons, ranging from anemia, asthma, varicose veins, or lack of funds.

Quarantine was a serious matter, necessary to keep infectious diseases out of Canada. On many voyages just one or two arriving passengers might be held, but inspectors were empowered to take whatever measures were necessary. In an unusual case, 350 passengers from *Tunisian* were held at Grosse Ile below Quebec in June 1912 after a case of smallpox was found on board. Those detained were all from that area of the ship where the case had been found. Similarly in June 1909, three cases of smallpox were discovered in *Tunisian*'s third class and it appeared that the disease had broken out during the crossing. On this occasion all passengers were landed at Grosse Ile while the ship was fumigated. The smallpox cases were held at Quarantine while the other passengers re-boarded and proceeded to Quebec.

If an immigrant was refused entry to Canada or the US, he or she was returned to Europe at the expense of the shipping line. As a result, shipping companies carefully screened their westbound emigrant passengers to make sure that they would be acceptable to the Canadian or US Immigration officers.

Two civil and two medical examiners usually boarded the *Empress* at Rimouski, when headed for Quebec, or at Halifax if bound for Saint John. The men would use the time before the ship docked to complete their inspection of passengers and baggage, thus speeding up the transfer to the waiting trains. To allay the fears of passengers, one CPR brochure described the Canadian customs officials as 'attentive, courteous, and obliging.'

Such inspections, it should be pointed out, were only for immigrants. First and second class passengers were quickly taken from the ship without formality and led to the waiting trains. Returning Canadians, US citizens, tourists and others were also spared a detailed Immigration inspection. Also boarding at Rimouski were a number of CPR baggage checkers, who would ensure that baggage was properly checked through to its final destination.

Passenger Manifests

One of the most cumbersome and time-consuming duties of the purser and his staff was filling out passenger manifest forms to comply with Canadian and British regulations. These documents consisted essentially of a listing of every passenger carried aboard the ship, along with other information. Canadian documents (for arriving passengers only) showed, in addition, sex, age, marital status, national origin, destination, occupation, religious denomination, ticket number, method of onward transportation, and the amount of money being brought into the country. Passengers on the manifests were segregated by class, as well as by those destined to Canada or the United States.

Manifests for British authorities were slightly different, and were filed for both arriving and departing vessels in accordance with the *Merchant Shipping Act* of 1906 and the *Aliens Act* of 1905. British documents showed the ports of embarkation and arrival, class, occupation, ages, and country of last permanent residence.

A birth or death aboard the *Empress* was recorded in the appropriate spaces in the British manifest and the Official Log Book. A separate form, Return of Births and Deaths, was filled out by the master and forwarded to the Registrar General of Seamen. Failure to do so was punishable by a fine of £5, under Section 254 of the *Merchant Shipping Act* of 1894. Births or deaths on westbound passages were usually in the form of simple marginal notations in the Canadian manifests. In some cases, deaths are not recorded in the Canadian manifests for the simple reason that they occurred *before* the manifest had been written up.

Once prepared by the purser's office, the Canadian manifest was signed off by the master and the ship's surgeon. On 9 June 1910, arriving at Quebec, Captain John Forster signed the following statement:

> I hereby certify that the above is a correct description of the RMS *Empress of Ireland* and correct list of all the Passengers on board the same at the time of her departure from Liverpool and that all the particulars therein mentioned are true.

Canadian customs agents checking baggage for first class passengers on the Lower Promenade deck, looking forward. The hose hanging from the railing suggests the photograph may have been taken while at the dock. (David Saint-Pierre)

The Ship's Surgeon was required to certify and date the following:

> I hereby certify that I have daily during the present passage made a general inspection of the passengers on this vessel, and that I have at least once during the passage made a detailed individual examination of each immigrant on board and that I have seen no passenger thereon who I have reason to believe is, or likely to become, insane, epileptic or consumptive, or who is idiotic, feeble-minded, or afflicted with a contagious, infectious or loathsome disease; or who is deaf, dumb or blind or otherwise physically defective or whose present appearance would lead me to believe that he or she might be debarred from Canada under the 'Immigration Act' *with the exception* of the ___ persons whose names are enumerated on the 'Ship Surgeon's List for Medical Examining Officer' which I have prepared for such officer giving my medical opinion on the cases therein dealt with; and that there were no deaths or births during the passage except those mentioned on said list.

Civil and medical examiners who had boarded the *Empress* at Rimouski or Halifax used the manifest as a check for immigration purposes, and Landing Cards for each passenger were cross-referenced to the manifest by page and line number. The civil and medical agents completed a summary section on the manifest, showing the ship's arrival date and time, the number of first, second and third class passengers.

Using as an example the arrival of the *Empress* in Quebec on 9 June 1910 (Mary Hill's arrival in Canada), the civil and medical examination of 442 second class passengers began at 9:15 a.m. and was completed at 11:30 a.m. There were no persons detained.

The examination of third class passengers, of which there were 982, took longer due to the sheer numbers involved and the rigor of the examination. The second team of examiners began the third class inspection at 6:00 p.m. (half an hour after the ship's arrival) and did not complete their work until 10:00 p.m. They detained – for medical reasons – two persons for Canada and two for the United States. The civil examiner detained five for Canada and one for the United States.

A final portion of the manifest summary sheet indicated that CPR passengers left by special train at midnight, six and a half hours after the ship had been made fast to the wharf at Quebec.

Manifests of the *Empress* make an interesting study in their own right, and the faded pages reveal a wealth of information of interest to genealogists and social historians. With an average complement of passengers, the typical *Empress of Ireland* manifest consisted of about thirty-five pages, though this could run to as many as fifty pages. Early Canadian manifests had forty-five names per page, but this was later standardized at thirty. *Empress* manifests are written in a variety of hands, sometimes indifferent and careless, not all of which are legible due to ink fading. Copies in the National Archives in Ottawa are on microfilm only, and many pages are almost illegible. Though arranged by class, names are not always in alphabetical order, which adds to the difficulty of finding a particular name.

Immigration and medical inspectors worked their way methodically through the manifest, checking each name and noting whether the person was a returned Canadian, British immigrant, or tourist. To save time, officers carried a series of rubber stamps. Entries such as 'Going to Husband' (or sometimes 'To Husband') and 'To be Married' provide hints of the happiness waiting for many women in the *Empress*. In such cases, the name and occupation of the husband or fiancé was noted in the manifest.

There were other stamps as well. 'Ret'd Canadians' was self-explanatory, as was 'S. Army.' 'British Bonus Allowed' and 'Continental Bonus Allowed' meant that the booking agent would be paid a bonus by the Canadian government for successfully delivering another new immigrant to the country. Worst of all was the finality of the dreaded '**DETAINED**'.

Empress manifests are a reflection of Edwardian times and values. Passengers in first class with titles were often entered with the title, and other personal information (like ages) was sometimes omitted. Lord Roberts, arriving in July 1908, is shown as 'Earl Roberts, VC, KCKP' and his occupation as 'F.M. Brit. Army.' Others, for example Alexander Hore-Ruthven and Reginald Pole-Carew (on the same 1908 voyage) describe their occupation simply as 'gentleman', as though the term said it all. In reality, Pole-Carew was a general in the British Army, and Hore-Ruthven, a former soldier, was Military Secretary to the Governor General of Australia. Still others on the same voyage, such as Sir Keith Fraser and Lord Lovat, show 'nil' in the column under occupation.

Manifests also provide some details of births and deaths at sea, and sickness among passengers. That of Lord Roberts' 1908 trip shows that seven Norwegians from third class were detained at the Quarantine station at Grosse Ile on 17 July. Four were children with measles, and all seven were released between 11-14 August.

Manifests also demonstrate that some arriving passengers, not necessarily all VIPs, were occasionally landed at Rimouski.

VIPs

During her career from 1906 to 1914 a number of important persons travelled in the *Empress* and, on such occasions the company rolled out the welcome mat, fully aware that such persons had alternative travel options via New York and Montreal, and that a favourable word from such people was worth a great deal.

'Please arrange to have him introduced to the Captain and Chief Steward and ask them to show him proper attention,' wrote Sir Thomas Shaughnessy in July 1906 in connection with the planned cross-

Canadian Pacific baggage checkers, checking first class baggage on the Lower Promenade deck, looking aft, a photograph used in every passenger list issued by the company. (David Saint-Pierre)

ing of a former US cabinet member. Such messages were not unusual in the least, and ensured that those who really mattered were given service that went beyond what normal first class service entailed. In addition to being invited to dine at the captain's table for all or part of the passage, itself an honour, VIPs were accorded other privileges if they wished or if the master had been so instructed by the CPR. Thus we note, for example, some passengers disembarking at Rimouski.

Some important passengers were met at Rimouski by a CPR representative. This was taken to an extreme when Rudyard Kipling and his wife were met at Rimouski in 1907 by Sir William Van Horne, then Chairman of the CPR, who accompanied them upriver to Quebec. Others enjoyed the privilege of boarding the eastbound *Empress* at Rimouski, rather than Quebec, one example being Lord Strathcona, then Canada's High Commissioner.

An invitation to dine at the captain's small table aboard the *Empress* was a singular honour. This might have involved from eight to ten people at a time, all carefully selected to ensure the right social mix and good conversation. It should be remembered that the Boer War had been the defining military event of the past two decades to most Britons and Canadians. Memories of the campaigns in South Africa were still fresh and, when important figures like Lord Roberts or Robert Baden-Powell were in the *Empress*, the master and his officers would have been interested to meet with men whose names had been household words.

Over the years the five *Empress* masters probably had mixed feelings about their role. No doubt some relished the company of the rich and famous; others probably loathed the duty, feeling they were mariners first and not entertainers. In such cases, masters could conveniently manufacture a pressing

SPECIAL NOTICE

Immigration Requirements

THOUGH the Authorities specify no particular sum, it is wise that all third class passengers have in their possession at least the sum of $10.00, otherwise the Immigration Authorities may deem them liable to become a public charge and order their deportation.   This applies to passengers destined to the United States as well as Canada.

Special Notice to third class immigrants, from a June 1906 CPR Rate Sheet. (National Archives of Canada)

reason to excuse themselves from the table and return to the bridge, leaving a chief officer to carry on.

Masters probably accepted it good grace, recognizing the value of the dining invitation in terms of public relations for the CPR. Among the duties of a master was that of host for his company's 'guests' and he had to ensure they were pleased enough with their treatment aboard ship to return.

Rudyard Kipling, whose privileged treatment has been noted above, also toured the ship with Captain Forster during the daily inspection, and went later to the Captain's room off the bridge – a rare honour. For their part, the VIPs knew how to reciprocate. Kipling and his wife signed Henry Kendall's autograph book, and Kipling inscribed two stanzas of one of his poems. Kendall, Forster's chief officer at the time, later wrote, '…I value these lines as among my most treasured possessions.' In other cases, VIPs presented small gifts to the officers or the chief steward on leaving the ship at the conclusion of the crossing.

Children

Several travellers observed that there were many children aboard the *Empress* on their particular trip. Passenger manifests allow us to determine the ratio of adults, children and infants by class. The following are wholly typical:

Westbound:

	Voyage	Adults	%	Children	%	Infants	%	Total
arrival at Quebec	12W	1,235	82.2	221	14.7	47	3.1	1,503
	47W	1,348	84.4	236	14.8	13	0.8	1,597
	64W	1,066	76.3	293	20.9	40	2.8	1,399
	88W	1,230	78.2	308	19.6	35	2.2	1,573
arrival at Saint John	20W	397	86.4	50	10.8	13	2.8	460
	45W	1,345	87.0	190	12.3	11	0.7	1,546
	68W	994	83.7	174	14.7	19	1.6	1,187

Eastbound, as one might expect, the ratio of children and infants was somewhat lower than westbound.

Using Voyage 93E from March 1914 as an example, the forty-eight children represented 9.9% of the total of 528 passengers. Twenty-two infants represented 4.1% of the total, a higher ratio than for westbound. As might be expected, few children or infants travelled in first class. The following data from voyage 74W, arriving at Quebec on 2 August 1912, shows a typical breakdown by class:

		Adults	Children	Infants	
1st class	– to Canada	196	22	1	
	– to USA	26	1	-	
2nd class	– to Canada	260	42	12	
	– to USA	17	1	-	
3rd class	– to Canada	619	203	15	
	– to USA	71	8	3	
Totals		1,189	277	31	= 1,497

American-Destined Passengers

With its westward rail connections from Montreal and Toronto, the CPR was well placed to serve passengers whose voyage originated or terminated in the American midwest. Between 1906 and 1914 the westbound *Empress* carried thousands of future American citizens from Britain and Scandinavia. Data from manifests shows that their proportion to the total passengers in the *Empress* remained fairly constant over time, as the following table illustrates:

Voyage 22W, arrived Saint John, 28 Mar. 1908

		Number	% of class	% of total
First class	to Canada	98	92.4	6.6
	to USA	8	7.6	0.5
Second class	to Canada	493	97.6	33.3
	to USA	12	2.4	0.8
Third Class	to Canada	776	89.2	52.5
	to USA	94	10.8	6.3
	total	1,481		

Voyage 80W, arrived Saint John, 31 Jan. 1913

First class	to Canada	115	96.6	9.1
	to USA	4	3.4	0.3
Second class	to Canada	357	97.3	28.2
	to USA	10	2.7	0.8
Third Class	to Canada	682	87.3	53.8
	to USA	99	12.7	7.8
	total	1,267		

Note: passengers with a destination beyond Canada, *e.g.* Hong Kong or Australia, were counted for Immigration purposes as Canadian-destined.

Other passages to Saint John in different years show similar results, as do mid-summer arrivals at Quebec.

On eastbound *Empress* crossings, the number of American citizens increased over time in absolute numbers and as a proportion of the total passengers, thanks to the CPR's promotional efforts and favourable publicity surrounding the St Lawrence as a viable alternative to New York. There may have been another reason as well. British vessels on the St Lawrence were less intimidating to the average American compared to the supercilious staff aboard prestigious vessels out of New York. Colin Simpson in *Lusitania* related that prior to the last voyage of the famed British liner, the pursers, chief steward, senior stewards from each deck, and Senior Third Officer John Lewis, were at the gangplank to welcome passengers in the traditional fashion. Lewis, catching sight of the throng of reporters and newsreel cameras, whispered to the purser, 'Who's the quality travelling with us, then?' Replied the purser, in a bored, condescending tone: 'We have no quality booked, just monied people.' Confirming that, Robert Ballard observed that third class cabin staff in *Lusitania* were worse snobs than the passengers in first class. Ample evidence from passengers confirms that the same attitude never existed aboard the *Empress of Ireland*.

Competition

Before the CPR established itself in the Atlantic steamship business in 1903 with the purchase of the Elder Dempster fleet, the best known company on the Britain-Canada route was the Montreal-based Allan Line. The Allan family's connection with shipping went back as far back as 1819 but it was not until 1852 that Sir Hugh Allan founded the line that bore the family's name and secured a government contract to establish a line of screw steamers on the St Lawrence. Allan's business prospered and, in time, expanded to provide passenger and freight service to Britain, Newfoundland, South Africa and South America.

With the first *Empress* voyage in the summer of 1906, the Allan Line began to feel the winds of serious competition. Newspaper advertising in the summer of 1906 promoted the fact that Allan steamers sailed from Montreal, and that the departure time had been arranged 'so as to give passengers a view of the noble St Lawrence by daylight. The trip down is a moving panorama the whole way.' It was a good idea, one that the CPR quickly incorporated into its own *Empress* material, though glossing over the fact that the *Empresses* did not sail the portion of the St Lawrence between Montreal and Quebec.

Snob appeal was alive and well in the summer of 1906. A postcard published by the CPR and showing one of the *Empresses* urged 'Go as your betters go and travel in safety and comfort by the Canadian Pacific Railway Company's Royal Mail SS Lines Atlantic Service.'

Realizing that not everyone wanted to take a train to Quebec, the Allan Line played up the fact its vessels sailed from Montreal, which the *Empresses* could not reach because of their draught. That advantage soon disappeared, for the CPR's other vessels on the Liverpool-Canada run – *Lake Manitoba*, *Lake Champlain* and *Lake Erie* – sailed as far as Montreal.

As the *Empresses* continued to steal traffic, the Allan Line began to cut its rates. Its rates in the summer of 1906 were as follows:

First class:	$70 and up; return tickets at reduced rates
Second class:	to Liverpool, $42.50 and up
	to London, $2.50 additional
Third class:	Liverpool, London, Belfast or Londonderry, including every requisite
	for the voyage, $27.50 and $28.75 according to the steamer.

Reducing rates to increase traffic was always a tricky business. But, for the Allan Line, it seemed to work for a while.

The CPR's advertising promoted the virtues of its *Empress* service. The 1906 Rate Sheet promised 'Cuisine and Attendance Unsurpassed' and 'The finest and fastest steamships in the Canadian service.' In its various promotional campaigns in Britain the CPR played to lower-class Britons' mistrust of strangers. '**NO FOREIGNERS THIRD CLASS** except Scandinavians' it promised would-be immigrants on the westbound passage, a fact picked up and echoed by the Salvation Army's large-scale emigration programme. Westbound manifests for the *Empress* confirm the CPR's rigid adherence to this policy. Rare indeed were other continental passengers in third class to Canada or the United States.

On 8 September 1907, at a time when the Allan Line was experiencing some financial difficulties, the CPR took over the Line's operations in a deal that was little-known at the time. Only later, during the First World War, was the Allan Line formally integrated into the CPR's marine operations, thus closing a historic chapter in transatlantic shipping.

From late 1907 onward, the nature of the competition between the two companies changed subtly, even though the outward face to the travelling public was that of two separate companies engaged in a struggle for passengers. In 1908 all the shipping companies involved in the passenger trade between North America and Europe agreed to honour each other's return tickets. Thus, a passenger booking on the Allan Line from Montreal to Liverpool could return on a CPR vessel, provided space were available.

There were a number of companies carrying passengers between Europe and Canada in those years and, given the number of emigrants, more companies entered this highly lucrative market. In 1911, Cunard purchased the Thomson Line and began serving the St Lawrence route with three vessels, *Albania*, *Ascania*, and *Ausonia*. By 1912, ten shipping lines served Canada on the Atlantic run to Europe. Of these, the two largest were the Allan Line and the CPR.

Competition was spirited but friendly. Officers and crews of the various ships knew one another, or at least had mutual friends. Many of them lived in the same neighborhoods in Liverpool, and in ports like Quebec, Montreal, Saint John and Halifax (as well as Liverpool) the men would have socialized.

More than one *Empress* passenger noted how the ship raced against the Allan boats, and Kipling commented on the 'friendly' wireless traffic exchanged between *Empress* and *Tunisian*.

Senior managers and directors of the CPR undoubtedly knew and socialized with their Allan Line counterparts and others in the shipping world. On at least one occasion the head of the Allan Line, Sir Montagu Allan, sailed in the *Empress of Ireland* in the company of Sir Thomas Shaughnessy.

Comparisons between the CPR and its competitors are difficult, inasmuch as the companies served a variety of ports with varying numbers of vessels. Data for 1911 show that the Allan Line carried the largest number of transatlantic passengers, followed by the Canadian Pacific and Canadian Northern.

In terms of the Liverpool-Canada route, the CPR held a slight overall advantage for total passengers carried, as shown below, and this was achieved with fewer sailings.

1911

	Eastbound	Trips	Westbound	Trips
Allan Line	17,682	50	52,787	52
CPR	25,214	45	48,711	44

The above numbers clearly reflect the large imbalance between west- and eastbound traffic. That same year, the *Empress of Ireland* carried a total of 9,881 eastbound and 15,886 westbound passengers, thus accounting for 39% and 33% respectively of the CPR's Atlantic passengers. Such numbers are typical for the ship's career between 1907 and 1913, excluding 1909 when she was out of service for the last two months of the year.

Passenger Lists

It was from the small but well-equipped print shop on the port side of Upper deck that *Empress*' two printers prepared first and second class passenger lists. These lists were made up as quickly as possible after the beginning of a crossing, so that the 'inhabitants' of the township might know their comp-anions. Separate lists were printed for each class. No list was prepared for third class passengers. There were probably too many of the latter to make it practical in any case and, in Edwardian times, those who travelled in third class were scarcely worth recording, despite the fact their large numbers supported the whole Atlantic trade.

Confirmation that such lists were printed quickly comes from the CPR Archives, which has copies of the first and second class passenger list for the ninety-sixth voyage of the *Empress* which departed Quebec on 28 May 1914. That such lists were printed less than seven hours after leaving Quebec shows that the printers went into action even before the last gangway was hauled away.

Atlantic *Empress* passenger lists consisted of a decorative color cover bearing the names of the company's two sister *Empresses*. This was used aboard both ships for west- and eastbound trips. Within this was an inside decorative cover, common to almost every voyage, and bearing the ship's name, master, ports of embarkation and arrival, and date, the whole enclosed within an intricate, stylized Celtic border.

Following this was a standard set of pages, common to all voyages and made up in advance. In the middle of the book came the actual list of passengers. Passenger lists were printed on good-quality paper, deep cream in color, with a dark brown type, and a cover in light cream. The booklets were $4\frac{1}{2}$ in wide and $6\frac{7}{8}$ in high, and held together by a double loop of red string. Passengers were listed alphabetically by surname, along with their hometown. It was all very formal, very proper, as the following from the second class list of 21 May 1909 illustrates:

Mrs L.A. Mountain, Guernsey
Miss G.I. Mountain, Guernsey
Master W.M. Mountain, Guernsey

Only rarely does a given name appear. Male children were denoted as 'Master' while 'Miss' was confusing, for it could refer both to young girls and unmarried women in their twenties. On occasion children were not named, but listed with their parents, as the following from August 1911 shows:

Hutton, Mrs L.M.D, London
and Three Children
or Hartshorn, Mrs, Nottingham
Infant and Two Children

Titles like 'Rev.', 'Dr', 'MP', 'Sir', 'Senator' and 'KC' were used, as were military ranks. In first class, it was common for servants to accompany their masters. The following entries from 2 June 1911 are typical:

Mrs Mary W. Fulford and maid, Brockville, Ont.
or His Highness Prince Leopold of Battenberg and valet

The 'standard' pages for the booklet consisted of the following: sailing dates for the next six months for the CPR's Atlantic Service to Liverpool; the ship's principal officers (chief officer, chief engineer, purser, surgeon and chief steward), information on and rates for sending telegrams from the ship; two maps, one showing the lights approaching Canada by the St Lawrence or Halifax-Fundy routes, and another for the Liverpool approach; information on CPR train services, and noting there was a CPR Ticket Office on board. These were followed by pages describing sports activities in Canada, a page (with photo) describing the land being sold by the CPR in western Canada; and a list of Canadian Pacific Hotels across Canada.

Last was a map of the Atlantic Ocean. Passengers who wished could plot the *Empress'* course and note the daily run for each day, which was posted by the Purser's Office.

The company recognized the souvenir value of the lists, for passengers treasured them as mementos of their trip, in many cases a once-in-a-lifetime experience. Mary Hill, growing up in Manitoba, used to take out her copy, reading the names and recalling her family's second class passage in 1910.

Given the numbers of people in second class and the need to consolidate lists of handwritten names, passenger lists contain occasional errors. One can imagine the disappointment in May 1909 of newlyweds Edwin and Millicent Lambe on discovering their names rendered as 'Lamb.' Still, it did not prevent them from saving the pamphlet. Their grandson shared it with the author ninety-one years later.

Press Coverage

The CPR was one of Canada's largest, most important, and influential companies. As a result, the comings and goings of its ships, in particular the two Atlantic *Empresses,* were well covered in newspapers in eastern Canada, particularly in Montreal, the country's financial and population centre, where the CPR had its headquarters.

The *Empress of Ireland* received good coverage in its three Canadian ports. Most major newspapers of the day had a column of marine news, for Canada was a sea-trading nation and Britain her largest trading partner, and the source of many thousands of new citizens every year. There was great interest also in eastern Canada in fast passages between Liverpool and Rimouski due to the mail delivery.

The Montreal *Gazette* and the *Daily Star* (whose front page bragged that the paper was in 'marconigrammic communication with the principal Canadian steamers on the Atlantic') often featured pieces on the two CPR sisters, perhaps goaded by the CPR's publicity staff. And, when an *Empress* was inbound to Canada, the papers often followed her progress once she had come within range of a shore-based wireless station. 'The *Empress of Ireland* was signaled 123 miles southeast of Cape Ray 1 p.m. yesterday and is due in Rimouski 5 p.m. today and in Quebec 2:30 a.m. tomorrow' is a typical example from the *Gazette* of 1 August 1912.

This is not to suggest that the CPR vessels were the only ones reported in the papers. In time, the Montreal papers reported on all fast passages across the Atlantic, as this example from October 1913 shows: 'Fast vessels do Another Spurt: *Royal George* and *Teutonic* Speeding Through Straits of Belle Isle.'

Though not a large paper, possibly the best coverage of the *Empress of Ireland* came from the Quebec *Chronicle*. The *Empresses* were, until 1914, the only large passenger ships that remained in the port of Quebec for a week – the others all heading to Montreal – during turnaround and, over time, the ships and crews came to play an important role in the life of the port.

The crews of the Atlantic *Empresses* integrated themselves into their Canadian ports in ways that were not possible in Liverpool. That was home, and once the *Empress* returned to her home port, the crew were paid off. Once they had signed the Crew List and Agreement for her next voyage, most men disappeared until the next sailing unless their duties required otherwise. In Canada the men (and women) joined the community in which they found themselves for a week at a time. They participated in various social, charitable and sporting activities, and made friends.

For most voyages, the arrival and departure of the *Empress*, regardless of port, was noted in the *Gazette*, along with passenger totals. Such numbers, though, need to be treated with caution for they do not always accord with the manifests.

Lists of arriving or departing first class passengers often (though not always) appeared in certain newspapers, though these were sometimes incomplete and did not reflect last-minute changes before sailing. Coverage in the French-language press was spotty at best, and passenger lists are conspicuous by their absence. While the *Gazette* applauded the fast crossing and large passenger list of the *Empress* in June 1910, the French papers took no notice of the event. Such lack of interest in the French press is understandable. Few passengers – with the exception of some French nobility in first class – came from France, and France was not a country from which many emigrated to Canada.

Toronto newspapers took scant notice of the Atlantic passenger ships, for Toronto had its focus on the Great Lakes. In Britain, the press treated the Canadian Pacific sympathetically. Though not as large or luxurious as the ships on the New York route, the two CPR sisters were the best available between Liverpool and Canada. They were sentimental favourites in Britain because they linked the country to

CPR Advertisement. c. 1909 showing the Empress of Ireland *and promoting the St. Lawrence route. (Marion Kelch)*

its largest Dominion, to which so many Britons now had family ties, as a result of growing emigration.

Passenger lists never appeared in *The Times*. However, the movements of the titled and other notables were printed faithfully in the society pages, and it is possible to track the arrivals or departures of men like Sir Thomas Shaughnessy and others. *Empress* stories appeared in Liverpool papers, though the ship was one of many in the port and did not generate the same level of interest as in Canada.

Why the Empress of Ireland?

In truth, few people probably cared whether they sailed in the *Empress*, her sister, or almost any other boat plying the route to Canada. Certainly to one-way, third-class emigrants, the choice of ships made little difference. Though the *Empresses* were slightly more expensive than other CPR vessels and those of competitors, there were many who could afford the difference. Value for the money could be found in all the steamers of the day and, even if the accommodations and food seemed spartan to those in first and second class, third class *Empress* passenger accounts make it clear they were clearly satisfied with what the company provided.

To second and first class passengers, if they wanted prestige accommodations between England and Canada, the best ships on the route were the two CPR sisters, though they were not all *that* far ahead of the competition, particularly in the later years. If the *Empress of Ireland* acquired a reputation for service or quality, it does not seem to have been enough to make people alter their schedules. In the various letters and diaries examined by the author, no passenger seems to have insisted on travelling in the *Empress* because of superior service or any similar reason, though in 1909 Governor General Earl Grey changed his schedule so that he could return in her. Nor was favourable word-of-mouth publicity a factor in booking passage in the *Empress*, for the CPR promoted its two *Empresses* with scrupulous equality.

In the case of 'name' passengers on the *Empress* who made a return crossing in her, the author found just three – Senator Frederick Thompson in 1906, Mackenzie King in 1908, and Sir Sandford Fleming in 1909. No doubt there were more but the low number is indicative. Most first class passengers,

Abstract of log,
RMS Empress of
Ireland, *Voyage*
18E. This
souvenir postcard
was made up in
the ship's print
shop on arrival and
sold to passengers
as a souvenir
(Stephen Brooks)

ABSTRACT OF LOG.

R.M.S. "EMPRESS of IRELAND."

J. V. FORSTER, R.N.R. COMMANDER.

St. John, N.B. to Liverpool 30th November, 1907.
VIA HALIFAX

Left Halifax 1-28 A.M. December 1st

DATE.	DIST.	LAT.N.	LONG.W.	REMARKS
Dec. 1	184	45.06	59.20	Moderate wind & choppy head sea.
,, 2	407	37.41	59.20	Strong head wind and rough sea,
,, 3	417	51.05	41.06	Strong to fresh wind, following sea
,, 4	400	53.37	31.08	Strong quarterly gale, high following sea,
,, 5	412	55.24	19.43	Strong quarterly wind, heavy sea
,, 6	425	55.28	7.20½	Fresh following wind, heavy confused sea
	195	To Bar Lightship		
Total	2440			

Arrived Bar Lightship 11-26 P.M. Friday, December 6th, 1907
Passage, Halifax to Liverpool   5 days,   17 hour,   58 minutes
Average Speed 17.68 knots

including the CPR's top management, were in a hurry to get somewhere, and they selected whatever vessel's sailing schedule best fitted their needs. In some cases that meant using a ship from a competing line, for many noted *Empress* passengers made a return passage in an Allan boat, even if it was slower and less opulent.

Many, even if they wanted to, could not change their schedules to fit that of the *Empress*, whose sailings from Canada or Liverpool occurred about four weeks apart.

Even Sir Thomas Shaughnessy, who made at least four crossings in the *Empress*, demonstrated no particular loyalty to his company's ships. He took whatever vessel he had to, including *Lusitania* to New York, where he could catch a train to Montreal and be back at his desk at the CPR's headquarters.

Two conclusions emerge. First, whether a passenger found himself or herself in the *Empress* appears to have been largely a matter of luck. Almost no one went out of his way to travel in her. Second, to only a relative handful of people – mostly second and third-class, and making one-way trips – was the *Empress* seen as anything more than a mere conveyance, the handiest means of getting from Point *A* to Point *B*. In that respect, things are much the same today. How many frequent flyers on British Airways or Air Canada really care whether they are on a 747-400 or an Airbus-340? First-time flyers, in contrast, will note all the details and recall their flights for many years.

Fortunately, some *Empress* passengers remembered.

4
Voyages I: 1906-1909

The *Empress of Ireland* was launched amid great ceremony by Katherine Gracie, wife of Alexander Gracie, Managing Director of the Fairfield works, at 2:30 in the afternoon of Saturday, 27 January 1906. January was an auspicious month for a launch, for the drab, cheerless month had taken its name from the old Roman god of beginnings. To cheers and the steam whistles of vessels in the river, the ship slid down the greased ways of Berth 4 for something like 925 feet, half again her own length, before coming to a bobbing halt in the chilly waters of the Clyde.

Five tugboats eased her into the fitting-out area, where she would remain for the next four months, while the distinguished guests trooped off for a champagne lunch and rounds of toasts. 'Success to the *Empress of Ireland* and prosperity to the Canadian Pacific Railway Company,' intoned Sir Digby Morant, a member of the Fairfield board.

That same day, Mrs Gracie cabled Thomas Shaughnessy in Montreal:

'THANKS FOR HONOUR OF NAMING *EMPRESS OF IRELAND* MOST SUCCESSFUL LAUNCH AND HAPPY DAY FOR ALL THE GODMOTHER WISHES PROSPERITY TO SHIP AND YOUR COMPANY.'

With the time difference, Shaughnessy was able to reply the same day: 'THANKS FOR KINDNESS IN CHRISTENING SHIP. TRUST THAT YOUR GOOD WISHES WILL BE REALIZED AND THAT VESSEL WILL IN EVERY RESPECT MEET EXPECTATIONS OF OWNERS AND BUILDERS.'

Archer Baker, the CPR's Liverpool manager, reported to his superior in Montreal: '*EMPRESS OF IRELAND* SUCCESSFULLY LAUNCHED TODAY REGRET UNIVERSAL ABSENCE YOURSELF AND LADY SHAUGHNESSY.'

Katherine Gracie had not been the CPR's first choice to christen the new ship. In December of 1905, five weeks before the launch, Thomas Shaughnessy had wired Baker with instructions to approach the Countess of Aberdeen. 'OUR NEW ATLANTIC STEAMER THE *EMPRESS OF IRELAND*,' Shaughnessy wrote in his telegram, 'WILL BE LAUNCHED AT FAIRFIELD GLASGOW JANUARY TWENTY-SEVENTH AND WE WOULD ALL FEEL HIGHLY HONOURED IF YOU COULD MAKE IT CONVENIENT TO ACT AS SPONSOR.'

The Countess, reached by Baker at her London home, had replied that she was regretfully unavailable on that date, due to a farewell party.

Over the next months a small army of labourers and artisans struggled to complete the ship, and sea trials began on the Clyde on 5 June. On hand for the trials were Arthur Piers, chief of the CPR's Marine Department, Dr Francis Elgar, who had designed the two *Empresses*, Alexander Gracie, and other observers. Even on the first day the new ship proved to be fast, reaching $20\frac{1}{4}$ knots at one point. That result must have pleased her builders, and not merely for the sake of pure speed. Fairfield was contractually committed to the CPR to provide a vessel with a guaranteed speed of $19\frac{1}{4}$ knots. That wasn't going to be easy, as the ship was also required to carry 6,500 tons of cargo on a mean draught of 27ft. 6in. To meet the cargo-carrying requirement, her hull had to be designed on more fuller lines than most other high-speed vessels. The CPR, figuring that the passenger business might one day fall off, had cannily ensured that the ship could make money hauling cargo if necessary. For the sea trial, the load was 6,900 tons, bringing the ship to her mean service draught.

The massive quadruple-expansion reciprocating steam engines behaved flawlessly, developing over

18,000 indicated horsepower at 81 revolutions per minute. So well, in fact, did they perform that one of the ship's three single-ended boilers was not even fired up during the test. In her speed trials off Ireland the *Empress* proved fractionally – a mere one-third of a knot – faster than the *Empress of Britain* in late April.

Off Greenock on 5 June, Arthur Piers sent the following telegram to the CPR's headquarters in Montreal: 'SPEED TRIALS TODAY SHORT ONE BOILER DID TWO MILES AT TWENTY AND QUARTER MEAN OF TWO MILES WITH AND AGAINST TIDE AND WIND OVER TWENTY CONSUMPTION TRIALS FOLLOW.'

Two days later he was able to report: 'ALL TRIALS SUCCESSFULLY CARRIED OUT CONDITIONS AMPLY FULFILLED.'

Press coverage was non-existent, British newspapers devoting their attention to the launch of the *Lusitania*, then the largest ship afloat, in Glasgow.

On 12 June the ship left the Clyde for her trial cruise around the Irish coast. That completed, the CPR ordered extra work to be performed on the *Empress* while she was made ready for her maiden voyage from Liverpool. The lengthy list of extra features, which cost £4,611 to implement, were mainly cosmetic, but some practical items were also ordered, including a remote helm control above the wheelhouse and additional electric lights.

As to the question of steering, the canard which would plague two formal *Empress* inquiries in the future, Fairfield's naval architect testified in 1914, 'On the trials of the vessel everybody was absolutely satisfied with her steering qualities.' Later, he added, '...on trials in our hands, [*she*] had steered very well indeed.'

On 21 June the new ship was formally taken over from her builders by the CPR.

The maiden voyage of any passenger steamship is a special occasion, when the hopes of her builders and owners are finally realized, and the new vessel begins its commercial career.

The opening sequence of James Cameron's epic *Titanic* captured unforgettably for millions the bustle and organized confusion surrounding the departure of a great Edwardian liner. There is no reason to believe that the maiden voyage of the *Empress of Ireland* was much different than any other of this era. The new ship that called the great port 'home' had arrived in the Mersey only a couple of days before, and the people of Liverpool had come in crowds to look her over with practiced eyes.

The *Empress* departed Liverpool on Friday afternoon, 29 June, with 1,258 passengers and general cargo, bound for Quebec via Moville, where she would stop for the outgoing mails. Appropriately, a Dublin-born master was on the bridge, Captain Francis ('Frank') Carey, a veteran of the St Lawrence and one of the best-known captains on the route. Carey, born in 1849, was the oldest of the men to take command of the Empress, but that was no drawback, for his experience at sea was second to none. One Canadian newspaper described him thus: 'Although of a modest and retiring demeanor he is a great favourite with those having the pleasure of his acquaintances [*sic*], being a thorough gentleman, a first class seaman and a practical navigator.'

First Officer was James Turnbull, 32, a capable, seasoned veteran who would remain aboard the *Empress* for seven months before transferring to the *Empress of Britain*. He would return to the *Empress* for four voyages in late 1913, this time as her commander.

The ship was by no means full. There were 119 first class passengers, 342 in second class and 797 in third, all of whom would have been awed by the newness of everything they saw. The beds they slept in that Friday night had never been slept in before. No one had played the piano or sat in the fine furniture in the public rooms, or opened a book in the library. And no one had ever eaten from the new china – Minton's 'Fontenay' pattern in first class, Minton's 'Alton' or 'White Fish' pattern in second, and plain china in third, each piece bearing in the centre the entwined letters CPR within a buckled belt containing the company's name.

While the passengers settled in and got to know the ship that would be their home for the next week, the *Empress* glided down the Mersey, guided by her pilot, cleared the Mersey Bar lightship and began picking up speed, setting a northwest course across the Irish Sea and bound for Moville and the rendezvous with the mail tender. The *Empress* arrived at Moville at 1:30 on Saturday afternoon, giving those on deck an opportunity to enjoy the views of the Irish coast and the last sight of land until Canada.

Captain Carey was a man keenly interested in the performance of the company's newest ship. He ordered speed – and got it. Daily noon-to-noon runs were as follows:

July 1   421 knots
July 2   460 knots (average over 18 knots/hour)
July 3   450 knots (average over 18 knots/hour).

At this point, the *Empress* ran into heavy weather and the speed slacked off. She made 302 knots on 4 July and, still in rough seas, 362 knots on 5 July. By this time she had entered the Gulf of St Lawrence via the safe southern route and made 404 knots on 6 July. The final run on 7 July, into Quebec, was 224 knots.

As they had done a less than two months before, with the maiden voyage of the *Empress of Britain*, the newspapers of Montreal and Quebec reported the departure of the *Empress* from Liverpool and, once in range of the Marconi shore stations in Canada, followed her progress through the Gulf of St Lawrence. Indeed, all that summer the press took a very active interest in the two new CPR vessels which so outclassed everything else on the St Lawrence route to Canada.

On 4 July the *Gazette* noted that 'The wireless is now searching for the *Empress of Ireland* and it is expected that the new liner on her maiden trip will be picked up today off Cape Race. The *Empress of Ireland* on her trial trips made such an excellent showing that great things are expected of her.'

The *Empress* checked in with the CPR on 4 July, some two hundred miles east of Cape Race. Arthur Piers, the CPR's steamship manager and one of the first class passengers, wired Thomas Shaughnessy via the Cape Race Marconi station: 'LAST LAND IRELAND SATURDAY FIVE ELEVEN P.M. RUNS 421 460 450 HOT BEARINGS LAST NIGHT NOW DENSE FOG ALL WELL.' In releasing the message to the press, the CPR mentioned a 'splendid' passage and noted the heavy fog off Cape Race, which had forced Captain Carey to reduce speed. No mention was made of the overheating shaft bearing – a problem that could easily be corrected and was not unexpected in a brand new ship.

By 5 July, at 7:30 a.m. the *Empress* was reported 180 miles SE of Cape Ray, experiencing clear skies and northwesterly winds. On the sixth, she landed her mails at 5:50 p.m. at Rimouski, and set off upriver, arriving at 5:30 Saturday morning. The arrival in Quebec of the *Empress* received less coverage than her sister ship, seven weeks earlier. Then, it had been front-page news. This time, the story was relegated to the shipping pages. 'Notwithstanding the early hour at which the steamer came into port,' wrote the Quebec *Chronicle*, 'there was a large number of people on the Breakwater awaiting her. Among them were representatives of the Customs and Immigration Departments, the Canadian Pacific and Grand Trunk Railways, and many who had assembled for the purpose of meeting friends who crossed on the steamer.'

Among the passengers was the famous Black Dike Band from England, making an 18-week tour of Canada and the United States, their first to North America. The manifest shows that the Band consisted of thirty-one men in second class, between the ages of 30 and 61, all from Yorkshire. As the men were neither returning Canadians nor settlers, they were listed in the manifest as 'Tourists'.

John Arthur Wood, 38, one the three euphonium players, (the euphonium was like a tenor tuba), kept a diary entitled *My experience with the Black Dike Band in Canada & America*, outlining events of his trip between 29 June and 16 November. It is the only known first-hand account of the *Empress'* maiden voyage.

> Friday June 29th
> We had no time to spare at Liverpool so went straight onto the ship, *Empress of Ireland*, a new ship 14,500 tonnage, which is her maiden voyage. We had a look around her & considered her to be a floating palace. About 5-30 we went onto the First Class deck &

played *Hearts of Oak, Rule Britannia, Lead Kindly Light*, & just as the anchor was weighed we played *Auld Lang Syne*, amidst cheers on the docks, & handkerchiefs waving, never shall I forget that sight, leaving my country & home, & there was scarcely a dry eye in the Band.

We had a beautiful dinner & then went on deck. We passed the Isle of Man about 11-5 p.m.

Saturday June 30th

Arriving at Moville in the North of Ireland, about 6-20 am where we waited for the mails till 1-30, thus already losing six hours. We lost sight of land about 6-30 at night, & it was a beautiful night on the sea.

Sunday July 1st

A beautiful morning, at 10-0 am a Service was held in the First Class Saloon, at which 8 of the Band played for the Service, I being one of the 8. After Service all the band played the *Hallelujah Chorus*. The Service was the most solemn Service I have ever seen, the Captain read all the lessons & prayers which were mostly for the safety of people on the sea. The rest of the day was spent sitting on deck in quietness.

Monday July 2nd

We awoke to find we were in a very heavy fog, the vessel was only going slow, & the fog horn was blown every minute. After dinner the fog cleared & it was a nice afternoon but rather cold. At night we gave a Concert in the 3rd Class Saloon, which was packed almost to suffocation, the concert was much enjoyed by the passengers, there was no collection.

Tuesday July 3rd

A very nice day all day but rather cold. We played games on deck, one was a kind of Hop Scotch, with long sticks. At night we gave a Concert in the 2nd Class Saloon for the benefit of the Sailors' Orphans, the collection amounted to £9-15-8.

Wednesday July 4th

Very foggy, the sailors were sounding for Sand [*Grand*] Bank & something had run hot in the engines, causing them to have to stand the biggest part of the night. We travelled 148 miles less than in the previous 24 hours, which I might say was marked on a chart every day exactly where we were in the ocean. The whole day we travelled slow & fog horn going continually, a very dreary day.

Thursday July 5th

Still the same as yesterday, but a heavy swell on the sea, a very funny thing when we went into breakfast, was a frame fitting onto the table to keep the plates &c from falling off. About noon the fog cleared & oh what a sight – big waves like mountains rising up & down. We passed a ship & we could see people on board quite plain. At dinner time about half the passengers were missing from the table, some on deck & some in their bunks. The Band were very lucky, only 2 men being sick & they were only sick one day. I never felt any effect, of course it is rather funny walking when the ship comes up to meet your feet, instead of you putting your feet down. About 3 o'clock we sighted land a long way off, with snow on the mountains. It was Newfoundland.

Friday July 6th

I went on deck about 5-0 am & I think it was a very pretty sight to see land about ¼ mile from the ship on the left hand side, with nice little white houses scattered all along the beach. They are French-Canadian fisheries. All day we ran up the Gulf of St Lawrence & at 6 p.m. we arrived at Rumuski [*sic*] where we put off mails, & those fellows called Custom Officers came on board & started to examine luggage. Some had duty to pay, one young man had a lot of cartridges in his box, but he had to pay. They did not trouble us much.

"Empress" Daily News

C.P.R. "EMPRESSES"

Hold the Atlantic Record between Liverpool and Quebec

6 DAYS, 2 HOURS, 30 MIN.

And Between Liverpool and Rimouski 5 Days, 14 Hours and 44 Minutes.

The "Empress of Britain" and "Empress of Ireland" are sister ships, being exactly alike in every particular, and were launched and completed within 3 months of each other. Each are 14,500 tons and have 18,000 horse-power. They make the voyage between Quebec and Liverpool in the same number of hours,

`. . R.M.S. "EMPRESS OF BRITAIN."`

often there not being more than fifteen or twenty minutes' difference between them in the run from Liverpool to Rimouski, or vice-versa. These voyages are always made well inside the six-day mark—the time being taken from the hour the vessel leaves the dock at Liverpool to the time she stops to discharge the mails at Rimouski in the St. Lawrence river on the westbound trip, or from Rimouski to the dock at Liverpool on the eastbound voyage. The fastest voyages between these places yet made by the "Empresses" are westbound—5 days, 14 hours and 44 minutes, eastbound—5 days, 15 hours and 20 minutes. From Liverpool to Quebec—dock to dock—the best time so far is 6 days, 2 hours and 30 minutes.

These steamers are bringing to Canada this season between 1,500 and 1,600 passengers a voyage, and do the largest business on the St. Lawrence route.

LESS THAN FOUR DAYS

Time Between Belle Isle and Tory Island, by the "Empresses."

The C.P.R. "Empress of Ireland" and "Empress of Britain" besides being the fastest and finest steamships in the Canadian service are easily the first favorites with the travelling public. The "Empresses" unitedly hold the records for the fastest passages in both directions from "land to land," the time between Tory Island off the north coast of Ireland and Belle Isle being—

Eastbound

"Empress of Britain"—3 days, 18 hrs. 45 min.

Westbound

"Empress of Ireland"—3 days, 18 hrs. 50 min.

These two steamships are sister ships being constructed on exactly similar lines and are identical in almost every detail. Each are 570 feet in length and 65 feet 6 inches in breadth.

HOW THE "EMPRESSES" REPAY THE DISTANT WIRELESS OPERATORS.

(Montreal Gazette, Sept. 13th, 1909.)

The "Empresses" of the C.P.R., in return for the service given them by the Marconi wireless stations in the Gulf and lower river, have devised a method of reciprocation which is somewhat unique. On the last voyage of the Empress of Ireland from Quebec, Captain Forster gave instructions that when the vessel was well within range of Point Amour, a cask should be set afloat with the Union Jack on top, containing the latest English and Canadian papers and magazines. The Point Amour station was advised of this new departure by wireless before the vessel arrived, and a boat put off from the lonely rock-bound station to get the cask filled with literature of all sorts. So much was the innovation appreciated by the wireless operators at that lonely Labrador point that when the Ireland was swinging across the banks, well out of sight of land, Captain Forster received a message of thanks from the men who were at the wireless key.

COMPARATIVE DISTANCES TO LIVERPOOL.

From New York		3108 mls
" Boston		2958 "
" St. John, N.B. { Can.	}	2723 "
" Quebec { Pacific }		2633 "

LONDON – HONG KONG

What the C.P.R. Is Doing To Bring Them Closer Together.

The line of the Canadian Pacific Railway extends across Canada from St. John, New Brunswick, on the Atlantic Ocean, to the city of Vancouver on the Pacific Ocean, and it is the only transcontinental railway in America whose passengers are carried without change of cars from tidewater to tidewater. It is the only system of railway from "Ocean to Ocean" under one management. Upon the Atlantic, this company operates a fleet of 14 ocean liners to and from Europe, and on the Pacific, a fleet of 10 steamships between Vancouver and China and Japan and Australia.

The recent great development of the Canadian Pacific System carries it beyond mere local interest to a position commanding the interest and admiration of the whole world. The Canadian Pacific Royal Mail Service, "The Overseas Mail" between London and Yokohama, Japan, and Hong Kong, China, is faster than by way of the Suez Canal. The voyage from London and across the Western Hemisphere to Vancouver is made inside 11 days; from London to Yokohama, 23 days, and from London to Hong Kong, 29 days. The voyage from Liverpool to Quebec (the point of debarkation on this side of the Atlantic in summer) is 400 miles shorter than from Liverpool to New York. The Company already land passengers from England to all interior points on the American Continent quicker than is done via New York.

The natural advantages of the Canadian Route, the excellence of the accommodation provided on the C.P. R. Steamships and Railway, under one control, combine to make the C.P.R. route between Europe and the Orient the most attractive.

RETURNING PASSENGERS.

During the season of the St. Lawrence River navigation Customs officials and Canadian Pacific Railway Baggagemen join the "Empresses" from Liverpool at Rimouski, and come up the river to Quebec, thus enabling passengers to have their baggage passed by the Customs and checked to rail destination before the ship comes to dock. During the winter season these officials board the "Empresses" at Halifax and go through to St. John, N.B. This arrangement relieves passengers of the annoyance and delay on landing at Quebec or St. John, N.B., as the case may be. Ticket agents also come on board at the above places and travel through to port of debarkation. Their object is to supply passengers with railway tickets, making sleeping and parlor car reservations through to their destinations. This feature of the C.P.R. service is very much appreciated.

Canadian Pacific Railway Company's Steamship Lines

'Empress' Daily News, 26 May 1910. (Canadian Pacific Archives)

> Saturday July 7
> We arrived at the dock at 5-30 am & after having a good breakfast we played the *Maple Leaf*, which is the national anthem in Canada, & *Auld Lang Syne*, & then shaking hands with the Captain & Officers we went down the gangway, and landed in Canada at exactly 9-0 am or 2-0 o'clock in the afternoon at home. It was very hot & we could feel the difference in the climate.

The *Chronicle* noted the Band's arrival in Quebec, its shipboard charity concert, and that the Band's rendition of Handel at the end of the Sunday service had been played 'with grand effect.' From Wood's account, it is interesting to note that word of the hot engine bearing had filtered down to the passengers.

The Band's first engagement was that same day in Quebec City, where its two concerts attracted good audiences. Over the next four months the Band would perform at a total of twenty-four cities, ending in New York. The Band, today numbering twenty-eight members, is one of the world's oldest and most famous brass bands. It still rehearses in the same bandroom as in 1855, in the West Riding city of Bradford. John Wood died in May 1938.

When the *Empress* was safely moored at the new extension to the breakwater, the task of unloading passengers' baggage began while passengers enjoyed a final breakfast on the ship. On this particular occasion, though customs officers had boarded at Rimouski, they had not managed to complete their work on the passage to Quebec, as the luggage of first and second class passengers had been placed in the same hold.

In the end, with 'Herculean' efforts by the customs staff and aided by CPR personnel, the first special train, containing the first class passengers, got away shortly before 9:00 a.m. The train for second class passengers departed at 11:00 a.m., and that for third class passengers by 1:00 p.m.

The Immigration buildings at Quebec were not used on this voyage, as the medical inspection of the passengers had been completed aboard ship, between Rimouski and Quebec. Instead, passengers stepped off the ship and into a new shed erected on the breakwater extension. Here, they merely pointed to their bags and anything not already checked was taken care of by porters. The passengers then entered the waiting trains and were soon on their way.

'Everything,' said the *Chronicle*, 'connected with the landing and entraining of the passengers worked most satisfactorily.' Indeed, the voyage itself had gone very well and, had it not been for two days of rough weather and the heavy fog, the ship would undoubtedly have set a record.

According to the manifest, there was one passenger who should have been landed at Grosse Ile, the quarantine station in the middle of the river and some twenty miles below Quebec. The *Empress* had not stopped and the passenger was brought on to Quebec, then sent back by launch.

On Saturday, following her arrival in port the ship was dressed with flags. Above her stem floated a British ensign on a green ground, with the golden harp of Erin on the fly. A newspaper was also published on the trip, containing wireless stories and 'packaged' news items. However, unlike in later years, the paper was titled the *Sea Gull*.

Observers were impressed with the new vessel's sailing capabilities. In two days of heavy weather, the *Chronicle* reported, 'she proved herself a fine, steady and comfortable seaboat, and passengers who were on their first sea voyage suffered very little from *mal-de-mer*.' Even on her maiden voyage the *Empress* showed promise of things to come, for the run of 460 knots constituted a one-day record on the North Atlantic route to Canada. Interviewed aboard his new ship, Captain Carey expressed satisfaction at the speed developed and pronounced the *Empress* a 'splendid sea boat.'

Arthur Piers provided a few more details, indicating that the *Empress* had reached a speed of $20\frac{1}{2}$ knots, and this with one of the boilers held in reserve. As with the *Empress of Britain*, there was an absence of vibration and the counterbalanced engines ran smoothly, and faster speeds could be hoped for once the engines had been properly broken in. It was what her builder, Dr Francis Elgar, had termed the 'stiffening' stage, the phase through which all new reciprocating marine engines had to pass before their performance could be optimized.

For some reason, the CPR at this point appeared uncertain as to what to do with its new ships. Arthur Piers, having crossed on the maiden voyage, talked publicly about a possible transfer to the Pacific, and noted that some interior changes would be necessary before the transfer could take place.

As the *Empress* also carried the mails from Moville to Rimouski, it is necessary to digress slightly at this convenient juncture, to consider the ocean mail service and the government subsidies that supported them. In 1855 the Canadian government signed a mail contract with Hugh Allan, agent for the Montreal Ocean Steamship Company, which later became the Allan Line. That contract called for fourteen fortnightly trips to Canada in the summer months, and five monthly trips to Portland, Maine, in the winter months. The inaugural run left Liverpool on 23 April 1856 and began a highly successful first year. Three years later the service was upgraded to a weekly one, and the mail subsidies contributed to the success and growth of the Allan Line.

Forty-five years later ocean mail service was still being provided by Allan's steamships. In 1904-1905, the Allan Line received a subsidy of £2,000 for each round-trip of the fast *Victorian* and *Virginian*, £1,000 for *Bavarian* and *Tunisian*, and £500 for the still slower *Ionian*, *Sicilian*, and *Pretorian*.

That arrangement changed the following year, once the CPR had announced it would begin construction of two fast liners to compete with the Allan's *Victorian* and *Virginian*. On 19 January 1906 the Allan Line negotiated a new transatlantic mail contract, for six years, with the Canadian Department of Trade & Commerce (which had responsibility for the postal service) for weekly service to be provided by four 17-18 knot ships, and with a subsidy of £3,000 per round trip. Though Allan had two ships capable of this speed, *Victorian* and *Virginian* (both triple-screw turbine vessels), it needed two more to fulfill the terms of the contract.

As Allan was at that time in some financial difficulty and unable to order new vessels, it agreed in April 1906 to subcontract a part of the mail contract to the CPR, which would use its new, fast *Empresses*. The winter mail port was, again, Halifax.

Some eyebrows were raised in government circles but, in the end, the subcontract was allowed to stand. The subcontract was an astute short term move for the Allan Line but provided the CPR with an entry into the mail business. In reality it spelled the beginning of the end for the venerable Allan Line. Less than three years later the CPR acquired *de facto* control of the Allan Line, though the company was not formally merged into the CPR until 1917.

In addition to the mail contract which the CPR shared for Canadian mail, the enterprising railroad also secured in the summer of 1906 a contract with the British government for mails via Canada to and from Hong Kong, China and Japan. The two-year contract was a good one for the CPR. For each trip, the company received $17,305, which would contribute to the steamships on two oceans and the rail link to Vancouver.

On the Atlantic, just two ships were designated by the British government for this purpose: the two fast *Empresses*. The terms of the contract were rather demanding. The mail had to be delivered to Japan in twenty-two days and China in twenty-nine after leaving London. The company was penalized $2,500 for failure to start a boat or train on time, with a further penalty of $500 for every 24-hour delay. The penalty for late arrival was $500 for every twelve hours. By September 1907 the times were relaxed – slightly. Westbound, the company had to deliver mail between Liverpool and Hong Kong in 28 days, 22 hours and 35 minutes via Quebec and Rimouski, and was allowed one extra day in winter via Halifax or Saint John. So, if the company chafed at delays at the Mersey Bar or the Crane Island Flats, or ordered its captains to make speedy passages, it had strong economic reasons for doing so. And it explained why the Orient mails were taken off at Quebec even before the first class passengers disembarked.

Canadian mails, whether off-loaded at Rimouski, Sydney or Halifax, were sorted on a railway mail car headed for Montreal. It was faster that way than waiting while the mail ship made her way upriver to Quebec. In general the Canadian postal service got good value for its money, and the CPR reaped a harvest of favourable publicity when its *Empresses* made an especially fast crossing.

On numerous occasions the restrictions of the mail contract must have irritated the masters of the two sisters *Empresses*. In late August of 1907, for example, there was an occasion when the *Empress of Britain*, eastbound to Liverpool, was obliged to wait seven hours at Rimouski for the European mail to arrive by train. In April 1908 the *Empress of Britain*, arriving at Halifax from Saint John, had to wait nine hours for the mail train to arrive. It was a frustration for passengers and crew, and a needless expense for the company. Sir Thomas Shaughnessy observed to a Saint John reporter that the *Empress of Britain* would be nearly a day late in arriving at Liverpool as a result of the enforced mail call at Halifax.

The problem arose in part because incoming and outgoing mails were treated differently by the Canadian Post Office. Mail from Europe, once landed at Halifax, was put on a special train that would arrive in Montreal twenty hours later. On the other hand, mail destined for Europe via Halifax was put on a regular train. If it was delayed, so was the sailing of the *Empress*.

Even before the *Empress of Ireland* began her maiden voyage, the Allan Line and CPR were endeavoring to arrange with the British Post Office and the Canadian authorities for an alteration of the sailing date with the British mails, and dropping the call at Moville. In the past, Canadian mails had been sent from London on Thursdays and loaded aboard the mail steamers at Moville on Fridays. The two Canadian shipping companies argued that, with the increase in vessel speeds, mails should be sent from London to Liverpool. Besides, the companies pointed out, the steamers had sometimes been forced to wait for hours at Moville for the Irish mail trains.

While the *Empress* was docked in Quebec City and making ready to return to Liverpool, a new mail arrangement was announced, the result of protracted meetings between the Canadian postal authorities and the two shipping companies. It was arranged that mail boats from Canada would depart on Friday mornings, and from Liverpool on Friday afternoons. As well, the call at Moville was dropped, a move welcomed by the CPR, '…because we believe that a source of danger to the vessels is removed.' wrote Thomas Shaughnessy to Postmaster General Rodolphe Lemieux.

With Moville no longer a mail port, the Canadian mails would be taken on at Rimouski and delivered in Liverpool, and vice versa. Sailing dates from Quebec for the *Empress* changed as well, from Thursday afternoon to Friday morning. Though the Allan Line announced its boats would continue to call at Moville for Irish passengers, the CPR was content to drop the port.

At Rimouski a further change was soon made. The government used one of its own boats as a mail tender, doing away with a boat provided for by private contract. Again, the steamship companies were pleased, as the previous vessel was antiquated and had caused delays in the past.

On Thursday, 12 July, prior to departure from Quebec, a Mr W.A. Phelan, Secretary of the Committee of Montreal Irishmen, presented Captain Carey with three handsome silk flags, as a mark of appreciation of the honour paid their nationality by the CPR in thus naming such a splendid vessel. The flags were 'greatly admired' and Captain Carey was delighted with the gift, asking Phelan to return his thanks to the donors.

Along with the flags, the Irishmen donated a magnificent parchment engrossed in old english script, containing an excellent picture of the *Empress*. In the decorated border were maple leaves showing fall colors, and shamrocks.

For the return leg of her maiden voyage, the *Empress* departed Quebec on Thursday, 12 July, with 517 passengers aboard, the new mail schedule not yet having gone into effect. Loading of the vessel had been completed earlier in the day, and she was drawing over 28ft forward and 29ft 6in aft.

A large crowd assembled on the different wharves in the vicinity of the Louise Basin to bid farewell to the new vessel, and they watched as the special train arrived from Montreal at 3:00 p.m., well in time for the planned sailing time of 4:00 p.m.

The Quebec *Chronicle* described the scene: 'At 4:15 the propellers of the big steamer commenced reversing, and she began to move slowly astern out of the Basin, assisted by two tugs. Fifteen minutes later, so easily is the ship handled, her head was downstream, the tugs cast off, and she started on her

Mail being loaded on the Empress of Britain *from the tender* Rhoda *at Rimouski, 1906. (National Archives of Canada)*

trip of over 2,000 miles across the Atlantic. Steam whistles sounded a parting salute, and a short time afterwards the *Empress of Ireland* disappeared around Indian Cove.'

On leaving, Captain Carey flew the flags presented to his ship. Somewhat unusually, a large number of friends of first class passenger Gustave Simard, having come aboard to bid the latter farewell, decided to stay aboard the *Empress* and disembark at Rimouski aboard the mail boat.

Also among those on board was a Canadian Pacific photographer. During the voyage he went about the ship, posing passengers for pictures that the company subsequently used for promotional purposes.

Even at this early stage of their careers a rivalry seems to have developed between the two sister ships, which left opposite sides of the Atlantic about the same time. The *Gazette* commented: 'The respective runs of the new liners will be watched with a great deal of interest by shipping men, and it will be a duel between Commodore Stewart and Captain Carey for the blue ribbon of the CPR Atlantic Services.' This was a rivalry that would persist for years, for both ships were evenly matched and, over time, they repeatedly broke each other's records on the North Atlantic route.

Having loaded the mails, the *Empress* departed Rimouski at 10:00 a.m. on Friday the 13th, arrived at Moville at 11:20 a.m. on Thursday the 19th, and arrived that evening in Liverpool. A passage of 5 days, 20 hours and 50 minutes to Moville was a new record and, coupled with a record set westbound by the *Empress of Britain*, caused 'great satisfaction' at the CPR's headquarters. The Irish of Montreal hoisted their glasses in salute.

The only negative note to the return trip was the death of an un-identified male, the first recorded death of a passenger aboard the *Empress*. It would not be the last.

The *Empress* returned to Quebec at 3:15 p.m. on Thursday, 2 August with 538 passengers aboard, having left Liverpool the previous Thursday, 26 July, at 6:35 p.m. Daily runs were as follows:

Fri.	195 miles
Sat.	405 miles

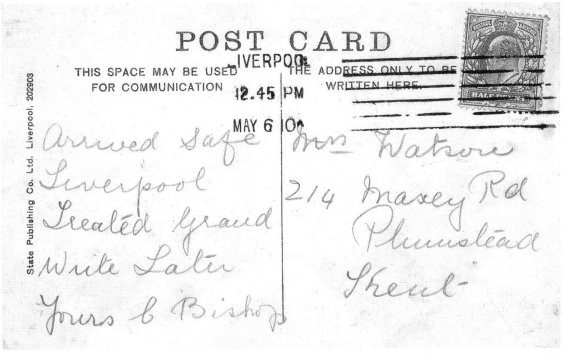

A typical message on the back of an Empress *card, May 1910.*

Sun.	430 miles
Mon.	440 miles
Tue.	451 miles
Wed.	431 miles
Thur.	324 miles (to Rimouski)
Fri.	154 miles (to Quebec).

When the weather was favourable, the *Empress* made good speed but, as the voyage progressed, she encountered headwinds up to Cape Race, and thick fog thereafter. Nonetheless it was a record-setting passage, establishing a new mark for the Moville-Rimouski route – and via the southern (or Cape Race) route, some 200 miles longer than through the Straits of Belle Isle.

First class passengers landed at once, and their train departed at 5:00 p.m. The second class followed an hour later, followed shortly by third.

There were changes on the social scene of Quebec City now that a new ship, the *Empress of Ireland*, called on a regular basis. On Saturday, 4 August, a social was held at the Sailors' Institute for the sailors and firemen of the *Empress*, *Philae*, *Nyassa* and *Coronel*. 'Every seat in the place was occupied,' reported the *Chronicle*, 'the windows were opened wide, cake and lemonade being passed through to the scores who were unable to enter.'

A hearty feast was provided for the attendees, followed by an informal concert, with crew members from the various vessels singing their favourite songs and dancing. The paper opined that 'Probably the best item was *How Do They Know I'm Irish* by a seaman from the *Empress of Ireland*.' Surprisingly, twelve of the men signed the pledge of total abstinence.

Crewmen appreciated the Institute and its work on their behalf. It sought magazines from Quebec citizens, and distributed them on the eve of sailing so the men could have some reading material. As well, the Institute collected old carpets and turned them into hand protectors and rags for the firemen and trimmers.

The Institute, located in a nondescript building in Lower Town, was a short walk from the Breakwater where the *Empress* docked for turnaround. It was a cosy and home-like place for off-duty crewmen, an alternative to the saloons of Quebec, if they wanted to read or write letters, and it was where shipping lines went to replace deserters. The main room, used for concerts, had a piano for the musically inclined, of which there were many. A separate room, for stewards and engineers, held a parlor organ. The visiting room was supplied with desks and writing materials for anyone who wished. During the week, Institute volunteers served tea every evening between 8:00 and 10:00, the charge for a cup of tea and a bun being one penny. Sundays featured evening song services (with free tea afterward), though it appears that men from the *Empress* were not regular attendees. A 1912 report for the Institute noted that 'we have… a better attendance from the Manchester steamers and the London boats than from the *Empresses*.' The Institute also provided a currency exchange service, '…for the stewards of the *Empresses*, and it seems to be appreciated.'

Three nights later at the St John Street YMCA there was another event, a concert featuring the various ships' crews, including officers. Announcing the evening, the *Chronicle* observed that 'As this is the second trip of the *Empress of Ireland*, unexpected talent is being discovered, and the concert will be a very enjoyable and amusing one.' Sailors were admitted free; civilians paid ten cents.

On her return trip (2E) the *Empress* carried no mails, for the first and last time in her career, due to some confusion arising from the change of sailing dates for the mail boats. The *Empress*' announced sailing date of Thursday, 9 August could not be changed at the last minute to Friday. This meant the ship would be well out to sea by the time the mails arrived at Rimouski on Saturday morning. As the CPR was obviously not willing to hold the *Empress* off Rimouski for twenty-four hours, it was arranged that *Tunisian* would carry the mails on this occasion.

The most notable of the ship's 980 passengers was Baron Komura, the eminent Japanese statesman and newly appointed ambassador to the Court of St James. Travelling in first class and accompanied by a valet, the baron, who was not in good health, was on his way to London to take up his post. Komura, who had represented his country at the peace conference convened by Theodore Roosevelt in September1905 which ended the Russo-Japanese War, had crossed to Vancouver aboard a CPR vessel and Sir Thomas Shaughnessy issued instructions that the Baron be well looked after on the transatlantic portion of his trip.

The special train from Montreal arrived on time for the scheduled 3:00 p.m. sailing, but the *Empress* was delayed over an hour due to the late arrival of the regular train from Montreal, which contained a number of passengers from the west. The Quebec newspaper reported one oddity: six Chinese in bond, presumably being deported.

Her progress to Liverpool was followed in the press. By 4:00 p.m. on the 15th she was eighty-five miles west of Malin Head, and arrived at Liverpool the following day.
Both sisters, it seemed, were performing very consistently, with one Montreal paper noting that fast passages were one of the principal features of the season.

As the summer progressed, the Allan Line found itself in a tough position. It promoted its service from Montreal and extolled the 'view of the noble St Lawrence by daylight.' Prices were just a few dollars less than in the *Empress*. But Allan ads also featured the record times of the Allan vessels, and these were all slower than the two new CPR boats.

As with any new undertaking, especially one as complex as provisioning large ships, problems inevitably arose, and these had to be dealt with by the CPR shore personnel. In the case of the two Atlantic *Empresses*, it appeared that food suppliers in Quebec City were not yet able to supply the highest-quality provisions that first and second class passengers expected. Complaints arrived in the company's offices, though no word of these complaints ever leaked to the press.

On 6 August, Archer Baker wrote to Thomas Shaughnessy expressing the complaints of one woman:

> I met last night at Dinner, Mrs Wilson, wife of Colonel Wilson commanding the Canadian
> Rifle team at Bisley. She told me that she had crossed in the *Empress of Ireland* July 12th and

This building, where the 'stewards of the Empress of Ireland *proved themselves exceptional entertainers' is the former Seamen's Institute at 13 St James Street (now Rue de la Barricade) in Quebec's Lower Town. Close to the Breakwater,* Empress *crewmen could relax here in their off-duty hours. (Author)*

she spoke in the most disparaging manner of the food; she said that all the passengers she knew were loud in their complaints and were longing for the voyage to be over, as she said – 'to enable them to get a decent meal', and that comparisons not in our favour were very loud and numerous on the L&NW Dining car from Liverpool to London. She said that in some instances the meat was uneatable, the fruit of the poorest quality – nuts, when opened, falling into dust. She had no complaint whatever as to the service which she said was good.

While the complaints may have had some substance, for they were echoed in the *Empress of Britain*, Mrs Wilson's complaints may have stemmed from sour grapes. On 20 August, Arthur Piers wrote that Mrs Wilson was known to the company's management by reputation. It transpired that she had occupied one of the side tables in the first class dining saloon, and that her first complaint had come on finding that the only vegetable served was potatoes. 'When it was ascertained,' Piers wrote, 'that she wanted another vegetable for lunch this was provided for her for the rest of the voyage.'
The lady seems to have been a chronic complainer. Piers continued:

She took great exception to the fact that small platters were not used for serving the meats etc. at table. Finally, the climax was reached when she saw on the Bill of Fare what struck her as being a dainty morsel, under the name of 'Yorkshire Rabbit'. She ordered some and when she found, as she expressed it, that it consisted of a piece of toast with some nasty stuff upon it that tasted more like cheese than rabbit, she had no good word for our table.

Never again, after the summer of 1906, were there complaints about the quality of the food in first or second class in the *Empresses*.

With a new vessel, and the experience of two complete voyages behind him, Frank Carey was prepared to test the *Empress of Ireland*, to explore her limits. Leaving Liverpool on Friday, 24 August at 11:20 p.m. with 1,455 passengers, the *Empress* arrived at Quebec at 2:10 a.m. on the morning of Friday, 31 August, setting a record of six days, eight hours and fifty minutes, beating the old record by more than six hours.

Daily runs for the crossing were: Saturday: 215 knots; Sunday: 422; Monday: 420; Tuesday, 431;

Wednesday, 444; Thursday, 454. In this period at sea, the ship encountered two days of heavy winds and seas. She carried an unusually large amount of general cargo in addition to the baggage of passengers and the two separate sets of mails. The cargo manifest alone filled forty-eight pages of foolscap. The only negative note to the remarkable journey was the death of an infant, who was buried at sea.

Canadian mails were landed at Rimouski, but the mails for China and Japan were carried to Quebec. The CPR was obviously proud of its newest ship and wanted to show what could be done on land as well. *The Times*, reporting the record, informed its readers that baggage and mails were transferred in less than forty-five minutes to the CPR's new special train, the 'Overseas Limited Express' which was intended to break the coast-to-coast speed record, and carry the Orient mail to Vancouver. The British Post Office as well was getting value for its mail subsidy. *The Times* noted that mails via the Atlantic route would be landed in China fully a week ahead of the Suez route.

Among the passengers in first class was Sir Sandford Fleming, one of Canada's foremost scientists and a true renaissance man of the Victorian era. He had designed Canada's first postage stamp, the three-penny beaver in 1851, had been an active promoter of the trans-Pacific cable system which was completed in 1902, was a charter member of the Royal Society of Canada, and served as Chancellor of Queen's University for thirty-five years. He was also a railroad builder, having surveyed western Canada for the CPR, becoming chief engineer and, later, a director of the company, and was present at the historic driving of the last spike on the transcontinental railway in November 1885. Little remembered today in Canada, Fleming's chief contribution to modern life still lives on, for he was the first to suggest standard time 'zones.'

Fleming, who at 79 ranks as one of the oldest passengers carried in the *Empress*, recorded his thoughts during the voyage in a small pocket diary, preserved today in the National Archives of Canada.

Fri., August 24	Left Liverpool 5:30 p.m.
	Delayed by low water 4 hrs
Sat., August 25	At sea
Sun., August 26	At sea
Mon., August 27	At sea – a little pitching
Tue., August 28	At sea – smoother sailing cold
Wed., August 29	At sea – sent Marconigrams to Ottawa – also to
	Principal [*Very Rev. David*] Gordon on *Tunisian* 70
	miles ahead and had reply
Thu., August 30	At Rimouski afternoon
Fri., August 31	Reached dock at Quebec 2:30 am. Train at 8 AM
	for Montreal

In the last week of September 1906 the *Empress* was plowing across the Atlantic, bound for Quebec, encountering stiff headwinds and pounded by violent gales for two days. She had left Liverpool on Friday, 21 September at 11:00 p.m., carrying 1,212 passengers and general cargo, along with the usual cargo of mails. This particular voyage would be notable for more than just the weather, for the *Empress* had reached the relative calm of the Gulf of St Lawrence on Tuesday, the twenty-fifth, when second class passenger Dalton Arnett of San Francisco, who had boarded at Liverpool in poor health, passed away. The ship's surgeon wrote later in the Passenger Manifest alongside Arnett's name:

2nd Class Cabin American citizen D. Arnett age 26. Deceased. Died 26th Sept. Buried at sea 27th Sept. Death due to choloemia.
(sgd) J.B. Winder Surgeon *Empress of Ireland*.

Cholemia is the presence of bile salts in the circulating blood, and might have been a difficult diagnosis for the *Empress* surgeon. By the time the Quebec *Chronicle* got the story, it showed 'jaundice' as the cause of death.

In accordance with the practice of the St Lawrence ships, the engines would be stopped for the burial. Many of the 281 passengers from first and 340 second class, lured as much by curiosity as anything else, attended the impressive service, along with the captain, all officers and numerous crew members. Archdeacon William James Armitage of Halifax, a distinguished Ontario-born theologian and author who happened to be travelling in first class, read the non-denominational service which concluded with the traditional, timeless words:

> Forasmuch as it hath pleased Almighty God of his great mercy to take unto himself the soul of our dear brother here departed: we therefore commit his body to the deep, looking for the resurrection of the body, when the sea shall give up her dead, and the life of the world to come, through our Lord Jesus Christ...

Wrapped in a Union Jack, the body in its weighted canvas shroud was lowered gently into the water. Reported the Montreal *Gazette*: 'the event cast a decided cloud over the rest of the voyage.

Despite the death of one passenger, the *Empress* docked in Quebec with as many passengers as she had started with. One third class passenger gave birth to a child soon after the voyage began, the first baby to be born aboard the *Empress*. Commented the *Gazette*: 'She was rewarded with the usual collection taken amongst the passengers.' Births at sea were not uncommon and, as one paper observed in 1907, it was an 'occasion of interest among the passengers, who, generally if the parents of the child are in humble circumstances, celebrate the event by collecting a sum for the child.' The tradition, though, was not always observed.

During the voyage Captain Carey was presented with a very handsome silver loving cup and flower bowl inscribed:

> Presented to Captain Carey by the passengers on board the SS *Empress of Ireland* on her maiden voyage from Quebec eastward, July 12, 1906.

It turned out that on that particular trip (on which she had set a speed record of 5 days, 20 hours and 50 minutes) first class passengers headed by Senator Raoul Dandurand and Gen. Sir George French had contributed a sum of money and arranged on arrival to have the silver pieces suitably inscribed. The presentation was made to the Captain by Archdeacon Armitage. The timing of the presentation was ideal, for this would be Frank Carey's last voyage in command of the *Empress*.

The *Empress* docked at Quebec on Friday, 28 September at 3:15 a.m. Despite the weather, the crossing had been a very respectable 5 days, 18 hours and 45 minutes, and she had averaged over 17 knots. Captain Carey, interviewed at the end of the voyage, commented that his engineers were confident that by next year, once the boat had found herself and the engines had accommodated themselves to the vessel, that it would be possible to keep up an average speed of nineteen knots.

Customs, medical and immigration officers had done their work well on the trip up from Rimouski, and all baggage had been examined. The train for first class passengers left at 8:00 a.m., second class followed at 11:00 and third class early in the afternoon. The CPR, meanwhile, collected the effects of Dalton Arnett and arranged to forward them to his mother in Los Angeles.

Over the years the *Empress* carried a number of valuable cargoes. Perhaps none was more valuable than the fifty-six boxes of specie from England, unloaded at Quebec at the conclusion of the trip. Though the cargo manifest has not survived, we can speculate that these boxes contained British gold sovereigns, which were legal tender in Canada at the time, though not widely circulated because of the country's decimal currency.

With the return of the *Empress* to Liverpool on 12 October, Captain Carey handed over command of the vessel to John Vernon Forster, who would command her for the next eighty-four voyages, spanning almost seven years. Born in 1874, Forster was the youngest of the five men destined to command the ship. Just thirty-two, command of the *Empress of Ireland* was a reflection of the confidence placed in him by the company. Before coming to the *Empress*, Forster's last command had been *Lake Erie*, Frank Carey's former ship and the one to which Carey was now returning.

Forster's first voyage departed from Liverpool on Friday, 19 October with 870 passengers aboard, and arrived at Quebec the following Friday, at 10:50 a.m. As before she discharged the Canadian mail at Rimouski, and transferred the China-Japan mails to a waiting special train at Quebec. Apart from rough weather, with strong headwinds and heavy seas, it had been an uneventful passage, an auspicious beginning for the new master.

At her stern, the *Empress* flew a new flag: the blue ensign of the British Naval Reserve instead of the ordinary red ensign of the British merchant marine. As John Forster was a Lieutenant in the RNR and as a sufficient portion of the ship's ratings were also reservists, the ship was entitled to the blue ensign, which would fly on her staff for the balance of her career.

At exactly 3:00 p.m. on Friday, 4 November the mooring lines of the *Empress* were cast off, but she experienced great difficulty getting clear of the wharf due to the rising tide and a strong easterly wind. However, by backing into the gap at the Breakwater and aided by three tugs at her head, the *Empress* was brought into the stream. Then, just as the ship was moving away from the wharf, a woman passenger arrived on the dock but was unable to board the steamer. Mel Brown, the CPR's General Passenger Agent, kindly offered her the opportunity to go down the river by the special train to catch the ship at Rimouski. Needless to say, the offer was gratefully accepted. It was a fitting gesture to end the season. The *Empress* would not be seen again in Quebec until the following spring.

In November, the Allan Line and CPR announced the schedule of sailings for the winter months. *Victorian* and *Virginian* would land mails and passengers at Halifax, while the *Empress* steamers would use Saint John as their terminal port, while still landing mail at Halifax. The CPR's plans had been the subject of considerable discussion in the Maritime provinces, for the early mail arrangement with the Allan Line envisioned that the two *Empresses* would use Saint John as the mail port. Halifax interests appear to have influenced the government to remind the two shipping companies that the Canadian mail contract stipulated all mail would go through Halifax. Thus, to satisfy the contract, the westbound *Empresses* had to call at Halifax on their way from Liverpool to land the mail, and call at Halifax on their eastbound passage from Saint John to pick up the mails.

Sniffed the *Saint John Globe*: 'While beyond doubt the arrangement is detrimental to the general interests of the rest of the Dominion, the only advantage accruing to Halifax is the sentimental prestige of being made a port of call and thus receiving the local European mails a few hours earlier than if they were carried to Saint John.'

The CPR claimed it was ready to abandon the mail subcontract in order to avoid inconveniencing its passengers with the additional delay. However, it could not even do that without the government's consent, which was not forthcoming. The CPR was stuck with Halifax for the time being, and bridled at the unfavourable comparisons between its route and the service to New York. Unlike the Canadian mails, mail to and from the Orient under the company's contract with the British Post Office, would be landed at Saint John and loaded aboard CPR trains for a fast trip to Vancouver.

The carriage of mail continued to give the company problems in terms of sailing logistics. On voyage 6W, having left Liverpool on 16 November 1906 at 8:10 p.m., for her first run of the season to Saint John via Halifax, the *Empress* duly arrived off Nova Scotia after a six day passage, which had been slowed by four days of stormy weather at the beginning, which made most of the passengers ill. Had it not been for the weather, she would have reached Halifax one day earlier.

Daily runs for this inaugural voyage to Halifax and Saint John were as follows:

November 17	278 miles
November 18	344 miles
November 19	409 miles
November 20	414 miles
November 21	426 miles
November 22	465 miles.

On Tuesday, 20 November, the *Empress of Ireland* passed her sister at close quarters in mid-Atlantic, and the two ships were close enough that passengers could exchange cheers as the 'mighty greyhounds of the ocean glided by each other swiftly' as the Halifax *Herald* recorded.

There was another death, this time a third class passenger, 36-year-old Annie Pretty of London, who had come aboard in ill-health. The rough weather did not help any. She died of a hemorrhage on the 20th and was buried at sea. Travelling alone, her effects were sent onward to her brother in Toronto, whom she intended to visit. The Official Log provides some clarification to the above, drawn from a Halifax newspaper account. Ms Pretty was a nurse by profession, 38 years of age, and her death was caused, according to Ship Surgeon Dr Winder, by 'heart failure.' On arrival in Halifax, an official named George Burck added the following: 'From inquiry made I certify the entry in the Official Log Book as to the cause of death to be true and am satisfied no further investigation is necessary.'

Off Halifax's Chebucto Head on the 22nd at 7 p.m., intending to offload the Canadian mails, a problem arose that no one had previously considered. No pilot was available and the *Empress* was obliged to wait outside the port. Signaling with lights and blasts from her whistle brought no sign of a pilot. After an hour, Captain Forster became impatient and took the ship in by himself, dropping her anchor off the ferry slip at 7:30. With a heavy sea running, making it difficult to keep the diminutive, 70-foot lighter *Pastime* against the side of the *Empress*, it took an hour and a half to offload the 1,124 sacks of Canadian mail, which were then put on a train.

A reporter from the Halifax *Herald* went aboard during this time and was introduced to some of the officers, whom he later described as 'exceedingly obliging and courteous.'

The *Empress*, none of her passengers having disembarked at Halifax, weighed anchor at 10:30 and turned for Saint John. On the bridge, guiding her out of the harbour, was the senior Halifax pilot, 67-year-old Capt. James Flemming. Aboard for the passage to Saint John were Arthur Piers, and a number of other CPR officials, as well as the immigration officials.

Responding to a complaint by the CPR, for nineteen pilots were on the roll for Halifax, the Department of Marine appointed a commission that sat at Halifax on the 27th and investigated the lack of a pilot. Evidence was taken, a report was made to the Department, and there the matter lay. There were no changes to the mail contract, but the pilot problem seems not to have recurred.

The mails at Halifax presented another problem as well, though this was more political in nature. Nova Scotian MPs, with an eye to port revenues, complained that the CPR steamers carrying mail – the two *Empresses* – should be compelled to tie up at the wharf at Halifax, instead of lying in mid-stream in the harbour and transferring mails to a tender. They also felt that passengers who so wished should be landed or taken on board at Halifax, instead of a few privileged people in first class. Neither of these proposals went anywhere at the time, for the company was sensitive to the potential for delays and realized that docking at Halifax would add yet more time to an already long voyage to or from Saint John.

The Nova Scotian parliamentary delegation was persistent, if nothing else. Discussions began in the Senate in February 1907 on the merits of Halifax over Saint John as a winter terminal for the Liverpool steamers. Nova Scotia advocates pointed out that fifteen hours less steaming time was required for Halifax, and that further delays of up to five hours were possible if the mail steamers happened to reach Saint John at low tide. New Brunswick boosters retorted they were confident the merits of Saint John would be borne out by a detailed study. Though the CPR might have been sympathetic to such arguments, it wisely stayed out of the inter-city fray.

Prior to the arrival of the *Empress* in Halifax, a sudden consternation had gripped the Board of Trade officials in the city. If the CPR had been compelled to land the Canadian mails there, no one had stated exactly *how* that should be accomplished. Rumors were rife that the CPR intended to land the mails by tender from outside the harbour, without actually docking. Inquiries by the company's Halifax agents, Messrs T.A.S. DeWolfe & Son, as to the facilities for landing mail by tender sparked the rumors, although nothing definitive would be settled until Arthur Piers, the company's steamships manager, and Marine Superintendent John Walsh arrived in Halifax. It was an important consideration, for the merchants of Halifax felt they would lose thousands of dollars of revenue if the *Empress* stood off the harbour to discharge the mails and a handful of passengers.

Piers let it be known he would like to transfer the mails to a ferry steamer, as it would be easier to effect the transfer than lowering mail sacks to the deck of a tug. As no ferries were available, Piers and Walsh came to a decision, and the Halifax Herald's headline on 23 Nov. said it all: 'MAILS TRANSFERRED IN STREAM FROM EMPRESS OF IRELAND.'

The Board of Trade at once lobbied the CPR to change its policy and land the mails at the pier, rather than anchoring in the stream. Piers made no comment but city officials seemed confident the company could be made to change its mind.

The arrival of the *Empress of Ireland* in Saint John on 23 November was front-page news in the New Brunswick port. She was the largest merchant ship ever to dock in the city and her arrival had the added benefit of turning the city into a mail point, though not for the Canadian mails. The *Saint John Globe* noted:

> CPR SS *Empress of Ireland*, the first of their fleet to come to St John this winter, is expected to reach port before 4 o'clock this afternoon, and as the tide will be within two hours of high, she should be able to come right up and dock.
>
> At Sand Point all preparations have been made to get the China mail and succeeding trains off promptly so that before 6 o'clock the first of these trains should be well on its way, for there will not be any delays over inspecting passengers or checking baggage, as the officials who boarded the steamer off Halifax last night will have that work all done.

The estimates proved accurate. The *Empress* docked before four, and the first train got away at 6:23 p.m. with first class passengers and the China mails, consisting of a further 551 bags. Two other trains followed with the second and third class passengers.

A large crowd gathered that Friday afternoon at Sand Point, and her size surprised even those who were expecting a large vessel. The arrival did not go as smoothly as the city would have liked. When the *Empress* came to her berth, she experienced a delay in docking because a schooner at the same berth had not been compelled to move, and the *Globe* fretted that this had delayed the departure of the mail train.

A second problem existed as well. Weeks beforehand, the CPR had informed the harbour authorities that it wanted a 20-foot pontoon between the ship and the wharf, to prevent any overhanging portions of the steamer from striking the conveyor posts. Despite the advance notice, the city managed to provide only a five-foot pontoon, and the inevitable happened. One of the posts was knocked over. The *Globe* commented that the city should have been better prepared to assist, rather 'than retard the great work of the CPR.'

The fact that the Canadian mail had been landed in Halifax, while the Royal Mails to the Far East were landed at Saint John provided a point of comparison for the city, and it avidly followed the progress of the mails to Montreal (19 hours and 15 minutes), compared to the mails destined for Vancouver. On the 24th, the *Globe* boasted, 'Saint John has every reason to feel well satisfied with the first trial made of it as a mail port.' and '…enough has been done to make it clear that this port can, if given the opportunity, land the mails in the west as rapidly, if not more rapidly, than by Halifax.' It noted, once again, that the call at Halifax created delay, danger and expense without serving any useful purpose.

On the occasion of her first visit to Saint John, the CPR opened the *Empress* to visitors on the weekend of 24-25 November. Several thousand people waited patiently to inspect the ship, and many who went aboard proclaimed themselves 'more than delighted with the accommodations and fittings.' Later the *Globe* observed that the *Empress* was 'in every detail… the superior of anything in the steamship line yet seen here,' and one experienced passenger commented that there were larger ships out of New York, but '…none more comfortably fitted, and none on which the wants of the passengers are more solicitously studied.

'All were charmed with the beautiful fittings and furnishings and surprised at the completeness of the arrangements to facilitate work. The culinary appliances were objects of special interest to the women visitors. There are many devices designed to make easy and simple the work and these were the object of much attention.'

A month later, when the *Empress* returned to New Brunswick on her next voyage, it was still front page news in the *Globe*, which reported that she carried 484 bags and 110 wicker baskets of Orient mail. After reaching Halifax with 470 passengers on Thursday, 20 December about 6:15 p.m., she got underway again three hours later. She arrived off Partridge Island about 1:00 p.m. the following afternoon, where she was obliged to wait for an hour for the docking 'window' to open. Partridge Island, where the quarantine station was situated, was less than two miles from the inner harbour where the *Empress* docked. A wait this close to her final destination must have been frustrating indeed.

That same month the company purchased from the Liverpool Steam Tug Company the vessel *Cruizer* to act as a tender for its steamers at Saint John and, during the summer schedule, at Quebec. The tug, built in Glasgow in 1895, would become a familiar sight to *Empress* passengers until 1913 when the CPR sold it to Halifax interests.

Off-loading the mails at Halifax proved to be a problem. The mail tenders owned by DeWolfe & Son were so small in comparison to the *Empresses* that mail sacks and parcel post baskets were thrown down from the ship, a height of twenty-five to forty feet. Inevitably, mailbags had ripped and the wicker baskets had been broken, strewing letters across the deck of the tender, where they were then walked on by the labourers. Not surprisingly, the Post Office complained to the CPR.

On 17 December the company wrote to DeWolfe. The instructions were quite explicit: 'Henceforth all packages of mail transferred from the steamers to the tenders must be lowered to the tenders in slings and carefully handled on the tenders.' DeWolfe did not want to antagonize the railroad. There were no further complaints.

Once the CPR's bookkeepers had tallied the company's passenger totals for 1906, management must have breathed a sigh of relief, pleased that the two *Empresses* had done well in their first year of service. In just six months the *Empress* had carried over ten thousand passengers. On the Liverpool route the CPR had carried 33,476 passengers westbound, and 13,965 eastbound, compared to the Allan Line's 45,260 and 14,304 respectively. These numbers gave encouragement for the coming year, when the two *Empresses* would be in service for a full twelve months.

Returning to Liverpool on 4 January 1907, the new year did not begin auspiciously for Captain Forster, for the *Empress* touched bottom in the Mersey and stuck fast in the alluvial mud. Early the following morning, with the rising tide, she was able to get off without injury. Though the incident was reported in the trade press a month later, CPR officials claimed that the 353 passengers on board were not even aware the ship had grounded.

Following the grounding, the *Empress of Ireland* skipped a sailing, and spent part of the month of January in dry dock at Liverpool, 'to have some repairs made and some overhauling done' as *Railway and Marine World* discreetly put it. During the period of repairs, the company chartered the Allan's *Tunisian* to fill the gap in the schedule.

It was probably at this time, while in dry dock, that the *Empress'* rudder was enlarged. This move, little publicized at the time, led to later controversy and unfounded allegations at inquiries in 1909 and 1914 that the ship steered badly. Some uncertainty exists as to the date when the rudder modifications were done. The Mersey Inquiry in 1914 stated that the work was done in 1908, and Fairfield's marine architect Percy Hillhouse wasn't absolutely certain. 'I think,' he testified, 'about 1908, but I do not know the exact date.' Later he said, 'The ship was built in 1906, and I think it was about two years later.'

Nonetheless, at the Inquiry held in the autumn of 1909, there was testimony that the rudder modifications had been made about two and a half years earlier, *i.e.* in the early months of 1907. Some support is lent to the 1907 date by Hillhouse who stated that 'some time later the fore part of her rudder got carried away accidentally and when that was being renewed advantage was taken of the change to slightly increase the area of the rudder.' Had the damage been caused in the grounding, it supports the idea that the rudder changes were done in January 1907, particularly as the 1908 winter overhaul for the *Empress* was shorter than in 1907.

As well, *Le Soleil* reported on 11 February '*La compagnie du Pacifique Canadien a reçu un message de Liverpool lui annonçant qu'on avait terminé les réparations au steamer* Empress of Ireland', thus giving further hints that the ship had undergone something more than just a routine overhaul.

The modification consisted of changing the shape of the rudder, increasing its area from 185 sq. ft to 227 sq. ft. The modification was made of $1\frac{1}{4}$ in steel plate, like the original rudder. The same modification was also made to the *Empress of Britain*, at about the same time.

In terms of the effect of the enlargement, Superintendent John Walsh in 1909 claimed it had made no difference to the *Empress'* steering and that, in his opinion, she steered perfectly before the modification. Hillhouse said much the same thing four and a half years later. 'The reason, as I understand it, was that they wanted to improve her steering qualities, but that she had previously to that, in trials in our hands, steered very well indeed.' Quartermaster John Murphy echoed that: 'The ship steered very good; as good as any ship I have ever been on.'

Perhaps feeling the spur of competition from the Allan Line, or seeking to deter other shipping companies from taking a portion of the lucrative North Atlantic passenger traffic, the CPR began floating trial balloons in the press. One report which circulated early in 1907 claimed that the *Empress of Ireland* and *Empress of Britain*, which had proven their worth in their first season, would be transferred to the Pacific routes, and that they would be replaced in the Atlantic by larger and faster vessels. It was the same 'speculation' that had been raised six months earlier on her arrival in Quebec City.

Recognizing that the *Empresses* (or any other big ship) required land-based logistical support beyond what had originally been envisioned, the CPR secured from the Mersey Docks & Harbour Board the use of the north side of Liverpool's Sandon Dock for its steamships. More importantly, the company also secured the right to construct cold-storage accommodations for provisions such as butter, cheese and other perishable items. This was an important move, as the company could now stockpile foodstuffs at the dock, and became less dependent on Liverpool ship-victualers. Work began immediately on the new cold-storage facilities, and they were officially opened on 4 October.

Having completed her repairs in dry dock, the *Empress* returned to service and sailed on 8 February with over a thousand passengers, a larger than normal contingent for this, the traditional slow period of the year. The trip had not been particularly rough for the season, but the ship had encountered heavy head winds all along the route to Nova Scotia and these had slowed her down. 'The voyage across was made without other event than the usual concerts and card parties,' was the way the *Saint John Globe* put it.

By this time residents of Saint John were used to the big CPR liners, and the arrival of the *Empress* was relegated to a back page of the *Globe*, which noted her arrival off Partridge Island at 2:30 a.m. on the 16th, and her docking at No.2 berth at Sand Point. Her time from Halifax was fourteen and a half hours, almost a record. Concerning the passengers, the *Globe* observed: 'In nationality the newcomers

The Empress *at Liverpool. The X on the hull was made by the sender of the postcard on Voyage 17W, who wrote: 'I have put a cross just opposite our cabin window.' (Stephen Brooks)*

are almost entirely English and Scandinavians, and the second class and steerage passengers are a very desirable-looking variety of citizens.'

Somewhat unusually, the paper also commented on the number of persons detained: 'Only two of the passengers were detained here by the immigration authorities. One of these was bound for Canada, and one for the United States. Both had eye disease.'

Even though Saint John was an ice-free port, the city experiences its share of the severe cold waves and snowstorms that hammer into the Maritimes on occasion. As the *Empress* departed on 24 February, the city was in the grip of a cold snap that sent temperatures plunging to -15° F. One envisions her ploughing around the Nova Scotia coast, her superstructure and masts thickly rimed with ice. Arriving at Liverpool on 2 March with just 355 passengers, the *Empress* established a record for the crossing between Halifax and Liverpool, 6 days, 1 hour and 45 minutes, lopping some 3 hours and 15 minutes off the record previously held by the *Empress of Britain*.

British newspapers of late March 1907, along with Canadian marine journals a month later, noted that the two-year mail contract between the Imperial government and the CPR had finally been ratified on 27 March by the British Parliament. It was merely a formality; the company had been carrying the Orient mails with great success since the previous summer and there was no reason for Parliament not to rubberstamp the arrangement.

On her fifth and last trip (8W) of the 1906-1907 season to Saint John, the *Empress* encountered head winds during most of the voyage and, off the Grand Banks, fog, both of which were usual for the spring months. She had left Liverpool on 5 April and arrived off Halifax in the early hours of the 12th. A thick fog hung in the harbour and she did not come up to the quarantine point until about 7 a.m. Docking at 8:00 a.m., Captain Forster wasted little time in Halifax. Less than forty-five minutes later, after disembarking the Canadian mails, amounting to 360 bags and 645 packages, and twenty-two first class passengers, she was outbound for Saint John.

Docking at Saint John, after a fast transit of fifteen hours, proved to be more of a problem. There was congestion at the CPR berth, and the *Empress* could not dock until *Montezuma* had gotten away, and *Lake Champlain* and *Montfort* shifted in order to make room for her.

When the winter of 1906-1907 drew to a close, the residents of Saint John could look back with pride on the numbers of passengers that had passed through their city. A total of 117 steamers had sailed, an increase of just four over the previous season, but arriving passengers had jumped to 30,125 compared to 19,912. Of the passengers, the CPR had landed 26,082 (86.6%), thanks largely to the increased capacity of the two *Empresses*. Of the twenty-six thousand, the *Empress of Ireland* had carried 4,795, or 18%. The *Empress of Britain* accounted for a comparable total.

Over the years, in terms of popularity as measured by actual passengers carried, virtually no difference exists between the two *Empresses*, either westbound or eastbound. This should come as no real surprise. The CPR publicized both ships equally, not favouring one over the other, and both were virtually identical in terms of appointments and speed. The CPR's advertising of the period conveys the clear impression that travellers should make no distinction between the two ships, and people should take whichever ship's sailing schedule best fitted their needs. As the passenger totals are nearly identical, one can conclude that word-of-mouth advertising was not a factor, nor did one ship have any particular 'cachet' over the other.

Even to the members of society who mattered, those in first class who presumably had some choice in their travel arrangement, there is no clear preference for one ship over the other. In 1913 (to get ahead of ourselves somewhat) the *Empress of Ireland* carried 1,946 passengers westbound, and 1,525 eastbound, while the *Empress of Britain* carried 1,976 and 1,358. These numbers clearly show that neither ship was favoured by first class passengers over the other, and also that the ratio between westbound and eastbound passengers was much more equal than for second and third class.

Having earlier floated the trial balloon of a possible transfer of the *Empresses* to the Pacific, it was now time to end the speculation – for the moment. In late April, from the CPR's highest levels, the previous rumors were strenuously denied, along with denials of the planned new ship construction. Over the ensuing years the balloons would be refloated at periodic intervals, in order to confuse other shipping lines as to the intentions of the CPR. In October 1910 *Le Devoir* carried an item attributed to the CPR claiming the company would built two Atlantic vessels capable of 21 knots, along with two others for the Pacific. In April 1911, *The Times* carried a report that Sir Thomas Shaughnessy had been discussing with officials in the United Kingdom the building of extra ships for the CPR, two of which would be for the Pacific trade, and that new vessels for the Atlantic were still under consideration. They would be, the article noted, faster and larger than the boats at present on the Atlantic service.

In July 1912, when the CPR faced nine competitors for traffic to Canadian ports, Arthur Piers, CPR's Liverpool-based Manager, arrived in Quebec and told the press that the main purpose for his visit to Canada was to discuss with his CPR officers the 'necessary arrangements for the additions to the Atlantic fleet which Sir Thomas Shaughnessy hinted at during his recent visit to England.' In the end, it all came to naught. But it certainly kept the competition guessing.

When the *Empress* returned to Quebec City on 10 May 1907 her arrival was noted in both the French and English press, and a large crowd was on hand at the Breakwater to see her dock. By this time she was just one of many vessels which, every week, disgorged thousands of immigrants, though the twin *Empresses* were favourites of Quebecers. The immigration buildings at the Breakwater had been improved over the winter months in an effort to speed up the flow of people, and customs officers were ready to 'perform their respective duties in a courteous and cheerful manner, which …is greatly appreciated by the people landed in this port.'

One of the 206 persons in first class who had boarded the *Empress* in Liverpool on 3 May was a straight-backed milit-ary man in mufti, Lt-Colonel Hardin Burnley-Campbell from the Scottish town of Ormidale in Argyll. Travelling alone, the 64-year-old officer and Justice of the Peace described himself on the passenger manifest as having no occupation, and giving his destination as Vancouver. These statements were only partly correct, for Burnley-Campbell was a man on an adventurous mission, and this was the first leg of a voyage he had planned meticulously.

On the first two days of the trip to Quebec, the *Empress* had run into strong westerly winds. These abated and thereafter she experienced moderate weather all the way to Rimouski. In its usual fashion, the Montreal *Gazette* – now that the ice had gone and the *Empresses* were returning to the St Lawrence – provided reports on the ship's progress, as she came within wireless range. On 9 May the paper noted:

> The *Empress of Ireland*... which left Liverpool last Friday at 7 p.m., is making a very fast passage for this season of the year, and was reported inward at Cape Race at 11:30 am yesterday. It was stated by the CPR offices yesterday that this is the earliest report ever received of one of the *Empresses* westbound, the *Ireland* being reported on Tuesday night as being 180 miles from the Cape. From Liverpool landing stage to within sight of land on this side in less than five days is remarkably fast going.

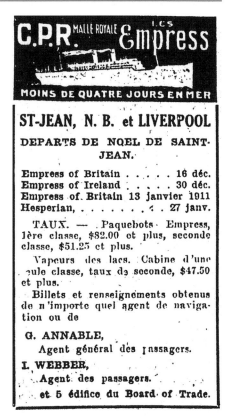

Typical CPR advertising in Montreal's Le Devoir, *December 1910. (Raymond Beaulieu)*

Despite the fast crossing, the *Empress* lost considerable time at Rimouski, where she arrived at 11:50 p.m. on Thursday night in a near-gale. The tug *Rhoda* went out to her to take off the mails but was forced to head back (with three of the *Empress* crew in her) on account of the heavy seas when only half the mailbags had been off-loaded. Left aboard the *Empress* were the Rimouski medical officer and three members of *Rhoda*'s crew. The *Empress* waited until 4:00 a.m. for the mail tender to return, then headed upriver in the same gale-like conditions, with the remainder of the mail still aboard. The *Gazette*, two days later, was somewhat cryptic, noting that there had been a problem with the tender which had come out to take off the mails. It later turned out that *Rhoda*'s machinery had broken, and that she could not have come out again to the waiting *Empress* under any circumstance.

She met with a further delay of ninety minutes at Crane Island, waiting while the tide rose sufficiently for her to cross the bar. Docking at the Breakwater in the early afternoon presented a problem, for there was a strong westerly wind and a rising tide. It had been, pronounced The *Gazette*, 'an exceptionally fast run for this time of the year, when the ice conditions are not all that can be desired from a navigation point of view.' The Quebec *Chronicle* saw it somewhat differently. Citing the needless delays, it called for a new mail tender at Rimouski.

Despite the minor delays, Lt-Col. Burnley-Campbell must have been a happy man, pleased with the progress of the voyage. In a letter to *The Times* published on 22 June, he explained why he had set out from England:

> Sir,—I landed at Dover on the 13th inst., completing the circle of the world in 40 days 19½ hours.
>
> Had I succeeded in catching the St Petersburg express at Berlin on the 12th inst., I should have reduced the time by several hours. But the trains do not run in connexion. I

do not know if my round is a record one as to speed. I am told that it is. But, as it may be interesting nevertheless in these high pressure record breaking times, to those who are fond of something exciting and out of the common, I annex full particulars of my journey.

I sailed from Liverpool on May 3 at 7:20 p.m., in the Canadian Pacific Railway Company's steamer *Empress of Ireland*, Captain Forster. I reached Quebec May 10, 3 p.m., left Quebec by the Canadian Pacific Railway 's oversea transcontinental mail train on the same date at 5 p.m., this train carrying the mails and first-class passengers only; arrived at Vancouver May 11, 5 am, departed Vancouver May 14, 12:30 p.m., by the Canadian Pacific Railway's mail steamer *Empress of China*, Captain Archibald.

Burnley-Campbell went on to describe the connections he made from Japan to Vladivostok, then the trans-Siberian to Moscow, thence to Warsaw, Berlin, Ostend and Dover. He explained the reason for his trip: 'An article on "The Speed of Travel" in the *Spectator* of March 16 tempted me to try what could be done, and should this letter catch the eye of the correspondent in the *Daily Mail* of March 12, whose most interesting letter I read with so much pleasure, will he kindly state if he knows of any case in which this route, just taken by me, or indeed any other route 'round the world' has been traversed in a shorter time or in so short a time?'

Burnley-Campbell had only one moment of anxiety along the way: the *Empress of China* went aground on an isolated rocky island in the Sea of Japan, and was lifted off by the rising tide. He had feared he would miss his railway connection in Vladivostok, and the next train would not come for four days.

A first class passenger on the same voyage sent his daughter a postcard showing the ship. He wrote on 9 May:

> Dear Ethel
> Arrived safe had a good passage.
> 'Boss' first class. Splendid weather.
> With love to all from Dad

Burnley-Campbell had some distinguished company in first class, for Lady Shaughnessy and Alice Shaughnessy were returning to Montreal aboard the *Empress*. Sir Thomas, one of those in the crowd on the Breakwater, welcomed them home. On 11 May, Sir Thomas wrote to Arthur Piers:

> I was at Quebec yesterday when the Empress of Ireland landed and we made a rather deplorable showing although it is probable that nobody was specially to blame. She had to be warped into the dock against the strong north wind; four or five of her cables snapped like woolen yarn when the strain came on them. Apparently these wire cables are absolutely unsuited to the handling of a vessel of that size… To the extent that I was able to judge the ship's officers did well.

Writing to Piers less than a week later, Sir Thomas noted that his wife and Alice 'were very comfortable and speak in the highest terms of everything connected with the ship.' Joining Burnley-Campbell and Lady Shaughnessy in the *Empress* was a new Chief Officer, whom the CPR had transferred from the *Lake Manitoba*. His name was Henry George Kendall and, though no one knew it at the time, he would one day play an important role in the history of the ship. Evidently pleased with his new ship, Kendall later wrote: '.all things were done most efficiently to a high standard.'

Kendall was a warm, outgoing mariner who possessed a good sense of humor. He enjoyed mingling with his passengers and had a knack for establishing an easy rapport with them, often entertaining them with anecdotes. His favourite poem was Rudyard Kipling's *If—*, which begins with the memorable lines:

HIH Prince Fushimi being presented to Captain John Forster by Archer Baker, the CPR's European Manager, 31 May 1907 (Voyage 12W), a drawing by A.C. Michael. The greeting took place at the main staircase on Saloon deck, only a short distance from the first class gangway. (Canadian Pacific Archives Image No. BR.29)

> If you can keep your head when all about you
> Are losing theirs and blaming it on you.

Recitation was another activity that Henry Kendall enjoyed and did well at. On 31 May 1908, though probably not serving aboard the *Empress* at the time, he delivered one speech that contained a prophetic warning:

> The Captain sleepless in his aerie stands,
> a thousand souls committed to his hands.
> Attentive, lest the lifting veil disclose
> some ghostly bark.

Departing Quebec on 17 May at 3:30 p.m., the *Empress* had 738 passengers and general cargo. A new arrangement was now in place for the mails. This time the *Empress* would stop at Sydney, Cape Breton, to take on board the Canadian mails, the first vessel to inaugurate the experiment, an attempt by Nova Scotia lobbyists to prove that Sydney was the logical mail point.

As she pulled away from the breakwater, there was a moment of excitement. The Quebec *Chronicle* explained:

> After the *Empress of Ireland* had left the wharf it was discovered that four men, who were seeing friends off, were still on board. The four of them rushed up to the bridge to see the captain and inform [*him*] of their plight. They saw visions of a trip to Father Point and return trip on the Intercolonial Railway, the latter journey at their own expense. The captain at once signaled the CPR tug *Cruizer*, which was lying at a short distance away, to come and take the dilatory visitors off. The tug ran alongside the big

steamer and relieved her of her unbooked passengers, and landed them on the break-water, much to their delight.

It was in Liverpool on the last day of May that two separate parties of very distinguished passengers boarded the *Empress* at Liverpool, bound for Quebec. The first to arrive that Friday was fifty-year-old HIH Prince Fushimi, cousin of the Japanese Emperor, who arrived at Liverpool's Riverside Station at 5:30 in the after-noon, having set out from Euston Station at 1:15. The Prince's high-profile visit to England had come to an end, and he had planned to tour Canada before returning to Japan, using the all-British route to Yokohama. This decision may have been influenced by Baron Komura, the Japanese ambassador to Britain. Komura had travelled in the *Empress* the previous year and, at Shaughnessy's express orders, had been well attended to.

The Prince's stay in England had been a successful and highly public one, marking the growing community of interests between Britain and Japan. He had been seen off at Euston by crowds of well-wishers, including an impressive list of British dignitaries (one of whom was Churchill) and a number of Japanese diplomats. Prince Arthur of Connaught, a future *Empress* passenger, also arrived at the station and the two had a lengthy conversation before the Japanese prince was handed a message from George V, wishing him a safe and pleasant voyage across the Atlantic. When the boarding whistle shrilled, the Prince shook hands with Prince Arthur, and the crowds cheered as he then boarded George V's personal coach, which the monarch had made available for the trip.

The weather on arrival at Liverpool could hardly have been worse. The correspondent of *The Times* described the scene as follows:

> Prince Fushimi has just said 'Goodbye' to these shores, and it could be wished that the last impression had been less dismal, though it was only too typical. Liverpool is well worth seeing from the river when you can see it, but the Mersey in a dull drizzle which allows nothing to be seen but the muddy water, the bedraggled Landing Stage, some serried ranks of umbrellas, and a warehouse or two in the background is not exhilarating, even to a native. That was all that could be seen this afternoon when the *Empress of Ireland* came alongside in readiness for the special train from London. The *Baltic*, which also sailed to-day, had to clear first, and she did not get away until past 5, so that very little time was left to bring the *Empress* up to the Landing Stage and make preparations for the arrival of the train due at 5:30. It had been expressly desired that there should be no ceremony, and there was none. As soon as the gangway was fixed the first class passengers who had been waiting rushed on board with their friends and filled the stairways with that indescribable confusion of aimlessly wander-ing humanity which marks the last moments of the departing liner.
>
> Ten minutes later the Prince arrived and walked on board with his suite, he having been met on his arrival at the Riverside Station by the Lord Mayor of Liverpool. It was just a little knot of Japanese and English gentlemen in tall hats with umbrellas up to keep off the rain; for the injunction to avoid ceremony had been so strictly obeyed that the passage across the Landing Stage to the ship was not even covered over, and, though the regulation strip of red carpet was laid across the brow, the whole party had to step in the puddles on the open stage. Mr Archer Baker, European Manager of the Canadian Pacific Railway, received the party on board.

The second distinguished passenger was Lord Grey, Governor General of Canada, accompanied by Lady Grey and their daughter Sybil. They had travelled to Liverpool in the same train as Prince Fushimi, but discreetly timed their arrival at the ship a few minutes later than the Prince's. In fact, the Governor General, in England on a private visit, had cut his own trip short in order to entertain the Prince aboard the *Empress*. It was still raining when the *Empress* slipped away from the Landing Stage shortly after six o'clock.

For the travellers, it hardly mattered. 'Once on board the ship,' the correspondent of *The Times* wrote, 'the weather was of no consequence.' The correspondent went on to provide readers with a description of the ship, and touched on a variety of other topics of interest. His text is reproduced below because it sheds light on a number of areas, and because the CPR must have benefited immensely from such favourable descriptions. One hopes that the CPR's publicity people in London took care of the correspondent in an appropriate fashion at Christmas.

> The great Atlantic liners of to-day are so vast, so splendid, and luxurious that the expression 'floating hotel' is quite inadequate to describe them. No hotel has such fine public rooms or is kept in such an immaculately spick and span condition, and none of these palatial vessels surpasses in these respects the two *Empress* boats of the Canadian Pacific Railway Company. They are not of the largest size nor of the highest speed, but they are of very large size – namely 14,500 tons, and of high speed – namely, over 17 knots; and they are more beautifully and bountifully appointed in the matter of public rooms than any of their rivals that I have seen.
>
> This beautiful ship was aglow with lights and flowers to welcome her distinguished passengers. The suites of rooms on the upper promenade deck assigned to Prince Fushimi and the Governor General were provided with exquisite flowers, and the dining salon was elaborately decorated in the same way. Bouquets were also presented to Lady Grey and Lady Sybil Grey by Mrs Archer Baker.

Having paid tribute to the ship, the correspondent dealt with the immigrants on the ship, in terms we would today regard as patronizing but in the Edwardian era were perfectly normal.

> Prince Fushimi will have an opportunity during the voyage of seeing the class of emigrants now going out in hundreds by day to Canada. Those in the *Empress of Ireland* are a very fine lot, healthy, well-dressed, clean, and pleasant. They include English and Scots, Scandinavians and Finns. A good many of the women and children are going out to join men who have already got good positions in Canada.

The ship, while not full, was close to it, with 186 first class, 476 second and 863 third class passengers. *The Times* added, 'the number of persons proceeding to Canada this year is quite unprecedented. For months all the cheaper accommodation has been taken up, and now the pleasure travel traffic is beginning to show a similar expansion. The accommodation for second and third class in the *Empress of Ireland* is, by the way, just as good in its degree as the first. Indeed the greatest changes which have been effected in recent years are in the cheaper classes of accommodation provided. The third class saloon has a piano, and, as for the second class, it is to all intents and purposes as good as the first, without the gilding.'

These distinguished passengers did not travel alone. The manifest for the trip shows the Prince was accompanied by an entourage of four persons, along with five valets in second class. And that Earl Grey was attended by an unnamed valet who accompanied his master in first class, and also that Lady Evelyn Grey and Lady Sybil were each attended by a maid, also unnamed.

Also in first class – on Lower Promenade deck – was sixty-year-old Sir Josiah Symon, a politician and former attorney general of the Commonwealth of Australia, who was invited to join Captain Forster's table. Symon was another multi-talented man of the kind the Edwardian period seemed to produce in quantity. He was a noted art collector, owned one of the best private libraries in Australia, and had published studies on Shakespeare's life and poetry. Two letters on *Empress* stationery written by Symon from the ship and held in the National Library of Australia shed light on this particular voyage and some of the interior furnishings of the *Empress*.

Selected portions of Symon's letters to his family appear below.

Sunday, June 2

... yesterday morning I wrote the enclosed Marconigram to be sent from Malin Head. It didn't go because the operator in charge of the Marconi office on board said he was having great trouble to get 'connected' & as we had almost passed the Head he was afraid it was no use trying to send it. I am sorry I did not know this ship had the Marconi system or I might have asked you to send me a message yesterday morning. It is very inexpensive – only 6/ or 7/ for 12 words. We shall know better another time.

As to myself – we left as I wrote from L'pool in wretched weather – wet & cold – but as I had a good dinner & was very, very tired, I slept well, & got up yesterday morning fairly fit, had bath, breakfast, walked about & sorted out my papers till lunch. After that it became colder & colder – I was glad to sit near the fires in the music room & Café – & a very heavy sea rose. This huge ship pitched most uncomfortably. As evening wore on the conditions became worse, & for the first time since leaving Adelaide I felt discretion was the better part of valour, & that if I did not care in advance, worse might happen. So instead of tempting providence & going down to dinner I went to bed.

It was a wild night. This morning I am told seas washed over the bridge. It must have been when we were rounding the north shore of Ireland. At any rate I escaped seasickness & being on my back in bed.

This morning it is beautiful – cold but fine with some sun. I had a cup of tea & some fruit: a fine hot bath, back to bed again: soon I am going down to lunch. Will resume afterward.

5 p.m. Lunch & afternoon tea have gone. We have just met & parted from a large steamer – the *Lake Champlain* – of this line but a mere pigmy compared to this one. She is homeward bound I suppose for L'pool. She is mostly engaged in taking immigrants for Canada from the Continent.

The dining saloon is amidships on the deck below that where my cabin is. It is very spacious and finely appointed but with no gaudy ornamentation, all small or moderate-sized tables, with a number of bays for parties along both sides. The Fushimi party occupy one of these bays & the Earl Grey party another. I sit at the Captain's small table. The seats are upholstered in crimson leather. Immediately above the dining saloon is a large, plain but very comfortable room called the Café where afternoon tea is served – each person gets a separate tea pot for himself or herself, with bread & butter cake & crisp brandysnaps. There also coffee is served after dinner & the men smoke cigarettes but a notice is up forbidding it here [*i.e. first class dining saloon*] …as a smoking room. It has bright electric stoves.

Then on the same deck further aft the regular smoking room – all in unpolished oak. Then still on the same deck further forward & next door to my cabin is the Library, where I am now writing – a most delightful room, paneled in polished mahogany, upholstered in green plush, with green carpet & plush & handsome mahogany writing tables. There seem always to be plenty of tables available – not the crush usual in Australian ships where there are only a few & everybody wants them at the same time.

Then immediately above the Café is the Music Room – most comfortable but in no way ostentatious. There also there are writing tables. It's quite sheltered from the weather, & with a regular drawing room, open coal fire. I found it very comfortable after lunch today – in fact, went to sleep reading the *Albany Review*.

I am saving a copy of the passenger list. My roommate is a young fellow called Green who is going to China direct. This ship connects with only the CPR Empress line from Vancouver to Japan & China.

Empress of Ireland *departing Liverpool with HIH Prince Fushimi and Earl Grey, 31 May 1907 (Voyage 12W), a drawing by Charles Wyllie,* The Sphere, *8 June 1907. (Canadian Pacific Archives Image No. BR.31)*

I was chatting at afternoon tea with a Japanese, who is also going direct through to Japan. He speaks English as well as you or I.

Symon's roommate can be identified from the manifest as Owen Green, a 31-year-old journalist from Lancashire, who was headed to Shanghai.
The weather then improved, so that the *Empress* was able to make average daily runs of 435 knots.

> Tuesday, 4 June 1907
> It's a bitterly cold though bright day – in that respect better than yesterday which was foggy all day, with the foghorn constantly going.
> There is a most excellent Library on board – admirably arranged and kept. Have read a very good little book – a criticism of Kipling by Rich[ard] Le Gallienne. Read it if you get a chance. Also *Penelope's Experiences in Scotland* by Kate Douglas Wiggins. It's delightful – she writes charmingly. There is a series – *England & Ireland* also.
> In the Café last evening after dinner I had a chat with a fine old Nova Scotian lady – a Mrs [Caroline] Pickford, whose husband [Robert] is partner in some line of steamers from Halifax to the West Indies.
> Prince Fushimi & his suite & Earl Grey & his folk come into the Café for coffee after dinner, with the rest of us here taken no notice of.

Not mentioned by Symon were the 'usual concerts and other entertainments during the trip' which had, according to the Quebec *Chronicle*, raised 'a handsome sum …for nautical charities.'
In his autobiography *Adventures on the High Seas*, Henry Kendall, Chief Officer at the time, recounted an incident following the sudden death of a Hungarian emigrant in third class.

Arrangements were made for the funeral to take place next morning at ten o'clock. By 6 a.m. the body had been stitched up in canvas, and deposited within the after wheelhouse; at 9.45 the six sailors who were to carry the corpse on a grating from the wheelhouse stood by; and I impressed the fat old Bos'n's mate with the necessity to have all things prepared that no hitch might be possible. Covered with a Union Jack, the body was to be moved at a given signal, the six men assuming a mournful aspect with head on breast and solemn tread. On reaching a certain spot, I was to join the procession, followed by the Captain, who would await the right moment and then the last ceremonies would begin.

Nothing seemed to have gone wrong, everyone in his proper station and the routine running smoothly, when my eyes caught sight of an awful error. Just as I joined to follow behind the Bos'un's mate, I glanced ahead. No Union Jack! But Earl Grey's private flag, which consisted of a modified Union Jack with crest in the centre, used by the Governor-General when in Canadian waters and flown from the masthead. That confounded assistant of the Bos'un had spent about ten minutes smoothing the crest out neatly over the Hungarian's stomach, and my remarks during the procession were not chosen for kindly sentiment. I called the stupid fellow every name that came to my tongue, promised to have him 'fired' on return to Liverpool; yet it was too late for changing the flag, and there was Earl Grey standing as a looker-on. The funeral ended, so when all had been cleared away I went up and reported to the Captain in his cabin. This is what he said by way of comment:

'…And when we have the next funeral in this ship, kindly moderate your damn language.'

The *Empress* arrived off Rimouski shortly after eight on Thursday evening and, for the second voyage in a row, she encountered rough seas. The ship spent two hours waiting for the mail tender *Rhoda* to get alongside before Captain Forster abandoned the exercise and headed upriver to Quebec.

There was a sad note as the *Empress* sailed up the Gulf of St Lawrence. A Mrs Jane Marshall, a second class passenger from Aberdeen, died of pneumonia. Unusually, her body was brought to Quebec for burial, as she was accompanied by her nine-year-old daughter, Jennie. This may be because, according to the manifest, Mrs Marshall was going to her husband in Montreal.

While the *Empress* was steaming up the St Lawrence, Captain Forster was called to the cabin of Prince Fushimi, where he was invested with the Order of the Rising Sun (fifth class), and presented with a handsome silver teapot and cigarette case, both inscribed with the Prince's crest. Prince Fushimi complimented the captain on the magnificence of the *Empress* and congratulated him on the 'admirable manner in which he had handled the ship during the voyage.' On 9 June Sir Thomas congratulated John Forster, writing: 'Personally and officially I am very much gratified His Imperial Highness was so favourably impressed by the discipline and service on the *Empress of Ireland* as to be moved to recognize it in this most marked and exceptional manner.'

Prior to disembarking, the Governor General presented Chief Steward Augustus Gaade with a valuable gold breast pin, bearing his crest and monogram, a gift to acknowledge the attention he and his family had received on the passage.

It was wet and disagreeable when the flag-bedecked *Empress* arrived in the harbour about 8:30 on Friday morning, 7 June and docked at the Louise Embankment. It was not until 11:00 that the government steamer *Druid* left the King's Wharf and came alongside the *Empress* to take off Earl Grey, his wife and daughter, along with his staff. Ten minutes later, the government steamer *Lady Grey* did the same for Prince Fushimi and his party, and they were ceremoniously welcomed to Canada.

Twenty Maritimers disembarked from the *Empress* in an angry frame of mind. As the Montreal *Gazette* explained:

Tea being served to first class passengers on Upper Promenade deck, starboard side, looking aft. (David Saint-Pierre)

They bought their tickets in London on the explicit understanding, they allege, that the *Empress* was to land them at Sydney. Two days after leaving Liverpool the captain announced that he had received orders to proceed to Rimouski. The passengers protested, but in vain. Off Cape Race they sent a protest by wireless to Sir Richard Cartright, acting premier, but got no reply. Then, at Rimouski, they were told the sea was too rough and the tender too small to disembark, and they were taken on to Quebec, where, they say, they were left to look out for themselves, while their baggage was all sent on to Montreal by mistake. Had they landed at Sydney, Halifax would have been reached Wednesday night. They talk of taking action at law against the CPR.

Two days later, the paper provided a follow-up:

The answer of the department is that the protestants have no cause for complaint, because it was distinctly understood that two days before the *Empress* sailed that she would not stop at Sydney, but would proceed direct to Rimouski. This was owing to the fact that HIH Prince Fushimi, and His Excellency the Governor General were passengers by the *Empress*, and it was therefore necessary that speed should be the first consideration. Under these condition[s] it is held that there is no ground for the complaint, inasmuch as the Maritime Province passengers must have known the conditions before they sailed.

On 14 June Glenn Clark and Wilbur Schilling boarded the *Empress* in Quebec City. They were outgoing, sociable young men from Iowa, and both had recently graduated from Grinnell College and had an urge to travel. They rewarded themselves with a trip to Europe – the Grand Tour – an inclination shared by many Americans in those years, looking for culture and their roots. Money was a concern, as it was to many young people, and they decided to travel third class. From a historian's point of view this was a fortunate development.

Twenty-five-year-old Glenn Clark proved to be a keen observer and faithful letter writer, for each day he wrote to a member of his family to recount his shipboard adventures, capturing events and details of which first and second class passengers would not have been aware. And, because he was Europe-bound, Clark's letters confirm the ethnic diversity of third class eastbound, compared to the uniformity of westbound passages. Clark and Schilling travelled by train from Iowa to Detroit, crossed to Windsor on a train ferry, and continued to Toronto, which they explored before heading onward to Quebec. For this particular trip, every berth in first and second class was occupied, and there were over five hundred in third class. In all, the *Empress* carried over twelve hundred passengers, the season's record for the St Lawrence. There were numerous passengers from the United States and Australia, and the local papers interpreted this as a sign that the St Lawrence was growing in popularity.

> On board SS *Empress of Ireland* 7 p.m. June 14, 1907
>
> Dear Father,
> …Up till this time I have been labouring under a rush and strain. We have had trouble getting our bunk to ourselves, but have finally accomplished it. I have been so busy sightseeing and so little used to it, that I have hardly had time to do other than write very meagre, awkward and tedious accounts of it.
> P.S. Everything is splendid. I like the plain simple food. Am in great shape. We already *feel* the deep swells of the ocean beneath us. I have this opportunity to mail a letter on the ocean, off the furthest east point of land. A ship from Sydney, Newfoundland [*sic*] meets us and takes the mail. So goodbye. I'm off for merrie England.

A larger number of people than usual had come to the Breakwater to witness the departure of the *Empress*. One reason for this was the presence aboard of the venerable head of the Salvation Army, William Booth. The Army band from Toronto was on the pier and, while the steamer was making ready to sail, the band played various numbers. After *God be With You Till We Meet Again*, General Booth, who was standing at the starboard railing, delivered a short address, exhorting the members of the Army to be true to their God, themselves, their families, their country, the poor, and the Army. As the lines were let go and the ship swung into the current, there was a loud cheer for the General and the band struck up a lively air. Glenn Clark's jaunty letters resumed:

> Saturday, June 15, 1907
> Dear Helen,
> Ship ahoy! We're off! One night has been passed and three meals. Head wind all the way. No one sea-sick.
> Everything O.K.
> Every nationality is found here. An old German Lutheran minister (with his family) who taught Ruth Roberts two years at Postville. My Danish friend of the train who was once taught in High School by our Principal Goodrich. An interesting Englishman and family who is returning disgusted (but cheerful) after nine months farming in Canada. A number of interesting families with little children who entertain us with their little games on the stern deck. A considerable number of Italians who have made their fortune in US are returning to a life of plenty in the old world.
> When we embarked from the wharf at Quebec a detachment of the Salvation Army

came to say goodbye to Gen'l Booth who was on our ship. They sang their songs and gave their music to us until we were out of hearing.

The meals are very plain, but pure, and nothing is kept to be served over again next day. The berths are as comfortable as we could desire. Also clean, for the straw in the mattress is burned at the end of every trip and fresh straw put in. The deck space is the best in the whole ship. We have the fo'castle, with a high and low open deck, besides our covered promenade. The poorer class who did not come prepared for cold weather are kept below and only the interesting and cultured people use the open deck. When it rains, Wilbur and I are the only ones who use it.

The feature of today was our race with the *Tunisian* of the Allan Line. It is a ship of the size of ours and met us when we started; it had started in the morning from Montreal. At suppertime it passed us amid great cheers. About eight we came up beside it and challenged it. A hard contest followed and we finally left it far behind.

SATURDAY – A beautiful day with banks of St Lawrence on either side. I found letter writing difficult as it made me dizzy. However, I wrote a hodge-podge of stuff to send on the mail off Sydney, Newfoundland [*sic*]. All day I talked with interesting people from all lands. A group of hearty Englishmen, women and children played 'Drop the Handkerchief' and other amusing games on the stern deck, which the 1st class passengers enjoyed watching. Later they struck up a Grand March, they attempted several songs but no one seemed to know them. Finally someone struck up our own *John Brown's Body* and they all joined in lustily and marched by it. At 9 p.m. lunch on cheese and sea biscuit, they began to sing and imagine my surprise when they sang *My Old Kentucky Home* best of all. Upon going near the fo'castle I could hear the familiar song, sung by the English sailors, of *In the Shade of the Old Apple Tree*.

Saturday evening we (Wilbur and I) joined in a game of slow ball with the pleasant German minister and his family of sweet little girls. In his party is a very refined and intellectual lady from [*Iowa*] State Normal College – an assistant on the faculty. Two refined young men joined our group. The sea was breathing heavily with long swells when we went to bed. Several people were sea-sick.

The Italians eat at the second table now. The people here are fine.

As before, the *Empress* called at North Sydney for the outgoing mails. This time there was a problem, for the fast ship entered the harbour at 2:45 a.m., only to find the mail train had not yet arrived. After waiting half an hour, she dropped her anchor and blew her whistle. At 3:15 the train finally showed up and, half an hour later, the government steamer *Montcalm* drew alongside with the mails. And, as well, six third class passengers, one second, and four first.

Said the Quebec *Chronicle*, 'At 4:25 a.m. the last of the mail bags disappeared through the yawning hole in the side of the *Empress*, and three minutes later the liner was away on the last lap home, via Cape Race. Three hundred and two bags of mail and 126 baskets of parcel post were handled by a gang of 25 of the *Montcalm*'s crew in 45 minutes. The men worked well, but there was some confusion, owing to the use of one gangway only.'

Sunday, June 16, 1907
Dear Eleanor,
We are in the fog-banks off Newfoundland. The fog horn blows at intervals and the bosun sounds the lead occasionally. On deck the fog is sifting down in drops and no one ventures upon it save Wilbur and me occasionally. This fog bank may enfold us two days. The swells are deeper and stronger, this huge ship rocks very slightly and many people are sea-sick.

Wilbur and I have both felt 'queer' – but have walked or slept it off. Last night while exchanging mails off Sydney, I hear that the *Tunisian* passed us again. Our powerful engines are now hurling us 20 miles an hour against wind and fog, and we will probably pass them again tomorrow.

Ugh! but it is cold. No heat in the third class apartments. The ladies sitting room is kept warm and a few refined gentlemen keep the ladies company here. The men's smoker on the opposite side of the ship is a refrigerator with all windows open. Twenty or thirty smoked bacons hang around in there, constantly playing cards or drinking watery beer. Wilbur and I go to the sitting room occasionally to get warm where there are four polished tables, eight cushioned chairs, a piano and a cushioned comfortable seat around the entire wall. Everything here is swept, polished and cleaned once a day. This is the cleanest ship I have ever been on. The toilet rooms beat any American hotel.

At dinner, after a splendid meal, we were served a rich plum pudding. Wilbur and I took it fearlessly. The daring of it! We attend regularly upon the four regular meals and eat as much as we want. We are sailors, we are! (Wait a minute 'til I rap on wood)!

At 8:30 we met in the dining room for Divine Service. The German minister, Rev. Buckleman, led and spoke a few sweet words in German in which he used Liverpool as our common goal. He spoke beautifully of the many races represented on the boat, and the many creeds with one common end. Schilling, my interpreter, gave me the gist of it. After this, my Danish travelling companion, Rev. Sanderson, spoke in English, drawing lessons from the Israelites' pilgrimage for the Promised Land.

After supper in the sitting room, Wilbur began playing softly on the piano. After playing *Come Ye Back to Old Grinnell* and some of our old college hymns, he began playing *Annie Laurie* and the old Scottish songs. Two pretty Scotch girls, sitting by, who talked so broad a Scotch we had almost taken them for foreigners, joined in and sang in entrancingly beautiful voices. After they had sung all the songs Wilbur knew how to play, I asked them to go on, and such beautiful strange songs they did sing! It was a feast; I never enjoyed music better.

Retiring to my shelf of straw with an extra blanket over me, I couldn't help thinking what a contrast in the two evenings just past. One with a German minister and family in some blustering German games, and the other with some Scotch girls with songs of bonnie Scotland.

This steerage trip is an excellent preparation for our European trip. We have one week's training in the simplest of beds and food. In our struggle against the possibility of sea-sickness, in regard to diet, exercise and sleep, we are fast hardening ourselves to the hardships of travel.

…I find myself averse to much reading or writing. The ancestor of the Stone Age is calling out in me for more hardship and more of the wild life of primitive man. I have developed a tremendous appetite for sailors' biscuit and smoked herring.

The enforced contact with all nationalities is also a great intellectual preparation. I am glad I have not read more. The young Scotchman of Ayr who paces the deck with me tells me of the points of interest in Scotland. A little London lad tells me just how to get around in London. From an Irish man last night I heard an interesting discourse on the different qualities of humour of different nations.

Monday, June 17 '07

Dear Mabel,

Rev. Sanderson and his bunk mate were absent from breakfast. Two more brave men have fallen by the wayside! Wilbur and I looked ominously at each other, felt our belts and immediately began to tuck away a bowl of porridge (with water and milk) and two huge pieces of roast meat.

The famous fog banks of Newfoundland are now behind us and we are in the open sea. A mist with a cold north wind off the icebergs still makes the stern deck uninhabited. Yesterday a small whale was seen. In a few days we may see more larger ones and icebergs also.

I stood a half-hour on the deck this morning, alone. Above – on a mast, in a coal-bucket shaped balcony stood the watch, sounding the bells. Behind me, on the bridge above, was probably a master, but I could not see him within his glass room. How strangely different was this huge, iron structure, so easily handled from the crude craft of John Cabot! As I watched the great, grey unceasing waves I felt that they were the very same, filled with the same water that met the eyes of John Cabot a few yesterdays ago. No land anywhere, and endless sea which merged into a misty sky a few leagues away. The sea is never at rest. It seems a living, breathing thing. Wonderful! Wonderful!

In the afternoon, the dense atmosphere condensed into rain, and together with the cold made things intensely disagreeable above. After supper, followed with a little candy purchased from the steward, Wilbur and I found ourselves in the parlor with Miss Landsburg, listening to the very interesting conversation of a young Scotchman, John Scott....

TUESDAY – we struck a rough sea today. I ate two hard-boiled eggs for breakfast.

Wednesday, June 17, '07
Dear Mother,
Today was beautiful. The sun was out for the first time since leaving Quebec. I wasn't exactly sea-sick yesterday. I was merely having a contest with two hard-boiled eggs, and I finally won out....

For the first time I noticed what an odor there was in the dining room. This comes from the silver and cups not being clean, being washed in the same water that the plates are washed in. Wilbur and I always clean off our tin (silver) on the table cloth which is changed every day, and we never have occasion to use the cups as the tea and coffee are awful! The rest of the food is always good and clean.

They scrub the floors all over the 3rd class apartments about once a day. I have not seen but five traces of sea-sickness, so quick are they to clean up.

This morning we got a Marconi-gram from the *Tunisian*, 100 miles behind us, that a man committed suicide upon that vessel today by jumping overboard. Last night we passed the *Empress of Britain* on her return passage.

Thursday, June 18
Dear Father,
Today at 6 o'clock, before Wilbur and I had roused ourselves from the heavy sleep of the night, two 3rd class passengers, who had died during the voyage, were buried. With a Union Jack about their bodies, sewed up in a canvas shroud, they were splashed into the sea, after a short service, a prayer and a song. Two life tragedies already before our trip is hardly started. Both of these were victims of a non-contagious disease contracted before they started. Wilbur was very sorry he was not up to witness the affair.

Today for dinner we had a dandy Irish stew (fresh meat), good baked beans, bread (no butter), barley soup, fruit pudding (heavy but good – a good 'ribsticker') and two dishes of ice-cream and two apples, which were very good and juicy. Taken altogether we are faring better than the 2nd class. They are over-crowded; we are only half-filled. Wilbur and I almost have a room (cabin) to ourselves, our other bunk mate being a splendid English guidebook for us.

The 2nd class have been almost exiled from their upper deck because of the snot from the stovepipes simply covering the stern of the ship. Their rooms are no cleaner than ours, merely more good-looking. To cap the climax they are continually 'kicking' about their food. Wilbur and I have a room above the water line, with a port-hole window always open, save on cool nights.

Yesterday we both took a hot sea-water bath – free! It was a luxury. We feel like fighting cocks. We only wish we had brought a little more fruit and also some candy for dessert. This plain fare is making us ravenous for Liverpool and 'Tenderloin steak with french-fried potatoes, etc., etc.'

Occasionally a bunch of us young fellows, the Scotchman, John Scott, the two Irish-American lads, George and Dick Gardner, and Wilbur and I talk it over and make our mouths water with what England can give us.

One of the Scotch girls who sang for us the other night is married. She has taken an interest in Wilbur, nevertheless, and he calls her, in sport, his 'Highland Mary.' Imagine our surprise when 'Highland Mary' told us she lived in Stirling and invited us to come up and take a dinner with them.

Rich milk and fresh eggs in abundance, she says.

Hurrah for bonny Scotland!

Hurrah also for Wilbur, who seems to have all the girls on board in love with him, particularly the young school teacher from Cedar Falls who knows some 'friends' of Wilbur's. I, alas, am raising a beard which is, alike, the envy and sport of all my friends. In the middle of the ocean I looked like Weary Willie [*a well-known British cartoon character of the period, who lasted until 1953*]. Today I look like a Russian nihilist…

Tonight we had an elaborate programme upon which Wilbur performed on a borrow-ed guitar. Particularly good was a bit of elocution exhibited by a sailor on board.

Goodnight.

One wonders whether the sailor giving the speech was none other than Henry Kendall, who excelled in this and is known to have spoken on other entertainment evenings. From the passenger manifest, the third class passengers who had died were both Finns, John Gyni and Johan Waikanen, who died of heart disease and hemorrhage of the lungs respectively.

Friday, June 19
Dear Morton,
Today at an early hour (about 5) we beheld the northern edge of the Giant's Causeway and knew the end was near. So splendid has been our run during the past two days of calm weather that it is apparent we shall reach Liverpool this afternoon.

…To the north we could see the hills of Argyllshire of Scotland. I cannot describe the beauty of the Irish bluffs to our land-famished eyes. Something in ruggedness to our own western mountains. Yet with a most beautiful coat of green extending down to the sea side. Here and there a group of white houses clustered in a hollow, little sea craft here and there on the ocean, and an increasing flock of gulls gathering in circles around our masts – made us feel that indeed the Old World was at our doors.

Finally nothing of the Scottish coast remained in sight save one immense rock – a mile in circumference, given in the map as Ailsa Craig, but called by the natives 'Paddy's Hilestone.' The giants of yore used it to reach Ireland from Scotland.

At 11 o'clock through a strong spyglass I viewed the beautiful Isle of Man. A Manxman on board told me that the graves of Danes and Irish and Scotch are all over it, showing that it was once the scene of great battles....

After packing and cleaning we found that Liverpool was in sight. I will never forget that first view: long white beaches, rows of dollhouse[s], built of brick with roofs of many gables and always of tile.

Presently a tug took us in tow up the river along miles of docks, finally to turn us around and alongside the wharf amid a wilderness of waving handkerchiefs from boat and Landing.

For one hour we stood and watched the rapid unloading of trunks and mail bags. Then with a wild rush the 3rd class were allowed down the gangway and into the Customs waiting room. Schilling and I said farewell to our neighbors of the voyage and sauntered along with our wheels [*bicycles*]. Once in the Customs room, when we saw an officer near, we opened our grips and told him to look.

'Shut 'em up,' he said without looking at or feeling them. After doing so he wrote something on the outside and went off – without having been asked to pay the $2.50 apiece for boat charges on our wheels. As this is an exorbitant and senseless rule, we sauntered along in high spirits, planning to spend at least 50 cents apiece for our 1st meal on land.

We were immediately assailed with a swarm (not of mosquitoes) but of small urchins who tried to snatch our luggage from our hands. After finding out that one could charge 6 pence and, being in agony under my awkward bundle, I let one lead us directly to the Glasgow station.

We missed the train by 12 minutes.

Then we went out to supper.

Glenn Clark returned to the United States in September aboard the *Deutschland*. Five years later he was offered a professorship in literature and creative writing at Macalester College in St Paul, Minnesota, where he also coached athletics. In 1942, after thirty years in St Paul, he embarked on a new career of speaking, publishing and writing, and devoted himself to help men and women become 'Athletes of the Spirit.' He saw fifty-five of his books published, mostly of a spiritual nature, and died in 1956 after a trip to Moscow.

In his letter of 15 June, Clark noted the presence aboard ship of the founder of the Salvation Army, 'General' William Booth. When the author contacted the Salvation Army Archives in London, they had no prior proof that the general had travelled aboard the *Empress*. His presence on the ship, with an entourage of four other senior Salvationists, further adds to the already great associations between the *Empress* and the Salvation Army. The aged General, travelling in first class, was concluding an arduous trip of seventeen weeks to the Far East, during which he met the Japanese Emperor. Unfortunately General Booth did not record his impressions of the *Empress*, although his secretary Commissioner Nicol said on arrival in Liverpool that the General had been suffering from insomnia.

Also aboard the ship, in first class, was the sixteen-member Canadian military shooting team, headed for competitions at Bisley. With their Canadian-made Ross Mark II rifles, they would go on to a number of second and third place scores in the British National Rifle Association matches over the next month. Rifle shooting at the time was a highly popular sport in Canada and the team's activities were followed with great interest in the press.

If Glenn and Wilbur were roughing it in third class, two newlyweds on the same crossing were enjoying the first leg of a honeymoon trip to Europe. Identified from their letters only as 'Kate' and 'Frank,' the couple seem to have enjoyed the *Empress*:

Place Viger Hotel
Montreal
June 10-'07

Dearest Mother

We are just leaving by the CPR train for Quebec. Montreal is charming in the early summer. Jack is a dear, tho' he roars over the rice which still showers from my belongings. Love to all,
Kate

Chateau Frontenac
Quebec
June 13-'07

Three days of romance (old & <u>new</u>!) in this delightful port. From my window in this hotel, I can catch a glimpse of the *Empress of Ireland* lying in the harbour below. We go on board tomorrow. Lovingly, dear Mother,
Kate

SS *Empress of Ireland*
June 14-'07

We're off! I scribble this sitting on deck as we glide down the river. The Chateau and the ramparts fade into the blue. I wonder if foreign shores will show anything more picturesque than old Quebec?
Lovingly,
Kate

SS *Empress of Ireland*
near Rimouski
June 14-'07

A last line, dear Mother, for the pilot to take ashore. I shall send you some *Empress* postcards as well as a letter, from Liverpool. The St Lawrence River is wonderful. We have another whole day before we leave sheltered waters and face the open sea. Fond love to all,
Kate

TELEGRAM sent 15 June 1907 from the *Empress of Ireland*
via Cape Ray and Fame Point Wireless Stations
TO: Mrs Esblay, St Louis, Mo
SEA LIKE OUR MARRIED LIFE WITHOUT A RIPPLE SHIP AND SERVICE LIKE OURSELVES SPLENDID
Jack

SS *Empress of Ireland*
June 17-'07

Jack played cricket on deck this a.m. and made 110 runs, before the bugle brought him down to lunch, when he ate straight through the menu. He says this route has all the others 'skinned to death', whatever that means.
Kate

SS *Empress of Ireland*

June 18-'07

Have just had a 'sun-bathe' on the upper deck. Many of the passengers are charming and everybody seemed so gay. Apparently old 'mal-de-mer' does not patronize this boat! I think everyone knows me for 'the bride.' Jack can't help a prideful air.

Kate

Liverpool

June 21-'07

Just leaving for London on the Empress Special. We had no trouble on landing, everything done for us. We did hate saying good-bye to the dear old *Ireland*. Hope your are enjoying this choice of 'picture posts' [*the* Empress *alongside the wharf at Liverpool*].

Yours lovingly,

Kate

After touring London, Amsterdam, and Paris, Kate and Jack returned to Liverpool and boarded the *Empress of Britain*. On 12 July Kate wrote in part: 'Everything seems so cheery and comfortable as on the *Empress of Ireland*.' Though she probably did not know it at the time, also travelling with them was Sir Wilfrid Laurier, Prime Minister of Canada, Lady Laurier and a small retinue.

Their postcards were collected and subsequently printed privately in a slim volume entitled *A Package of Postcards and a 'Wireless' – A Bride's Story*. The couple seem to have valued their privacy. The book was published anonymously and 'Kate' and 'Frank' cannot be matched against any first or second class list on the *Empress*, nor against the manifest for the *Empress of Britain*. One suspects, but cannot prove, that the book was actually a clever promotional device printed by the Canadian Pacific.

On her next voyage (13W) from Liverpool, which commenced 28 June, the *Empress* made a fast crossing and reached Quebec on 5 July at 11:45 a.m., carrying a total of 1,482 passengers. Sir Thomas Shaughnessy was again one of those waiting on the dock, for his son was aboard in first class, along with a number of colonial statesmen headed home after the Imperial Conference in London. Fifty ratings from the Royal Navy, headed for Canada's west coast, were also aboard, though not in first class.

One *Empress* passenger in first class on that passage who scarcely needs an introduction was Guglielmo Marconi, the Italian entrepreneur whose invention and perfection of wireless telegraphy in the closing years of the nineteenth century transformed the world and how it saw itself. Thirty-three that year, he was already world famous and his wedding two years earlier in London had attracted some of the leading establishment figures in Britain and representatives of the political and diplomatic world. But Marconi was not well; under stress from work and constant travel, he also suffered from a recurrence of malaria that summer. When he recovered, he sailed in the *Empress*, headed to Nova Scotia to conduct tests at his company's transmitting stations. He was accompanied by his wife Beatrice ('Bea'), Bea's sister Eileen O'Brien, and brother Barney.

In *My Father, Marconi* his daughter Degna later wrote:

Eileen carried her camera with her and took innumerable photographs of Marconi posing with the captain and, again, with Bea, whose coat just clears the deck and whose brimmed hat is winged, just like Mercury's. The sea air made him feel immeasurably better and he worked on the crossing but his nerves were still unreliable and he worried all the way over at the speed the captain maintained. Twice in the middle of the night he woke the other three to say, distractedly, it was sheer madness for the captain to risk everyone's life by going full speed in fog through an iceberg zone just to arrive on schedule.

They did arrive, for all that.

TRAVEL BY CANADIAN PACIFIC

ROYAL MAIL
" EMPRESS "
STEAMERS.

LARGEST AND
FASTEST TO
CANADA.

EMPRESS of IRELAND, Apl. 17
LAKE ERIE ..., ... Apl. 22
Weekly Service from Liverpool.

Only four days open sea. Luxurious accommodation at moderate
fares. In view of the heavy booking for the Prince of Wales's visit
and the Quebec Tercentenary, passengers should secure berths at
once.

Inclusive fares from LIVER- } { JAPAN (22½ days).
POOL, *via* Vancouver   } to { CHINA, AUSTRALIA,
(All British Route.)

RAIL TOURS IN CANADA. Through the World's
Grandest Scenery.

Pamphlets and all information supplied at Canadian Pacific
Railway, 62-65, Charing-cross, S.W.; 67, King William-st., E.C.;
24, James-st., Liverpool; 92, Cross-st., Manchester; 67, St. Vincent-
st., Glasgow; 18, St. Augustine's-parade, Bristol; 41, Victoria-
street, Belfast; 33, Quai Jordaens, Antwerp, or local Agents.

Typical CPR advertisement, The Times, *10 April 1908.*

One can imagine the thrill of the two operators when Marconi visited the wireless shack and introduced himself to his employees. Marconi shared the Nobel Prize for Physics in 1909 for his contributions to the development of wireless telegraphy. The father of modern telecommunications died in
Rome in July 1937, mourned by a world whose frontiers he had done so much to shrink.

The Gazette provided some details of the 28 June trip the following day in a column headed 'Made
Very Fast Passage':

> The special train of nine coaches arrived at the Windsor Station at 7:30 last night. The
> *Ireland* left the bar lightship, in the Mersey, at 10:35 p.m. on June 28, reaching Rimouski
> at 10:40 Thursday night. Owing to the attempt to call at Sydney with the mails, which
> project had to be abandoned due to the dense fog and the grounding of the Government
> steamer *Montcalm*, the course covered by the *Ireland* was longer than usual, being 2,721
> miles. The time of the passage was 6 days 5 hours 5 minutes, the average speed, allowing
> for stoppages, being 18.3 knots an hour.

It was an uneventful trip as far navigation was concerned, with fine weather and a calm sea, and it was
only as she neared the coast of Nova Scotia that the fog set in. The daily noon-to-noon runs were:
Saturday, 251 knots; Sunday, 452; Monday, 457; Tuesday, 453; Wednesday, 454; Thursday, 454; and 202
to Rimouski. 'Had it not been for the fog encountered on the last two days, the CPR claim that the
Ireland would have come near breaking the record,' though there was also the usual delay as the *Empress*
steamed slowly up river from Rimouski, to await the rising tide.

The Quebec *Chronicle*, always more useful than the big-city papers for the human side of the trip, added:

> Dominion Day [*July 1*] was patriotically observed on board the *Empress*, the ship being gaily
> decorated with flags. Conspicuous among the decorations were the set of silk flags presented
> to the steamer by the Irishmen of Montreal. In the afternoon there were games and different
> kinds of sports, which were greatly enjoyed by all on board, many of the passengers declaring
> that the birthday of the Canadian Dominion was never more joyously celebrated anywhere.

That summer held a busy round of social engagements for the men of the *Empress*. On Saturday, the day following her arrival in port, a social took place at the Seamen's Institute, 'patronized by scores of the men' of the *Empress*, followed by an informal concert. On the Tuesday another concert was held at the Institute, also well attended by the men of the *Empress*. The social column of the Quebec paper noted that *Empress* steward F. Sullivan 'was in excellent voice, and his song was much appreciated.'

Even during turnaround it is good to note the Victualing Department managed to find a few hours off from the routine of cleaning and getting ready for the next crossing.

Departing from Liverpool on 26 July (Voyage 14W), the *Empress* carried 1,467 passengers, with a distinguished group in first class that included Lord and Lady Strathcona, Lord and Lady Hindlip and Lord Vivian. Lord Strathcona was Canada's High Commissioner to Britain and one of the builders of the Canadian Pacific Railway. Eight members of the Canadian Bisley team, who had left for England in the *Empress* in June, were also aboard, speaking highly of their experiences at the competitions.

Captain Forster had been lucky, for he reported hazy weather nearly all the way across, followed by intermittent fog in the Gulf. The daily runs had been good enough – 268, 437, 451, 450, 450 and 422 knots – to break the record set by the *Empress of Britain* just two weeks previously. On this passage the mails were landed at Rimouski, for the Sydney experiment had been less than a success. Following the mail drop, the *Empress* headed upriver and stopped off Grosse Ile to land some cases of measles, and docked at Quebec at 11:30 p.m.

Also on board was the largest number of passengers ever brought from Europe to Quebec and bound for the Far East – eighty-five, all headed to China, Japan and the Philippines. These passengers were whisked away from the ship, along with the British mails, less than an hour after docking by the Oversea Special, a fast through-train consisting of two baggage, three sleepers, and one dining car.

Lord Strathcona and other passengers, before disembarking, ascended to the boat deck to congratulate Captain Forster on the fast passage and to thank him for the great attention paid to them during the crossing. Before entering his private railway car, Lord Strathcona looked around and commented to a nearby reporter that more people arrived in Quebec in a week than in a year compared to when he had first come to Canada, seventy years earlier.

Below decks, a serious problem lurked for Captain Forster and the CPR, though this did not become evident until after the ship had docked at Quebec. The following handwritten letter from the Quebec Immigration Agent to his superior in Ottawa, L.M. Fortier, explained:

DOMINION OF CANADA
IMMIGRATION OFFICE
Quebec, 3rd August 1907

Sir,

I beg respectfully to make the following report for your information and action.

The manifest of the SS *Empress of Ireland* arrived on 2nd instant, certifies that there were on board, 294 Saloon, 335 Second Cabin and 838 steerage passengers.

After medical and civil examinations of the 838 steerage in the Immigration buildings, five passengers by this vessel, *viz.* Baurs Wiltinas aged 36, Davis Willins, 27, A. Liten 27, David Doitz 21, and Benjamin Nautoz 24, Russian Jews, (men) were found in the building.

They state they paid no ocean passage, had no ticket for the voyage, their names are not on the ship's manifest, no report was made by the ship's officers to the Medical Inspection or to this office of their being on board (which is in violation of Secs. 12 and 13 of the *Immigration Act*), were provided with berths, meals and were treated same as all the other steerage passengers on board.

I have a certificate from several English steerage passengers that these Russians occupied and slept in the same open berth with them.

Upon their examination by the Medical Inspectors, four of them were found to be Trachoma cases. All were sent to the Detention Hospital.

After discussing the case with the CPR officials here, they offered to deport these men by the SS *Lake Manitoba* sailing today, but it was agreed to keep them over for the SS *Empress of Ireland* or until a full investigation by the Department was made with the CPR Head Office, Montreal.

I have the honor to be, Sir,

Your obedient servant.

(sgd) P. Doyle

Imgt. Agent

The matter was treated seriously by Ottawa, for the problem of stowaways had grown to alarming proportions. Early the previous year the Donaldson Line's *Athenia* had arrived in Montreal with what proved to be a record number of stowaways on a voyage to Canada: twenty-six. Thereafter, shipping companies kept a closer watch. Stowaways found after the ship was well out to sea were compelled to work for their board, and were then handed over to the Canadian authorities for stealing their passage. Commented the Montreal *Gazette*: 'The stowaway evil is growing and there is a determined effort on the part of steamship companies to stamp it out.'

No line on the North Atlantic seemed immune to stowaways. The CPR's *Mount Temple* was discovered with twelve stowaways in June 1906; the Allan's *Tunisian*, four in August the same year; and *Montfort*, twelve in May 1907.

On August ninth, as the *Empress* was leaving for Liverpool, Fortier wrote to David McNicoll, a CPR Vice-president in Montreal and a member of the board, saying, in part, 'I am instructed to ask whether you can show why the Department should not immediately take legal proceedings against the Master of the ship.'

As well, the matter must have been regarded as serious by the *Empress'* doctor, for trachoma, a chronic infection of the cornea, is one of the oldest contagious diseases known to mankind and can be spread by poor sanitation. In the cramped (though clean) third class quarters, there was a small chance of the disease being spread, but he would have ordered extra cleaning to be safe.

McNicoll replied by telegram the following day, promising to investigate the matter and asserting that neither the company nor its masters would countenance such 'irregularities.' After what was certainly a hectic investigation over the weekend, McNicoll provided the following letter to Fortier on Tuesday, the thirteenth:

With reference to your favour of the 9th instant.

I find that the five passengers in question were stowaways. They have been returned by the *Empress of Ireland* and we will arrange to prosecute them on reaching Liverpool.

I regret that they were not discovered. There was certainly no intention on our part to import any passengers without showing them on the ship's manifest.

Unfortunately for the CPR the matter didn't end there. The *Empress of Britain* arrived on the 16th at Quebec and six more males, again identified as Russian Jews aged from 24 to 44, were found. A further round of similar correspondence followed: Doyle to Fortier, and Fortier to McNicoll, though more pointed this time and expressing the hope that '…you will have a very thorough and searching investigation of the whole matter with a view to seeing where the fault lies, and punishing any officers or employees of your Company who may be culpable in this matter.'

Stung, McNicoll promised that the CPR would return the latest batch of stowaways and prosecute them as well on arrival in Liverpool. He concluded his short response to Fortier: 'We are also taking every possible step we can think of to avoid any recurrence and if we find that any of our crew has in any way aided these people in getting on board they will be severely dealt with.'

Meanwhile, the press was having a field day. On 20 August the *Morning Citizen* printed an item headed 'Dishonest Stewards/ Passengers Smuggled on Steamers Without Paying Company.' The opening paragraphs of the article alleged that a wholesale system of fraud had been carried on by stewards and other employees on board. Under the scheme, it asserted, potential stowaways would pay a fraction of the fare – half or less –to – dishonest stewards who were in collusion with one another and were in a position to let the stowaways mingle with legitimate third class passengers. When tickets were being collected, the dishonest stewards would arrange to have the illegal passengers someplace where the ticket collectors or pursers were not. Provided with berths and meals, they would look like legitimate passengers.

On the 28th, McNicoll was able to write to Fortier, reporting the company's progress and the disposition of the stowaways: 'I would say that six [*sic*] of the stowaways on the *Empress of Ireland* were prosecuted on the return of the steamer to Liverpool and got a term in jail. Those now on the *Empress of Britain* will be prosecuted on arrival and I hope this will be the means of preventing others from attempting the same means of reaching this country. We will leave no stone unturned to get at the bottom of it, and prevent it.' In the event, the CPR got off easily. The Canadian government required only reimbursement of the amounts spent at Quebec for the board of the stowaways pending their return to Britain. In the United States, a shipping company would have paid a fine of $1,000 per illegal immigrant discovered – a stringent penalty that ensured masters scoured their vessels for illegals.

Stowaways on such a scale on the two *Empresses* were clearly the result of an organized group at work. Investigations in Britain led to the arrest and prosecution of a number of individuals from London and Liverpool who had conspired to pass into Canada, in an irregular manner, Russian Jews and other transmigrants who were suffering from diseases that prevented them from entering the country in a regular manner.

A letter to Lord Strathcona in London, written in October 1907 by H. Steevens Dudir, Assistant Prosecutor for the city of Liverpool, explained how the scam functioned:

> There have been two Jews having premises in the East End of London, who have advertised in Yiddish papers, and by means of handbills, several premises at which arrangements could be made whereby emigrants suffering from Trachoma and other specified diseases would be passed into Canada without a medical examination, at prices varying from £8 to £12. Upon the emigrants calling at the addresses given, they were medically examined by one or other of the occupiers of the houses and on payment of a deposit and the amount of their railway fare to Liverpool, they were taken to a railway station and sent to Liverpool with instructions to go to the premises of another alien who acted as the Liverpool Agent.
>
> It was then stated by the Liverpool Agent that he required payment of the balance of the sum agreed upon and on receiving payment he then, with the connivance of the steerage stewards on board steamers belonging to the Canadian Pacific Railway Co., passed the diseased emigrants into the steerage quarters of those steamers without any payment to the Company or its agents. The emigrants were then taken charge of by the steerage stewards and concealed either in the steward's room or in the quilt storeroom during the times at which the examinations by the ship's doctor, or by the Ticket Inspectors, were taking place.
>
> On arrival in Canada the emigrants appear on a number of occasions to have success-fully landed and avoided the immigration authorities; but in the case to which I am now referring emigrants on two steamers, the *Empress of Britain* and the *Empress of Ireland* belonging to the Canadian Pacific Rly. Co., were detected by the Immigration Officers at Quebec and sent back to this country. The stewards of the ship disappeared upon the fraud being discovered at Quebec. A medical examination has disclosed the fact that nearly all the emigrants are suffering from trachoma.

The parties in Liverpool were initially charged with defrauding the emigrants, but the charges could not be sustained and a charge of attempting to defraud the CPR was substituted. As for the *Empress of Britain* stewards who had participated in the affair and had fled on its discovery, they were caught in Canada in November, deported and tried in Liverpool in December.

That did not stop the stowaways. The next major 'catch' came in May 1911 aboard the *Royal Edward*. No stowaways were reported again for the *Empress* until the spring of 1914.

While the CPR's senior management was preoccupied with the stowaway scandal, the *Empress* crewmen in Quebec slipped into a familiar round of friendly social activities at the Seamen's Institute. The regular Tuesday night concert of 6 August was a 'very successful affair' and the account on the following day mentioned twelve of the *Empress* crew who had performed songs, and singled out McBride for special mention 'for his ready response to many encores.'

On Thursday, 8 August, a day before departing for Liverpool, the *Empress* received a handsome clock, a gift subscribed for among the Irishmen of eastern Canada. The clock, made of Irish bog oak, was originally intended to be given to Sir Thomas Shaughnessy, and had been first talked about in the Irish community in the late summer of 1906.

The occasion began with a luncheon on board for the delegation of Irishmen. The ship's print ship produced a handsome souvenir menu card for each guest, and the Irish-themed meal shows what the galleys of the *Empress* were capable of, even amid the bustle and confusion a day before sailing.

Eggs à la St Patrick
Salted Almonds   Lax on Toast

———

Consommé Peter the Great
Potage à l'Irelandaise
Salmon King Edward VII
Sole à la Tipperary

———

Grilled Lamb Cutlets à la Friar Tuck
Chicken à l'Tyrone

———

Ribs and Sirloin of Beef   Horse Radish
Roast Turkey and Sausage

———

Cold
Roast Beef   Benoist Beef
Ox Tongue

———

York Ham   Capon   Roast Mutton

———

Ballanhay Potatoes

———

Killarney Pudding
Dublin Tart   Monaghan Jelly
Phoenix Park Biscuits

———

Ice Cream and Wafers
Coffee

When the cigars were passed around after this modest Edwardian repast, Captain Forster proposed the first toast. 'The King,' he said simply, and lifted his glass. A round of speeches followed, and then came the actual presentation of the clock by William Lee to Arthur Piers, filling in for the unavoidably absent Shaughnessy.

'Please accept this clock,' Lee began, 'presented to the *Empress of Ireland*, as a small token of esteem and affection from the subscribing Irishmen of Quebec, Montreal, Ottawa and Toronto, to a fellow-country-man who has showered such lustre on our race and rendered such distinguished services to Canada.'

Piers, rising to accept, regretted the absence of Sir Thomas Shaughnessy. He spoke briefly of the CPR and concluded by thanking the Canadian Irishmen for their 'handsome token of esteem', and promised it would always occupy a prominent place on the *Empress of Ireland*. Marine Superintendent John Walsh then proposed the health of 'Our Guests' and made a short humorous speech. Another toast followed, this time to Captain Forster, who in reply again thanked the subscribers, among whom were some of the most prominent men in the country, for the gift.

After that the guests went on deck, where they were invited to witness the weekly inspection of all officers and crew, some 400 in number, and the manning of the boats. The guests departed about 4:00 p.m., thoroughly pleased with their afternoon on board.

The clock was a 'superb' piece, made by the Howard Clock Company of Boston, one of the most eminent makers of marine timepieces, and ordered through Birks of Montreal, the city's leading jewelry store. The bog oak frame was custom-carved with a wreath of shamrocks, and on the dial plate was a large maple leaf. A polished plate at the bottom bore the following inscription:

Presented to
RMS *Empress of Ireland*
by Irishmen of the Cities of
Quebec, Montreal, Ottawa and Toronto,
in token of esteem and respect to
Sir Thos. H. Shaughnessy, President
1906

When the *Empress* sailed for Liverpool on 9 August, there was one steward less aboard ship, and his absence had nothing to do with jumping ship, itself a fairly common occurrence. Returning to the dock late at night on Monday, 5 August, a young steward named Payne had apparently tripped and fallen into the water and was seen no more. His body was recovered in the Louise Basin two days after the ship departed.

In late summer that year, the CPR announced in Montreal that its Atlantic steamships would again make Saint John their winter quarters. As in the winter of 1906-1907, Halifax would be visited by the *Empresses* only for the purposes of embarking and disembarking the Canadian mails. Nova Scotians quietly gnashed their teeth and mustered more arguments in favour of their capital as the termination point for the ships. At the same time, the railway announced it was looking at the possibility of having the two *Empresses* abandon Quebec in favour of steaming a hundred and fifty miles further up the St Lawrence to Montreal. This was a response to the Quebec-based Ship Laborers' Society, which had recently increased its rates for night and Sunday work. The threat by the CPR was a hollow one: the channel up the river was not deep enough to accommodate the draught of 31ft 1¾in of the two *Empresses*.

Arriving in Quebec on 29 August , the *Empress* disembarked a total of 1,532 passengers (although another source claims 1,554), the largest number of passengers ever landed at Quebec from any steamship. In either case, the number was a large one and would stand as a record for the *Empress of Ireland* for another year, until 1,550 were landed in September 1908. That total would be eclipsed on 1 September, 1910 when the astonishing total of 1,606 were landed on the westbound leg of Voyage 50. The year 1910 witnessed a record for the *Empress of Britain* as well, carrying 1,617 westbound passengers to Quebec on 15 September, and eclipsing the record set by her sister. That record by the *Empress of Britain* would remain unsurpassed in the pre-war years.

The crossing was another fast one, five days, 11 hours and 40 minutes from Liverpool to Rimouski, and broke the *Empress'* own mark, thanks to fine weather almost all the way across. She would have been faster up the river after dropping the mails at Rimouski, but the tides were wrong and so she steamed slowly upriver so there would be sufficient water at Crane Island and the St Thomas flats. Daily runs were very good: 308 (Sat.); 445 (Sun.), 459 (Mon.), 465 (Tues.), 463 (Wed.), and 332 knots to Rimouski on Thursday.

Possibly the most famous of the 186,848 passengers ever carried by the *Empress* was the prolific English author and poet Rudyard Kipling, whose writings gave Britons a sense of Empire, destiny and duty. As a popular verse of the post-Boer War period put it:

> *When the Empire wants a stitch in her,*
> *Send for Kipling and Kitchener.*

Kipling's name is today still widely recognized and universally respected, thanks to works like *The Jungle Book*, *Captains Courageous* and *Kim*.

On 20 September 1907, Kipling and his American-born wife Caroline boarded the *Empress of Ireland* in Liverpool for a tour of Canada, during which Kipling would be awarded an honorary degree in Montreal, meet prominent local citizens across the country, and make speeches in various cities, this latter a task he did not particularly relish.

Devoted to their two children, John and Elsie, the couple wrote two fascinating letters from the *Empress*, and Kipling, himself no stranger to ships and the open ocean, drew pen and ink sketches to illustrate aspects of life aboard ship. As well, in later published works he recounted more experiences from his sea journey to Canada. In all, they make one of the most memorable accounts of what it was like aboard the *Empress*, although their experiences could scarcely be called typical.

s.s. *Empress of Ireland*
Monday morning, September 23rd

A cold grey foggy morning with a south-west swell: the ship pitching a little and a great many chairs empty at breakfast.

Very dear Family,

This North Atlantic ocean is a silly thing. I left it ten years ago in a thick fog with a lumpy grey cold confused sea and now I have come back to it, it is doing the very same things as it did then. The same old fog-horn is making the same husky throaty noise and the decks are all damp and dripping.

Mother is telling you in her letter how we were shifted out of Cabin 123 – the one Elsie wrote the labels for. It was really very funny. I was lying in my cabin reading when my cabin steward came with a piece of paper in his hand and said:– 'The Purser says that you are to shift.'

I was almost asleep, and naturally I grew angry. 'Shift? Shift?' I said. 'What the deuce for? Where the deuce to? Confound your shiftings.'

'Please, Sir', said he, awful humble, 'it's a Suite.' ('Suite' means a set of rooms, and is pronounced like sweet.) Then he showed me the piece of paper, on which was written 'Mr Kipling to shift to 119-121'. Then it was my turn to grow humble and I followed him to the port side of our deck and we opened a little door marked 'private' – and this is the plan of what I saw.

1 = bedroom
2 = sitting room
3 = bathroom

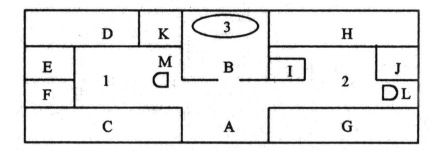

A. Beautiful little hall – leading into
B.   "   " bathroom with private bath etc.
C. Sumptuous bunk for Mummy and one above for me: ornamented carved ends to bunk – not common iron
D. Large and splendid couch under window – furnished pale green.
E. F. Wash stands for Mummy and me
K. Magnificent white wardrobe with large mirror.
2. Sitting room – white wall paper
H. G. Two superb pale green couches – one with ornamented wooden ends
I. Writing table
L. Real chair
M. Another real chair in bedroom.

Talk about luxury! Just think of the joy of having your own private bath at any hour you want instead of having to cut about the passages in your dressing gown the minute that the Bath Steward tells you that your bath is ready. I feel like the Duke of Connaught and Mummy feels like the Duchess.

The ship is a wonderful concern. I went all over her with the Captain at Inspection this morning. She has one deck more than the *Walmer* and she carries about a thousand third class passengers. I am sorry to say that most of them are sea sick. I was nearly sick myself while I was going over their quarters. There are decks deep down below where the men passengers lie in iron bunks three deep – no, two deep. Not exactly a nice place. We went over the kitchens and saw the machine which takes a barrel of flour and turns it into dough for bread, and an electric machine for washing dishes (Nellie would like that) and an electric machine for roasting meat. It was all more wonderful than you can imagine – and so were the smells – THE SMELLS – THE SMELLS!!!

Last night I went up to see the Captain in his cabin on the boat deck. It wasn't like the Cape Boats. The wind blew: there was a cold moon and a chilly wrinkled sea and I wrapped myself up in my great coat and felt cold.

Kipling's comment about the Duke of Connaught is interesting. Four years later the same suite on Lower Promenade deck, located on the port side and immediately aft of the first class café, was occupied by another distinguished visitor. Refurbished specifically for the voyage, it would be occupied by the HRH Prince Arthur, Duke of Connaught, heading to Canada to take up the post of Governor General.

First class passengers reading in the alcove in the after portion of Upper Promenade deck. The original photograph was taken on Voyage 1E, the maiden voyage eastbound, and subsequently retouched for promotional purposes. The alcove was also an area for conversation: 'We discussed this [Imperial policy] ... under the lee of the wet deck-house in mid-Atlantic; man after man cutting in and out of the talk as he sucked at his damp tobacco' – Rudyard Kipling. (Stephen Brooks)

The Duchess would have a similar suite on the starboard side.

In all, the Kiplings received a substantial upgrade. Room 123, the outside room they had originally booked, cost $100 for double occupancy in that low-season period; the outside *en suite* room 119-121 with bath and toilet would have cost $450 for two persons.

In his 1910 book *Letters to the Family*, Kipling observed that '...a C.P.R. steamer can not be confused with anything except Canada,' and went on to provide several insights into his journey in the *Empress*:

> We discussed this [*Imperial policy*] ... under the lee of a wet deck-house in mid-Atlantic; man after man cutting in and out of the talk as he sucked at his damp tobacco. The passengers were nearly all unmixed Canadian, mostly born in the Maritime Provinces ... but scattered about their businesses throughout the wide Dominion. They were at ease, too, among themselves, with that pleasant intimacy that stamps every branch of OurFamily and every boat that it uses on its homeward way. ...These big men, smoking in the drizzle, had hope in their eyes, belief in their tongues, and strength in their hearts.
>
> ...Just at the end of the talk one of our twelve or thirteen hundred steerage-passengers leaped overboard, ulstered and booted, into a confused and bitter cold sea. Every horror in the world has its fitting ritual. For the fifth time – and four times in just such weather – I

heard the screw stop; saw our wake curve like a whip-lash as the great township wrenched herself round; the lifeboat's crew hurry to the boat deck; the bare-headed officer race up the shrouds and look for any sign of the poor head that had valued itself so lightly. A boat amid waves can see nothing. There was nothing to see from the first. We waited and quartered the ground back and forth for a long hour, while the rain fell and the seas slapped against our sides, and the steam fluttered drearily through the escapes. Then we went ahead.

Somewhere in mid-ocean Rudyard and Carrie Kipling signed Chief Officer Henry Kendall's album. As Kendall later recounted, '...he graciously wrote a stanza of a poem in my album, whilst the ship hurried over the mid-Atlantic. Both author and his wife signed it, and I value these lines as among my most treasured possessions.'

From his 1902 poem *The Sea and The Hills*, Kipling had written the third stanza, which began, somewhat prophetically:

Who hath desired the Sea? Her menaces as swift as her mercies?
The in-rolling walls of the fog and the silver-winged breeze that disperses?'

In the following letter, the first two paragraphs were written by Caroline Kipling, and her husband completed the letter. Unlike the first letter, this was written on cream-colored letterhead, with 'CANADIAN PACIFIC RAILWAY ATLANTIC SERVICES' printed in red, along with the company's house flag at left.

R.M.S. *Empress of Ireland*
Wednesday Sept. 25th 1907

Dear John

This is our flag and I enclose a picture of this ship which is a great beauty. We are so sorry not to have sent you a wire but we lost communication with England very soon and it was no fun to send it to Canada and then back.

Last night after dinner Daddy had two wires from Canada and today he answered them. It's most amusing to hear the *click click* at the top of the big pole which is aft near the hold hatch and on the open deck the telegraph man has his office. We think and talk of you a lot and were glad to have a wire from Mr Stanford to say you were making a good start.

The weather has been perfectly beastly. Yesterday it was cold and clear but today it is thick and cold – one of the heaviest fogs that I have ever seen. If you look up the map you will see that our course is from Liverpool round the North of Ireland through the Straits of Belle Isle and down the mouth of the St Lawrence River. Well, last night about midnight we were nearly up to the Straits of Belle Isle expecting to pick up the light-house there when the fog came down like a blanket. We had to stop altogether for about four hours blowing our siren until we heard the foghorn blow from a lighthouse on the shore. (You see I don't know this run so I can't explain it to you as easily I could the Cape run.) Then we knew we were in the Straits of Belle Isle. They are only ten miles wide in one place. I thought that the fog would lift after we got through but it came down thicker than ever and this morning it was like the steam of a laundry. We are pushing through it slowly with our fog horn blowing like a sick cow and every one is very wet and moist and angry. They are getting up the passengers' luggage and putting it on the decks exactly as they do on the Cape steamers.

One of the most interesting things on the ship is what you and I talked about – the Marconi telegraph. As you know, people can send telegrams to ships at sea by sending the electric current through the air. They don't need telegraph poles or wires.

First class passengers playing on Lower Promenade deck, looking forward. (David Saint-Pierre)

There is a little square cabin on the after deck – just like the boatswain's cabin on a Cape boat. It stands just at the foot of the mizzen-mast. You look down upon it from the passengers' deck.

All you see is a little wire coming out of the square house and going up the mast and ending in a sort of cross piece with two wires hanging between the mizzen and the main mast. I have tried to draw it up above. Well you go in there and find a young man all surrounded by most wonderful telegraph instruments which buzz and click and spit out long blue sparks. He wears a sort of bridle on his head like this – so that he can listen to the clicks [*Kipling drew front and side view sketches of the Marconi operator wearing headphones, and added a note: 'The round things over his ears are telephone ear-pieces!'*].

Outside the cabin there is nothing but grey fog and a slow crawling sea. Inside the cabin instruments buzz and click and messages come in for passengers sent by their friends in Canada two or three hundred miles away.

When there are no messages coming in the telegraph operator sends all sorts of private messages to other ships on the sea – funny messages from officers to officers.

I was in there this morning and the second officer of this ship and the telegraph officer were laughing like anything. I said:– 'What is the joke?' They said:– 'We have been guying the *Tunisian*.' (That is a steamer of the Allan Line.) The *Empress of Britain* [*sic*] usually overtakes the *Tunisian* (who is a slow boat) just about the Straits of Belle Isle. They thought they would overtake her as usual yesterday and so, when they were about seventy miles behind her they sent her a message saying: – 'Hurry up, you old tramp.' The *Tunisian* wired back: – 'Don't be proud. We'll beat you yet' or something of the kind. Well, *then* down came the fog I told you about and we had to slow down and never passed the *Tunisian* after all. She got past the Straits of Belle Isle in a little bit of clear weather and away she went down the gulf of St Lawrence, throwing out cheeky messages to us and asking who was the old tramp now, and recommending to us to be patient and good. Just the sort of chaff you and I might throw about playing on the pond. Well, right in the middle of her chaffing *she* got caught in a fog lower down the gulf and wired us that she had to stop and she was in an awful temper about it and we wired back telling her to keep her hair on and that we were coming down and would get into Quebec first after all.

Just as I had finished that line, the Stewardess came in with telegrams for me from Montreal and St John New Brunswick, asking me to dine in two places there. Isn't it all very wonderful! Here are we in a thick white fog with messages and chaff coming in and going out all the time.

I do hope we shall beat the proud old *Tunisian*.

There isn't very much else to tell you about. The food is not bad but the weather as I may have remarked before is VILE! I met a man in the smoking room who spends his time hunting seals and catching whales in the polar seas. He goes as ship's doctor in a dinky little three hundred ton barque and he enjoys it awfully.

…He told me that whalers are the most superstitious people in the world. If a boat pushes off from the ship's side any way except bow first, she must row back, be hauled up again to the davits, her crew must get out of her, step in again, and be lowered down all over again!

And you must *never* pass anything into a boat *through* anything. I mean if you are handing a gun or a harpoon to a man in a boat you must not push it out of a porthole or through the rigging but must lift it clear over the bulwarks and put it in the man's hands. If you handed a man a knife through a loop of rope or through one of the ratlins of the rigging you would spoil his luck for the day.

… I'm awfully glad you are not on this misty moisty trip. There's a girl on board rather like Elsie but bigger. She comes from Sevenoaks and goes to school there and she can run like a young rabbit.

I haven't seen any nice boys. There aren't many children as they are usually left in Canada or England. There are any amount of grown ups and they are awfully nice to us. But I shall not be sorry to come home again.

Thursday 1 o'clock. We have come through the fog. It is *very* cold, bright & clear and we are running along the shores of the St Lawrence River. It looks rather like Tews woods. We shall stop at a place called Rimouski to put off the homeward mails. I'll write again.

Ever your most loving

Dad

P.S. We passed the *Tunisian* this morning at 8 o'clock. She was very angry about it.

Despite Kipling's comments, *Tunisian* was not *that* bad. Built in 1900, she was a 10,000 ton vessel capable of 17 knots which had been chartered by the CPR on two occasions in the previous year. When passed by the *Empress*, she was inbound to Montreal with 1,150 passengers.

Kipling's narrative is continued in the following extract from *Letters to the Family*:

The St Lawrence on the last day of the voyage played up nobly. The maples along its banks had turned – blood red and splendid as the banners of lost youth. Even the oak is not more of a national tree and the sight of its welcome made the folks aboard still more happy. A dry wind brought along all the clean smell of their Continent-mixed odours of sawn lumber, virgin earth, and wood-smoke; and they snuffed it, and their eyes softened as they identified point after point along their own beloved river–places where they played and fished and amused themselves in holiday time. It must be pleasant to have a country of one's very own to show off. Understand, they did not in any way boast, shout, squeak , or exclaim, these even-voiced returned men and women. They were simply and unfeignedly glad to see home again, and they said: 'Isn't it lovely? Don't you think it's beautiful? We love it.'

The next letter to the children was written in Montreal:

> Place Viger Hotel,
> Montreal.
> Sunday night. Sep. 29. 1907
>
> Very dear Family,
> We have been in Canada now since Friday morning; and our adventures would fill a book. Just as soon as we got up in the morning when the steamer had reached Quebec, I heard a voice outside our cabin door saying there was a private car waiting for us to take us to Montreal.
> … We left the ship and found this stately splendour of a private car … tacked on to the end of the passenger train.

The private car (named 'Dalton') – complete with porter – though the Kiplings did not at once realize it, had been put at their disposal by Sir William Van Horne, Chairman of the CPR. Van Horne had met the *Empress* at Rimouski, a singular honour, and entertained the Kiplings in Montreal at the beginning and end of their trip. 'You may find her useful,' was Van Horne's off-hand comment about the coach, 'to knock about the country. Hitch on to any train you choose and stop off where you choose.'

The Kiplings took Van Horne at his word. In the next four weeks they travelled to Vancouver and back, a distance of more than six thousand miles. Kipling observed, 'When we wished to sleep in peace, it slid off into still, secret freight-yards till morning. When we would eat, *chefs* of the great mail trains, which it had honoured by its attachment, asked us what we would like.'

The Kiplings returned to England on 24 October from Montreal aboard the Allan Line's RMS *Virginian*. Two months after his trip in the *Empress*, Rudyard Kipling was awarded the 1907 Nobel Prize for Literature, the first English author so honoured. The writer whose nearest claim to a formal education was travel on three continents, and whose later writings would help Britain heal the wounds of the Great War, died in 1936.

Statistics for the five months ended 30 September 1907 showed the following passenger arrivals at the port of Quebec:

	1st	2nd	3rd	total
CPR	2,832	6,100	36,518	45,450
Allan	3,300	13,221	24,000	40,521
Dominion	3,657	4,793	9828	18,278
Donaldson	-	1,424	2,991	4,415

Clearly the CPR had something to be pleased about as the second year of *Empress* service progressed. While first and second class passenger totals were still lower than the Allan's, the all-important third-class trade, which supported the rest of the operations, was fifty percent higher than the Allan traffic. It augured well for the future.

In October a rate war broke out on the North Atlantic and the CPR joined in a general reduction of rates, first for eastbound passengers, and later, for westbound. For sailings on and after 1 November the new rate structure was as follows:

Empress of Ireland & Empress of Britain	1st	£11 and up
	2nd	£8 10s and up
Lake Manitoba	1st	£9 and up
	2nd	£7 10s and up
Lake Champlain & Lake Erie	1st	£9 and up
	2nd	£8

As it did every year, the Canadian Pacific organized an autumn excursion to Montreal for the various officials of the port of Quebec. It provided a special coach attached to the regular train, provided a theatre evening and put the men up at the swank Place Viger Hotel as a way of saying 'Thank You' as the shipping season wound down. The two-day trip ended with a ride from Montreal to Quebec aboard the *Lake Manitoba*, outbound to Europe. The group of forty-four that left Quebec on 25 October included men from the US Customs, the Canadian Immigration Service, Medical Inspectors, the Harbour Master, Chief of Police, newspapermen, and anyone in a position of importance in the city. It was all part of doing business at the port, and perhaps a way of making amends for the stowaway problem of August.

For the crossing that began at Liverpool on 18 October (17W) and arrived at Quebec on the 25th, Captain Forster reported heavy weather throughout the passage, particularly from Longitude 30 W and up past the Strait of Belle Isle, though that was to be expected for the autumn months. Coming up the river, the *Empress* was forced to anchor for four hours below Crane Island to await the rising tide, a delay that would have to be made up for somewhere along the way to Hong Kong for the British mails.

Sailing on 1 November, her last departure from Quebec for the season, the *Empress* had 643 passengers, 'a very large booking for this season of the year,' according to the *Chronicle*. 'The *Empress of Ireland* has had a very successful season on the St Lawrence and it has been nip and tuck between her and the *Empress of Britain* for the blue ribbon of the Canadian route.'

Two days before their ship sailed, the men of the *Empress* gave a farewell concert at the Sailors' Institute. There were seven performers from the ship, with many of their shipmates in the audience.

Toward the end of the year, Arthur Piers, the company's general manager of steamship services, moved from Montreal to Liverpool, for by now the British port was the focal point of a fast-growing business. Piers, fifty-five that year, a man who was already spending much of his time in England or commuting on the company's two *Empress* steamers, must have welcomed the move. In reporting Piers' transfer, *The Times* took note of the planned transfer of the two *Empresses* to the Pacific, and the anticipated construction of two new *Empress*-type boats for the Atlantic Service. While the company's headquarters staff in Montreal could feed rumors to the Canadian papers, Piers would now be in a position to do so in the United Kingdom, seeking to promote the company's stock and throw the competition off guard.

Fares on the Atlantic were reduced again in January 1908, as the rate war escalated further, with shipping companies trying to attract business in a normally quiet period. The CPR's new rates, valid until 25 March, for westbound passage were as follows:

All steamships	2nd	£4 adult; children 1-12, £2; infants, £1
Empress of Ireland & *Empress of Britain*	3rd	£4 10s adult; children, half-fare; infants, 10s
Lake Champlain & *Lake Erie* & *Lake Manitoba*	3rd	£4 adult; children, half-fare; infants, 10s

The voyages of the *Empress of Ireland* continued in the new year, each much like another, yet different in subtle ways. It was in February 1908 that the officers of the *Empress* bid farewell to a Chief Officer whose skills and competence they had come to respect. The CPR had just given Henry George Kendall his first command, as master of the steamship *Milwaukee* in the European coastal trade. Kendall could add the coveted fourth gold stripe to the three he already wore on his sleeve.

The year 1908 also witnessed another milestone for the CPR in Liverpool, for the company opened its first boarding house to accommodate the growing numbers of emigrants bound to Canada. This wasn't a radical move. Other shipping lines had done the same thing, and the CPR was merely keeping up with the competition.

Eastbound on Voyage 20, a girl was born to the Lancaster family of England. The proud parents named her Alexandra Evelyn, then added one more name, this time in honour of the master of the ship. Alexandra Evelyn Forster Lancaster was the first child to be born aboard the ship since the autumn of 1906.

Westbound on her 21st voyage, another death occurred aboard the *Empress* before she arrived in Saint John on 29 February. Violet Morgan, the four-year-old daughter of emigrants Thomas and Jane from Shropshire, was buried at sea in the usual solemn ceremony.

Fresh from her winter overhaul, the *Empress* departed Liverpool on 20 March 1908, bound for Saint John via Halifax. Among those on board was a Japanese named Saukisi Komura, who had spent enough time in England to form some lasting friendships. In a card postmarked at Halifax on 28 March, he composed the following message to the Nesbitt family of Lewisham:

> My dearest friends,
> We were so sorry not to be able to see you once more before we left but we found everything too much of a rush at the end. We hope you are all much better.
> We left Liverpool on the 20th & have been having continuous rough weather, which will make us one day late in reaching St John N.B. This we expect to be on 26th inst. We leave Vancouver on 14th prox., reaching Yokohama on 27th idem. Please take care of yourselves & we wish you all every happiness. Looking forward to seeing you again soon.
> Yours very sincerely
> (sgd) S. Komura 26/3/08
>
> P.S. My all others are yet sea sick. For all the size of this str. she is pitching about like cork!

The manifest of the trip allows a more complete picture to be constructed. Komura was a 45-year-old merchant, accompanied by his wife Leyi (age 31), son Haru (3½) and servant Shizue Nakawo (25), all travelling first class. They were the only Japanese in first class; in fact, they were the only Japanese on board, in a total of 1,481 passengers.

Among the few who made a round trip on the *Empress of Ireland* was a 35-year-old Canadian civil servant. In the spring of 1908, although a protégé of Prime Minister Sir Wilfrid Laurier, William Lyon Mackenzie King was all but unknown to the Canadian public. The capable young man had been sent to London to confer with British authorities on the subject of immigration to Canada from the Orient and, in particular, from India.

King left Canada on 7 March 1908 (Voyage 21E) from Saint John, carrying personal messages to Sir Edward Grey from President Theodore Roosevelt, whom King had met in Washington a month earlier. A prolific, life-long diarist, the sea air seems to have stilled the pen of the civil servant, whose occupation was described in the manifest as 'Political', for there were no entries in his diary until the ship reached England on 16 March.

Two postcards from Voyage 22W:

Dear Nell:
We are on board just now & sailing away at a great rate. You would not know we were at sea. Not a bit sick.

Dear Uncle
We are delighted with the boat & have got good company in our cabins.

The following is an abstract from the log of the *Empress* for Voyage 22E, from Saint John to Liverpool. The abstract was printed aboard ship prior to arrival in Liverpool in a postcard format and sold as a souvenir to passengers before they left the ship.

ABSTRACT OF LOG.

R.M.S. 'EMPRESS of IRELAND'
J.V. FORSTER, R.N.R. COMMANDER
St John N.B. to Liverpool, April 3rd. 1908.
VIA HALIFAX

Left Halifax 9-30 P.M. April 4th.

DATE	DIST.	LAT.N.	LONG.W.	REMARKS
Apl. 5	261	43.28	57.48	Moderate quarterly wind & sea
Apl. 6	419	44.27	48.15	Moderate wind & smooth sea
Apl. 7	427	47.48	38.58	Mod. quarterly wind & slight sea
Apl. 8	407	49.31	29.13	Mod. quarterly wind & slight sea
Apl. 9	433	50.51	18. 9	Gentle breeze smooth sea
Apl. 10	430	51.54	7.10	Gentle breeze, smooth sea
	187 to Liverpool Bar			
Total	2564			

Arrived Liverpool 10-21 P.M. Friday, April 10th, 1908
Passage Halifax to Liverpool 5 days, 19 hours, 41 minutes
Average Speed 18.35 knots

His business in England completed, Mackenzie King was able to return on the *Empress* a month later. Although there is another gap in his diary for the voyage, the following entry for 17 April, Good Friday, provides some details of the departure:

I went to the Princess Wharf some distance from the hotel to see about the luggage that had come on from Liverpool, but as the *Empress of Ireland* was still out in midstream, and had not been brought alongside the wharf, was unable to get any information on its whereabouts. I spent an hour or more on the docks watching the crowds and the various ships leaving for the day's holiday. At twelve went to the Adelphi Hotel and wrote a few letters to persons in England, and on the way back to the wharf had a hurried lunch at one of the hotels en route.

The *Empress* was alongside the wharf and I found on going aboard that all our luggage was safely put away in the staterooms, and that we had been given the finest suite on the ship, the companion suite being given to Judge Girouard and his family. It has been newly fitted over and is beautifully decorated with red and blue, a charming little sitting room, with several chairs, desk, table, comfortable bedroom and bathroom. About eighty first class on board, second class and steerage well filled.

At 9:00 p.m. on Thursday, 23 April, on her last night at sea before reaching Saint John, there was the traditional evening of entertainment for first class passengers. On this particular evening the entertainment was in aid of the Liverpool Seamen's Orphan Institution, and the Chairman for the evening was none other than W.L. Mackenzie King. The programme was divided into two parts, and featured a variety of acts including vocal solos, mandolin, violin and piano solos, and recitations. Among the personal papers of Mackenzie King in the National Archives is a copy of the programme from that night, carefully preserved as a memento of the voyage.

The reverse of the programme contained a description of the Institution and explained its purpose: 'to feed, clothe and educate the destitute or necessitous children of all classes of seamen or seafaring men.' Passengers were also given a subtle reminder that '…no more fitting tribute of gratitude can be shown to the Almighty hand, who brings the ship in safety to her journey's end than by helping to support the children who are left fatherless by the necessities of the seamen's life.'

With the aid the passenger manifest, almost all the performers can be identified as passengers travelling in first class, probably recruited over the previous few days by the Chairman to perform for the benefit of their fellow travellers. Passengers would have entered into the spirit of the evening, little caring whether the talent was second-rate or not. It was their last night at sea and they were determined to make it a memorable one. One can assume that on most voyages a similar practice was followed, unless the number of first class passengers was too small, in which case the passengers would have been supplemented by crew members.

On King's voyage, even with just ninety-one first class passengers, there were enough talented amateurs to assemble such a varied programme; the talent pool from voyages with over 200 first class passengers must have been remarkable. On this voyage, W.G. Reilly was a 31-year-old Canadian manager; Mabel Downing, 35, an English musician; Andrew Betts-Brown, 29, an engineer from Scotland; Charles Dalziel, 31, a broker from Canada; Laura McMeans and Pearl Montague, 17 and 18 respectively, were students from Winnipeg; Bernard Weiler, 41, a British merchant headed to New York.

Hayes and Tunstall were both members of the crew, whose fine voices helped round out the programme. Harold Tunstall was a frequent (and popular) performer at various charity events at the Quebec Seamen's Institute, and also sang for the second class entertainment programmes.

By long-established custom, the proceeds of ship's concerts went to the Liverpool Seamen's Orphan Institution (a 'Royal' designation was added in 1922), and in each year between 1906 and 1914, the *Empress of Ireland* contributed to this worthy charity. The institution, founded in 1869, still continues its good work today, looking after the children of deceased British seafarers. Though the orphanage closed in 1949, the Institution provides finances for education and welfare of the children.

Making a fast run and enjoying a fine voyage, the *Empress* came within five hours of the fastest time ever recorded between Liverpool and Halifax, and carried 1,506 passengers, a large number, given the season.

First Class Programme of Entertainment, 23 April 1908, under the
chairmanship of William Lyon Mackenzie King (Voyage 23W).
(National Archives of Canada)

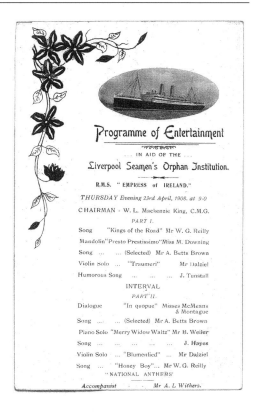

Arriving off Halifax on the 23rd about 7:00 p.m., the *Empress* docked at Halifax's Deepwater Terminus, where the Canadian mails and a few first class passengers were disembarked. Less than an hour later, she sailed for Saint John. The short transit to Saint John was marred by the death from diphtheria of a 9-year-old Russian girl, a third class passenger. She was hastily buried at sea off the Nova Scotian coast.

The CPR's public relations people evidently knew their jobs, and had correctly identified Laurier's protégé as someone who merited special treatment. On the fourteenth, while still in London, King had visited the company's offices to thank their manager for having arranged the suite of rooms 'at the ordinary passage rate for return.' The historian can only regret that this man, who compiled one of the most remarkable diaries every written by a Canadian, did not write more about his time on board the ship. Presumably King used his time on the return to work on his report, which was submitted on 2 May 1908.

William Lyon Mackenzie King won a seat in Parliament in 1908 and entered the Laurier cabinet as the first Minister of Labour. He was chosen leader of the Liberal Party and became Prime Minister in 1921, a position he held until 1930 (with the exception of three months in 1926). When the Liberals returned to power in 1935, he served as Canada's most enigmatic Prime Minister until his retirement on 15 November 1948.

In third class on the same crossing were two brothers, Edgar and Reginald Chapman, from Brighton, emigrating to Canada. Though actually fifteen, Reginald's age was entered on the manifest as seventeen and his name is shown as 'Robert'. During the crossing, the young schoolboy proved to be an easy mark or had a streak of bad luck, for he managed to lose all his money in gambling, probably (as his granddaughter speculates) in the classic 'shell-game', where a player has to guess which of three walnut shells covers the pea.

Fortunately for Reginald, his elder brother had enough money to satisfy the immigration requirements for both of them. On arrival at Saint John the brothers headed westward to seek their fortune on the frontier.

King's voyage presents an unsolved question with respect to a collision involving the *Empress*. The Lloyd's Register for Captain John Forster records for 22 April 1908 a collision in which the ship sustained

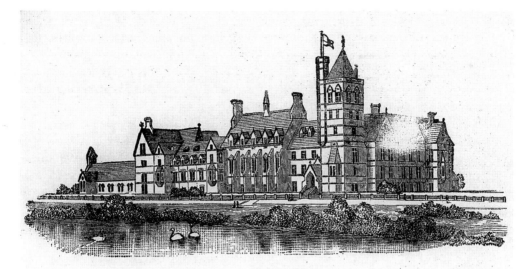

THE LIVERPOOL

Seamen's Orphan Institution.

WAS founded in 1869 to feed, clothe and educate the destitute or necessitous children of all classes of seamen, or seafaring men. From that date to the 1st July, 1907, over 6,400 children have received the benefits of the Institution, and many poor widows have been enabled to keep a roof over their heads, and their little ones from the workhouse; there are at present over 900 children upon the books.

The benefits conferred are not restricted to any nationality, or to any form of Religious Worship, though children of seamen, who have sailed five years out of the Port of Liverpool, have a preference. The frequent recurrence of such names as Agirre, Bengoa, De Cruze, Freimuller, &c., testifies to the Foreign paternity of many of the children.

A very large number of these Orphan children have lost their fathers by the perils of the sea in crossing the Atlantic, and conveying passengers and cargo to and from America. A still larger number of seamen die from diseases contracted by exposure to the weather, in all seasons and at all hours; *and no more fitting tribute of gratitude can be shown to the Almighty hand, who brings the ship in safety to her journeys end,* than by helping to support the children who are left fatherless by the necessities of the seamen's life.

The returns from the Board of Trade are appalling in their evidence of the loss of life at sea, for they show that in thirty-five years following the establishment of this Orphanage, no less than 139,525 seamen died in English ships **abroad**, of whom 92,197 were drowned. This number does not include those who die in the United Kingdom.

The Orphanage is open for the inspection of Visitors every day except SATURDAY and SUNDAY, from 2 till 4 p.m.; whilst those who are in Liverpool on SUNDAYS can have no greater treat than by attending the Children's Service at 11 a.m., or at 3.30 p.m. A card with visitor's name handed to the Verger will always command attention.

During the year **1906, 1176** Children received the benefits of the Institution, of this number there were:—Children of

CAPTAINS, OFFICERS, PURSERS and PILOTS.	SEAMEN, including CARPENTERS and SAILMAKERS.	ENGINEERS and FIREMEN.	STEWARDS, COOKS and BUTCHERS.
167	466	357	186

Liverpool Seamen's Orphan Institution, on the reverse of the Programme of Entertainment. (National Archives of Canada)

no damage. On that particular date the *Empress* would have been south and east of Newfoundland but there is no mention in any newspaper or other source of a collision or other incident involving the ship.

Normal rates went into effect in the spring to coincide with an increase in westbound passenger traffic, for April and May were the two busiest months for the CPR's Atlantic service. First class rates in the *Empress* reverted to the usual $80.00 and up, second class was $48.75-50.00, and third class, $28.75, according to an advertisement in the Halifax *Herald*.

In early May the Canadian Pacific issued a directive amending the color scheme of its vessels. Henceforth, all the company's ships on the Atlantic, Pacific and Great Lakes would have a black band painted at the top of the previously all-yellow funnel. The company found that coal smoke had marred the appearance of the funnels, and decided that a black band was the simplest way to fix the problem.

In the late spring of 1908, at the instigation of a family friend, a young boy looking for a job walked up the gangway of the *Empress* while she was docked in Liverpool. Seventy years later, Arthur Owen recounted his experiences:

> Home life was not too pleasant and at the age of fourteen (when students finished their schooling) my brother Gerald and I became interested in the passenger liners which sailed from Liverpool. The Princess Landing Stage was a very busy place with many ships coming and going, and the lure of the sea appealed to us. My brother was only on the *Empress of Ireland* for a very short time and then joined the *Mauretania*.
>
> On May 6, 1908 I signed on the *Empress of Ireland* as a Bell Boy. On signing up at the age of 14½ I was told to go to the firm of Lewis' in Liverpool where I lived and, at my expense, fitted me out with my uniforms. On May 15 I had to be on board ship at 7:00 am. The ship was docked at Sandon Dock, Liverpool. I was kept busy helping to prepare for the embarkation of the passengers in the afternoon when we would be sailing for Saint John.
>
> On my first day out to sea, we were in the Irish Sea and the call came: 'Man overboard!' The ship circled around for quite a while, having thrown out a life belt but the man drowned.
>
> When I was a boy at school, I never knew what it was like to be without a headache and once I joined the ship, my headache disappeared. I attribute it to the fact that every morning before going on duty, I used to walk around the deck with another member of the crew, and we had to be on duty at 5:15 a.m.
>
> I was one of six Bell Boys. Every other day we were on duty from 5:15 a.m. to 11:00 p.m., the other evenings we were off duty after dinner. We had one hour off duty during the day.
>
> We sailed to Saint John during the winter and to Quebec City during the summer. Being a Bell Boy I received lots of tips and was thrilled to go home with pockets full of silver and gold. My mother took all my pay, which in those days seemed a natural thing to do. My pay was 3 pounds 16 shillings per month.

Arthur Owen remained in the crew and received a promotion in 1909, at which time we will follow the young man again. The tall lanky youth was an accomplished soccer forward, and found a place on two of the ship's teams. He played for the Stewards, and for the composite team that represented the ship in outside matches.

The *Empress* returned to Quebec on 22 May in the evening, her passage and progress duly noted in the maritime pages of the *Chronicle*. North Sydney was again the mail destination, and she landed the Canadian mails there in the *Lady Evelyn* before heading toward Quebec. She carried 1,392 passengers, a most respectable total, as April and May were always the busiest at Quebec in terms of passenger numbers. Weather conditions reported by Captain Forster were typical: strong head winds for most of the trip, with haze in the pack ice off Newfoundland. And there was the usual delay of several hours below Crane Island waiting for the rising tide.

When the ship had docked, a number of Quebecers – all former *Empress* passengers – went on board to welcome Captain Forster on his return to the St Lawrence. Coaling began on Saturday morning, just twelve hours after the *Empress* had docked at Quebec's Breakwater. The operation was always a dirty business. Sometimes it could be dangerous as well, for on this occasion a coal company employee named Henry Harding lost his footing and fell into one of the *Empress'* bunkers. Stunned by the fall, Harding managed with difficulty to extricate himself, whereupon it was found he had badly injured one of his shoulders.

If the ship was welcomed back in Quebec, so too were some of the crew. On the Tuesday after her arrival, the ship's band participated at a well-attended seamen's concert at the YMCA. An article on the local news page titled 'Feature was Unique Band of *Empress of Ireland*' described how the evening's attraction had been the ship's five-man band and its bandmaster, Owen Shehyn. Rather than their normal instruments, the band performed two numbers, 'played on the inexpensive instruments one usually purchases on being imbued with an early desire to attain some practical knowledge of the musical profession.' Whatever the instruments, the band's efforts 'brought fourth repeated rounds of applause.' The bandsmen had other talents as well; two of them also sang two solo numbers.

It was in 1908 that composer-arranger Myrtie C. Wallace wrote a work for solo piano. Entitled *The Empress of Ireland Waltz*, it was published in Cambridge, Vermont (and, in 1910, in Montreal by John Harrison) as six pages of sheet music, and subtitled 'With Honour to the Canadian Pacific Railway Company's Atlantic Steamship.' The link, if any, between Wallace and the ship or the CPR remains to be established, although he had written other earlier works including the *Lord Strathcona March*. No similar tribute was ever written for the *Empress of Britain*.

On Friday, 29 May 1908 William Symons, a Salvation Army Staff-Captain and band leader boarded the Empress Special at Windsor Station in Montreal, heading for Quebec. Symons had been on a visit to Canada to see his relatives and was now returning to England and his wife, Emily, and their two children. By chance, the Army's Lt-Col. Addie of the United States and his wife were travelling to England on the same voyage, along with Adjutant Sturgeon, and they looked forward to meeting their colleague once the train arrived alongside the ship. Col. Addie had no trouble spotting the 29-year-old Symons, for he stood apart from the other passengers thanks to his uniform. Symons stood patiently on the wharf, waiting at the gangway, preparing to hand his ticket to the collector.

The *War Cry* of 13 June continues the story:

> Here it was the accident took place. A tidal movement of the vessel pushed the gang-plank on to the Staff-Captain's foot, and before he could be extricated his leg had been very badly crushed.
>
> The ship's doctor temporarily dressed the wound, and Staff-Captain Symons was carried to the ship's surgery, where, with the assistance of two Canadian doctors, who were on board, the wound was properly dressed, and he was then conveyed to his cabin.
>
> Nurses were appointed for day and night duty, and everything possible was done to make him comfortable, and to relieve the intense pain from which he suffered.
>
> Colonel and Mrs Addie and Adjutant Sturgeon were with him much of the time and he appeared to be progressing favourably. Serious symptoms did not, indeed, manifest themselves until noon on Sunday, and even after that the doctor thought he had a fighting chance for his life. Later in the day, however, he grew rapidly worse. He passed away on Monday [*June 1*], four days after the accident occurred, and was buried the following morning.
>
> To Colonel Addie fell the mournful duty of informing the Staff-Captain that his race was run. At first he could not believe that he was so seriously hurt, and suggested that at the worst he could lose his limb.
>
> But when, at last, he recognized that the end was drawing nigh, he smiled with beaut-iful resignation, and, looking into Colonel Addie's eyes, said, 'Ah, well, it must be so. Say

good-bye to my darling wife and children. Tell my wife that this all harmonises with God's plan for us.'

Then he spoke of his work – the work he loved so well, and in which he had been engaged from boyhood. 'They have always told me at Headquarters that my prospects were bright for the future,' he said, 'and when it comes to sacrifice and devotion, I have always endeavoured not to play second to any man.'

Once Colonel Addie asked him to what he referred as he spoke half unconsciously. 'Oh!' he said. 'I was thinking about that poor fellow in our emigrant party who lost his money going out, and I wanted to help him find it.'

'Kiss the children for me,' he said at last. 'Tell Emily not to fret.' Then he stopped a moment, and finally concluded, 'And ask the Staff band to play.'

Staff-Capt. Symons was the first Salvationist to be 'promoted to Glory' aboard the *Empress*. Fate decreed he would not be the last.

Also aboard were sixteen ministers who were impressed by Symons' firm faith and the courage with which he faced the end. They wrote the following letter to Emily Symons, and asked Col. Addie to deliver it:

RMS *Empress of Ireland*
June 6, 1908

Mrs Symons,
Dear Madam,
We, the undersigned, fellow passengers with your late husband on board the RMS *Empress of Ireland*, in view of the sad circumstances connected with his death, desire to express to you our most sincere sympathy with you in your sorrowful bereavement.

It is a matter of real satisfaction to assure you that, in your loved one's last hours, his steadfast faith in his Saviour never faltered, and that he fell asleep at last in full possession of joy and peace in believing.

We pray that the God of all comfort and grace, the Father of the fatherless, and Husband of the widow, will be your increasing Comforter, abiding with you and yours for ever.

The letter was signed by the Bishops of Montreal, Qu'Appelle, North Dakota, and Yukon, and by thirteen other clergymen, ministers, and missionaries.

Voyage 25W, departing Liverpool on 12 June, was somewhat out of the ordinary. The *Empress* encountered strong north-westerly winds all the way from Liverpool to Sydney, with hazy weather in the ice track. The time between Liverpool and Sydney was a very respectable 5 days and 9 hours. The passenger complement of 1,045 included a party of 100 brought out under the auspices of the Salvation Army, including a number of wives coming out to their husbands, and domestic servants. The unusual feature of this particular crossing was that the passenger list increased by two souls, 'a fine boy and a pretty girl' having being born at sea.

Returning to England, the *Empress* picked up the mails at Rimouski, making for a shorter trip than if she had stopped at Sydney. At least two special groups sailed on the eastbound passage. The first, a party of young ladies who, having won a newspaper contest in Illinois, were now happily embarked on the European trip they'd won.

The second was 'The Cuthbert Houseparty', a private group organized by E.M. Cuthbert of Toronto, and evidenced a growing middle class with the money and inclination to travel. Their itinerary for a two-month escorted tour of Britain and the continent was printed in a 14-page souvenir brochure whose deep-purple cover bore the caption 'Don't Worry. !!! Smile!'.

In addition to a minutely detailed schedule that would have done honour to a military planner, the brochure contained numerous practical instructions for the party:

> Be sure and take warm clothing on the ocean; woolen underwear and warm jackets.
> Gentlemen will require a light overcoat for the British Isles. No dress clothes necessary.

And, as the group had its own special train at Liverpool to take them to Euston station, members were advised:

> To facilitate matters, *carry your own suit case and wraps off the boat across the wharf to the train*. The stewards will want to carry them off the boat for you. To allow them to do so means to get them mixed up with a thousand other pieces, and may delay our train two hours to search for them. Take them yourself, from the stateroom and either carry them to the baggage car of our train or to the truck we will have waiting to receive them as soon as you are off the boat on the landing. That is the last handling of your luggage you will have for weeks.

The brochure also noted that provision had been made for entertainment during the voyage and, somewhat ominously, warned 'No one allowed to be sea sick more than one day.'

In the year 1908 Canada celebrated the tercentenary of the founding of Quebec City. A great celebration took place that summer in the Ancient Capital, attended by political and military dignitaries from Canada, other dominions, and Britain. Many of these latter sailed in the *Empress of Ireland* and formed the largest and most impressive company of men and women ever gathered aboard the ship.

The Times, mindful of its social obligations, devoted considerable space to the departure and the upcoming celebrations in Quebec. On 11 July, the paper noted: 'The Canadian Pacific Company's steamer *Empress of Ireland*, which left England yesterday, had on board a distinguished company of passengers bound for Quebec.' Next came a lengthy listing of the delegation, headed by Irish-born Field-Marshal Lord Roberts, C-in-C of British Forces in the Boer War. The following is a partial list of the delegation, and conveys an idea of its importance:

Lord Roberts, Commander in Chief, British Army; his daughter, Lady Aileen Roberts; two ADCs, Capt. the Hon. Hugh Dawnay of the 2nd Life Guards and a Canadian, Col. Septimus Denison; the Duke of Norfolk; Lord Lovat, head of the Fraser clan and having historic links to Wolfe's campaign of 1759, representing Scotland; the Rt Hon. the Earl of Ranfurly, representative of New Zealand; Capt. the Hon. Arthur Cecil Murray, MP, a descendent of British General James Murray, who fought with Wolfe and became the first British governor of Quebec; Lord Bruce; Lady Donegal; and Capt. the Hon. Dudley Carleton.

Despite the delegation, first class was by no means full, for there were only 186, making a total of 1,066 passengers. Among these were a number of tercentenary visitors as well, including correspondents of major British periodicals and newspapers, two artists from *The Sphere*, and representatives of the Reuter News Agency. The tercentenary attracted considerable interest in Britain since the Prince of Wales, the future George V, was also participating in the ceremonies at Quebec, although he would arrive by Royal Naval warship only on the 22nd.

Describing the passage of the *Empress*, the *Gazette* noted that the distinguished party had enjoyed an 'excellent trip,' and added: 'the field marshal, with his easy manners and good nature, was the most popular man aboard ship.' During the voyage, the field marshal had many questions on Canada and Quebec and had 'found many on board who were willing to supply him with all the information at their disposal.' The Quebec *Chronicle* claimed that the field marshal and Lady Eileen 'were well pleased with the arrangements made for the comfort of passengers on board the *Empress of Ireland*.' *The Times* noted as well that the visitors in the delegation 'expressed themselves much impressed by the St Lawrence route.'

Unusual was the fact that the *Empress* carried two winners of the Victoria Cross, Britain's highest military award for gallantry in the face of the enemy. One recipient was Lord Roberts himself, who had won the award in 1858 as a lieutenant during the Sepoy Mutiny. The second, scarcely mentioned in *The Times*, was Captain Alexander Hore-Ruthven, who had won the award in September 1898 as a lieutenant in Sudan for the rescue of a wounded Egyptian officer, while under fire by the advancing Dervishes. In full dress uniform at dinner aboard ship, the two men with the $1\frac{1}{2}$in wide crimson ribbon of the Victoria Cross would have commanded the respect of every military man aboard.

Hore-Ruthven, thirty-six, described in the manifest simply as 'gentleman', was actually the military secretary to Lord Dudley, the governor general of Australia, and the two were headed to the south Pacific. Hore-Ruthven was the second son of the 8th Baron Ruthven and, after being educated at Eton, joined the Highland Light Infantry in 1891. Newly married in 1908, he scrawled a ten-page letter to his wife in which he described his feelings on leaving her and provided some impressions of the sea crossing.

Empress of Ireland
Tuesday 13 [*sic*] July

My own little darling child:
We have had such a beastly voyage up to now – wild & wet & wavy & the last 2 days a thick mist – we have had to slow down. The wind is Arctic; today we are very far north, N. of Newfoundland but are not into the straits between N'foundland & Labrador [*until*] tomorrow, when they say the weather will improve.

This ship is very comfy & the food is good & I have done nothing but eat non-stop since we left. It's been too wild & wavy to do anything & I have hardly spoken to anyone but Callan – most of them are sick!

The card sharpers have not appeared yet – the weather has been too rough but the last 2 days are always fine and I expect they are lying low till then.
Wed.
Weather improved at last but was icy cold all yesterday afternoon. We came through a lot of icebergs, some of them quite close to the ship & the fog was so thick last night that we lay to for 5 hrs as they want no chance of running into the icebergs.

We have turned the corner now & are in the Straits between N'foundland & Labrador & it is getting fairer & warmer every minute.

We played cricket this m[*ornin*]g 1 & 2nd class. BD Zalter a success as a bowler but no luck with the bat. John played for 2nd class but his keenness is greater than his skill! He is very happy I think & feeling so at home on board ship.

We get in to a place called Rimouski tomorrow morning where I shall post this & you ought to get it next Sat. week. Oh my darling child I can hardly believe I have only been away from you 5 days – it seems years & years.

In his unpublished draft autobiography, Hore-Ruthven later wrote about some of his fellow passengers and recounted a joke played upon a pompous member of Parliament:

We travelled by sea with many celebrities, including descendants of Wolfe himself, and of those who had fought by his side. Others in the party were descendants of families whose names were famous in the history of the development of Canada. Surveying the heirs of those departed heroes, one could not but marvel at the tricks of heredity. One could hardly believe that these ordinary, conventional people were in any way connected with the men of enterprise and daring, whose exploits had been told and retold for generations.

Two proud symbols of the Edwardian era: RMS Empress of Ireland and the motor car. The picture was probably taken at Saint John, c.1911. Note the steel bars protecting the first two portholes in the crew's quarters in the forecastle, one of the few ways to distinguish the two sister ships. (Maritime Museum of British Columbia)

Among the better types was the most famous and beloved Field Marshal of our day, Lord Roberts. We had not been long at sea when Marconigrams began to arrive inviting him to visit and accept the freedom of the most important cities of Canada, and it soon became evident that he would be subjected to an extremely strenuous and exacting time.

Among the lesser descendants, a somewhat pompous MP was rash enough to express the opinion that he too, on account of his own distinguished ancestors and claims to fame, would probably have to submit to similar ordeals. Some of the younger, more frivolous passengers saw no reason why this should not prove true. They concocted a Marconigram, purporting to come from the Mayor of Rimouski, asking him to accept a formal address from the loyal citizens of his town as a mark of respect and admiration for the bearer of such an historic name. Our friend accepted at once, and immediately went to his cabin to prepare a suitable reply. We then chose an eminent journalist, whose figure and features suited the part, to represent the Mayor, and the portly young scion of a noble family was given the part of Mayoress.

Soon after the ship berthed at Rimouski, 'His Worship and Milady', suitably attired, entered the crowded saloon where our friend had been asked to await their arrival. In his loyal address, the 'Mayor' enlarged on the pleasure it afforded the good people of the Dominions to welcome to their shores such a distinguished individual, and spoke of the respect and admiration in which he was held by the loyal citizens whom he had the honour to represent. Our hero's reply was a masterpiece of rhetoric and eloquence. At every point the delighted spectators, vainly endeavouring to hide their mirth, cheered him to the echo. At length 'His Worship' retired amidst mutual good wishes and sentiments of esteem and regard, and the steamer proceeded on her way.

Hore-Ruthven went on to a distinguished career. He saw service in France and Gallipoli, was mentioned in despatches five time, and achieved the rank of Brigadier General in 1917. From 1920 to 1924 he comm-anded the Welsh Guards, and was appointed Governor of South Australia from 1928 to 1934. He served as Governor General of Australia from 1936 to 1944 and was named the first Earl of Gowrie in 1945.

Another member of the delegation was Lt-General Sir Reginald Pole-Carew, known to many Canadians who had served in South Africa. The general's wife, Lady Beatrice, kept a diary while on board, from which the following extracts are taken. Lady Beatrice, whom Hore-Ruthven described as 'affable', was another member of the group involved in the practical joke on the MP, referred to above.

July 10th 1908 p.m.
We sailed from Liverpool 5:30 on board Canadian Pacific ship *Empress of Ireland* – found many friends going on same expedition – printed list gives names. We were given two most comfortable cabins – & arranged for our 'table party' in dining saloon following: Duke of Norfolk, Lord Ranfurly, Lord Lovat, Sir Keith Fraser. We left Liverpool in a squall – grey sea, white horses – generally un-propitious & our hearts sank as the wind & sea increased – however dinner was got thro' with quite an honest hunger – for these big ships take the seas easily but about 9 we were in for a moderate gale, and plunged in & out of unpleasant abysses – & most of our fellow passengers retired in haste to bed – personally felt bad – it was bad – then slept till morning.

July 11
Gale over – but sea sullen & ugly & not calm – no special appetite for breakfast – took exercises up & down deck – excellent chicken broth taken round at 11: – couldn't face lunch. Other women of our party didn't appear all day – took more exercise after tea – made the acquaintance of more fellow passengers & paced the deck till dinnertime – enjoyed this as sea was calm.

July 12 Sunday
Service and nice hymns – largely attended – sea kind & calm but weather overcast & coldish day spent walking, talking, eating, reading & sleeping. Everyone very cheerful & the 'sick' are resurrected once more.

July 13
Still grey & cold – there is a Captain Murray on board, who is busily impressing us all of the importance of his visiting Canada – as a descendent of the first Lord Elibank who was governor general years ago. Some of us have decided that it will be for his good, that some harmless joke be played at his expense – and we are busily thinking out a plan – Lord Lovat being our ring leader.

July 14
Heavy fogs at intervals – but no responding echoes to our fog horn. Our practical joke is forming itself & tomorrow Captain Murray will receive a Marconigram from the Governor of Halifax, as a preliminary – in the evening we attended a 2nd class concert but slipped off early – Some of us saw all over the ship in the afternoon – such an enormous hotel – engine room wonderful – all the accommodation so well thought out & most interesting.

July 15
Bad fog – in afternoon sports took place – Hugh Dawnay hurt his knee, falling heavily in a race – Captain Murray has received a Marconigram to the effect that a deputation will be sent

to welcome him at Rimouski where the ship stops at for an hour tomorrow – he swallowed the whole thing & goes around telling everyone abt it – too conceited for words – he is now writing out an address in answer to the one he is to receive & we are all trying not to laugh in his face – fog cleared at 5:45 & we saw some great icebergs, one like a big white church with a spire – several small ones in vicinity of large ones – some are 100 feet high and 200 feet below the water – after dinner we attended a concert in the 1st class saloon – quite nice music – Lord Roberts took the chair – about 9 o'clock before the concert we came in right off the Island of Anticosti, bought by one of the Meniers, it stood out, a long stretch of dark blue-indigo with the sunset flaming red & orange behind it – a wonderful brilliancy of colour & all the water between our ship & the island – like a sheet of glowing gold.

July 16th

Such a delight on waking to find ourselves gliding along in the beautiful St Lawrence with scenery that reminded me of Scotland on our port side – the other we could not see for the width is enormous – we have got Mr Maxwell, correspondent of the *Daily Mail*, to impersonate the mayor of Rimouski & Lord Bruce is to dress up as his wife. Captain Murray has issued instructions to some of us to be present at the deputation ceremony & has hired a cabin in which to receive the Mayor – He announced that he intends to wear a new grey frock coat which, we assured him, was the *very* thing. Lord Bruce came to my cabin as Rimouski hove in sight & aided by Polly, Capt. Kincaid-Smith, Lord Lovat, Sir K. Fraser, Mrs John Hope who lent a smart Paris cloak & some curls – & the artist of the *Illustrated London News* who painted Lord B's lips – we turned out a marvellous lady mayoress with a blue straw motor bonnet, lined silk curls, a grey coat trimmed with lace – a white silk skirt & a white lace veil. 'She' carried a large bouquet of faded asters and looked a rare oddity. Mr Maxwell had been 'got up' by the barber & was completely disguised by a false moustache, an 'imperial' – & his hair brushed straight up – he wore a red ribbon round his neck and & looked the part of a provincial mayor to perfection – then most of those concerned in the plot went to the cabin where stood Captain Murray arrayed in the frock coat & looking nervous but pleased, he assigned us to our places & we noticed with amusement that wine & cakes etc. had been prepared for the honoured guests. 'The Mayor is just coming' said someone & a few minutes after Capt. K-Smith announced, 'His Worship the Mayor of Rimouski.' Capt. Murray bowed to them both & then the Mayor read an address here enclosed – Violet Elliot laughed out loud – even then Capt. Murray didn't see – but gave her a withering glance – & then he proceeded to read his thanks to the Mayor – and make himself pleasant to Mrs Mayor who merely smiled & bowed – they refused refreshments & were hustled out with the excuse that the Captain was anxious to show the Mayor round the ship – Capt. M. was anxious to accompany them but we dissuaded him.

The whole afternoon he harped on the subject – & said how ugly he had thought the Mayoress – 'I think she was dumb,' he also said, 'as she never answered any of my questions – merely smiled.' So passed off a most excellent joke.

Another lovely sunset we had, as we were going thro' mountainous country & islands – lovely effects of light & colours – later we danced for a little – at 11.30 came to Quebec – all the lights on the hill looked like a brilliant illumination.

The passenger manifest for the trip provides more details on these 'conspirators'. General Pole-Carew, 59, and Lady Beatrice, 31, were travelling with a valet and maid. 'Captain Murray' acquires a given name – Arthur – and an age, 29. 'Maxwell' becomes 41-year-old William Maxwell, while Mrs John

Hope is revealed as a 29-year-old Canadian, travelling to Victoria in the company of Mrs R. Dunsmuir, from one of the wealthiest families in British Columbia. Also in first class was William Armitage, the Halifax theologian who had conducted a burial service aboard the *Empress* in September 1906. This time, fortunately, his services were not needed, although perhaps they would have been had Arthur Murray ever discovered the originators of the prank.

Another first class passenger, of whom the 'society' people would have taken little note, was a 34-year-old British artist named Frank Craig who already enjoyed a considerable reputation. His illustrations had found a ready audience in magazines such as *Scribner's*, *Harpers* and *McClures* in the US, along with *The Graphic*. He was respected also as a historical painter and book illustrator, his work having accompanied some of the era's best known authors including Rudyard Kipling. Craig had exhibited at the Royal Academy and various Paris salons, and had won a gold medal for portraiture in Paris. Designated 'Special Artist' he even went to South Africa with British forces to paint the campaigns of the Boer War.

On this particular occasion he had been engaged by *The Graphic*, a London weekly news magazine, as Special Artist-Correspondent, with the task of illustrating some aspects of the ceremonies and important visitors at Quebec. During the journey up the St Lawrence Craig had an opportunity to witness the reaction of immigrants viewing their new homeland from the *Empress*. *The Land of Promise: St Lawrence River*, executed later, is an emotional and highly realistic work, which succeeds because it is exactly the scene one *expects* to see. A variety of third class passengers, some hastily summoned from below, have gathered on the portside fore Shelter deck, their faces showing a range of emotions as they survey the green, wooded hills along the south shore of the St Lawrence, their first close-up view of Canada.

The Canadian Pacific liked the picture as well, later using it in the daily diaries, though this time under the generic title 'Emigrants on an *Empress*'.

The *Empress* docked at Quebec on Thursday, 16 July after 11:00 p.m. As she had been expected at 7:00 p.m., the ceremonial arrival of Lord Roberts was put off until the following morning. Since they would not be needed on the Friday morning, several members of the delegation decided to disembark that evening and were taken to their rooms at the Chateau Frontenac. Lord Roberts, along with most of the passengers, remained on board for one more night. In the morning, the resplendent Field Marshal, accompanied by his daughter and secretary, descended the *Empress*' gangway to a government launch, which ferried them to the King's Wharf, about a mile upriver from the Breakwater. Here, in the official ceremony of welcome, he was greeted by civic leaders and a delegation of the Royal Canadian Regiment, of which he was honorary colonel. Then, to the accompaniment of a nineteen-gun salute, Lord Roberts proceeded through the old city to the Citadel atop Cape Diamond, where he was greeted by Governor General Earl Grey.

During the following week, while the *Empress* was being turned around for her next crossing, she played no further role in the festivities. On the 22nd, two days before she sailed to Liverpool, all hands must have paused at their various activities and rushed to the rails to witness the gala arrival of the Prince of Wales aboard the cruiser HMS *Indomitable*, escorted by HMS *Minotaur*. Moored in the river, ships of three navies – British, French and American – thundered out a 21-gun salute, along with the batteries in the Citadel. Vantage points in Quebec overlooking the harbour, like Dufferin Terrace below the Chateau Frontenac hotel, were reported by *The Times* to be 'black with spectators.'

A day later, *Empress* crew members were ideally placed to watch the re-enactment of Champlain's arrival in his ship *Don de Dieu* and, that night, a programme of fireworks at 9:45.

Prior to the summer of 1908, Beaujeu Bank off Crane Island in the St Lawrence below Quebec City could delay deep-draught vessels if they arrived at low water. Two years of work by the dredge *Galveston*, purchased by the Canadian government for the purpose, had created a channel thirty feet deep and 600 feet wide through Beaujeu Bank which would enable liners like the *Empress* to pass at all times. No longer, claimed the government, would the departure or arrival of the *Empress* at Quebec be determined by tide tables.

In parallel, further dredging at the St Thomas shoals had removed another impediment for large vessels. Before dredging, there had been just twenty-four feet of water at low tide, far less than the

Empress needed. By the time dredging had finished, there was a 30-foot channel at low water, extending to a width of 1,000 feet.

Departing Quebec on 24 July, the *Empress* carried the year's record number of eastbound second and third class passengers, a fact duly noted in the Montreal papers. The *Gazette* noted that in a slumping passenger season for both east and westbound traffic, the two *Empresses* had done well, adding 'one of the features being the increasing number of travellers from the United States, chiefly from the middle and far west.'

In 1908 the Atlantic Shipping Conference was set up, in order to consider all aspects of transatlantic steamship travel. Although beyond the scope of this work, suffice it to note that three lines with routes to Canada were represented, *viz.* the Allan Line, CPR and Donaldson. All the participants hoped to fix rates for first and second class passages based on various criteria, and they hoped to establish a pool for emigrant traffic in order to eliminate the ruinous rate wars that had previously played havoc with company profits. Like any cartel, for that was what it amounted to, it worked as long as its members wanted it to. The arrangement remained in place until 1914, when the two German lines, NDL and Hamburg-Amerika, quit over the question of Austro-Hungarian emigration via Trieste and the CPR's poaching of traffic.

Fog in the St Lawrence was a common occurrence at any time in the shipping season. Some fogs, though, could be much worse than others, as 1,066 passengers discovered on the westward leg of Voyage 27. Making good time from Liverpool, the *Empress* (along with *Corsican* and *Ottawa*) entered the Gulf and ran immediately into fog, which became very dense between Father Point and Quebec. 'The utmost caution had to be taken and the *Empress* had to creep up very slowly.' stated the *Chronicle*, noting that the trip up the river to Quebec had occupied eleven hours more than normal, so that the ship arrived at Quebec on 14 August. Apart from fog, according to Captain Forster, the crossing had been uneventful, with the usual concerts and games among the passengers.

Uneventful passages, it seemed, were becoming a matter of routine.

As on every voyage, benefit concerts for the Liverpool Seamen's Orphan Institution were held in first and second class. For the latter, held on Tuesday, 11 August, a surviving programme and the passenger manifest confirm that the entertainers were largely drawn from the 339 passengers in second class, and represent a good cross-section of the population. Dorothy Doane, 40, was a British teacher bound for the United States; Lily Jones, 34, whose occupation is shown on the manifest as 'Theatrical' was also headed to the US; Annie Belling ('GOING TO HUSBAND') was travelling with her three children and destined to Hamilton, Ontario. George Lister, 24, was a clerk, while Lizzie Allen was an 11-year-old Canadian schoolgirl.

With the pageants of the tercentennial over, life in Quebec City returned to normal, and concerts resumed once again at the Sailors' Institute. On Tuesday, 18 August, the band of the *Empress* (composed of eight firemen, using mainly home-made instruments) performed a 'splendid' concert, and regular singers like Harry Tunstall also played to an appreciative audience. 'The choruses,' said the *Chronicle* the next day, were 'carried up to the rafters by the crowd of merchant sailors who thronged the hall.'

The year 1908 opened with the voyage of a future prime minister of Canada. On 18 September it was the turn of former prime minister Sir Charles Tupper to travel in the *Empress*, as he and Lady Tupper returned to their retirement home in Bexley Heath. The native of Nova Scotia, then in his 87th year, was among the oldest passengers ever carried aboard the ship.

As the shipping season on the St Lawrence drew to a close that year, a new problem arose for vessels: blinding smoke from forest fires that raged unchecked along both banks of the river. September had been an exceptionally dry month and the drought had continued into October, making the coniferous forests tinder dry. Though rains came occasionally, they were insufficient to put out the fires or prevent them from spreading. Many ships were held up in their transit of the river, or else delayed their departure from Montreal or Quebec. When vessels did venture out on the river, the results could be disastrous; two ships collided below Quebec City in the heavy smoke and were badly damaged. After a rain cleared the air somewhat, there was a crush of vessels on the river, each bent on making the open sea as quickly as possible. Then with little warning, the smoke would shut down navigation, and the vessels were obliged to anchor.

Only with the first snows of winter did the situation on the St Lawrence improve. By that time, the ocean-going vessels had already departed for their winter ports.

That autumn the *Empress* seemed to enjoy a streak of good luck, for none of her sailings was affected by the smoke. In fact, she broke new records for speed in a season when records were not expected.

Arriving at Quebec on 8 October with 817 passengers, the *Empress* set a speed record for the year and wrested the blue riband from her sister. Departing Liverpool at 6:30 p.m. on Friday evening, 2 October, the *Empress* arrived at Quebec at 4:00 p.m. the following Thursday, thus shaving three hours off the old record. Despite strong head winds in the Gulf and on the river, it was an otherwise uneventful crossing.

Two special trains left the quayside shortly thereafter and reached Montreal in time to make the westward connecting trains. Said the *Gazette*: 'All this season there has been the closest possible kind of rivalry between the respective skippers of the two vessels, Captain Murray, of the *Britain*, and Captain Forster, of the *Ireland*.' The paper (and others) commented also on the advantages of the St Lawrence route, and noted (not for the first or last time) the speedy delivery of the mails by the CPR vessel. The similarity of the language in various papers suggests that editors were working from a CPR press release.

While the *Chronicle* congratulated Captain Forster for 'having achieved with his fine vessel such a rapid passage across the Atlantic, and taking the record by such a good margin, from an equally as fine a steamer.' the paper also extended its praise to pilot Adélard Bernier for 'bringing the vessel up from Rimouski in record time and in hazy weather.'

A month later history repeated itself.

In a stretch of fair and clear weather on Voyage 30W, the *Empress* shaved fifty-five minutes off the record established only two weeks before by the *Empress of Britain*, which had broken the previous mark set by the *Empress*. As usual the newspapers followed the ship's progress once she came within wireless range, and speculation was rife as to whether the weather would change and slow the ship down, for blinding snowstorms were expected in the lower parts of the river. Still, the papers did not imagine that Captain Forster would allow the weather to snatch a record from his hands.

'If the CPR Co.'s greyhounds… continue snatching the blue ribbon of the Atlantic from each other, there will soon be very little of that interesting piece of dry-goods left,' commented the *Chronicle*. Arriving at Quebec on 5 November at 2:30 p.m., the *Gazette* described the last few minutes of the voyage thus:

> …and when the crack boat of the fleet rounded the bend at the Island of Orleans yester-
> day afternoon, and swept up to her berth, her decks crowded with cheering passengers,
> and with the naval reserve flag of her doughty commander, Captain Forster, fluttering
> proudly at the peak, a new chapter was written in the history of St Lawrence navigation.

As the clocks of the old city struck three, she was warped to her dock and the first passenger came down the gangway a few minutes later. Captain Forster, somewhat unusually, was quickly surrounded by enthusiastic passengers who congratulated him on the fast passage and the honour of commanding the fastest ship on the route to Canada. All the passengers sported blue ribbons in their button holes to symbolize the ship's achievement. The blue ribbons were still in evidence when the passengers made their connections in Montreal, the *Gazette* noting 'that a better pleased lot of travellers never passed through Windsor Station.'

The *Chronicle* joked that Forster and the crew would receive 'enough of blue ribbon favours before leaving Quebec to start a good sized millinery store.'

While the CPR could spend its money promoting the beauty of the St Lawrence route, popular attention focused on one thing: speed. The Gazette correctly observed that 'the fast voyages of the *Empresses* this year are recognized to have done more to bring the St Lawrence route into prominence than any other known factor.'

After the ship had docked, more details of the trip emerged. It transpired that as soon as the *Empress* had left the Bar Lightship in the Mersey, 'every man, from the captain to the grimiest stoker in the belly of the vessel had but one object in view, and that was to regain the blue ribbon.' Day after day the ship churned its way across the Atlantic, averaging 18.3 knots per hour. Daily runs to noon were: Saturday, 328 knots; Sunday, 458; Monday, 462; Tuesday, 450; Wednesday, 462; Thursday, 312 to Rimouski. Encountering snow and gales – meaning wind velocities in excess of 35 miles per hour – in the lower Gulf, she arrived at Rimouski at 4:25 on the Thursday morning. A total of 1,308 sacks of mail and 362 bags of parcel post were unloaded in record time, and the *Empress* set off again at 5:50 a.m. for the final 150 miles to Quebec City. Despite a delay of forty-five minutes at Quarantine off Grosse Ile, the *Empress* still managed to set a new mark.

All in all it was a remarkable trip – just 5 days, 22 hours and 20 minutes – and the Montreal paper likened it to the speed feats achieved on the New York run by bigger and faster vessels. It was also a fine way to end the season in Quebec, for the *Empress* and her crew would not see the Ancient Capital again until the following spring.

Among the ninety-one passengers in first class were members of the Canadian Olympic lacrosse team, returning from a month-long trip to England where they had played South African and English teams for the world championship. Four days before leaving Liverpool, the Canadians had defeated Great Britain 14-10 to retain their world title. The manifest provides some details of that long-forgotten team: Alfred Turnbull, 36, a civil servant from New Westminster, whom *The Times* described as 'always prominent' in the championship match; goaler Frank Dixon, 30, a clerk from St Catherine's ('kept goal well'); and George Rennie, a 26-year-old clerk from New Westminster.

When the *Empress* departed Quebec at 3:20 p.m. on 13 November, she carried 1,406 passengers, among whom were a contingent of Royal Navy men returning to England after serving at Esquimalt, in British Columbia. Third class, with 1,101 passengers, was completely full; it was the largest number of third class passengers the ship would carry in her eight-year career.

Bookings on eastbound vessels to Britain in December of 1908 were extremely heavy, a measure of the success of Christmas rates instituted by the major shipping companies. Outbound from Saint John on 12 December, the *Empress* carried the impressive total of 1,480 passengers, a number that would be the ship's highest-ever for an eastbound crossing. It was a fine way to end the year, except that passengers had exceptionally rough conditions throughout the trip, very likely the worst sustained weather ever encountered by the *Empress*. The postcard Log Abstract conveys only a faint hint of their misery:

Dec. 13:   ...heavy conf'd sea
Dec. 14:   ...heavy to rough sea
Dec. 15:   Mod. to strong full gale, very heavy sea
Dec. 16:   Strong gale & tremendous N.W.'ly sea
Dec. 17:   ...heavy q'ly sea
Dec. 18:   ...heavy q'ly sea.

By the end of 1908 it was clear that the Allan Line had lost its position as premier carrier on the Liverpool route to Canada. The venerable carrier had been elbowed aside by the upstart CPR, whose *Empress* steamers had helped tip the balance with their increased capacity for third class passengers and faster speeds. In that year the Allan Line had carried 29,711 passengers on the westbound leg, compared to the CPR's 34,744. More importantly, the CPR had carried 20,282 third class – the bread and butter passengers – compared to the Allan's 16,112. Eastbound, the CPR's lead was even greater: 30,031 compared to 20,354.

New Canadian immigration regulations had greatly reduced the westbound third class passenger traffic in 1908 compared to 1907. Each immigrant was now required to have at least $25 in his possession and work to go to immediately on arrival. Shipping circles estimated that since the new

The Library, Empress of Ireland. '*...next door to my cabin is the Library, where I am now writing – a most delightful room, panelled in polished mahogany, upholstered in green plush, with green carpet and plush and handsome mahogany writing tables*' – *Sir Josiah Symon. (Stephen Brooks)*

orders had taken effect, more than 2,000 men had been turned back at the port of landing, or deported shortly after their arrival. Somewhat unfairly, the new regulations punished the shipping companies for the subsequent actions of new arrivals. If an immigrant got into trouble within a year of landing in Canada, the steamship company which brought him out was required to return him to the port from which he had sailed. After a year, if an immigrant became a public charge, the government paid the shipping company a small sum to return him to Europe.

The physical condition of new arrivals was monitored more closely than ever before, and even those with adequate funds but no immediate job could find themselves turned back.

Such policies explain the second and third class *Empress* passenger totals in the table below, where westbound totals declined in both classes in 1908, and increased in the eastward direction.

Westbound			Eastbound	
II	III		II	III
4,385	8,798	**1907**	2,002	5,048
3,879	7,101	**1908**	2,255	7,736

Overall, the *Empress* totals fell off much less than the 1908 totals for the CPR, Allan and other lines. Westbound third class totals for the CPR, for example, fell from 34,036 in 1907 to 20,282, a reduction of 40%. The Allan's numbers fell even more precipitously, from 35,846 to 16,112, a drop of 55%, while the *Empress of Ireland*'s second and third class passengers declined just 17%.

It was 26 February 1909 when a twenty-five-year-old carpenter named Henry ('Harry') John Brown boarded the *Empress* in Liverpool, heading for a new life in Canada. He was typical of many British emigrants in that he left his sweetheart, Maggie Sherman, at home in the London suburb of Wandsworth. The following three postcards, all showing the *Empress*, convey the thoughts typical of a young man leaving a woman behind him for an indeterminate period.

Liverpool
[postmarked Feb. 25]

Dear Maggie
Arrived safe. Cheer up 6 hrs gone. Ireland next.
Harry

Liverpool
26th 1909 [postmarked Feb. 26]

Dear Maggie
Boat leaves dock about 4 P.M. Fri. Am getting ready for the fishes. Will let you have another from Ireland if possible.
Harry

The last postcard shows the *Empress* entering Saint John harbour:

Dear Maggie
Arrived safe. Fri. night will write when I get to Toronto. 1 week 1 day.
Cheer up.
Harry

Harry settled in Toronto, where he worked as a carpenter for the rest of his life. In 1910 Maggie emigrated to Canada aboard *Tunisian* and married her sweetheart. Harry's postcards have been carefully preserved by one of his grandchildren in British Columbia.

Following is a postcard souvenir log extract for Voyage 35W, from Liverpool to Saint John.

ABSTRACT OF LOG.

R.M.S. 'EMPRESS of IRELAND'
J.V. FORSTER, R.N.R. COMMANDER
Liverpool to St John N.B. March 26, 1909.
VIA HALIFAX

Passed Bar Light-ship at 6-5 p.m. Friday March 26th.

Date	Dist.	Lat. N.	Long. W.	Remarks.
Mar. 27	316	51.21	10.30	Fresh breeze, moderate sea
Mar. 28	444	50.22	22.08	Fresh gale & squally, heavy head sea
Mar. 29	421	48. 3	32.18	Fresh to mod. sea, heavy head sea
Mar. 30	425	45.53	42.11	Strong unsteady winds, heavy confused sea
Mar. 31	443	43.48	51.43	Fresh head to strong following wind, confused sea
Apl. 1	423	43.42	16.23	Gale of hurricane force to mod. head wind
	109	to Halifax		
Total	2581		274 to St John	

Arrived Halifax 6-5 p.m. Thursday April 1st 1909
Passage… Liverpool to Halifax 6 days, 4 hours, 0 minutes
Average speed 17.5 knots

ABSTRACT OF LOG.

R.M.S. "EMPRESS of IRELAND'
J. V. FORSTER, R.N.R. COMMANDER

:0:

St. John, N.B. to Liverpool December 11th 1908
VIA HALIFAX.

:

Left Halifax 11-48 p.m. Suturday December 12th.

DATE.	DIST.	LAT, N.	LONG. W.	REMARKS.
Dec. 13	207	44.54	58 41	Fresh gale to mod. breeze, heavy conf'd se
,, 14	414	47.44	48.41	Fresh to to mod. breeze heavy to rough s
,, 15	408	50.28	40.18	Mod. to strong full gale, very heavy sea
,, 16	426	53.19	29.45	Strong gale & tremendous N. W'ly sea
,, 17	426	65.06	17.58	Strong gale to strong breeze, heavy q'ly s
,, 18	423	55.09	5.58	Strong breeze to mod. gale, heavy q'ly se
	141	To Liverpool		
	2445			

Arrived Bar Light-ship 7-35. p.m. Friday December 18th 1908.
Passage—Halifax to Liverpool 5 days, 15 hours, 47 miutnes.
Average speed 18. knots

Abstract of log, RMS Empress of Ireland, *Voyage 31E. This souvenir postcard was made up in the ship's print shop on arrival and sold to passengers as a souvenir. The 1,480 passengers, the highest-ever total for an eastbound crossing, experienced rough conditons, particularly on 16 December. Note the mis-spelling 'miutnes', evidence of hurried preparation.*

The passenger who purchased that particular Log Abstract postcard sent the following message:

> Dear Mother:
> I arrived hear at St John today. Will write when I see Willie.
> PS – this card was printed on board.

Bell Boy Arthur Owen must have made a favourable impression on his superiors in the Victualing Department. His narrative continued:

> I did twenty trips as a Bell Boy and then was promoted to Officers' Steward April 10, 1909. I shared my quarters with the 'Captain's Tiger' in a cabin on the Boat Deck. I was responsible to all the officers. On September 23, 1910 I was moved to Assistant Steward and continued in the position until I left the ship. The Chief Steward was [*Augustus*] Gaade; he was a fine man, heavily built and very strict.
>
> The ship did not have an orchestra, so on every trip the ship's crew and some of the passengers used to make up a concert. One of the crew who was one of the stewards, 'Curly' Tunstall, was a wonderful singer and in great demand.

The *Empress* returned to Quebec at 2:55 a.m. on Saturday, 1 May with 1,455 passengers, the mails and 2,780 tons of general cargo, the bulk of which was destined to western Canada. The Breakwater that morning was a busy place, for she was followed a few hours later by the Allan's *Corsican* and the Dominion Line's *Canada*. All told, over three thousand passengers funneled through Quebec in the space of a few hours.

EMIGRATION.

Donations earnestly solicited to assist

DR. BARNARDO'S HOMES

in their Emigration Scheme this year.

1,082 Boys and Girls emigrated in 1907 (at small cost of £10 per head), making a total of 19,727 emigrants, of whom 98 per cent. have been successful.

241 Young People left for Canada on 12th ultimo.

.*.Mark Gifts " Emigration Fund." Cheques and P.O.'s payable to " Dr. Barnardo's Homes " crossed same way and remitted to the Honorary Director, William Baker' Esq., M.A., LL.B., 18 to 26, Stepney Causeway, London, E."

Typical appeal for donations to assist emigration to Canada, The Times, *10 April, 1908. Barnardo's brought more than 30,000 British children to Canada before child emigration ended in the 1930s.*

First and second class *Empress* passengers were landed early and took their waiting trains; third class passengers were taken into the Immigration building and, after undergoing the usual examination, left about 10:00 a.m.

With the opening of navigation to Quebec, the Sailors' Institute on St James Street re-opened for the season on 1 May. It was well patronized that day by men from the *Empress*, along with a handful from other steamers in port, who were pleased to note that in their five-month absence, the Institute had acquired a piano. On the Saturday night tea and biscuits were served to about sixty men, and on Sunday about forty attended the evening song service. With the sailors back in Quebec, the usual call went out in the newspaper for magazines and periodicals for the Institute.

On 7 May, one day before the *Empress* departed for Liverpool, a new ship sailed up the St Lawrence on her maiden voyage. This was the White Star-Dominion's *Laurentic*, constructed by Harland & Wolff in Belfast. She reflected the latest thinking in liner technology, a combination of reciprocating engines and low-pressure turbines. In several respects she outclassed the CPR's two Atlantic *Empresses*. *Laurentic* was now the largest vessel in the Canadian trade, measuring 565ft and 15,000 tons, and could carry about 1,700 people. She included all the luxuries the Edwardian public had come to expect in great liners, along with separate libraries for first and second class, and an electric elevator for passengers between the Saloon and Upper Promenade decks. Passengers, so the papers claimed, would 'find the provision made for their comfort second to none on the Atlantic.'

The CPR took due note, determined to ensure that the cachet of the *Empresses* would not be lost.

Days off in port could provide a variety of amusements for crew members. Arthur Owen described one incident of youthful hi-jinks:

> Being a young boy, I naturally looked for adventure, so when we were docked in Quebec one day, four of us took the ferry over to Point Lévis. Then we took a streetcar to where we knew there was a derelict boat moored in the St Lawrence River.
>
> Being adventurous, we decided to board her. To do so, we found there were two steel hawsers attached with planks across. We climbed on them and they rocked perilously,

then we climbed up the rigging into the crow's nest and carved our initials on the mast.

After that we went to the bosun's locker which was in the bow of the ship and found two distress rockets. We put them under our jackets and got back to Quebec.

As we approached our ship we did not know what to do with the rockets, as we could not take them on the ship, so we decided to set them off. One of the boys lit a cigarette, laid the rockets on a horse's watering trough and lit them. All hell broke loose! We ran for our lives back to the ship as the Quebec authorities came running to the spot. Sparks and stars were flying everywhere.

They never found out who was responsible for doing such a thing!

On Friday evening, 21 May 1909 Edwin and Millicent (Cresswell) Lambe boarded the *Empress* in Liverpool along with 1,462 other passengers on the ship's second voyage of the season to Quebec. Married just two days before in Darlaston they were bound for Toronto and a new life together in Canada. Each day they took the list of Second-Cabin passengers, in which their names had been mis-spelled as 'Lamb', and carefully copied the Daily Run into the back of the book and traced their curved route across the Atlantic from the charts posted by the Purser's Office. Belle Isle Strait being still dangerous, Captain Forster had opted for the southerly route around Cape Race.

DAILY RUN

Date	Distance
May 22	256
May 23	435
May 24	454
May 25	440
May 26	410
May 27	451

On the same trip as the Lambes, though in third class, was a group of ninety-five British women whose occupation was listed in the manifest as 'Domestics.' They were English, Scottish and Irish, whose ages ranged from 18 to 35, and all were bound for Winnipeg. Against each name was stamped 'Bonus Allowed Mrs Sanford', and therein lies the story of another group of immigrants. Mrs Sanford was Matron of the Girls' Home of Welcome in Winnipeg, where the women went until they found a job and a place to live. Mrs Sanford was associated with the Girls' Friendly Society that helped its members (mostly domestics and factory workers) to emigrate.

This was by no means the first occasion that parties of Mrs Sanford's had travelled in the *Empress*. That distinction belongs to a group of some eighty women who had booked on her maiden voyage in June 1906.

The *Empress*, with the Lambes and Mrs Sanford's party, arrived at 2:10 p.m. on Friday, 28 May, just an hour after *Corsican*, which meant that Immigration officials had to deal with almost 3,000 passengers. Things worked smoothly. An hour after the *Empress* arrived, her first class passengers departed by train, and second class followed soon after. Mrs Sanford's party and other third class passengers went through the usual arrival formalities and did not get away until the evening.

Weather for the passage had been fine, and passengers observed several icebergs but no field ice. The *Empress* was delayed two hours at Grosse Ile to land a couple of cases of measles.

Empire Day, 24 May, had been celebrated aboard the *Empress* in mid-ocean in grand style – in first class, at any rate. Captain Forster ordered the ship dressed with flags, and the first class saloon was decorated specially for the occasion. In first class, 'A most sumptuous dinner… was served and done ample justice to', and reflected the diversity of the British Empire:

Eggs Victoria   Olives   Sardines Territorial

———

Consomme Alexander   Potage Prince of Wales

———

Sole à l'London   Halibut à l'Ottawa

———

Grilled Lamb Cutlets à l'Australia
Chicken à l'South Africa

———

Roast Beef of Old England
Saddle of Mutton à l'Windsor
Goslin à la Asquith
Capon à la Chancellor

———

Grouse Edward VII

———

Empire Pudding
Devonshire Tart   Jelly St George
Killarney Tartlets   Pride o'Scotland
Royal Glaces

———

Rarebits à l'Wales

———

God Save the King

Dinner had been followed by a programme of entertainment, under the chairmanship of Senator Melvin Jones of Toronto. The *Chronicle* termed it 'excellent' and added '…many of the items being warmly applauded.' One of the evening's speakers was Colonel J.P. Grant, who spoke at length of the CPR and paid tribute to the Atlantic *Empresses*. The Colonel, who had made more than fifty crossings in the New York boats, claimed that the saloons of the CPR's *Empresses* were not excelled by any of the New York steamers, while second and third class in the *Empress* were far superior to any other. With unsolicited comments like those of Colonel Grant's, which later found their way into the press, the CPR management could worry less about the threat from *Laurentic* and the White Star-Dominion Line.

Richard B. Angus, a director of the CPR and president of the Bank of Montreal, then moved a vote of thanks to Captain Forster, his officers and crew for 'their unselfish endeavors to do all in their power to promote the comfort and well-being of all the people committed to their care.' The motion was carried by a standing vote and, following a vote of thanks to the evening's chairman, the programme came to a close.

Departing for Liverpool at 3:35 p.m. on 4 June, the *Empress* carried a distinguished passenger list that included Governor General Earl Grey and Finance Minister William Fielding. In honour of the Governor General, the *Empress* was bedecked with flags. Just before the first class gangway was removed, His Excellency expressed his admiration for the handsome style in which the ship had been dressed, and went on to complement the CPR on the arrangements made for the comfort and accommodation of its passengers.

One voyage later (38W), outbound from Liverpool, a passenger mailed a postcard which was off-loaded at Rimouski and postmarked on 25 June. He (or she) wrote:

Still in the same boat. Two more days and the long journey over. Had a lovely passage with the exception of [*word missing*] days seasickness. Love to all of you.

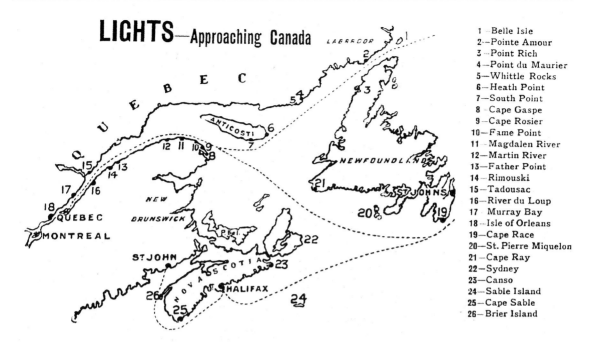

LIGHTS—Approaching Canada

1 — Belle Isle
2 — Pointe Amour
3 — Point Rich
4 — Point du Maurier
5 — Whittle Rocks
6 — Heath Point
7 — South Point
8 — Cape Gaspe
9 — Cape Rosier
10 — Fame Point
11 — Magdalen River
12 — Martin River
13 — Father Point
14 — Rimouski
15 — Tadousac
16 — River du Loup
17 — Murray Bay
18 — Isle of Orleans
19 — Cape Race
20 — St. Pierre Miquelon
21 — Cape Ray
22 — Sydney
23 — Canso
24 — Sable Island
25 — Cape Sable
26 — Brier Island

Lights – Approaching Canada, from the second class passenger list, 21 May 1909 (Voyage 37W). (Barry Lambe)

Perhaps the above passenger was too ill to have noticed the icebergs off the coasts of Newfoundland and Nova Scotia, for that summer was a particularly bad one for icebergs. Captain Clark of the Red Cross liner *Florizel*, which docked in New York, estimated there were more than a thousand 'bergs in the area, many 200 feet high and 1,000 feet long. The *Empress* herself radioed the following ice warnings:

49.00 N,	44.45 W,	two small bergs, several small pieces
46.00 N,	52.46 W,	numerous small pieces
46.43 N,	55.54 W,	one small berg.

Megantic, the latest addition to White Star-Dominion's fleet, also in the same area as the *Empress*, reported 'many large bergs.'

Once again the *Empress* made a fast trip from Liverpool, having left on 18 June at 8:00 p.m. Moderate weather and intervals of fog brought her to Rimouski in six days and eight hours. A thick fog between Rimouski and Quebec forced her to anchor for six hours, spoiling what was otherwise a fast crossing from port to port.

During the turnaround, the *Empress* soccer team played its final match of the season in the Quebec District Association Football League on 1 July. In order to win the trophy, the *Empress* team had to win or tie against the Garrison Artillery. A record crowd turned out, and even Captain Forster and several deck officers managed to find time before sailing to watch the late afternoon match, along with a number of officers from the garrison. It was the game of the season. The RCGA led 1-0 after 45 minutes of exciting play and, on resuming, the pace picked up, despite the wet field. The *Empress* team tied the game part way through the second half, only to have the RCGA score again. With just two minutes to go, the *Empress* tied the game, 2-2. The tying goal had been set up by steward Arthur Owen, the 'Empress Sharpshooter.' The tie gave the *Empress* team the one point they needed to clinch the championship of the six-team league. For the first time, the league cup would travel across the ocean. Of their ten games that season the *Empress* team won eight and drew two, giving them eighteen of a possible twenty points.

On the return trip, the *Empress* departed Quebec City for Liverpool on 2 July with 744 passengers – along with over four hundred hoarse crewmen and one soccer trophy. Other ships, like *Corsican*, departing Montreal on the second, and *Megantic*, sailing on the third from Montreal, all carried good numbers of passengers. *The Times* noted that 'a feature of this season's travel from Canadian ports is the large number of Americans from all part of the Western States who are travelling to Europe by way of the St Lawrence.'

Sir Sandford Fleming, who had first sailed in the *Empress* in August 1906, had an opportunity to renew old acquaintances aboard the vessel. In his pocket diary he recorded the following for the trip to England:

Fri., July 2	*Empress of Ireland* leaves Quebec today. Charlie and I sailed in *Empress of Ireland* The ship full of passe[n]g[er]s
Sat., July 3	At Rimouski
Sun., July	Fog nearly [*all*] day
Mon., July 5	Fog. Ice to the North Banks during the night
Tue., July 6	Almost a smooth sea
Wed., July 7	A fine passage so far – a good deal of fog. Horn blowing each night
Thu., July 8	Another nice warm day. Cleared up a little A great bundle of letters sent on board
Fri., July 9	Station at Liverpool

Earl Grey, the Governor General, returned to Canada in the *Empress* on 24 July after an extended trip to England. The Earl was no stranger to the ship, for he had first sailed in her in June 1907 with Prince Fushimi, and he had crossed to England in her again from 4-12 June 1909. That particular crossing had been so enjoyable that the Governor General decided to return to Canada in her, and he rearranged his schedule accordingly. The *Empress* left Liverpool on Friday, 16 July at 6:40 p.m., and made her fastest crossing of the season, using the Cape Race route, having encountered considerable hazy weather. Detained for an hour at Quarantine to disembark a family with measles, she nonetheless arrived in Canada just thirty minutes short of the record via Cape Race. Arriving at Quebec, the ship was dressed from stern to stem (man-o'-war fashion) in honour of the Governor General.

Earl Grey's home-coming to Canada was quiet and unofficial. There was no salute of guns from the Citadel, and just three men were on hand to meet him at the dock: the Chief Justice of Canada, Prime Minister Wilfrid Laurier, and the Lieutenant Governor of Quebec. On arriving, Grey stated his passage had been 'most agreeable.' In fact, during the voyage the Governor General had taken a great interest in the ship and her crew. Impressed by the athletic prowess of her crew, he was surprised to learn there was no field in Quebec City where the men could indulge in exercise without paying for it. At once, he headed a subscription list to provide funds for their expenses in this respect, a thoughtful and unexpected gesture that all crew members appreciated.

Death at sea could occur at any time and to anyone. When the *Empress* arrived at Quebec City she carried one less passenger, for 36-year old Henrietta McMillan had died of heart failure on Monday, 19 July. She was buried at sea, an event that cast a gloom over the vessel for the remainder of the trip. The manifest shows that George and Henrietta were in second class, accompanied by their two daughters and bound for Vancouver.

Concerts at the Seamen's Institute continued that summer, as they had in previous years, and the men of the *Empress* were welcomed performers. On Tuesday, 27 July the 'stewards of the *Empress of Ireland* proved themselves exceptional entertainers. The audience, though not nearly so large as the programme deserved, made up for any lack in numbers by the enthusiastic applause which they tendered the many excellent items. Encores were demanded repeatedly, and several of the performers were forced to reply more than once to the rounds of applause.' The reviewer for the Quebec *Chronicle* went on to single out some of the *Empress* performers. 'Mr Tunstall and Harry Thomson also received well-merited and unstinted praise. The former revived and inspired with new life and humor such songs as *The Lass o' Killiecrankie* and *Just Because She Made Those Goo-goo Eyes*, while his rendering of *Days of Old* and *Queer Questions* was well received. Harry Thomson sang *The Blind Boy* and *Sing Me to Sleep* in his clear, boyish voice, and was called back in both. Those who have not heard a sailor's concert of this kind certainly ought not to miss the next opportunity.'

Sporting events continued as well. On 29 July a cricket match, Quebec *vs.* the *Empress of Ireland* took place at the usual 4:00 p.m. time, and that evening the Stewards and Engineers fought to a 1-1 tie on the QAA grounds.

Sir Sandford Fleming's business in England concluded in such time that he and his wife could return to Canada in the *Empress* on 13 August, one of the few instances of a first class passenger making a return voyage in the ship. His diary provides some inkling to the voyage with a total of 1,327 passengers:

Fri., August 13	In the afternoon Charlie and I sailed in *Empress of Ireland*. Ethel my grand-daughter Uncle B and Cary saw us off
Sat., August 14	At sea. Many pleased passengers
Sun., August 15	At sea. Fine weather. Busy answer[ing] letters these days on the voyage
Mon., August 16	do.
Tue., August 17-18	do. Enter Straits of Belle Isle. No ice [on] sea – only a few bergs on busy day and beautiful smooth water on the Gulph [sic]. A little rain & fog afternoon.
Thu., August 19	Had about 20 letters to send ashore at Rimouski. Reached the Landing at Quebec just after dark about 7:45. Left by 11 p.m. train for Montreal.

The fog which Fleming glossed over was described by Captain Forster as 'thick as a hat' and was responsible for spoiling what otherwise would have been a record trip. So thick was the fog off Rimouski that the mail tender *Lady Evelyn* twice missed the *Empress*, although people on the tender could hear those on the liner talking. Transferring the mails thus took longer than usual, and there was intermittent fog from Rimouski to Cap Saumon. Two cases of measles had to be landed at Grosse Ile, causing a further delay of forty-five minutes.

Sandford Fleming returned to Canada in good company: a large number of delegates to the meeting of the British Society for the Advancement of Science, to be held in Winnipeg. And, in an ironic twist, also on board was E.C. Newcombe, Deputy Minister of Justice, who would be counsel for the Crown at the Mersey Inquiry, five years later.

If distress rockets had earlier provided a relatively harmless outlet for Arthur Owen's youthful energies, the following incident could well have had more serious consequences:

Around August 1909, my first month in the Officers' Mess, we were docked in Quebec and it was very hot. Four of us young Bell Boys decided we wanted to go for a trip on the St Lawrence if we could find a boat. There were always row boats anchored in the St Lawrence and this day we took one, a flat-bottomed French Canadian boat which was tied up to a barge in the basin. We started to row in the St Lawrence down to the Isle of Orleans. We did not realize we had a current behind us taking us down the St Lawrence. This was around 7:00 p.m. and thunder and lightning started so we decided to turn back but found that we were rowing two strokes and going back three owing to the current, so we decided to keep the bow into the waves as the St Lawrence was getting very rough and the waves were high. Naturally we drifted to the breakers off Montmorency Falls. We were actually thrown on them but managed to get off. At this time it was pitch dark when suddenly we came smack into something which we grabbed and it happened to be a yacht anchored to a buoy.

We climbed aboard then and went down to the hatch, took off our jackets which were soaked, then covered windows and lit the oil lamps. With the rough water one of the boys, Eric Stokes, became terribly sick. We had a job to keep him on board. We just sat in the cabin hoping the storm would abate.

At daybreak, we started to row back. We got nowhere owing to the tide; our hands were bleeding with the struggle to keep with the tide. It all seemed hopeless. We felt doomed and all shook hands and said our prayers and told each other what to tell our parents should we be saved and others lost.

After a struggle we got to Point Lévis. A French Canadian saw us and told us that the Coast Guard was looking for us. We decided to row back to the ship. The tide changed again and it was taking us back to where we were originally. We saw a lifeboat from the *Empress of Ireland* in the distance and it was the Second Officer [*Mansfield*] Steede and his crew out looking for us.

In the meantime a tug from Quebec was dispatched to look for us and they spotted us. They threw a lifeline and pulled us aboard. None of us were able to stand on our feet, we were so exhausted. They delivered us to the ship. The crew were watching and cheering for us as we came aboard, as they feared we had been lost as we had been away from the ship all night.

We were escorted aboard and told to go to the pantry, and get a good meal. I happened to be looking out of the porthole where the lifeboat was being hoisted. Officer Steede was in charge. When he saw me he called me an SOB and said if he had found us, he would have keel-hauled us all the way back to the ship. He was furious as it had caused considerable trouble as the ship was sailing that day.

After we sailed, around 4:00 p.m. and around the Isle of Orleans, Captain Forster called me to the bridge, gave me his binoculars and said, 'Where were you last night?' and I pointed it out to him. He said, 'You know, you have caused the CPR considerable expense, phone calls, tugs, etc. in the search for you boys. We shall deduct the expenses off your paysheet.'

As a young boy I had always turned my wages over to my Mother. This worried me that she would find out why my pay had been deducted. I asked Mr [*William*] Hughes, who was a friend of hers, not to tell her and he never did. He was saved when the *Empress* went down. Naturally I promised the Captain we would never do such a thing again and he said he would not deduct from our pay.

I told the boys and they were overjoyed.

On occasion the Breakwater at Quebec had witnessed late-arriving passengers frantically trying to get aboard the departing *Empress*. On 27 August there was a sensation as the *Empress* pulled away from her berth. All but one of the hawsers holding her to the dock had been let go when a man was seen running along the ship's deck. To the amazement of the large crowd of onlookers, he grasped the sole remaining hawser and, hand-over-hand, made his way down the thick rope. Helped onto the wharf, he was exhausted from his exertions.

When it was found that he was a member of the crew, and not some late-staying visitor, he was taken into custody by the police and charged with deserting his ship.

A passenger from that eastbound trip (Voyage 40E) wrote on 2 September: 'We are now off Ireland & expect to be at Liverpool early tomorrow. Had an excellent passage on a very comfortable boat. We only regret we have not seen more sunshine. It is very grey today.'

In the late summer of 1909 the wireless system aboard the *Empress* was upgraded with higher-power transmitters, giving it a greater transmission range than before. It was also about this time that both *Empresses* were equipped with electric masthead signaling apparatus, similar to the equipment adopted some years earlier by the Royal Navy with great success. The system was basically a simple one, consisting of an ordinary telegraph key, located on the bridge, and connected to an electric lantern on the masthead. The Morse system was used and, explained *Railway and Marine World*, '…the vessels are thus enabled to keep in communication with shore stations and report ice and weather conditions. This equipment, which is additional to the wireless telegraph installation already on these vessels, places the CPR steamships first among the vessels on the St Lawrence route as regards communication with the land.'

It was also about this time that captains of the CPR's Atlantic fleet began to supply newspapers and periodicals to the isolated wireless telegraph stations along the St Lawrence. During the navigation season, and depending on the voyage leg, papers from Montreal and Quebec, or Liverpool and London, were packed in barrels, to which a flag was attached, and thrown overboard.

Thus it was in September, eastbound to Liverpool from Quebec, while coming up to Point Amour at the western approach to the Strait of Belle Isle, Captain Forster ordered a sealed cask to be set afloat, containing the latest English and Canadian newspapers and magazines. On top floated a Union Jack for easy visibility. Alerted by wireless, the crew from the lonely, rock-bound Marconi station set off in a boat to retrieve the cask. Later, out of sight of land, John Forster was handed a message of thanks from the men at the wireless key.

In September 1909 the Allan Line's turbine-powered *Victorian*, arriving at Rimouski, set a new record for the Line, making a time of 5 days 18 hours between Liverpool and Rimouski. The record, noted in *Railway and Marine World*, was still considerably slower than the best time of the *Empress* at that time, 5 days 15 hours, set on 5 November 1908. The crew of the *Empress* could still hold their heads high with pride.

The westbound leg of Voyage 41 began on Friday, 10 September 1909 when the *Empress* swung down the Mersey with a total of 1,571 passengers on board. It would be the largest number of people landed at Quebec that year, a fact duly noted by the Canadian papers. The number of third class passengers, 943, caused some surprise as it was generally considered late in the season, when the tide of immigration had normally fallen off. The weather was generally unsettled with northwesterly winds through most of the crossing, and the ship encountered gale-like winds as she neared Belle Isle. Still, on the whole she made fast time, for the best day's run was 450 knots. Once in the Gulf, reporting in by wireless to Heath Point, she found good weather up to Rimouski.

Departing from Quebec on 24 September for the return leg, the *Empress* carried Rodolphe Lemieux, the Canadian Postmaster General, on his way to Berne for a meeting of the International Postal Convention, and thence to London to resume negotiations with the British government aimed at reducing cable rates.

Most *Empress* passengers would not have been aware of a bearded, elderly man who boarded, some-what unusually, in the mail tender at Rimouski, a privilege accorded to only a few. This was Lord Strathcona, Canadian High Commissioner in London. Strathcona had left Montreal by special train for Rimouski, and a large crowd of well-wishers, including the pipe band of the Royal Scots, had assembled at the Windsor St Station to bid him farewell.

Inbound from Liverpool the *Empress* encountered dense fog in the Gulf of St Lawrence on 13 October, near the conclusion of an otherwise routine run from Liverpool with 1,211 passengers. Fog at this time was nothing unusual and that morning at 9 o'clock she reported her position as inward of Point Amour, and that she expected to reach Rimouski the following afternoon. Haze and fog had hung in the area between the Straits and Anticosti for several days, causing delay to all incoming steamships.

Emerging from the fog, the *Empress* picked up speed, and headed into a fresh southwest wind.

On the 14th, Thursday, between Cape Chatte and Matane she was about two miles offshore and a mile off Roix Rock, an obstruction some 500 feet long and 400 feet wide. Making up for time lost in the Gulf, the *Empress* was moving fast. Allowing for headwind and current, Captain Forster estimated that her speed of $18\frac{1}{2}$ knots translated into 16 knots over the ground. At that rate, the *Empress* was two and a half hours away from picking up Pilot Bernier at Father Point.

Having left the bridge at 10:50 a.m., Forster was in his room, just off the chart room. Both were level with the bridge and his windows looked out onto the bridge, where the Second and Fifth Officers were in charge. Besides the two officers, the bridge watch which came on at 10:00 a.m. consisted of Quartermaster John Murphy at the wheel, a second QM, William Richards, and a bridge messenger.

Murphy, 43, had been a QM for twenty years and his time at sea also included eight years as an AB in the Royal Navy. Though he had joined the *Empress* just eighteen months before, he was possibly one of the best QMs on the St Lawrence route, and was said to be capable of steering the *Empress* to one degree accuracy. His is a name to remember. In a curious coincidence, Murphy was one of the QMs on the bridge of the *Empress* on the fatal night of 29 May 1914. In the crow's nest was able-bodied seaman Albert Giblan, who had also come on duty at 10:00 a.m.

The *Empress* at this point in her crossing, having consumed the major portion of her coal, was riding fairly high, and according to later testimony, was drawing $26\frac{1}{2}$ ft aft and 25ft forward. Then without warning, at 11:04 a.m., the *Empress* struck an object on the port side. The liner heeled slightly to starboard, accompanied by a rumbling and grating sound.

Captain Forster rushed to the bridge. 'What's the matter?' he barked at Second Officer Harry Waite. 'I do not know!'

'Is anything the matter below?' Forster demanded again, thinking a problem existed in the engine room. 'Port the helm,' he ordered, an order that would turn the ship to starboard, away from the shore. He countermanded that order almost at once, seeing that the *Empress* had already swung three points – about 33° – to starboard. 'Steady and keep your course.'

Third Officer Julian Duck entered the time of the collision in the scrap log. Later, the Chief Officer would make an appropriate entry in the regular log. On the bridge telegraph, the command 'Slow Ahead' was rung, although the engine room had already, on its own initiative, reduced speed.

'Take a bearing of Matane!' Forster ordered. Duck complied at once, taking cross bearings off Matane Lighthouse and the Ste Felicite Fog Station, while issuing his own orders to QM William Richards: 'Cast the lead.'

Sounding with the seven-pound lead was done from a platform at the after end of Lower Promenade deck. Richards reported no bottom up to the red mark indicating seventeen fathoms. Like most aboard the *Empress*, he was an experienced hand, with nine years as QM and two years in the *Empress*.

Duck later described the collision as 'a kind of grating rumble', a shock that came in jumps. Second Officer Harry Waite termed it 'a gentle shock. Something rubbing – it was not a violent shock.'

Saloon waiter Robert Fayle felt three light bumps, and then walked aft. Looking over the starboard propeller he glimpsed a piece of timber, some 18-20ft long. It was of light color, with one end broken and jagged, possibly a pine mast. Edward William Braine, a bedroom steward, also went up on deck. On the starboard side, close alongside the *Empress*, he saw a large piece of wooden wreckage, also about 20ft long, but dark in color. Other passengers at the rail saw fragments of wood on the port side which they then pointed out to him.

After the *Empress* cleared the obstruction, a hasty examination of the vessel took place. Chief Engineer William Sampson, whose first orders had been to close watertight doors and draw the fires,

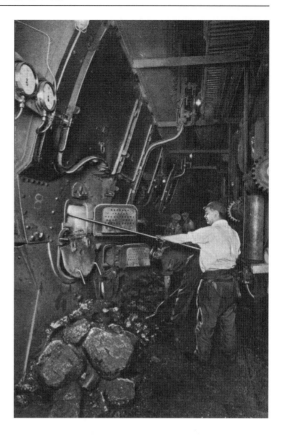

Boiler Room of the Empress of Britain, *c.1914. This is the only known authenticated photograph showing the boiler room of either of the* Empresses. *(David Saint-Pierre)*

discovered she was taking water in the No.1 and No.2 stoke holds, just forward of the boiler room. Officers' Steward Arthur Owen explained what happened next:

> She took on twenty feet of water in the forward stoke hole. How those men worked in the stoke hole to put out the fires under the boilers! They were exhausted and afterwards the Captain gave them all bottles of beer. I myself closed one of the watertight doors.
>
> There was panic among the foreigners aboard ship in third class but they were eventually quieted. We just limped into Quebec City into what they called 'The Basin.'

Once the situation had been stabilized, Forster telegraphed the CPR's office in Montreal to advise of the accident and the damage sustained. Forster ordered a notice to be posted, telling passengers to be ready, in the event it was decided to disembark them at Rimouski.

Playing it safe, the company telegraphed Forster to disembark all passengers at Rimouski, whereupon Forster wired back that the damage was not as great as had been first thought and that the ship was in no danger. Placated, the company allowed the mails to be off-loaded at Rimouski as usual. This process took an hour and a half, following which the *Empress* set off at 4:45 p.m. at a slow pace for the last leg to Quebec.

Superintendent Walsh, having taken a fast train from Quebec, boarded the *Empress* at Rimouski, along with the usual contingent of customs and baggage officials. On the 14th, rumors began to fly in Quebec City that the inbound *Empress* had either run aground or met with an accident. Questioned by the *Chronicle*, the CPR denied the rumor, stating the ship had met with no accident. A day later the truth could no longer be hidden. The Montreal *Gazette*, in reporting the story, observed that 'Captain Forster …is well-known on the St Lawrence route as a careful and skillful navigator.' The papers also offered their readers the suggestion that the obstruction 'must have been a submerged wreck of a schooner or lumber barge which came to grief during the equinoctial gales on the gulf during the past weeks.'

A portion of the 2,330ft Breakwater at Quebec, where the Empress *docked. The shed at left occupies the site of the former baggage shed. (Author)*

The CPR, putting on a brave face (a risky tactic in the absence of firm information), issued a statement by Fourth Vice-President George Bosworth that a diver would evaluate the damage once she arrived in Quebec. And, that the company believed the *Empress* would be able to leave as usual for the homeward passage to Liverpool on the following Friday.

It was not to be, for a variety of reasons.

The stricken ship arrived at Quebec at 4:40 a.m. on Friday, 15 October, and tied up at the Breakwater in its usual place. Passengers were landed as soon as possible, and then the marine specialists began to arrive. The tug *Cruizer*, summoned from Montreal, began pumping water from the No.2 compartment as soon as she had come alongside the wharf.

At five the following afternoon, to facilitate the inspection work by divers, the *Empress* was moved from the Breakwater into the outer, or tidal, portion of the Louise Basin, and she was moored at the Reford Wharf on the Basin's south side. Before the diver and his support team arrived, another problem was discovered. The hawsers had been overtightened, thus bringing the ship up tight against the wharf. While this may have been a security measure, to keep the ship as stable as possible while the divers inspected her, someone had forgotten that the steel oval step under each gangway door protruded six inches from the hull. As the tide ebbed, these oval steps snagged on the wharf, causing the liner to heel to starboard. Finally the iron steps slipped off the dock and the *Empress* rolled suddenly back to port. The portside hull scraped the wharf and the ship settled back on an even keel, though not before a few dishes in the dining saloons were broken.

At 6:00 p.m. dock workers began to remove the cargo, none of which had suffered any water damage. An hour later, after a hundred tons had been unloaded into Shed 19, the men stopped for the night. That same evening, 140 *Empress* stewards were sent back to Liverpool aboard the *Lake Erie*, whose master, ironically, was Frank Carey – first commander of the *Empress of Ireland*.

At 8:17 that night, a constable Mercier of No.10 police station on the Louise Embankment first noticed flames coming from a window of one of the conveyors leading from the Canadian Northern Railway grain elevators on the Pointe-à-Carcy pier. Mercier telephoned the nearby fire station and, eight minutes later, a second alarm was sent in. Even before the first firefighters arrived on the scene, the flames had made their way through the conveyor and into the elevator itself, containing 140,000 bushels of grain. A strong west wind fanned the flames, carrying sparks and cinders toward the river. It was soon evident that Shed 19 would be the next to go, posing a direct threat to the *Empress*.

The Lévis fire brigade from across the river managed to put a fire engine aboard the passenger steamer *South*, which helped fight the fire from the waterside, along with the government steamer *Lord Strathcona*.

Arthur Owen related, 'We on board ship had to keep the hoses played on the side of the ship. She became badly blistered because of the intense heat and portholes were cracked. We were in difficulty because we had no steam up owing to the damage below.'

Superintendent Walsh telephoned frantically for a tug. At length the tug *Belle* arrived and pulled the *Empress* away from the burning docks, assisted by the CPR's *Cruizer*, and over to the north side of the Basin. It was a timely move. Within a few minutes the fire reached the Reford Wharf. Shed 19, 450ft long and packed with 1,500 tons of bagged Scottish anthracite coal, lumber, provisions and general merchandise, was consumed, along with the elevator and almost everything else, including the police station. Spared, thanks to the Lévis firefighters, were the CPR sheds on the Breakwater and the adjacent immigration buildings on the Princess Louise Embankment.

And, fortunately, so was the *Empress*, in great part due to the skill of her officers and men, many of whom had been assisting the Quebec firemen on the Reford dock. The next morning, with small fires still smoldering on the dock, veteran diver Joseph Begin began his inspection of the *Empress*' hull. With twenty years' experience as a hard-hat diver, he knew his trade. Working in near-zero visibility and cold water for six consecutive days, Begin reported to the CPR that the major damage extended for about twenty-five feet in length on the port side, beginning some 40ft forward of the bridge on the third lap of the keel plate under the bilge keel, and that the garboard strake was also cracked and open, and that the rivets had been broken off.

In layman's terms, it meant that there was damage to the third range of hull plates on the left side, at the bilge keel. As well, the first range of steel plates (the garboard strake) next to the keel had been cracked, and that the rivets holding them together had been broken. Later, during the formal Inquiry, he stated, 'I never saw a ship damaged like that before.' Begin concluded that the damage sustained was caused not by a rock, but by the *Empress* having come in contact with submerged wreckage.

On the 18th, Begin succeeded in stopping some of the leaks. As pumping of the forward stokehold continued and the remaining cargo was unloaded, the *Empress* rose nearly two feet in the water, drawing something over 23ft forward.

With each day that passed, it became apparent that the *Empress* had been more severely damaged than previously imagined, and that she would not be able to sail to Liverpool as planned on Friday, the 22nd. The CPR then arranged to put the outbound *Empress* passengers aboard *Corsican*, also scheduled to leave the same day, along with the mails and some of the perishable freight.

It was also apparent that if permanent repairs were to be made, it would not be in Quebec City. The *Empress* was too wide to go into the city's only graving dock, and the nearest one that would accommodate her was in Halifax. Hearing the diver's report, and following inspection of the damage by naval engineers, the company decided to fill the puncture in the keel with a patch of cement and wooden wedges, a common and inexpensive way to make temporary repairs to vessels. Permanent repairs, it was further decided, would be done in England. The temporary patch was completed under the supervision of Jules Lepage, repair foreman for George T. Davie & Sons shipyard. George Davie himself took a personal interest in the repairs and visited the ship as work went on. Cement, three to four feet thick, depending on the location and extent of the damage, was poured into the damaged areas.

At the same time, diver Begin returned to work, inserting pine plugs to replace the broken rivet heads. The plugs would help keep out the water until the *Empress* could be drydocked.

Bosworth, the CPR vice-president, began an inquiry at Quebec on behalf of the company. It was a purely internal affair, with no official status. A formal Inquiry convened in Quebec on 26 October, with Capt. L.A. Demers, acting Wreck Commissioner, and aided by two Nautical Assessors, Capt. James Bain and Capt. Charles Von Koenig. At the first sitting, the panel heard testimony from Captain Forster, Second and Third Officers, the two QMs, lookout Albert Giblan, Chief Engineer William Sampson, along with diver Joseph Begin, pilot Adélard Bernier, and Superintendent John Walsh.

Questions were raised, not for the last time, in connection with the steering characteristics of the *Empress*, and the enlargement of her rudder two and a half years earlier. The allegations of poor steering were dismissed as unfounded.

Based on the preliminary evidence, the Canadian Minister of Marine and Fisheries ordered a survey of the area around Roix Rock, looking for the submerged wreckage which the *Empress* was presumed to have struck. The government ordered its steamer *La Canadienne*, under Commander I.B. Miles RN, to the Matane area. Miles, who had been with the department for four years, was in charge of surveying the lower St Lawrence. The survey began on 28 October, was interrupted by bad weather for two days, and wrapped up on the 31st. In that time, Miles surveyed a patch of water measuring 15 square miles, a rectangle centred on Roix Rock and extending $2\frac{1}{2}$ miles east and west, and $1\frac{1}{2}$ miles north and south. He found no obstruction, not even the slightest vestige of a submerged or sunken wreck, and observed that the soundings on the chart were exactly as represented.

The CPR, not content to leave the matter in the hands of the government and not having been invited to accompany Commander Miles, had meanwhile dispatched Capt. Murray to the same area as Commander Miles. Murray's team combed the area around Roix Shoal, presumably with the same result, though the outcome was never reported.

On the 27th, the *Empress* departed at 12:30 p.m., manned by a skeleton crew, headed for drydock in Liverpool. She carried no passengers, but had an ordinary cargo load. Arriving on 3 November, the *Gazette* noted that she 'has made a good run home.'

Arthur Owen's narrative continued:

> They decided… they would send the crew home and only return to England with a skeleton crew. I was one of that crew as I was a Steward and experienced in handling the officers.
>
> …It took us ten days to arrive in England and it was the calmest trip I had ever experienced since joining the ship. The ship was put in the Hercules Dock in Liverpool and when I went to have a look at the damage to her, had I seen the extent to the damage I don't think I would have appreciated having to go back to England in her. She was laid up for three months so I stayed at home.

Owen's account appears to be mistaken in two respects. The ship arrived in Liverpool on 3 November, after a trip of eight days. As well, he identifies the 'Hercules' [*i.e.* Herculaneum] dock in Liverpool as the destination of the *Empress*. In fact, she entered the Brocklebank Dock, one of the port's larger docks, with an area of 11 acres.

In Liverpool, the CPR had retained several consulting firms to examine the ship and submit their opinions on the nature and extent of the damage sustained, as it was important for the company (and its insurers) to determine whether the *Empress* had struck an uncharted rock or derelict. In general, their reports corresponded closely with that of the diver.

The Ministry of Marine and Fisheries also wanted its own independent survey. On 8 November the following cable was sent to the High Commissioner in London:

> Inquiry *Empress of Ireland* adjourned – vessel docked Liverpool – would Board of Trade examine vessel to ascertain cause of damage: rocks or derelict.
> (sgd) Brodeur

The High Commissioner, Lord Strathcona, contacted the Board of Trade's Marine Department on 10 November. The Board sent its reply to the High Commission on 29 November, noting that the damaged ship had been examined by a Surveyor at Liverpool. As the Board could not form a firm opinion on how the damage had occurred, it had secured the views of its Principal District Officer at Liverpool and its Principal Ship Surveyor, both of whom submitted typed reports which were later entered into the record.

Surveyor Thomas Miller wrote on the 19th, in part:

> From the appearance of the damage, which is of a particularly intermittent nature, the vessel must first have been struck on the port side of the bottom plating by two separately projecting objects; the one coming in contact with the landing edge between strakes B and C at a distance of 137 feet from the stem, and the other striking strakes E & F about 40 feet further aft. In each case the bottom, including frames and floors is set up and buckled and the platings scrubbed and slightly scored for a width of about two feet and a length of 78 feet in the case of B & C strakes, and a distance of 58 feet along strakes E & F. The damage at these points terminates gradually as if the vessel had heeled over to starboard and then rolling back again the same two objects again came into violent contact with the ship's bottom about 50 feet abaft midships, severely setting up and buckling the plating, frames and floors for a length of 29 feet along strake E and 74 feet along strake B the lower banding of strake C also being slightly affected.
>
> These two objects evidently did no further damage to the hull but another of the same nature must have come into contact with the bottom close up to the port side of the keel amidships severely buckling and setting up strake A for a length of 153 feet and the keel plate for almost the entire after half of its length. The keel plate was also broken longitudinally and burst in at places along the line of damage.
>
> The flat bar keel which is 11 inches wide and 3 inches deep was scored and worn away on the lower port corner for a length of 42 feet commencing at a point 108 feet from the after end, the bar for a length of 30 feet being tilted up on the port side through an angle of 15 degrees. The vessel then seems to have risen clear of the object for a length of 16 feet and to have struck it again sliding over it for the remaining 50 feet of the keel bar which was heavily scored and worn away on the port lower corner. The keelson was also buckled and set up and the keel bar at a distance of 50 feet from the after end was tilted up on the port side.
>
> On the starboard side B strake was set up slightly for a few feet in length abreast of a point about midway between the forward and after damage on the port side; this apparently being done when the vessel presumably rolled over to starboard. The only other damage so far as can be ascertained at present consists of the tips being broken off two blades of the port propeller.

Miller went on to consider the probable cause of the accident:

> Judging from the extent and nature of the damage it is very difficult to say what substance was struck and it seems hardly possible that the damage could be caused by the vessel passing over the submerged hull of a derelict vessel of ordinary construction, but the absence of deep scoring and fore and aft cutting and tearing of the plates which is usually found when vessels have stranded on rocks seems to preclude the possibility of the damage to this vessel being caused by passing over rocks unless they were of a very smooth boulder like surface.

The Board of Trade's Principal Officer at Liverpool, A.H.F. Young, concurred in the main with Miller's report, but disagreed with Miller's contention that the *Empress* had not hit a submerged wreck. Young believed that the evidence supported exactly the *opposite* conclusion. He said, in part, in his letter also dated 19 November:

> It seems to me that the very nature of the bursting in of the flat bar keel and keel plates in the after body is suggestive of the strong probability that the object struck was some substantial body in suspension such as a waterlogged timber ship. …Looking at the whole of the damage aft it is suggestive of an upward blow having been delivered by the sunken object rather than an ordinary case of a vessel striking.
>
> However after careful examination of the marking and scoring of plates I failed to find the least indication that the object struck was of a rocky nature.

David Archer, Principal Ship Surveyor, writing a week later, found it hard to reconcile this theory with the damage to the keel slab, which had been ground away for a depth of half an inch on the port side at the after end of the vessel. He concluded, 'I think the evidence is not conclusive either way but incline to the view that she struck a waterlogged iron vessel.'

The Inquiry sat for a second time at Quebec on 23 November, at which time Frederick Meredith, representing the CPR (and who would do so again in 1914 at the Mersey Inquiry), presented various affidavits from marine surveyors who had examined the hull at the graving dock. As well, there were two further witnesses from the *Empress*, saloon waiter Fayle and bedroom steward Braine, who described what they had felt and seen on the morning of the collision, corroborating written affidavits submitted previously.

Foreman Lepage from the Davie yard, who had overseen the temporary repair, testified that it was his opinion the *Empress* had struck a submerged wreck.

Meredith read into the record the 'Certificate of Survey' dated 11 November, submitted by George Hepburn & Son, Consulting Engineers and Naval Architects, whom he described as one of the best-known consulting firms in the world:

> We carefully examined the damage and in our opinion it has been caused by vessel striking submerged wreckage composed of Timber and Iron or other hard substance.
>
> The nature of the damage, and the fact that it is in five distinct patches, and that while there is a little local scoring in places, there is no scoring in other places where the worst damage occurs even to the bursting of heavy hull plates, indicates in our opinion that it must have been caused by something other than rocks which would have scored the plating and torn it open in continuous lines of damage, more particularly as the vessel at the time she met the obstruction was said to be travelling at about full speed.

The CPR was evidently eager to spend money on consultants, for the above opinion was also concurred in and signed by George R. Brace, an independent Surveyor, as well as by Edward C. Hill, a Surveyor to the Salvage Association and the Underwriters.

As if all this was not enough, the company had also engaged Messrs Flannery & Given, Consulting Engineers, for the same purpose. They submitted a lengthy report, dated 11 November, concluding that '…we are of the opinion that the vessel has passed over some submerged waterlogged, wooden derelict, as the absence of fore and aft continuous scoring indicates that the damage was not caused by passing over rocks or other fixed hard substances.'

Messrs H.&C. Grayson, Shipbuilders and Engineers, submitted a report on 12 November saying substantially the same thing and arriving at the same conclusion. Meredith's most interesting comments came in connection with two pieces of wood found in the ship's bottom, unconnected with the temporary repairs made at Quebec. One piece of wood had been found by Harry Mowatt, CPR's Marine Superintendent at Liverpool, and, in his Declaration, Mowat stated:

That I found on the port side of the ship wedged in the forward outer corner of the fifth butt strap of the keel plate counting from aft and between frames 64 and 65, a sliver of wood about five or five and one-half inches long. The butt strap was damaged and the forward outer corner sprung off.

Again, for the layman, a butt strap was a strip of steel plating that overlapped and held together two other adjacent plates whose edges butted together.

The second piece of wood had been found by George Herbert Butterworth, CPR's Superintendent Engineer and Dock Superintendent at Liverpool. In his Declaration, Butterworth stated:

That on the 9th day of November 1909 I made an examination of the S.S. *Empress of Ireland* in the Brocklebank Graving Dock, Liverpool.

That in the course of my examination I found in a fractured keel plate at frame 47 about 18 inches on the port side of the centre line of the ship a small piece of old wood jammed hard into the fracture in a fore and aft direction.

The pieces of wood proved to be conclusive.

At its third sitting, on 18 December, after hearing from Commander Miles the results of his survey, the Inquiry decided that, 'In view of the almost unanimous opinion of various experts who thoroughly examined the damaged hull of the *Empress of Ireland*, setting forth that said injuries were incurred by vessel coming in contact with the submerged hull of a derelict probably held in suspension, the Court is therefore of [the] opinion that no blame can be attached to anyone for the casualty.'

The presence of a half-submerged hulk might seem strange to the modern reader, but wreckage of this nature was common enough a century ago. The Saint John *Standard*'s Shipping News routinely featured Dangers to Navigation, with three or four such items each day. A typical item: Str *Ems* (Ger) from Emden, reports May 11, lat 46° 55' N, lon 30° 11' W, passed a large portion of a wooden vessel covered with marine growth and several smaller pieces of wreckage in the vicinity.'

In 1901 the steamer *Kildona* had met with a similar accident near the same place as the *Empress*, and just eleven months after the *Empress* had hit the wreckage, the CPR's *Montreal* signaled that there was such a wreck just to the west of Father Point. Though the Department of Marine at once followed up on the report, the results of the investigation are not known.

Faced with the temporary loss of one of its premier vessels, the CPR hastily arranged to charter the Allan's *Hesperian* while the *Empress* underwent repairs. *Hesperian*, a twin-screw vessel from the Stephen yard in Glasgow, had entered service just the year before and was a worthy, though somewhat slower, replacement for the *Empress*, since the Glasgow route did not require vessels of the same speed as the mail boats. That winter, the CPR arranged for further Allan charters, including *Corsican* and *Tunisian*, the railway having cancelled a number of its winter sailings.

When the *Empresses* were on the winter schedule to Saint John, special trains departed from Montreal's Windsor Street Station the day previous to the sailing. In the 1909-1910 winter season, there was no precise departure time and the CPR advised *Empress* passengers that departures could be anytime between 3 p.m. up to the time of the regular express to Saint John at 7:25 p.m. Early on the day of the train departure the company posted notices in the station to show when the special train would leave. CPR ticket agents were instructed to make sure passengers travelling through Montreal knew to look out for the posted departure time to Saint John.

The *Empress* remained in dry dock for three months to complete repairs before returning to service with a voyage to Saint John on 11 February 1910, by which time the twentieth century had entered its second decade. There was every reason to hope, and no reason to doubt, that the coming decade would be as successful and prosperous as the first.

5
Voyages II: 1910-1914

If some passengers were unlucky with respect to weather even in the summer months, there were others who enjoyed calm weather in the least likely time of year, mid-winter and the westbound run from Liverpool to Saint John. One such lucky passenger, whose name was Charlie and who probably travelled in first class, sent a postcard which was cancelled at Saint John on 19 March 1910. He wrote:

We had a grand voyage. The water was like a mill pond right away across. It was alright. There are nearly 1,400 passengers on board. We are winding up tonight with a grand farewell concert.

In fact, Charlie under-stated the passenger total. It was 1,491, an unusually large number for that time of the year, but 1910 was destined to be the best year to date for the *Empress* in terms of passenger totals in the westbound direction, with a total of 16,196, a record that would survive until 1913.

Nine-year-old Gladys French, in second class with her parents and their two other children, recalled the same unusual weather. Interviewed in March 2001, shortly after her hundredth birthday, she said, 'It was a remarkably good trip at that time of year, because we came in March and there were no rough seas. We children thoroughly enjoyed it. We did have a day when we were seasick …we weren't seasick very long.'

The family, headed to Kelowna, British Columbia, from Sussex, shared a 'big cabin. The way I remember it,' she said, 'it was all bunk beds. And so we all had a bed to ourselves.' When asked about the food, she admitted with a laugh, 'The day we were feeling a bit seasick, nothing looked good to us.'

On the return leg of that voyage, the forty-fourth, sailing from Saint John on 26 March 1910, the *Empress* established a dubious career record for the least number of passengers carried: just 300, with 39 in first class, 58 in second and 203 in third. Of the two sister Atlantic *Empresses*, the *Empress of Britain* had a pre-war career low of 276 passengers, departing Saint John on 26 February 1909.

Passengers departing from Saint John on that March day must have been surprised to find themselves outnumbered by the crew, who perhaps relished the tranquillity as a time to catch up on needed cleaning and other tasks. Service, always good, would have been even more attentive than usual.

Emigrants who travelled to Canada in groups were nothing new, but the *Empress* crew would have taken special note of a group of over a hundred boys who boarded the ship in Liverpool on 8 April bound for Saint John. The boys, all in third class, were from Mr Fegan's Boys Home, and ranged in age from 9 to 17. It was the only Fegan group of the year and, according to the manifest, they were headed for the Toronto region where they would find farming positions in foster homes. James William Fegan, the philanthropist and founder of the programme was also aboard, though he travelled in first class. Known as 'Fegan of Deptford' for his work among the impoverished youth of this section of the British capital, Fegan had established receiving homes in Brandon and Toronto for the children he brought to Canada. Fegan was a man who did not believe in sending his boys to Canada un-prepared. On a farming estate of eighty-four acres at Goudhurst in Kent, he provided appropriate training to the city boys destined to Canada, where they learned farming by Canadian methods, planting Canadian crops and using Canadian implements.

Like some other emigrant groups, Fegan's boys were encouraged to repay the cost of the passage, so that others in turn could come to Canada. To give 'some lad left behind the same good chance in life', was the way one grateful Fegan boy put it. The ticket, which cost fifty dollars, was almost exactly the annual wage for a boy of fourteen who was placed on a farm.

In the December 1910 issue of *Loving and Serving*, the journal of Mr Fegan's Homes, James Fegan described his trip in the *Empress*:

> The voyage to Canada was a very favourable one as regards weather. The arrangements made by the Canadian Pacific Railway both on sea and shore were most satisfactory.
>
> It may be well for me to explain here that with each party of boys over a certain number, free transit, to and fro, is granted by both the steamship and railway companies concerned to the person or persons travelling in charge according to the size of the party. I went in personal charge of this party and therefore had free passes out and back both on ship and train.
>
> It is not in any sense 'a holiday' to take charge of such a party on such a long journey, especially as one's assistant is generally 'under the weather' for the best part of the voyage – and very few of the boys escape sea-sickness. It may be a labour of love, but it is no pleasant experience to be down amongst a large number of sea-sick boys and no light task to get them–some hardly able to stand, and others utterly helpless – up on deck, and comfortably settled on a crowded ship – and encourage them to face their meals time after time.
>
> …the voyage affords me very special opportunities of spiritual ministry of which I seek to take advantage to the fullest extent, and on my last trip held services on deck or between decks twice a day.
>
> We left Liverpool on Friday … and on the Sunday evening very few of our boys were able to attend the evening service I had arranged in the Third Class Dining Saloon, but I was surprised to find such a good attendance of the steerage passengers and the staff, although many of the former were hardly able to hold up their heads.
>
> At the close a bright, pleasant woman came up to me and said, 'You don't remember me, I suppose, Mr Fegan, I'm Mrs —. When I was a widow in deep difficulties you took my boy. I am going out to him now. I am married again and he has sent the money for me and my husband and our boy to come out to him. He has his own farm and has got a home built and furnished to receive us.'
>
> I thought it would cheer the many anxious and depressed ones before me to hear such an interesting story, so I just, on the spur of the moment, introduced her to the gathering and she very happily told them of her son's success and goodness. The effect was magical. The whole crowd brightened up, and Mrs — sat down amidst hearty clapping and was soon the centre of warm congratulations.
>
> … We made a very rapid passage to St John, N.B. The Canadian Pacific Railway filled the train to which our reserved carriages were attached first of all and rushed us as 'a special' right through to Toronto, not even running into Montreal. …Of course the railway journey is a very tiring experience. The seats are just hard boards – the trains jolt a great deal more than our own – the brakemen pass through the carriages continually slamming the doors with all their might … but the only thing in a Colonist Car to do is bear the inconvenience and weariness and be thankful it is all only for twenty-four hours to Toronto and not for six days or so to British Columbia.
>
> In a few days the boys were all drafted off to their new homes.

By coincidence, George Bogue Smart, longtime Chief Inspector of British Immigrant Children and Receiving Homes for the Canadian Department of the Interior, inspected the Fegan Home on George Street in Toronto shortly after the boys had arrived. In his report to the government, Smart mentioned meeting Fegan himself, and commented: 'They were a fine, bright lot of boys, well clad and suitably outfitted for farm life and work. I was pleased to note that they were all inculcated with the idea that farming was to be their future occupation. Mr Fegan advised me that they were to be apprenticed only with approved farmers, many of whom had received in previous years his boys, who had now out-grown their minority and were doing for themselves. The characters and dispositions of these young immigrants were known to Mr Fegan before their selection for Canada, and he looked forward with confidence to their success in the Dominion.'

A year later, Smart could report to his superiors that fully 95 percent of the boys had rehired with their old employers for another year. This was a measure of the programme's success, for the boys had the option of changing if they wished.

Smart's work often took him to England. He appears to have been a regular CPR customer and always travelled in first class. It is one of life's ironies that on 28 May 1914 he embarked from Quebec in the *Empress of Ireland*. One of the thirty-six survivors in first class, he later testified at the Mersey Inquiry.

On the Fegan voyage the *Empress* made a particularly fast stop at Halifax. The Montreal *Gazette* noted that she had arrived at Halifax at 11:40 a.m. and had sailed for Saint John at 12:35 p.m. The manifest revealed also that an unnamed infant died during the voyage.

Arriving at Quebec on 13 May (Voyage 46W) via the Cape Race route, Captain Forster reported a fast and uneventful passage for the first trip of the season to Quebec, apart from fog in the ice track, which caused a delay of three hours. Perhaps the most remarkable feature of the trip was the speed with which the 190 first class passengers were disembarked and sent on their way. 'Eleven minutes after the *Empress* was moored,' recorded the *Chronicle*, 'a special train with the saloon passengers and their baggage, and having Sir Thomas Shaughnessy's private car attached, left for the west.' Among the 190 in first class had been Lady Shaughnessy and two of her children.

Second class passengers were also fortunate; their train got away fifty minutes later.

A postcard cancelled at Rimouski on 27 May tells us something about Captain John Forster:

> The Captain of this ship has a tame canary which he keeps in his pocket & it never thinks of flying away.

On 3 June 1910 a sleeping five-year-old Scottish girl, Mary Hill, was carried aboard the *Empress* in Liverpool by her parents, John and Elizabeth. John, forty-eight, a tenant farmer in Scotland, was determined to move to Canada so he could own a farm of his own. Along with Mary, the Hills brought their second daughter, Jane, two years older than Mary; their eldest, Lizzie, 17, had already left for a new life in the United States. The family travelled with only a couple of trunks, containing a few family treasures and photos. Only chance had brought the Hills aboard the *Empress*: she happened to be the next boat going to Canada.

The *Empress* began her 47th voyage at 6:30 p.m., pulled out into the Mersey by the usual tugs. Though first class contained only 173 passengers, second class held 442 persons, while third class fairly bulged at the seams with 982 people, which would be the highest number for the year. Of the 1,597 passengers, there were 236 children and 134 infants, the bulk of the children and infants being in third class.

Travelling second class, the family was broken up for the voyage, as only two berths had been paid for. That was a common enough situation. Elizabeth Hill got one berth; Mary and Jane were small enough to share a berth. The remaining berths in the cabin were assigned to two other women. John Hill bunked with other men in a second class cabin and spent the daytime hours with his family.

For a five-year-old, it was a grand adventure. Ninety years later Mary (Hill) McCullough recalled some of the aspects of her trip. The memories were still fresh, undimmed by time:

> It was quite a delight for my sister and I to go and sit down where we wouldn't be hardly seen and watch those fancy [*first class*] ladies all dressed up with their fancy gowns on.
> We got down at the end of the stairs… If you behaved yourself, and sat nice and quiet

LOVING AND SERVING. 9

As soon as a lad is able to pay for board, lodging, &c., in some respectable family, he will be placed out in this way and thus a vacancy be created to help another lad on in life.

We shall also help any lads who may

£539 15 0 **Still Needed for Proposal II.** Now I want to ask my readers if this Proposal II. commends itself to their judgment as kind and helpful and economical. Then I want to explain that in my estimates it was set down for £1,650 altogether, that

EUSTON STATION.

eventually seem eligible to emigrate on the understanding that they will, as speedily as possible, honourably repay the cost of their emigration.

in gifts and promises we have just £1,110 5 0 in hand, and therefore still need £539 15 0 to make up the entire cost.

* * * *

* * * *

LOVING AND SERVING. 11

We left Liverpool on Friday, 9th April, and on the Sunday evening very few of our boys were able to attend the evening service I had arranged in the Third Class Dining Saloon, but I was surprised to find such a good attendance of the steerage passengers and the staff, although many of the former were hardly able to hold up their heads.

An interesting Story. At the close a bright, pleasant woman came up to me and said,

"You don't remember me I suppose, Mr. "Fegan, I'm Mrs.——. When I was a widow "in deep difficulties you took my boy. I am "going out to him now. I am married again and "he has sent the money for me and my husband

SERVICE ON DECK.

Left: *Future Canadians: emigrant boys from Mr Fegan's Boys Home, waiting for the Empress Boat Train, Euston Station, 8 April 1910 (Voyage 45W). 'They were a fine, bright lots of boys...' – George Smart (Fegans). Right: Service on the deck of the* Empress of Ireland *(Voyage 45W), conducted by J.W. Fegan. '... on my last trip held services on deck or between decks twice a day ...'. Note the fog bell on the forward mast. (Fegan)*

there, and didn't say anything, you could watch them. We didn't talk, because…mother had told us, 'Don't make a sound and they'll not see you.' We would talk about the dresses, because they were elegant. They were…first class and they were dressed to sit at the captain's table that night. Then the next night he had different ladies and gentlemen, and, of course, the gentlemen were all dressed up with those cutaway coats.

At one point, the *Empress* passed an eastbound vessel, most likely the *Empress of Britain*, which had left Quebec City on 3 June. Mary related: 'We happened to be up on deck and this ship was coming. [W]hen we were passing, they blew the whistles…and the other ship answered him.'

Though 249 children and infants were on board, the two Hill children were not allowed to play with them. 'We were people that sort of kept to ourselves,' Mary explained.

There's one thing I will never forget, the sight of the icebergs. …the purser or whatever you call them, came down and said, 'Come up on deck! We're in the icebergs!' Of course, I didn't know that nine-tenths of that iceberg was below the water…because it was such a big sight of ice, and there was more than one. We were in the iceberg field and everybody was coming up on deck to see the icebergs, never thinking that if you hit one of those…

The icebergs made such an impression that she told the author, 'I don't even have to close my eyes… they're floating by, behind you.'

As the author knows from personal experience, 747 captains will sometimes call the attention of westbound passengers to the icefields in the North Atlantic. From 38,000 feet they are tiny diamonds against a blue sea. At sea level they must be awe-inspiring.

> Anytime I was up on deck, I never went near the rail. That was too close to the water. When you looked as far as you looked this way or that way, you couldn't see anything – only water. It was such a vast expanse of water for a little kid to look at…
>
> …one night I woke to the sound of the purser saying, 'Oh, Mary, you've wet the bed.' And I knew *I* hadn't wet the bed. Apparently in the night time the wind got up and Mary that slept in the top bunk – one of the two ladies – she had the porthole. The waves started coming in…the porthole, and she had called for the purser to come, 'cause she couldn't close it, and that was how her bed got wet.
>
> They had to bring in fresh, dry bedding. The mattress and everything was wet.
>
> …the food was okay. But we were used to plain food. We were used to our oatmeal porridge in the morning.
>
> Mother was [sea]-sick. In fact, I think mother got sick before us kids. Mother had taken the top bunk when we got sick. [*The steward*] was very good to us when we were sick. That's when he brought in the…picture books…crayons and books and things like that. You see, you didn't pack an awful lot of stuff to entertain you on the way, because you [*were*] only allowed so much.
>
> I had a white furry coat…I remember mother giving me half an orange to eat up on deck, and I no sooner got it down than I threw it back up, and it dribbled down my white coat, and I remember crying about that part.
>
> …[*W*]e stopped at a place, I think the name was Rimouski, and some of them had to go off in quarantine.

The *Empress* docked in Quebec at 5:30 in the afternoon of 9 June, three days after Mary's sister had celebrated her birthday aboard the ship. Once the first class passengers had disembarked, second class travellers were allowed off. There was the usual rush of people who wanted to feel solid ground under their feet once again. Mary recalled:

> …[*W*]hen we were coming off the boat, I walked down the gangway part way, and I guess I wasn't walking fast enough, and somebody picked me up and carried me off. I remember I looked back after we got off and saw that it was just as big as the boat that sailed past us. But…when you're on it, you don't see the bigness of it.

The *Gazette*, in Montreal, as usual, followed the ship's progress up the Gulf, once she was in wireless range of the shore stations. Coverage began on 9 June, under a column titled '*Empress of Ireland* Making Fast Run.' Reporting in by wireless, the ship was 118 miles east of Fame Point at 2:30 p.m. on 8 June, and the *Gazette* offered the opinion that she would dock at Quebec that night. It continued: 'The *Empress of Ireland* came through the Straits of Belle Isle and now that the northern shortcut is being used by passenger vessels the competition for fast passages will grow apace,' and added, 'The passenger list in all departments being a bumper one.'

Slowed down for two hours by fog in the Gulf of St Lawrence, the *Empress* did not succeed in breaking her old record.

On 10 June, the paper's readers were informed that Mayor Guerin and an alderman, Montreal's official delegates to the funeral of Edward VII, had returned to the city on the special *Empress* train at 12:24 a.m. Once further details of the trip were available, coverage continued the following day. In an item headed '*Ireland*'s Fast Run – Record for the Season', readers learned that:

> The *Ireland* left Liverpool at 6'oclock on Friday evening and was reported off Belle Isle early this week, being the first *Empress* to make the northern passage inwards this season. Her progress up the Gulf and lower river was made at a speed averaging over 18 knots, reaching Rimouski at 7 a.m. yesterday. Quick work was done discharging the heavy mail and before 9 o'clock the *Empress* was steaming on the last lap of the voyage to Quebec. She swung into her berth at the breakwater at 6 o'clock and shortly before seven the first special with the saloon passengers pulled out from the ship's side, reaching the Windsor Station at midnight.

The paper offered the opinion that the ship's fast passage and a capacity list of passengers so early in the season would mean some new records for the St Lawrence before the close of navigation.

There was also an interesting observation on the rivalry between the masters of the twin sisters: 'The fight between Captain Murray of the *Britain* and Captain Forster of the *Ireland* for the season's blue ribbon promises to be particularly keen this year. The *Empress of Britain* has made an excellent run, arriving in Liverpool from Quebec. Both the CPR flyers appear to be tuned up for the season and something interesting in the shape of record passages is looked for during the summer.'

Mail was a topic of interest to the general public and to the CPR management, which needed to impress the Post Office with the performance of the company's vessels. The shipping page article touched on the subject of mails as follows:

> As a result of the splendid run of the *Empress of Ireland*, the English mails which left Liverpool at 6 o'clock last Friday reached the Bonaventure station at 10 o'clock last night and will be delivered both in the city and in Toronto by the first of the morning today. This is far and away the best performance of the season and means that letters posted in Euston Station last Friday at noon are today lying on the breakfast tables of Montrealers and Torontonians, having taken considerably less than seven days. The CPR flier, even at this early stage of the season, seems likely to hold the record for quick mail carrying which she won last year.

John Hill, the aspiring landowner who described himself as a 'farmer' in the manifest for the 3 June sailing, got his wish. In his adopted country, under the British flag he was loath to abandon, he soon found a job on a farm after the family arrived in Winnipeg and, in a few years, the family bought its own farm. The Hills saved the second class passenger list showing their names. As she grew up, Mary would often take out the list, like a talisman, and recall their trip. 'In there,' she said, 'I could read 'John Hill' and 'Elizabeth Hill' and 'Jane Hill' and 'Mary Hill.' It was my delight to read my name in there and know I had come over from another country. I used to tell the kids at school, 'Oh, I came over on the *Empress of Ireland*.' But it didn't mean anything to them. Their people were born here.'

On 15 June, while the *Empress* was in Quebec and making ready to return to Liverpool, the steamer *Royal Edward* of the Canadian Northern Railway arrived in Quebec City from Bristol, setting a new port-to-port record for the westbound trip of 5 days, 23 hours, and thirty minutes, thus breaking the *Empress of Ireland*'s record of 6 days, 1 hour and forty-five minutes. Though nothing was said officially, every *Empress* crew member knew their captain would do whatever was necessary to regain the title. And, that he had the full support and encouragement of the CPR, which would not lightly be upstaged by a competing railroad.

Inbound from Liverpool on 6 July, Captain Forster reported by wireless that he had experienced hazy weather but no ice east of Belle Isle, though he had found four icebergs on the north shore and one on the south shore thirteen miles east of Cape Norman, at the eastern end of the Strait. The departure of the *Empress* from Liverpool had been somewhat unusual. Owing to very heavy weather, it had proven impossible to land the pilot outside the Bar, the normal practice, and the *Empress* had been obliged to proceed to Point Lynas off the Welsh coast to put him ashore.

Arriving at Quebec on 7 July at 7:00 p.m., first and second class passengers were landed almost immediately, and their trains departed for Montreal. The 965 third class passengers remained on board and were not disembarked until the following morning. As in previous summers, concerts at the Sailors' Institute were held on an occasional basis. It was through the medium of competitive sports that the crew of the *Empress* was brought into closer contact with the community of Quebec.

Two events made the local paper that week. On Wednesday the thirteenth, the first annual *Empress of Ireland* sports meeting was held, 'and proved a great success in every way.' The day's highlight was the tug-of-war, where eight engineers gained an unexpected victory over the stewards, each of the winners being awarded a briar pipe for his efforts. Events included the quarter-mile (open to officers, engineers and heads of departments), 220- and 100-yard races, and various novelty events like a sack race, three-legged race and an obstacle race. The *Chronicle*, which devoted considerable space to the event, summarized: '...the events proved that the *Empress* men have some very good talent among them, which would put up a respectable showing with the best company.' In the Boys' race, young steward Arthur Owen took first place, winning a silver keyless watch.

The next day at 4:00 p.m. the two *Empress* soccer teams met on the grounds of the Quebec Athletic Association. In what was termed a 'good' match, the Stewards defeated the Engineers 3-1, all three goals for the stewards being scored by the tall, slender centre forward Arthur Owen, whose story we have been following. Having scored eight goals the previous Monday against the team from the Chateau Frontenac, Owen was now being called the 'Empress Sharpshooter' in the *Chronicle*.

Departure, on Friday the fifteenth, must have seemed an anti-climax to the men and women of the *Empress*.

For years the CPR had promoted the St Lawrence route as an alternative to the New York route, hoping to attract passengers from the American midwest. By the summer of 1910 it appeared as though the company's efforts had at last borne fruit. In early July the *Gazette* noted with approval that the majority of the passengers aboard the CPR's *Lake Champlain*, bound to Liverpool from Montreal, were from the United States. 'The CPR,' the paper observed, 'would seem to have solved the mystery of how to attract the American tourist, and in spite of the fact that the New York vessels are both speedier and far more ornate than anything they have as yet been able to offer, the fact remains that the St Lawrence route is today getting quite a hundred per cent... more traffic from the American side than was the case last year.'

The CPR, of course, was not the only beneficiary. The paper noted a few days later that the Allan's Glasgow-bound *Pretorian* carried 147 cabin passengers, of whom 111 were Americans.

An item from the shipping news of the Montreal *Gazette* of 15 July 1910 shows how appealing international travel was to young Americans.

> Sailing on the *Empress of Ireland* today, from Quebec, is a party of youths, who, banded together under the cognomen of the American Boys' Touring Club, are bent on seeing as much of England and the Continent in as short as time and at as small a cost as may be possible. They number fifteen and in point of age vary from 13 to 22 years, while they have a guide and friend travelling with them in the person of Mr G.A. Rieder. The club is composed almost exclusively of Chicago youths and is promoted by the YMCA of that city. They have planned to take in, amongst other items of interest which are going on in Europe this summer, the Passion Play at Oberammergau, and they will be away altog-ether for about seven weeks. The passed through the city yesterday and left on the afternoon train for Quebec, which they will explore before the boat sails.

Intense pressure on the North Atlantic route helped to keep passage rates competitive. In the summer of 1910, with no fewer than eight lines carrying passengers to Montreal or Quebec, second class aboard the *Empress* was $51.25 and up. Second class in the Allan's turbine ships *Virginian* and *Victorian* was $50.00 and up. While still reasonable, prices had crept upward in the four years since the *Empresses* had started service. Second class *Empress* tickets had risen from $45.00 in 1906, while second class in the Allan boats had increased from $42.50.

Despite the price hikes, the summer of 1910 was an excellent one for all the passenger lines in eastern Canada. Ships were booked weeks in advance with tourists returning from Europe, and the CPR boats were almost fully booked as the summer came to a close.

After Rudyard Kipling and Guglielmo Marconi, the next most famous passenger carried by the *Empress* was Lt-Gen. Sir Robert Baden-Powell, hero of Mafeking in the Boer War, though he is now best remembered as the founder of the Scout movement. Baden-Powell arrived in Quebec on 4 August accompanied by sixteen Scouts to promote scouting in Canada.

The siege of Mafeking, lasting from 13 October 1899 to 17 May 1900, was one of the turning points of the Boer War and gave Britain a much-needed moral victory. Mafeking, a city of no strategic importance on the Transvaal-Bechuanaland border, had been defended by a British garrison of 745 and 450 irregulars, under the command of then-Colonel Baden-Powell. Besieged by a force of some ten thousand Boers, Baden-Powell's real achievement lay in tying up so many Boers at a critical period of the war. His energetic and imaginative defensive tactics made him a national hero in Britain.

The General evidently used his time aboard the *Empress* to relax. The only entries in his daily journal for the voyage are laconic: 'At sea.' Baden-Powell travelled simply and without ceremony. The manifest showed him simply as 'Robert Baden-Powell.' When interviewed by the *Gazette*, the tanned and fit-looking general was standing at the gangway of the *Empress*, watching his contingent of scouts preparing their kit and retrieving bags from the hold. 'Look at that,' he commented with evident pride. 'Is not that a justification of my movement? You see how quickly and carefully and methodically they do their work compared to the dock labourers.'

Baden-Powell and his scouts returned to England aboard the White Star Line's *Arabic* in early October, their mission to Canada a success.

On this particular crossing, the *Empress* had enjoyed good weather conditions and set a new record for the land-to-land (Tory Island to Belle Isle) passage, which the newspapers liked to quote, of three days and eighteen hours. The *Daily Star* noted that Captain Forster had been 'heartily congratulated on the ship's fine performance' by the company's management. 'In the run from land to land,' the *Chronicle* claimed, 'she is far ahead of all compeers on the western run.' Daily runs to noon each day were: Saturday, 326; Sunday, 459; Monday, 460; Tuesday, 456; Wednesday, 460; Thursday, 312.

The *Empress* had arrived at Rimouski at 4:14 a.m. on the 4th and transferred her mails (1,816 bags), along with at least one first class passenger. As always, the CPR was willing to accommodate a certain class of people, and allowed Charles Marcil, the MP for the Bonaventure riding, to disembark. She left Rimouski at 5:40 a.m. and made a good passage up the river to Quebec and docked at 2:30 p.m. Even the docking was fast, taking just fifteen minutes and breaking the record of the *Empress of Britain* by three minutes.

Three special trains were required; the first, for first class passengers arrived in Montreal at 9:00 p.m., followed by two more, for second and third class passengers. Arthur Piers, the CPR's Liverpool-based steamships manger was also on board, making one of his periodic voyages to Canada, and no doubt profiting from his voyage in the *Empress* to judge the state of the company's Atlantic *Empress* service and the degree of customer satisfaction.

First class also carried a number of other persons of some importance. One of these was thirty-nine-year-old Alexander Edward Murray, 8th Earl of Dunmore, identified in the manifest as 'Alexander Ed. Earl of Dunmore.' He was described as 'TOURIST' and listed Winnipeg as his destination in Canada. Though a retired captain of the Scots Guards, he is the third VC known to have travelled in the *Empress*.

Delegates to the Eucharistic Congress, August 1910 (Voyage 50W). Left, Irish-born Rt Revd H. MacSherry, Bishop of Port Elizabeth (South Africa); right, Cardinal Vincenzo Vannutelli, legate of Pius X. (Sheila Taipale)

He had won the Victoria Cross in 1897 in Afghanistan when, as a Lieutenant in the 16th Lancers, he had gone to the rescue of a wounded officer of the Lancashire Fusiliers.

The westbound land-to-land record of the *Empress* did not last long. Her new nemesis, *Royal Edward*, set a new mark on 10 August of three days and sixteen hours, two hours faster than the *Empress*, and also broke the Britain-to-Canada record by five hours. It was a notable achievement, especially given that the distance from Bristol to Quebec was forty-two miles greater than Liverpool to Quebec.

The westbound leg of the *Empress'* fiftieth voyage set a record in terms of passengers, 1,606, a record that would stand for the balance of her career. Many on this crossing were coming to Canada to attend the 21st International Eucharistic Congress, which was to take place in Montreal from 7-11 September. It was the first Congress to be held outside Europe, and first class in the *Empress* was nearly filled with Europeans headed to the event. The manifest shows that titles such as 'Clergyman', 'Abbot', 'Priest', 'Bishop' and 'Cardinal' are appended to a score of names.

On leaving Liverpool the *Empress* had again encountered a fierce gale, and the ship had once more been obliged to detour to North Wales to land the pilot. After that the weather had been fine and clear all the way to Rimouski, where the *Empress* arrived at 6:45 a.m. on 1 September. After dropping off the mails, along with eight first class and seven second class passengers, the *Empress* departed at 7:15 for Quebec.

At Rimouski, Archbishop Paul Bruchesi of Montreal boarded the *Empress* in order to greet one of the first class passengers. His Eminence Vincenzo Vannutelli, Cardinal-Bishop of Palestrina and the legate of Pius X, was the most notable of the distinguished passengers in first class. Vannutelli, seventy-three, was the Holy See's foremost diplomat, one of the most widely travelled and respected princes of the Church. In his honour the Papal flag flew at the *Empress'* fore-truck and she was gaily decorated with flags. All the way up to Quebec, from both sides of the river, the *Empress* was saluted by church bells, waving flags and cheering people. Lightships and other vessels were dressed with flags in honour of the man who would preside over the forthcoming Congress. The Breakwater and other vantage points like Dufferin Terrace were thronged as the *Empress* drew alongside and moored at 3:30 p.m.

Every ship in the harbour was 'dressed' with flags and their whistles added to the noisy welcome. On the Upper Bridge stood the Cardinal and other distinguished prelates, a courtesy extended to them by Captain Forster. The Cardinal, who stood head and shoulders above most men, bowed repeatedly to the assembled crowds, acknowledging their cheers.

Once the *Empress* was secured, the CGS *Lady Grey* came alongside and a gangway was lowered between the two vessels. At the top of the gangway stood Captain Forster and John Walsh, to bid farewell to the Cardinal and his entourage of two secretaries and a valet, along with other distinguished clerics. As the Cardinal Legate left the *Empress*, the papal flag was hauled down and replaced with the Canadian ensign. Once aboard *Lady Grey* the Cardinal was officially welcomed by two government ministers. The formal ceremony of welcome took place at King's Wharf, where an enthusiastic crowd of 20,000, along with civic officials, Papal Zouaves, the band of the Garrison Artillery, bishops and other church dignitaries waited. There was no doubting the sincerity of the welcome. Over five hundred Canadians had fought as Zouaves in 1869 to defend the Papal States against Garibaldi and the *Risorgimento*, and Vannutelli himself had been in the front lines as chaplain, tending to the wounded soldiers.

Addressing the crowd, the Cardinal paid tribute to the land he had seen from the *Empress*: 'As we came along the shores of the St Lawrence, which were the finest in the world, and as we saw the countless churches on its banks, we had recalled the pioneers of the faith in Canada, the settlers from France.'

While the Eucharistic Congress may not have changed history, the lavish (and very visible) reception of the Cardinal by the Canadian government may have. In the Canadian general election the following year, the Conservatives under Robert Borden defeated Sir Wilfrid Laurier's Liberals over the issue of reciprocity with the United States. The *New York Times* speculated that the attention bestowed by the Liberals on Cardinal Vannutelli had upset Protestants in Ontario, leading them to abandon Laurier.

For sportsmen, the return of the *Empress* signaled a friendly renewal of sporting rivalries. On Saturday afternoon, the Quebec Cricket Club played the men of the *Empress* on the historic Plains of Abraham, just outside the city walls.

Although the return crossing (50E) set a new eastbound speed record for the *Empress*, the most interesting aspects of the trip took place at Quebec as the ship was leaving. On hand to say farewell to a party of English and Australian Boy Scouts was Baden-Powell. From the Breakwater, Baden-Powell signaled 'Good-bye, boys' to the Scouts on deck. Delighted with the honour of being seen off by the founder of the movement, the boys signaled back, and messages were exchanged until the ship slipped down the river. Before the *Empress* departed, Baden-Powell had gone on board to inspect them and bid them a safe journey home.

Just as the ship was pulling away from the Breakwater, an excited man appeared on the dock, waving his hands in agitation. In the crowd his signals were unnoticed and the ship continued to pull away. A CPR official noticed the man's distress, and the situation was quickly explained. The man had missed the *Empress* by twenty-four feet, but absolutely had to get on board.

The *Chronicle* explained what happened next:

> The obliging and energetic officials of the CPR, however, quickly grasped the possibilities of the situation. Sam Vezina, the well-known boatman, with his men, who had been engaged with the lines of the steamer, was still in sight. He was quickly called into requisition, and, after a perilous descent down one of the ladders which face the dock, the belated passenger was quickly rowed out by the willing arms of the boatmen to the *Empress*. A rope ladder was thrown over the side, and he clambered over the side with celerity if not gracefulness, his actions being viewed with the deepest interest by the large crowd on the dock. But he caught his steamer, even if it cost him labour and money – a roll of bills in the passenger's hands and the passing of one of them to the boat's crew being plainly visible to the interested spectators on the wharf.

CPR advertisment, c.1912, showing the Empress of Ireland leaving Quebec. (Marion Kelch)

There was also at least one unwilling passenger aboard the *Empress*, a twenty-three-year-old Scot named James Rae who was being deported from Canada. During the eastbound passage, Nilo Latvala, a three-year-old Finn, died of acute laryngitis. A second death occurred, the ship's third (and last) crossing with a double fatality. James Rae, the deportee, jumped overboard rather than return to Britain.

Over the years, the comings and goings of the *Empress of Ireland*, her sister, and the other vessels that called Montreal or Quebec their summer home ports were featured in the Montreal papers. Of all the vessels, the *Empress* seems to have been a sentimental favourite, though perhaps the CPR press relations people had something to do with that.

The following item from the shipping pages of the *Gazette* illustrates the coverage that was typical of the period, and sheds light on the voyage – the fiftieth – that began in the Mersey on 23 September and ended in Quebec on the 29th.

IRELAND'S FAST RUN
SIX DAYS ON THE WAY

The *Empress of Ireland*, of the CPR, which has been a very consistent performer this season, again accomplished an excellent performance, by reaching Quebec yesterday afternoon shortly before 4 o'clock. The first special train reached the Windsor Station at 11 o'clock last night.

This run of the *Ireland* is the more remarkable when the squally and foggy conditions now prevailing in the Gulf of St Lawrence are taken into consideration. For the past few days equinoctial gales have been sweeping the lower river, from Quebec to Belle Isle, but the CPR flier came through gale and dirty weather with ease and speed. For the entire voyage she averaged well over eighteen knots.

The *Ireland* brought one of the largest passenger lists ever landed on Canadian shores. She left the landing stage at Liverpool at 6 o'clock last Friday night, and last night her

Montreal passengers were at home, six days after the liner swung down the Mersey. The passengers for the West went through last night.

Perhaps spurred by the CPR's publicity section, who wanted to make sure the Post Office knew it was getting value for the mail subsidy, the report continued:

The mails from the *Empress*, consisting of 244 bags and forty-six wicker baskets, reached the Montreal Post Office shortly after 11 o'clock last night. An extra staff of sorters worked all night and by 6:30 this morning the letters will be ready for house to house delivery. The consistent manner in which both the *Empress of Ireland* and her sister ship, the *Empress of Britain*, have landed their mails on Thursdays has been one of the features of the St Lawrence season so far.

On this particular trip she carried 1,557 passengers, a fact that the papers did not take much notice of. By that time large passenger lists were somewhat routine for all the steamers, and the year 1910 threatened to break all previous records for passenger landings at Canadian ports. One CPR official admitted, 'While we have carried our share, the other lines have not been by any means idle. The CPR can still claim to have carried more passengers than any other line this year.'

The large number of passengers late in the season was also attributed to a growing preference on the part of Americans for the St Lawrence route. The *Chronicle* noted that 'A considerable number of the first class are returning to their homes in the United States, and choose the St Lawrence route in preference to any other.' Emigration organizations in Britain were always anxious to ensure that the vessels on which their groups travelled maintained certain standards, especially with respect to cleanliness and, for female emigrants, security and propriety. On 29 September 1910 a self-possessed forty-four-year-old widow walked down the *Empress'* gangplank at Quebec, and spoke to a reporter from the *Gazette*. Though the manifest described her purpose for coming to Canada as 'Tourism' it was not strictly true. Two days later the paper ran the following story on its inside pages, not a part of the daily marine page:

TRAVELLED SECOND CLASS
Lady Briggs was Anxious to Study Conditions on St Lawrence Route
Among the second cabin passengers who arrived on board the RMS *Empress of Ireland* yesterday afternoon was Lady Briggs, of England. Lady Briggs travelled second class in order to personally ascertain the treatment which passengers on ocean vessels coming to Canada are given. During the trip she visited all three departments and expressed herself as being highly pleased with her experience. Lady Briggs, during her stay in Canada, will pay particular attention to the opportunities here for capable young women of good moral character.

A few days afterward the Quebec *Chronicle* found her travelling incognito and staying at the city's Women's Christian Association. Since departing the *Empress*, she had inspected the detention hospital, interviewed various immigration officials, and expected to travel all across Canada on her one-woman fact-finding mission.

Lady Briggs was no ordinary woman. Elizabeth Charlotte Gruar, then twenty-three, had become the second wife of Sir John Henry Briggs in 1889, despite the fact her husband was eight-one. Widowed in 1897, she had great literary talent and had edited her husband's works, including *Naval Administrations 1827-1892*, and *The Experience of 65 Years*, and *The Staff Work of the Anglo-Boer War, 1899-1901*. As well, she had a flair for adventure, and contributed articles to the *Morning Post* describing the Sudan campaign of 1899 and the Boer War, and wrote articles on naval and other subjects for various magazines. Her biography in the 1914 edition of *Who's Who* listed her recreation as 'an extensive traveller in Europe and Africa.'

It is tempting to link Lady Briggs to Henry Kendall, for there is a copy of Kendall's 1939 biography inscribed 'To Mrs Caroline[*sic*] Briggs with happy memories of bygone days 1902-1939. From the Author H.G. Kendall Dec. 1939.' Lady Briggs was still alive in 1939, by which time *Who's Who* had added 'America' to her travel destinations. One is left to wonder whether Captain Kendall had made her acquaintance at some point and the two had remained in contact with one another. Yet another *Empress* mystery.

On Thursday, 6 October, one day before departure, a soccer rematch took place between the Engine Room Department and the Stewards. The *Chronicle*, announcing the event, noted 'the rivalry between the above teams is very keen,' and explained that winner would be given a place in the Quebec Football League. That same day, the *Empress* hosted a luncheon for a convention of passenger agents, meeting in the city that week. More than 250 people trooped on board and spent an hour inspecting the ship before luncheon was served in the first class dining saloon. Captain Forster welcomed the delegates warmly and spoke of his ship and the care given to the thousands of people who patronized the CPR. John Walsh also spoke, taking the occasion to talk about the great progress in ocean transportation. Walsh also paid tribute to the press of Canada, praising them for publicizing the advantages of the St Lawrence route, and their coverage of the CPR. The event concluded with the presentation to Captain Forster of a silver match box, a token of the convention's appreciation for his hospitality.

In that summer season of 1910, the of arrivals and departures for the *Empress* seemed to settle into a predictable routine. Looking back on 12 October the *Gazette* said:

> A noteworthy feature of the present season of St Lawrence navigation has been the clockwork regularity with which the Canadian Pacific Railway *Empress* steamers have been arriving and leaving from this side. Since the opening of navigation, via the Belle Isle route, their time of arrival at Quebec has been within forty minutes of 3:30 Thursday afternoons and their departure has not varied ten minutes from 3:30 p.m. of the following Friday.

In England that autumn a Sunday newspaper published a sensational article dealing with 'the horrors of emigration' and the hardships and discomforts of a passage across the Atlantic. The Quebec *Chronicle* complained that 'No one who has ever made the journey would be deceived by the melodramatic rubbish contained in such articles, but untravelled people who contemplated migration might be misled and distressed by it.' A well-known Canadian clergyman, Rev. A. Thorold-Eller, who happened to be in England at the time, saw the article and subsequently recounted his own experiences to the *Chronicle*:

> Having occasion to return to England for a few months, and having had a very pleasant trip out second class by the *Empress of Britain*, I was determined to return by one of the CPR boats.
>
> I was advised by my friends not to think of sailing third class. It will be very rough, they said, also the food was scanty and none too good. However, partly on account of the cheaper rate, and also being anxious to see what the third class was really like, I determined to try it.
>
> I came on board prepared to endure the worst, and consoled myself by thinking that after three and a half years in the West, one could put up with roughing it.
>
> I was agreeably surprised from the moment I set foot on deck.
>
> After delivering up our tickets we were at once shown to our cabins. These are spotlessly clean, and are scrubbed out every day by the stewards. The food is good, well cooked and varied each day. The dining saloon is large and comfortable, and the table appointments clean. The stewards are civil and attentive, and do their work well, under capable management. There is a large smoking room for the men, and a room, contain-

ing a piano and well furnished, set apart for the use of the ladies. There is also a piano in the dining saloon, which is used for concerts in the evening. A large expanse of covered deck is available for the use of the third class passengers in wet weather, and there is also plenty of deck space for exercise in the open air. Every section of the boat is visited each day by the captain and other officers of the company.

I am thoroughly satisfied with everything on board, and feel sure that anyone wishing to have a speedy and enjoyable voyage could not do better than sail on the *Empress of Ireland*.

Weather, always an important consideration to queasy passengers, was the subject of a postcard mailed at the conclusion of the outbound passage from Liverpool on 21 October 1910. An unidentified writer observed:

We certainly are going 'splish splash row row.' We have had a rough voyage. Ursula has been ill but soon got better. There are so many children on board, they have a grand time playing about.

There were any number of reasons the *Empress* could be delayed in the long trip across the Atlantic, though most often it was the fault of the weather, particularly fog. Arriving in Quebec on 29 October, a day later than usual, the *Empress* had experienced heavy weather – but that wasn't the problem. This time, the delay was directly attributable to coal. It transpired that she had coaled at Liverpool with an inferior brand of coal, due to a strike of coal miners in Wales. The poorer-quality coal provided less power, and made her fully twenty-four hours late docking in Quebec.

It didn't help any that the ship had been delayed for a couple of hours by low water at Crane Island, whose channel had supposedly been dredged in 1908 to a full thirty feet at low tide. The *Empress* arrived only at 12:30 a.m. on the 29th, which meant that the 1,318 passengers – a record for the late season – did not get away until the morning. As it was the last trip of the *Empress* to Quebec for the season, the usual round of farewell visits, sporting events and concerts took place. The Empress Engineers defeated the Quebec Corinthians 2-0 on 31 October at the QAA grounds, and another soccer match took place the following day, with the Stewards losing 4-6 to the team of HMS *Cornwall*. As the Stewards had previously lost another match (1-2) to the Garrison Artillery, the *Empress* teams were no longer in contention for the Quebec League Cup. The lone goal for the Stewards had been scored by the young sharpshooter, Arthur Owen.

On 1 November a Seamen's Concert took place, with men from the *Empress* and HMS *Cornwall* contributing the talent. As always, seamen were admitted free; adults were ten cents, and children five cents. On 3 November, the day before sailing, the Empress Engineers played the last soccer match of the season at the QAA grounds against the Garrison Artillery. Described as an 'exciting' game, it resulted in a 1-1 tie.

No one ever recorded the exact time or place, but it was around this time that the *Empress* acquired a cat, a marmalade-yellowish tabby named Emmy, who quickly settled into shipboard life. Emmy proved to be a good sailor over the next three and a half years and made friends with the crew.

With her return to Saint John, eastbound *Empress* departures were on Friday, as in the past. That meant the Empress Special to West Saint John left Montreal at 8:00 p.m. on Thursday prior to the sailing of each *Empress*. Trains consisted of tourist, dining and standard sleeping cars, and ran directly to the ship's side, and were intended to carry only *Empress* passengers. Anyone destined for points in the maritime provinces was steered to the company's daily service leaving at 7:25 p.m.

The pre-Christmas period was always a busy season on the North Atlantic, as travellers sought to return to Britain or other continental destinations for the holiday. In order to spur traffic even more, shipping lines often offered reduced fares. It was a good policy, for all those North Americans would have to return home early in the New Year, at a time when steamships would be nowhere near capacity with immigrants.

Le Devoir announced on 3 December that the *Empress* had left Saint John the previous afternoon with fifteen hundred passengers who had taken advantage of special fares to spend the Christmas and New Year's holidays with their families, adding that more than 300 people had been unable to find a place on board. Like other newspapers of the time, *Le Devoir* was somewhat unreliable when it came to passenger totals. The actual number of *Empress* passengers was 1,216, still an impressive number for the season and the direction.

With the conclusion of five seasons on the North Atlantic run to Liverpool, it is instructive to look at the Canadian Pacific's performance, and that of the *Empress of Ireland*, particularly in the face of increased competition.

In 1910 the *Empress* carried 16,196 passengers westbound, and 7,825 eastbound. Westbound, the total was the highest number carried in any twelve-month period to date, but the eastbound results must have been somewhat disappointing, as they were considerably lower than the best result, 11,513, achieved in 1908. However, in defense of the *Empress*, she had missed one (or perhaps two) sailings in the winter of 1909-1910 as a result of the October 1909 incident. The missed sailings might have added perhaps another 3,000 to her 1910 totals.

In that year, ten shipping lines served the ports of eastern Canada, linking them to a variety of British and continental destinations. Of the European ports, the most important was Liverpool, served by the CPR, Allan Line and White Star-Dominion. Allan had carried more than 54,000 passengers westbound from Liverpool, compared to the CPR's 45,000, and White Star's 43,000, and Liverpool was the point of embarkation for 47.8% of all westbound passengers arriving in Canada, amounting in all to over 302,000. For the CPR, about one-quarter of the line's westbound Liverpool passengers travelled on the *Empress of Ireland*, and a similar number were carried on the *Empress of Britain*.

For eastbound passengers, Liverpool was by far the most important destination. Of some 90,000 eastbound passengers, 62,000 or 68% went through the Mersey port. In terms of Liverpool passengers, the CPR ranked second of three, with the Allan Line enjoying a margin of some 9,000 passengers in the westbound direction. Eastbound, the two lines were almost equal, and White Star was not far behind.

Overall, including the CPR service from the ports of Antwerp and London, the Allan Line still held a significant edge in terms of total passengers carried, 96,000 to 71,000.

'Success to the *Empress of Ireland*' Sir Digby Morant had toasted at her launch, 'and prosperity to the Canadian Pacific Railway Company.' By the close of 1910 it seemed that both of those wishes had become reality.

In 1911 the *Empress* made her first voyage from Liverpool only on 27 January, having completed a short period of overhaul. She carried a good number of passengers, 1,017, considering the time of the year. The following postcard, cancelled at Halifax on 3 February, gives the impressions of a passenger named George:

> Just a word letting you know that the voyage is nearly over. We have got as far as Halifax (N.S.) 1 more day on the water thank goodness. The food on the boat is not bad but you do not need it all.
> I have missed six meals. Remember me to all at home. Mother has address of [*illegible*].

On 10 March 1911 on the eastward leg of her 56th Voyage, the *Empress* welcomed aboard Sir William Van Horne, the legendary builder of the CPR and one of Canada's richest men. Van Horne, who had retired as Chairman of the company only the previous year, was still a member of the board, a position he would hold until his death in 1915. Departing from Saint John, Van Horne wrote one letter to his daughter Adeline, on the leg between Saint John and Halifax, and posted it in time to be taken off with the pilot and mail bags. Written on CPR letterhead, the letter dealt with the need to purchase a variety of trees for Covenhoven, the family's summer home at St Andrews in New Brunswick, and sheds no light on his impressions of the *Empress*.

A second letter, also on CPR letterhead, is more interesting to the maritime historian.

Off Queenstown

CANADIAN PACIFIC RAILWAY
ATLANTIC SERVICE

RMS *Empress of Ireland*
St Patrick's Day 1911
in the morning

My very dear daughter

…we have now reached Ireland with hardly a wave on the way. We shall be at Liverpool this evening but probably not early enough to land: so I don't expect to get to London before noon tomorrow. The voyage has been very pleasant in every way. The ship is not crowded and there are some very nice people on board. Mr & Mrs Buddan of Montreal with three bright little boys, Mr & Mrs & Miss James Reid Wilson, Mrs K.W. Blackwell and Mrs D. McL. Brown. From St John Mr & Mrs J.T. Robertson, friends of the Hazens and from Toronto Mr Armour and Mr MacMurchey.

The others I don't know, save Miss Gwendolin E. Foreman of Grand Rapids Michigan, aged eight months, whom I have estranged from her parents.

There is now a billiard table on this *Empress* and I have had the novel experience of playing billiards at sea which could be done every day – real English billiards. I expected to have to wait for my ferry-boats for that. The attendance on this ship is very perfect and the meals are very good. The ventilation and temperature are just right and everybody is pleased.

I shall probably return by the *Empress of India*, sailing from Liverpool on the 7th April. There is no good ship that I can catch earlier. This will bring me to Montreal about the 14th, a little later than I expected.

I shall wire Bonnie from Liverpool and I hope to see him and Edith tomorrow afternoon.

All the people on this ship that I have mentioned have inquired about Small William who seems to be extensively known and admired. His whisper to me at the table just before I left home is constantly in my mind:- 'Grandpa, take me with you.' I wish he were here.

With very much love to all

Your affectionate

Father

This is the first (and only) reference to a billiard table aboard the *Empress*. No one knows where the table was located.

The envelopes of Van Horne's two letters are interesting in their own right. The first, mailed aboard the *Empress* and taken ashore at Halifax, bears the following cancellation:

PAQUEBOT
POSTED AT SEA
RECEIVED
MR 12 11
HALIFAX

The second, posted aboard ship somewhere between Queenstown and Liverpool, and marked in Van Horne's hand 'Via New York', carries a similar cancellation:

PAQUEBOT
POSTED AT SEA
RECEIVED
18 MR 11
LIVERPOOL.

The post office aboard the *Empress* evidently held large stocks of Canadian and English stamps for sale to passengers. Although Edward VII had been dead for some eleven months, both of Van Horne's letters bore stamps with the likeness of the former monarch, Canada's two-cent carmine and the one-penny scarlet of the British Post Office.

In April 1911 the prestigious British magazine *Railway and Travel Monthly* featured a nine-page color article on the Canadian Pacific's maritime activities. Tracing the company's history for its well-heeled readers, the magazine stated:

> The year 1906 marked the establishment of the service between Quebec and Liverpool by the superb *Empresses of Ireland* and *Britain* which have been such a strong factor in popularizing the matchless St Lawrence route, not only among Canadians, but also among the people of the United States, especially those of the middle and western sections. These steamships, carrying a maximum of 1,600 passengers of all classes, and sailing once a fortnight, since their advent to the St Lawrence route have created so much new business, that the existing lines, both the Canadian Pacific and their competitors, have experienced no falling off in their carryings.

In April 1911 the CPR allowed its agents, for the first time, to make through-fares to Europe by the *Empresses*. Agents were instructed in a company bulletin to add the rail fares to Montreal to the appropriate steamship fares from Quebec, and then issue rail tickets to Quebec.

With their ship's return to the port of Quebec on 28 April, the men of the *Empress* wasted no time in renewing their sporting contacts in the Ancient Capital. On 3 May the *Empress* soccer team played a practice match against the Quebec Corinthians, the former winning by a lopsided 5-1. The sporting season was off to a good start.

And so was the shipping season, for the *Empress* had made five consecutive passages to Canada in 1911 with over a thousand passengers, and that total would run to ten before it ended in November. The flood of immigrants to Canada showed no sign of letting up.

For more than two hundred years Scots have traditionally favoured Canada as a place of emigration, and the CPR's advertising of the Canadian west as a land of promise and opportunity struck a responsive chord in the hearts of many enterprising Scots in the Edwardian era. Thus it happened that the Craw family of Edinburgh, with relatives already in Winnipeg, decided in 1911 to leave Britain. It was a small family by the standards of the day: John, thirty-eight, a printer by trade, his wife Violet, a part-time music teacher, and two boys, James born in 1896, and Donald, born in 1900. Economic conditions in Scotland had not been good for some time, with layoffs and shortened work weeks being common in many industries, and John was determined to provide a better future for his sons than Britain could offer. Spurred by the CPR's advertising campaign, John Craw booked a passage on the *Empress of Ireland*, using his own money from a Scottish cooperative society. As did many other emigrants who knew they might never see their friends and relatives again, the days prior to departure were filled with a busy round of farewell social events, for Violet was well-known and respected in Edinburgh's musical circles.

The Empress Juniors 1912/13 soccer team. Front row, middle, Arthur Owen, the 'Empress Sharpshooter'; front row, left, Ken Williams. Owen and Williams left the ship in Saint John in April 1913, halfway through Voyage 83. (John Owen)

Interviewed in Manitoba by an oral historian in 1980-1981, Donald Craw looked back fondly on his trip as an eleven-year-old. Like others, he found it a memorable experience. 'We came on the old *Empress of Ireland*,' he recalled after seventy years. 'It was a beautiful ship. It was one of the better line ships at the time. They were very fussy on the *Empress* boats. They would only take British or Scandinavian passengers, and there was no steerage. We travelled second class.'

The Craws were not alone from Scotland. The manifest for the voyage showed that Scottish emigrants composed almost three-quarters of the second class passengers.

The family boarded the *Empress* on a dull, drizzly day after a train-ride from Edinburgh. The ship was moored in the Mersey, some distance away, and they were obliged to board her by tender. 'I remember looking up at the ship; I had seen big ships in the distance, but I had never been close to one before, and I wondered 'How am I ever going to get up there?' It so happened they had a door in the side of the ship.

'We had quite a stormy voyage and, speaking to one of the stewards afterwards, there were a number of Salvationists on board at the time, and he told us that every time there's a group of Salvationists on board, we always had a bad storm!'

'The food was 'excellent', an observation made by numerous other passengers over the years. 'We were very friendly with the steward, who used to come along and bring us biscuits and cheese late at night.'

Several events stuck in the mind of young Donald:

I remember the storm at sea. It was quite exciting at the time. It was a nice calm day... beautiful... the sun was shining, and all of a sudden, the ship took a dip. Over the loudspeaker, the communications system [*Craw is probably incorrect in this recollection*], they told everybody they had to go down below deck. They came down and they battened all the portholes shut, except one or two for air. It was amazing to see the height of the waves; she was a big ship, and she would just rise over the crest of one wave and into the deep trough before the next one. The ship would shudder and she would take a cant up, and you could hear the propellers racing until they got back in the water again.

Another incident that was amusing was we were sitting in our cabin and worried about things at home. Mother all of a sudden says, 'Do you hear what the Salvationists are singing?'

'No, what?'

'*God Be With You Till We Meet Again!*'

Later, as the ship reached the waters off Newfoundland they saw icebergs and other things that the young boy would remember with total clarity. 'In the distance, we saw these spots on the water. Stewards came along and told us they were whales. That was my first sight of a whale!'

'We arrived in Quebec City at night. It was too late, and we had to go through Immigration, of course, and everything was closed up. I remember going up on deck; everything was calm, the water was calm. The stars were shining – a beautiful night. It was very peaceful.'

His recollections were correct. The manifest showed that they docked at 3 a.m. on 19 May. The Craw family passed through the usual Immigration inspection, presided over by policemen with white helmets and gloves.

[*The Inspection*] was quite cursory. They asked you how much money you had; you had to have fifty pounds. We had the necessary fifty pounds. ...[B]efore we went on the ship we were inspected medically, that was quite cursory – they felt your pulse and looked into your eyes. The same when you were coming off the boat. You were asked, of course, if you had your inoculations, one thing they were particular about. There wasn't much trouble at all.

Having completed the formalities, Mrs Craw waited with Donald for her husband and eldest son. 'My mother and I were waiting for Dad and my brother to come to us, and father came dashing up. 'Look what I got!' and he handed over a package of 'Bull' Durham tobacco. 'Don't worry. I didn't have to pay for it.' That appealed to his Scotch thrift. Then my brother came along. 'Look. I just stepped off the boat and this lady gave me a real book!' It was the Gospel of St Matthew. I always said that they had two consolations: one for the spirit and one for the mind.'

Summing up the *Empress* experience, Donald Craw said, 'I must say the treatment on the ship was excellent. Beautiful boat. We thoroughly enjoyed the voyage across.' In the interview he still remembered the name *Storstad* and the circumstances surrounding the sinking of the *Empress*. Even into later life, he kept his autograph album, and always knew that some of the stewards who had once signed his book had died with their ship.

The Craws travelled by a slow Colonist Train to Winnipeg, and settled down in the same city as their relatives. Canada, at the outset, proved to be a slight letdown to the two boys. Like most youngsters of the day, they had been reared on *Boy's Own Paper*, and the adventure stories of George Henty. James and Donald were disappointed to find Canada wasn't wild enough and Winnipeg, with paved streets, was a real city and not some frontier post.

For the same westbound trip of 19-25 May, a postcard sent by 'PQR' provides some corroborative details: 'we have had rough weather on Sunday [*the 21st, the third day out from Liverpool*], but have had a very good passage on the whole.'

It was in this same time period that rumors were rife in the shipping world that the CPR was planning to leave the Atlantic Shipping Conference. Several reasons for this were advanced, the main one being that the company was disconcerted by the encroachments of its foreign rivals in the Canadian trade. While Conference rules clearly spelled out that one line was forbidden to trespass on the territory of another, ways around this restriction could be found. Though lines like Cunard, White Star and German-American were not permitted to serve Montreal, there was a loophole: they could do so through surrogates. Thus, Cunard served Canada through the Thomson Line, White Star by the Dominion Line, and German-American by the Canada Line.

In the end, the CPR remained in the Conference, but there was no love lost between the company and the other members of the industry cartel that controlled the North Atlantic.

When George V was crowned at Westminster Abbey in June 1911, the Coronation featured official delegations and military contingents from every corner of Britain's global empire. Canada was well represented, sending by far the largest force to the elaborate ceremony. On 2 June 1911 the *Empress* departed Quebec with a contingent of 703 soldiers from Canada and nine from Bermuda, along with a distinguished company of first class passengers. The Gazette described the scene:

> The *Empress of Ireland*, to the echo of cheers from the thousands that lined the wharf and counter cheers from her crowded decks, sailed from here this afternoon for Liverpool with the Canadian Coronation contingent, in command of Col. Hugh H. McLean, ADC. The *Empress*, wholly dressed with flags, her decks lined with bright uniformed soldiers, and with the band of the Royal Canadian Regiment playing on deck, made one of the most impressive sights witnessed in this old garrison city, so accustomed to the gaiety surrounding military functions.

On this voyage the *Empress* carried 251 passengers in first class; the officers and men seem to have taken over second and third class, for the ship carried almost twelve hundred passengers in all.

The contingent had been carefully selected to represent all branches of the army, and to represent all areas of the country and included more than fifty French-Canadian officers and men. Selections were also made 'according to character, physique and seniority' and many of the militia members were travelling to England at considerable sacrifice. Although the Canadian government paid their travel expenses and the British government fed and housed them, the men would not be paid for time off work. A number of the officers, still of relatively junior rank, would later go on to important command positions in the Canadian Expeditionary Force. Of these, the most notable was Major David Watson, publisher of the Quebec *Chronicle*, who ended the war as a Major General in command of the 4th Canadian Division in France.

Almost overlooked in the military ceremonies were a number of other distinguished people on board. They included His Highness Prince Leopold of Battenberg (a twenty-two-year-old cousin of George V, and a nephew of the Duke of Connaught), and Archbishop Paul Bruchesi of Montreal, making his second trip in the *Empress*.

To mark the occasion, the ship's print shop published a special passenger list, with an elaborate embossed front cover in full color, and an inside cover bearing a photograph of Westminster Abbey. The type font changed as well, to Old English, and carried the additional notation: 'Carrying the Canadian and Bermudan Contingents to The Coronation of George V and Queen Mary.' Two inside pages, also in Old English type, described the actual coronation service and were followed by two pages with the first class passengers, in all numbering 209, including one child, one maid and one valet.

Among the personal papers of then Lt-Col. John Taylor Fotheringham, a distinguished Toronto physician and Medical Officer from the Army Medical Corps, today held in the National Archives in Ottawa, is a copy of that passenger list, bound in blue string and measuring $6\frac{7}{8}$ in by $9\frac{3}{8}$ in. Though Fotheringham went on to achieve the rank of Major General, serving in 1917 as Director General of the Canadian Army Medical Service, his voyage in the *Empress* was evidently an occasion to be remembered.

When the ship arrived in Liverpool on 9 June, *The Times* provided some insights into the voyage and the activities of the soldiers while onboard:

> While England lay basking in the heat of a Canadian summer, the Canadian troops on their way to England for the Coronation were having a cold and rainy trip across the Atlantic, with a taste of fog. Otherwise the voyage that ended at Liverpool yesterday was pleasant enough, the sea being smooth, the accommodation in the *Empress of Ireland* excellent, and the whole company cheerful in the extreme.
>
> Every day the troops went through their physical exercises in detachments; concerts were of nightly occurrence; and dances and cinematograph exhibitions of Canadian scenery were held. Every afternoon the whole force assembled to practise Canadian songs with full band accompaniment.

The paper then described the arrival in Liverpool: 'It was nearly half-past 11 before the Canadian Pacific liner came into sight, for a slight mist hung over the Mersey. In a few minutes the great ship, dressed rainbow-fashion, stood motionless, towering above the landing stage.'

To greet her were the Lord Mayor and Lady Mayoress of Liverpool, an impressive delegation of military officers, and the band of the 4th West Lancashire Howitzer Brigade, pipers of the Liverpool Scottish, and the bugle band of the Liverpool Rifles. As the ship came alongside, the band struck up the *Maple Leaf*. *The Times* continued:

> The civic and military party immediately went on board, and in the saloon Colonel McLean and his officers received a very warm welcome to Liverpool from the Lord Mayor. By 1 o'clock the whole force had disembarked and set off, bands playing, on a march through the central parts of the city.

In July the CPR announced that it had leased nearly all of the ground floor of the Royal Liver Insurance building in Liverpool, the new office tower that dominated the city's riverfront near the Landing Stage. While some of the space would be for offices, the main beneficiaries of the move would be third class passengers, for the company intended to provide waiting space for up to 800 emigrants on their way to Canada. This was welcome news. The proximity of the new waiting area to the Landing Stage made life easier for non-English-speaking emigrants, especially those travelling in large family groups.

The summer of 1911 was a particularly bad one in the United Kingdom in terms of labour unrest. A strike by British dock workers in May spread so that, by August, twenty thousand men in the London docks were on strike, supported by carters, and more than twenty ocean liners in the port were unable to sail. As well, dock activities at Manchester and Liverpool had also come to a halt, paralyzed by workers looking for wage increases to keep up with the rising cost of living, and in mid-June sailings from Southampton had been disrupted by the Coal Porters' Union.

In Liverpool in mid-June, the CPR agreed to a general wage increase for all its employees amounting to $2.50 (*i.e.* 10s) per month, an example that was followed by White Star and others. The $2.50 was exactly one-half of what the men had demanded, and industry sources predicted that the settlement would enable the *Empress of Ireland*, *Teutonic* and *Baltic* to meet their sailing schedules. The company felt some urgency to meet the *Empress* sailing dates, as she was a mail carrier and contractual obligations had to be met.

In the event, the *Empress* sailed from Liverpool on the 16th, the scheduled date, but the company made a further last-minute concession. As the *New York Times* put it: 'when the time came for the signing of a crew for the *Empress of Ireland* today the company was forced to concede an additional $1.25.'

Labour scored another victory that June. On the 29th, Cunard, the CPR and Allan Lines all agreed to recognize all seamen's unions, including the dockers' organization. Stewards of the *Empress of Britain*

Two different designs of gold and enamel souvenir pins sold in the gift shop aboard the Empress, *from the collection of Philippe Beaudry. (Author)*

returned to work and loading of *Tunisian* was resumed. That wasn't the end, of course. The docks at Liverpool, which normally handled one-quarter of Britain's food imports, were already littered with rotting food, and dock hands still prevented the carters from handling foodstuffs.

On 15 July, the various transatlantic steamship lines announced fare increases, effective two days later, of $2.50 for both eastbound and westbound traffic, for first and second class tickets. Third class and steerage rates remained unchanged. The explanation was simple: the companies were merely offsetting the wage increase which had been granted to the strikers.

'Another Fast Run From Liverpool' announced the Quebec *Chronicle* when the *Empress* arrived on 20 July with 1,381 passengers, including twenty Scouts returning from the Coronation ceremonies. The ship had enjoyed fine weather up to the ice track, where she ran into thick fog and had to slow down.

That summer, as the *Empress* traversed the Atlantic, her crew monitored with special interest the wireless broadcasts from Poldhu. Even as the carters accepted a wage settlement, railway workers across Britain went on strike and the lockout of dockers in Liverpool continued. And, it was also at this time that the mutiny aboard *Virginian* took place, discussed above, with fifty-seven of her stewards imprisoned on arrival at Montreal.

The *Empress* sailed from Liverpool on 11 August at 8:10 p.m. with 1,433 passengers who were, no doubt, relieved to get away, for there were thousands of others, including many Americans, whose sailings from the Mersey had been cancelled or delayed.

While the ship was still at sea, the strike escalated to a new level. In Liverpool, at a meeting of transport workers on 13 August, two hundred people were injured in a clash with the police. Troops were sent to restore order and, two days later, when stones were thrown at them, they opened fire, killing two. Armed sailors were landed from a cruiser in the Mersey to protect the docks. By the 15th, with the lockout of 40,000 dockers and others in Liverpool continuing, Merseyside was deserted. Canada-bound liners like *Virginian* and White Star's *Megantic*, without crews and no one to load the mails, cancelled their sailings. Shipping companies, among them the CPR, then circulated joint letters giving notice that they could not be held responsible for delays or damage due to the disruptions in the sailing schedules caused by the labour dispute.

The ship's fast arrival in Quebec on 17 August, after a trip marked by good weather, was scarcely noted.

Departing from Quebec on the 25th at 3:30 p.m., the *Empress* had 640 passengers, mail and a light cargo load. She was, however, chock full of coal, having enough on board to steam to Liverpool and back without replenishing her bunkers. It was a wise precaution. Without the assurance of adequate coal in Liverpool or men to load it, the ship would be effectively stranded – an expensive asset with fixed costs yet earning no revenues for whatever time she was stuck in Liverpool. During a normal crossing the *Empress* consumed about 2,400 tons of coal. Normally she could carry up to 4,000 tons in her bunkers, but additional coal in bags could be stored in her holds and this would give enough of a margin to cross the Atlantic and back.

In third class she carried just 394 passengers. Much of the forward space on Lower deck, between the first and third watertight bulkheads, normally housing almost 200 people in convertible accommodations, would have been converted to cargo space for additional bags of coal. What little cargo the *Empress* carried was low-priority and non-perishable, like lumber. If not unloaded in Liverpool, it could be brought back and forth across the Atlantic several times, until the strike was settled.

While the *Empress* sailed from Quebec on the 25th, her sister was delayed four days at Liverpool, finally sailing on 29 August.

By the time the *Empress* returned to her home port on 1 September, peace had been restored on Merseyside. A settlement was reached on 25 August and the city and its waterfront were largely back to their normal routine, with the exception of 30,000 dockers who remained locked out by the ship-owners. Seamen, firemen, cooks and stewards were able to board their ships, and *Virginian* departed that same afternoon for Quebec. The shipping companies then agreed to end their lockout of the dockers, who returned to work the following day, and the long, acrimonious dispute was finally over.

Only as the summer slipped into September did the Atlantic steamship companies increase their third class rates to Canada and the United States, this time by five shillings. The companies again justified the hike by pointing to the wage increases granted to the crews over the summer.

Illness at sea was always a concern to the ship's doctor. An infectious disease could spread rapidly in the close confines of a vessel like the *Empress*. Arthur Owen recalled one incident where he was required to go beyond the normal duty for an Assistant Steward:

> One anxious time I endured happened on one of our outward-bound trips. A young child (I never asked whether boy or girl) was very ill and the ship's doctor feared small-pox or diphtheria.
>
> When we arrived at Rimouski I was picked to take the child ashore – evidently as I was young and very nimble on my feet. I had to take the child in my arms, the tug [*sic*] drew up alongside and both ships dropped their gangplanks. I had to watch myself and jump from the *Empress* with the child in my arms onto the tug. This I did successfully.
>
> For days afterwards I was examined by the doctor but fortunately I developed nothing in the line of infection.

If the *Empress of Ireland* had been good enough for Baden-Powell in the summer of 1910, Scout leaders decided that it would certainly be good enough for a Canadian contingent of Scouts returning from Britain. Among the 801 passengers in third class on Voyage 61W were fifty-seven Scouts, all but three from Alberta and Saskatchewan. The boys enjoyed fine weather up to the ice track, whereupon fog had set in, and the *Empress* had been obliged to slow down. Arriving at Quebec at 5:45 p.m. on 20 July, there was an inexplicable delay in disembarking passengers, and the special train did not leave until 1:00 a.m. the following morning.

In Liverpool a woman named Esther visited the *Empress* on 3 September, prior to sailing. In a postcard she described the ship thus: '*Quel colosse! Peut embarquer 350 voyageurs de 1ere classe, autant de 2e et 1,000 de 3e classe.*' She continues: 'Once aboard it is easy to lose one's way and the passengers have great difficulty finding their cabins [Author's translation].' The consequences of this would be realized on 29 May 1914.

On Voyage 63W, the *Empress* was nearly full, with 1,563 passengers, among whom were the Welsh Female Choir, a 'talented musical body' embarking on a tour of Canada. On the whole the weather was clear and fine, though the ship encountered the usual headwinds. The crossing was marred by one tragedy: a man in third class jumped overboard. Though the ship was stopped and the crew made every effort to save him, he disappeared without a trace. Halting the ship in mid-ocean and searching for a man overboard was a hopeless enterprise, and everyone involved knew it. Still, the shipping companies were obliged to make the effort, a face-saving exercise.

In June 1910 the British government had announced that Canada would get a new governor general, Field Marshal HRH the Prince Arthur, 1st Duke of Connaught and Strathearn, who would take over from Earl Grey. The Duke, third son and seventh child of Queen Victoria, was a professional military officer, appropriate for a man whose godfather had been the Duke of Wellington. Already familiar with Canada from previous visits in 1869 and 1906, the Duke had developed an affection for the country and its people. His nomination as the country's tenth governor general was greeted with enthusiasm.

The Duke's appointment, though, was unusual. He was the first royal governor general in any Dominion of the British Empire, and his name had been proposed at the behest of his late brother, Edward VII. For a variety of reasons the Duke did not take up his appointment until 1911. The Duke and Duchess (formerly Princess Luise Margarete of Prussia) embarked from Liverpool on 6 October aboard the *Empress of Ireland* in two suites which the CPR had redecorated specifically for the royal couple. This kind of treatment was nothing new for the Duke. When he had returned to England in *Virginian* in May 1906 at the conclusion of a Canadian tour, he had taken over a suite of six rooms on upper deck though, since the ship was so new, the rooms had needed only minor re-decorating.

Pomp and ceremony for royal personages was nothing unusual but, in London on 6 October, there was a special excitement as the Duke and Duchess embarked from Euston Station for Liverpool, and the London & North Western Railway issued a large number of invitations to witness their departure. The couple were popular with the British public and the royal party was seen off by a large crowd of friends, relatives and well-wishers who gathered at the station for the boat train's noon departure.

The train was a special one, consisting of six saloon coaches and the royal carriage, which had been decorated for the occasions with ferns, and vases of lilies and carnations. As their train pulled away, the Duke and Duchess stood until the station was out of sight, bowing to acknowledge the cheers of the crowd.

At Liverpool the scene was a familiar one, for the city was used to seeing off dignitaries at the Riverside Station. While the royal train was still some distance from Liverpool, the *Empress* steamed up to the Landing Stage from her anchorage in mid-stream, 'dressed rainbow fashion' as *The Times* correspondent described her.

A large crowd had gathered on the Landing Stage along with a guard of honour supplied by the 6th Battalion of the Liverpool Regiment. When the train pulled into the station, the royal couple were welcomed by a gaggle of civic and military officials. From the Station, they crossed the road and walked down a gangway to the Landing Stage. Here, the band played the national anthem and *The Maple Leaf* as the Duke inspected the guard. Crossing the narrow gangway and entering the *Empress* by a door in her side, the royal couple were welcomed by Captain Forster. Once aboard, the Royal Standard with the Duke's arms was broken out at the masthead.

At 5 p.m. the signal to cast off was given and the *Empress* glided gently away from the Landing Stage. The Duke, wearing an overcoat and cap, appeared on the upper bridge with Captain Forster. Visible at last to the assembled crowds, they cheered again and again as the ship drew away, even the passengers on the forward deck joining in the cheers. At the same time, *The Times* correspondent added, 'the steam sirens of the ferry steamers and all the other small craft in the river gave vent to a terrific and long-drawn outburst of affectionate discord.'

This was probably the first time a merchant vessel had ever left a British port flying the Royal Standard from her foremast – 'a distinction of which Lieut. Forster and his officers, no doubt, feel justly proud' observed the Quebec *Chronicle*.

If anyone in Britain worried that the Duke and Duchess might find the *Empress* not to their taste, *The Times* hastened to reassure its readers that the ship was fully adequate:

Although a number of fine vessels have been put on the Canadian route in the last few years, the twin *Empresses* still deserve all the admiration that they won years ago. Their internal arrangements are superb. In the *Empress of Ireland* the Duke and Duchess occupy a suite of rooms on the starboard side of the lower promenade deck, close to the café, overlooking the grand saloon. The Royal apartments have been decorated and furnished for the occasion by Messrs A. Blain & Son, of Liverpool. The one private sitting room is furnished in Sheraton style, and a green Axminster carpet with an inconspicuous design has been specially made for the occasion.

The CPR had little in the way of renovations to do. Some partitions had been removed to make two cabins into one, and the rooms were decorated with hangings selected by the royal couple. The royal party had engaged all the rooms opening on one corridor, so that all could be accommodated together. 'All' meant the Duke, Duchess, Miss Pelly, Lady-in-Waiting to the Duchess, Lt Col. H.C. Lowther, Military Secretary to the Duke, and two Aides-de-camp, Capt. W. Long and Lt Hon. A. Ramsay. Added *The Times*: 'The members of the Royal party will take their meals in the general saloon, like the other passengers.'

In the diary written by the Duchess, now in the Royal Archives in Windsor Castle, she recorded simply on 6 October: 'Our cabins are most comfortable & specially done up & two made into a very nice sitting room.' One is left somewhat disappointed that the Duchess could not find more time in which to record her impressions of the ship.

Sharing the *Empress* with the Duke and Duchess were 867 passengers in third class and 333 in second. Included in the latter were four emigrants to Canada: Richard Jackson, sixty-six, a retired Liverpool merchant, his wife Edith Mary, fifty, and his daughters Margaret ('Maggie'), a thirty-one-year-old teacher, and Edith Alice ('Edie'), a twenty-four-year-old clerk. The family's furniture and other belongings had been shipped earlier by a Blue Funnel Line cargo vessel to Vancouver, where they planned to settle. Mrs Jackson was a faithful diarist and recorded her trip over the following days. Her entries provide an unparalleled insight into a westbound crossing in second class:

Saturday, October 7th
Clock retarded 35 minutes last night so we were up betimes this A.M. On deck by 7 o'clock. Breakfast at 8:00. Get a book from Library and sit on upper deck until luncheon, which we had at 12 noon. Steward brings around a cup of soup about 11:00 and afternoon tea about 4:00.
Saw six rainbows during the day.
Not feeling well. Do not go up to dinner – instead the stewardess brings me a little boiled fish. Retire at 7:00 P.M.

Sunday, October 8th
Have a fairly good night, but cannot eat anything at breakfast. Have some fruit during the morning. Attend Divine Service at 10:45 in First Class Saloon. Sit just behind the Duke & party. No sermon, just the Morning Service and hymns:
All People that on Earth do Dwell
Oh God our Help in Ages Past
Onward Christian Soldiers.
Luncheon at 12:00. Sit on deck afterwards reading. Chief Steward comes along with Mr Allcroft and have a chat. Afternoon tea follows and then come down to make myself tidy for dinner. Am not able to go up for dinner. Dad and Maggie go. No dinner for me. Afterwards I attend Divine Service in 2nd class Saloon. Sermon by a clergyman from 1st class. I retire at 7:30.
Clock retarded 54 minutes at midnight.

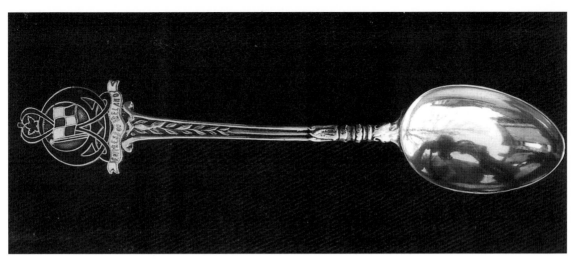

Silver and enamel souvenir spoon sold in the gift shop of the Empress, *from the collection of Philippe Beaudry. (Author)*

Monday, October 9th

6:00 A.M. cup of tea & biscuits. Afterwards go on deck, finding it very stormy. Go back to my berth where I stay all day. Ill all Monday. Sick many times and feel very bad. Dad & Maggie stay on deck until lunch. Dad is blown over deck chair and all. Am rather sorry at missing the spectacle! One lady got her thumb broken. No one allowed on deck after luncheon. Nearly all the passengers are ill, <u>even</u> <u>Maggie</u>, and very few people turn in for dinner. Only one, and at most four, at many of the tables. Daddy comes to bed at 7:00. Stewardess brings me some arrowroot, but can't manage to take it.

Can truly say I have been 'rocked in the cradle of the deep', being tossed from one side to the other and sometimes my head being lower than my feet. In spite of which I felt <u>no fear</u> owing, I believe, to the prayers of so many dear ones in 'the dear home land.'

Clock retarded 54 minutes at midnight.

Tuesday, October 10th

Awake 5:00 A.M. Steward brings tea and biscuit at 6:00. Ask him to take the girls some. Felt better after the tea. Get up and dress as soon as dad goes up on deck. Go up for breakfast which consists of tea and toast. Come up on deck, sit & write in my diary, then read until beef tea comes around, then a chat until luncheon. After luncheon, walk up & down, then Mr Allcroft come along and marches Dad & Maggie off to his room for a smoke and afternoon tea. Also takes them to see the engines. Edie & I sit & read until we get cold, then go down & rest until dinner.

After dinner rest until 8:00 when there is a concert in the Dining Saloon in aid of Mariners' House. It was not quite a success owing to several artists not appearing. Over by 10:20 when we retire for the night.

Belle Isle in sight about 11:00 P.M.

Clock retarded 60 minutes at midnight.

Wednesday, October 11th

Steward brought tea & biscuit at 6:00 A.M. Dad had a bath 6:15. Breakfast 7:30. See land both sides of the ship & keep Newfoundland in sight all morning. It was grand on deck and we kept walking about to keep warm.

The luggage has all been brought up and we spotted ours and it looks all right.

Luncheon at 12:00 after which a wash & brush up. I should say we were all photographed on deck at 10:00.

This afternoon we all went down & had tea with Mr Allcroft and spent a very pleasant time with him. Came up on deck and sighted land again as ship sailing up St Lawrence River. Just going to dinner. The sunset on the Isle of Anticosti was glorious. My dinner today was a full course – *viz.* soup, boiled fowl, plum tart, jelly dessert, plums & grapes. Am beginning to feel quite at home on the boat.

Write letters & diary. Bath 9:15 then bed after a most enjoyable day.

Clock retarded 60 minutes at midnight.

Thursday, October 12th

Tea 6:30 as usual. Dress, go up on deck to view land and then into Dining Saloon to write until breakfast time. After breakfast finish letters, then go up and see pilot come on board. Also see passengers land for Rimouski. Duchess comes out and stands close to me for a few minutes.

We are now steaming along merrily again and everyone is busy getting their luggage packed up and ready for Customs Officer & Doctor. It is a very misty morning, at present can scarcely see land.

12:40 – just had lunch, got our baggage passed and saw Doctor about 11:30. Some lovely hills in sight, just passed a Coast Guard station & a pretty village.

Our dinner is 4:45 so we shall not have much longer on board to look round. Am just going on deck for a final sniff of ozone after making up these diaries for posting at Quebec. It is grand this afternoon, but everyone seems to be intent on their baggage.

Hope you enjoy reading this scrawl & with much love from us all,

Edith M. Jackson

As Edith noted, after four days at sea, second class passengers were treated to a programme of entertainment in the second class dining room. As usual, the talent for the evening was drawn, to the extent possible, from the second class passengers themselves. And, as Edith Jackson recorded, if several of the 'artists' did not appear for their performance, it may have been due to seasickness.

Canadian newspapers like the *Montreal Daily Star* booked their own reporters aboard the *Empress* to file stories via wireless on the Duke's activities. The following are extracted from the correspondent's reports.

On board the steamship *Empress of Ireland*, via steamship *Saturnia* and Belle Isle and Cape Ray October 10 –

A severe squall struck this steamer on Monday. Heavy seas broke over the main deck continually, and the promenade was awash from sunrise to almost sunset. The wind dropped towards evening, however, and the swell calmed down to a long steady roll – the regulation Atlantic breaker – which was quite pleasant after the sudden jerks, jolts and bruisings of the day.

HRH the Duke of Connaught was on deck through the worst portion of the storm, watching from behind the shelter of a wind screen the huge breakers come rolling on board. There were very few passengers who cared to face the tempest, but the Duke appeared to be enjoying himself hugely and once, when an extra big comber came crashing on board and drenched him with spray, he laughed as he shook himself free and turned to light a fresh cigar.

Both the Duke and Duchess are enjoying excellent health. They are good sailors, and remain absolutely unaffected by the weather. The Duke spends most of his time strolling about on deck chatting with the passengers generally.

He is one of the first on deck in the morning, long before his staff are up, taking his constitutional in the shape of a sharp walk to and fro the full length of the promenade deck, setting an example to the other passengers of early rising.

On board the *Empress of Ireland*, 12 noon Wednesday, October 11 –

At noon today the *Empress* is about 100 miles from Heath Point and making good progress. There is every indication that the ship will arrive at Quebec on schedule time.

On board the steamship *Empress of Ireland*, via Point Riche and Cape Ray, October 11 –

Glorious weather greeted the arrival of the Duke in Canadian waters this morning. The misty drizzle of last night had cleared away and today broke fine, but rather cold.

We entered the Straits of Belle Isle in the early hours of the morning, but the Duke was on deck at 7 a.m., admiring the coast scenery through the latter part of the Straits.

During the rough weather preceding this fine spell a lady passenger fell down the companionway, severely injuring her head, but not suffering otherwise. This was the only accident during the trip. The fine weather has brought the passengers up on deck by the dozen.

On board steamship *Empress of Ireland*, via Fame Point, October 11 –

Their Royal Highnesses are receiving messages of welcome from every passing station and every passing vessel. Among them was a greeting from Earl Grey. The Duke has already Marconied about twenty replies.

The Duke and Duchess are evidently both greatly pleased at the greetings they have received. The Duchess is making a tour of the ship this afternoon, visiting all classes on board. The Duke has already made a similar tour, and met with a most cordial reception everywhere.

The *Empress* is assuming a festive air, gay decorations of bunting, bannerettes, flags, flowers, and drapings appearing everywhere. Everybody on board seems infected with the general gaiety, and none more so than the royal passengers.

On board steamship *Empress of Ireland*, via Cape Ray, October 11 –

After a few hours of splendid weather approaching the Straits of Belle Isle, keen winds began to blow, bringing in their train a heavy drizzle and wet mists, while the sea became choppy. Their Royal Highnesses, however, persisted in promenading the deck together, afterwards taking tea in the cafe.

The Duke afterwards continued on deck, chatting with various passengers who, following his example, stayed to walk until dinner time.

In deference to His Royal Highness' expressed desire, there is a continuance of the absolute lack of formality which marked his first appearance on board. He mixes freely with the passengers every day, and enjoys nothing more than a chat about Canada or something Canadian. So far, the trip has been a singularly uneventful one, wholly devoid of any untoward incident with the exception of the accident already related. Owing to the general inclement weather, even the usual sports on deck were not organized.

The Duke's activity promenading the decks is surprising everybody on board. The officers declare it would be creditable even in a much younger man. His Royal Highness easily outwalks the members of his staff. Indeed he is hardly below at all during the day time, except when driven down by the heavy seas which have from time to time broken over the vessel and made many of the passengers most unhappy people.

Despite the weather, the *Empress* made another fast crossing, six days and four hours from port to port. Daily runs to noon were: Saturday, 314 knots; Sunday, 444; Monday, 443; Tuesday, 419 in heavy gale; Wednesday, 452; Thursday, 395 to Rimouski. At the conclusion of the trip, the Duke bestowed a small gift of appreciation on Chief Officer Mansfield R. Steede, a diamond-studded gold tiepin. Steede's grandson today treasures the pin as a memento of his seafaring grandfather.

Ablaze with light, the *Empress* rounded the point at Indian Cove and arrived off Quebec on Thursday, 12 October 1911 at 6:45 p.m. A large crowd, chilled by the northerly wind, had assembled at the Breakwater to see the Duke, and it broke up in disappointment once it was learned that the royal party would remain aboard until their official landing at the King's Wharf the following morning. The Duke, whose swearing-in ceremony was scheduled for noon the next day, remained in his quarters and received only half a dozen visitors.

The CPR left nothing to chance. Superintendent John Walsh personally supervised the placing of the gangways, and no one was allowed on board except various officials, members of the press, and those having friends among the passengers. At the request of the Harbour Master an extra detachment of police was on hand to keep order, but their task proved to be a light one, for the crowd was orderly. First class passengers disembarked almost at once and boarded their special train, followed shortly by second class. Third class had to wait until the following morning before entraining for Montreal and the west.

Under normal circumstances an outgoing governor general would have left Canada before the new one arrived, but pressing matters in Ottawa had blocked Earl Grey's departure. As it happened, the Earl and Lady Grey were also in Quebec City aboard the government steamer *Earl Grey*, intending to sail the next day for England in the Allan's *Victorian*.

Hearing of this, the Connaughts invited the Earl and Lady Grey aboard the *Empress*, and the foursome sat dining and chatting in the Duke's cabin for some time before the Greys returned to their vessel. It was the last time the Earl, who had made three trips in the *Empress*, set foot on the ship. Later, as *Earl Grey* cleared Quebec and headed for her rendezvous with *Victorian*, the *Empress* sounded her horn in salute to the departing governor general. The crew had not forgotten the man whose interest in their welfare had started the sports fund two summers earlier.

The retinue of household servants that attended the Duke and Duchess did not accompany the royal couple. Instead they had departed from Liverpool in the *Victorian* and arrived at Quebec on 6 October, enough time for them to properly organize the governor general's residence in Ottawa. Incredibly, the Duke and Duchess brought over an entourage of twenty-seven staff members (including children), comprising cooks, housekeeper, footmen, maids, sculleryman, French chef, chauffeurs, valet and clerk. Such skilled persons were evidently not available in Canada at the time.

For this particular royal passage, the ship's print shop came up with a special cover for the first class passenger list, combining the CPR's name with the royal arms, and appropriate linked symbolic devices like the rose, shamrock, thistle, leek and maple leaves. The six names in the royal party, along with titles and positions, took up more than half a page.

Also in First Class was artist Frank Craig, whom we first encountered in July 1908. Craig, making his second trip to Canada aboard the *Empress*, was bound for New York, though engaged by *The Graphic* as Special Artist. Somehow, perhaps walking on the Upper Promenade deck, Craig met the Duke of Connaught and persuaded the royal passenger to sit for him. Craig executed a fine pencil and water-color portrait of the Duke, and signed the work, adding, 'SS Empress of Ireland Gulf of St Lawrence.' The work, measuring $22\frac{1}{2}$in x $14\frac{1}{2}$in can be dated to 11 October. Research for this book thus helped date the portrait, now in the National Archives of Canada. Unlike Craig's 1908 picture of emigrants, the portrait of the Duke is sober and restrained, and conveys only a hint of the artist's abundant other talents.

In ill health for much of his life, Frank Craig moved to Portugal in 1916. He died of tuberculosis at Cintra, a spot favoured by artists and writers, in July 1918. The Jacksons, from second class, settled in Vancouver where Richard died in 1919. Edith Mary continued to live with her step-daughter Maggie, and died in British Columbia in 1955 at the age of 94. The Duke of Connaught served as Canada's Governor General until 1916, whereupon he returned to England. He died in 1942 at the age of 92.

The *Empress* returned to Quebec on 10 November, after encountering 'terrible weather with strong head gales and rough seas.' Eight hundred and thirty-two people were aboard to share the misery of the last trip for the season to Quebec.

The ship's Pierrots were booked into the Auditorium on Wednesday, 15 November to close off the season, and the event was promoted extensively in the *Chronicle*. The public were promised new acts, and Auditorium manager Fabré was quoted as saying, 'For an organization of this kind there is talent far above the average. I had the pleasure of seeing a rehearsal today and some of the members were so good that I will book them in the vaudeville at a generous salary if I can possibly secure them.' Though the term 'Pierrot' originally denoted pantomime acts, where the players usually had whitened faces and wore loose white clothing, the *Empress* company had enough talent to stage a full-fledged revue. The troupe lived up to its advance billing. Captain Forster, the ship's officers and many of Quebec's leading citizens witnessed an evening of magnificent singing, humorous quips and jokes. The performance was well received, the *Chronicle* claiming the following day: 'If all the encores that had been demanded could have been responded to, the performance would very likely be going on still.'

The Duke and Duchess of Connaught were evidently pleased with the treatment they had received aboard the *Empress*. On 12 November the CPR announced in Montreal that HRH Princess Patricia of Connaught would sail in the *Empress* for Canada to join her parents. The Princess, the youngest daughter of the Duke and then 24, would depart from Liverpool on 1 December and, once in Halifax, would proceed to Ottawa aboard a special CPR train. The company also announced that Her Royal Highness would occupy the same suite as her parents. Though the announcement itself was highly impersonal ('It is announced at the Canadian Pacific Railway offices…') one senses the barely concealed gloating at the CPR's offices, a feeling of pride that the *Empress* had won out over the competition's boats.

The Princess duly arrived in Canada on 9 December accompanied by Miss Adam, her Lady-in-Waiting, and Major Malcolm Murray, Comptroller of the Household to the Duke of Connaught. Unfortunately the Princess had no sense of history for, as her daughter-in-law told the author, she never kept any letters and she never kept a diary.

For the winter of 1911-1912, the Canadian Pacific continued to make Saint John the winter port for its Atlantic fleet. 'Empress Specials' again left Windsor Station either at 8:15 p.m. or 6:40 p.m. on Thursdays, one day prior to the departure of the mail steamers. The 6:40 p.m. train, for the convenience of those arriving from the west, connected at Montreal Junction with Train 6 from Winnipeg and Train 18 from Toronto.

The CPR also established an 'Allan Special' for the benefit of Allan passengers with tickets out of Saint John. This was only good business on the part of the CPR. First, it generated more rail traffic for the CPR and, given that the CPR had de facto control of the Allan Line, it made sense to give passengers an easy way to access the ships. As well, the railway set up special connections for the benefit of passengers on White Star-Dominion, Royal (Canadian Northern), Cunard (formerly Thomson) and Donaldson steamships, all with the idea of promoting traffic for the railway and providing convenience for people who might later need the CPR.

In 1912 the *Empress* continued to make her regular crossings, and John Forster marked five and a half years as master of the best steamship in the company's North Atlantic service.

Ralph Carrington boarded the Empress on 5 April 1912 in Liverpool, destined for Saint John. Prior to leaving Britain, he wrote a postcard to his sister, a nurse at High Peak Hospital in the hills of Derbyshire, reflecting the fears of a first-time sea traveller and a less-than-complete knowledge of English spelling:

> Dear Sister,
> A disappointment sorry i couldnt see you i adent time to turn round befor i goot to go i
> hope i dont start feeding the fish i think we shall half a nice voge
> i send my best love to you so good by remember me to all from your Brother Ralph by by

Also aboard the ship was the Knight family from Somerset. Attracted by the CPR's land promotion, the family had sold its home and purchased a CPR farm in Strathmore, Alberta. John and Jane Knight, together with their four children, boarded at Liverpool. They were just one of fourteen families – English, Scottish and Irish – all bound for the Western Irrigation District and brand-new farms. None of the families had any particular reason for sailing in the *Empress*, apart from the fact she happened to be sailing at the right time.

Vera, then a girl of five, recalled their second-class voyage in an interview in March 2001. Her seven-year-old brother, Jack, had been given a football as a farewell gift. Once the *Empress* was at sea, 'He was up on deck kicking it, and he kicked it overboard, and he said, 'Daddy! Jump in the ocean and save my ball!''

'I thought the food was wonderful,' she recalled, then added, 'of course, kids would.' Vera and Jack proved to be better sailors than their two older siblings, Cyril and Hilda, who 'were never out of their bunks the whole way over. Jack and I never missed a meal.'

Off Newfoundland the *Empress* passed into an icefield dominated by an immense iceberg. 'They were all raving about the iceberg and everybody was looking at it. I said, 'Daddy, lift me up so I can see it.' He said, 'It's a white floating palace.' That iceberg was so big …I can still see it in my mind, as little as I was.'

Captain Forster prudently went around the iceberg, telling passengers the ship had detoured seventeen miles to avoid it.

From Saint John the Knights took the train westward. At one point newsboys 'were running up and down the platform yelling, 'Read all about it! The unsinkable *Titanic*'s gone down.' Everybody was thankful we didn't have the money to be on it.' The *Empress* passengers on the train were convinced *Titanic* had struck the same iceberg Captain Forster had carefully gone around.

On that same voyage, the ship's seventieth, there was a group of boys from Mr Fegan's Boys' Home in third class. This time the group numbered 115, mostly between 14-16, though the youngest was just eight. Under RELIGIOUS DENOMINATION on the manifest, all were shown as 'C of England.' Led by 'Jimmie' Taylor and John Bryant, age 45, the boys were destined to the Fegan Home on George Street in Toronto, and thence to foster farm homes in the area.

George Bogue Smart, seeing them in Toronto on his round of inspections, observed: 'I was much struck by their good appearance. They were a bright, hopeful-looking lot of boys, splendidly outfitted and soon taken up by the farmers of Ontario. I found that arrangements had been made for situations for nearly all of them before they reached Toronto.'

Also in third class was Josephine Israelson from Sweden, along with her five children ranging in age from six years to three months. They were headed to a homestead at Metiskow in Alberta, where Josephine's husband, Victor, had constructed a nice log home. With five young children to look after, Josephine was in desperate need of help. Fortunately, her eldest brother volunteered to accompany her to Canada. *Titanic* had been the family's first choice but they luckily booked the *Empress* from Liverpool instead.

Relatives in Sweden began knitting and sewing so there would be enough warm clothing for the children, and soon barrels and boxes were packed with everything Josephine and the children would need to begin a new life – linens, dishes, coffee grinder, churn, wool carders and even a spinning wheel.

Liverpool and the ship they embarked on must have seemed alien to the 31-year-old Swedish woman who spoke no English. Years later, the children remembered snippets of their voyage in third class. 'Uncle August would take the three oldest children up to the top deck to play. One day, as they stood looking out at the ocean over the railing, George's hat blew off his head. When he saw it floating on the water, he thought he could climb over the railing and retrieve it from the ocean. Luckily his older brother John grabbed him and pulled him down.' Third class was recalled as 'rather dark, poorly ventilated, and overcrowded.' 'The children …were not accustomed to some of the food served and refused to eat it, which may have accounted for their hunger.'

With the summer sailing schedule to Quebec set in the spring of 1912, the CPR published its train information to agents at the end of April. This time there would be two 'Empress Specials', one leaving Montreal's Windsor Station at 8:30 p.m. on Thursday, previous to an *Empress* departure, and a second train on Friday morning at 9:45 a.m. Both trains would run direct to the ship's side at Quebec. Another change had been made as well: 'Allan Specials' would run on Friday mornings from Windsor Station at 9:45 when *Virginian* and *Victorian* were the mail ships, and would take passengers direct to the ship's side, even though these two ships were departing from Montreal.

In May 1912 the Canadian government renewed the mail contract, valued at $600,000, with the Allan Line for a further twelve months. By extension, it meant the CPR's subcontract with the Allan Line, involving transport of the mails by the two *Empresses* would continue, along with *Virginian* and *Victorian*. With four ships, it meant there was effectively one mail trip per week in each direction. However, in renewing the contract, the government warned that it expected future contracts would be negotiated on a radically different basis.

At some point, after six years, it must have seemed to almost everyone – the company's management, crew, officers and shore personnel – that the voyages of the *Empress* had entered into a predictable, stable and almost boring routine.

Still, nothing at sea could ever be taken for granted, as the following incident showed. Having left Liverpool on Friday, 3 May 1912, the seventieth voyage began as normally as any other, with 1,550 passengers. On Monday, the third day out, the throttle valve spindle of the high pressure cylinder of the starboard engine blew out, scalding one crew member and striking another on the knee. Chief Engineer William Sampson determined that his men could begin temporary repairs, but the starboard engine would have to be shut down. Rather than return to Liverpool, the ship could still continue, but at reduced speed. Using just the port engine, progress averaged 250 miles a day, down from the usual 440.

Out of range of the shore Marconi stations on either side of the Atlantic, the CPR did not learn of the ship's problems until the ninth, when the *Empress* radioed Cape Race, by which time she had been further delayed by fog for twenty-four hours, and was proceeding under reduced speed.

With typical circumspection, *The Times* informed its readers of 'a slight derangement of the spindle valve' necessitating a reduction in speed.

Superintendent Walsh departed by the *Lake Champlain* in order to meet the *Empress* in the Gulf, and the company's tug *Cruizer* was told to stand by at Father Point to render assistance if necessary. Though none was needed, the sturdy tug accompanied the *Empress* upriver to Quebec. By the time the ship docked in Quebec at 9:00 a.m. on the thirteenth, the scalded crewman had almost recovered and plans had been made to complete the necessary repairs at Quebec, in such time that the planned sailing date of 17 May could still be met. Arriving passengers were described by the *Chronicle* as 'well' and 'in the best of spirits notwithstanding the unavoidable delay on the passage.'

It marked an interesting beginning to the *Empress'* season in Quebec, and the *Chronicle* noted 'the many friends of Lieut. Forster, his officers and crew are much pleased to see them back in Quebec again.'

Among the passengers in second class were the wife and four young children of Charles James Thompson, bound for Edmonton where Charles had settled the previous year. Intending to become a farmer in Alberta (thanks to a successful CPR poster campaign), he had soon found that he and horses

Left: *Inspection card for Elisa Sathre, third class passenger who landed at Quebec on 30 August 1912 (Voyage 75W). Note that the card is cross-referenced to the Manifest, p.23, line 2, for ease of inspection on arrival.* Right: *Reverse of the inspection card. (Eunice Gulbraa)*

'did not speak the same language.' Instead he had settled in Edmonton and became a pipefitter. Here he built a primitive tar-paper shack for himself and sent for his wife Edith, one son and three daughters – the youngest just nine months.

The family travelled up to Liverpool by train from the Sussex village of Mayfield a couple of days before sailing. At last, the day of departure came and they climbed the gangway onto the 'huge ship which had a strange smell – oil and fish and salt and oranges.' Unlike many bound for Canada, they were not accompanied by friends, and for this reason Charles Thompson had booked his family in second class, all in a single cabin. Though he could have afforded first class, he felt second would be friendlier. 'Mother said we would take a cheaper cabin because the ordinary folks (like us!) are always helpful.'

Joyce, Charles Thompson's second daughter, wrote the following account in 1993 of their trip:

> The little Thompson family was to sail on the *Empress of Ireland* about two weeks later [*than* Titanic]. Friends were anxious about us, but others said, 'After that disaster the next ships would be twice as safe.'
>
> I was just five years old, but memories of that journey are still vivid, eighty years later. I remember taking a tour of the ship, and seeing the beautiful rooms for the captain and the best first class passengers. Then we were disappointed at our second class cabin with bunk beds and one tiny round window that was seldom opened.
>
> Two days out Mother was terribly seasick and spent the next week in bed. Other second class passengers were very helpful, took the three children up for meals and helped to look after baby Nancy.
>
> The two-year-old boy, Phil, was a problem. He was very quick and full of curiosity, and the two little girls could not keep track of him. He explored the whole deck and we looked for him in vain. At last Mother stitched a large card to his jersey's back – 'Please return Phil to Cabin 202' – and everyone who saw him trotting around brought him back to us.
>
> I remember going on deck day after day. We liked to watch the foamy track the ship left behind. We even liked the constant sound of the engines.
>
> There were always many grown-ups pacing the deck and gazing far out to sea. We asked the friendly cabin boy, 'What is everyone looking for?'

Canadian Pacific Railway Co.
ATLANTIC STEAMSHIP LINES.

448 Stav.

KONTRAMERKE PAA REISEEFEKTER.
Hermed ultlevnes till indehaveren ved ankomsten till CANADA. Reiseefekter nummer.

Ansvarighetsgräns per Kontract, Kr. 50.

2090

JOH. G. SANDSMARK, Stavanger.
E. L. DAVIS, Paragon Station, Hull.
CANADIAN PACIFIC RAILWAY CO., 24, James St., Liverpool.
CANADIAN PACIFIC RAILWAY CO., Quebec and Montreal.
☞ VÄND

BAGGAGE NOTICE.

Upon landing in Canada from the steamer, passengers should immediately claim all their baggage and, after Customs examination, get it checked by the Railway Officials to inland destination.

BAGAGE NOTICE.

Passagerer som gaar iland i Canada fra Damskipet, maa oieblikkelig fordre udleveret alle sine sager og efter Toldvisitationen hos vedkommende Jernbanefunktionær faa dem indregistrerede for bestemmelsestedet inde i landet.

Left: *Baggage receipt 2090 issued to Elisa Sathre, Voyage 75W. (Eunice Gulbraa)* Right: *Reverse of baggage receipt. (Eunice Gulbraa)*

'Icebergs, of course,' he said.

I thought he said 'ice-*birds*.' 'What do you do when you catch the ice-birds?' I asked.

He laughed and said, 'I will crush them up and make some ice-cream for your tea.' When we ate the ice cream (a big treat) I still almost expected to see some feathers!

One very scary day there was *no* noise of the big engines that drove the ship. There was a big noise. The ship stopped right then. There was no wake behind the stern. People were terrified for a few minutes, thinking we had struck an iceberg.

But soon the stewards brought the news that one of the big boilers had burst, but there was no danger. The *Empress* would have to stop for three days while repairs were made. The six-day trip finally took almost ten days.

It seemed a long time before people excitedly pointed to 'land' in the distance. 'What is it?' I asked. 'Is it Canada?' But the answer was, 'No, it's just New-found-land' – which I thought meant land we had just found and did not want.

But at last it seemed Canada was close. We were sailing down a huge river – the banks were so far apart we couldn't even see them at first.

But days later there were trees and little towns, and at last the engines stopped again, we packed all out belongings, held hands, and stepped carefully down the gang-plank to solid ground. We were in Canada!

We little girls were almost sorry to leave the kind people who had helped us on the *Empress*. It had begun to feel like home. We were never to forget it.

Nor, when interviewed in February 2001, had she forgotten the abundance of oranges available at breakfast time. Terming the trip the 'first adventure of my life' she told the author, 'Parts of it are still vivid – like an old movie.' Then she added, 'Mother was seasick the whole ten days. My sister and I ran freely on deck and watched the waves and made friends with the crew.'

The manifest shows that Edith Thompson and her four children arrived in Canada with a pre-paid rail ticket to Edmonton and forty dollars. Joyce Thompson eventually became a teacher in rural Alberta, where she married Stanley Gould, a farmer fifteen years her senior. She still lives in Alberta and takes pride in doing her own cooking. In 1993 she attended a performance of the play *Empress of Ireland*, written by Alberta playwright Marion Kelch and performed in the town of Czar.

Inspection certificate issued to third class passenger Elisa Sathre at CPR's Liverpool Boarding House, 22 August 1912, one day prior to boarding the Empress. (Eunice Gulbraa)

As a result of her late arrival, the concert of the *Empress'* Pierrots, scheduled for Monday the 13th, was postponed until the Wednesday. Despite a shortened turnaround, it seemed many crewmen had time to take an evening off to watch their shipmates at the Auditorium Theatre. Captain Forster and other officers watched a two-part programme whose performers were all from the *Empress*.

Part I

1– Opening Chorus	The Troupe
2 – Humorous Song: Popping In and Out	P. Laycock
3 – Song (bass): Roll on Thou Dark and Deep Blue Ocean	J. Myers
4 – Duet: Bai Jane	Messrs Jones and Gray
5 – Humorous Song: Me	R.A. Kennedy
6 – Humourous Song: Mother Machree	H. Tunstall
7 – Humorous Song: Paper Bag Cookery	J.L. Jones
8 – Song: Good-Bye	C. Lewis
9 – Song and Dance	Messrs Crean and Taylor
10 – Humorous Dialogue: You Can't Sing Here	Messrs Terry and Laycock
11 – Quartette: Soldier's Farewell	Messrs Terry, Tunstall, Gray & Lewis

Part II

1 – Martyrs of the Arena	Empress Male Voice Choir
2 – Song and Dance	Master L. Smith
3 – Humorous Song: Poor Thing	H. Laycock
4 – Song: Alexander's Ragtime Band	H. Tunstall
5 – Humorous Song: Standing at the Corner of the Street	J.L. Jones
6 – Humorous Song: I Can't Reach the Top Note	R.A. Kennedy
7 – Farcical Sketch: The Hero	Messrs Terry, Laycock and Tunstall
God Save The King	

The evening was a success, the *Chronicle* reviewer declaring 'the theatre-goers of Quebec were greatly pleased to welcome back to Quebec the performers of the *Empress of Ireland*.'

The *Empress* departed Quebec, as planned, on 17 May at 4:15 p.m. with 654 passengers, few of whom were probably aware of the engine problem she had sustained on the westbound leg.

Fog off the Grand Banks proved to be a problem for a number of vessels in early June. Returning to Quebec via Cape Race with 1,516 passengers on Voyage 72W, the *Empress* was delayed twenty-four hours by fog. After leaving Liverpool at 8:19 p.m. on Friday, 31 May, the ship had encountered strong headwinds, which yielded to thick fog on Wednesday. Among the passengers was Sir Thomas Shaughnessy, and Sir Montagu and Lady Allen.

Congestion at the Immigration area in Quebec was nothing new, but the following shows how busy the port could get and how efficiently immigrants could be processed. The *Empress*, westbound on her 73rd voyage, arrived at the Breakwater with 1,506 passengers at 2:45 p.m., just an hour after *Tunisian* had arrived with 1,100. Still, with inspectors boarding the large liners at Rimouski, the arrival process was not as bad as it seemed. In short order, the first special train got away quickly with the first class passengers and the Orient mail.

Two second class passengers were in less of a hurry to leave the ship. They were the Thomases, Owen and Annie, whose daughter Jean Sophia Alice had been born on 4 July and baptized aboard ship. The manifest records her birthplace as 'At sea' and notes that mother and daughter were taken to Quebec's Jeffrey Hale Hospital.

While the Salvation Army often chartered an entire vessel for its emigrants, it happened also that smaller numbers of people would need to be accommodated, either new settlers to Canada or Army personnel going about their work. Almost from her maiden voyage, members of the Army had travelled aboard the ship, including General Booth himself in June 1907, though no one seems to have attached any significance to that at the time. The voyage of 26 July 1912 was one more link in the chain binding the *Empress* and the Army inextricably together; on this occasion about fifty Army staff embarked from Liverpool.

They had a calm voyage, illustrated by the following postcard, dated 1 August and addressed to The Rev. M.E. Atlay at St Matthew's Clergy House in Westminster:

> We are in the Gulf of St Lawrence and hope to make Quebec early in the morning. Absolutely unruffled passage. Trevelyan on board: we have chummed.
> (sgd) J.B. Atlay

The manifest showed James B. Atlay was a British civil servant, aged fifty-one, headed to Toronto as a tourist. The 'Trevelyan' referred to is Rev. William Bouverie Trevelyan, a noted clergyman and author who was destined to British Columbia as a tourist. Trevelyan had served earlier as vicar of St Matthew's and was obviously known to the recipient of the postcard.

One of the rare occasions when the two sister *Empresses* were in Quebec together occurred while the *Empress* was being turned around between her arrival on 2 August and departure on the ninth.

The *Empress of Britain*, after colliding in dense fog with the fully laden collier *Helvetia* in the Gulf of St Lawrence on 27 July, had limped back to Quebec on the 29th, her bow badly damaged. Struck amidships by the *Empress of Britain*, the collier had been impaled on the liner's bow for half an hour, allowing the collier's crew of forty-three and two female passengers to be rescued. The 375-foot *Helvetia*, a coal boat for the Dominion Coal Company, sank quickly after the two ships separated. Ironically, both *Helvetia* and *Storstad* were built just a year apart in the same Newcastle shipyard. Both were loaded with Cape Breton coal, bound for Montreal.

Taking advantage of the unusual opportunity, soccer teams from the two *Empresses* took to the field on Saturday, 3 August. On a hot afternoon, the *Empress of Ireland* team was outplayed 0-2 by the *Empress of Britain*.

A postcard showing the ship and mailed from Liverpool to a young boy in Wrexham in August is typical of many notes jotted before the ship's departures, and a reminder that the problems of parents have not changed much in the intervening years:

> Dear David —
> This is the boat I am sailing in today.
> Be a good boy to your mother. I am sure Gladys will.
> Your loving father

That same month a young widow from Haugesund, Norway, and her fourteen-year-old son Ludvig boarded a ship in Stavanger, bound for Liverpool and new lives in Alberta. The family's history was a tragic one, for Elisa Satre was a seamstress whose husband, a sea captain, had been washed overboard from his vessel in 1901. Arriving in Liverpool, they stayed at the CPR's boarding house near the Landing Stage and embarked in the *Empress* on 23 August, along with 1,548 other passengers.

The Satres, in third class, were just two of several hundred Scandinavians – Finns, Danes, Swedes and Norwegians – all bound to Canada. Ludwig's memories of the trip remained with him for the rest of his long life. He recalled that the food was just average. He found their cabin small and, to make things worse, many of the almost 900 people in third class were seasick, as it had turned into a very rough voyage. The young boy made his way up to the deck in heavy weather, where the air was clean and fresh. He liked it so much that he fell asleep in a coil of ropes. Eventually a sailor found him, chastised him, and sent him below, whereupon Ludvig became sick like everyone else.

The *Empress* encountered icebergs and thick fog off Belle Isle, and lost six hours by steaming at reduced speed. Once through, the weather moderated somewhat and they enjoyed fine weather up the Gulf and river. When the *Empress* arrived at Quebec on 30 August, a boy, born on the passage to Scandinavian parents in third class, was taken with his mother to the Detention Hospital.

Meanwhile, Elisa and Ludvig Satre were processed through immigration. After their cards were duly stamped, they collected their baggage and boarded the waiting CPR train, bound for Sedgewick in east central Alberta. One day after arriving in the town, Elisa married Erik Johnson, a friend from Norway with whom she had corresponded for many years. Ludvig, who later became a farmer, was a guest of honour at the play *Empress of Ireland*, staged in Czar in February 1993. Though he never spoke much of his trip, Elisa carefully saved their tickets, landing cards and other papers connecting them to the ship.

From a postcard cancelled on 20 September 1912 at Liverpool:

> Just a line to let you know that I had arrived safe on the boat and we have got a good berth. It sails at 7 p.m. & we are waiting for it to start. I have just finished up my dinner on the boat.
> Your loving gr. son Ralph

If seamen had managed to wrest a pay hike from the shipowners as a result of their strikes the previous summer, it took until November 1912 before lines like the CPR and Allan raised the salaries of officers and masters. The Allan management had offered an across-the-board increase to its officers, and had evaluated the salaries of its masters. The CPR, meanwhile, made what *The Times* termed 'a substantial increase' in the pay of its officers, while other lines increased officers' wages by £1 per month.

It is interesting to use the *Empress of Ireland* passenger totals for 1912 to compute load factors for the vessel. In that year the *Empress* made twelve trips westbound and thirteen eastbound. Assuming a maximum capacity of 350 in first class, 350 in second and 1,000 in third, we can construct the following tables:

		1st	2nd	3rd
Westbound	Theoretical capacity	4,200	4,200	12,000
	Actual passengers	2,046	4,445	9,409
	Load factor (%)	48.7	105.8	78.4
Eastbound	Theoretical capacity	4,550	4,550	13,000
	Actual passengers	1,451	2,159	5,712
	Load factor (%)	31.9	47.5	43.9

While load factors vary with the season, they show that eastbound loads were always lower than westbound, with the least difference being in first class. An overall load in third class westbound of 78% is very respectable, and contributed to the operating success of the *Empress*. The load factor of 105% for second class westbound can be explained by putting half-fare children in the same bunk, and thus carrying more than the nominal capacity.

Even in the winter months, the voyages and passenger counts of the *Empress* continued to be monitored in the Montreal papers. In January 1913 the *Gazette* told readers that the ship had sailed from Liverpool on 24 January 'after her customary winter overhauling' and that she carried 120 first, 350 second and 1,257 third class passengers, 'an exceptionally heavy list for the time of year.'

On 18 April, for the ship's 83rd westbound crossing, twenty-seven-year-old Florence ('Florrie') Morgan boarded the *Empress* in Liverpool, heading for Saint John where she would meet her fiancé, Ernest Arthur Baker. Together, the two planned to proceed to Brandon, Manitoba, where they would be married. Arthur had left Cardiff in 1912 along with his brother and had come to Canada, where he found a position with the Canadian Pacific Railway and settled in Brandon.

On 22 April Florrie wrote a four-page letter to her family in Cardiff on stationery bearing a photograph of the ship and the caption 'R.M.S. 'Empress of Ireland.'

My Dear Mother & Father, Sisters & Brothers,
I expect you are wondering how we are getting along. Well up till now we have all been terribly ill with seasickness. What an awful thing it is, you feel as though you would give the world if the boat would go down, or else that you have never started the journey. It certainly is no joke to go to Canada. How some girls can go, with no one to go to, I cannot understand. Suppose they have more nerve, or pluck, than I have. Do wish I were able to rough it more, but you cannot expect from a person what is not there.

I don't know what Father would do if he could hear the people reaching [*retching*] their hearts of them almost, and then when you see their poor faces, well you would wonder how they could live the journey through.

We have four beds in our berth. I have the one on top and Flo & B, the bottom one. On the other side is a mother and her three children, the father and two other of the children are in another berth. They are going a long way, the other side of the Rockies. No house or anything else to go to, they have to wait at the nearest railway station, which is some eighty-odd miles away from their destination – (Such a life would kill you Mother, I am sure) – until they get a house roughly built.

I shall never forget the feeling when we crossed the ferry [*from Cardiff to Avonmouth*]. Oh it was awful, such a lonely feeling & then the worst part of all, crossing on the tugboat to embark on the *E of I*. But there it will be all right when I am with my Arthur & will have his care until I get stronger.

All this awful dry reaching I have had, I cannot touch food, and of course have nothing to bring up, but I have reached until the water has streamed out of my eyes and it makes you feel so weak.

Tuesday.

My Dear Mother

You will be pleased to know that we are all getting better & strong enough to get out of bed & take a meal in the dining-room. We have found our sea-legs at last and able to get up on deck for a breath of fresh air. We have indeed been rocked in the cradle of the deep on this voyage, for you would imagine you were in a very high swinging boat, when you are in bed, it is a horrid swimmy feeling. You will be glad to hear that we have not had to pay excess on luggage so far. Everybody on board is exceedingly nice and kind. Nothing too much trouble. Stewards & Stewardesses very nice. We have very good food and as much as ever you like to have – no scarcity.

Last night we had a meeting in the dining room (Salvation Army). It was very nice and we had some lovely hymns. It was quite an uplift by the way. We all sleep very well, considering the boat rolls so terribly.

Now we are getting well, the journey is full of interest as you can quite imagine. Such different faces and characters. There are over 900 3rd class passengers, more than 300 of the better class. She is a huge boat.

…Must not forget to tell you Mr & Mrs Hewitt were very kind, what we should have done without them I do not know.

We hope to land on Saturday. At present we are in the iceberg region, it is bitterly cold but the foam is simply lovely….

Well now, I must close. With Fondest love & thanks to you one and all for your kindness towards me.

Ever remaining your most affectionate Daughter,

Florrie

The *Empress* arrived in Saint John on Friday, 25 April. No one knew it at the time, but this was the last time the great ship would ever sail to the New Brunswick port that had been her winter home for seven seasons.

Florrie travelled on to Manitoba by train, where she married Arthur on 30 April. In 1919 Florrie and Arthur, along with their son, moved back to Cardiff where Arthur joined the family coal business. Florrie, in poor health, died in 1920.

'Swallowing the anchor' was a Liverpool seaman's expression meaning to jump ship, and for most men it could not have been an easy decision. In the case of Arthur Owen it was made somewhat easier, as his parents had decided to emigrate to Canada, there being plenty of jobs for bricklayers. In April 1913 Arthur decided to join them. He explained later how it was done:

A chum of mine [*Ken Williams*] aboard ship decided he too would jump ship with me. The *Empress of Ireland* arrived at Saint John on Friday. It was our duty to assist passengers to disembark and to put their luggage on the dock. We used to have to put luggage stickers with the passengers' initials on their luggage. In this way we put our own luggage with theirs, having obtained the necessary stickers. In this way it went through the Customs. The Customs Officer knew us and knew we were jumping ship so checked the luggage. When the opportunity arose we grabbed our luggage and got to the freight doors on the dock. From there we could drop our luggage onto the railway tracks below.

At an opportune time we got the bags and took them to a corner store and asked the man to hold them for us until we called for them. We reimbursed him, told him that we would pick them up at 5:30 p.m. Saturday when we were off duty. We left the ship in our private clothes and left the rest of our belongings on the ship.

As I was Assistant Steward, I was well known and friendly with the crew. In this way I managed to obtain our Board of Trade Certificate of Discharge book which recorded all our sailings, from the Assistant Purser. Usually this book would not come into my hands until I returned to England at the end of the return trip, as I started from there. In jumping ship, I only completed half of the trip. The whole crew knew of our intentions and wished us good-bye in secret. They all hated to see us go. We went to the corner store and retrieved our bags, and then caught the train for Montreal and there met my father, and on to Toronto.

For years afterward the 'Empress Sharpshooter' was reluctant to mention he had jumped ship, feeling he had abandoned his shipmates. Dictating some of his *Empress* experiences to his wife in 1978, he observed wryly, 'I realize now the gods were good to us as, had we stayed on the *Empress*, we too would have gone down with the ship.' He spent the rest of his life in Toronto, working first as a bricklayer with his father. He married in 1920, had two children, and subsequently learned the printing trade. At one point he was hired by the Canadian Pacific, though he never admitted he'd previously worked for the company aboard the *Empress*. Later he worked for the local electric utility and retired in 1960. He maintained a lifelong interest in soccer and died in 1989 at the age of ninety-six.

In the late spring of 1913, responding to the needs of its bread and butter clients, the westbound third class passengers who comprised almost sixty percent of the *Empress'* manifest, the CPR opened large third class waiting rooms in the dock area of Liverpool. There was even a nursery area, capable of accommodating twenty children. In this, the company was not alone. All the Liverpool-based shipping firms were going out of their way to look after passengers whose needs, only a decade before, would have been sniffed at and dismissed as unimportant.

In the spring of 1913 some of the *Empress of Ireland*'s first class passengers found a pleasant upgrade in their accommodations. The company fitted electric radiators in all outside first class staterooms, as well as the library and first class smoking room. It was, no doubt, a welcome addition for those obliged to suffer the rigors of a first class passage aboard the *Empress*. The radiators were in the form of miniature fire grates and were intended to give the same comfort and cheerful glow as open fireplaces.

A CPR bulletin of 1 March 1913 explained that the accommodations of the *Empress* were un-surpassed and no effort or expense had been spared to provide every new appliance for the comfort and enjoyment of passengers.

There was another change as well that spring. The CPR announced a modification in the summer schedule for trips eastbound from Quebec. Henceforth the Atlantic *Empresses* would sail from Quebec and Liverpool on Thursdays, instead of Fridays as had been the practice for previous years.

Two 'Empress Specials' from Montreal would serve the ships. One train, consisting of baggage, colonist, first-class coaches and standard sleeper, would leave Windsor Station on Wednesday at 8:30 p.m. and proceed directly to the ship's side. A second train, the 'Empress Mail Special', having baggage, colonist, first-class coaches, dining and parlor cars, would leave Windsor Station at 9:50 a.m. on Thursday and run direct to the ship's side.

A colonist coach was a no-frills coach with spartan furnishings and designed to accommodate third class passengers. Such coaches, equipped with potbellied stoves for cooking and heating, took thous-ands of new arrivals westward to their new homes and figure prominently in the recollections of many immigrants to Canada.

On 7 April 1913 the Postmaster General announced in the House of Commons that a contract had been entered into for the transport of mails between Canada and Britain. Unlike the previous contract, which involved just four vessels (two Allan liners and the two *Empresses*) the new contract provided for mail service three times a week in summer, and twice in winter, instead of once a week as in the previous contract. And, instead of four vessels, there were now twelve, from four steamship companies: Allan and the CPR, as before, along with Canadian Northern and White Star-Dominion.

In a complex arrangement, the Allan Line was permitted to use, in summer, *Victorian*, *Virginian*, *Corsican*, and *Tunisian* and, until the new *Alsatian* and *Calgarian* were ready in the early months of 1914, *Grampian* and *Hesperian*. The CPR, as before, would use the *Empress of Ireland* and *Empress of Britain*. Canadian Northern would use *Royal Edward* and *Royal George*, while White Star-Dominion would use *Laurentic* and *Megantic*.

Winter arrangements called for the Allan Line to use *Alsatian*, *Calgarian*, *Victorian* and *Virginian*. The CPR would use both *Empresses*; Canadian Northern would use its two vessels, while White Star-Dominion would get no part of the winter service, as it used Portland (Maine) as a winter port, although it was permitted to have *Teutonic* as a stand-by vessel in case one of the others should be laid up.

Valued at a subsidy of $1 million per year, the contract allowed the use of either Montreal or Quebec in summer, and Halifax and Saint John in winter, and landing points in Britain were at the option of the companies, the choices being Liverpool or Bristol, though *Hesperian* and *Grampian* could continue to serve Glasgow over the short term. The subsidy would be divided among the companies in a manner that remained to be agreed upon.

In all, it was a typical Canadian arrangement, with the government not wanting to appear to favour any of the shipping companies, while recognizing how dependent the companies were on the mail subsidy to help pay the operating costs of the vessels.

With 1,586 passengers on her eighty-fourth voyage, the *Empress* returned to Quebec on 23 May 1913, her latest-ever date to go up the St Lawrence. The *Chronicle* commented: 'This is the *Empress of Ireland*'s first trip to Quebec this season and despite the disagreeable weather there were a large number of people on the dock to welcome her popular commander, his officers and crew back to Quebec.' Although the ship had faced headwinds and seas for the greater part of the trip, the paper noted, 'The trip across was altogether uneventful.'

Atlantic crossings, it seemed, were getting rather commonplace and routine.

A month later, a pleasant function took place on board the *Empress* as she steamed upriver from Rimouski in the closing hours of her 85th voyage. Chief Steward Augustus Gaade was summoned to his cabin to meet some friends who wished to discuss 'a certain important matter with him.' On reaching his room he was surprised to find representatives of the Canadian and US Customs and Immigration departments, the Post Office, and railway companies, all of whom were accustomed to going up and down between Quebec and Rimouski.

Once Gaade had entered, the door was shut. George Moore, the CPR's Quebec City passenger agent, stepped forward, cleared his throat and, after a short speech, presented Gaade with three sets of carvers – meat, fish and game – and concluded by wishing the chief steward and his new bride a long and happy voyage over the sea of life.

Regaining his composure, Gaade thanked the donors for their valuable and unexpected gift. Customs Agent Bolger then made a witty speech and proposed long life, health and happiness to the couple. This was drunk, as the *Chronicle* put it, 'with Highland honours, the company singing *For They Are Jolly Good Fellows*.' After again congratulating the bridegroom, the party broke up. There were jobs to be done and 1,496 passengers to be attended to before the ship docked in Quebec.

This time, the *Empress* had a new berth at the Breakwater, a bit further to the west than her former docking area. There was now enough room to accommodate two large steamers between the *Empress* and the north end of the Breakwater.

First class passengers were landed at once from the midship gangway, while the mails were sent ashore forward.

Sometime between 20-26 June, while their ship lay at Quebec, the officers of the *Empress* gathered on Lower Promenade deck for a group photograph. A year later, all but two of the main officers were

EMPRESS SPECIAL TRAINS

Will leave Windsor Street Station at 8.30 p.m. Thursday, June 13, and 9.45 a.m. Friday, June 14, connecting with R.M.S. Empress of Ireland which sails from Quebec Friday, June 14.

Trains run direct to the ship's side.

Typical newspaper notice for Empress Special trains. Montreal Gazette, *13 June 1912.*

still aboard her. Only the master and ship's surgeon had changed.

Departing on Thursday 26 June the *Empress* left Quebec with 1,089 passengers, a very considerable number, among whom were many Americans. First class held a special party of doctors from Chicago bound for a medical convention in Germany, and a group from Cincinnati on a European tour. The St Lawrence route was enjoying a renaissance in popularity.

With so many of the *Empress'* crew drawn from the Liverpool area, it was natural that the CPR and her crew took a great interest in local charities. In July 1913 Arthur Piers, the company's Liverpool manager, arranged for two additional hammocks in the Lancashire and National Sea Training Home for Boys, at Liverpool, to be known as Empress Hammocks. They would, he announced, be supported by the officers and crews of the company's steamships *Empress of Ireland* and *Empress of Britain*.

While anchored in the Mersey on the afternoon of 11 July 1913, a few hours before she was due to sail on her 86th voyage, the *Empress* was part of a large flotilla of merchant vessels inspected by George V, Queen Mary and Prince Albert (the future George VI) from the Dock Board's tender, *Galatea*. A total of 109 ships of every description were arranged in two lines stretching over ten miles, with *Mauretania* in the middle of the line. With only two Royal Navy ships present, at the end of the line, HMS *Liverpool* and HMS *Lancaster*, it was an impressive demonstration of the power of Britain's mercantile marine. The waterborne tour was the high point of the Royal Family's state visit to Liverpool. The official opening of the new Gladstone Dock, 1,020 feet in length – nearly 140 feet longer than the *Olympic* – later in the day, which was the reason for the monarch's visit, must have seemed somewhat of an anticlimax.

The *Empress* was thirteenth in line and, as *The Times* noted in its coverage, 'had her passengers on board, and left for Montreal [*sic*] half an hour after the close of the review.'

Though it was midsummer, Captain Forster elected to take the Cape Race, or southerly, route and the *Empress* made a fast trip of just 6 days and 16 hours from port to port. Passengers interviewed at the wharf in Quebec expressed delight with the trip across and 'the excellent treatment they received on board from all the employees of the company.' One New Yorker who claimed to cross the Atlantic several times a year stated that on no other ship had he 'found more attention, care and consideration paid to passengers than that given by the stewards and waiters of the *Empress*.'

Arriving at Quebec in the morning of 18 July to conclude the passage, the manifest contained an unusual entry: 'Corpse.' This was identified as passenger James Simeon, age 71, a Canadian bound for Toronto. Presumably Simeon had died aboard ship while on the last portion of the trip up the St Lawrence River, and could not be buried appropriately at sea.

Making the return trip to England was General Sir Ian Hamilton, one of the most experienced soldiers in the British Army. Serving as Inspector-General of Overseas Forces, the sixty-year-old general was returning to England after a whirlwind tour of Canadian military installations and meetings with militia and army officers. He had taken the morning boat train from Montreal and it had arrived earlier than expected, with the result that the guard of honour, ordered for 3 p.m., had not yet shown up. Hamilton took the gaffe in good stride. He and his aide waited in their railway carriage until the guard, forty members of the 9th Voltigeur Regiment of Quebec, were in place. He then made a quick inspection, complemented the men on their appearance, and bid goodbye to a large number of senior Canadian officers gathered on the quayside. Hamilton then boarded the *Empress*, which departed almost immediately thereafter.

Two military bands on the wharf proved to be an unexpected treat for the *Empress*' eight hundred passengers, who showed their appreciation by frequent applause as the ship slowly pulled away from her berth. On the dock Colonel Sam Hughes, Minister of Militia, called for three cheers for General Hamilton, and they were given with an enthusiastic roar. Invited to the bridge by Captain Forster, Hamilton waved to the officers on the quayside and stayed on the bridge until the *Empress* was in the middle of the river, her bow pointed toward the sea.

Once settled, the man who would, two years later, lead the ill-fated British campaign against the Turks at Gallipoli, began writing a series of reports on his impressions of Canada's military readiness. The general's diary made no mention of his passage, apart from noting that they had passed through an icefield before entering the Strait of Belle Isle.

Also on board was Charles Taze Russell, the sixty-one-year-old founder of Jehovah's Witnesses. In a letter on *Empress* stationery dated 24 June, he wrote: 'Here we are on board – all well! Nearly all the baggage is missing so far–but not my trunk.' Evidently the perils of travel were not much different ninety years ago than in the jet age.

The usual routines of summer turnaround in Quebec City continued as in the past. On 16 August, a Saturday, the Quebec Cricket Club defeated the *Empress* by a score of 78 to 52, and on the 19th, *Empress* singers performed at the Catholic Sailors' Club – 'in every particular most successful' claimed the *Chronicle* the next day.

Another link in the chain with the Salvation Army was forged that summer. Arriving at Quebec on 11 September 1913, part of the 1,573 passenger total (second highest for the year), were about seventy-five Salvation Army immigrants. It was another fast crossing for the *Empress*: six days and two hours from dock to dock. Captain Forster reported fine weather and an uneventful voyage. This time, it seemed, the presence of a Salvation Army group failed to produce the usual stormy weather.

Docking at Quebec was getting to be a routine affair as well. Arriving at Quebec at 4:15 p.m., the ship ran up the harbour, turned smartly in her own length, went alongside the dock and was safely moored in just fifteen minutes. It was fast work, although some claimed it could be done faster if not for the harbour regulations against speeding.

On Monday night, 15 September, the Amateurs of the *Empress* gave a concert at the Seamen's Institute. Over the years the *Empress* men had supported a variety of charitable causes at the Institute. On this particular night, the concert was in aid of St Bridget's Home, which looked after more than 400 orphans and the elderly poor. It was one of the most deserving charities in the district of Quebec and the men had rehearsed their programme of music and songs for months, in anticipation of a large crowd. Admission, given the nature of the evening, was twenty-five cents.

While junior officers were regularly rotated through the *Empress* by the CPR in preparation for other commands, many crew members had known no other captain than John Forster, who had been described in 1909 by Third Officer Julian Duck as 'a particularly careful navigator' and 'always cool.' Thus the crew must have been somewhat apprehensive when, on 17 September, it was announced that the popular Forster was retiring from sea duty and would assume a shore position with the CPR at Liverpool.

Learning of the news, hundreds of Quebecers found an opportunity in the next two days to make their way aboard the *Empress* to bid Forster goodbye and wish him luck on his well-deserved promotion. The *Chronicle* noted that he had 'won the admiration of one and all, not only as a thorough seaman and navigator, but as an upright and perfect gentleman, who at all times looked after the safety and welfare of all committed to his charge.'

When the *Empress* cleared the Breakwater on 18 September at 4:05 p.m. with 871 passengers, her whistle sounded three farewell blasts, to which the tug *Cruizer* replied. John Forster handed command over to Captain James Turnbull in Liverpool on 1 October 1913. When the ship sailed down the Mersey two days later with 1,473 passengers aboard, she had a new master on the bridge, a man whose habits and idiosyncrasies would have to be learned. Turnbull was no stranger to ships of the *Empress* class, for he had served as chief officer in both Atlantic *Empresses*, and was well known to the people of Quebec. Said the *Chronicle*: 'Possessed of most affable and pleasing manners, Lieut. Turnbull is sure to become most popular with the travelling public.'

Despite rough weather in the Atlantic and fog in the Gulf, James Turnbull's inaugural voyage (89W) as master of the *Empress* was a fast one, even though the ship had been delayed by tides at Liverpool and did not get away until just before midnight on 3 October. The voyage was marked by a happy event, the birth of a boy on 5 October to Mrs Margaret Cornthwaite, a third class passenger en route to Sudbury to join her husband William, a miner. On arrival at Quebec, mother and the newborn were sent to Jeffery Hale Hospital, while her four other children, ranging in ages from nine to three, were taken to the Detention Hospital. In honour of the captain, the boy was named James Turnbull Cornthwaite; his birthplace is recorded in the manifest as 'at sea'.

Soccer fans were treated to an excellent match on Saturday afternoon, 11 October. The *Empress* eleven played a charity match at the Exhibition Grounds against a team composed of the best players from the four Quebec teams in the league. In what was termed an 'interesting' game, the men of the *Empress* went down to defeat, 3-1.

On leaving Quebec on 16 October with 868 passengers, the *Empress* met with a slight mishap that delayed her by five hours. Owing to a strong northeasterly wind, she had considerable difficulty in getting away from the Breakwater. The tugs *Belle* and *M.E. Hackett* took ropes from her bow, and a hawser from her port quarter was attached to a post on the inside of the Breakwater to bring her stern into the gap in the Louise basin. As the *Empress* swung clear of the wharf the tugs cast off their lines and the hawser on the dock was also let go. The latter fell into the river and fouled the *Empress'* port propeller.

Once she was bought back to the dock and moored in her usual place, the CPR secured the services of the diver from the salvage tug *Lord Strathcona*. After some work the diver succeeded in clearing the propeller and the *Empress* finally departed at 8:00 p.m.

On 1 October 1913 the CPR announced that it had decided, for the forthcoming winter at least, that its *Empress* steamers would make Halifax their winter port, and would not merely call there to disembark passengers and mail on their way to Saint John. At the same time, the Allan Line confirmed that its new mail boats, *Alsatian* and *Calgarian*, would not be calling at Saint John. While the Allan decision had been suspected for some time, the CPR's decision on the *Empress* mail steamers came as a complete shock. Both lines had previously advertised sailing dates from Saint John, and some form of political interference was suspected at first.

The decision was confirmed the following day at the CPR's headquarters, when a press release was handed out. The CPR tried to mitigate the news by pointing out, first, that the arrangement was for this year at least, thus seeming to hold out some hope that Saint John might again become the winter port and, second, the remainder of the company's Atlantic fleet would sail to and from Saint John as usual. Though the press statement was silent on the reasons for the change, company officials noted that Halifax could better handle the mails and passengers, although Saint John was a better port for freight.

That was probably true, although facilities at Saint John were being upgraded as rapidly as possible, and this offered the city hope for the future. But, as the *Standard* astutely noted in an editorial, 'everything cannot be done in a day' and Halifax would not be idle in the meantime.

CONCERT

In Aid of

St. Bridget's Home

Given by Amateurs of the

Empress of Ireland

IN SEAMEN'S INSTITUTE,
Champlain Street.

On Monday Evening, 15th Inst.

Doors open at 7:30 o'clock.
Entertainment at 8 o'clock sharp.

TICKETS 25c EACH,

Sold at P. J. Evoy's, John street; St. Patrick's Presbytery, Emmet and St. Lawrence Clubs, and at door of Hall.

sept12x3

In the New Brunswick port there was predictable outrage and indignation, though the city's case wasn't helped any by the fact that only a week before, Local 273 of the International Longshoremen's Association had submitted to the city's shipping agents a wage schedule for the coming season that would have put the city ahead of other east coast ports like Boston, Portland, Halifax, Montreal and Quebec. The longshoremen, who the previous season had worked for 35 cents an hour in summer, with a nine-hour day, and 30 cents in winter with a ten-hour day, were now seeking 40 cents an hour. And, while they had previously worked nights at the old day rates, they now wanted 45 cents an hour for nights, with heavy premiums for Sunday work. And they were demanding a nine-hour day. In Halifax, by comparison, the rates were 25-27 cents an hour, 35 cents for nights, and double time on Sundays.

As Saint John was a winter port, this created a problem for all the shipping companies, for vessels found it difficult to keep to their schedules in rougher weather. That meant the companies often needed the longshoremen at nights and on weekends to meet their planned sailing dates – and thus would incur additional costs.

On top of this the Marine Freight Checkers' Union and the Coal Handlers' Union in Saint John were ready to jump on the bandwagon, and planned to notify the shipping companies of wage increases to catch up with inflation.

Interviewed in Montreal on his return on the 5th, Sir Thomas Shaughnessy commented that the company had given the matter grave consideration, observing that 'The call at both Halifax and Saint John involved undue risk to the vessels in making the trip between the two ports along the coast of Nova Scotia in all sorts of weather, and eastbound passengers, who embarked at Saint John, were necessarily subjected to a delay at Halifax of from twelve to twenty hours on each voyage.' As well, he argued, the company's other vessels would continue to go to Saint John, which was the company's traditional winter port and, in view of the large number of vessels using Saint John, the CPR considered the port infrastructure would be overtaxed if the *Empresses* continued to dock there.

'This arrangement is only a tentative one and will be subject to revision when West Saint John has the harbour and wharf facilities to properly accommodate the ocean traffic.' Shaughnessy had thus left the door open for the New Brunswick port. The new arrangement with Halifax was merely temporary and would be reviewed once the Saint John harbour and wharf facilities could accommodate the increased traffic.

A Saint John delegation to Ottawa of twenty prominent citizens of all political stripes failed to sway the politicians or persuade them to lean on the CPR and have the decision reversed. Though the delegation was given a polite hearing in the capital, Prime Minister Borden did not commit himself. Despite optimistic headlines, the citizens of Saint John resigned themselves to the loss of the two *Empresses*.

For one year, at least.

There was just one small consolation. Saint John would still see a portion of the mails, for the Royal Line (owned by the Canadian Northern Railway) steamers *Royal George* and *Royal Edward* would make Saint John their winter home, and the Allan Line kept its mail boats *Virginian* and *Victorian* on the run to Saint John as well. Thus, each of the two cities would see four mail steamers, though the bigger and faster vessels would head to Halifax.

Despite ongoing harbour improvements at Saint John, the city would still have to work hard to secure the return of the two *Empresses*. At the end of November, the government let a contract worth over $5.2 million to upgrade the harbour facilities in Halifax. In Halifax, the mood was upbeat. 'Halifax Can Move the Ocean Traffic' was the *Herald*'s headline on 8 October, referring to the port's ability to handle the passenger traffic, and the Intercolonial Railway's ability to move passengers and freight.

In quantitative terms, what did the switch to Halifax for the *Empress of Ireland* mean to the port of Saint John? A column in *The Standard* of October 6 provides some interesting answers.

– food suppliers lost approximately $5,000 per trip
– coal suppliers lost about $6,000 or more per trip
– labour lost the unloading and loading of some 5,000 tons of freight per trip, and at an estimated cost of fifty cents per ton, this meant a further loss of $5,000 in wages
– freight handlers lost a similar sum in wages per trip.

In all, each lost trip of the *Empress of Ireland* represented a direct loss to Saint John of over $20,000, and that did not include wharfage charges, pilotage fees, passenger and immigration agents, clerks, checkers and others. Saint John suffered an intangible loss as well, something harder to swallow: a loss of prestige for the port.

Regardless of what was happening on land and the political battles between the two winter ports, the men of the *Empress* had a ship to run, passengers to convey safely and a schedule to meet. On her last trip to Quebec for the year (90W) the ship encountered adverse weather up the Gulf and docked at 2:00 a.m. on 8 November, some eight hours later than expected.

After a turnaround of five days, the ship left Quebec on Thursday at 3:30 p.m., 13 November, with 1,270 passengers, general cargo and the mails. It was a good passenger load for the season, though more could be expected on the next sailing, the pre-Christmas return by Europeans to their homes. As always a crowd gathered to wave goodbye to the *Empress*. She was a sentimental favourite and Quebecers would not see her again until May 1914.

With the transfer to Halifax it became necessary to set up new arrangements for the 'Empress Specials'. Accordingly the company's Bulletin No.59, dated 1 December 1913, informed agents of the change of terminal port, and advised that the two *Empresses*, along with the Allan mail steamships, would sail from Halifax on Saturdays, on arrival of the special train. Trains would leave Montreal's Windsor Street Station each Friday at 12:00 noon, commencing 5 December, and run direct to the vessel's side at Halifax, arriving about 1:00 p.m. local time. Only steamship passengers for the *Empresses* and Allan vessels would be carried; passengers could board also at Sherbrooke, Megantic and Brownville Junction, on the way to Halifax.

Most passenger steamships companies of the era took safety very seriously and had developed guide-lines or principles for their officers to follow. Cunard cautioned its masters against the 'folly' and 'stupidity' of those commanding other ships at sea, and White Star informed its masters 'No precaution which insures safe navigation is to be considered excessive.' International Mercantile Marine's *Instructions to Captains* stressed that 'no risk is to be run which can be avoided by the exercise of caution …and by choosing, whenever a doubt exists, the course that tends to safety.' And, of course, the Canadian Pacific had its book of Rules, discussed above.

Sometimes, though, the rules could be an inconvenience.

On 5 December 1913 the *Empress* arrived in Halifax, her first arrival of the season in Nova Scotia and different inasmuch as she would not, this time, continue on to Saint John. She had departed Liverpool on 29 November under the command of James Turnbull, with 717 passengers. It was a light westbound load, typical of the pre-Christmas season, for fewer immigrants came to Canada in the cold winter months. In first class – with just 43 passengers – the service would have been even more attentive than usual. In the run-up to Christmas, the mail service was working flat out. The *Empress* had brought out almost 4,000 postal packages, enough to fill twelve mail cars.

While the Halifax *Herald* welcomed the first arrival of the CPR *Empress*, the paper was more interested in what had transpired on the high seas. Breathless with excitement, a front-page story informed readers how, after leaving Liverpool a race had developed across the Atlantic:

> Steaming bow upon bow on courses parallel and two miles apart, the White Star steamer *Teutonic* and the royal mail steamship *Empress of Ireland* fought for supremacy since early Thursday morning and not until they made Sambro was it decided which should enter first. Altho begun upon the departures from Liverpool, the thrills of the race of these two ocean greyhounds did not come until the *Empress* overhauled a three hour handicap the *Teutonic* enjoyed until striking a fog bank Wednesday evening. She then slowed down until daylight. Thereafter it was neck and neck to Halifax with the *Empress*, her officers say, giving way to avoid collision. The *Teutonic*, which set out three hours earlier than her rival, was 4 days 5 hours and 3 minutes on the voyage.

The paper also commented on the grand sight of four big liners all in port at the same time, the four largest ever to be docked simultaneously at Halifax. 'Perhaps equally imposing,' it said, ' was the spectacle at the terminals as side by side the 'Big Four,' *Virginian*, *Scandinavian*, *Empress of Ireland* and *Teutonic* slung out their gangways and derricks to debark and embark their wealth in human and merchant freight.' The paper noted with satisfaction that the four vessels brought the daily transoceanic tonnage totals up to 56,640, though there were some negative side effects to having captured the big liners from Saint John.

Port facilities were being taxed as never before, and less important vessels were forced to wait at anchor until a berth could be found. The promised improvements to the port facilities would not be completed for some time, although temporary sheds were expected to be erected shortly, in time for the Christmas passenger rush. In the meantime, there was little anyone could do but grin and bear it. White Star's *Megantic*, expected the following day, would only add to the congestion.

A new chaplain for Church of England immigrants took up his post in Halifax that December. His name was Rev. J.V. Young, and one of his duties was to meet each incoming boat and provide to those entering Canada whatever moral comfort and assistance they required. The chaplain's duties had been provided previously by a Reverend Cunningham who noted with pleasure, on handing over the assignment, the air of prosperity surrounding the Christmas contingent, leaving for the old country for a holiday.

That winter the CPR constructed new offices at the Halifax Immigration Building, a sign perhaps that the company intended the new arrangement at the port to be a permanent one.

As if the mail squabbles between Halifax and Saint John were not enough, the Montreal Board of Trade waded into the mêlée in early December 1913, claiming that the winter arrangement with Halifax was insufficient, and that service would be better if the Canadian mails were routed via New

York. Such an arrangement was clearly not acceptable to the Canadian government, and it ignored the resolution of the Board of Trade.

Early in the new year of 1914, once the transatlantic passenger movements for the previous year had been tabulated, men such as John Walsh and others in the company's offices in Liverpool and Montreal had much to be proud of.

The year 1913 marked a high-water point for the *Empress* and the Atlantic passenger trade in general. The *Empress* bested her previous results and carried a total of 16,614 westbound and 10,280 eastbound passengers. In itself this was an impressive achievement, as it demonstrated that emigrant ships need not return to England almost empty, and that the ships could cover their costs in both directions. Passenger totals (Appendix 1) revealed also that the CPR had at last managed to market its transatlantic services to an ever-larger audience, and that the traditional low bookings in the winter could be overcome.

If the CPR had done well in 1913 on the Liverpool run (with 40,015 westbound and 23,235 passengers), the Allan Line had done even better on the same route, carrying more than 52,000 and 25,000 respectively. The Allan Line, with more vessels serving the route, made fifty westbound trips and fifty eastbound trips to achieve its impressive totals; CPR ships made forty-two westbound trips from Liverpool and thirty-eight eastbound trips. As well, the Allan Line benefited from the close co-operation between the CPR and itself, a result of the de facto ownership which was still carefully hidden from the public. In reality, the CPR was as happy to see passengers travel on the Allan Line as its own boats. It amounted essentially to the same thing.

After her return to service 21 February 1914, following the annual refit that had kept her off the North Atlantic for a month, the crew of the *Empress*, on returning from leave, were surprised to find Captain James Turnbull had been replaced by James Murray, himself no stranger to ships of the class, for Murray had commanded *Empress of Britain* for eight years, and would have been familiar – by reputation if not by sight, since the schedules of the two ships did not overlap – to many of the crew.

James Turnbull was headed for Murray's old command, the *Empress of Britain*. Turnbull and Murray thus became the only men to command both of the CPR's Atlantic *Empresses*, and Turnbull was fated to command the *Empress of Britain* again in the early 1920s.

In the early spring of 1914, thirty-eight-year-old Leonard Grout of Vancouver booked passage to England for himself, his wife Mab and two sons, Bill and Ted, age eleven and five respectively. After seven years in Canada, working in the wholesale fruit and vegetable business, he later wrote, 'our family has done well and the country has been good to us.' Even though his adopted country had been in an economic depression for over a year, the young family had managed to save enough money for the second class fare. It was, he reasoned, time to go visit the family in Gravesend in Kent and show off the children to their grandparents. And, though British Columbia was beautiful, it wasn't… well, England.

Leonard Grout had booked a crossing from Quebec on the RMS *Empress of Ireland*, sailing on Thursday, 28 May for Liverpool. One day, strolling in the streets of Vancouver, Grout met an old friend, who happened to work for a shipping line, a rival of the CPR. Learning of the family's planned trip on the *Empress*, the friend persuaded him to change from the CPR. Had it not been for a chance meeting with a friend, the author's family tree might today look very different. Leonard Grout, great-uncle of the author, lived until 1952 and never had to experience the frigid waters of the St Lawrence.

Last-minute booking changes were not unusual in the least. The CPR was very flexible in that respect and accepted new bookings even up to the last day before sailing. The company knew that for every passenger like Leonard Grout, there would be another who decided at the last minute, for one reason or another, to switch his booking to the *Empress of Ireland*. Two such were the noted English actor Lawrence Irving and his wife, Mabel Hackney, who decided to return to England in advance of the rest of their touring theatre company. Booked on the *Empress* for 28 May, both perished in the sinking.

For some time the CPR's bulletins to its agents had featured letters of commendation from rail passengers concerning the service they had experienced. In early 1914 two unsolicited letters from *Empress* travellers provide an insight into how passengers viewed their treatment aboard ship.

From Bulletin 61 (1 February 1914), from a Montreal newspaper man to the general Agent of the Atlantic Line:

On board the *Empress of Ireland* – This trip has been an exceptionally fine one, and I am bound to say that taking the accommodation, the food and the service, this beats anything I have seen.

One assumes he was travelling first class.

A month later, Bulletin 62 carried a testimonial from a Tennessee college professor who had recently returned from a trip around the world, purchasing point-to-point tickets and using the CPR steamships only on the Atlantic. In a letter to the company's general Agent in Cincinnati, the professor wrote that 'the best service [I] received during the whole trip was on the *Empress of Ireland*.'

On Friday, 20 February 1914, one day before beginning her 93rd voyage, the *Empress* received her renewed Passenger's Certificate from the Board of Trade. The survey had been conducted by a Mr J. Dow, a BoT engineer and ship surveyor, and he also signed the Certificate. The Certificate, enabling her to carry a total of 1,860 passengers in the foreign trade, would remain in force, unless previously cancelled, until 7 February 1915. According to the Certificate, the *Empress* carried a total of 1,950 adult life jackets, and 150 for children, along with eighteen life buoys, nine of which were fitted with lights. The buoys were carried in prominent places and distributed around the ship.

An unusual birth occurred aboard the *Empress* on the return leg of Voyage 93. On the eastbound passage there were four deportees, one Finn and three Swedes. Of the Swedes, one was a thirty-year-old woman, a domestic helper named Ellen Skoglund who was very pregnant. She gave birth to a son, Carl Erik Skoglund, while at sea. The boy's father, a twenty-seven-year-old labourer named Karl Olsson, was also being deported. Despite the family's probable need, passengers in first and second class did not take up a collection for the boy.

The North Atlantic could be rough in winter, as 1,354 passengers discovered on the 94th crossing, westbound from Liverpool. The following is extracted from a postcard dated Saturday, 25 March 1914, mailed by a passenger named Frank when the *Empress* arrived at Halifax on 28 March:

You will see that I have landed safe and well after a VERY ROUGH VOYAGE (not sick). Will write after I see some friends. Love to all.

On that same voyage was a family whose thirteen members made it one of the single largest family groups carried in the *Empress* at one time, even in a period when large families were commonplace. Christopher Blades, then fifty, was a farmer in the tiny Lincolnshire village of Goulceby, who had seen the ads describing the need for farmers in western Canada. Talking it over with his wife Jane, they concluded there would be greater opportunities and more space for farming in Canada than England. Their decision was reinforced by the examples of two men in the hamlet, who had already gone to Alberta while their families waited in England.

Selling their farm, they headed to Liverpool, accompanied by the remaining members of the Wedgewood and Toole families, and all embarked in the *Empress* on 21 March 1914. Like almost everyone else, they had no special reason for booking the *Empress*: she just happened to be available when they needed it.

Bernard, the seventh child, was ten years old when the family emigrated. Interviewed in February 2001, he recalled seeing the ship pass alongside one iceberg. The food in third class he described as 'very good' and remembered three calls for dinner. In particular he remembered the sandbox for third class children. The family was in three cabins and most of them, including Bernard, were seasick. The manifest for that particular voyage shows that the family arrived in Canada with more money than most emigrants: two thousand dollars, raised from the sale of the farm in Lincolnshire. Christopher, Jane and their children homesteaded in Ohaton in north-central Alberta, as did their friends from Goulceby. Bernard served as an electrician in the RCAF in the Second World War and still lives in the same area where the family settled eighty-seven years earlier.

It may have been on the return leg of that voyage, as the *Empress* neared the Welsh coast and ready to pick up her pilot at Point Lynas, that Captain James Murray invited one of his passengers to the bridge, for Murray had a point to prove. His guest, a Mr Bowles, had been one of the junior counsel employed at the 1912 Admiralty Division hearing into the sinking of the collier *Helvetia* by the *Empress of Britain*. Sir Samuel Evans, who headed the British inquiry into the accident, had doubted Murray's testimony when Murray estimated the *Empress of Britain* had hit *Helvetia* at just three knots. Murray had ordered full astern from half-speed, and Murray's estimate was that the liner had slowed to three knots in one minute and forty-five seconds, and to a full stop in two and one-quarter minutes.

This time, in a demonstration, Murray issued the same command, with Bowles on the bridge. When the *Empress* slowed exactly as he had described, Murray asked Bowles to convey the information to Sir Samuel.

After leaving Liverpool on 17 April and bound for Halifax, the *Empress* enjoyed smooth sailing until the 21st when, off the Newfoundland coast, she encountered a great icefield. George Shaw, emigrating from England aboard Canadian Northern's *Royal George*, described in a letter the same ice conditions experienced by the *Empress*, a day or so before:

> …we began to get near ice and before long hardly any water was to be seen. The boat had to keep cutting the great field of ice all the while. Wireless messages informed us we had 64 miles of thick ice to go through and the boat could not have been travelling, at times, more than 2 miles an hour; in fact, at times she was stationary. I think she then altered her course for at about 2 o'clock a.m. she was clear of the ice.
> I was informed that at 12:15 midnight she had a nasty knock removing some of her plates.

This letter in the National Archives has another significance as well from an *Empress* perspective. Postmarked at Montreal on 27 May, it was one of the letters put aboard the *Empress of Ireland* at Quebec on 28 May, bound for England. The envelope bears the stamp 'RECOVERED BY DIVERS FROM WRECK OF S.S. EMPRESS OF IRELAND.' The letter, in black ink, was perfectly legible after many weeks under the St Lawrence and was returned to George Shaw by the Canadian postal authorities.

Two young stowaways, the first since 1907, were discovered at the conclusion of the trip. Thomas Young and William Jones, who had hidden in the coal bunkers, were returned to Liverpool and turned over to the authorities. They were liable for a term of three months in prison.

It was at Halifax on 1 May 1914 that Henry George Kendall, formerly master of *Ruthenia*, took command of the *Empress*, relieving James Murray. Kendall thus became the fifth man to command the *Empress of Ireland*, the third in just seven months, and the second former Chief Officer of the *Empress* to become her master, James Turnbull being the first to achieve that distinction. Murray, having decided to leave the CPR, had accepted the position of harbour master at Quebec, and the transfer of command was more conveniently effected in Halifax than Liverpool. He had the satisfaction of knowing that from his office in Quebec he would be able to see the two *Empress* liners he had been privileged to command.

The Times later commented that Kendall was 'popular alike with the travelling public and the men who have served under him,' and reminded its readers that he was more widely known because of his association with the Crippen case. In 1910 Henry Kendall, while master of *Montrose*, had played a leading role in the capture of a fugitive wanted for murder in Britain. Kendall, suspecting one of his passengers was the fugitive, sent a wireless message to Scotland Yard. The Yard's Inspector Walter Dew, having taken a faster ship from England, arrested the unsuspecting Harvey Crippen at Rimouski while Kendall looked on.

Kendall, some of the long-serving crewmen recalled, had served almost a year as Chief Officer in the *Empress* under John Forster in 1907-1908, and in the intervening years he had not lost his talents to entertain passengers and take the time to understand their needs. A passenger aboard *Ruthenia* in late 1913, writing a testimonial that the CPR printed in its Bulletin No.60, explained that she had 'appreciated the Captain's efforts to make the journey such a pleasant and interesting one.'

In his autobiography Kendall later described his feelings about the appointment to the *Empress*:

> The year 1914 for me personally promised to be more than ordinary, for I had been trans-ferred to the Liverpool-Montreal route and given command of the finest ship in the CPR fleet – the *Empress of Ireland*. It was no small honour to be Master of such a magnificent vessel.

This would be the *Empress*' last visit to the Nova Scotian capital until the winter schedule. Just before the ship departed for Liverpool, the ship's violinist John William Furness had a bizzare premonition. Furness, thirty-two, who had once played in the Pier Head Band at Southport, had made five voyages in the *Empress* and more than fifty on various ships, enough time at sea to make him as superstitious as any sailor. Accompanied by a Mr Davies of the Church of England Institute, Furness visited the graves of *Titanic* victims in Halifax's Fairview cemetery. There, he asked Davies to take his photograph.

The photograph, not a particularly good one, appeared a month later in the Halifax *Herald*, just one of many news items dealing with the lost liner, for the people of Halifax had much to remember about the ship that had called their city home in Canada for less than six months. The violinist, a tall man with a full moustache, stared back at the camera in a somewhat awkward fashion, surrounded by headstones from the 1912 disaster. There was another photograph too, of the violinist playing a game of billiards. His body was never recovered.

The citizens of Halifax waved fond good-byes to the *Empress* as she sailed on 2 May, bound for Liverpool. They were confident they would see the ship and her crew again in November, as the CPR seemed pleased with the new sailing arrangements. In five visits to Halifax that winter of 1913-1914, many of the *Empress*' crew had formed lasting friendships. Crewmen had donated their time and services to local charities, as they did in other ports, and they would be missed at some of the local clubs. The ship's five musicians, especially, would be missed. When the *Empress* was in port, the orchestra members could be found most nights at a popular cafe named The Maze. Halifax had become a second home for these men and they, in turn, took an active interest in the city and its people.

The citizens of Saint John, concerned that the loss of the two *Empress* mail steamers might become perm-anent, began collecting statistics to prove that mail service via Halifax was no faster than via Saint John, and the Board of Trade resolved to send another delegation to Ottawa to present the city's claims as a mail port.

At sea, on the way to Liverpool, a fifty-five-year-old Finnish woman named Maria Helakoski entered a diabetic coma and died. She was buried with the usual solemn rites, the first death aboard the *Empress* under her new master.

On 8 May, as the Empress came opposite Point Lynas, on the Isle of Anglesey which lies off the Welsh coast on the approach to Liverpool, Captain Kendall decided to evaluate the ship's stopping capability. From full speed – 18 knots – he ordered the engines to full astern. Two minutes later, in a distance of just twice her length, the *Empress* came to a full stop, bobbing gently in the swell. James Murray had conducted the same test in the same place just weeks previously.

Having brought his ship into Liverpool, Henry Kendall was handed the following message from the CPR's Maitland Kersey:

> From: Manager-in-Chief, Ocean Services
> To: Captain Henry Kendall
> Date: May 9, 1914
>
> Dear Sir:
> In handing over the command of this vessel to you, I desire to particularly call your attention to the importance of your command and to the value of the ship, and to emph-

asize to you the instructions of the company relative to the care of your vessel and the lives of your passengers.

It is to be distinctly understood that the safe navigation of the ship is to be in all instances your first consideration. You must run no risk, which by any possibility might result in accident; you must always bear in mind that the safety of the lives and property entrusted to your care is the ruling principle by which you must be governed in the navigation of your ship, and that no saving of time on the voyage is to be purchased at the risk of accident.

I cannot sufficiently emphasize my desire that these instructions shall be carried out to the letter.

It is expected that all the officers of your ship will bear this in mind, and will be specially cautioned by you, and, furthermore, that everyone on board will do their utmost to please and to gratify the company's patrons.

One wonders whether such a letter went out to each new master assuming command of a CPR vessel, and what was Kendall's reaction to the letter, for he was a prudent master and familiar with his responsibilities. The captain kept his copy of the letter in his stateroom. Three weeks later it lay at the bottom of the St Lawrence.

On 15 May, hours before her departure from Liverpool, Emigration Officer Thomas E. Thompson conducted an emigration survey aboard the *Empress*, a process witnessed by Maitland Kersey. Thompson later reported that he was 'perfectly satisfied with everything found on board the vessel,' and that the *Empress* was in all respects fit for the intended voyage.

In a letter dated 4 June he reported his findings to the Board of Trade Surveyors' Office in Liverpool. Thompson's letter, reproduced below, illustrates the thorough nature of the inspection and sheds light on the organization and state of preparation aboard the *Empress*.

SS *Empress of Ireland*										Off. No. 123972

Sir,–I have the honour to report that on May 15th last I conducted the clearance M.S.A. Part III of the above steamer.

I inspected all the steerages, compartments 1, 2, 3 and 4 on No. 1 Passenger Deck and compartments 1, 2 and 3 on the lowest Passenger Deck, the total number of beds 802. In each of these beds lifebelts were laid out for inspection and they all appeared to be in good order; these belts are kept in racks overhead whilst at sea and are always handy.

I also examined the fire appliances in these compartments and saw the watertight doors closed as I passed from one to the other. All the ladder-ways, etc. were in order, direction (oil) lamps being placed where necessary.

On examining the crew who were mustered on the saloon deck I found that each man had a badge pinned to his coat with the number of his boat on it, and that the sailors were divided so as to provide at least two for each boat under davits.

As soon as the muster was over the bugle was sounded and all hands repaired to the boat deck when the order 'out all boats' was given. All the boats under davits, sixteen in number, were at once swung out. Two sailors were in each and they shipped the tholepins, passed the ends of the painters out and shipped the rudders, the rest of the boats' crews setting up the guys and clearing away the falls. From the time the order was given to the time the boats were ready for lowering about four minutes had elapsed.

Two of the Englehardt collapsible boats were also opened up, the canvas sides being rigged and all gear shipped.

I then went round with the chief officer and inspected the equipment of all the boats and I found these to be in order and to comply with the regulations.

After swinging in the boats the crew was called to fire stations by bell and bugle, hoses were stretched out and the water turned on, a number of stewards were mustered with buckets and blankets and provision men were told off to attend the boats. A number of stewards were also told off to control the passengers in case of need. Two fire annihilators picked at random from the steerages were turned on and were in order.

The Captain then took me through all the passages and showed me the fire appliances in the first and second class accommodation and as we came to each watertight door it was closed to my satisfaction. Direction (oil) lamps were placed where necessary.

I then went down the engine room with the chief engineer and saw all the watertight doors in the engine room, tunnel and boiler room; these all worked perfectly.

The second officer went with me to the signal locker and I found the fog and distress signals to comply with the regulations. The sounding gear also I found to be in good order.

With regard to the boat and fire drill, each member of the crew appeared to know his duties and both were carried out quickly and without confusion.

The life-buoys which were attached to the bridge and rails were in good order and easy to get at, floating lights being attached to half the number.

The vessel cleared for Quebec her draught of water being 27 feet 9 inches F. and 29 feet 2 inches aft, Freeboard 12 feet $5\frac{1}{2}$ inches.

I am, sir,

Your obedient servant,

(sgd) Thomas E. Thompson

Somewhere between 20 February survey and 15 May, the *Empress* acquired a few more lifesaving appliances. The Emigration Survey showed 2,212 lifebelts, 150 childrens' belts and 24 life buoys (six more than she was required to have), somewhat more than the 1,950 adult life jackets listed in the February certification.

On 16 May, one day after the *Empress* had left Liverpool, Thompson approved her certificate as an emigrant ship. The certificate would be collected on her return to Liverpool.

The ninety-sixth voyage of the *Empress* commenced at 3:00 p.m. on Friday, 15 May, carrying a total of 1,173 passengers, a lighter load than normal for mid-May, and somewhat fewer than her previous two westbound trips. Her sea passage was normal in every respect, though she had encountered ice in the Gulf. Coming up the Gulf she had been delayed for seven hours by fog and heavy smoke from brush fires. She arrived off Rimouski light in the water, as might be expected after the consumption of almost 2,500 tons of coal. The depth forward was 25ft 2in, and aft 28ft.

The *Empress* was brought upriver by Adélard Bernier, her regular pilot, and no doubt pleased to see many familiar faces among the bridge watch. Off Grosse Ile she passed the eastbound RMS *Calgarian*, and tied up at the Breakwater overlooked by Dufferin Terrace at 3:15 p.m. on Friday, 22 May.

That year the St Lawrence season had opened on 29 April, ten days later than in 1913 and six days later than in 1912. Though the *Empress* was the last of the big liners to make the trip up the St Lawrence, she was greeted warmly by the people of Quebec, to whom she had become a familiar fixture in the harbour.

A change had taken place in the five-man orchestra during the last turnaround in Liverpool. Thirty-year-old Albert Naylor had been replaced by a younger man, George Baxter, age twenty. Baxter was destined never to see England again.

Second class steward Alexander Craik, a large, well-built man with a flowing moustache, must have breathed a sigh of relief on arriving in Quebec, thankful that the first half of the ninety-sixth voyage had been completed without incident. Craik, whose marriage certificate described him as a 'Licensed

Victualler' had been at sea long enough to acquire the superstitious beliefs of sailors. He had a lucky charm that always accompanied him to sea – a small, crudely struck bronze coin from ancient Judaea. For this particular voyage, Craik had forgotten it on the mantle in his home in Wallesey, outside Liverpool. Alexander Craik never returned to his home in Cheshire, and his body was never found. Devastated at their loss, his family later moved to Canada. Craik's grandson still has his grandfather's lucky charm, probably the oldest item ever carried aboard the *Empress*.

On Saturday, 23 May, one day after the *Empress* docked in Quebec, Captain Hugh Staunton, CPR's Superintendent of Life-Saving Appliances, carried out an inspection of the liner's safety appliances, to ensure they were all in good order and condition. Staunton's duties were wide-ranging. He was responsible for all boats, fire hoses, life buoys, lifebelts, watertight doors, life-saving apparatus. As well, he tested the men in rowing proficiency. According to Staunton's later testimony, he went into various cabins, took lifebelts out of their racks, tried the strings and inspected the canvas around the cork. Everything was in good condition. Staunton would have been surprised had it not been. The same day a boat drill was held. Three boats were lowered into the water, and only the presence of coal lighters alongside the *Empress* prevented more from being lowered. As well, two of the twenty collapsible Englehardt lifeboats were opened and rigged out on deck. Staunton ordered two boats to be left in the water, so that the seamen could practice rowing.

In addition to the boat exercise, Staunton ordered a surprise watertight door exercise. He noted that it took just three seconds in the engine room and $3\frac{1}{2}$ to four minutes on deck to close the doors. In daylight, on an even keel, without passengers, it all seemed so simple.

Soccer fans were pleased by the ship's return to Quebec. On Monday, 25 May, the *Empress* team handed Montmorency its first defeat of the young season. Montmorency, the 1913 champions, lost 1-0 to the sailors who were described as 'fast' and having 'a splendidly balanced line-up.' A few days later, paying tribute to four of the eleven men who died with their ship, the *Chronicle* called the team 'about the best football eleven that was to be found on any of the big ocean liners coming to this port.' One of the dead, Augustus Pierce who was a cook, intended to settle in Quebec on the ship's return, having signed to play with the Montmorency team.

It was not uncommon for men from the Black Gang to jump ship in North America. It was hard work and the pay was poor, and a stoker or trimmer had no difficulty finding a better paying, easier job ashore. Thus it happened that before the *Empress* returned to Liverpool, five firemen and two trimmers decided to 'swallow the anchor' – to use Arthur Owen's phrase. The CPR was used to this. The company signed on at least eight men for the return trip. One, a French-Canadian named Henri Fournier, would survive and testify before the Mersey Inquiry, though three others would not be so lucky.

One of the three, fireman Bernard Tumilty, was no stranger to the engine room of the *Empress*, for he had shipped aboard her in mid-November 1906 as a last-minute replacement, and possibly on other subsequent occasions as well, an inexpensive (though arduous) way to cross the Atlantic. On 25 May the native of Crosby wrote to his brother Thomas in Vancouver, using stationery from the Quebec Seamen's Institute.

> …I may go out to Vancouver as the steam boating is better out here than at home, as you are under Navy discipline in the boats out of L'pool all work now & no liberty only at the discretion of the Master some get ashore one night & some the other it is not the same as it used to be not by half.
>
> I am in the *Empress of Ireland* but I am only on for one trip as she is no good & the talent is worse all from Scotland Road [*a poor section of Liverpool*] you know….

Four days later Bernard Tumilty was dead. Like so many others, his body was never recovered.

Another replacement was a down-and-out English boxer, Edward ('Ted') Fitchett. His ring career in Canada had taken a turn for the worst ever since Darky Allen had fought him to a draw in Montreal's

Stewards on the Empress, May 1914, from the Montreal Daily Star, *30 May 1914.*

Canadian Club and after that fiasco, he'd been reduced to a stint as trainer at the Hochelaga Club. He'd even taken on some pupils before becoming a trainer at the National Sporting Club. It paid the bills but it wasn't as exciting as prize fighting. And it was tough making a living in Montreal, where every ring fan now regarded him as a has-been.

Fitchett had made many friends in Montreal, especially with the Royal Highlanders, where he turned up at every training fight to help instruct the men. He had also taken two privates under his wing and had the satisfaction of seeing the regiment win the Dominion championship. Ted Fitchett was a determined man. On Monday, 25 May he made a snap decision. He would make a comeback in England, then return to Montreal in the autumn and re-launch his career. He left Montreal on the Wednesday, seen off at Windsor Station by his former manager and a few boxing friends. To save passage money, Fitchett signed on as a stoker aboard the *Empress*. It would be good exercise, he probably reflected, and by the time the ship docked in England, he would have shed a few pounds in the stifling heat of the boiler room.

Ted Fitchett's body was never recovered. His name appeared on no crew list.

6
Black Friday and the Aftermath

At 4:27 in the afternoon of Thursday, 28 May 1914, the last hawsers holding the *Empress of Ireland* fast to the Breakwater at Quebec are let go and the great ship slowly pulls away, her funnels belching black smoke as she heads for Liverpool on a rising tide. Winds are light and the weather is clear. It is the beginning of the eastbound return-leg of the *Empress'* ninety-sixth voyage, Henry Kendall's third crossing as master, and it promises to be another routine crossing. The twin screws bite the water and the great ship moves slowly into the current, as Pilot Adélard Bernier on the bridge quietly issues steering orders to the quartermaster.

The departure has gone smoothly, much like any other, an old and familiar drama played out in any port where passenger vessels begin their long journeys across an ocean. There is a feeling of organized chaos, of hustle and bustle as the last bags and trunks are brought aboard, sorted out, and over a thousand passengers assigned to their respective quarters along with the luggage needed on the passage. The transfer of passengers and bags from the 'Empress Special' to the ship has gone so smoothly that Salvation Army Capt. Edward Dodd, a sub-editor of *The War Cry*, would later write from the ship:

> From the train to the *Empress* was but a few steps, and the transfer of passengers and baggage was so silent and so swift that one would have thought the party was entirely composed of seasoned globe-trotters instead of people many of whom had never crossed the Atlantic before.

Though those about to embark do not know it, preparations for this departure had started the day before, when the fires were first lit in the cold furnaces, coaxed back to life by plenty of pitch pine and bushels of charcoal. Now, down below, the members of the black gang have got the steam up, and they await only the engine orders from the bridge.

That morning, as he does every day, Henry Kendall made his inspection of the ship accompanied by his officers. At 10:45 a.m. the watertight doors are inspected; the crewmen assigned to each are at their appointed stations. No problems are reported.

Other inspections have also taken place, for they too are routine daily events. At 11:00 a.m., for example, Engineer George O'Donovan inspected the steering gear and the telemotor on the bridge, as he has done every day for eight months. Twice each voyage, in Quebec and in Liverpool, he adds a small amount of glycerine and water to the hydraulic steering system. As well, he inspects the engine and tightens any valves that are loose.

Coaling ports are closed and screwed down, and duly noted in the log, as required.

A vast machine has sprung into action, both on the ship and ashore, to ensure that all proceeds smoothly and the *Empress* will meet her planned sailing time. Four hundred and twenty crew members are on board and, at this particular time, almost all of them are busy, making sure that last-minute items are properly attended to, that all is in readiness. In the library, the latest Canadian newspapers and periodicals are carefully set out. Down in the galleys, butchers are cutting up meat and dressing poultry, and the first loaves of bread are already being baked.

One man who is not busy is senior wireless operator Ronald Ferguson, twenty, whose shift will not begin until 8:00 p.m. In a 1981 audio recording, he related how he had taken a deck chair up to Boat deck, where he could observe the final preparations for boarding. It was a lucky decision: the deck chair he had selected would later save his life.

Cranes swing the last of the cargo, totaling 1,160 tons, valued at over $1.25 million, while manifests are checked and double-checked. Neatly stowed in the holds, the cargo consists mainly of general goods valued at $250,000, and a shipment of 212 silver bars from the Nipissing Mine at Cobalt and consigned to Mocatta & Goldsmid, a major bullion dealer in London. The ingots are in two lots. One, consisting of 163 bars, is valued at $824,000; the second, with forty-nine bars, $275,000. With London silver prices of 26$\frac{1}{4}$d. per ounce, there is about five tons of silver in the ship.

As if losing seven men through desertion is not bad enough, there is another last-minute deserter from the *Empress*. Emmy, the ship's cat, runs down the gangway and cannot be coaxed back, despite having a litter of kittens on board (Ship's cats probably deserted their vessels all the time but, in a curious coincidence, a four-year-old black cat named Dowie, mascot of the stokers, walked off *Lusitania* in New York on 1 May 1915. Seven days later, *Lusitania* was torpedoed off the south coast of Ireland.) Hearing of Emmy's desertion when their ship later docked at the Breakwater, the men of the Allan liner *Alsatian* regard it as a striking omen.

At last a bugle sounds and stewards began circulating on each deck, calling the traditional warning 'All ashore that's going ashore!' Companionways are suddenly mobbed. On deck there are last-minute photographs, kisses, final words, and tender embraces. At length the last gangway is retracted.

As it has done for most *Empress* departures, the Montreal *Gazette* provides a short, typical comment in its shipping pages, based on day-old information. Bearing the title EMPRESS HAS GOOD LIST (how ironic, in retrospect!), the piece notes simply: 'The *Empress of Ireland* sails from Quebec this morning [*sic*] for Liverpool, carrying ninety in the saloon and 250 and 650 third class passengers. An Empress Special in two sections left the Windsor Station with the passengers from Montreal and the West.' For the papers there is nothing particularly newsworthy about this particular crossing. It is, by now, a routine affair, just one of several sailings to Europe in that particular week.

On the wharf a large, colorful crowd has gathered, as it always does on the day of departure, regardless of the season or the weather, for the sailing of a large steamship, especially an *Empress*, is something special. There are final waves of farewell, paper streamers and handkerchiefs, blown kisses, shouts of 'Bon voyage!', and, this time, an impromptu concert offered by the Salvation Army band, who have somehow managed to collect their instruments from the mountain of luggage. The ship carries general cargo, mail and 1,057 passengers – 87 in First Class, 253 in Second and 717 in Third. Of the passengers, one hundred and sixty-seven are Salvation Army members, headed for the Third Internat-ional Congress in London. Almost ten percent of the third class passengers are Europeans from Ford plants in Detroit, returning to Europe for a vacation during a plant shutdown.

On the Promenade deck, the Army's thirty-nine-member Territorial Staff Band, garbed in stetson hats and scarlet tunics, plays *O Canada* and *Auld Lang Syne*. There is no one present to comment on the unintended, yet appropriate, symmetry of the latter, no one to recall that the Black Dike Band had played the same traditional Scottish song when the *Empress* arrived at Quebec on her maiden voyage. Then, as the Staff Band switches to *God Be With You Till We Meet Again*, there is a long blast from the whistle of the *Empress*, a farewell to the hundreds along the wharf whose upturned faces are rapidly becoming an indistinguishable blurred mass. Once the *Empress* is in mid-river, the crowd on the dock drifts away slowly. In a few minutes she swings around the point at Indian Cove and is lost to view.

On the bridge, in addition to Captain Kendall, two officers of the watch and two quartermasters, is Pilot Adélard Bernier. The fifty-four-year old pilot, the only man entrusted by the CPR to bring the two sister *Empresses* up and down the river, has made this trip to Father Point hundreds of times before, and he is relaxed. He has piloted the *Empress of Ireland* for almost eight years without mishap, and this is his 102nd trip aboard her. He knows her habits better than any man aboard.

The *Empress* moves ahead, aided by the current. Her engines settle into a steady, rhythmic beat as she accelerates slowly up to her full speed, just over 18 knots, her props spinning at 72 revolutions per minute. She rides low, with a mean draught of 27 feet, for her water ballast tanks are full, and the river at Quebec is still fairly fresh.

For one thousand and fifty-seven passengers, it is a time to settle into their accommodations, lay out their things, and introduce themselves to the people who will be, for the next six days, their cabin mates. Then they emerge in small groups, wandering about the ship, for the most part awed by what they see. For those on the bridge, the familiar landmarks down the St Lawrence click by with metronomic precision and are entered into the log.

...*St-Laurent*...

...*St-Jean*...

...*7:00 p.m. – Traverse St-Roch*...

At 8:00 p.m. the watch changes in the wireless shack, and junior operator Edward Bamford gives the headphones to Ronald Ferguson. Outside, dusk slowly gives way to night.

...*9:15 p.m. – abeam Cap Saumon*...

By this time, passengers in each class have finished their evening meal, and have settled down for a relaxing evening. By tradition, the first night at sea is a casual one. Many passengers retire early, having almost no idea of the layout of the ship or how to move from one deck to another.

...*Dog Light*...

Those strolling briefly on deck notice a young moon and stars shining, though they would not have tarried there long, for even in late May the nights are cool. The ship's musicians put down their instruments at 9:00 p.m., their last number being Charles Gounod's *Funeral March of a Marionette*. At any other time, the choice of music would hardly be noticed; on this night, in hindsight, it assumes the status of an omen.

Salvation Army Major George Attwell writes a postcard to his son Cecil in Toronto

> Lovely trip so far. I will post this at Rimouski.

The irrepressible Salvation Army band organizes an impromptu concert, and Adjutant Harry Green dazzles listeners around the piano in the second class social hall on Saloon deck. Parties spring up in different parts of the ship. Others scribble notes hastily before the last call for mail, to be off-loaded at Rimouski while the Europe-bound mail is brought aboard.

Kendall, under examination at the Inquiry, describes the evening thus: 'A young moon, stars shining.'

> Q. A clear night?
> A. A beautiful clear night.
> Q. You could see the land?
> A. Yes.
> Q. And see the shore lights all about?
> A. Yes.
> Q. And you could see the lights on a ship approaching at what distance?
> A. I should say at about eight miles.

First class passenger Clayton Burt in an affidavit sworn in Liverpool corroborates Kendall's statement. 'I was on deck shortly before retiring and it was beautifully fine weather.' Nonetheless, in compliance with the company's *Rule 40*, she carries a double watch while travelling on the St Lawrence. Two officers are on the bridge; there are two lookouts, one in the crow's nest, another in the stand at the forecastle head.

About 9:45 p.m., with a four-knot current helping her downriver, the *Empress* passes the Norwegian-registered *Alden*, a collier upbound for Montreal, under charter to the Dominion Coal Company. The two ships pass port-to-port – red-to-red – at a distance of three-quarters of a mile off Cap-aux-Chiens. Bernier has a snack on the bridge, never leaving his post beside the quartermaster at the wheel. Kendall, whose stateroom is on the same level, comes and goes several times.

Most passengers retire for the evening. As second class steward Frank Harrison said later, 'they were pretty nearly all turned in at 10 o'clock', that being the time when he went off duty. Chief Steward Augustus Gaade makes his accustomed round at 10:00 p.m., checking the second and third class quarters. The Salvation Army band packs up its instruments. In the first class smoking room, the bartender wipes a few glasses and watches a desultory game of bridge.

...Red Island Lighthouse...

At 11:00 Gaade makes another tour of inspection, this time in first class. The reading room and music room are deserted; in the smoking room the card game is still going on, but winding down.

Night watchmen come on duty, three in second class.

Slowly, the weather changes, not unusual for this time of year. The *Empress* encounters two slight patches of fog on the river, the first between Red Island and Bic, the second between Bic and Father Point. Kendall orders a reduction in speed, varying from eight knots (half speed) to slow, and the whistle is used. *Rule 51* reminded masters of the peculiarities of fog in the St Lawrence. Both reductions are for about ten minutes each although, in a departure from normal practice, neither is entered in the log.

At midnight, the *Empress* watch changes. First Officer Edward Jones comes to the bridge, along with Third Officer Charles Moore, relieving Second Officer Roger Williams and Fourth Officer Tunstall. Kendall and Pilot Bernier are still there, concentrating on their tasks. Quartermaster James Galway yields the helm to John Murphy, while QM Sharples stands by. There is also a deck boy present.

All is routine. Everything is normal. The men have done this many times before and each knows his job perfectly. There is no hint of impending disaster.

In the boiler room, Ted Fitchett is stripped half-naked, heaving coal and no doubt hoping for a speedy crossing to Liverpool.

Off Rimouski, on the south side of the river, the government steamer *Lady Evelyn* loads the overseas mail and takes off the North American mails that have been posted by passengers on the short trip from Quebec.

The *Empress*, her keel tasting water that is now more salt than fresh, has risen nine inches since leaving Quebec. Of this, seven inches are due to salt water, and two to the consumption of coal, fresh water and other stores.

A few minutes later, about a mile north of Father Point gas buoy, the CGS *Eureka*, a converted tug under the command of Capt. J.B. Bélanger, comes alongside the *Empress* to take off Pilot Bernier and one CPR ticket agent, whose identity is never firmly established. On the bridge, Bernier shakes Kendall's hand. 'I don't think you'll run into much fog,' he says. The departing pilot and ticket agent descend the first-class gangway, which is then raised and secured for the voyage. It will not be needed again until Liverpool. Bernier is assisted by Ordinary Seaman Price, who had won the Albert Medal as a seaman aboard *Devonian* for having rescued two sailors from the burning *Volturno* the previous October.

The ship is stationary for five to ten minutes, moving slightly in the current, about a mile and a half offshore. The weather has cleared again; the wind has died and the sea is calm.

At the same time, Able Seaman John ('Jock') Carroll, a veteran of thirty years at sea, climbs into the crow's nest, replacing AB Bruin. On the bridge, QM John Murphy hands the wheel to Sharples, then leaves the bridge to stream the log.

At 1:20 a.m. the mighty engines rumble and *Empress* begins to move once again. Kendall orders a course of N. 47 E. magnetic to clear the shore, and Full Ahead – between 17 and 18 knots.

The crow's nest lookout sights, and reports, the Cock Point gas buoy.

At about the same time, a few miles down river and Metis Point behind her, still invisible to the *Empress* lookouts, a black-painted collier plods upstream at 8½ knots, riding low in the water. She is the 3,561-ton (net) *Storstad*, 452ft long and with a beam of 58.2ft, outward from Sydney and bound for Montreal. *Storstad* is not far off the south shore of the river, approaching Father Point for her pilot.

Storstad's black-painted, single mid-ship stack bears a large white 'K', signifying her ownership by the Klavenes Line of Norway. Constructed in 1910 at the Armstrong, Whitworth & Company yards at Newcastle-upon-Tyne, she is built on the new Isherwood longitudinal system, designed to give great fore-and-aft strength to the hull, a useful feature for places like the St Lawrence where pack ice can occur in the late spring months. Her designers, intending that she be able to slice through ice and shove it aside without damage, had also given *Storstad* a heavy, sharp vertical stem that had been riveted together, thus adding to an already strong system.

Storstad's hull was divided into eight watertight compartments by seven transverse bulkheads. In the event of a head-on collision, Armstrong engineers estimated that the bow could crumple back safely to the first watertight bulkhead, some 24ft aft of the bow. They would be proved right. The stem of the *Storstad* was damaged to a length backward toward the stern of 14ft 6in.

At the Mersey Inquiry, the naval architect Percy Hillhouse from Fairfield estimated that the *Storstad* penetrated about eighteen feet into the starboard side of the *Empress*, punching a gaping hole below the waterline of some 350 sq.ft., and allowing 265 tons of water per second – over 50,000 gallons per second – to flood into the stricken *Empress*.

Under time charter to the Dominion Coal Company, and loaded with 10,800 tons of Cape Breton coal, *Storstad* is under the command of Thomas Andersen. Andersen, in his mid-forties, is no stranger to the St Lawrence route. He has sailed in Canadian waters for seven years and has commanded *Storstad* for nearly three years. At this moment Andersen is asleep in his cabin, having retired from the bridge and leaving orders to be called in case of fog. In his place is thirty-three-year-old Chief Officer Alfred Toftenes, who began his career at sea nineteen years earlier. On duty with Toftenes are Third Officer Jacob Saxe, a quartermaster at the wheel, a lookout on the forecastle head and one sailor on deck.

Aboard the *Empress*, up in the crow's nest, John Carroll spots masthead lights ahead, at a distance of about six miles. It is 1:38 a.m. He strikes the 10-inch brass bell once – 'Lights on the starboard side.' The signal is a standard one; two bells from the crow's nest would mean 'Object to port'; three bells, 'Object dead ahead.'

Kendall, feeling he is now far enough from shore, orders a change of course: N. 73 E. magnetic. It is almost the same track that the two *Empresses* have used for years when outbound for Liverpool. Quartermaster Murphy makes the necessary adjustment of the wheel and the great ship turns obediently to her new heading. The masthead lights off the starboard side are still visible, four miles away. Kendall intends to pass starboard-to-starboard.

With this, the setting is complete. The cast of unsuspecting characters and the two ships are in the places assigned to them by Destiny on the watery stage of the majestic St Lawrence River, for this is where it will end, after seven years and eleven months, having carried 186,848 passengers and steaming more than half a million miles.

A bank of fog comes up suddenly off the land, a thin curtain separating the actors, for their inexorable, tragic rendezvous with history must yet wait a few more minutes, until the last grains of sand have emptied from the hourglass.

In less than thirty minutes the proud *Empress of Ireland* will lie at the bottom of the St Lawrence, rammed on the starboard side below the waterline by *Storstad*. In the dark she will roll over and sink in fourteen minutes, taking 1,012 passengers and crew with her in the worst maritime disaster in Canadian history.

To Henry Kendall fell the task of informing his superiors in Quebec the news of the disaster. Initially too dazed to give a lengthy account of the sinking, from Rimouski he cabled Marine Superintendent John Walsh, one of the most heart-rending messages a master can send: 'SHIP GONE.' Only later, from Rimouski, did he cable a follow-up message: '*Empress of Ireland* stopped dense fog, struck amidships vital spot by collier *Storstad*.'

By this time, with global communications, the world was rapidly becoming aware of the unthinkable disaster that had taken place on the St Lawrence. For a maritime nation like Britain, whose empire was bound together by fleets of merchant vessels, death at sea was expected, part of the price of empire and greatness. But the loss of the *Empress*, in terms of the cause, the place, and the scale of loss, was wholly unexpected. Anxious crowds soon formed outside the CPR's offices in Liverpool and London, waiting for news.

Quebec City was staggered by the news and flags everywhere were half-masted. The *Empress*, said the *Chronicle*'s editorial, 'was one of the first ocean greyhounds to make Quebec her summer terminal point in Canada, and with her sister ship …had come to be considered as somewhat of a local institution.'

In Ottawa, Conservative Prime Minister Robert Borden rose in the House on the morning of the twenty-ninth to brief the assembled members. It was, he said, his 'duty to refer to the appalling disaster of which tidings came to us this morning,' and continued, 'In its awful suddenness, and the enormous toll of human lives which was taken, the disaster comes to us with a shock which, I suppose, was never experienced in this country before.' Borden hoped that later reports, indicating more passengers had been saved, would prove to be true, then added, 'I do not believe, from the reports which have come, that the disaster is one that could have been prevented by anything that the country could have done in the way of rendering the navigation of the St Lawrence more safe. It appears that it occurred in a fog and was one of those accidents which are almost if not wholly unpreventable by any possible means that we could devise for the safety of navigation.'

That was an insightful observation, and not one to everyone's liking, though it would essentially be borne out by the Mersey Inquiry.

Borden closed his remarks by noting that he had brought the disaster to the attention of Parliament so that 'we may have the opportunity of expressing not only our deep regret for the disaster itself, but our profound sympathy with those who have been bereaved in this way.'

The Liberal opposition leader, Sir Wilfrid Laurier, who had travelled both ways in the *Empress of Britain* in 1907, spoke briefly, knowing that it was not a time for partisan politics. He noted, 'Our sympathies will go to the relatives and friends of those who have been lost.' He concluded, 'I join my own voice to the voice of my Right Hon. friend the Prime Minister of Canada in extending to the victims and their families – all that we can offer to them under the circumstances – our most sincere and deepest sympathy.'

Following their ordeal, surviving passengers and crew were brought on the 29th by rail from Rimouski to Lévis, where they were ferried across the river to Quebec. Crew and third class survivors were put up in the *Alsatian*, while first and second class passengers were brought to the Chateau Frontenac and cared for at the CPR's expense. Many were dressed in ill-fitting clothing donated by the people of Rimouski.

On the river bodies were being collected and brought to Rimouski, where caskets were hastily constructed. John Walsh organized patrols along the south shore of the St Lawrence to recover bodies that had drifted downstream. Meanwhile, the CPR, recognizing the scale of the catastrophe, enlisted the services of undertakers and embalmers in Quebec, and even brought in fifteen embalmers from Montreal. A temporary morgue was set up in Shed 27 on the waterfront in Quebec, and 188 caskets arrived at Quebec on Sunday, 31 May amid solemn ceremony, on board the CGS *Lady Evelyn*, the whole event being recorded by a gaggle of newsreel cameramen.

Identification of many of the bodies would prove difficult over the next few days.

In a Rimouski schoolhouse on the 30th, a jury was sworn and coroner J. Rinault began an inquest that heard testimony from Henry Kendall, Chief Engineer William Sampson and Capt. Bélanger of *Eureka*, among others. It was slow going. Testimony was in English, with sequential translation into French for the jury.

The jury moved to continue the proceedings in a week's time.

Outside events soon made that impossible.

Special legislation, necessary because the *Empress* was a British-registered vessel, was hastily enacted in Ottawa on 2 June, to authorize a formal commission of inquiry. On 3 June, the British government, at the invitation of the Canadian government, appointed Hon. John Charles Bigham, Lord Mersey, as President of the Commission, though a decision on the venue was not announced in Ottawa until 5 June. The Inquiry would convene in Quebec City, which was the logical choice.

Mersey departed England on 6 June for Canada via New York in *Mauretania*. Knighted in 1897, the seventy-three-year-old Lord Mersey had excellent credentials and his appointment was received with general approval. As a member of the bar he had extensive experience in maritime cases. He had been President of the Admiralty Division of the High Court of Justice from 1909 to 1910, and presided over the *Titanic* inquiry in London in 1912. As one of nine delegates for Great Britain, he was selected as President of the International Conference on Safety of Life at Sea in 1913-1914.

Two other commissioners were soon named, Ezekiel McLeod, Chief Justice of New Brunswick, and Sir Adolphe Routhier, ex-Chief Justice of Quebec. Appointed as nautical assessors were Captain L.A. Demers, Dominion Wreck Commissioner; Commander P. Howe of the Dominion Naval Service; Professor John Welch, naval architect; and Commander W.F. Caborne of the Royal Naval Reserve. George Vaux was named by the British Board of Trade as an advisory member. Commented the *Daily Telegraph* on the members of the inquiry: 'The composition of the tribunal affords every guarantee that it will be conducted with ability and complete impartiality.'

The Rimouski inquest ended officially on 20 July, the jury unable to render a verdict due to insufficient evidence.

On the St Lawrence the search for bodies continued for days. The log book of the *Empress* was recovered on 29 May by Captain François-Xavier Pouliot of the government steamer *Lady Evelyn* while picking up bodies. A syndicated Canadian Press story, reprinted in several papers, announced the find and said, 'The book is not damaged, being found in a watertight metal box. It is supposed that the First Officer, whose body was identified here last Sunday, leaped with it from the sinking boat and that when he drowned he loosened his grip on the box, leaving it to drift.'

Just four of 138 children survived the sinking. One of these was eight-year-old Florence Barbour from second class, who was left an orphan. She was the subject of the following letter sent to Fred McMahon, manager of the Chateau Frontenac hotel.

> Augustus Street
> Cornwall, Ont.
> May 31st, 1914
>
> Dear Sir, – I trust you will kindly pardon this liberty I take in writing you, and I think you will, if you continue to read on.
>
> I read in the press last night about a little girl of 8 years, by name of Florence Barber [*sic*], Cumberland, England, who is now, through the sad and terrible loss of the *Empress of Ireland*, an orphan and without relatives in this world and is now under your care, or at least an inmate of your beautiful hotel.
>
> We are without children and although we belong to the working class, we could give her a comfortable, respectable and I am sure, a happy home.
>
> To those whom it may concern or who have interested themselves in the little girl's case, we shall be pleased to have them make enquiries regarding our standing here, as I am an English woman, my great sympathy goes out to this child and, indeed, to all of them.
>
> I passed through Quebec in 1911 on a visit to England, and I greatly admired your beautiful hotel.
>
> And, now, if you will kindly consider the contents of this letter and grant us an early reply, by wire if it is not too much to ask.
>
> Should we be chosen to have the girl, I am sure many will be willing to put her safely in the train and in care of the officials and on her arrival at Cornwall station, my husband

and myself will take future charge of her.

Awaiting your reply,

I am respectfully yours

(sgd) M.E. Goreau

P.S. – In either case a reply will greatly oblige – M.E.G.

Sir Thomas Shaughnessy refused point-blank to get the CPR involved in an adoption case, and ensured that the matter was turned over to the proper authorities. Records show that Florence Barbour was adopted by a Quebec family.

Other vessels plying the St Lawrence paid tribute to the *Empress* and her dead. At 6:00 a.m. on Sunday morning, 31 May, White Star-Dominion's *Teutonic*, bound for Liverpool from Montreal, stopped her engines at the wreck site while the bugler played *Taps* and the ship's company mustered on deck. Among *Teutonic*'s first class passengers were the late Lawrence Irving's theatrical company, returning to England from their tour of Canada. Irving and his wife Mabel had decided to take the *Empress*, in order to arrive home sooner.

That same afternoon *Megantic*, inbound from Liverpool, halted at the scene of the wreck and stopped her engines for a few minutes. Passengers and crew gathered on the port side and bared their heads for a short prayer, led by her captain, Hugh David, and concluded by singing *Abide with Me*.

In the days following the sinking, crew members of the *Empress*, along with many passengers, were deposed by lawyers. It was a condition of the *Merchant Shipping Act* of 1894 that surviving crew members of a foundered vessel had to make a formal deposition as to the circumstances surrounding the loss as soon as practicable after the event. In the case of seventy-three of the crew, who returned to England in *Corsican*, the Board of Trade (which had responsibility in such cases) declined to take depositions, feeling perhaps that men who had been belowdecks at the time of the collision would not add much to what was already known.

Among those embarking aboard *Corsican* was fireman John Ryan, thirty-one. He was a veteran member of the black gang, having joined the merchant navy at an early age and served aboard various vessels out of Liverpool, including *Lusitania*. He had made only one previous voyage aboard the *Empress*, the 94th, in late March, though he was familiar enough with the Canadian route, having sailed aboard various White Star liners like *Megantic*, *Teutonic* and *Laurentic*, and the *Empress of Britain*. His Certificate of Discharge book shows he was well regarded by his officers, for 'VERY GOOD' is stamped throughout his book where he had been rated 'For ability' and 'For general conduct'. Perhaps owing to an injury sustained in the sinking, Ryan did not return to sea until October, when he signed aboard *Indian* as a fireman. Though Ryan had managed to cheat Death aboard the *Empress*, he died at sea in 1923 under mysterious circumstances aboard *Cliftonhall*.

The first funerals for crew members took place on 4 June in Quebec City. An impressive service was held at 9:00 a.m. at the city's Anglican cathedral for seven of the crew, following which they were buried in the Mount Hermon Protestant cemetery. A parallel service took place at St Patrick's, the Irish Catholic church, for five more crew, who were interred at the parish cemetery. Present were representatives of the Governor General, the federal and provincial governments, and the CPR, including Captain Walsh and Captain James Murray, the Harbour Master at Quebec and a former master of the *Empress*, along with Royal Navy bluejackets from HMS *Essex* and Quebec's police in dress uniforms. Also present were Henry Kendall, 'his face set and stern, but haggard and pale with grief,' and James Grant, the ship's doctor whose work had saved many lives.

The floral tributes were lavish. The CPR's was in the shape of a large anchor, and flowers had also been provided by HMS *Essex*. A spray of flowers for each coffin was provided by the Ladies' Committees of the Protestant and Catholic Seamen's Institutes.

Other interments occurred later in Quebec. Twenty-one *Empress* victims were buried in St Patrick's, of whom sixteen were unknown; the Jewish cemetery holds nine adults and one child; and other crew and passengers were laid to rest at Mount Hermon, high atop the bluffs overlooking the St Lawrence a short distance upstream from the old city.

In the early morning hours of 6 June the *Empress of Britain*, inbound from Liverpool, slowed and stopped at the spot where her sister had gone down. There, although it was 2:00 a.m., some of the officers and crew, along with a few passengers, held a short service of prayer. They were joined by a weary James Turnbull, who had spent the greater part of the journey on the bridge, after a trip marked by fog and very heavy seas.

In the days after the sinking, many stories of the passengers and crew appeared in the press on both sides of the Atlantic, in some cases offering a wealth of mis-information.

The following two letters, never before in print, were written by Frank and Henrietta ('Hetty') Brooks, Salvation Army members from Toronto who were to attend the Congress in London. Frank Brooks was in second class; in third, Hetty and her young daughter, Dolly. The poignant letters describe the couple's experiences and the loss of their young daughter. Mrs Brooks, ill in hospital in Quebec after the sinking, was never interviewed by reporters, nor was her husband. The letters somehow convey more of the crushing sense of loss than any number of sensational newspaper articles:

> June 11, 1914
>
> My Dear, Dear Father and Mother
>
> I had hoped ere this to have been privileged to see & kiss your dear faces but it has been ordained otherwise. I know you are disappointed but I hope ere very long to be able to come & see you all.
>
> I am very grateful that Frank and I are spared to each other but at present my heart is aching very badly over the loss of our precious little Dolly. I had looked forward so much to bringing her to see you all but it was not to be and, dear little soul, while she wanted to see you all, she did so dread crossing the water. All she wanted was to come all the way by train.
>
> After the collision she did everything she was told and never made a murmur till we found ourselves in the water, when she said 'Oh Mama, Oh Mama,' and in another moment we were both sucked under and I lost her. But after a while I came up and clung to some wreckage and was picked up. I was not in the water long but dear little Dolly, when we recovered her body, her spirit had gone to God and we are desolate. Still, when we look around and see the whole families that have been wiped out, we do try to be grateful that we are spared. Of course we lost everything we had with us including our money so we must just wait & see what recompense the shipping company are prepared to make. Everybody we have met since the accident have been kindness itself and more than anxious to do anything they can to be of service. We, or rather Frank, wired as soon as ever he could to his mother saying he & I were safe & asking her to let you know but there was such a crush of telegrams that I am afraid they were a long time in getting sent out. But I do hope you were not in suspense long. I am glad to say Frank & I are pretty well as I truly trust this will find you each one.
>
> Give our love to family & Jack and also to Nathan & his wife. I would like to write to them both but just at present I am too restless to do much in that line so please give them our best love.
>
> Of course you have heard George Felstead & wife & two children were all lost. I did not see any of them after the accident although Lou & the children were in a berth quite near me. I don't somehow think they ever got out of the boat. Of course the band boys were mostly all quartered together and George Felstead was in the same cabin as Frank and got

out before Frank but I think he went to try to find his family & not knowing the boat very well, as we had been on her only a few hours, I think when the lights went out he lost his way and probably never got to them. This is what we think; of course, we do not know.

Now, dear ones, you must not worry about us; we are quite alright ourselves. Our only grief is the loss of our darling and that is bitter indeed although it is better she should go than have been left without father or mother as others have been.

Now I really must close with heaps of love & kisses to you each one & please write soon to your loving children.

(sgd) Frank and Dett

P.S. I am enclosing a bit of fern picked from my girlie's grave.

Frank Brooks wrote the following undated letter to his mother in England a few days later:

My Dear Mother

I can imagine how you are looking to get a line from us. We received your letter the other day and I can quite understand the very trying time you must have had. Well, Mother, it seems very hard and strange why we should have to pass thro such a terrible disaster; it hardly seems possible such a thing could have taken place but still we are reminded of it very much by the loss of our precious girlie. Truly the best flower has been plucked from our little home but there come[s] one sweet consolation & altho it is a hard blow to us, we feel she is enjoying the sweets of heaven where no more sorrows or trials will befall her.

Of course you will have read quite a lot about the disaster but to have the experience is more than one can really explain; in our case, we had no time to do anything but take a chance. It seems a wonderful thing why Det. & I should be spared when you think I had no idea where she was & could not even think w[h]ere she was & the terrible position of the ship made it impossible to walk & in total darkness I was compelled to give her & Dolly up & so I, being able to swim, just jumped into the water & swam till I was pulled up into a boat that was upside down and there the thought came to me if I sit here I shall be frozen or die of exposure & just as if I was being guided by an unseen power, I jumped into the water and swam to a boat which was picking up people and safely landed into it & was finally taken to the *Storstad* as naked as the day I was born. However the heat from the engine room seemed to drive the cold out of me & apart from an attack of rheumatism which came on afterwards, I have not suffered much, apart from a little nervous shock but I assure you that now I feel in good [*spirits*] again.

As for Det. she has proven herself to be a brave little woman; if she could only tell you her experience, you would do as I do – look at her and marvel at her being here. But she did well and held on to Dolly till the boat went down & she was carried into the water & lost her hold on Dolly & then she hardly remembers much until she found herself ashore again at Rimouski. She must have lost consciousness, for she can just remember a sort of dream. So, you can see she was almost gone when it seems that the same power that was pushing me along and helping me to fight for my life must have been watching over her & I imagine when she came to the surface she must have come up near a boat & been picked up. But, as I have said, she remembers nothing.

During all this I had given her up as lost & about 3 hours afterwards, we bandboys, 8 in number, were standing, talking about our experience when someone said, 'Here comes Mrs Brooks,' & when I turned to look, there was [*Det.*] being carried around the end of the building. You talk of your joy when you got that telegram. Well, try to imagine mine at the

Page from fireman John Ryan's Certificate of Discharge book. The last line shows the final voyage of the Empress of Ireland, *and carries the handwritten notation, 'Ship Wrecked 29 May 1914, Discharged 5 June 1914, L'pool'. One of 73* Empress *crewmen repatriated to Liverpool aboard* Corsican, *Ryan's next voyage was aboard* Indian *to Galveston in October. (Carol Sheldon)*

sight of seeing her again. It was a big surprise & relief. Of course, she was in a terrible cond-ition but I did the utmost I could & with the kindness of the people she soon began to feel herself alive again. We stayed over the next night at Rimouski and were sent to Quebec next day. On arriving there I did not feel satisfied with her cond-ition so I called a doctor to the hotel & he ordered her to the hospital with pl[e]urisy in her lungs but, with good treatment, she was soon on the way back to good health & is now feeling as well as you could expect.

Now don't you consider it a wonderful thing how we should have come thro where so many have lost their lives. God has indeed been mindful of us & I would write you pages & pages concerning our experiences but I feel you are satisfied with the fact that we are spared a little longer for some purpose & therefore do not want too much of the adventurous side.

We have not given up the hope of coming home and I shall try as soon as possible to arrange for a trip. You see, we lost every stitch we had & every dollar has gone. But things will come out alrig[h]t in time. So, don't worry; we are alright. Mr Eaton called to see us in the hospital at Quebec and, since getting home, I have started work again at Eaton's. The shop also gave me a nice donation and lots of good clothes & in fact everywhere we have been shown the best of kindness. I want you to go round to Mr Westwood's & show this letter as, of course, he is so anxious, as you are. But cheer up. That's what we are doing in spite of such a blow. We cannot understand these things but He has promised

to guide us with his eye & I fully believe God has been watching over us & will yet bring
us to realize why this has happened.
Give our love to all & accept the best we can send.
Your affect. Children
(sgd) Frank & Hetty

The sinking of the *Empress* was worldwide news for days, and generated messages between many people
who were connected in some way or another to the CPR, or to its directors. Most people in Canada
admired and were proud of the CPR *Empresses*, and of the enterprise and ideas of the men and the
company which stood behind the ships. The following is extracted from a letter from Paris to Sir William
Van Horne's daughter Adeline. Dated 29 May it shows how quickly the news spread about the disaster.

> Dear Miss Addie,
> I am quite shocked by the horrible news about the *Empress of Ireland* and her crew and
> passengers. Such a catastrophy is awful in itself; but in this case, it appeals to my feelings
> still more, because the ill-fated boat is connected with the CPR, and the CPR in my eyes
> identifies itself with my dear Van Horne friends.

At Lloyd's the sinking of the *Empress* was greeted with disbelief, coming just two years after the *Titanic*,
for the accident need not have occurred at all. The monetary loss to insurers was one of the heaviest ever
incurred, with the exception of *Titanic*. Total insurance coverage amounted to over £500,000 as shown:

General insurance on the vessel (so-called 'hull' insurance)	£280,000
additional insurance on total loss	100,000
cargo	150,000
total	**£530,000**

The loss, according to Lloyd's sources, would be shared among some thirty marine companies and
about a hundred underwriters' syndicates.

The true wonder of the *Empress* disaster is not that so many died, but that *anyone* was saved. In the
near-freezing waters of the St Lawrence, at night, in a darkened ship turned on her starboard side and
rapidly filling with water, survival was largely a random affair.

If it took great luck to survive the *Empress of Ireland*, imagine what it took to survive not only the
Empress but also *Titanic*, as did one man. Fireman William Clark, a quiet, matter-of-fact forty-three-
year-old with a grey moustache and kindly eyes, was an unlikely survivor. A veteran of the war in South
Africa, the lucky Irishman from County Louth had escaped *Titanic*'s stokehold in 1912, and aboard the
Empress he had been ordered out of the stokehold moments after the collision. He ended up in a life-
boat and was taken aboard *Storstad*.

Returning to Glasgow via Greenock on 9 June in the Allan Line's *Corsican* accompanied by seventy-
three other surviving crew members (all but one from the black gang) and sixty-one third class passengers, Clark was interviewed by reporters, intrigued by the story of a man who had survived the two
greatest maritime catastrophes of modern times. Though *Corsican* proceeded directly up the Clyde to
Glasgow, reporters and a few family members were ferried out to the ship by tug from Greenock.

'I was a fireman on both the ships,' Clark told *The Times*:

> It was my luck to be on duty at the time of both accidents. The *Titanic* disaster was much
> the worst of the two. I mean it was much the most awful. The waiting was the terrible
> thing. There was no waiting with the *Empress of Ireland*. You just saw what you had to do

Making money from the sinking of the Empress of Ireland, *an advertisement from the Quebec* Chronicle, *30 June 1914.*

and you did it. The *Titanic* went down straight like a baby goes to sleep. The *Empress* rolled over like a hog in a ditch.

I was shoveling coals when the *Empress* was struck. I heard the engines stop. I ran up to my boat, No.5. We swung her down, but the list of the ship threw her out from the side into the water and then the hooks of the davits loosed off and she floated away. I had to dive into the water to catch her. By that time the ship was just going. I heard screaming and then helped to pull people out of the water. We were picked up by the *Storstad*.

Despite his two narrow escapes, Clark remained optimistic. The resident of Derby Road in Bootle said, 'There is a sort of superstition among sailors and I believe it applies on land as well that the third is fatal, but that does not worry me. I'm going back to Liverpool to find a job on another steamer.'

Having arrived in Glasgow, passengers and crew members, who were dressed in such clothing as they could obtain in Canada, were allowed to select from a large store of clothing provided by the CPR. From the Glasgow docks, crew survivors – who ranged in age from 18 to 51 – from the *Empress* had a special train organized to bring them to Liverpool's Exchange Station on 9 June. The Manchester *Guardian* described the scene:

Long before the train arrived the station platforms were crowded with hundreds of people, who climbed to all points of vantage in order to get a glimpse of the rescued crew. The train arrived shortly before seven, and as it steamed into the station, there was a wild cheering and waving of hands.

Seventy-three survivors stepped from the train and were welcomed by mothers, wives, sweethearts, children, and friends. The scene was very touching. Old women who welcomed back their sons wept and shouted for joy. Two Roman Catholic priests were on the platform and spoke kindly words to the survivors as they made their way through the throng. All the belongings the crew had with them were wrapped in red handkerchiefs and paper. The majority are stokers and firemen. They made their way quickly through enormous crowds into the streets, where they were followed by still greater crowds of interested people.

Printing companies soon came out with a variety of memorial postcards for the *Empress*, showing the ship, the date of loss and the number of deaths. Other postcards showed the *Empress* and a separate photograph of the *Storstad*, her bow crumpled. Rumsey & Co. of Toronto urged wholesalers to write, wire or phone their bulk orders for memorial cards priced at two dollars per hundred. What is surprising is the speed with which postcard companies printed the memorial cards. The earliest cancellation date noted is 7 June!

While some of these found ready purchasers, regular *Empress* postcards continued to be sold. One such card, postmarked 15 June from Canada, comments on Dr Murdoch Alexander Lindsay of Halifax:

> This is the *Empress of Ireland* which was wrecked in the St Lawrence May 29/14 with over a thousand lives. What a terrible tragedy it was – one can hardly realise to look at her that she could go down in ten minutes. We had only one person from our city, a Dr Lindsay, who was going to England to get married. How sad it was. Imagine the ones that were asleep never to awaken again – only in the world beyond.

At the Canadian Pacific offices, large stocks of promotional literature for the Atlantic *Empresses* remained on hand. Rather than scrap those depicting the *Empress of Ireland*, the company adopted the simple expedient of merely blacking out the name.

'BIG MONEY FOR HUSTLERS' announced an advertisement from a Boston company that appeared at intervals in the Halifax *Herald* in mid-June. It encouraged would-be agents to order 14x22 prints of the *Empress* suitable for framing. Samples were available for fifteen cents.

Out of respect, flags were flown at half-mast on all vessels in the port of Montreal for a week after the sinking, and the Canadian Pacific ordered flags to be flown at half-staff at its offices and agencies around the world.

Memorial services were held in various cities in North America, England and elsewhere, along with funerals for those whose bodies were recovered and identified. Once released by the authorities in Quebec, coffins were sent off by rail to grieving relatives in cities like Montreal and in small towns and villages. Some Britons, like Sir Henry Seton-Kerr, were buried in Quebec following cabled instructions from the family. Others, like first class passenger Charles Goldthorp, were returned to England for burial. Goldthorp's coffin was shipped aboard *Alsatian* to his family in Bradford.

The largest of the public funerals took place on Saturday, 6 June, at Toronto's Mutual Street Arena, where the funeral for sixteen Salvation Army victims was attended by more than ten thousand, including many civic dignitaries, while the processional route to Mount Pleasant Cemetery was thronged by 150,000.

In England, at a memorial service in the Royal Albert Hall, there were 148 empty seats, for the lost Canadian Salvationists. Each one bore the white mourning badge of the Army with its crown and red letter *S*.

To John Walsh fell the task of informing families of the fate of their loved ones. Typical of the telegrams sent in early June by the chief marine superintendent is this one, to the relatives Bernard Tumilty, who had been engaged in Quebec City as a last-minute replacement.

> Montreal Que June3rd 1914
> Thos Tumilty Victoria, BC
> Your wire late sorry to inform you Tumilty not among saved
> J T Walsh
> Chief Marine Supt

For many in that long summer of 1914 there was an agonizing lack of information about their loved ones. The following letter from the National Archives and addressed to Walsh on 25 July from a café owner in Vancouver is probably typical of the letters written by distraught families:

Dear Sir, –

We are extremely anxious to get some reliable information from a source that can be depended upon.

Our only child (William H. Wakefield) was lost on the ill fated 'Empress of Ireland'. From the moment we first learned of the disaster, we have been hoping that we could recover the body of our son. Up to now, we have had no word, and any word that has come, seems to be only guessing.

What we are anxious to know is this, – What are the prospects of recovering the bodies of those who have been trapped in the boat? Are the divers still working under your direction for the recovery of bodies? Do you purpose to continue, or abandon the work?

You may easily imagine the state of desperation we are in, and I assure you, my wife and self will be deeply grateful for any information you may be able to forward to us.

Thanking you in anticipation,

Yours sincerely,

(sgd) W.J. Wakefield

The Mersey Inquiry convened in Quebec City at the Court House across from the Chateau Frontenac on 16 June and, over the next eleven days, sifted through a mass of often conflicting evidence. Four parliamentary stenographers from Ottawa and the chief editor of Hansard worked in shifts to take verbatim proceedings. The Inquiry called sixty-one witnesses, and examined more than seventy exhibits. The printed report of the Inquiry, which appeared in 1914, runs to 615 pages and upwards of 250,000 words.

Despite this, it was Joseph Conrad who perhaps best summed up the reasons for the accident, a month before the Inquiry delivered its judgment. Commissioned by the *Illustrated London News* to write on *The Lesson of the Collision* as part of its issue of 6 June 1914 devoted to the disaster, the man who had held a master's certificate for twenty years and was the celebrated author of such nautical works as *Typhoon* and *Twixt Land and Sea* penned a one-page article, from which the following are abstracted:

We have been accustoming ourselves to put our trust in material, technical skill, invention, and scientific contrivances to such an extent that we have come at last to believe that with these things we can overcome the immortal gods themselves.

You can't get the better of the immortal gods by the mere power of material contrivances.

It seems to me that the resentful sea-gods never do sleep, and are never weary.

As long as men will travel on the water, the sea-gods will take their toll.

The famous front-line war correspondent and author Philip Gibbs (later knighted), writing in *The Graphic* of 6 June, penned a similar essay entitled *Out of the Darkness – The Tragedy of the* Empress. In it, he compared the loss of the *Empress* to *Titanic*. 'It was,' he wrote bluntly, 'not an "act of God", to use the old sea-phrase, but men's blundering. Her loss was not due to the great natural forces mightier than all our human skill, but to an error of judgment, a stupid 'accident.' This is what gives the worst sting to the agony of our regrets.' His essay continued, 'No science and no skill could dodge that death that lumbered up through the night... In spite of all our victories, all our pride of skill, all our science, we are but children playing in the dark.'

The similar verdicts of Conrad and Gibbs helped to shatter some of the last, lingering illusions of *la belle époque*. Theirs were not answers that Edwardians, imbued with the ideas of progress and scientific achievement, would have liked.

In Quebec a passenger about to embark on the *Empress of Britain* on 12 June sent a postcard depicting the *Empress of Ireland* arriving at Quebec, and wrote: 'This is ship as she was once, seems almost impossible to sink her but all done in 14 minutes. Quebec almost went wild, getting over it now. I was loading at her sister ship today and wondering how she could sink.'

At Rest: Watercolour impression of an Empress *grave in Montreal's Mount Royal Cemetery. The cemetery holds victims of* Titanic, Empress *and* Lusitania. *(Patricia Kirby)*

The CPR moved quickly to fill the gap in the summer schedule, chartering *Virginian* from the Allan Line. *Virginian* was a good choice, with a proven record on the North Atlantic route. Launched in 1904 from the Stephen yard on the Clyde, she was a 538ft, triple-screw vessel and was, along with her sister *Victorian*, the first turbine liner on the North Atlantic and the first with triple screws. *Virginian* made her first voyage under charter to the CPR, arriving at Montreal on 21 June from Liverpool with 699 passengers, and departing on 25 June with 756. It was the end of an era on the St Lawrence.

In a memo of 24 June, Sir Thomas Shaughnessy authorized plans to be drawn up for two first-class passenger ships about 600 feet long for the Liverpool service. The company began making inquiries on the Clyde, letting shipbuilders know it might be interested in constructing a replacement for the *Empress*, depending on delivery dates and prices.

With the outbreak of war, everything changed.

There would be no new ships, and *Virginian*'s charter by the CPR was soon terminated. She sailed from Liverpool on 4 September, and on her return passage *Virginian* was one of the large flotilla that transported the first Canadian contingent to England in October 1914, carrying 1,394 troops of the 7th Battalion, along with ammunition, medical stores, flour and lumber, and other support staff.

After that she was taken over by the Admiralty as an armed merchant cruiser, being returned to the CPR in 1917. Sold by the CPR in 1920 to the Swedish America Line, she was renamed *Drottningholm*. Sold again, she was renamed *Brasil* in 1948 for the Home Line, and renamed yet again in 1951 as *Homeland*. She was scrapped at Trieste in 1955 after a fifty-year career, a record for continuous service unequaled by any liner on the North Atlantic, and a tribute to the many vessels built on the Clyde in *la belle époque*.

Hundreds of messages of sympathy poured each day into the CPR's offices in Montreal even as late as ten days after the sinking. There were two main themes to the messages: sorrow at the loss of life, and sympathy for the railway company. Those that were addressed to Sir Thomas Shaughnessy, and there were many, were answered in person. Shaughnessy's letters convey the impression of a man profoundly moved by the loss. Replying on June 2 to Sir Thomas Tait in Toronto, Shaughnessy wrote simply:

> My dear Sir Thomas:
> Many thanks for your kind and sympathetic letter.
> The loss was appalling and the sadness of it all overwhelming.

Three days later Shaughnessy wrote to the mayor of Rimouski, and concluded, 'The sad catastrophe, which cast a gloom over the whole world, brought to the front the best attributes of human nature, as illustrated by you and the people of Rimouski. You have the sincere gratitude of the Company, and of myself personally.'

Like many, Shaughnessy was quick to apportion blame for the collision. Replying on 30 May to a sympathy letter, he wrote: 'That the Company was not at fault in any way, does not lessen our sorrow for those who lost their lives, and for their families.'

Shaughnessy, who knew many of the *Empress* men, was moved by their plight. He authorized clothing advances to William Sampson and Henry Kendall of a hundred dollars each, and contributed generously from his own pocket to the relief funds that soon sprang up. As well, he arranged for the CPR to provide some special services to a few first class families who had suffered losses. The family of Sir Henry Seton-Kerr, the big-game hunter whose body had been recovered, received photographs of his grave in Quebec's Mount Hermon cemetery.

Newspapers reported that in Montreal Thomas Andersen had a considerable number of supporters who felt that the veteran captain had been made a scapegoat in the sinking, even before the Mersey Inquiry completed its investigation.

The Norwegian government convened an 'inquiry' of its own at its Consulate General in Montreal, with a panel consisting of the First Secretary from the Norwegian Legation in Washington, and two Norwegian captains familiar with the St Lawrence route. Testimony was taken only from persons aboard *Storstad*; there were no witnesses from the *Empress* or the CPR. This investigation completed its work on 29 June, before the Mersey Inquiry delivered its findings. The Norwegian government, not surprisingly, exonerated *Storstad*'s crew.

The log book of the *Empress* was the subject of a brief discussion at the Inquiry in Quebec City. It proved to be of little use, for it was complete only until midnight on the night of the disaster. The watch officers had been slow to enter the extracts from the various temporary (or 'scrap') logs kept in various departments of the ship. The log was entered into evidence as Exhibit V. Unfortunately, almost all of the Exhibits and charts produced for the Inquiry have disappeared from the National Archives in Ottawa – assuming they even got there in the first place. It is possible that they may be mis-filed but this seems a slim hope. Another of the enduring, unsolved *Empress* mysteries.

The Times lauded Lord Mersey and his efforts in conducting the Inquiry. The paper's Montreal correspondent reported: 'The skill with which Lord Mersey has handled the whole subject is praised by every one. The opinion is freely expressed that his clear-sightedness, incisiveness, and expertness in dealing with the witnesses and eliciting points which counsel had failed to reveal and the refusal to allow prejudicial statements contributed immensely to the speed with which the inquiry has been conducted.'

That report, by chance, shared a page dealing with the assassination of Archduke Franz Ferdinand and his wife in Sarajevo.

Lord Mersey, reading portions of the judgment of the Commission of Inquiry at the Court House on the morning of 11 July, said:

We regret to have to impute blame to anyone in connection with this lamentable disaster, and we should not do so if we felt that any reasonable alternative was left to us. We can, however, come to no other conclusion than that Mr Toftenes was wrong and negligent in altering his course in the fog, as he undoubtedly did, and that he was wrong and negligent in keeping the navigation of the vessel in his own hands and in failing to call the captain when he saw the fog coming on.

It is not to be supposed that this disaster was in any way attributable to any special characteristics of the St Lawrence Waterway. It was a disaster which might have occurred in the Thames, in the Clyde, in the Mersey, or elsewhere in similar circumstances.

That closed the matter from an official point of view. The government of Canada could step back, satisfied it had done all it could and that the safety of the St Lawrence route had not been questioned.

'The verdict speaks for itself,' Sir Thomas said in Montreal on 14 July. 'It is a source of great satisfaction to the CPR to know that no blame attaches to any of the company's officers and that Canada's great waterway is equally free from reproach.'

Storstad, sold at auction on 8 July for $175,000 at Montreal, sailed down the St Lawrence for repairs and arrived at Quebec on 9 July.

Thomas Andersen, predictably enough, disagreed with the Inquiry's verdict. In an interview on 20 July in Quebec, and printed in *Le Devoir*, he observed bitterly that the president of the tribunal preferred the version of an Englishman than that of four honest Norwegians (*'le président du tribunal a préféré la version d'un Anglais à celle de quatres honnêtes Norvégiens.'*)

After that, lawyers for the CPR would pick at the case for the next years, for the Mersey Inquiry had no binding legal effect. Counsel for *Storstad*'s owners promised to secure another finding in Admiralty Court. *Canadian Pacific Railway Co. vs. SS Storstad* was heard in Admiralty Court in Montreal on 15 February 1915, and Hon. Justice Dunlop rendered his decision on 27 April, finding in favour of the plaintiff, the CPR. Though in 1919 the courts allowed the CPR claims to be admitted, it was a symbolic victory. For the Maritime Steamship Company, its liability had ended with *Storstad*'s sale.

Though the *Empress of Ireland* was – and remains – Canada's worst maritime disaster, there is no general agreement on the exact number of deaths. This should come as no surprise. As early as 2 June, the CPR issued a list showing 'the final complete official figures' – some 1,024 names, the number used in the *Illustrated London News* in its 6 June issue on the sinking. The Saint John *Standard* commented that day, 'New list adds to confusion regarding number of persons lost,' and correctly concluded, 'Exact death toll in *Empress* Catastrophe may never be known.' The Quebec *Chronicle* echoed the same feeling, noting that confusion surrounding the number lost was one of the most distressing aspects of the tragedy.

At the outset of the Mersey Inquiry, E.L. Newcombe, counsel for the Crown, stated, 'I am informed that they [*the CPR*] have experienced very great difficulty in getting out an exact list owing to the discrepancies in the names of the passengers, particularly in regard to the continentals, shown on the manifest, and the names given by the survivors.' In his opening statement Newcombe claimed a total of 1,014 fatalities, a number that is often cited by many sources. However, a few days later, John Walsh provided yet another total, 1,012, broken down as follows:

First class	87	of which 51 lost
Second class	253	of which 205 lost
Third class	717	of which 584 lost
Crew	420	of which 172 lost
Total	**1,477**	**of which 1,012 lost**

Walsh confessed that the number was correct 'to the best of our ability. It is hard to find out the exact truth, but the only discrepancy would be in the names. The numbers are correct.'

In its findings, the Inquiry ultimately agreed with the total of 1,012, publishing the following breakdown:

		Total	Saved
First Class	Adult, males	49	24
	Adult, females	34	11
	Children, males	-	-
	Children, females	4	1
	total	**87**	**36**
Second class	Adult, males	114	33
	Adult, females	107	13
	Children, males	11	-
	Children, females	21	2
	total	**253**	**48**
Third class	Adult, males	446	115
	Adult, females	169	17
	Children, males	54	1
	Children, females	48	-
	total	**717**	**133**

Of the	609	adult male passengers,	172 were saved
	310	adult female passengers,	41 were saved
	65	male children,	1 was saved
	73	female children,	3 were saved
total	**1,057**	**passengers,**	**217 were saved**

The total number of the crew saved was 248, as follows:

	Total	Saved
Deck Department	59	36
Engine Department	130	92
Sup. Engineers ex *Empress of Asia*	4	3
Victualing Department	212	113
Matron and stewardesses	10	1
Musicians	5	3
total	**420**	**248**

While many works on the *Empress* quote the Mersey total of 1,012, others offer a wide range of fatalities, and no backup to support their various claims. In this book, the figure of 1,012 is used for the simple reason that no other source can adequately support a different number.

As Appendix 8 shows, the Mersey total is wrong. But how wrong?

In the aftermath of the sinking, there were many who commented on the fact that almost sixty percent of the crew had been saved. It was Captain James Murray, one-time master of the *Empress*, who explained there was a standing order that when a collision occurred, the crew were to immediately take their stations at the boats. Thus many crew members found themselves on deck, in the process of trying to perform their duties, when they were thrown into the river. 'I am certain,' Murray said in an interview on 1 June, 'that there was no better crew on any vessel afloat than that which manned the *Empress of Ireland*, and all of them stuck to their posts in a manner that is a credit to their race and profession, and there certainly can be no reflections truthfully on their conduct.'

On stock markets in Europe and North America, the *Empress* was the main item for discussion on 29 May, as word of the disaster flashed around the world. The following day, the Montreal *Gazette* commented that 'The shock of the *Empress of Ireland* disaster reduced interest in the stock market, already at a low ebb.' and went on to observe that the CPR had shown better resistance to the news of the disaster than had been expected. In Montreal, the Friday morning close was only a point lower than the Thursday close, while in London, the stock dropped two points initially and then recovered much of the loss in later trading.

Other papers noted the same thing. 'CPR STRONG IN SPITE OF DISASTER' said the Saint John *Standard* on 30 May. The paper went on to explain the market considered the monetary loss, which amounted to over two million dollars, comparatively small compared to the company's reserves and surplus.

In the aftermath of the *Empress of Ireland*, one can advance several reasons why the CPR's shares didn't suffer more than a 1.7% loss.

First, the company was a large and diversified one whose marine operations represented only a portion of its overall activities. Even though the company had become one of the largest shipping companies in the world, operating on two oceans and the inland lakes of Canada and using a total of seventy-two steamships of twenty different types, its success did not depend on a single vessel, which was only the third in terms of size after the *Empress of Russia* and the *Empress of Asia*.

The CPR's diversified rail and other operations buffered it against a collapse. In the weeks before the *Empress* disaster, for example, oil had been discovered in the Calgary area and speculators imagined that one of the prime beneficiaries of this would be the railway, which owned substantial tracts of land in the region and would move goods and people to the new oilfields.

Second, the company was insured against loss and its insurers swiftly paid in full the company's claim of $2 million, about the same amount as the *Empress* had cost to build in 1906.

Third, by the spring of 1914 the twin *Empresses* were no longer the largest, fastest or most luxurious vessels serving the Canadian route. Those honours now belonged to the Allan Line's *Alsatian* and *Calgarian*, which had made their maiden voyages earlier that same year. Immigration in 1914 had fallen by 50% from the 1913 levels as a result of a recession in Canada and rising unemployment. That meant there was an excess of capacity on the Britain-Canada route, and the loss of the *Empress* was less severe than it seemed. And, though the public didn't know it, by 1914 the CPR and Allan Lines were being run as an integrated operation, though there was still an outward facade of competition.

Last, the company paid a dividend of ten dollars a share. At 194 per share (on 8 June), it yielded a respectable 5.13% annually. In other words, the CPR was still a good buy compared to many other equities.

Over the next two months, stocks in Europe and North America drifted lower in an apathetic market. The CPR, which had traded as high as 219 5/8 earlier in the year, was already well down from that level when the *Empress* sank, and the stock continued downward throughout June and July, with almost none of the decline attributable to the loss of the *Empress*. On 31 July, with Europe already at war (though Britain would not enter the war for another four days) the stock tumbled to $171\frac{1}{2}$ British equity markets were closed by the government and investors in New York began baling out of shipping companies whose assets could be taken over by the Admiralty. 'WAR SENDS STOCKS TO NEW LOW LEVELS' was the headline in the *New York Times* as investors dumped their holdings.

The Edwardian era, the age of innocence, was over.

7
Salvage and the *Empress of Ireland*

Following the sinking of the *Empress*, there was an early (and misplaced) optimism that the wreck could be raised. On 3 June, *The Times* confidently told its readers that 'should the company abandon the vessel to the underwriters, the latter will certainly make every effort to raise her. The officials of the Canadian Pacific Railway have, it is known, received offers from several salvage companies in the United States. No decision has been made on the point, but it is considered by marine experts here [*i.e. Montreal*] as in the highest degree probable that some effort will be made to raise the ship.' Within a couple of days that rosy picture had changed radically.

On 4 June the company abandoned the ship to its underwriters, who made their first payment to the CPR the following day, exactly a week after the disaster, and the payment was made on the basis of a total loss. The CPR's claim had been processed remarkably quickly. As a rule, losses were not settled until the captain's protest, duly sworn before a notary, had been received by the underwriters.

The underwriters soon realized that the *Empress*, badly holed and lying on her starboard side in over 150 feet of water, would be impossible to raise. Attention thus focused on raising the 212 silver ingots, the purser's safe, and recovering some of the bodies still trapped inside the hull. As the Halifax *Herald* crassly (though accurately) observed, 'One million and ninety-nine thousand dollars is worth the employment of scores of divers.'

The CPR, too, was under pressure to recover bodies from the wreck, in order to placate public opinion which demanded that *something* be done.

The CGS *Druid*, a lighthouse and buoy tender, steamed to the vicinity to study the wreck site. The grave of the *Empress* was not difficult to locate. Air was still leaking out of the hull and an oil slick bloomed at the surface. *Druid*'s captain, Michel Gagnon, placed a buoy about half a cable (some 300ft) northeast of the wreck, and four miles off Ste-Luce. This was not the first buoy on the site, for a spar buoy had been set up on 29 May, though it had blown away by the following day. On 30 May a proper marker had been put in place, a green buoy showing an oscillating white light.

The first dive on the *Empress* took place on 7 June, a little over a week after the sinking, from a small boat that was moored with kedge anchors. A helmeted diver descended at the end of a weighted line to establish the position and orientation of the wreck. He found the ship lying on her starboard side, canted over at a sharp angle. The bottom was reported as soft mud, and 12-15ft of the hull was buried in the mud. Depth to the port side of the ship at low water was seventy-five feet. Conditions were less than perfect. A current of $2\frac{1}{2}$ knots swept over the wreck. The water was cold and dive times, due to the depths involved, would be limited to reduce the risk of decompression sickness or 'the bends' as it was commonly called. Ascents to the surface would be in slow stages, allowing the divers sufficient time to breathe out the excess nitrogen in their bodies, and thus avoid the bends. As well there were innumerable projections on which a hard-hat diver's air hose and rope could get snagged. In all, the diving conditions could be summed up as difficult and dangerous. But not impossible.

Diving operations halted temporarily on 8 June, when a strong easterly gale sprang up. On board *Druid* were several embalmers, who were to prepare any bodies for burial as soon as they were brought to the surface. Also aboard *Druid* were two keen observers, John Walsh of the CPR and William Wallace Wotherspoon, who had been engaged to head up a team of American and Canadian divers. Wotherspoon, whose name often appears incorrectly in newspapers of the day as 'Weatherspoon', was a highly qualified professional diver and salvage expert with his own company in New York. He had considerable experience with deep-diving operations, which were considered very hazardous in the days before the physiology of decompression was fully understood. One of Wotherspoon's previous assignments had been to recover bodies from the USS *Maine*, whose sinking in Havana harbour in 1898 had precipitated the Spanish-American War. He was no stranger to the St Lawrence. In 1905 he had worked on the Allan Line's stranded *Bavarian*, and had helped re-float the *Royal George* when she had gone aground below Quebec in late 1912.

Wotherspoon, testifying later at the Mersey Inquiry, identified himself as an engineer of the Canadian Salvage Association. The chief of diving operations described his engagement as three-fold: 'first to attempt to obtain the bodies, then the mails and then a quantity of silver.' In fact, he had been engaged by three separate parties for the three distinct tasks: by the CPR, to make every possible effort possible to recover the bodies in the ship; by the Postmaster General, to recover the mails; and by the Insurers, who wanted to recover the bullion.

No one expected that all the bodies would be recovered, for the risks to the divers would have been too prohibitive. In the lower deck where third class passengers had been accommodated, and in the close confines of companionways, there was a great danger that air hoses could be fouled, and the divers could not exchange rope signals with their tenders at the surface. And, though no one was tactless enough to say so, the costs would have been enormous. All that was expected was a token effort. In the end, the divers did better than anyone would have foreseen.

As far as recovery of the mails was concerned, the divers had no formal contract with the Post Office. A loose arrangement was struck with the salvors, which one postal official later clarified. 'If,' he explained, 'whilst carrying out their Contract with the Insurance Companies, they were successful in recovering the mails, we would later on decide what remuneration would be proper to give them.

'In other words, we asked the Company which had the contract with the other parties not to leave our mails at the bottom of the river, if in the performance of that contract, they could at the same time recover them.'

Diving began in earnest once the antiquated British cruiser HMS *Essex* arrived on the scene on Friday, 19 June. *Essex*, on a goodwill visit to Canada, had assisted in the initial recovery of bodies from the river following the sinking of the *Empress* and, by chance, she had a small team of Royal Navy divers on board with some of the most modern equipment.

Chief Gunner John MacDiarmid, who was also a Royal Navy diving instructor, had three divers under his command: leading seaman Wilfred Whitehead, and two men identified as Kellier and Macdonald. Whitehead, with four years of diving experience, was the first of the *Essex* team to visit the wreck. He made his initial descent at 1:00 p.m. on the 19th, shortly after *Essex* arrived on the scene. His instructions were simple: to walk fore and aft, so that the stream of rising bubbles would indicate the direction of the wreck. Observers at the surface noted the *Empress* lay NE to SW, her bow facing northeast. The dive lasted about forty minutes.

Whitehead testified at the Inquiry that visibility at thirteen fathoms (78ft) was about ten feet. He estimated he travelled 18-20 fathoms along the side of the ship, though he admitted readily that he had no idea where he was, or that he was even on the port side. He estimated that the ship lay at an angle of about sixty degrees, and reported seeing no open portholes in the lower tier of portholes.

After just three weeks in the water, the sea was starting to claim the *Empress*. Whitehead described it thus: 'There is a thin coating of slime so that as you draw your fingers over it, it leaves finger-marks.'

The three RN divers made a total of five dives, each man diving alone. They waited for periods of low wind and calm surface conditions. John MacDiarmid gave his divers specific orders not to enter the wreck. They were to examine the exterior and hull only. Lord Mersey later complemented the Chief Gunner: 'You were very wise,' he said at the Inquiry. The divers reported seeing portholes open, though the Inquiry did not make much of this fact. And, because they were forbidden to enter the hull, they could not determine whether the watertight doors had been closed.

Wotherspoon's team had also been busy at the site, now crowded with three support vessels, *Essex*, *Lord Strathcona* and a small chartered steam schooner named *Marie Josephine* which had been rigged for diving operations. Captain Hugh Watson, commander of the *Essex*, placed his ship's modern dive gear at Wotherspoon's disposal. Most usefully, the *Essex* gear included a recompression chamber. More and better equipment was soon ordered, and it arrived on 3 July. This new gear included divers' hard-hat helmets which were fitted with an innovation: simple British-made telephones that enabled a diver to communicate to the surface via the umbilical cable. A patch-box at the surface enabled a diver to communicate with other divers working below. In all, Wotherspoon concurred that the equipment he had, with that from *Essex*, was the best that money could procure and science suggest.

Wotherspoon's team consisted of six experienced divers, along with a large gang of men for the surface support team. On Friday the 19th, Edward Cossaboom, described as 'one of the continent's best experts in his strenuous calling', secured a marker buoy on the stern of the *Empress* and recovered the first body, which was tethered to a rope and hauled to the surface by the tenders. The divers then fixed two moorings on the wreck, one at the stern and the other at the after end of No.4 hatch. Work continued at all cycles of the tide, though the divers preferred to dive at slack water, when the current was lessened.

Tragedy struck on Sunday, 21 June. High winds and choppy seas had prevented dive operations in the morning, but conditions improved in the afternoon and Cossaboom descended at 2:00 p.m. Working at a depth of about 75 feet near the forecastle head, Cossaboom had sent two bodies to the surface when he apparently lost his footing on the slippery hull and fell over the side of the ship into deeper water. In doing so, he suffered what is termed a 'squeeze', caused by an imbalance of pressure. While working at 75 feet, the air supplied to him by a hand-operated surface pump and a long hose was slightly over the ambient water pressure at that depth. In falling to a deeper depth, he was no longer in equilibrium, and the increased water pressure literally jammed the unfortunate diver into his own helmet, the only part of his rubberized canvas suit that was not compressible.

When Cossaboom failed to respond to rope signals from his tender, two divers went down to look for their companion. They returned empty-handed. At that point Wotherspoon's team was out of divers, the others going through surface decompression to rid their bodies of accumulated nitrogen.

Essex diver Wilfred Whitehead then volunteered to look for Cossaboom. He succeeded in less than fifteen minutes, finding Cossaboom at 130 feet and lying prone on his life line. Though Cossaboom was hauled quickly aboard *Marie Josephine*, there was nothing Dr Moreault, the on-board physician could do. Cossaboom never recovered consciousness and died thirty minutes later, the first diving fatality on the wreck.

Diving operations were temporarily suspended and *Essex* left the site. Cossaboom had been a favourite among the men because of his good disposition and intrepid nature, and his death cast a pall of gloom over the operation. Walsh then met with Captain Watson and, after a period of discussion, the pair agreed to continue the recovery of bodies. Accordingly, *Essex* returned to the scene of the wreck. Chief Gunner John MacDiarmid, after testifying at the Mersey Inquiry, returned to the site aboard *Lord Strathcona* and the team of eight divers resumed its grisly work. Feeling the press of time and knowing the *Essex* team could not remain on site indefinitely, Wotherspoon sent telegrams to other expert divers in New York and Chicago.

The grisly work went on, day after day. In *Men Under The Sea*, Edward Ellsberg described it in graphic terms: 'the divers worked their way through the ship, with men and women, suddenly overtaken by death, staring at them with sightless eyes and agonized faces almost at every turn. To make matters worse, the ship was soon alive with shellfish attracted by the feast, and many a corpse went up so badly eaten as to be forever unrecognizable.'

As the divers reported to Wotherspoon at the conclusion of each shift, the diving chief was able to build up a coherent picture of the wreck. Asked at the Inquiry whether the divers could provide an actual description of the damage that was caused by the collision, Wotherspoon replied, 'I very much doubt it. ...I think it would be a very hazardous and perhaps impossible undertaking. While the rail may be above the mudline I think the injury would be covered by mud.'

Recovery efforts continued into July, the results being followed avidly in the daily press. *Le Devoir* noted on 8 July the recovery of the bodies of Brigadier-General James Hunter and his son and, two days later, the recovery of four more bodies. '*Dans la coque de l'Empress*' *Le Devoir* noted on 17 July, along with the recovery of three more bodies. The names of the divers – Jack Devine, Edward Tuck, Henry Chinchen, Lutz and J. Laty – became familiar to an audience enthralled with the highly dangerous and macabre operation.

Wotherspoon, by now in sole charge of the diving activities, made a fast trip to New York to get more help and electric lights for the dive team, and returned on 14 July. On 22 July strong winds hampered the recovery efforts, and *Lord Strathcona* departed the wreck site. The following day, wind, rain and fog shut down the efforts completely, and shipping in the St Lawrence was delayed. By this time the divers had recovered more than 250 bodies, a relief to certain families, a heartbreak to others whose relatives still remained trapped in the steel coffin. Many of the bodies, after prolonged immersion, could not be identified and a good number of them were buried in a mass grave between Rimouski and Father Point, on a site purchased by the CPR and maintained to this day by the company.

As the initial phase of their work came to a mostly satisfactory conclusion, the team's attention turned to raising the purser's safe.

The safe posed two problems. First, it had to be recovered unopened, so that no one could later claim its contents had been rifled by the divers. Second, there was no way the massive safe could be manhandled through the labyrinth of passageways. It would have to be extracted vertically through a hole blown in the side of the ship, and winched to the surface.

On 3 July, Wotherspoon and his team headed to Rimouski aboard *Lady Evelyn* to rendezvous with the *Empress of Britain*, inbound from Liverpool. In the early morning hours, while the ship stood off Rimouski discharging the Canadian mails, the salvage master and his divers were led about the ship. They measured the purser's safe, and plotted a pathway, making hasty notes as they walked around. They had little time. After barely an hour, the *Empress of Britain* steamed upriver and the divers returned to the *Marie Josephine*.

Back on the portside hull of the sunken *Empress*, the divers carefully began counting rivets to make sure they were in the right place, a side cargo port almost directly over the purser's office. Once that was done, the divers began drilling into the steel hull, seven-eighths of an inch thick. Chains secured to the bow rail held L-shaped angle irons, which the divers used as a working platform. A pneumatic drill, fed by two Rand compressors at the surface, was used to bore closely spaced holes around the perimeter of a 6ft x12ft rectangle.

The first holes were the most difficult. In conditions of near weightlessness, the divers had nothing to push on, to give the drill purchase. Once the first few holes had been drilled, things got a bit easier. Hook bolts could be inserted and these would support a steel beam.

After the rectangle had been outlined, a small charge of dynamite was used to blow out the hull plating.

This was not the first hole the divers had made in the hull of the *Empress*, although it was the largest and the only one to be blasted. At least four smaller rectangular holes had also been cut to give the divers easier access to key parts of the ship. For each side of the rectangle a row of holes was drilled as close together as possible. After the corner holes were drilled, hook bolts were inserted and a support beam for the drill installed. When the four sides of the opening had thus been defined, hooks were inserted in a number of holes along one side and a powerful pull from a hoisting engine on the support boat did the rest. The hull plating was not torn completely off, but merely pulled out of the way, like the lid of a sardine can.

After dynamiting, the real work began, as two teams laboured in parallel. One team unbolted the safe from its bulkhead, while a second began clearing a pathway for the safe.

When all was ready, a surface winch began pulling, and the massive safe started to move toward the opening in the hull. Divers levered it into position for the final lift, then got safely out of the way. The safe bumped and twisted against the hull as it was lifted toward the surface. There was a heart-stopping moment when the safe broke the surface and the assembled men realized, with mounting horror, that the lifting line was within a few inches of the top of the safe. If it slipped off, all their work would have been in vain.

Letter recovered by divers from the Empress, *and returned by the Dead Letter Office in Ottawa to the sender in British Columbia. Note the stamp 'Recovered by divers from wreck of SS* Empress of Ireland'. *This letter has remained in the sender's family since 1914. (Nikki McConnell)*

Slowly – ever so gently – the load was swung inward and the safe lowered gently to *Marie Josephine*'s deck. Once the rigging lines were removed, the safe was sealed by a government agent. It was 20 August and the hardest part of the job had been completed.

Amid great hoopla, the safe was opened in Quebec on the 22nd. To the great relief of the insurers, the overwhelming majority of claims filed against the company had been grossly overstated. Claimants, never expecting the safe could be recovered, inflated their losses, expecting a windfall from the insurance companies. Though the safe had been costly to recover, it had all been worthwhile.

Back on the St Lawrence, the divers could now concentrate on the mails.

On the first day, the 21st, they recovered twenty-three bags. The next two days were slow, but things picked up on the 26th with twenty-two bags, ten on the 28th and thirty-three on 1 September. The last recovery, twenty-two bags, was made on 15 September. In fourteen days of diving the divers recovered a total of 318 bags for the Post Office. Each day, the bags were turned over to postal officials and a typed receipt was issued showing 'Rimouski Wharf', the date, and 'Received for Canada.'

Along with the mails, the dive team recovered all 212 of the silver ingots from the cargo hold. Compared to the safe, it had been a relatively easy task.

The mail matter, once it was recovered, was spread out at Rimouski to dry. Newspapers, spoiled by their immersion, were disposed of as waste. Once dry, the letters were repacked into sacks, amounting to nineteen in all, and forwarded to the Dead Letter Office (DLO) in Ottawa for disposition. According to a DLO memorandum, over 20,000 letters required processing.

Unlike the newspapers, the letters had not deteriorated. The addresses were still perfectly legible after some four months underwater, thanks to indelible india ink. The contents of one such letter have been quoted above in the context of the icefields encountered by the *Royal George* in May 1914.

Obviously proud of its efforts, the salvage company forwarded to the Postmaster General on 19 September a photograph of some of the recovered letters, along with a comment indicating how pleased the Bank of Montreal had been with the return of its mail.

The DLO, in a departure from normal practices, decided that letters should be returned to senders where possible. As the Deputy Postmaster General explained in a letter to his counterpart in Britain, 'It was thought that the senders would prefer to have the letters returned to them so that they might know what had happened to their correspondence rather than that letters should simply be sent forward after such an interval of time had lapsed since they were posted.'

Where the name of the sender could not be established, letters were forwarded to their destination.

In all cases, each letter was endorsed by the DLO 'Recovered by divers from wreck of SS *Empress of Ireland*.'

It was slow work, for the letters needed to be thoroughly dry before the DLO could begin sorting them. By 21 September, while sixteen sacks had been received in Ottawa, only two sacks, with some 2,100 letters, had been processed.

Not all the mail was recovered before diving operations ceased for the season on 18 September – never to be resumed, as it turned out. Left aboard the *Empress* were thirty-two baskets of Canadian-originated parcel post, and thirty-three empty baskets, along with other first-class Canadian and trans-Pacific mail. Still, it was an excellent performance.

Of the 20,000-odd recovered letters, 1,438 contained financial instruments of various types. Two hundred and seventy nine contained Canadian and various foreign currencies equivalent to C$788.87. The cash was mostly in small amounts, with ten dollar bills being the most common. The highest single sum, by far, was thirty dollars.

Number	Type	Value (C$)
938	Money Orders	8,107.16
279	Currency	788.87
54	Drafts	38,699.98
8	Bills of Exchange	20,299.20
4	Promissory Notes	714.75
1	Postal Note	0.50
154	Cheque	22,231.55
1438	**total**	**90,842.01**

For the successful recovery of His Majesty's mails, the divers invoiced the Post Office the sum of $15,000 on 16 November 1914. In its covering letter, the Canadian Import Company, acting as agent for the divers, pointed out the hazards involved in working at a depth of 175 feet, and noted that the divers of HMS *Essex* had been instructed by the Admiralty to make no further dives due to the great risks attached. The company also pointed out that it had lost one of its best divers in the recovery operations.

The letter concluded optimistically, 'We feel, however, we have established a record, and further, the salvage of the mails demonstrates to the whole North American public, that mails shipped by Canadian steamers, via the St Lawrence river, are always recoverable from any accidents in our river and gulf.'

The invoice, interesting because it gives an idea of the scope of work involved, read as follows:

The Dominion Government,
Postmaster General's Department.
To The Canadian Salvage Association Limited.

==

For expenses, time, and services, in connection with the Salving and delivery at Father Point, P.Q. of Three hundred and Eighteen (318) bags of mail, rescued from on board S/S *Empress of Ireland*, while wrecked and submerged in the Gulf of St Lawrence, from May to October 1914, at a hazardous and risky depth of some 175 feet, wherein we lost the life of an experienced diver, besides other accidents to our plant.

Remuneration, including personal attention of experienced wrecking master, use of valuable plant, imported from England, Hospital Locks for the recuperation of Divers, and other expensive and risky operations involved, Freighting expenses of plant, to and from risk, railway fares, wages, and other cash disbursements, including personal supervision of Mr W.W. Wotherspoon, experienced Compressed Air authority, Marine Diver and operator, $15,000.00

219 Board of Trade Building,
Montreal, 16th November, 1914.

The work at the DLO in Ottawa dragged on, and the last of the recovered letters was not disposed of until 13 January 1915. Once the envelopes started to arrive at their intended destinations, the work of the divers was acknowledged in England. The *Daily Mirror* of 8 January 1915 contained a photograph of one such recovered envelope.

Even then some people weren't satisfied with the Post Office's efforts.

The National Archives in Ottawa contains a letter from a Bertram Adamson, dated 5 January 1915, referring to two letters recovered from the wreck which had been returned to him. Bertram wrote in part, 'As in each case the address on the envelope is perfectly legible and the postage has been duly paid, I am at a loss to understand why they were not forwarded to the respective addressees.'

There was also a complaint from a customer who demanded to know why it took so long for the recovered letters to be delivered. The response, dated 9 February 1915, from the Chief of the Dead Letter Branch in Ottawa to the Deputy Postmaster General, noted that the letter had reached Ottawa early the previous October and had been date-stamped when received, 'but, as some thousands of letters were recovered and as they required particular handling and special treatment, it took considerable time before they could be treated, and the letter in question has evidently been one of the last to be sent forward.'

Today, the recovered letters are sold occasionally at Internet auction sites. Prices are higher for marked envelopes which are contained in the covering DLO envelope (the so-called 'ambulance envelope'), itself also duly stamped with the recovery notation.

In April 1916 the Post Office submitted a claim of $5,000 for salvage operations against the proceeds of the sale of the *Storstad*.

Proposing new life-saving devices or raising the wreck seemed to be a particular personal obsession to many that summer, including some people who evidently had little idea of what marine salvage entailed. The following is a letter sent to the Minister of Marine and Fisheries:

> Alameda, Sask. June 15, 1914
> Dear Sir,
> I will undertake to raise the *Empress of Ireland* and put her up on dry land, or furnish the plan for raising it. I may say my plan for raising it would be to build a scow on empty barrels then run a cable from the scow down to the *Empress* and then from there out on to the land three miles and by that means tow it to the land.
> Yours truly,
> (sgd) J.J. Brealey

An Ottawa bureaucrat responded a week later:

> Sir:-
> I have to acknowledge receipt of your letter of the 15th instant addressed to the Minister of Marine and Fisheries, stating that you will undertake to raise the *Empress of Ireland* and indicating your plan for doing this work.
> I am, Sir,
> Your obedient servant
> (sgd) Wm. P. Anderson
> For Deputy Minister

Getting paid for their super-human efforts proved to be a problem for the salvagers. After invoicing the government $15,000 for recovering the mails, the government finally settled for $10,000. The Canadian Pacific paid $35,000 for recovery of the purser's safe, an expensive proposition but one which avoided millions in grossly inflated claims. As for the silver, the salvagers were paid $36,172 for their expenses, but nothing for the bullion itself. After taking the insurance companies to court, the Canadian Salvage Company obtained a judgment for a further fee of $22,685.

At least fourteen of the *Empress'* lifeboats were recovered. These were of different types and some may have broken free from the sinking ship and drifted downriver. Once surviving passengers and crew had been taken aboard *Storstad*, no one gave any immediate thought to the lifeboats. Zeni notes that two were picked up more than twenty miles downriver by the Allan's *Grampian*. Another was recovered by the lighthouse keeper at Métis-sur-mer.

Edward Curotte, a Rimouski entrepreneur whose company sold marine and other engines, recovered three *Empress* lifeboats on 29 May, eight miles north of Ste-Luce. One of these was No.3 lifeboat, of steel, the same boat which had picked up Henry Kendall. It was one of the five lifeboats on the starboard side that had been launched successfully. Curotte's two other lifeboats were wooden, and fully equipped. Curotte towed them to Rimouski and declared them to the Collector's office. At that point, Capt. J.B. Belanger of *Lady Evelyn* took the boats from Curotte, over his vehement protests, without paying the salvage. Upset, Curotte referred the matter to his lawyers.

By mid-November six lifeboats had been collected at Rimouski. In a letter dated 14 November, the local Marine & Fisheries agent requested permission from his superiors in Quebec to spend $50 to haul the boats, which he valued between $4-5,000, out of the water to avoid their destruction by ice.

In June 1915, just over a year after the disaster, eight recovered lifeboats were purchased by the Robert Reford Company, steamship agents. The boats were sent to the Davie shipyard at Lauzon for repair, though the shipyard was instructed not to deliver the boats until such time as the customs dues were paid, for the boats were of British origin and had been brought into Canada without payment of duty.

Curotte, his salvage claim still unpaid, wrote to the government and was brushed off, the government informing him that claims were being settled by Lloyd's agents in Quebec. Five months later, in February 1916, disturbed by the private sale of the boats, Curotte wrote again to the government, requesting his salvage fee. His letter ended, 'I earnestly hope you will kindly give this matter your immediate attention as I spent time & money to get these boats and also to guard them during the time they were here and I do not honestly see why they did not pay me at least for the salvage of same.'

Curotte's claim for salvage of three lifeboats was not settled until mid-1917, when the government's legal advisor supported his case.

After its discovery on 17 July 1964 by a group of five divers from Montreal and Gatineau, the *Empress* became a magnet for local divers, despite the difficult diving conditions and the relatively primitive scuba equipment available then. Inexplicably the wreck at first managed to escape the attention of commercial salvagers, and it was left to sport divers to recover many of the objects now on display in the Musée de la mer at Rimouski and the Musée Maritime du Québec at L'Islet.

As the CPR had abandoned the ship to its insurers, the *Empress* was basically fair game for anyone looking for souvenirs. All a diver had to do from a legal point of view was declare his finds to the local Receiver of Wreck. Most of the things divers brought up in the first few years were small items that could be carried easily, or brought up with simple lift bags. That changed in 1967. A 30-year-old professional hard-hat diver and salvage expert from Montreal named Brian Erb, with the assistance of Rimouski diver Donald Tremblay, put together a six-man team to salvage the bronze propellers of the *Empress*. Using a small, 64-year-old freighter, the M/V *Morrisburg*, as a workboat, the team dynamited off the port propeller and raised it on 28 September 1968.

There was no thought of recovering the four-bladed prop for a museum. Scrap bronze was worth 55 cents a pound, and Erb had visions of making a fortune from all the brass in the *Empress*, along with bottles of vintage champagne and cognac. Despite this, Erb protested he was not a scavenger. 'I would not like to see these propellers melted down into scrap,' he was quoted as saying. 'They have far more value historically.'

The massive prop could not be lifted aboard the *Morrisburg*: its 20-ton weight would have capsized the 93-foot vessel. Instead the recovered propeller was slung below the workboat and lashed with cables.

As *Morrisburg* plodded back to Rimouski at one knot, the propeller struck bottom, nearly capsizing the boat. One of the blades hit a rock and snapped off.

Once Erb's team had the prop – minus one blade – back in Rimouski more than 3,000 people came to stare at the massive artifact, measuring over twenty feet from tip to tip. For many it was the first tangible evidence of the shipwreck they had heard about for years.

In the end, Erb's efforts were a costly commercial failure. The team earned just $5,000 for the propeller, paid by a scrap dealer. Twelve and a half cents per pound was a poor return for the danger and the time invested over two summers. The salvage team disbanded and never pursued the starboard propeller or the rest of the *Empress'* brass fittings.

After Erb's misadventure, commercial salvagers did not return to the *Empress* for some years, and it became once again the playground and *chasse privée* of local scuba divers, some of whom, like Philippe Beaudry gained an encyclopedic knowledge of the wreck.

In 1970 Beaudry, then twenty-five, made his first dive on the wreck. Over the next thirty years the one-time Montreal accountant and dive shop owner would log more than 600 dives on the ship, probably more than anyone else, and accumulate an unparalleled collection of *Empress* artifacts and memorabilia. The ship, and helping to preserve her, became his obsessions. Beaudry travelled widely over the years, meeting and interviewing former *Empress* passengers and crew members, and contributed his time and knowledge to various expeditions interested in the remains of the ship.

With time, word of the wreck and the relatively easy pickings spread through the diving community, and each year more divers arrived in Rimouski seeking to visit the wreck and recover an artifact. The wreck itself is the only one of the great passenger liners from Edwardian times that can be dived. Although conditions like current, low light, depth and cold can make for a dangerous dive, the risks can be managed by experienced scuba divers. Improvements in dry suits and the introduction of mixed gas for scuba divers has also helped make the wreck more accessible to sport divers.

What comes as a surprise is how long it took for some of the prime artifacts to be removed from the ship. A sextant, for example, was recovered only in 1971 by Donald Tremblay, as was the wheel in the same year. The twenty-five brass letters, weighing 154 pounds, which spell EMPRESS OF IRELAND and LIVERPOOL were recovered from the silt during a two-year period beginning in 1995 by two divers from Victoriaville, Danny St-Cyr and Pierre Lepage. Lepage became, in June 2001, the most recent diving fatality on the *Empress*.

After thirty years, while not picked clean, the *Empress* achieved the dubious distinction of being the 'most pillaged shipwreck in modern history,' and artifacts disappeared into the collections of divers all over Canada and the United States.

In May 1980 Philippe Beaudry helped establish the Musée de la mer in Rimouski, using many of the artifacts he had recovered to form the nucleus of the collection, along with objects loaned by other divers.

Commercial salvors returned to the *Empress* in June 1993, when a salvage operation got underway to recover the *Empress'* valuable teak. In retrospect it is odd that no one had thought to go after it earlier, for the wood was in excellent condition despite being underwater for seventy-nine years, and it had a significant commercial potential.

A team of seven divers, employed by 30915243 Quebec Inc., worked on-site, using the 127ft *Gesmer 1*, a former Dutch-built trawler converted to support diving and recovery operations. The boat was owned by Michel Tadros, a commercial fisherman from Madeleine Centre on Quebec's Gaspé coast. In a matter of weeks the divers managed to remove more than five thousand 2in x 4in and 2in x5in teak planks, measuring anywhere from eight to twenty-two feet in length.

A court challenge was initiated by Philippe Beaudry, founder of the Empress of Ireland Historical Society, a non-profit corporation he had set up after a disagreement with the other museum co-founders in 1983. Beaudry won a temporary injunction on 13 August, but a Rimouski judge turned down the request for a permanent one just two weeks later, claiming that the Society had no ownership rights in the wreck.

Beaudry put forth two arguments against the salvage. First, that removing the teak would seriously disturb the wreck. Second, that recovery on this scale represented an act of disrespect to the 400-plus bodies still estimated to be inside the ship.

Tadros countered that he and the team were making it safer for other divers. 'By removing all that loose teak,' he claimed in an interview, 'we're doing other divers a favour – we're clearing away the rubble and making it safer for them.' Despite that assertion, there was little doubt serious damage was being done to the wreck. The hull, already in poor condition and succumbing to the effects of time, corrosion and gravity, was slowly collapsing. Lines of gaping bolt holes along the under-decks, formerly anchoring points for the teak planking, now admitted more water into the interior of the wreck and accelerated the corrosion process.

Following the judge's ruling, salvage work resumed immediately and continued for the balance of the dive season.

Losing in court, Beaudry then shifted to the political arena, lobbying the federal government to declare the wreck off-limits to salvagers. His pleas for support from the people of Rimouski found little interest and nothing further was done. Commented Beaudry, 'I don't think the local population is ready yet to accept the *Empress* as a historical site.'

Commercial salvage on the scale undertaken by Michel Tadros and his team is an expensive proposition, and their venture eventually went bankrupt. The company's main financial backer, businessman Jacques St Onge, received most of the salvaged teak in compensation. St Onge, who also owns one of the *Empress'* anchors and a bell, has sold just three 18ft lengths of teak, and remains undecided as to what to do with the balance of the wood. Meanwhile, the planks remain stored outside, exposed to the elements, on the south shore of the Gaspé peninsula.

In the spring of 1998 stories began to circulate in the Rimouski area that a team of underwater demolition experts and a marine salvage company intended to dynamite the wreck of the *Empress* in order to salvage a load of nickel amounting to some 130 tons, and valued at about C$1.3 million. That was news to most *Empress* experts. No one had ever heard of a cargo of nickel ingots, and most doubted there even *was* nickel on board.

After that, things started to get interesting. A team of four Nova Scotia divers was questioned at the Rimouski docks by Quebec Provincial Police in connection with their dives on the *Empress*. The divers explained that they had been hired by a company to film the interior of the *Empress*. The company, it soon developed, wanted the images in order to find where the nickel had lain since 1914.

First class cabin, Upper Promenade deck, looking forward. (David Saint-Pierre)

Jacques Saint-Onge, who had already earned the ire of many for the teak harvest, told journalists in early April 1998, 'I have in my possession documents that prove there really is nickel on the ship. We think we've found the spot where the ingots should be. We have already invested nearly half a million dollars in this venture.' He went on to say that his team had received a mandate from a European insurance company, historically linked to the sinking.

True or not, the rumors managed to galvanize a number of people into action. Concerned about the possible destruction of the wreck by blasting, or the desecration of the final resting place of so many people still entombed inside the hull, various individuals and groups (including the Salvation Army) began to lobby the government of Canada to take action. Among those who spoke up was Bertrand Blanchet, Bishop of Rimouski. 'It is like a big coffin,' he observed. 'We have a moral duty to ensure respect for this shipwreck as for any cemetery.'

In response to the pressure tactics, the government agreed to block the proposed salvage operation. It was an important victory, but many realized it was only a short-term solution to a longer-term problem. Lobbying continued, seeking to have the government declare the wreck a protected site, which could still be visited by recreational divers.

The pressure continued, though the salvagers, by now perhaps realizing the animosity they had stirred up, kept a low profile. On 24 April 1998 the Quebec Minister of Culture and Communications issued a notice of intention to proceed with the classification of the wreck of the *Empress of Ireland* as cultural property. It was a recognition of the venerable ship's symbolic value and was intended to stop the uncontrolled looting of a cultural resource. On 10 June that same year, the Canadian Coast Guard moored a large white information buoy over the wreck to indicate the wreck's protected status, and that any recovery is to be authorized by the Quebec government. Scuba divers are allowed to visit the site and, in a typical year, they make about a thousand dives. Recovery of objects is prohibited.

On 15 April 1999 the Quebec government finally declared the wreck a historic site, protecting it from further plundering. The *Empress of Ireland* thus became the first underwater heritage site in the province.

In September 2000 the latest chapter in the *Empress* saga began to unfold when longtime *Empress* diver and artifact collector Beaudry announced he had applied to Heritage Canada for permission to export his artifacts to Leonard Lyons, described in the press as a St Augustine collector and dealer. The announced price was US$1.5 million, for some of the gems of Beaudry's collection including the fog bell, starboard navigation lamp and brass staircase fixtures. Beaudry, who claimed to have spent over $225,000 of his own money defending the wreck, explained he was looking for a return on his investment over the years.

There was predictable outrage in Quebec and the rest of Canada. Many were stunned by the hypocrisy, Beaudry having earlier declared to Robert Ballard on the TV programme *Lost Liners* that he 'had a mission to protect' the *Empress*. Serge Guay, director-general of the Musée de la mer, which Beaudry himself had helped found two decades earlier, was quoted in the Montreal *Gazette* as saying, 'He has often spoken about the historical importance of these objects and of keeping them in Quebec.'

Under pressure, the Canadian Culture Export Review Board blocked the sale temporarily, so that a Canadian buyer could be found. In theory, if no Canadian buyer came forward, Beaudry would then be free to sell his collection in the United States. In December, acting on a request by the Musée de la mer, the Board agreed to determine a fair cash offer for the collection. A Board spokesman explained that it had two objectives: 'To safeguard the cultural property, and at the same time to ensure a fair price, so it is a win–win situation for all involved. There is a price on the table and the Board will determine if that is a fair cash offer.'

In March 2001 Beaudry explained himself to a reporter from the Toronto *Globe and Mail*. 'I've devoted my life to the *Empress of Ireland*. I risked my neck every time I dived,' he said. 'But there's not enough interest or recognition here. People have no attachment to their history.' Disillusioned the previous year when he had been unable to secure funding from the federal or provincial governments to stage an exhibition of his artifacts, he continued, 'I said to myself, 'If Canadians don't care, why should I?' To me this is the history of Canada, not the history of a simple boat. This story belongs to Canadians.'

The matter is still unresolved.

The teak of the *Empress* is a fascinating subject in itself and merits further discussion.

Rather than subcontract out the interior furnishing of its vessels, Fairfield had a small army of carpenters, cabinetmakers and furniture makers as part of its large workforce. The woodworkers were consummate craftsmen who excelled at their trade.

Ships like the *Empress* used as many as twenty different types of wood, and this was received at the Fairfield yards in the rawest possible form, usually as giant timbers from around the world. Massive saws and planing machines were used to reduce the timber into board lumber, veneer and paneling.

The interior of the *Empress of Ireland* was a treasure trove of decorative wood and a showcase of the woodworker's art. To take one example, over 46,700 square feet of mahogany was installed in the ship, and the *Empress* was by no means the most luxurious vessel of the period. In keeping with its traditions of quality and excellence, the Glasgow shipbuilder spared no expense, and accepted few compromises in terms of quality. Solid wood was always the first choice, wherever possible. When that wasn't feasible, veneers were used. In addition to mahogany, other exotic woods found their way into the ship: satinwood, alderwood, and bird's eye maple, for example, in paneling in the passenger areas. Large-scale, hand-carved moldings of mahogany, oak and yellow pine framed the panels, creating an impression of strength and opulence. Even the CPR's advertising noted the varieties of wood used. A 1906 brochure referred to the mahogany-paneled dining room, mahogany frames in the library, and waxed Italian walnut in the café.

One of the most useful woods that Fairfield employed was teak, primarily for decking. Of the *Empress*' eight decks, the two lowest, Orlop and Lower, were of steel. Main deck had planks of white pitch pine, each plank being five inches wide and three inches thick. Upper deck was also covered in planking of white pitch pine, but not throughout. Teak began to appear in the alleyways and open passages.

Successively higher decks had richer appointments. Shelter, Lower Promenade, Upper Promenade and Boat decks were covered in teak planks of various lengths. Pitch pine was used inside and teak was used in all open areas of these decks. In all, Fairfield records show a total of 18,027 cu.ft of pitch pine and 12,283 cu.ft of teak was installed in the *Empress*.

The teak (*Tectona grandis*) could have come from several areas, including Central America, Africa and Southeast Asia, where the trees grow to heights in excess of 150 feet. It is most likely that the teak originated in India or the Straits area, as it is native to these areas and both were British possessions when the *Empress* was constructed. The wood is durable and strong, noted for its tight grain, and has long found a market in marine applications, where its ability to withstand moisture is highly prized.

Teak today has almost disappeared from large-scale marine use due to its prohibitive cost and scarcity. Burmese teak, for example, costs about $12 per square foot, and this for wood one inch thick. By contrast, the planks used aboard the *Empress* were almost three inches thick.

The decking of the *Empress* would have required logs which are almost unobtainable in today's market. Counting the rings on surviving teak pieces indicates that some of the trees which went into the *Empress* decks began growing between 1680 and 1700. There are few old-growth teak forests except in remote areas like Borneo, and the wood today is cultivated on plantations. Teak has become so scarce that most modern 'teak' furniture uses only a thin veneer, with solid teak pieces commanding hefty prices from furniture makers.

This explains why the teak decking was a prime target for the salvage team in 1993.

 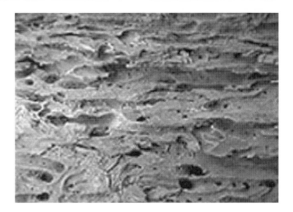

One could be excused for thinking that the *Empress* teak, after almost eighty years underwater, would not be worth salvaging. Such is not the case. The photo (above left) shows a portion of a teak plank raised by diver Raymond Beaulieu a few years ago, with the plank being sawn to illustrate a cross-section. The water has affected less than a millimeter of the teak's surface. Underneath, the wood has retained its hardness and strength. The wood, when oiled and polished, betrays no hint of its years under the sea. Running a plank through a planer to remove the top layer of wood would yield thick boards of varying lengths, with a variety of possible uses.

Compare the teak to the photo (above right) showing a pitch pine deck plank from the *Empress*, also recovered by Raymond Beaulieu. The pine shows the typical 'honeycombing' indicative of massive attack by marine worms, which are found in salt water. These planks have no structural strength.

The teak photo also shows a 'plug' covering the screw or bolt which once held the plank to the deck. After being bolted to the deck, a teak plug was glued into the bolt hole, forming a watertight covering. The plugs were selected with great care by the carpenters, so that their color and grain perfectly matched the surrounding wood. Installed so that the grain of the plugs followed that of the planks, the plugs were almost invisible from a distance.

THE ILL-FATED C.P.R. STEAMSHIP "EMPRESS OF IRELAND"
Went down with over 1,000 souls, May 29th, 1914.

'No. 494. God be with you!

"The grace of our Lord Jesus Christ be with you."—ROMANS xvi. 20.

J. E. RANKIN, D.D. (CLOSING HYMN.) W. G. TOMER.

649 J THE LATE MR. LAURENCE IRVING & BEAGLES POSTCARDS
THE LATE MISS MABEL HACKNEY.

8
Disaster Relief Funds

In 1914, governments in English-speaking countries were not in the habit of providing funds for disaster victims or emergency relief. Instead, following the well-entrenched principle of 'voluntarism', this task was left largely to public-spirited social and business leaders, pillars of Edwardian society who were expected to set an example for the lower classes. Thus, literally within hours of the sinking of the *Empress*, a well-oiled machine sprang into life. Over the next six weeks, thousands of people gave their names, talents and time to a host of fund-raising activities, just as they had done before on behalf of *Titanic* victims and would do so almost a year later for victims of the *Lusitania*.

On 29 May Sir Thomas Vansittart Bowater, Lord Mayor of London, set up a fund for the families of *Empress* victims and appealed to the general public for donations. In launching what would become known as the Mansion House Fund (after the Lord Mayor's official residence, a Palladian-style palace in the heart of The City), Bowater wrote, in a letter reproduced in *The Times*:

> I feel I shall be anticipating the wishes of the benevolent public and following the tradition of the Mansion House on occasions of great public calamity, if I intimate, without delay, that I have opened a fund for the relief of the widows, orphans and dependent relatives of the crew and passengers of the ill-fated liner *Empress of Ireland*, whose loss in such distressing and pathetic circumstances, has caused widespread sympathy and grief throughout the Empire.
>
> I shall be glad to receive the offerings of the charitable public for a cause which must appeal to everyone, and I invite the assistance of my brother Lord Mayors and mayors throughout the kingdom in the collection of an adequate fund. The help of the newspaper Press will, as in the past, be warmly welcomed, and, I know, readily extended.
>
> I should like to add that in the distribution of the fund I propose to avail myself of the services of the Public Trustee, whose administration of the large sum collected two years ago on the loss of the *Titanic* has given universal satisfaction.
>
> Donations may be sent to the Secretary's Office, Mansion House, or to the Bank of England.

In short order, cash began flowing into the Mansion House Fund.

On 2 June, readers of *The Times* were informed that the King had contributed £500, Queen Mary £250, the Prince of Wales – the future Edward VIII who would rule for 326 days in 1936 before abdicating – £250, and Dowager Queen Alexandra, widow of Edward VII, £200.

The letter from the King to the Lord Mayor was simple and direct and echoed the feelings the monarch had expressed in his official letter of condolence (Appendix 2):

> Privy Purse Office, Buckingham Palace
> June 1, 1914
>
> My Lord:
> I have it in command from the King to inform your Lordship that his Majesty subscribes the sum of £500 to the fund your Lordship is raising for the help of those stricken by the

loss of the *Empress of Ireland*. For them, on their overwhelming sorrow, the King feels most deeply.

I remain, my Lord, your Lordship's most obedient servant.

William Carrington

George V, who had trained in the Royal Navy, must have felt an empathy toward the sailors, one who had shared with them the perils of the sea. He may also have recalled seeing the *Empress* in the St Lawrence in connection with the Tercentenary celebrations, and the previous summer during the review of merchant vessels at Liverpool.

Over the next days the Fund did very well, and its progress was reported daily in *The Times* and other British newspapers. The Fund grew to £8,000 on 2 June, rose to £21,500 (4 June), £24,000 (5 June), £28,000 (6 June), £29,000 (8 June) and £31,000 (9 June). Thereafter, progress was slower but by 22 June had reached £39,000.

Donations came from companies, banks and individuals from all walks of life and stations in society. Among the notable donors, all of whose names were published in *The Times*, were Norway's King Haakon VII and Queen Maud (daughter of England's Edward VII) – 100 guineas, as well as many individuals and companies involved with the shipping industry, the Canadian Pacific Railway, or having other ties to Canada or the *Empress* herself.

Thus, we find, for example, Lloyd's Register (£210); Fairfield Shipbuilding & Engineering Co. Ltd. (£105); members of the London Stock Exchange (£1,109 17s); the Corporation of London (£525); Cunard Co. (£250); Oceanic Steamship Co. (£250); Elder Dempster Co. (£100); the Steamship Owners' Coal Association (£105); the Strathcona family (£500); Lord Mount Stephen, first president of the CPR (£1,000); Sir Thomas Shaughnessy (£500); Mrs Hugh Allan, of the Montreal-based Allan shipping family (£50); and Sir George Perley, acting Canadian High Commissioner (£100). Alexander Gracie and his wife Katherine, who had launched the *Empress*, contributed £100. There was even a donation of £100 by A.F. Klavenes, managing owner of the *Storstad*. London banks were generous. Baring Brothers gave £1,000, as did N.M. Rothchild & Son.

Fittingly, the largest single donation (£5,000) was made by Canadian Pacific.

Sir Thomas Shaughnessy was no stranger to the *Empress*. He and family members had travelled aboard her on numerous occasions, and he knew many of the officers and crew personally.

A special collection at St Paul's Cathedral garnered £46 7s 6d. A box set outside the Mansion House, in the centre of The City's financial district, collected small change from passers-by. In just five days the box netted an almost identical sum from people who may have heard the refrain of a song written immed-iately after the sinking. *Gone Are The Friends We Know*, published in London by E. Marks & Son, urged:

> *But give a helping hand in the old Homeland*
> *Help for the ones they leave behind.*

A similar fund was launched in Liverpool, also on 29 May, by Lord Mayor Herbert Rathbone. Fund-raising went well in the ship's home port, devastated by the disaster in the same way South-ampton had been two years earlier with the loss of *Titanic*. According to a statement made by the Lord Mayor on 9 June, all but seven of the 206 crew members dead or unaccounted for had come from the Liverpool region. Although this number was incorrect, for the Mersey Inquiry set the number of crew deaths at 172, there was no hiding the fact that the great port had been hard hit.

In five days the Liverpool fund stood at £13,758 and grew, over time, to some £25,000. As in London, contributions came from corporations and individuals. The CPR and Sir Thomas Shaughnessy, each having contributed generously to the Mansion House Fund, and sensitive to the suffering of Liverpool

Canada Mourns, Halifax Herald, *2 June 1914.*

families, made further identical donations to the Liverpool fund. The National Seamen's and Firemen's Union, of which many of the crew were members, sent £300 in a gesture of sympathy. The Earl of Derby sent £200, and his wife a further £25.

In London the Salvation Army opened a special fund for the families of Salvationists lost in the disaster.

Through notices in newspapers, the Public Trustee in Britain invited applications from members of the crew or passengers of the *Empress* or their dependents who had been placed in dire circumstances. Claim forms could be obtained by writing to the Public Trustee at Clement's Inn.

It was soon evident that a substantial amount of money would be required. On 3 June Duncan Fraser, who had previously acted as honorary actuary for the *Titanic* Fund, in response to a request by Lord Mayor Rathbone of Liverpool, estimated that about £180,000 would be required. Of this, he estimated, about £80,000 would provide for dependents of the lost crew and £100,000 for passengers.

Rathbone's appeal for money appeared in various newspapers the following day, and he urged that 'as soon as the [*Whitsuntide*] holidays are over, all who can afford to do so will contribute according to their means.'

Duncan Fraser's estimates were based on his experience with the *Titanic* Fund. There, after considerable debate, it had been decided that distributions to passengers' dependents, other than third class, would be made on a lump-sum basis, ranging from £150 to a widow with children to £24 for a father.

Crew dependents, on the other hand, would be given weekly allowances, the exact amounts of which varied according to a number of factors. A widow, for example, received anywhere from 12s 6d to £2 per week, with extra amounts for children, again determined by various factors. Of course, the biggest variable in all of this was how much could be raised. Obviously, the more money raised, the greater the individual payments.

It is interesting to note the paternalism inherent in the way payments were made. The widows of crew members could evidently not be counted on to handle the sudden arrival of a lump-sum payment, and so had to be protected from their own financial inexperience by doling out the money through a weekly distribution.

In parallel to the outright solicitation of donations, various benefit theatrical and orchestral perform-ances were staged in the capital and other cities over the next weeks, with all proceeds being given to either the Liverpool or the Mansion House Fund. The first of these was a special matinee performance of *Pygmalion* on 1 June at His Majesty's Theatre in tribute to Lawrence and Mabel Irving, the two noted actors who had been lost in the tragedy. The benefit, for which the actors and members of the orchestra donated their services and George Bernard Shaw donated his author's royalty, raised the sum of £92 4s. The matinee must have been a great success, for it had been planned originally as the first performance of a People's Theatre, with special low prices to attract the working and trades classes. Shaw's sparkling comedy was still new to the London stage, having opened only in April at His Majesty's, and the theatre was almost sold out. Not surprising, for even the stall seats were just 2s 6d and standing room in the gallery was 3d. This imposing, copper domed theatre in the Haymarket was built in 1897 and has changed little in the intervening century. It is easy to imagine the largely working-class audience, along with a few Labour Party members of Parliament, settling down in their seats on that holiday Monday afternoon with an expectant hush as the house lights were dimmed.

Sir Herbert Beerbohm-Tree, proprietor of His Majesty's, starred as Henry Higgins, while Eliza Doolittle, the Cockney flowerseller, was played by Mrs Patrick Campbell. There is little doubt that these two fine, experienced actors lived up to the review filed by the critic for *The Times* who, when the play had first opened, wrote 'Mrs Campbell's Eliza is a delicious thing' and 'Sir Herbert Tree makes quite a rich character of Higgins.' In their acting careers both Mrs Campbell and Tree had played opposite Lawrence Irving and, on that particular afternoon, each must have felt a mixture of emotions, including a keen sense of loss for a capable actor and valued colleague. At the close of the previous night's performance, Tree had paid a special tribute to the lost actor: 'We actors were proud of Irving in life and we are no less proud of him in death…. His work was always like the man – original.'

Shaw's play is still performed regularly, but it is probably more familiar to millions as the inspiration for the smash 1956 Broadway musical *My Fair Lady* and the 1964 movie starring Audrey Hepburn and Rex Harrison.

On 5 June Princess Bariatinsky (whose stage name was Madame Lydia Yavorska), an actress and owner of London's Scala Theatre off Tottenham Court Road, offered the theatre for a 2:30 matinee of *Anna Karenina*, in which she was currently featured in the title role. The play was adapted from Tolstoy's classic novel of a love affair that destroys an upper-class Russian woman, and is still per-formed in various forms. There is no indication of how much the performance, then at the end of its London engagement, raised for the Mansion House Fund, but every bit helped. With seats costing from 2s 6d to 10s 6d, it may have done reasonably well.

Joint patrons for the Scala benefit were ex-king Manoel II of Portugal, Lord Mayor Bowater, and the Honourable John Burns. Manoel, twenty-four, and an intimate of the British royal family, was a fixture of London's social scene, for he had selected Britain as his residence in exile after being deposed in 1910. Burns was President of the Board of Trade, a member of Parliament, and the first Labour repres-entative to achieve cabinet rank.

Despite the fact that the *Empress* was now old news, elbowed rudely aside by other pressing issues like Home Rule for Ireland and unrest in the Balkans, the fund raising went on. In Paris the Boston Opera Company, on tour in Europe that summer, gave a special performance at the Théâtre des Champs-Elysées on 17 June in aid of the Mansion House Fund. The correspondent of the *New York Times* reported that 'the house was crowded with a brilliant audience, including the American, British and German ambass-adors.' Also present were representatives of French President Raymond Poincaré, who had originally planned to attend. Poincaré was no doubt needed elsewhere, for torrential rains in the past day had left more than twenty-five dead in the capital, and portions of streets had washed away.

The Company offered two works, the first being *Il Segreto di Susanna* (*Susanna's Secret*), a 1909 one-act comic opera by Ermanno Wolf-Ferrari that called for two voices and a mime. The second was Giuseppi

Verdi's 1859 *Un Ballo in maschera* (*A Masked Ball*), whose setting was, fittingly, eighteenth century Boston. This work featured soprano Felice Lyne in a minor role as the court page Oscar. She had asked permission to take part in the performance, to celebrate her good fortune. Originally booked on the fateful *Empress* voyage, Miss Lyne had taken an earlier boat to Europe following an urgent cable summons.

Both works from that evening have disappeared from the current repertoire for good reason. Verdi wrote better operas and a modern audience would find Wolf-Ferrari's work somewhat ludicrous, for Susanna's great secret is that she smokes. At the time though, that was something to be hidden; in 1904 a woman had been arrested on New York's Fifth Avenue for smoking a cigarette.

An afternoon concert of popular orchestral works and excerpts took place on Monday, 29 June, at the Royal Albert Hall. This was an appropriate venue, as the public memorial service for *Empress* victims had been held here on 5 June. The concert, another of the events under the Lord Mayor's direct patronage, was not particularly well attended, perhaps (as *The Times* speculated) due to a local heat wave, a phenomenon that would prove common in that last summer of peace.

Four hundred instrumentalists donated their services, as did a total of seven conductors from London's leading orchestras. Of the seven, the most familiar to a modern listener was Thomas Beecham, conductor of the Covent Garden Opera House. Knighted in 1916, Beecham died in 1961 at the age of eighty-two, acknowledged as one of England's foremost conductor-arrangers. Two others, Sir Henry Wood and Landon Ronald (later knighted) were well regarded as conductor-arrangers, though their names are unfamiliar to today's audiences. The remaining four have faded into obscurity. Boxes for this event cost up to 63s, while seats ranged from 2s to 12s 6d. For those who could not afford these prices, there was standing general admission at 1s.

The Times provided a brief (and favourable) review the following day, while also carrying stories about the assassination of the heir to the Habsburg throne, Archduke Franz Ferdinand, and his wife in the obscure Bosnian capital of Sarajevo. Though no one yet knew it, the fuse for the Great War had been lit and the old order in Europe was about to self-destruct.

The following day, the hottest thus far of the summer in London, featured a 2:15 matinee at the Aldwych Theatre under the patronage of HM Queen Alexandra and other members of the royal family. The Aldwych, an elegant, well-proportioned theatre off Drury Lane, has changed little over the past nine decades and it takes little stretch of the imagination to recreate that sweltering afternoon, with well-dressed patrons arriving by motor car to witness a programme of poetry recitals and tableaux featuring various artists. Programmes involving *tableaux vivants* – scenes depicted by silent and cost-umed participants–are almost unknown to today's theatre audiences but were immensely popular at the time. Among the many artists who donated their services for the occasion was *Fraülein* Janotha, court pianist to the German emperor. Tickets for the event were moderately priced, ranging from 2s 6d to £2 2s, in order to appeal to as wide an audience as possible.

On 8 July, Princess Louise, Duchess of Argyll, was the patron of a 2:30 performance of a play entitled *Grumpy* at the New Theatre, just off Leicester Square. The play was a popular one, described later by one critic as an 'engagingly artless little thing.' Again the players donated their services for the Mansion House Fund. The same evening featured a benefit concert at Queen's Hall near Shaftsbury Avenue, with an audience drawn largely from the leading shipping firms in London. Other benefit perform-ances took place in London as well, usually smaller in scope and with less august patrons, such as *The Mikado* at the Cripplegate Institute Theatre, and in other provincial cities. Even if these could not match the size or prestige of mainstream London theatres, they were all driven by a common feeling of compassion and generosity toward those who had suffered losses.

In North America similar activities were also underway. On 1 June in Quebec City the Seamen's Institute requested the *Chronicle* to accept subscriptions to aid the destitute seamen of the wrecked ship. It was a fitting gesture, as over the years the men of the *Empress* had performed at the Institute on numerous occasions. Now the crew's past generosity would be repaid in a tangible fashion. Heading the subscription

No. 2140

LOSS OF "THE EMPRESS OF IRELAND."

Mansion House Relief Fund.

Blades, East & Blades, Printers, 23, Abchurch Lane, E.C.

Received with thanks this _____ 21 AUG 1914 _____ 1914.

of _Collected at Special Service at Holy Trinity Church. Stratford. New Zealand._

the sum of **£ 2 : — : 6**

T. VANSITTART BOWATER,
Lord Mayor,
Treasurer.

Receipt for £2 0s 6d sent to the Mansion House Fund. This money was collect at a special service at Holy Trinity Church in Stratford, New Zealand, and sent to Canadian Prime Minister Robert Borden, who then forwarded it to London. (National Archives of Canada)

list was John Ross, president of the Seamen's Institute, who gave $250. Funds needed to raised quickly, as it was intended to distribute the money collected to the seamen prior to their return to England on 4 June. When the men did not depart on *Alsatian* as originally planned, the fund was kept open for a few more days. Among the contributors were the maids of the Chateau Frontenac, who sent in $16.60.

By the time the *Empress* crew departed, the Institute had collected enough money to give each of the 227 survivors the sum of nine dollars each, and the men appreciated the timely assistance as most had lost everything.

The Corporation of Pilots, Quebec and below Quebec, sent $100 to the CPR. A subscription at the Ross Rifle factory on the Plains of Abraham in Quebec raised $160. This money was cabled to Captain John Forster in Liverpool for distribution to the widows and orphans of the lost crew. Forster presumably added the money to the Liverpool fund.

The first subscriber to the fund set up by the Quebec Board of Trade on 12 June was the Duke of Connaught, the Governor General, who donated $500 on 13 June. The Duke and Duchess evidently remembered the ship and her crew with particular affection. The City of Quebec voted $1,000 and, by 10 July the fund reached $2,621.

The Quebec Football Association, remembering many fine soccer matches against men they would never see again, sent ten dollars to Sir Thomas Shaughnessy. Sir Thomas forwarded it to the fund. Under the patronage of the Duke of Connaught and Andrew Allan, the orchestra of the *Calgarian* performed at a well-attended charity concert at the Quebec YMCA. The proceeds went to aid the widows and orphans of the lost seamen. On 20 June a highly successful musical and dramatic benefit took place at the parish hall of Quebec's Anglican cathedral, featuring the orchestra of the Chateau Frontenac, along with amateur recitations, songs and dialogue. Local caterers donated the refreshments, while others contributed plants and decorations. The event raised $258.50 which was duly sent to the Quebec Board of Trade.

On 4 July, the variety troupe from the *Empress of Britain* staged a benefit before a packed house at the Quebec Auditorium. On their return to Liverpool, the troupe gave a similar benefit on 22 July.

The Montreal city council voted $10,000 for relief on 2 June, and the money was subsequently turned over to the fund established on 9 June by the Montreal Board of Trade. The Montreal Fund started off well, raising $30,000 on its first day, the main contributions coming from the city, the Bank of Montreal ($7,000) and the Canadian Manufacturers' Association ($2,000). The Board named a general committee, consisting of leading citizens, representatives of the newspapers and the churches, and appealed for funds. Having noted the amounts raised in England, for the results were carried in local Canadian newspapers, the organizers expressed their confidence '…that the citizens of Montreal will not be found lacking in similarly generous contributions.' In a week, the fund had grown to $36,000 through corporate and individual donations. By late June when the fund was closed, it held almost $50,000.

As to the disposition of the money, the Montreal committee wisely recognized the need to avoid duplicating efforts in Britain. It therefore promised to '…forward the total amount to whatever central committee may be finally charged with the distribution of the funds now being raised in the United Kingdom.'

In Toronto, home to a considerable number of the lost passengers, the city's Board of Control recommended $25,000 for relief funds, and this was ratified on 8 June.

The largest single contributor to the relief funds was the American oil magnate and philanthropist John D. Rockefeller who, on 21 June, contributed $11,000 (£2,200).

On 4 June, Prime Minister Robert Borden committed his Conservative government to aid those who had suffered in the disaster. Typically, Borden did not specify the form or amount of such aid. Only later, perhaps shamed by the generosity of private citizens and aware of how much would be needed, did the government pledge £10,000.

From New Zealand came a donation of £2 0s 6d collected at a special service of Holy Trinity Church, in the town of Stratford. This particular donation arrived at the Mansion House in a roundabout fashion, forwarded by the Prime Minister of New Zealand to Prime Minister Borden, who passed it in turn to London.

On 6 July, Lord Mayor Bowater convened a meeting at the Mansion House to deal with the problems of administering the sums collected in London and Liverpool, now amounting to £43,000 and £25,000 respectively, and not including the amounts pledged by the Canadian government and other groups. The meeting, with representatives from the Public Trustee, Canadian High Commission, CPR, Salvation Army and other interested parties, led to a number of decisions.

First, the Liverpool Fund would be used for the claims of dependent crew members and, in this respect, it soon began making payments for temporary relief. On the other hand, the Mansion House Fund, along with the Canadian funds, would be used to settle claims from passengers. The last day of September was established as the cut-off date by which all such claims should be filed, and notices to that effect appeared in various newspapers.

Less than a month later Great Britain and her colonies went to war, expecting that the troops would be home for Christmas. A host of national priorities and competing claims for public charity – Red Cross, Belgian refugees, and a host of others – pushed *Empress* fund-raising into the background. In truth, it hardly mattered, for 'Empress Fatigue', as a later generation might have termed it, had set in. *Empress*-related benefits had ended and donations had fallen off rapidly.

Letters, some on black-bordered mourning paper, requesting claim forms or information poured into government offices before the 30 September deadline. One typical letter from Saint John, addressed to the Minister of Marine & Fisheries in Ottawa on 11 September, is preserved in the National Archives:

> Honourable Sir:-
> I understand that notice has appeared in the local press intimating that all applications of claims for relief in the matter of the *Empress of Ireland* disaster, have to be filed before the end of September.

My son, Frank W. Hamilton was employed on this ship in the capacity of Ticket Agent and is one of the members of the crew who perished. I am consequently desirous of obtaining any portion of the fund subscribed for the relief of the sufferers, to which I may be entitled. If there are any papers which it is necessary for me to fill in, I will be very glad if you will furnish me with blanks, so that I can have them taken care of.

While I understand that this matter may not be in your hands, yet I would appreciate it very much in such an event, if you would kindly pass this letter over to the Department interested. Your kind attention will be much appreciated by,

Yours truly,

(sgd) John W. Hamilton

The forms were simple enough. Prospective claimants had to provide the full name and address of the person lost, along with age, occupation, and income, as well as further details of the deceased's dependents. These additional details included date of birth, income, amounts received from insurance, employer or other sources, and particulars of the degree of support provided by the deceased. The form was then required to be certified by a Justice of the Peace, clergyman, qualified medical practitioner, banker or solicitor, who would have to certify to the following: 'I am satisfied that the statements made on this claim form are true, and that the persons claiming relief were actually dependent at the time of the Disaster upon a passenger on the *Empress of Ireland*.'

Some cases would be refused, however worthy, because the applications were not received in time. Dated 3 October, the following letter from Edmonton was sent to the Department of External Affairs in Ottawa:

Gents,

Please forward me a copy of claims form respecting *Empress of Ireland* Relief Fund.

My wife Mrs S. Bronken, and child Ella Bronken, were lost in *Empress of Ireland* disaster, 29th May 1914, and oblige

Yours truly

(sgd) Samuel Bronken

Inevitably, some people had the wrong idea about the Relief Fund, feeling that it was a general fund against which any sort of claim could be made. Writing to the Canadian High Commissioner in London, Mr H.A. McGachen from London, Ontario, who had lost his wife and three children in third class, requested information as to how to recover the value of the lost baggage (estimated at $450), the family jewelry ($250) and the value of the 'shock I received at the time' (which he estimated at $1,300).

On 11 December, the County Court in Liverpool awarded widows of the *Empress* crew a pension of 15s 6d a week, for life, to be paid from the accumulated funds. At the time this was a reasonable sum and would help a family make ends meet, but wartime inflation in Britain soon reduced its real value.

A month later, Sir Charles Johnston, elected Lord Mayor the previous September and in office only since November, closed the Mansion House Fund and turned over to the Public Trustee the sum of £45,364. To this was added more than £36,000 raised in Canada. In all, 353 widows, children and other dependents received settlements.

Although the amounts collected were impressive, and sufficient to pay modest lump-sum settlements and pensions, they were a long way from the £430,780 raised two years earlier for the *Titanic* Fund. But then the *Empress* wasn't *Titanic* and its sinking lacked the high profile of the latter. It was far short of the £180,000 that the actuary Duncan Fraser had earlier estimated would be required.

With this, however inadequate it might seem to the victims' families, for no amount of money could replace a loved one, the *Empress* file could be closed. Those who were left had to carry on with their lives as best they could.

It was left to bureaucrats to deal with the administration of the relief funds and their distribution. That work continued even into the 1960s, as long as there were dependents receiving relief. Over time, as dependent recipients died off and the funds continued to earn interest, payments could be increased slightly. At 31 December 1950 there were still thirty-three dependents and the value of the *Empress* Fund stood at £61,766, with grants for the year amounting to £4,171.

At the end of July 1951 the allowance was increased. The weekly allowance to widows went up by four shillings and, to other dependents, two shillings. In 1958 the Public Trustee purchased annuities for the beneficiaries and, with effect from 1 September, this yielded an increase in the payments.

For beneficiaries in Canada, the Public Trustee paid the owed amounts to the Canadian High Commission in London, for conversion and remission to Canada. In the early 1960s there were still three dependent widows receiving a pension, all residents of the Toronto area. The weekly pension consisted of two parts, a widow's allowance of £3 5s 0d and a compassionate allowance of 10s 0d. This was supplemented, on occasion, by special grants at Easter.

Every six months the High Commission was required to reported the continued existence and widowhood of the three Canadian recipients.

A 1914 Canadian-published disaster postcard.

9
Remembering the *Empress of Ireland*

Just two months after the worst maritime disaster in Canadian history, Britain and her Empire were at war. The initial enthusiasm for war in all combatant European capitals tended to push all unrelated events aside, as men were called up or volunteered for service in a war widely expected to be over in a matter of months.

But the war that began in Europe in the summer of 1914 was different. It was the first total war in history, affecting virtually everyone in the warring nations, and on a scale few could have imagined. Warfare had become an industrialized process and the death tolls were staggering in terms of their size and how little was achieved on the battlefield. On average between August 1914 and November 1918 in this tragic and unnecessary war, five thousand soldiers died *every* day – five times the number who died in the *Empress* on 29 May 1914.

In time the horrors of stalemated trench warfare on the western front and the horrific casualty lists led in England to a popular feeling that everything which had gone before and contributed to the old order deserved to be forgotten. Old political certainties and social conventions changed as well, and the world that emerged after four years of world warfare was different than that of 1914.

Thus it was the fate of the *Empress* to be lost just before the most destructive war in European history, and to be overshadowed by all that came afterwards in the turbulent twentieth century.

What were the odds that one ship and 1,012 victims would be remembered?

In 1998 David Zeni selected *Forgotten Empress* as the title of his ground-breaking work on the sinking of the *Empress of Ireland*. While it makes an eye-catching title, it stretches the truth somewhat. In the book's epilogue, Zeni advanced a variety of reasons why the *Empress* may have been forgotten, including the First World War, the *Titanic*, and a lack of internationally famous personages aboard, and claimed that 'Interest in the *Empress* was non-existent from 1915 until dives on the wreck in 1964.'

Here we must politely disagree with Zeni, even though we recognize he was speaking somewhat metaphorically. Neglected, yes. Un-appreciated, yes. Overlooked, certainly. But *forgotten*? Never.

This book contends that the *Empress*, happily, was never really forgotten on either side of the Atlantic.

Though the flame of memory flickered low, it could not be completely extinguished. The ship continued to live in the minds and hearts of those who had once sailed in her, as the interviews conducted with living *Empress* passengers in connection with this book amply proved. Persons now in their mid-90s still recalled with precision events that had occurred when they were young children, and in many cases had passed these memories and memorabilia down to their children and grandchildren. It is not just the stories themselves, but their accuracy, as confirmed by the manifests, that demonstrates the *Empress* was fondly remembered.

The families of immigrants, at least, had good reason to remember her with affection. They grew up knowing that parents or grandparents had come over on the *Empress of Ireland* and, though they might not know exactly what that sea journey had entailed, the name of the ship was familiar to them, something that marked a turning point in the family's history. And, if the family had saved a postcard or a souvenir passenger list, or some small trinket, there was some tangible link back to the ship, something to point to with pride.

Donald Craw, disappointed as a boy to find Winnipeg was too much of a city for his liking, kept his autograph album, filled with the signatures of men who had died on their ship. Others kept the postcards and passengers lists that marked a high point in their lives. For families like the Cornthwaites of Sudbury, the *Empress* was held in special esteem. Although James Turnbull Cornthwaite, a member of the select club of *Empress* babies, died in 1980, he was proud to tell his three children of being born aboard the ship and how his name honoured her captain. James' six siblings also knew the unusual circumstances of their brother's birth and passed the story on to another generation.

Reginald Chapman, the young immigrant who had lost all his money gambling on the westbound crossing in April 1908 never forgot the *Empress* or his experience, and taught his grandchildren the shell-game that had nearly been his undoing.

Nor was the *Empress* forgotten by surviving or former members of the crew. They remembered her with particular affection and pride, recalling their service in her as something special in their lives. They kept their Board of Trade Discharge Books and told stories of the ship. That pride, undiminished, survives to this day in the families of several crew members with whom the author spoke in the year 2000.

Even before the 1914 disaster there was ample evidence of pride among the crew. 'This is my new home!' proclaimed a postcard showing the ship, and sent by crewman Jim Keegan to his family when he joined her in 1907.

In the research for this book the author found just two negative comments about the *Empress*, one from a 1906 first class passenger who didn't like the food, and the second from a replacement fireman who complained about the discipline and the crew in May 1914. Perhaps naysayers did not commit their impressions to paper, but one is left with the impression that the overwhelming majority of people who sailed in the *Empress* as passengers or crew liked the experience and remembered the ship fondly. Their memories, not easily forgotten, would last a lifetime, as though they had some final duty or obligation to discharge by remembering the *Empress*.

For the twenty thousand businesses and homes to which letters recovered from the wreck were returned, remembering the *Empress* was a fairly simple matter. In most cases the letters were kept by the senders, regarded as curiosities. While many are still held by families, numerous others found their way into archives and maritime museums, so that today they are among the most common items of *Empress* ephemera.

Even in 1964, as the fiftieth anniversary of the sinking approached, the ship and the disaster were featured prominently in Canadian newspapers – a month and a half before the wreck was relocated by scuba divers. Prior to that anniversary, a number of Canadian interests had even tried to persuade an ailing Henry Kendall to make a final visit to Canada, to commemorate the event.

The ship lived on, though for very different reasons, in the minds of the Salvationists who had survived the sinking, and who gathered every year at Toronto's Mount Pleasant Cemetery on the Sunday closest to 29 May to pay tribute to their fallen comrades and loved ones. With 133 dead from its contingent of 167, there could be no forgetting, and the members were joined together in a shared grief. In 1916 the Army erected a handsome granite memorial in the cemetery, paying tribute to all those who had been 'Promoted to Glory'. A regular attendee at the memorial service was Grace (Hanagan) Martyn, who had survived the sinking as a seven-year-old and was raised by an uncle in Toronto. She missed only four of the services before she died in May 1995 at the age of 88, the last known survivor of the sinking.

If the Army took the time every year to mourn its losses, the public at large in Toronto found little occasion to remember. Almost from the outset, newspaper coverage of the memorial ceremonies was tepid at best and, by 1924, the tenth anniversary, papers like the *Globe* made no mention at all of the ship or the Salvation Army's commemorative service.

To mark the fiftieth anniversary of the sinking, the Army commissioned a painting by William Wheeler, showing the *Empress* in her final moments, canted ninety degrees to starboard and only a minute or so before her final plunge.

Only in recent years, as David Creighton notes, was the annual memorial service discontinued, a deision that was not an easy one to make. The last service in Mount Pleasant was held on the 85th anniversary in 1999. But, as Creighton shows in his warm and highly personal book, three successive generations of Creightons were all familiar with the *Empress* and the story of the disaster that had robbed him of his grandparents.

The Creightons were not alone in remembering. The *Empress* blighted the memories of many other families, passengers and crew, who had lost loved ones. They too would remember this ship, though with sorrow and not affection, a dark shadow in their collective past.

Try though they might, they would never be able to forget, as the following letter by survivor Hetty Brooks shows:

> May 29, 1915
>
> I guess when the war is over things will brighten up here. (We hope so, in case not anyway.) We are having a very cold spring and after such a long winter as we have had, I guess we are rather impatient for the good weather. Frank has got the garden dug and planted but things want sunshine to bring them on.
>
> Do you know it is just twelve months ago today that we started on our ill-fated trip home, and somehow it will keep recurring to one's mind. It has been a year full of sorrow to hundreds of homes and when you read and hear of all that is happening these days, we are almost inclined to think that our dear ones who have been gathered home are better off. They are safe from sorrow, though our hearts are sore for their loss.
>
> (sgd) Hetty Brooks

Other surviving passengers remembered the ship and their ordeal. As late as October 1934 Henry Kendall, in correspondence with former first class survivor Mrs P.J. Adie of Birmingham, wrote '[S]ome day I hope to meet and even under the tragic circumstances of 1914 have a laugh.' The loss of the *Empress*, one feels, haunted Kendall for the rest of his life.

Those who received a cheque every month from the Public Trustee or the Canadian High Commission did not forget the *Empress,* nor did their families.

Though the CPR lost no time in distancing itself from the ship, and at some point disposed of most of its *Empress*-related files and other material, some people refused to let go of the memories. A travel agent in Hallock, Minnesota, a few miles south of the Canadian border and home to a significant number Scandinavian-Americans, hung an original CPR framed poster of the *Empress* on the wall of his office in 1915. Measuring $40\frac{1}{2}$in x $26\frac{1}{2}$in, the poster was finally taken down in the late 1940s and put into storage. When the building was demolished in 1995, the sign and many other salvaged items were sold at auction.

Songs were written about the sinking in both French and English. Published in sheet form for home consumption, they helped perpetuate the memory of the ship for a short time. *Gone Are The Friends We Know (The Loss of the* Empress of Ireland*)* with words and music by F.V. St Clair is wholly typical of the era, with lyrics of excessive sentimentality and outright chauvinism. *'The women and children first' was Captain Kendall's cry…* was scarcely credible even in 1914, and *'The belt he wore – he tore it off/a White Man to the core'* reflects the common prejudices and attitudes of the time.

Le Naufrage de L'Empress of Ireland, with lyrics by A.S. de Pierreville and music by Philias Champagne is somewhat of an improvement over its English counterpart. So is *La Catastrophe de l'Empress of Ireland*, whose lyrics by Gaston Charles were written to the melody of *Minuit, Chrétien*. The first of these two works was published in New Hampshire, the second in Montreal.

Up and down the south shore of the St Lawrence, especially in the Rimouski area, the people knew of the great ship that lay a scant four miles off their coast. Their parents had told them stories of survivors at the dock and bodies stacked like cordwood. In school, young children like Adrienne Dionne, mother of future *Empress* diver Raymond Beaulieu, memorized the lyrics of *La Catastrophe de l'Empress of Ireland*:

Le Saint-Laurent à l'onde chanteresse
Suivait son cours lent et majestueux…

Memorial to Empress *victims, St Patrick's Cemetery, Quebec. (Author)*

In time these schoolchildren would teach their own children about the *Empress* and pass on what they knew of the events of 1914.

Mary Ann Sutton of Toronto published a six-page booklet in 1914 containing a 92-line poem she had written entitled *The Loss of the Empress of Ireland*:

> 'Twas misty before the dawn of the 29th of May,
> The *Empress of Ireland* was wending her way;
> Bound for the old land – fourteen hundred souls aboard;
> A happy, hopeful, singing crowd who trusted in the Lord.

The poem disappeared from sight even more rapidly than the *Empress*. The few surviving copies are in the hands of dedicated ephemera collectors.

Radio played a role in keeping the name of the *Empress* alive, for an interview with Henry Kendall was broadcast in the autumn of 1934. Kendall's 1939 autobiography *Adventures on the High Seas* resurrected a brief interest in the ship, even though Britain and Canada were again at war with Germany. In a September 1939 review, the Montreal *Daily Star* critic called it 'one of the most thrilling life stories of the year…' and added that 'Captain Kendall has a great yarn to tell.'

And, for anyone who came, there were other memorials and graves of victims. The CPR erected a grey granite memorial between Rimouski and Father Point that identifies the burial place of eighty-eight victims, sixty-eight of whom were unidentified. To this day the site is maintained at the railway's expense. St Patrick's Cemetery in Quebec has a memorial to twenty-one dead, while nearby Mount Hermon has an impressive monument paid for by the CPR, along with two simpler stones in other portions of the cemetery. These latter, of lichen-encrusted weathered marble, bear the inscription 'CANADIAN PACIFIC', mark the graves of crew members.

In Ottawa, unsold copies of the Mersey Inquiry in English and French translation, formed another

Empress *sailings that would never take place. Canadian Pacific advertisement, Halifax* Herald, *30 May 1914. The advertisement was pulled by the next edition of the paper.*

CANADIAN PACIFIC
EMPRESSES AND OTHER STEAMSHIPS

LIVERPOOL SERVICE

FROM QUEBEC.
EMPRESS OF IRELAND, May 28
EMPRESS OF BRITAIN, June 11
EMPRESS OF IRELAND, June 25
EMPRESS OF BRITAIN, July 9
EMPRESS OF IRELAND, July 23

For Rates, Reservations, Plans, Literature, Tickets, Etc.. apply to W. B. HOWARD, General Agent, St. John, N. B., or J. D. Chipman, C. P. R., 37 George Street, Halifax.

type of monument. Printed in quantity by the King's Printer, copies from 1914 were still available for sale in the early 1960s. Today they are avidly sought after by collectors.

If the *Empress* came close to being forgotten, historians are partly to blame, and sloppy scholarship has not helped either. Martin Gilbert, a leading contemporary historian, wrote in Volume 1 of his three-part *A History of the Twentieth Century*:

> On February 8, in a disaster that in the scale of loss recalled the fate of the *Titanic* two years earlier, the Canadian Pacific steamer *Empress of Canada*, on its way from Quebec to Liverpool, was run down in fog by a Norwegian collier, and sank in seventeen minutes; 1,023 passengers were drowned.

Readers familiar with the *Empress* story should be able to pick out the wrong date and, worst of all, the name of the vessel.

Thomas Bonsall, in *Great Shipwrecks of the 20th Century*, made the claim that twenty people died aboard *Storstad* in the collision with the *Empress*, perhaps the first to make this strange assertion. In fact, no lives were lost aboard *Storstad* and the crew performed in an exemplary fashion in saving the lives of many *Empress* passengers.

Newspapers have never been particularly reliable sources of information, and modern papers are not much better than their Edwardian predecessors. A May 1994 Canadian Press feature on the 80th anniversary propagated a new batch of factual mistakes, claiming, for example, that *Storstad* had been built in Norway and fireman William Clark had testified before an inquiry.

A great deal of fantasy has unfortunately acquired the status of truth in connection with the *Empress*, and this hasn't helped the process of remembering. Perhaps the most notorious of these fantasies is the story of stoker Frank Tower, known as 'Lucks' Tower, 'The Man Who Cannot be Drowned', who was reputed to have survived the sinkings of *Titanic*, *Empress of Ireland* and *Lusitania*. Frank Tower never existed, though the myth was perpetuated in a number of *Empress* books. Robert Ballard, in *Exploring the Lusitania*, finally put the myth to rest.

So, too, with the story of chief stewardess Jackson aboard the *Empress*, who, according to several 1914 newspapers, had survived the *Titanic* but not the *Empress*. Repeated often enough, this story long ago assumed the mantle of truth, even though there never was a chief stewardess named Jackson.

The story of the *Empress* never really disappeared from newspapers in the half century after her sinking. Yellowed clippings in the vertical files of various libraries and archives bear witness to the fact that the *Empress* was not forgotten, even into the 1950s and early 1960s. Newspapers on both sides of the Atlantic managed to keep the ship in the public mind, with articles on the disaster appearing with the death of a noteworthy passenger or crew member.

Two typical examples should suffice, though there are many from which to choose. '*Empress of Ireland* Tragedy Is Recalled by Death of Survivor Who Vividly Related Catastrophe' was the boxed headline from a two-column article in the *Quebec Chronicle-Telegraph* of 10 November 1934. The article noted the death of Montreal barrister Louis Gosselin, a first class passenger on the last voyage whose sensational interview with *Le Progrès du Golfe*, a Rimouski newspaper, a few hours after the sinking, was the first published account of the disaster and which appeared in translation in the New York *Herald Tribune*.

Another typical article came from the *Chronicle-Telegraph* of 29 May 1937, a three-column item titled 'Twenty-Three Years Ago Today *Empress of Ireland* Disaster Shocked Quebec.' The article recounted details of the last voyage for a new generation of readers. Why the paper picked the twenty-third anniversary to run the story is anyone's guess but, by 1939, the twenty-fifth anniversary, war clouds again hung over Europe, as they had in 1914, and the story might not have received the same attention anyway.

Despite sporadic coverage in newspapers, the true keepers of her memory were those who had once sailed in the cheerful and popular ship. Out on the Manitoba prairie, when told of the sinking of the *Empress of Ireland*, a horrified nine-year-old schoolgirl burst into tears. Fiercely proud of the vessel that had once borne her family to a new land, Mary Hill explained, 'That was *my* boat.'

Eighty-six years later, it still was.

10
Masters of the *Empress of Ireland*

No history of the *Empress of Ireland* would be complete without a brief look at the men who, between 1906 and 1914, walked her bridge and assumed responsibility for the safety of the ship, her passengers and crew. The men who commanded the *Empress* were at the peak of their profession, highly respected mariners whose capabilities had been proven over a period of years on the North Atlantic, to whom the CPR entrusted the pride of its Atlantic Service. It was Superintendent John Walsh, himself a captain, who testified at the Mersey Inquiry, '...suitability and ability and seniority lead them to the *Empresses*, and the *Empresses* are our best.'

Francis ('Frank') Carey

Perhaps appropriately, the first master of the *Empress of Ireland* was born in Dublin in 1849 and educated in Ireland. Like other experienced masters, Frank Carey came into the service of the CPR when it acquired the Beaver Line, and in 1906 had the honour to become the first master of the *Empress*. He began his long career at sea in 1863 and, after obtaining his certificate (No.92875) in Dublin in 1874, served aboard *Lord Byron*, in the Mediterranean and Atlantic.

Captain Carey joined the Allan Line in 1877, and served as master of its vessels on the North Atlantic before joining Elder Dempster & Co. where he was employed on a variety of lake-class vessels. When Elder-Dempster sold its Atlantic fleet to the CPR, Frank Carey continued in his position as master of *Lake Erie*, which he had commanded since June 1902. After thirty-eight voyages in *Lake Erie*, he was picked by the CPR to command the *Empress*. Captain Carey made just four voyages as master of the *Empress* before returning to the *Lake Erie* in October 1906.

Still in command of *Lake Erie* in January 1913, the ship was renamed *Tyrolia* and used by the CPR to bring Austro-Hungarian emigrants from the port of Trieste to Canada. After many years on the Atlantic, this was a welcome change for Captain Carey and he made twelve further voyages as master of *Tyrolia*.

Appointed Marine Superintendent for the CPR in early 1914, he retired in June 1914 as Commodore of the CPR's Atlantic fleet, after more than fifty years at sea. During his career he made more than six hundred Atlantic crossings, an impressive achievement. On his retirement from *Tyrolia* he received a number of gifts subscribed for by the ship's officers, engineers and stewards. On 16 November 1914 the Mercantile Marine Services Association in Liverpool honoured him with a presentation to commemorate his long service.

During his career Frank Carey had been awarded a medal and vote of thanks from the Liverpool Shipwreck and Humane Society, a medal and vote of thanks from the Mercantile Marine Services Association, a medal from the Norwegian government, and a pair of binoculars from the Canadian government for saving life at sea.

In November 1892, while in the Beaver Line's *Lake Huron* and bound from Montreal to Liverpool, *Lake Huron* encountered the North German Lloyd liner *Spree*, disabled with a broken propeller shaft and with water in her after compartment. Over a period of five days, *Lake Huron* towed *Spree* 800 miles into Queenstown, and earned a salvage fee of £25,000.

In February 1885 Carey had been aboard the Beaver Line's *Lake Winnipeg* when it assisted the disabled steamer *Alaska*, having lost its rudder, into New York, earning £5000 in salvage money.

He died at Wallasey, near Liverpool, on 30 December 1933.

***Empress* voyages**: four (1-4 inclusive) (Appendix 1)

John Vernon Forster, RNR, OBE

Born in Sunderland on the North Sea coast in 1874, John Forster spent the early part of his nautical career in the ships *Highfield* and *Milton Stuart*. In 1889 he entered Elder Dempster & Co.'s service as second mate on the SS *Yola*, and three years later was given command of the steamer *Ashanti*, both of which were engaged in the West African trade.

He obtained his certificate (No.028972) in October 1898 at Liverpool and continued in the service of Elder Dempster on a variety of ships, beginning his service on the St Lawrence route at this time. He transferred to the *Mount Temple* in 1903.

It was at this time that he helped rescue the crew of the three-masted schooner *Percy & Lillie* when the 141ft US-flagged wooden schooner foundered in mid-ocean. For his services, he was later pres-ented with a gold watch and chain by President Theodore Roosevelt. Retained by the CPR following the purchase of the Elder Dempster Atlantic vessels in 1903, Captain Forster was soon thereafter appointed Chief Officer of the *Lake Manitoba*, and the same year achieved his first CPR command, aboard the same ship. In the following years he served as master of, successively, *Mount Temple* (1903-1906) and *Lake Erie* (1906).

Like other masters, he held a commission in the Royal Naval Reserve, and he was also a Younger Brother of Trinity House, the London-based association of British mariners whose origins go back to 1514, which was concerned with lighting, buoying and piloting on the coast of England.

Named to command the *Empress of Ireland* in October 1906 at the age of 32, the youngest of the ship's five captains, John Forster served as master of the *Empress* until September 1913, completing eighty-four voyages. He was a highly regarded master who was known on the St Lawrence route as a careful and skillful navigator.

Relinquishing command of the *Empress* in October 1913, he 'went ashore', becoming the CPR's Chief Marine Superintendent at Liverpool, and in late 1915 was appointed General Superintendent for Canadian Pacific Ocean Services Ltd., the company formed by merging the marine operations of the CPR and the Allan Line. Later he became assistant manager and, later, manager for Canadian Pacific at Liverpool. From 1933 until his death he was agent at Southampton for the Canadian Pacific Railway. In addition, he held the rank of Lt. Commander in the Royal Naval Reserve.

He was appointed Officer of the Order of the British Empire in 1918 for services rendered during the war. Captain Forster died on 3 August 1938 at Southampton, aged 64.

***Empress* voyages**: eighty-four (5-88 inclusive) (Appendix 1)

James Turnbull, RNR, CBE, RD

Born in Chester, the county town of Cheshire, in 1874, James Turnbull made his first voyage in command of the *Empress* in October 1913, sailing from Liverpool on 3 October. Like many other mariners of the time, his career spanned both sail and steam. Educated at the Liverpool Institute, Turnbull first went to sea in 1889 as an apprentice on the barque *Iredale*, owned by the famous sailing company Iredale & Porter, and served in her for four years and nine months. On passing his exams as second mate, he was appointed in that capacity to the I&P barque *Cumbrian* and, on obtaining his chief's ticket, promotion was rapid. He sailed first as second, then as chief officer on the ship *Cockermouth*.

In 1897 he received his master's license (No.027800) and joined the Elder Dempster Company, and was appointed Third Officer on the ship *Dahomey*, his first steam vessel. Shortly thereafter, Captain Turnbull was given command of the screw steamer *Ibaden*, engaged on the African coastal trade. In 1900 Turnbull transferred from the coastal services to Elder Dempster's Atlantic service, and became chief officer of the Beaver Line steamship *Lake Superior* and, later, *Lake Megantic*.

Following the CPR's acquisition of Elder Dempster's Atlantic fleet in 1903, Captain Turnbull became the first of the company's Atlantic officers to obtain permission to undergo naval training. Taking a two-year leave of absence from the CPR, he served as acting-Lieutenant aboard HMS *Flora* in the Pacific squadron, and then on HMS *Swiftsure* of the Channel Fleet. In 1905 he was promoted to Lieutenant in the Royal Naval Reserve, obtained his Extra Master's certificate, and resumed his career with Canadian Pacific on the Atlantic run, receiving a series of increasingly important promotions.

Captain Turnbull served as Second, then Chief Officer on *Lake Manitoba*, then Chief Officer on the *Empress of Ireland* beginning with her maiden voyage on 29 June 1906. In March 1907 he transferred to the *Empress of Britain* as Chief Officer and in 1911 was appointed to his first CPR command, *Monmouth*. In January 1913 he commanded *Montcalm* and in March the same year, *Mount Royal*, from which he was posted to command of the *Empress of Ireland*.

Captain Turnbull served as master of the *Empress* for five voyages, until February 1914, when he took over the *Empress of Britain*, and handed the *Empress* to James Murray. Turnbull was also a Younger Brother of Trinity House. He was promoted to the rank of Commander in the Royal Naval Reserve in 1915, advanced to Captain (1920) and Commodore, 2nd class (1928), serving also as a member of the Royal Naval Reserve Advisory Board.

Early in the Great War he commanded an armed yacht, and was mentioned in despatches in 1917 for services in vessels of the Auxiliary Patrol between 1 February and 31 December 1916. In 1917 he was appointed Port Convoy Officer at Sydney, Nova Scotia. He received the RNR Officers' Decoration in 1918, and was made an Officer of the Order of the British Empire.

After the war, Captain Turnbull returned to the Canadian Pacific, where he commanded a variety of vessels including *Grampian*, *Metagama*, *Melita*, and *Montnairn*. There were a number of incidents in his later career with the CPR. While in command of *Grampian*, the ship hit an iceberg off Cape Race in July 1919, and the *Metagama* grounded in fog in the St Lawrence in September 1920, being refloated the following day, and no blame attaching to the officers.

In 1921 he was made a Commander in the Order of the British Empire. During the 1920s he continued to command CPR vessels, including the *Empress of Britain* again, *Empress of Scotland* (1927-1929), *Duchess of Richmond* (1929), *Empress of Scotland* (1930) and *Empress of France* (the former Allan Liner *Alsatian*) (1931), *Montclair*, and *Duchess of Bedford*.

He was one of the founders in 1926 of the Honourable Company of Master Mariners, of which he was made a Liveryman, a body formed to promote the interests of the maritime profession. In addition, he enjoyed a number of other honours including being made a Freeman of the City of London. In early 1927 he was appointed as an aide-de-camp to George V, a position he held until 1929. He also performed social work for the Croydon Council of Social Services.

After a distinguished career, his last command was the CPR's *Duchess of Bedford*. He retired from active service with the company on 6 December 1934, having also achieved the rank of Commodore in the Royal Navy Reserve. He died in London on October 16, 1964.

Empress voyages: four (89-92 inclusive) (Appendix 1)

James Anderson Murray, RNR

A native of Manchester, James Murray was born in 1860. Educated at the Hulme Grammar School, he first went to sea in 1879 at the relatively late age of nineteen. He received his certificate (No.09829) in

1887 in London, and served aboard a variety of Elder Dempster vessels plying the West African coast, Indian Ocean, and South American and West Indies routes over the next fifteen years.

Beginning in 1904 he served aboard *Lake Manitoba*, and was appointed to command the *Empress of Britain* in August 1906. He remained in that capacity for many years, and was in command of when she rammed and sank the collier *Helvetia* in July 1912 in the Gulf of St Lawrence. In February 1914 he was transferred to the *Empress of Ireland*, making two and one-half voyages in her before resigning from the CPR, and handing over his command on 1 May 1914 at Halifax.

He was appointed Harbour Master at Quebec at a salary of $4,000 per year, and testified briefly at the Mersey Inquiry in connection with the performance of the *Empress*. Murray was a Lieutenant Commander in the Royal Naval Reserve and a Fellow of the Royal Geographic Society. He was killed in the explosion in Halifax harbour on 6 December 1917, one of almost two thousand fatalities when the munitions carrier *Mont Blanc* was struck by the steamship *Imo*.

Empress voyages: $2\frac{1}{2}$ (93-95W inclusive) (Appendix 1)

Henry George Kendall, RNR

The most familiar of the *Empress'* masters, although for the wrong reasons, Henry Kendall's career as an officer was spent almost exclusively on the North Atlantic between Britain and Canada. He assumed command of the *Empress of Ireland* from James Murray on 1 May 1914 in Halifax, and completed only two crossings prior to the ill-fated trip of 28 May.

Born in the London borough of Chelsea on 30 January 1874, Henry Kendall spent his boyhood in Liverpool and went to sea at the age of fifteen aboard the *City of Berlin*, a steamer of the Inman Line plying between Liverpool and New York. The steamer was a good one, the first Atlantic steamer to be fitted with electric lights and capable of 16 knots – good enough to have captured the Blue Riband briefly in 1875. The same year he joined aboard the Blue Funnel steamer *Agamemnon*, engaged on the Orient run.

Kendall then switched to *Iolanthe*, a 255ft sailing vessel engaged in the Australia trade. After a series of adventures he stowed away on *Yaralla*, a coastal mail steamer and ended up on Thursday Island in the Torres Strait. Here he spent more than a year, working on a support boat for hard-hat pearl divers. He returned to England as an able-bodied seaman, rounding Cape Horn in a leaking 350-ton Norwegian barque with a cargo of sea-bird guano, a harrowing voyage that took 197 days and included a gale off New Zealand in which the ship nearly foundered. Kendall's next berth, where he was destined to serve three years, was aboard the four-masted clipper *Liverpool*, at one time the largest sailing ship in the world. In her, and in other vessels over the following years, he sailed to the West Coat of the United States, West Africa, and South America. His last voyage in a sailing ship as first officer of the *Liverpool*.

He received his certificate (No.029896) in 1901 in London. Shortly thereafter his career took a more conventional turn, for he joined the Beaver Line as Fourth Officer aboard the steamer *Lake Superior*, engaged on the run between Liverpool and Quebec City. Later Kendall wrote that the cold weather of the North Atlantic and the fogs of Newfoundland made him wonder whether he had made the right decision, and whether he ought to find a route promising blue, sunny skies. The Canadian route won out.

Kendall was second officer of the Elder Dempster's 3,912-ton *Lusitania* (not the famed Cunarder torpedoed in 1915) when she piled onto the Newfoundland coast on 26 June 1901, and was complemented for the way in which he helped allay panic among the passengers following the accident.

He was second officer in *Lake Champlain* in 1901 when that vessel became the first British merchant ship to have wireless apparatus installed, and obtained an Extra Master's certificate in 1902. Kendall survived the absorption of the Beaver Line by Elder Dempster, and the subsequent 1903 sale of Elder

Dempster's Atlantic vessels to the CPR. His service with the CPR began in April 1903 as Second Officer aboard *Lake Champlain*.

In May 1907 he was named First Officer on the *Empress of Ireland*, serving under John Forster for almost a year. He was an outgoing, gregarious officer who liked to make sure that his passengers enjoyed themselves, and was described also as popular among the men who served under him. In April 1908 he was given his first command, the steamer *Milwaukee*, then engaged in the European coasting trade. After less than a month he was assigned to the steamer *Monmouth*, at about the same time as he was commissioned as a Lieutenant in the Royal Naval Reserve. In the summer of 1908 he was in charge of *Monmouth* when the ship struck an iceberg in the Strait of Belle Isle. In the next six years his commands included *Montrose*, *Lake Manitoba, Lake Erie, Lake Champlain*, and *Ruthenia* (ex *Lake Champlain*), the latter, like *Tyrolia* (the renamed *Lake Erie*), engaged in the Austro-Hungarian emigrant business out of Trieste.

It was while in command of *Montrose* that Kendall gained widespread recognition by identifying a passenger bound for Canada as the notorious murderer Harvey Crippen, and it was Kendall who sent the wireless message to Scotland Yard which resulted in Crippen's arrest at Rimouski on 31 July 1910. For his role in bringing Crippen to justice, Kendall received a reward cheque for £250 from the British government, the first such award by the government in forty years. The captain never cashed the cheque. It hung on his stateroom bulkhead as a souvenir, moving with him from ship to ship.

In August 1912, in command of *Lake Champlain*, Kendall came to the aid of the Allan liner *Corsican* when the latter struck an iceberg off Belle Isle. Henry Kendall was a lifelong teetotaler, and non-smoker, and a man with a philosophical bent. 'Be prepared for the worst' was his watchword. He also possessed a good sense of humor. As Master of *Ruthenia* in October 1913 he autographed the diary of Ottawa artist Florence Biddle, and wrote: 'Life is full of disappointments. Nothing ever comes off but buttons.'

Returning to the *Empress of Ireland* in May 1914, in which he had formerly served as Chief Officer, Henry Kendall was in command of the ship when she was rammed in fog in the Gulf of St Lawrence on 29 May 1914, and sank with the loss of 1,012 lives, the worst maritime disaster in Canadian history. It was a slow-motion nightmare that would haunt the captain for the rest of his long life.

Though absolved of blame by the Commission of Inquiry headed by Lord Mersey, Captain Kendall never again held command of a vessel. After testifying at the Inquiry, Kendall was attached to the operating department of CP Ocean Services in Liverpool on 27 July 1914. It was during this time, as Marine Superintendent, that he was temporarily in Antwerp supervising operations. While there, the Germans crossed the Belgian frontier, part of a broad pincer move designed to strike against Paris. With German armies fast closing in on the pocket of resistance around the Belgian port, Captain Kendall managed to escape the city aboard *Montrose*, his old command, along with 600 refugees, while *Montreal* was hauled down the Scheldt by tugs. It had been a narrow escape, for *Montrose* was waiting to coal, while *Montreal* was undergoing engine repairs. Hastily transferring coal and supplies to *Montrose*, the two liners escaped the Germans. Once at the North Sea, *Montrose* towed *Montreal* safely to England.

On 17 September 1914 Cmdr Kendall was transferred to *Calgarian*, the Allan Line steamship that had made its maiden voyage to Quebec just three months earlier. Requisitioned by the Admiralty and converted to an armed merchant cruiser, *Calgarian* was first used for blockading neutral ports to bottle up German liners. Later *Calgarian* was used for patrol duties and, subsequently, she escorted convoys on the North Atlantic. "I have no cause to complain," he wrote to a former first class *Empress* survivor, "except the life is very monotonous, though at times we have exciting bits to keep our minds busy."

Henry Kendall was still serving as second in command aboard *Calgarian* when she was torpedoed and sunk on 1 March 1918 seven miles NW of Rathlin Island, off the coast of Northern Ireland while escorting a thirty-vessel convoy from Canada into the Clyde. Hit by torpedoes from *U-19*, the ship sank quickly and two officers and forty-seven ratings were lost. Kendall and other survivors were rescued by a British patrol boat. 'They gave it to us good,' he wrote six months later, 'they put no less than four torpedoes into her....'

Following this, in June 1918 he became Commodore of Convoys ('...the best and most responsible job in the Royal Naval Reserve,' Kendall termed it), and escorted 196 ships across the Atlantic without loss. The largest of the convoys for which he had responsibility consisted of forty ships, moving at a glacial six knots. In August 1918 he wrote: 'I arrived from America last Saturday after having brought a large convoy of twenty-seven ships across safely, and it is going to take more than Fritz to give me cold feet.' Kendall was mentioned in despatches for services in Patrol Cruisers between 1 January and 31 December 1917.

At the end of hostilities, he retired from active duty and was appointed (on 19 November) Marine Superintendent for the CPR at Southampton, a post he held until 1924. Following that he served as Marine Superintendent at Brunswick Yard in the Surrey Commercial Docks until his retirement on 1 February 1939. He was also a Younger Brother of Trinity House.

Henry Kendall wrote a 256-page biography entitled *Adventures On The High Seas*, published in the United Kingdom in the late summer of 1939 by Hurst & Blackett. Although it went into a second printing, the book has become somewhat of a rarity because most of the copies appear to have been destroyed in a German attack on London on 29 December 1940.

Despite pleas by various Canadian groups to return to Canada as part of the fiftieth anniversary of the loss of the *Empress of Ireland*, Captain Kendall refused. He died in November 1965 in London. His obituary in *The Times* of 29 November consisted of five lines and, as many writers have pointed out, made no mention of the *Empress of Ireland*. It read simply: 'CAPTAIN HENRY GEORGE KENDALL, who in 1910 as master of the liner *Montrose* radioed to Scotland Yard that the murderer Crippen was on board, died in a London nursing home yesterday. He was 91.'

Henry Kendall was buried in Chiselhurst, Kent. His epitaph reads: 'First person to use wireless telegraphy for crime.' Though he had chosen the words, they give the unfortunate impression *he* was the criminal.

***Empress* voyages**: 1½(95E and 96 incomplete) (Appendix 1)

APPENDIX 1
Voyages of the *Empress of Ireland*

Bold indicates a record passage (see details in Appendix 3)

No.	From	To	Departure	Arrival	Master	1st	2nd	3rd	Total
1W	LPL	QUE	1906/06/29	1906/07/07	F.J. Carey	119	342	797	1258
E	**QUE**	**LPL**	1906/07/12	1906/07/19	F.J. Carey	191	185	141	517
2W	**LPL**	**QUE**	1906/07/26	1906/08/02	F.J. Carey	202	240	538	980
E	QUE	LPL	1906/08/09	1906/08/16	F.J. Carey	145	127	223	495
3W	**LPL**	**QUE**	1906/08/24	1906/08/31	F.J. Carey	299	324	832	1455
E	QUE	LPL	1906/09/07	1906/09/14	F.J. Carey	116	134	175	425
4W	LPL	QUE	1906/09/21	1906/09/28	F.J. Carey	260	341	611	1212
E	QUE	LPL	1906/10/05	1906/10/12	F.J. Carey	73	107	201	381
5W	LPL	QUE	1906/10/19	1906/10/26	J.V. Forster	123	253	494	870
E	QUE	LPL	1906/11/04	1906/11/09	J.V. Forster	85	115	292	492
6W	LPL	STJ	1906/11/16	1906/11/23	J.V. Forster	52	92	324	468
E	STJ	LPL	1906/11/30	1906/12/08	J.V. Forster	63	130	624	817
7W	LPL	STJ	1906/12/14	1906/12/21	J.V. Forster	65	81	324	470
E	STJ	LPL	1906/12/28	1907/01/05	J.V. Forster	63	93	197	353
8W	LPL	STJ	1907/02/08	1907/02/16	J.V. Forster	76	336	631	1043
E	**STJ**	**LPL**	1907/02/24	1907/03/02	J.V. Forster	58	62	215	335
9W	LPL	STJ	1907/03/08	1907/03/16	J.V. Forster	145	478	799	1422
E	STJ	LPL	1907/03/22	1907/03/30	J.V. Forster	96	65	228	389
10W	LPL	STJ	1907/04/05	1907/04/13	J.V. Forster	124	467	801	1392
E	STJ	LPL	1907/04/19	1907/04/27	J.V. Forster	106	92	224	422
11W	LPL	QUE	1907/05/03	1907/05/10	J.V. Forster	206	488	815	1509
E	QUE	LPL	1907/05/17	1907/05/24	J.V. Forster	209	218	311	738
12W	LPL	QUE	1907/05/31	1907/06/07	J.V. Forster	184	459	860	1503
E	QUE	LPL	1907/06/14	1906/06/21	J.V. Forster	324	300	416	1040
13W	LPL	QUE	1907/06/28	1907/07/05	J.V. Forster	182	450	850	1482
E	QUE	LPL	1907/07/12	1907/07/19	J.V. Forster	257	323	415	995
14W	LPL	QUE	1907/07/26	1907/08/01	J.V. Forster	294	335	838	1467
E	QUE	LPL	1907/08/09	1907/08/16	J.V. Forster	148	204	366	718
15W	LPL	QUE	1907/08/23	1907/08/29	J.V. Forster	327	337	868	1532
E	QUE	LPL	1907/09/06	1907/09/13	J.V. Forster	115	133	405	653
16W	LPL	QUE	1907/09/20	1907/09/27	J.V. Forster	270	339	863	1472
E	QUE	LPL	1907/10/04	1907/10/11	J.V. Forster	152	154	413	719
17W	LPL	QUE	1907/10/18	1907/10/25	J.V. Forster	104	449	645	1198
E	QUE - LPL		1907/11/01	1907/11/08	J.V. Forster	123	110	410	643
18W	LPL	STJ	1907/11/15	1907/11/23	J.V. Forster	66	126	451	643
E	STJ	LPL	1907/11/30	1907/12/06	J.V. Forster	92	211	1025	1328
19W	LPL	STJ	1907/12/13	1907/12/20	J.V. Forster	88	121	377	586
E	STJ	LPL	190712/27	1908/01/03	J.V. Forster	46	130	620	796
20W	LPL	STJ	1908/01/24	1908/02/01	J.V. Forster	55	193	212	460
E	STJ	LPL	1908/02/08	1908/02/15	J.V. Forster	80	102	842	1024

No.	From	To	Departure	Arrival	Master	1st	2nd	3rd	Total
21W	LPL	STJ	1908/02/21	1908/02/29	J.V. Forster	78	384	438	900
E	STJ	LPL	1908/03/07	1908/03/14	J.V. Forster	57	87	765	909
22W	LPL	STJ	1908/03/20	1908/03/28	J.V. Forster	106	505	870	1481
E	STJ	LPL	1908/04/04	1908/04/10	J.V. Forster	62	113	447	622
23W	LPL	STJ	1908/04/17	1908/04/24	J.V. Forster	91	475	940	1506
E	STJ	LPL	1908/05/02	1908/05/08	J.V. Forster	132	114	266	512
24W	LPL	QUE	1908/05/15	1908/05/22	J.V. Forster	137	451	804	1392
E	QUE	LPL	1908/05/29	1908/06/06	J.V. Forster	191	282	657	1130
25W	LPL	QUE	1908/06/12	1908/06/19	J.V. Forster	117	301	627	1045
E	QUE	LPL	1908/06/26	1908/07/03	J.V. Forster	307	332	526	1165
26W	LPL	QUE	1908/07/10	1908/07/16	J.V. Forster	186	296	584	1066
E	QUE	LPL	1908/07/24	1908/07/31	J.V. Forster	166	183	511	860
27W	LPL	QUE	1908/08/07	1908/08/14	J.V. Forster	283	339	444	1066
E	QUE	LPL	1908/08/21	1908/08/28	J.V. Forster	103	132	506	741
28W	LPL	QUE	1908/09/04	1908/09/11	J.V. Forster	317	333	900	1550
E	QUE	LPL	1908/09/18	1908/09/25	J.V. Forster	150	120	503	773
29W	**LPL**	**QUE**	1908/10/02	1908/10/08	J.V. Forster	150	271	396	817
E	QUE	LPL	1908/10/16	1908/10/23	J.V. Forster	85	125	681	891
30W	**LPL**	**QUE**	1908/10/30	1908/11/05	J.V. Forster	91	156	351	598
E	QUE	LPL	1908/11/13	1908/11/20	J.V. Forster	100	205	1101	1406
31W	LPL	STJ	1908/11/27	1908/12/04	J.V. Forster	45	116	314	475
E	STJ	LPL	1908/12/12	1908/12/19	J.V. Forster	89	460	931	1480
32W	LPL	STJ	1908/12/25	1909/01/02	J.V. Forster	36	59	221	316
E	STJ	LPL	1909/01/08	1909/01/16	J.V. Forster	120	111	287	518
33W	LPL	STJ	1909/01/29	1909/02/05	J.V. Forster	49	181	452	682
E	STJ	LPL	1909/02/12	1909/20/02	J.V. Forster	36	73	148	257
34W	LPL	STJ	1909/02/26	1909/03/06	J.V. Forster	98	359	761	1218
E	STJ	LPL	1909/03/13	1909/03/20	J.V. Forster	59	81	173	313
35W	LPL	STJ	1909/03/26	1909/04/02	J.V. Forster	92	455	883	1430
E	STJ	LPL	1909/04/09	1909/04/17	J.V. Forster	68	115	219	402
36W	LPL	QUE	1909/04/23	1909/05/01	J.V. Forster	112	472	871	1455
E	QUE	LPL	1909/05/07	1909/05/14	J.V. Forster	70	232	273	575
37W	LPL	QUE	1909/05/21	1909/05/28	J.V. Forster	149	417	898	1464
E	QUE	LPL	1909/06/04	1909/06/12	J.V. Forster	165	228	389	782
38W	LPL	QUE	1909/06/18	1909/06/25	J.V. Forster	147	314	728	1189
E	QUE	LPL	1909/07/02	1909/07/10	J.V. Forster	259	244	241	744
39W	LPL	QUE	1909/07/16	1909/07/23	J.V. Forster	180	307	778	1265
E	**QUE**	**LPL**	1909/07/30	1909/08/06	J.V. Forster	154	124	175	453
40W	LPL	QUE	1909/08/13	1909/08/19	J.V. Forster	255	337	735	1327
E	QUE	LPL	1909/08/27	1909/09/03	J.V. Forster	59	138	193	390
41W	LPL	QUE	1909/09/10	1909/09/16	J.V. Forster	302	326	943	1571
E	QUE	LPL	1909/09/24	1909/10/01	J.V. Forster	141	125	159	425
42W	LPL	QUE	1909/10/08	1909/10/15	J.V. Forster	160	312	739	1211
E	QUE	LPL	1909/10/27	1909/11/03	J.V. Forster	nil	nil	nil	
43W	LPL	STJ	1910/02/11	1910/02/19	J.V. Forster	76	232	747	1055
E	STJ	LPL	1910/02/26	1910/03/04	J.V. Forster	44	98	338	480

No.	From	To	Departure	Arrival	Master	1st	2nd	3rd	Total
44W	LPL	STJ	1910/03/09	1910/03/18	J.V. Forster	120	461	910	1491
E	STJ	LPL	1910/03/26	1910/04/02	J.V. Forster	39	58	203	300
45W	LPL	STJ	1910/04/08	1910/04/15	J.V. Forster	144	458	944	1546
E	STJ	LPL	1910/04/23	1910/04/29	J.V. Forster	140	123	179	442
46W	LPL	QUE	1910/05/06	1910/05/13	J.V. Forster	190	481	958	1629
E	QUE	LPL	1910/05/20	1910/05/27	J.V. Forster	176	196	310	682
47W	LPL	QUE	1910/06/03	1910/06/09	J.V. Forster	173	442	982	1597
E	QUE	LPL	1910/06/17	1910/06/24	J.V. Forster	304	218	351	873
48W	LPL	QUE	1910/06/30	1910/07/07	J.V. Forster	173	413	965	1551
E	QUE	LPL	1910/07/15	1910/07/22	J.V. Forster	191	198	301	690
49W	LPL	QUE	1910/07/29	1910/08/04	J.V. Forster	257	329	931	1517
E	QUE	LPL	1910/08/12	1910/08/19	J.V. Forster	118	145	222	485
50W	LPL	QUE	1910/08/26	1910/09/01	J.V. Forster	341	318	947	1606
E	**QUE**	**LPL**	1910/09/09	1910/09/16	J.V. Forster	150	133	360	643
51W	LPL	QUE	1910/09/23	1910/09/29	J.V. Forster	269	326	962	1557
E	QUE	LPL	1910/10/07	1910/10/14	J.V. Forster	133	114	389	636
52W	LPL	QUE	1910/10/21	1910/10/29	J.V. Forster	151	349	818	1318
E	QUE	LPL	1910/11/04	1910/11/11	J.V. Forster	91	165	558	814
53W	LPL	STJ	1910/11/18	1910/11/25	J.V. Forster	74	157	425	656
E	STJ	LPL	1910/12/02	1910/12/09	J.V. Forster	89	267	860	1216
54W	LPL	STJ	1910/12/16	1910/12/23	J.V. Forster	64	167	442	673
E	STJ	LPL	1910/12/30	1911/01/06	J.V. Forster	66	127	371	564
55W	LPL	STJ	1911/01/27	1911/02/04	J.V. Forster	91	328	598	1017
E	STJ	LPL	1911/02/10	1911/02/17	J.V. Forster	84	170	318	572
56W	LPL	STJ	1911/02/24	1911/03/04	J.V. Forster	70	455	718	1243
E	STJ	LPL	1911/03/10	1911/03/18	J.V. Forster	70	83	235	388
57W	LPL	STJ	1911/03/24	1911/03/31	J.V. Forster	149	484	852	1485
E	STJ	LPL	1911/04/07	1911/04/15	J.V. Forster	75	141	300	516
58W	LPL	QUE	1911/04/21	1911/04/28	J.V. Forster	188	457	818	1463
E	QUE	LPL	1911/05/05	1911/05/12	J.V. Forster	150	202	332	684
59W	LPL	QUE	1911/05/19	1911/05/25	J.V. Forster	160	484	785	1429
E	QUE	LPL	1911/06/02	1911/06/09	J.V. Forster	251	324	605	1180
60W	LPL	QUE	1911/06/16	1911/06/23	J.V. Forster	127	447	810	1384
E	QUE	LPL	1911/06/30	1911/07/07	J.V. Forster	298	282	439	1019
61W	LPL	QUE	1911/07/14	1911/07/20	J.V. Forster	232	348	801	1381
E	QUE	LPL	1911/07/28	1911/08/04	J.V. Forster	130	141	388	659
62W	LPL	QUE	1911/08/11	1911/08/17	J.V. Forster	237	335	861	1433
E	QUE	LPL	1911/08/25	1911/09/01	J.V. Forster	115	131	394	640
63W	LPL	QUE	1911/09/08	1911/09/14	J.V. Forster	284	336	943	1563
E	**QUE**	**LPL**	1911/09/22	1911/09/29	J.V. Forster	90	133	502	725
64W	LPL	QUE	1911/10/06	1911/10/12	J.V. Forster	210	333	867	1410
E	QUE	LPL	1911/10/20	1911/10/27	J.V. Forster	125	123	535	783
65W	LPL	QUE	1911/11/03	1911/11/10	J.V. Forster	85	261	486	832
E	QUE	LPL	1911/11/17	1911/11/24	J.V. Forster	67	204	1033	1304
66W	LPL	STJ	1911/12/01	1911/12/09	J.V. Forster	96	170	444	710
E	STJ	LPL	1911/12/15	1911/12/22	J.V. Forster	98	558	755	1411

No.	From	To	Departure	Arrival	Master	1st	2nd	3rd	Total
67W	LPL	STJ	1911/12/29	1912/01/06	J.V. Forster	58	141	337	536
E	STJ	LPL	1912/01/12	1912/01/20	J.V. Forster	82	173	452	707
68W	LPL	STJ	1912/02/09	1912/02/17	J.V. Forster	102	393	692	1187
E	STJ	LPL	1912/02/23	1912/03/02	J.V. Forster	69	105	284	458
69W	LPL	STJ	1912/03/08	1912/03/16	J.V. Forster	158	474	731	1363
E	STJ	LPL	1912/03/22	1912/03/30	J.V. Forster	67	94	319	480
70W	LPL	STJ	1912/04/05	1912/04/13	J.V. Forster	173	474	905	1552
E	STJ	LPL	1912/04/19	1912/04/27	J.V. Forster	93	106	343	542
71W	LPL	QUE	1912/05/03	1912/05/13	J.V. Forster	180	488	882	1550
E	QUE	LPL	1912/05/17	1912/05/25	J.V. Forster	98	224	332	654
72W	LPL	QUE	1912/05/31	1912/06/08	J.V. Forster	219	410	887	1516
E	QUE	LPL	1912/06/14	1912/06/22	J.V. Forster	218	210	315	743
73W	LPL	QUE	1912/06/28	1912/07/05	J.V. Forster	167	407	932	1506
E	QUE	LPL	1912/07/12	1912/07/19	J.V. Forster	188	199	333	720
74W	LPL	QUE	1912/07/26	1912/08/02	J.V. Forster	246	332	919	1497
E	QUE	LPL	1912/08/09	1912/08/16	J.V. Forster	111	139	263	513
75W	LPL	QUE	1912/08/23	1912/08/30	J.V. Forster	335	332	883	1550
E	QUE	LPL	1912/09/06	1912/09/13	J.V. Forster	118	157	355	630
76W	LPL	QUE	1912/09/20	1912/09/27	J.V. Forster	221	372	911	1504
E	QUE	LPL	1912/10/04	1912/10/11	J.V. Forster	135	79	292	506
77W	LPL	QUE	1912/10/18	1912/10/25	J.V. Forster	151	452	798	1401
E	QUE	LPL	1912/11/01	1912/11/08	J.V. Forster	87	143	1025	1255
78W	LPL	STJ	1912/11/15	1912/11/23	J.V. Forster	25	151	426	602
E	STJ	LPL	1912/12/01	1912/12/07	J.V. Forster	109	396	830	1335
79W	LPL	STJ	1912/12/13	1912/12/21	J.V. Forster	69	160	443	672
E	STJ	LPL	1912/12/27	1913/01/04	J.V. Forster	76	134	569	779
80W	LPL	STJ	1913/01/24	1913/01/31	J.V. Forster	119	367	781	1267
E	STJ	LPL	1913/02/07	1913/02/15	J.V. Forster	101	125	358	584
81W	LPL	STJ	1913/02/21	1913/03/01	J.V. Forster	129	480	840	1449
E	STJ	LPL	1913/03/07	1913/03/13	J.V. Forster	103	110	368	581
82W	LPL	STJ	1913/03/21	1913/03/28	J.V. Forster	152	477	850	1479
E	STJ	LPL	1913/04/04	1913/04/12	J.V. Forster	79	162	358	599
83W	LPL	STJ	1913/04/18	1913/04/25	J.V. Forster	189	448	865	1502
E	STJ	LPL	1913/05/01	1913/05/08	J.V. Forster	96	116	289	501
84W	LPL	QUE	1913/05/16	1913/05/23	J.V. Forster	184	477	925	1586
E	QUE	LPL	1913/05/29	1913/06/05	J.V. Forster	180	225	600	1005
85W	LPL	QUE	1913/06/13	1913/06/20	J.V. Forster	174	442	880	1496
E	QUE	LPL	1913/06/26	1913/07/03	J.V. Forster	319	296	474	1089
86W	LPL	QUE	1913/07/11	1913/07/18	J.V. Forster	167	347	890	1404
E	QUE	LPL	1913/07/24	1913/07/31	J.V. Forster	174	162	470	806
87W	LPL	QUE	1913/08/08	1913/08/14	J.V. Forster	216	360	894	1470
E	QUE	LPL	1913/08/21	1913/08/28	J.V. Forster	118	170	518	806
88W	LPL	QUE	1913/09/05	1913/09/11	J.V. Forster	290	354	929	1573
E	QUE	LPL	1913/09/18	1913/09/25	J.V. Forster	142	175	554	871
89W	LPL	QUE	1913/10/03	1913/10/10	J. Turnbull	119	453	901	1473
E	QUE	LPL	1913/10/16	1913/10/23	J. Turnbull	71	161	636	868

No.	From	To	Departure	Arrival	Master	1st	2nd	3rd	Total
90W	LPL	QUE	1913/10/31	1913/11/08	J. Turnbull	67	190	599	856
E	QUE	LPL	1913/11/13	1913/11/20	J. Turnbull	56	174	1040	1270
91W	LPL	HFX	1913/11/29	1913/12/05	J. Turnbull	43	132	542	717
E	HFX	LPL	1913/12/13	1913/12/20	J. Turnbull	86	458	756	1300
92W	LPL	HFX	1913/12/27	1914/01/02	J. Turnbull	97	94	151	342
E	HFX	LPL	1914/01/10	1914/01/17	J. Turnbull	70	156	594	820
93W	LPL	HFX	1914/02/21	1914/03/01	J.A. Murray	94	347	620	1061
E	HFX	LPL	1914/03/07	1914/03/14	J.A. Murray	24	113	386	523
94W	LPL	HFX	1914/03/21	1914/03/28	J.A. Murray	85	467	802	1354
E	HFX	LPL	1914/04/04	1914/04/11	J.A. Murray	53	109	752	914
95W	LPL	HFX	1914/04/17	1914/04/24	J.A. Murray	74	496	889	1459
E	HFX	LPL	1914/05/02	1914/05/09	H.G. Kendall	45	93	371	509
96W	LPL	QUE	1914/05/15	1914/05/22	H.G. Kendall	115	310	748	1173
E	QUE	LPL	1914/05/28	incomplete	H.G. Kendall	87	253	717	1057
TOTALS						**26,265**	**48,985**	**111,598**	**186,848**

Source: author

Tables compiled from passenger manifests in the National Archives of Canada and Public Record Office, Lloyd's Captains' Registers, various newspapers, and *Report of the Trans-Atlantic Passenger Movement*.

Notes:

1. 'Voyage' means one complete round trip. The *Empress* made ninety-five voyages, and was in the process of completing a 96th, the eastbound return leg, when she sank on 29 May 1914.

2. As with much else concerning the *Empress*, there are discrepancies between various passenger totals. To the extent possible, the above totals are based on manifests in the National Archives of Canada.
Discrepancies arise because some sources did not count non-paying 'passengers' who were being deported from Canada, and manifests may not have been corrected for births or deaths at sea, especially on eastbound voyages. Deportees on eastbound voyages were recorded only in 1911 and thereafter. The *Empress of Ireland* carried seventy deportees in 1911, forty-six in 1912, 176 in 1913 and thirty-four in 1914. Stowaways are not included.

Discrepancies in arrival dates stem from possible confusion between actual arrival at a port and when passengers were disembarked. With late night arrivals, passengers often disembarked the following morning.

Passenger totals reported in newspapers are, generally, unreliable.

SAILINGS

	1906	1907	1908	1909	1910	1911	1912	1913	1914
Liverpool to:									
Quebec	5	7	7	7	7	8	7	7	1
Saint John	2	5	6	3	5	5	5	4	-
Halifax (direct)	-	-	-	-	-	-	-	2	3
total	**7**	**12**	**13**	**10**	**12**	**13**	**12**	**13**	**4**

Earliest arrival in Quebec: 28 April 1911
Latest arrival in Quebec: 23 May 1913
Earliest arrival in Saint John: 23 November, in 1906, 1907 and 1912
Latest arrival in Saint John: 19 February 1910

PASSENGERS CARRIED BY THE *EMPRESS OF IRELAND*

Westbound				**Year**	Eastbound			Grand	
1st	2nd	3rd	Total		1st	2nd	3rd	Total	Total
1,120	1,673	3,920	6,713	**1906**	736	891	1,853	3,480	10,193
2,066	4,385	8,798	15,249	**1907**	1,726	2,002	5,048	8,776	24,025
1,692	3,879	7,101	12,672	**1908**	1,522	2,255	7,736	11,513	24,185
1,544	3,480	7,788	12,812	**1909**	1,131	1,471	2,257	4,859	17,671
2,032	4,133	10,031	16,196	**1910**	1,541	1,842	4,442	7,825	24,021
1,987	4,579	9,320	15,886	**1911**	1,553	2,492	5,836	9,881	25,767
2,046	4,445	9,409	15,900	**1912**	1,451	2,159	5,712	9,322	25,222
1,946	4,621	10,047	16,614	**1913**	1,525	2,334	6,421	10,280	26,894
368	1,620	3,059	5,047	**1914**	279	724	2,820	3,823	8,870
14,801	32,815	69,473	117,089		11,464	16,170	42,125	69,759	186,848

Selected Maximums and Minimums for the *Empress of Ireland*

Most passengers, westbound:	1,606	Voyage 50W
Most passengers, eastbound:	1,480	Voyage 31E
Fewest passengers, westbound:	316	Voyage 32W
Fewest passengers, eastbound:	300	Voyage 44E
Maximum first class passengers:	341	Voyage 50W
Minimum first class passengers:	24	Voyage 93E
Maximum second class passengers:	505	Voyage 22W
Minimum second class passengers:	59	Voyage 32W
Maximum third class passengers:	1,101	Voyage 30E
Minimum third class passengers:	141	Voyage 1E

APPENDIX 2
Messages of Sympathy

The following is a selection of the hundreds of messages of sympathy sent from around the world in the aftermath of the sinking. Those marked with an asterisk (★) were read into the parliamentary record by Canada's Prime Minister Robert Borden.

★Telegram from King George V to the Duke of Connaught, Governor General of Canada:

> London, 30th May, 1914
> I am deeply grieved at the awful disaster to the *Empress of Ireland* in which, alas so many Canadians have lost their lives. The Queen and I assure you of our heartfelt sympathy with those who mourn for the loss of their relatives and friends.
> (sgd) GEORGE, R.I.

★Telegram from Queen Alexandra to the Duke of Connaught:

> London, May 30, 1914
> The terrible disaster that has occurred to the Atlantic liner, *Empress of Ireland*, in the St Lawrence river grieves me more than I can say. Up to last night we had hoped in London that most if not all of the lives had been saved, but this morning I learn that the first report was true and that over 1,000 people had been drowned. I wish to express to you my intense sorrow in this awful catastrophe and beg of you kindly to see that my heartfelt sympathy may be conveyed to the relatives of all those who have perished.
> (sgd) ALEXANDRA

★Telegram from the Right Hon. the Secretary of State for the Colonies to the Duke of Connaught:

> London, 29th May, 1914
> I have learned with the deepest regret of wreck of SS. *Empress of Ireland* and the disastrous loss of life which has occurred. Please take what steps are possible to make known my sym-pathy with relatives in Canada of those who have perished.
> (sgd) HARCOURT

★Telegram from the Duke of Connaught to Prime Minister Borden:

> Toronto, May 29, 1914
> On behalf of the Duchess and myself I desire to express to you our deep grief at the terrible disaster to the *Empress of Ireland* and our heartfelt sympathy with the families of those who have perished.
> (sgd) ARTHUR

★Telegram from Prince Alexander of Teck (the governor-general designate of Canada) to Prime Minister Borden (received at the office of the High Commissioner):

> Grieved to hear of disaster *Empress of Ireland*. Kindly convey sympathy of Princess and myself with relatives of victims.
> (sgd) TECK

★Telegram from the Prime Minister of New Zealand to Prime Minister Borden:

> Dunedin, May 29, 1914
> On behalf of Government and people of New Zealand desire express sincere sympathy with our sister dominion in appalling loss of life which has taken place in the foundering *Empress of Ireland* and our heartfelt condolence with relatives and friends of those who have perished.
> (Sgd) MASSEY, Prime Minister

*Reply by Borden to the Prime Minister of New Zealand:

> On behalf of Government and people of Canada I send our deep and sincere appreciation of your message and our profound sympathy for those in your dominion who have been bereaved by the loss of relatives and friends in this appalling disaster.
> (sgd) BORDEN

President Woodrow Wilson to George V:

> Deepest sympathy on the occasion of the appalling catastrophe to the steamship *Empress of Ireland*, which has brought bereavement to so many English homes.

Reply of George V to the President:

> I thank you sincerely for your sympathy in the terrible disaster to the *Empress of Ireland* and for your kind thoughts for the families of those who have perished.
> (sgd) GEORGE R.I.

Kaiser Wilhelm II to his cousin, George V:

> Let me express to you my deepest sympathy at the terrible catastrophe which overtook the *Empress of Ireland*. The loss of so many valuable lives is indeed deeply to be deplored, and I feel sincerely for the poor bereaved relatives.

Prince Henry of Prussia to Sir Thomas Shaughnessy, President of the CPR:

> Princess and myself wish to express our heartfelt sympathy in view of terrible and loss of so many valuable lives. We often admired your lovely boats at Hong Kong.
> (sgd) HENRY, PRINCE OF PRUSSIA

George V to Sir Thomas Shaughnessy:

> In the appalling disaster which has befallen your Company by the loss of the *Empress of Ireland*, in which, alas! so many lives have perished, I offer you my sincere sympathy.
> (sgd) GEORGE, R.I.

President of France Raymond Poincaré to George V:

> *C'est avec profonde émotion que j'apprends la terrible catastrophe de l'*Empress of Ireland *qui met tant de familles en deuil.*
> *J'ai à coeur d'adresser à votre Majesté les sincères condoléances et l'expression de la vive sympathie du peuple français.*

To the above, the King replied:

> I hasten to send you, M. le Président, my sincere thanks for the expression of sympathy you have been good enough to send me on the occasion of the terrible disaster to the *Empress of Ireland*. The sympathy of the French people in this sad event is particularly precious to me.
> (sgd) GEORGE

Swiss Foreign Minister to Sir Edward Grey:

> *Sur l'ordre de mon Gouvernement, j'ai l'honneur de venir présenter à celui de Sa Majesté, par l'entremise de votre Excellence, les vivres condoléances du Conseil Fédéral de la Confédération Suisse à l'occasion de la terrible catastrophe dont le vaisseau* Empress of Ireland *a été la victime.*
> *Profondément ému, le peuple Suisse tout entier s'associe au deuil cruel qui frappe de si nombreuses familles. En étant auprès de votre Excellence l'interprète de ces sentiments, je vous prie d'agréer aussi l'ex-*

pression de ma douloureuse sympathie personnelle et de celle de la Légation.

Duke of Connaught to Governor of the Bahamas:

> Your telegram 13th of June: on behalf of the Government and people of Canada please convey to the Government of Bahamas deep appreciation of their message of sympathy in the recent appalling disaster. Generous contribution has been sent to Lord Mayor's Fund.
> (sgd) ARTHUR

Duke of Connaught to Sir Thomas Shaughnessy:

> The Duchess and I desire to assure you and the Canadian Pacific Railway of our great grief in the terrible loss of life that has attended the sinking of the splendid ship which brought us out to Canada three years ago. We should be most grateful for any further particulars.
> (sgd) ARTHUR

The Duke also sent a message to the Salvation Army, and replied to telegrams of condolence from the Mayor of New York and the Prime Minister of New Zealand.

General Bramwell Booth, leader of the Salvation Army, to the Salvation Army at Toronto:

> My heart is stricken with grief in the great loss and sorrow which have fallen upon us in this appalling disaster. Our comrades were so true, so brave, so devoted. Their places will be so difficult to fill. I am sending Commissioner McKie to-morrow to stand by you, and I assure you of the prayers of the whole army world. Mrs. Booth joins me in deep sympathy with all the bereaved, both in Canada and the Homeland.

Bramwell Booth to Sir Thomas Shaughnessy:

> We sympathize with you on account of the great disaster to the *Empress of Ireland* in the St Lawrence. We have sustained a great loss. It is a great grief to us, but God is with us.

Lord Mayor of Manchester to CPR's Manager, Liverpool:

> Citizens of Manchester are appalled by the immensity of loss of life by wreck of *Empress of Ireland*, and I desire to express their sincere sympathy.

There were a plethora of other messages as well. The Diocesan Synod of Newfoundland sent its condolences. The Governor General of Australia cabled the Colonial Secretary in London, for onward transmission to Canada, expressing Australia's sympathy for her sister Dominion, and the Imperial Japanese government sent a message of condolence, as did Mexican President Victoriano Huerta to George V. In addition there were probably hundreds of messages exchanged between officials at slightly lower levels, along with personal visits. The Norwegian Chargé d'Affaires called at the Foreign Office on Saturday, 30 May, to express the profound sorrow of the Norwegian Government, as did the American Ambassador. Various British and French officials traded messages, and the Mayor of Cape Town sent the following to the Lord Mayor of Liverpool: 'The citizens of Cape Town tender heartfelt sympathy with sufferers by dire disaster *Empress of Ireland*.'

People all over the empire were moved to send messages of sympathy. The mayor and town council of the South African city of Bloemfontein sent the following telegram: 'Please convey to the proper authorities expression of deep regret for citizens of Bloemfontein at terrible disaster 'Empress of Ireland' and sincere condolences with relatives of victims.'

As well, telegrams and letters flooded into the CPR offices in London and Montreal, from prominent individuals in the railway and transportation industries.

APPENDIX 3
Speed Records Set by the *Empress of Ireland*

Prior to the arrival of the two *Empresses* in 1906 on the North Atlantic route to Canada, the speed records were held by the Allan Line's *Virginian*, whose fastest westbound passage was in May 1906 (5 days, 20 hrs., 40 min. from Liverpool to Father Point) and eastbound, July 1906 (6 days, 5 hours between) between Father Point and Moville. After that the Allan liners, despite being equipped with turbine engines, never seriously challenged the CPR boats.

Only in 1914, once the new Allan vessels *Calgarian* and *Alsatian* began service, was there a renewed threat to the records held by the CPR vessels. With the outbreak of war, all interest in records vanished and, by the war's end, the two former rival companies had merged.

The term 'Records' is somewhat misleading, for there was never an official Blue Riband for the Britain-to-Canada route, as there was for the prestige run to New York, despite the mention in newspapers of the day of a 'St Lawrence Blue Ribbon.' Suffice to say that a variety of 'records' exist, depending upon what, exactly, was being measured.

As this book shows, there was a rivalry between the *Empress of Ireland* and the *Empress of Britain*. During their careers, the *Empress* and her sister set several marks, breaking their own records and passing the distinction between themselves. Previous records set by one ship were later shattered by the other, sometimes only by a matter of minutes. Records, though, were as much due to weather and tides as other factors, for the two sisters were fairly evenly matched in terms of speed.

Shown below are records for the *Empress of Ireland*.

Note: the ocean distance is measured between mail points. In the early years, these were Moville in Ireland and Rimouski in Quebec. After Moville was dropped as a mail point in favor of Liverpool in late 1906, the record points changed accordingly.

The following is taken from *The Times* and other sources and, as will be seen, conflicts with information presented in Bonsor, Vol. 5, Appendix G.

Eastbound
Rimouski to Moville

1E	19 July 1906	5 days, 20 hrs, 50 min.

Set on return leg of maiden voyage

Rimouski to Liverpool

39E	6 Aug. 1909	5 days, 14 hrs, 28 min.
50E	16 Sept. 1910	5 days, 10 hrs, 58 min.

Quebec to Liverpool

63E	28 Sept. 1911	5 days, 13 hrs, 45 min.

Halifax to Liverpool

8E	2 Mar. 1908	6 days, 1 hr, 45 min.

Westbound
Moville to Rimouski

2W	26 July 1906	5 days, 10 hrs, 30 min.

(which eclipsed the *Empress of Britain* record of 5 days, 21 hours, 17 min. set in June)

Liverpool to Rimouski

3W	31 Aug. 1906	6 days, 8 hrs, 50 min.
29W	8 Oct. 1908	6 days, 2 hrs, 30 min.
30W	5 Nov. 1908	5 days, 15 hrs

Liverpool to Quebec

29W	8 Oct. 1908	6 days, 20 hrs
30W	5 Nov. 1908	5 days, 22 hrs, 20 min.

Bonsor lists the following records for the *Empress of Ireland*:

Westbound
Moville to Father Point
August 1906   5 days, 10 hrs, 30 min. (voyage 3W)

Eastbound
none

APPENDIX 4
Diving Fatalities on the *Empress of Ireland*

Name	Date	Home	Type
Edward Cossaboom	21 June 1914	New York, N.Y.	Hardhat
Hector Moisin	24 June 1981	Rimouski, Que.	Scuba
Lise Parent	28 Sep. 1996	Laval, Que.	Scuba
Xavier Roblain	28 Sep. 1996	Sainte-Foy, Que.	Scuba
Pierre Lepage	24 June 2001	Victoriaville, Que.	Scuba

APPENDIX 5
Births and Deaths Aboard the *Empress of Ireland*

The following is a list of persons who died during their passage in the *Empress*, extracted from passenger manifests and newspapers. There are probably some omissions. Some names of the deceased do not appear in the manifests, probably because the death had occurred *before* the manifest was completed.

1E   – male, unidentified, non-British
3W   – Math. Hissa, 3rd class, Finnish
4W   – Dalton Arnett, 26, 2nd class, American, cholemia
6W   – Annie Pretty, 36, 3rd class, English, hemorrhage
12W   – one Hungarian
        – Jane Marshall, 2nd class, Scottish, pneumonia (body brought to Quebec)
12E   – John Gyni, 39, 3rd class, Finnish, heart disease
        – Johan Waikanen, 29, 3rd class, Finnish, hemorrhage of the lungs
16W   – one person, overboard
19E   – E.N. Jordan, 30, clerk, Irish, consumption
21W   – Violet Morgan, 4, English
22E   – infant Andrews (born and died at sea), mal-development
23W   – girl, 9, Russian, diphtheria
24W   – one person, overboard
24E   – William Symons, 32, English, result of injury sustained on boarding the *Empress*
35E   – Annie Kanock, 30, housewife, Polish, heart failure and complications following childbirth
39W   – Henrietta McMillan, wife, English, heart failure
43E   – Maria Mattinen, 24, wife, Finnish, tuberculosis
45W   – infant, unnamed
48E   – Tyson Miller, 76, farmer, English, asthenic pneumonia and heart failure
50E   – James Rae, 23, Scottish, deportee, committed suicide by jumping overboard
        – Nilo Latvala, 3, Finnish, acute laryngitis
56E   – Kari Djorkham, 33, housewife, Norwegian, heart disease
63W   – man, unidentified, third class, committed suicide by jumping overboard
66E   – Florence Strutt, 38, wife, English, diabetic coma
69E   – Harold Carter, 27, bank clerk, English, pulmonary phthisis
78E   – Victor Drew, 32, painter, English, phthisis
83E   – Ivan Karuna, 18, laborer, Russian, phthisis and heart failure
86W   – James Simeon, 71 (body brought to Quebec)
95E   – Maria Helakoski, 55, wife, Finnish, diabetic coma

On a happier note, at least eleven children were born aboard the *Empress*:

4W   – boy??
20E   – Alexandra Evelyn Forster Lancaster (parents: J.H. and Mrs. Lancaster, English)
22E   – infant Andrews (died shortly after birth aboard ship)
25W   – one boy, one girl
73W   – Jean Sophia Alice Thomas (parents: Owen and Annie Thomas; born July 4, 1912)
75W   – boy (parents Scandinavian, third class)
76E   – Marie Repp (parents: John and Marie Repp, Hungarian)
89W   – James Turnbull Cornthwaite (mother: Margaret Cornthwaite, English)
90E   – Hesel Bustad (parents: Rasmus and Marie Bustad, Norwegian)
93E   – Karl Erik Skugland (parents: Karl Oskar Olsson and Ellen Elizabeth Skoglund, Swedish)

Regardless of their parents' nationalities, children born in a British-flagged vessel became British subjects.

APPENDIX 6
Postcards

The Edwardian era was a time of cheap, efficient and frequent mail delivery, and relatively few people had telephones. 'Drop me a postcard' was said in the same way later generations would say 'Give me a ring', and people sent cards as an easy and inexpensive way to stay in touch. Postcard collecting became a craze in Europe and the Americas, and many middle-class families had a postcard album into which they put cards from friends or relatives, such albums typically being kept in the parlor so that they could be shown to guests. So popular were postcards that in 1913, Canada's eight million people sent more than sixty million cards. Postcards were also low-cost souvenirs, and were valued as well in the days before cameras were common.

Even before her keel hit the waters of the Clyde, the *Empress of Ireland* began to be featured on postcards. These early cards or 'postals' as they were called, were based on artists' impressions of the ship, usually from seeing the plans drawn up by the Fairfield naval architects.

Throughout her career the *Empress* was featured on a large variety of postcards, artist impressions as well as photographic cards. Representations of the *Empress* were often accompanied by devices such as clasped hands and the legend 'Hands across the Sea', the CPR's red-and white checkerboard house flag, or the crossed Canadian ensign and the Union Jack. There was even a high-quality black-and-white photograph card in 'bas-relief', which sought to give a three-dimensional feel to the ship.

An attractive series of special cards on silk did not show the *Empress* at all, but featured her name and the allegorical motifs of crossed flags and clasped hands.

Though the illustrations of the *Empress* on postcards are interesting, to a social historian the messages are more important, for they are a reflection of the times and convey the impressions of passengers. Messages on *Empress* cards are often banal, advising friends or relatives of the writer's safe arrival or imminent departure, written in a variety of languages reflecting the diversity of her passengers: English, German, Swedish, and Welsh.

The following, dated 5 April 1907 from a passenger about to embark on the *Empress*, is typical of most postcards:

> Dear M,
> arrived at Liverpool 8 this morning all night's traveling this is our ship
> Love from us both

Sometimes, though, passengers felt a need to share with the recipient some details of what must have been the voyage of a lifetime, and a number of such messages have been included in this work.

Among the best of the postcards depicting the *Empress* were those of Raphael Tuck & Sons, whose cards often featured the royal warrant and the legend 'Art Publishers to Their Majesties the King and Queen.' Tuck produced a series of 'Oilette' color cards depicting famous liners. Postcard 9625 in Series II showed the *Empress* in a high-speed dash at sea (cover illustration). Other noteworthy publishers included C.W. Hunt of Liverpool, Warwick Brothers & Rutter, and Valentine & Sons of Montreal and Toronto, though their cards were usually printed in Britain at their Dundee factory.

The cards were sold on board the ship, as well as at shops on the Landing Stage in Liverpool, and in Quebec City, Halifax and Saint John, where arriving or departing passengers could buy them easily.

No one know how many different postcards there are of the *Empress of Ireland*, for there is no formal catalog. Our best guess is over two hundred, based on two years' observation. A number of Quebec-based experts, whose knowledge of the *Empress* and related ephemera is unsurpassed, estimate the number is possibly as high as one thousand, though this includes all color variations and re-impressions.

Even after the sinking, publishers found ways to sell cards, issuing a series of memorial cards. These typically are bordered in black, and show the *Empress*, often along with the damaged *Storstad*, or a poem, accompanied by some statistics of the sinking. Publishers reacted swiftly to the loss of the *Empress*, sensing a market opportunity. It seems to have taken only a short time to design and print suitable cards and get them into the hands of distributors. The earliest example seen by the author is postmarked 7 June 1914 from North Bay, Ontario.

As a means of reducing costs, card publishers often used identical images of the *Empress of Ireland* and the *Empress of Britain*, since the two sisters were virtually copies of one another. Most passengers probably never noticed. Another series of cards marked 'Empress of Britain and Empress of Ireland' merely had the latter portion of the legend inked through after the sinking.

There are occasional printing errors. One series shows the *Empress of Ireland* with the house flag of a rival line, and another series shows the *Empress of Britian* [*sic*].

For convenience, *Empress of Ireland* postcards can be classed in five categories:
  External views: photographs: at sea; in port (Liverpool, Quebec City, Halifax, Saint John)
  External views: artist impressions; early; late
  Internal views: photographs; artist impressions
  Memorial postcards: *Empress* alone; *Empress* and *Storstad*; other (*e.g.* poem)
  Special types: *e.g.* bas-relief; silk.

APPENDIX 7
Genealogy and The *Empress of Ireland*

During the preparation of this book, the author received numerous letters or e-mails that usually began with something like 'My grandparents emigrated to Canada about 1910 on the *Empress of Ireland…*' or 'My great-uncle was a steward in the *Empress….*' and asking for help in locating documents.

Appendix 1 contains the first-ever systematic voyage record of the *Empress of Ireland* and is a starting place to begin tracking a family member with a link to the *Empress*.

The National Archives of Canada holds microfilms of manifests for the **westbound** passages of the *Empress of Ireland* between 1906 and 1914. These are arranged by port in chronological order, and are mixed in with the manifests of all other passenger vessels arriving at the same port. The microfilms are located in a self-service reading room, and reader-printers are available. Manifests are arranged by class, and by destination (*e.g.* Canada or the United States). Within a class, the lists are not always arranged alphabetically.

Many manifests are not well microfilmed and are difficult, if not impossible, to read for a variety of reasons – poor handwriting, faded ink, etc. Note that manifests are not always accurate guides to ages; errors have been noted and, in the pre-passport days, no one could really verify the ages people supplied to the purser. Although names can also be misspelled, the manifests are still a valuable research tool. When searching for an ancestor, an approximate date of the voyage is useful or, at least, a port. Otherwise, searching manifests can be a frustrating and time-consuming process. For hours, check the website of the National Archives at *www.archives.ca*.

The Public Record Office (PRO) in Kew, a London suburb, has passenger manifests for all **westbound** and **eastbound** passages of the *Empress of Ireland*. These are filed in chronological order for the port of Liverpool. The British manifests are considerably easier to read than the Canadian documents; still, it is a good idea to have the approximate sailing date. Manifests are generally arranged by class, though passengers' names are not necessarily arranged in alphabetic order. All passenger manifests in the PRO for the *Empress* are in Class Lists BT 26 and BT 27 respectively, for inward and outward passages. Copying facilities are available. For details on the PRO, check the website at *www.pro.gov.uk*. The PRO website also has a list of professional researchers who can do research for clients unable to go to London.

Genealogists should understand that the names of passengers in first and second class are well documented, particularly for British subjects. For third class passengers, particularly in the early years, the information may be much scantier. A typical entry might read as follows: 'Jozef Wiznewski, Warsaw, with wife and two children.' Note as well that the manifests in England are **not** the same as those in Canada. The manifests in Ottawa generally contain more detailed information on passengers than their British counterparts.

The PRO also maintains Agreement and Crew Lists for the *Empress of Ireland*. Crew Lists are filed, as might be expected, by ship name. Crew Lists are not cross-indexed, so it is impossible to follow the career of a crewman without knowing the ships on which he served, and the dates. As well, the PRO has a number of Official Log Books of the *Empress*. These provide, *inter alia*, a list of crew members and changes through discharge or desertion; arrival and departure dates; marriages, births and deaths. Note, though, that these Official Logs are not the voyage log books for the ship, showing positions and times.

If an ancestor served as an officer in the *Empress*, his career can be tracked through Lloyd's Captains' Registers, available in various maritime libraries. One library that is prepared to conduct such research (for a fee) is the Maritime History Archive, at Memorial University of Newfoundland. For details, check the website at: *www.mun.ca/mha*.

If an ancestor emigrated under the auspices of a particular British emigration organization such as the Salvation Army, Dr Barnardo's Homes, or Mr Fegan's Homes, these organizations (which are still in existence) may also be able to provide assistance.

Some contacts:

> The Salvation Army
> International Heritage Centre
> 117-121 Judd Street, King's Cross
> London WC1H 9NN   website: *www.salvationarmy.org/history*

The Salvation Army offer a tracing service. Details are available from:
> The Salvation Army
> 101 Newington Causeway
> London SE1 6BN

> Barnardo's After-Care Department
> Tanner's Lane
> Barkingside, Ilford
> Essex IG6 1QG
> England

Records for Mr Fegan's Home in Canada are held by:
> Mr Douglas Fry
> 503 King George
> Brantford, ON
> Canada N3T 5L8

Note that Mr Fry charges a fee for searching his records.

> Mr Fegan's Homes Inc.
> 160 St James Rd
> Tunbridge Wells
> Kent TN1 2HE
> England   website: *www.fegans.org.uk/history.htm*

However, Fegan's does not have the resources to undertake tracing or research work.

APPENDIX 8
Crew List 96th Voyage

In listing the victims of the ninety-sixth voyage of the *Empress*, *Forgotten Empress* – along with certain Canadian newspapers of the day – presented only a passenger list. The omission in 1914 is perhaps understandable in the context of the times and the fact that most of the crew were British, but the unfortunate implication is that somehow the fates of over 420 crew members were less important in comparison to the passengers.

As would be expected, most major British newspapers printed more complete crew lists, though these contain errors and it is next to impossible to reconcile the various lists of crew members. At least seven of the *Empress*' crew deserted in Quebec prior to the voyage, and at least eight last-minute replacements were hired on.

Listed below are the names of 425 crew members on the last voyage of the *Empress*. In a separate list are the seven firemen who were not aboard. First names are given where these are known, since individuals often signed the Crew Agreements with initials instead of full first names.

Names in **bold** are those who lost their lives (total, 175).

Names in *italic* testified before the Mersey Inquiry (total, 24).

A.B. = Able-Bodied Seaman; O.S. = Ordinary Seaman.

Crew Members

Absolom, V.	B.R. Steward	Campbell, John	Fireman
Ainge, Edward	Linenkeeper	Campbell, Michael	Trimmer
Anderson, J.	Trimmer	Canepa, William	Assistant Steward
Baker, S.	Bell Boy	*Carroll, John*	A.B.
Baker, Harry	Assistant Steward	Chadwick, G.A.	Assistant Steward
Bailey, George	Fireman	Challis, M.E.	Assistant Steward
Bamford, Edward	Assistant Marconi Operator	**Chance, William**	Captain's Steward
Barber, John	Fireman	**Cheetham, John**	Assistant Sal. Steward
Bell, R.	Deck Boy	Clague, R.	Assistant Steward
Bent, J.	O.S.	Clandon, Henry	Cook
Bishop, T.	Assistant Cook (Ship's)	**Clare, W.**	Assistant Steward
Boyd, E.	Fireman	Clark, William	Fireman
Braine, Edward	B.R. Steward	Clarke, J.	A.B.
Braithwaite, J.	2nd Baker	Clarke, John Joseph	Trimmer
Bray, W.	Kitchen Porter	**Cochrane, Andrew**	Engineer's Boy
Brennan, Robert H.	Junior Second Engineer	**Cody, M.**	Trimmer
Brown, John	Assistant Steward	Connor, James	Donkeyman
Brown, Patrick	Trimmer	Connor, John	Greaser
Brown, W.	O.S.	Cooke, Thomas	Assistant Steward
Bruin, Thomas	A.B.	Coombs, C.	Second Sal. Pantryman
Burns, Charles	Assistant Storekeeper	**Cooper, Walter**	Assistant Steward
Burrows, T.	B.R. Steward	**Cope, Hector**	Assistant Steward
Byrne, John	B.R. Steward	Cope, John	Assistant Pantryman
Caley, F.J.	Junior Ninth Engineer	Copplin, G.	Assistant Pantryman

Corfe, John	Scullion	File, O.	Ex. Second Officer
Corrigan, Thomas	A.B.	**Fisher, Samuel**	Bell Boy
Cox, S.A.	Writer	Fitzgerald, H.	O.S.
Crabb, Joseph	Assistant Steward	**Fitzpatrick, Alexander**	Assistant Steward
Craik, Alexander	Second Steward	Fitzpatrick, J.	A.B.
Crayton, Robert	Seaman	**Flagel, J.**	A.B.
Crellin, R.W.	Assistant Steward	Flinn, Roy	Assistant Steward
Crowther, J.	Leading Fireman	Flood, Thomas	Leading Fireman
Cunningham, J.	Cook	Foster, Ernest	Trimmer
Cure, A.	Assistant Steward	*Gaade, Augustus W.*	Chief Steward
D'Arcy, Patrick	Greaser	**Gale, Thomas**	Assistant Steward
Davidson, George	Storekeeper	**Gallagher, William**	Deck Boy
Davies, John	Trimmer	*Galway, James F.*	Q.M.
Davies, John	Fireman	**Gardner, William**	Scullion
Davies, Peter	Fireman	**Gavigan, Bernard**	Assistant Steward
Davis, J.	Barkeeper	Gee, Percy	Assistant Sal. Steward
Dawson, Alfred	Third Butcher	**Gerrard, Thomas**	S.R. Steward
Dawson, Edward	Assistant Steward	Gibson, J.	Assistant Steward
Dehnel, Henry	Interpreter	Gill, H.	Sal. Pantryman
Delaney, Austin	Assistant Sal. Steward	**Gill, J.**	B.R. Steward
Dennehy, E.	A.B.	**Gillespie, R.**	Senior Fourth Engineer
Dennis, T.	A.B.	Glasberg, Rudolph	Barber
Derbyshire, A.	B.R. Steward	**Glover, Thomas**	Cook
Dewey, J.	Trimmer	**Grant, E.**	Trimmer
Dinwoodie, Agnes E.	Stewardess	Grant, J.	Electrician
Disley, John	O.S.	Grant, James.F.	Surgeon
Dixon, A.H.	Assistant Steward	Gratwick, T.	O.S.
Dixon, Harold	B.R. Steward	Gray, Arthur	Assistant Sal. Steward
Dolan, Paul	Trimmer	Gray, W.W.	Assistant Steward
Donaldson, John	Trimmer	Green, Fred	Assistant Steward
Donegan, James	Assistant Steward	Gregory, Fred	Assistant Steward
Douglas, S.	Fifth Baker	Greives, G.	Assistant Steward
Downey, Thomas	A.B.	**Gutcher, James**	Q.M.
Duckworth, W.B.	Electrician	**Hadfield, William**	Assistant Sal. Steward
Duffy, John	Fireman	Haigh, Samuel	Assistant Steward
Duggan, James	Assistant Printer	**Hamilton, A.**	Bell Boy
Duggan, Patrick	Greaser	**Hamilton, Frank W.**	Ticket Agent
Dumbell, Thomas	Assistant Steward	Hampton, W.	Junior Second Engineer
Dunn, John	Trimmer	Haran, Patrick	Cook
Durkin, John	Café Steward	Harford, N.	A.B.
Eliott, A.	Third Baker	*Harrison, Frank*	B.R. Steward
Evans, Albert.	A.B.	**Harrison, F.**	Grill Cook
Evans, John	A.B.	**Harrold, W.**	B.R. Steward
Faulkner, R.	Assistant Pantryman	Hayes, Ernest C.	First Assistant Purser
Fawcett, W.	O.S.	Hayes, Edward	Trimmer
Fayle, Robert	Assistant Sal. Steward	*Hayes, Joseph A.*	Assistant Steward
Fereday, Arthur	Assistant Steward	**Healey, J.**	Greaser
Ferguson, Ronald	Senior Marconi Operator	**Hepburn, J.**	Fireman

Herbert, William	Assistant Steward	**Lawrie, James**	Assistant Steward
Highfield, W.D.C.	Printer	**Learmouth, G.**	O.S.
Hird, W.	Engr. Steward	**Leary, C.**	Cook
Hobson, S.	Bugler (Assistant Steward)	**Leders, Lily**	Stewardess
Holden, George S.	Greaser	Lee, S.	Cook
Hollies, Helena	Stewardess	**Lennon, George**	Assistant Steward
Holt, Robert	B.R. Steward	**Leonard, Thomas**	A.B.
Hopwood, William	Assistant Steward	**Leonard, W.**	O.S.
Houghton, James	Trimmer	**Lewis, Charles**	Chief Third Class Steward
Hudson, John	A.B.	**Lewis, Henry**	Assistant Steward
Hudson, W.D.	Barkeeper	Lewis, John	First Assistant Cook
Hughes, Hugh	B.R. Steward	*Liddell, Robert*	Junior Second Engineer
Hughes, William H.	Assistant Steward	**Lightfoot, G.**	Officers' Steward
Hughes, William L.	Assistant Steward	**Lyons, W.**	A.B.
Hunt, Thomas	Assistant Steward	Macdonald, L.A.	Assistant Steward
Hutchison, George	Fireman	**Madden, B.**	Stewardess
Jackson, Charles E.	Fireman	**Madden, Frank**	Assistant Steward
Jacob, Alfred	B.R. Steward	Maguire, Joseph	Fireman
Jaques, Henry	Assistant Steward	Maguire, Joseph	Trimmer
Jeffries, James	A.B.	Maguire, J.	A.B.
Johnson, J.	Cook	Maher, Patrick	Greaser
Johnson, K.	Cook	Malone, Bernard	Leading Fireman
Johnston, John A.B.	Eighth Engineer	Malone, Peter	Leading Fireman
Jones, Clasrke	Assistant Steward	**Manderson, George**	Assistant Sal. Steward
Jones, Daniel H.	O.S.	Mathews, J.L.	Chef
Jones, Ellen	Stewardess	Matthews, John	Trimmer
Jones, Edward J.	First Officer	McAdam, William	Greaser
Jones, Harold	Assistant Steward	McAleavey, Michael	Greaser
Jones, H.	Barber	McAleavey, Patrick	Scullion
Jones, Harold	B.R. Steward	**McBride, William**	Trimmer
Jones, Henry Andrew	Saloon Steward	McCabe, James	Fireman
Jones, John	Assistant Steward	McCabe, Richard	Trimmer
Jones, J.M.	Senior Second Engineer	McCabe, Thomas	Trimmer
Jones, Miriam	Matron	McCowan, James	Fireman
Jones, Owen	Assistant Steward	McCoy, James	A.B.
Jones, Percy Reginald	Bell Boy	**McCoy, R.L.**	Assistant Pantryman
Jump, Joseph	Fireman	McCready, Thomas	Fireman
Jump, J.	Trimmer	**McDonald, Alexander**	Purser
Kane, T.	Trimmer	McDonald, C.K.	Junior Fourth Engineer
Keegan, John	Trimmer	McDonald, M.J.	Chief Butcher
Kendall, Henry G.	Master	McDougall, D.	A.B.
Kerwin, J.	Trimmer	**McEnroe, Edward**	Trimmer
King, John	Trimmer	*McEwan, James*	Junior Fourth Engineer
Knight, Robert	Second Butcher	*McEwan, John*	A.B.
Knill, A.	Cook	McGuinness, John	Trimmer
Lally, J.	Fireman	**McGuinness, Michael**	Leading Fireman
Lang, B.	Seaman	**McGuinness, R.**	Fireman
Lappin, W.H.	Cook	McGuinness, Thomas	Leading Fireman

McGrath, John	Assistant Steward
McMahon, Peter	Fireman
McManus, Henry	Fireman
McOnie, George	Junior Third Engineer
McSherry, J.	Assistant Steward
McWilliams, R.	Assistant Sal. Steward
Megson, John	Greaser
Mellor, H.	Deck Steward
Metcalfe, G.	Assistant Sal. Steward
Metcalfe, Thomas	Assistant Steward
Mitchell, James	Trimmer
Mitchell, Robert	B.R. Steward
Mohring, George	Assistant Pantryman
Moore, Charles	Third Officer
Moran, James	A.B.
Morgan, James	Trimmer
Morl, William	Boots
Morland, Harold	Assistant Steward
Mountain, Thomas	Fireman
Muir, C.W.	Assistant Steward
Mulvaney, W.	Trimmer
Munroe, William	Second Class Pantryman
Murden, Reuben	Trimmer
Murphy, John	Q.M.
Murphy, John	Assistant Steward
Murphy, Peter	Leading Fireman
Murphy, William B.	Trimmer
Murray, Peter	Trimmer
Murtagh, Matthew	B.R. Steward
Murtagh, W.	Bell Boy
Myers, Frank	Assistant Steward
Myers, John	Assistant Sal. Steward
Neal, Henry	Trimmer
Negus, Matilda	Stewardess
Nelson, Cornelius	Greaser
Nelson, George	Assistant Steward
Newham, Henry	Assistant Sal. Steward
Nugent, W.J.	B.R. Steward
O'Connell, Daniel	Trimmer
O'Donnell, Daniel	Greaser
O'Donovan, George	Junior Third Engineer
O'Neil, H.	Fireman
Orford, G.L.	Assistant Steward
O'Sullivan, James	A.B.
O'Toole, Patrick	Trimmer
Owen, Robert	Pantryman
Owen, W.S.	Assistant Steward
Page, Clarice	Stewardess
Parkinson, C.	Assistant Steward
Parkinson, Fred	Assistant Steward
Parry, D.	Assistant Steward
Passmore, Charles	B.R. Steward
Paterson, John	Fourth Butcher
Pearson, Sophia	Stewardess
Pelton, Benjamin	Assistant Steward (Died at Jeffrey Hale Hospital, Quebec, 11 June)
Perry, Harold	Assistant Steward
Peterson, V.	Carpenter
Phenna, F.	Assistant Steward
Pierce, Aug.	Cook
Pinner, C.	Assistant Steward
Pitts, W.H.	Assistant Steward
Powell, Leonard	Assistant Boots
Preston, John	Inspector
Price, J.H.	O.S.
Price, W.	Assistant Pantryman
Prince, William	Assistant Sal. Steward
Pritchard, Ernest	Assistant Cook
Pritchard, John	Assistant Steward
Pritchard, Oliver	Assistant Steward
Prowse, James B.	Assistant Steward
Quinn, John	Trimmer
Quinn, William	Trimmer
Radley, Alexander C.	Boatswain's Mate
Rankin, A.C.	Second Writer
Ratcliffe, John	Assistant Steward
Reardon, Daniel	Greaser
Regan, M.	Fireman
Reich, Joseph	Assistant Steward
Reid, H.	Fireman
Reid, James	Fireman
Reid, James	Trimmer
Rice, Edward	Fireman
Richards, Edward	Second 2nd Class Steward
Riddell, Alice	Nurse-Stewardess
Riley, John	A.B.
Roberts, James	Engineers' Steward
Roberts, Wolliam	Assistant Steward
Robertson, John	Second Class Steward
Robinson, William	Trimmer
Rockford, Moses	Fireman
Rohr, Arnold	Confectionery man
Ross, W.	Greaser
Rowan, William	Assistant Steward
Rowland, Joseph	Fireman
Rushton, Joseph	Assistant Steward

Ryan, John	Fireman	**Terry, John**	Assistant Steward
Ryan, Thomas	Trimmer	**Thomas, William**	Assistant Steward
Sampson, William	Chief Engineer	**Thompson, G.J.**	Plumber
Saunders, Robert	Master-at-Arms	Thomson, Archie	Assistant Steward
Shannon, Edward	Fireman	Toole, John	Fireman
Shannon, F.J.	Assistant Steward	**Trainer, Nicholas**	Boots
Sharkey, M.	Cook	**Tunstall, B.**	Fourth Officer
Sharples, W.H.	Q.M.	**Tunstall, Harold**	Assistant Steward
Shaw, H.	Fourth Baker	Turner, J.	Assistant Cook
Sheridan, Robert	Greaser	Ventro, J.	Cook
Simms, J.	A.B.	**Vivian, B.**	Assistant Steward
Simon, Albert	Assistant Cook	Wakeford, C.	Second Assistant Purser
Singer, Joseph	Assistant Steward	**Walden, D.**	Fireman
Skarratt, L.	Assistant Steward	**Walker, Thomas**	B.R. Steward
Smith, A.E.	Assistant Steward	**Welsh, Thomas**	Trimmer
Smith, A.E.	Sixth Engineer	White, H.	Trimmer
Smith, Charles	Assistant Steward	White, J.B.	Seventh Engineer
Smith, Harry	Assistant Sal. Steward	Whitty, John	Leading Fireman
Smith, H.K.	Assistant Steward	Whitty, James	Fireman
Smith, James	Trimmer	**Wildman, J.**	Storekeeper
Smith, Joseph	Assistant Steward	Williams, A.C.	Second Sal. Steward
Smith, T.J.	Sixth Baker	Williams, David	Cook
Smith, W.B.	B.R. Steward	**Williams, G.C.**	Assistant Steward
Smythe, James	Fireman	Williams, Joseph	Assistant Steward
Snowdon, John	Assistant Steward	**Williams, Roger**	Second Officer
Somers, Matthew	Fireman	Williams, R.	B.R. Steward
Spencer, Charles	Bell Boy	*Williams, Thomas*	Chief Sec. Cabin Steward
Sprague, T.	Boatswain	Williams, William	Greaser
Starr, Edmund	Greaser	**Williams, William**	Lamp Trimmer
Steede, Mansfield R.	Chief Officer	**Williamson, P.**	Senior Fifth Engineer
Stephens, John	Fireman	**Willis, George O.**	Smokeroom Steward
Stephens, John	Greaser	**Wilson, F.**	Assistant Steward
Stratton, Lucilla	Stewardess	Wilson, John	Fireman
Summers, John	Greaser	**Wilson, J.**	Trimmer
Swan, J.H.	Tenth Engineer	**Worthington, P.**	Fireman
Swinton, Alec	Chief Baker	**Wright, A.**	Assistant Steward
Taylor, W.	Carpenter's Mate	Wynne, T.	Scullion

Supernumerary Engineers ex-*Empress of Asia* (CPR's Pacific Service) who signed on for passage to England

Briard, H.	**Scott, W.**
Rankin, James	Smith, Albert

Musicians

Baxter, George	Norman, Frank S.	Bandmaster
Childs, Harold Bert	Pemberton, Albert	
Furness, John William Violinist		

Substitutes signed on at Quebec in place of Deserters

Cottle, Samuel	Trimmer	Wilson, James	Trimmer
Kerwin, J.	Trimmer	but not included in any other 'official' list:	
Neale, H.	Trimmer	*Fournier, Henri*	*Trimmer*
Tumilty, Bernard	Fireman	**Fitchett, Edward**	Stoker
White, H.	Trimmer		

Crew members who failed to make the sailing date of 28 May, the so-called 'Deserters'

Caldwell, J.	Trimmer	Freel, C.	Fireman
Casey, J.	Fireman	Gray, J.	Trimmer
Cooney, J.	Fireman	Sheridan, F.	Fireman
Doolan, J.	Leading Fireman		

Source: author

Compiled from various primary sources including National Archives (RG 42, Box 229, Vol. 35532 Part 2), contemporary newspapers, Crew Agreement Voyage 96.

The following data from the Mersey Inquiry shows the survival rates for various departments. Note that the data, based on a crew total of 420, does not reconcile exactly with the above lists.

	Total	Saved	% saved
Deck dept.	59	36	61.0
Engine dept	130	92	70.8
Supernum. Engineers	4	3	75.0
Victualling dept.	212	113	53.3
Matron + 9 stewardesses	10	1	10.0
Musicians	5	3	60.0
Total	**420**	**248**	**59.0**

Statistically, female stewardesses had by far the lowest survival rate, followed by the victualling department. Overall, however, the crew far did better than passengers: 59% of the crew survived, compared to just 217 of 1,057 passengers (20.5%). This is probably due to the fact that the passengers had not been aboard ship long enough to know their way about and thus were unable to escape from the lower decks. In third class, for example, just 133 of 717 (18.5%) survived, almost the same percentage as second class, a long way from the 43% survival rate in first class.

APPENDIX 9
Storstad

Following the collision with the *Empress* in the early hours of 29 May, after dropping off the rescued passengers at Rimouski, the crippled *Storstad* picked up pilot Archille Lachance at Father Point and sailed under her own power to Montreal, escorted by the salvage tug *Lord Strathcona*. She skipped a planned stop at Quebec, halting long enough to disembark pilot Lachance and pick up the Montreal pilot. She arrived about 2:00 p.m. on 31 May, her Norwegian flag at half-mast, and was impounded by the authorities at the insistence of the CPR, which had filed a suit for damages of $2 million against her owners, Actienelskabet Maritime (Maritime Steamship Company) of Christiania, Norway.

In Montreal, her cargo of coal was unloaded at the Dominion Coal Company's dock. Captain Andersen and his officers were besieged by reporters but, cautioned by counsel, refused to make any statements.

In turn, the owners of *Storstad* on 2 June in Montreal denied all liability and initiated a countersuit against the CPR for $50,000 for 'damage occasioned by a collision which took place in the River St Lawrence on the 29th day of May last, and for costs,' alleging the *Empress* was at fault and had been negligent in her navigation.

The first hearing took place in Montreal on 4 June, in Quebec Admiralty Division of the Exchequer Court. *Storstad*'s owners petitioned for release of the vessel and offered a bond in the amount of $234,609.67, although they stressed this was done without prejudice and was not an admission of liability. The odd-looking sum was calculated by the owners as their maximum liability, at $38.92 per ton of *Storstad*'s gross tonnage. Using a figure of 6,028 tons, without deduction on account of engine rooms, they arrived at the above number.

The bond was duly refused and, on 22 June, the Exchequer Court ordered that *Storstad* be sold at auction and the proceeds be deposited with the court pending final resolution of the matter. Accordingly *Storstad* was sold in Montreal on 7 July for $175,000. The purchaser was identified by the *New York Times* as a Mr Charles Cornell of the Prudential Trust Company, acting for O. Wicksburg of Norway. Though the paper claimed 'her former owners had had nothing to do with the purchase', she was ultimately re-acquired by the Klavenes Line.

The $175,000 was deposited with the Court against any future claims (including the CPR's $2 million). Claims would be paid only if, ultimately, *Storstad* was found legally to blame for the sinking. The Mersey Inquiry was merely that, an inquiry. Blame for the accident would have to be determined in an appropriate court of law. And, of course, claims would be paid only from the amount collected from *Storstad*'s sale. Her owners were absolved of further financial responsibility.

Held as security in the lawsuit initiated by the CPR, the ship was released on payment to the court of ten percent of the purchase price. The remaining $157,500 was paid to the court on 23 July. *Storstad* sailed downriver from Montreal on 8 July and arrived at 5:00 p.m. at the government dock at Lévis, awaiting entry to drydock at the George T. Davie & Sons yards at Indian Cove, on the south shore of the St Lawrence. Entering drydock on 11 July, a team of workmen began cutting away the damaged bow section, an operation which took four days to complete. A constant stream of visitors flowed through the Davie yard, anxious to see for themselves the collier that had sunk the *Empress*. During the time his ship was in drydock, Captain Thomas Andersen lived aboard her, inspecting progress and meeting with the press.

Repairs took a month, with two hundred men working day and night, and cost some $50,000. The whole fore section of the ship was completely rebuilt, over a length of twenty-eight feet. Some shipyard workers refused to work on Sunday, leading Davie & Sons to complain that this would make them uncompetitive with American and other Canadian yards. In general, once a ship entered drydock, work continued around the clock in order to free up the drydock as quickly as possible. Davie estimated it was losing a thousand dollars for each additional day that *Storstad* remained in drydock.

In the third week of July, as repairs neared completion, her officers were re-engaged by the ship's new owners, including Captain Thomas Andersen and Chief Officer Alfred Toftenes, who had been blamed by the Mersey Inquiry for sinking the *Empress*. *Storstad* returned to service on the St Lawrence as a collier after emerging from Davie's drydock.

Storstad's role changed on the outbreak of war, although the spring of 1917 found her still flying the flag of neutral Norway and owned by the Klavenes Line. At this time the Imperial German Navy's campaign of unrestricted submarine warfare was in full swing, having started on 1 February, a last desperate attempt to bring

England to its knees. No longer would the former maritime code prevail, whereby German U-boats would stop merchant ships, allow their crew to take to the boats, provide them with food and water, and assist them to the nearest land before sending the target to the bottom.

Despite the fact she was a neutral ship, with a crew from neutral powers, flying the flag of the American Commission for Relief in Belgium and bearing the designated markings of a relief vessel, *Storstad* was now a target for German U-boats. In early March the ship was nearing the end of a long voyage from Buenos Aires to Rotterdam, loaded with 10,000 tons of maize. Thomas Andersen, still master of the *Storstad*, had taken the precaution of obtaining from the German Consul at Buenos Aires a declaration that she would be given safe conduct through all waters, and that she would not be interfered with in any way by submarines.

Storstad made a coaling stop at Gibraltar prior to heading north toward the neutral Dutch port through which relief supplies were being channeled. On 8 March she was battling heavy seas at 51° 20'N 11° 50'W, off the southern end of Ireland. At about 10:00 in the morning a U-boat, invisible to *Storstad*'s watch even though it was lying on the surface, began shelling the hapless steamer with two deck guns from a distance of about four miles, while bearing down on her at speed. The U-boat fired some twelve rounds before submerging. Moments later the ship was rocked by a huge explosion as a single torpedo smashed into her port side. The Isherwood system was no match for a standard German torpedo.

John Roy Christian, born in the US of Norwegian parents, and the sole American on board, recounted his experiences in the *New York Times* four days later:

> When the *Storstad* entered the danger zone we put up a big lamp bearing the letters 'B.R.' [*Belgian Relief*]. At night the lamp was lighted by electricity and the letters could be plainly seen by day, and on the sides of the vessel the usual Belgian relief signals were painted. I was down below and somebody said we were under submarine shellfire. Most of us thought it only a joke. I went on deck and saw shells falling near us, fired by a submarine at least three miles away.
>
> The shelling continued some ten minutes, but the *Storstad* was not hit. Suddenly, the submarine ceased firing and our captain ordered four very big Belgian Relief flags to be flown and another big signboard bearing the words 'Belgian Relief Committee' to be placed forward. There was thus no chance of the Germans mistaking our ship.
>
> We could see the submarine getting nearer and thought the trouble was at an end for sure. Instead, the *Storstad* suffered an awful shock. Tons of water fell upon the ship, which rolled badly. She had been torpedoed on the starboard side and I saw cargo floating away out of her side.
>
> Our boat pulled straight for the submarine, as the Captain said he thought they would give us a tow. Then the German officer bellowed out in English: 'Come alongside.'
>
> As we got alongside the submarine, a sailor came out of the conning tower and mockingly held up the German flag. The German commander refused to answer our Captain when he asked for a tow. We were told to clear away and join our other two boats. The submarine fired two more shells at the *Storstad* and so sank her. The U-boat then disappeared and we did not see her again.
>
> At midnight we sighted a ship not more than half a mile away, and as we could find no dry matches, every man shouted as loud as he could.
>
> Immediately all lights in the ship went out and, although we hollered ourselves hoarse, she kept on her course. There was no rudder to our boat.
>
> During the next day we dried some matches in the sun and at nightfall rigged up a piece of rag soaked in paraffin to make a flare signal. At 10 o'clock that night we had been thirty-six hours in the open boat and perished with cold and hunger and wearied out, we and the other boats were picked up by a patrol boat. Our fourth engineer, a Norwegian named Sorensen, was taken off in a dying condition from exhaustion and exposure and died a few minutes later.

The U-boat which sank *Storstad* was never identified from the after-patrol reports which commanders filed on return to port.

In that month of March, German U-boats sank 593,841 tons of allied and neutral shipping. *Storstad*, only a minute portion of this grim statistic, and with just one fatality from her crew of thirty-eight, had finally joined the RMS *Empress of Ireland* in a cold, watery grave.

BIBLIOGRAPHY

Books

—. *A Package of Postcards and a 'Wireless' – A Bride's Story*. Private printing, undated, probably 1907. Reproduced by the Canadian Institute for Historical Microreproductions, No.74491

—. *Report and Evidence of the Commission of Inquiry into the Loss of the British Steamship 'Empress of Ireland'. Commission of Inquiry into the Casualty to the British Steamship 'Empress of Ireland'*. Canadian Sessional Paper No.21b, 5 George V, 1915

—. *Annual Report of the Department of the Interior. Report of the Superintendent of Immigration*. Canadian Sessional Paper No.25, various years

—. *Le Naufrage de l'Empress of Ireland*. Musée de la mer de Pointe-au-Père, 1999

—. *Report of the Trans-Atlantic Passenger Movement*. James Kempster Printing Co., printed annually, New York

—. *Official Report of the Debates of the House of Commons*, Vol.CXVII, 1914

Appleton, Thomas E. *Ravenscrag – The Allan Royal Mail Line*. McClelland & Stewart, Toronto, 1974

Bairati, E. et al. *La Belle Epoque*. William Morrow Co. Inc., New York, 1978

Ballard, Robert D. and Dunmore, Spencer. *Exploring the Lusitania*. Madison Press, Toronto, 1995

Ballard, Robert D. and Archbold, Rick. *Lost Liners.* Hyperion, New York, 1997

Bonsor, N.R.P. *North Atlantic Seaway, Vol.5*. Brookside Publications, Jersey (CI), 1980

Brinnin, John Malcolm. *The Sway of the Grand Saloon*. Delacorte Press, New York, 1971

Burggraf, Marjorie L. *The* Empress of Ireland, *A Canadian Marine Monument to Twentieth Century Immigrant History*. Marine Museum of the Great Lakes at Kingston, Kingston, 1996

Canadian Pacific Railway Company. *A Brief Description (with a few illustrations) of the Canadian Pacific Railway Co.'s Royal Mail Steamships, the 'Empresses.'* Undated

Canadian Pacific Railway Ocean Services. *Uniform Regulations*. Harrison & Sons, London, 1914 (Reproduced by the Canadian Institute for Historical Microreproductions, No.76340)

Creighton, David. *Losing the Empress – A Personal Journey – The Empress of Ireland's Enduring Shadow*. Dundurn Press, Toronto, 2000

Croall, James. *Fourteen Minutes – The Last Voyage of the Empress of Ireland*. Michael Joseph, London, 1978

Daniel, Clifton (ed.). Chronicle of the 20th Century. JL International Publishing, Liberty (Missouri)

Dear, Ian. *Great Ocean Liners: The Heyday of Luxury Travel*. B.T. Batsford, London, 1977

Ellsberg, Edward. *Men Under the Sea*. Dodd, Mead, New York, 1939

Gilbert, Elliot L. *O Beloved Kids – Rudyard Kipling's Letters to His Children*. Harcourt Brace Jovanovich, Orlando, 1984

Howard, Michael and Louis, Wm. Roger. *The Oxford History of the Twentieth Century*. Oxford University Press, Oxford, 1998

Kemp, Peter (ed.). *The Oxford Companion to Ships and the Sea*. Oxford University Press, London, 1976

Kendall, Henry. *Adventures On The High Seas*. Hurst & Blackett, London, 1939

King, William Lyon Mackenzie. *The Mackenzie King Diaries 1893-1931*. Microfiche, University of Toronto Press, 1973

Kipling, Rudyard. *Letters to the Family*. Macmillan, Toronto, 1910
—. *Something Of Myself*. Doubleday, Doran & Co., New York, 1937

Lee, Charles E. *The Blue Riband – The Romance of the Atlantic Ferry*. Sampson Low, Marston, London, undated

Marconi, Degna. *My Father, Marconi*. McGraw-Hill, New York, 1962

Marshall, Logan. *The Tragic Story of the Empress of Ireland*. Patrick Stephens, London, 1972 (reprint of the original edition by L.T. Myers, 1914)

Maxtone-Graham, John. *The Only Way to Cross*. Macmillan, New York, 1972
—. *Crossing & Cruising*. Charles Scribner's Sons, New York, 1992

Musk, George. *Canadian Pacific. The Story of the Famous Shipping Line*. Holt Rinehart and Winston, Toronto, 1981

Perry, Hobart. *Ship Management*. Simmons-Boardman, New York, 1931

Phillips, Alan. *Into the 20th Century 1900-1910 Canada's Illustrated History*. National Science of Canada, Toronto, 1977

Pinney, Thomas. *The Letters of Rudyard Kipling, Volume 3 1900-10*. University of Iowa Press, Iowa City, 1996

Ransome-Wallace, P. *North Atlantic Panorama, 1900-1976*. Ian Allan, London, 1977

Rasky, Frank. *Great Canadian Disasters*. Longmans Green & Co., Toronto, 1961

Roy, Karino. *Le drame de l'Empress of Ireland – Pointe-au Pére, 29 mai 1914*. Editions du Plongeur, Vanier, 1993

Simpson, Colin. *Lusitania*. Longman, London, 1972

Wall, Robert. *Ocean Liners*. Collins, London, 1978

Wood, Herbert. *Till We Meet Again – The Sinking of the Empress of Ireland*. Image Publishing, Toronto, 1982

Zeni, David. *Forgotten Empress*. Halsgrove, 1998

Periodicals

The Shipbuilder, No.1, Summer 1906
Canadian Railway and Marine World (after 1912; previously titled *The Railway and Marine World*)
Diver Magazine, Vol.8, No.1 (Jan.-Feb. 1982)
Railway & Travel Monthly, 1911, Vol.2 (April)
The Graphic
Illustrated London News

Newspapers
Halifax: *The Halifax Herald*
Liverpool: *Echo*
London: *The Times*
Manchester: *The Guardian*
Montreal: *The Gazette*; *The Montreal Daily Star; La Presse*; *Le Devoir*
New York: *The Times*
Ottawa: *Evening Journal*
Quebec City: *The Quebec Chronicle; Quebec Chronicle-Telegraph; Le Soleil*
Saint John: *The St. John Standard; Saint John Globe; The Evening Times Star*
Toronto: *Globe*

Videos, Films
Lost Liners, PBS Home Video (2000)
Voyage to Oblivion, Merlin Films (2000), the English-language version of *Sombré dans l'oublie*, 1999
St Lawrence, Stairway to the Sea, Cousteau Video Library, Time Life (1992)

Interviews with former *Empress* Passengers
Mary (Hill) McCullough, taped 18 September 2000
Vera (Knight) Way, taped 23 March 2001
Gladys (French) Smith, taped 26 March 2001
Bernard Blades
Joyce (Thompson) Gould
Interview with Donald Craw (C2310) from the Andrew Ross McCormack fonds, at the Provincial Archives of Manitoba

Unpublished Material held by Institutions
Diary of HRH Prince Arthur, Duke of Connaught (Royal Library)
Letters of Sir Josiah Symon, 2 June and 4 June 1907 (National Library of Australia, MS 1736/1/1130-32)
Letter of Earl Gowrie, 13-14 July 1908 (National Library of Australia, Series 7/1/4)
Earl Gowrie, extract from draft autobiography (National Library of Australia, Series 15/2)
Letters of Rudyard Kipling (University of Sussex)
Letters of Sir William Van Horne (National Archives of Canada, MG 29, A 60, vol.90)
Letters and diaries of Sir Sandford Fleming (National Archives of Canada, MG 29 – B1, vol.82)
Diary of Lady Beatrice Pole-Carew (CP 80, Antony House, Torpoint, Cornwall)
Letterbooks of Sir Thomas Shaughnessy (National Archives of Canada, microfilms M-2983 to M-3069)
Department of Marine. *Formal Investigation Held at Quebec on Thursday October 26 1909 in re Accident to SS* Empress of Ireland (National Archives of Canada, RG 42 Vol.547)
Department of Marine. Various items (National Archives of Canada, RG 42 Series B-1, Vol.229, Files 35532 & 35566; RG 42, Vol.232, File 35762; RG 42, Vol.230, File 35628)
Immigration Branch. Correspondence (National Archives of Canada, RG 76 Series 1-A-1, Vol.459, Reel C-10400 File 703849)
Immigration Branch. Microfilms of passenger manifests for vessels arriving at East Coast ports. (National Archives of Canada; Saint John, Reels T-507 & T-508, and T-4820 to T-4828; Halifax, Reels T-4751 to T-4753; Quebec City, Reels T-487 to T-493, and T-4759 to T-4808)
Post Office. Various items (National Archives of Canada, RG 3, Series C-2, Vol. 633, File 69265)
External Affairs. Various items (National Archives of Canada, RG 25, Series G-2, Vol.6676; RG 25, Series B-1-b, Vol.252, File P-1-66; RG 25, Series A-3-a, Vol.1143G-1)

Drawings
Deck and Rigging Plans of the *Empress of Ireland*, Reproduced by Ship Reproductions, 1995 (website: *www.rmsempressofireland.com*)